Reference
and Subscription Books
Reviews

Reference and Subscription Books Reviews 1972-1974

Reprinted from *The Booklist*

Volumes 69-70

September 1, 1972-August, 1974

Prepared by the
American Library Association
Reference and Subscription Books Review
Committee

AMERICAN LIBRARY ASSOCIATION

Chicago 1975

Copyright © 1972, 1973, 1974 by the
American Library Association

Permission to quote any review in full
or in part must be obtained from the
Office of Rights and Permissions of the
American Library Association.
Permission to quote a review in full
will be granted only to the publisher
of the work reviewed.

Library of Congress Catalog Card
Number 73-159565

International Standard Book Number
0-8389-0194-8

Manufactured in the United States
of America

Contents

Preface, xvii

REVIEWS

Almanac of World Military Power, 1
The American Peoples Encyclopedia, 3
American Reference Books Annual 1970-   , 7
The Barnhart Dictionary of New English Since 1963, 9
Bowker's Medical Books in Print, 1973, 12
Britannica Junior Encyclopaedia for Boys and Girls, 13
Britten's Old Clocks and Watches and Their Makers, 16
Butterflies of the World, 17
Cassell's Encyclopaedia of World Literature, 19
Chambers's Biographical Dictionary, 20
The Collectors' Encyclopedia of Antiques, 21
The College Blue Book, 26
Collier's Encyclopedia, 28
The Compact Edition of the Oxford English Dictionary, 32
Constitutions of the Countries of the World, 33
Cram Modern World Atlas, 35
A Dictionary of Literature in the English Language, from Chaucer to 1940, 36
Dictionary of Science and Technology, 37
Documents of American Theater History, 39
Dynamics of World Power, 41
The Earth and Man: a Rand McNally World Atlas, 43
Editorials on File, 45
Encyclopaedia Britannica, 48
Encyclopaedia Judaica, 56
Encyclopaedia of Occupational Health and Safety, 60
Encyclopedia of Associations, 61
The Encyclopedia of Education, 63
The Encyclopedia of the Horse, 70
Encyclopedia of Psychology, 71
Encyclopedia of World Literature in the 20th Century, 72
The Environment Film Review, 74
The Environment Index 71, 75
Environment Information ACCESS, 75
Exotica: Series 3, 77

v

Foundations of Colonial America, 79
Glenn G. Munn's Encyclopedia of Banking and Finance, 62
Granger's Index to Poetry, 81
Great Britain: Foreign Policy and the Span of Empire 1689-1971, 82
Great Soviet Encyclopedia, 84
Grzimek's Animal Life Encyclopedia, 86
Guide to Atlases, 88
A Guide to Critical Reviews, 89
Guide to Reference Material, 92
Harper's Dictionary of Music, 95
Harver Junior World Encyclopedia, 97
Harver World Encyclopedia, 103
Historic Documents 1972, 108
History of American Presidential Elections, 1789-1968, 109
History of U.S. Political Parties, 111
House and Garden's Antiques: Questions and Answers, 112
The Illustrated Encyclopedia of the Animal Kingdom, 117
The Illustrated Libraries of Human Knowledge, 118
Illustrated World Encyclopedia, 122
In Black America, 126
Index to Fairy Tales, 1949-1972, 129
The International Encyclopedia of Dogs, 130
The International Encyclopedia of Film, 133
International Library of Negro Life and History, 135
International Visual Dictionary, 140
The International Wildlife Encyclopedia, 143
Irregular Serials and Annuals, 146
Kobbe's Complete Opera Book, 148
Lands and Peoples, 151
Larousse Illustrated International Encyclopedia and Dictionary, 153
The Law of War: A Documentary History, 155
The McGraw-Hill Encyclopedia of World Biography, 156
McGraw-Hill Encyclopedia of World Drama, 159
Magazines for Libraries, 160
Makers of America, 162
Man, Myth & Magic, 164
Masterpieces of Chinese Art, 167
Merit Students Encyclopedia, 168
Modern Century Illustrated Encyclopedia, 171
Music of the Middle Ages to the Renaissance, 173

Music in the Modern Age: A History of Western Music, 173
The Musician's Guide, 174
National Geographic Atlas of the World, 175
The Negro in American History, 179
The New Book of Knowledge, 181
The New Century Handbook of Classical Geography, 186
The New Century Italian Renaissance Encyclopedia, 187
New International Illustrated Encyclopedia of Art, 189
New Scribner Music Library, 191
The New York Times Atlas of the World, 193
New York Times Book of Antiques, 195
The New York Times Directory of the Film, 196
The New York Times Directory of the Theater, 197
The New York Times Film Reviews: A One-Volume Selection, 1913-1970, 199
New York Times Guide to Continuing Education in America, 200
The New York Times Guide to Federal Aid for Cities and Towns, 201
Notable Names in American History, 203
Oxford Economic Atlas of the World, 204
Patterson's American Education [1973], 206
The Penguin Dictionary of Science, 208
Pergamon World Atlas, 209
Phaidon Dictionary of Twentieth-Century Art, 211
The Practical Encyclopedia of Good Decorating and Home Improvement, 212
Profiles of Involvement, 214
Purnell's History of the 20th Century, 216
Rand McNally Cosmopolitan World Atlas, 220
Rand McNally Premier World Atlas, 221
Rand McNally World Atlas, 221
Rand McNally Worldmaster Atlas, 222
The Random House Encyclopedia of Antiques, 22
The Realm of Science, 228
The Romantic Movement Bibliography, 1936-1970, 231
St. Martin's Dictionary of Twentieth-Century Composers, 232
Science and Technology Research in Progress, 1972-1973, 233
Scientific and Technical Books in Print 1972, 236

Selective Guide to Materials for Mental Health and Family Life Education, 237
Sources and Documents of United States Constitutions, 239
The Standard Directory of Newsletters, 240
Statutory History of the United States, 242
Studio Dictionary of Design and Decoration, 244
A Supplement to the Oxford English Dictionary, 245
Tapestry and Embroidery in the Collection of the National Palace Museum, 248
Taylor's Encyclopedia of Government Officials, 249
Time-Life Encyclopedia of Gardening, 250
The Times Atlas of the World, 254
The Times in Review: 1960-1969, 255
Treasury of American Design, 257
Ulrich's International Periodicals Directory, 258
United Nations Resolutions, 260
The Ways of Game Fish, 262
The Ways of Wildfowl, 262
Webster's New Collegiate Dictionary [8th ed.], 264
Webster's New World Dictionary, 267
Who Was Who in the USSR, 270
Who's Who in Government 1972-1973, 272
The World Book Encyclopedia, 272
World Chronology of Music History, 279
The World Encyclopedia of Dogs, 130
The World Encyclopedia of the Film, 133
Worldmark Encyclopedia of the Nations, 281
The Xerox Intermediate Dictionary, 283
Young People's Illustrated Encyclopedia, 285
Young Students Encyclopedia, 287

NOTES AND COMMENTS

Acronyms and Initialisms Dictionary, 294
African Authors, 294
Afro-American Artists, 295
American Art Directory 1974, 295
American Black Women in the Arts and Social Sciences, 296
American Book Publishing Record, 297
The American Heritage Book of Great Historic Places, 297
American Indian Women, 297
American Malacologists, 298
American Men and Women of Science: Discipline Index, 298
American Women, 298
An Annual of New Art and Artists '73-'74, 299
Annual Register of Grant Support 1973/74, 299
Annual Review of United Nations Affairs, 1971-1972, 299
The Archaeologists' Year Book, 300
ARTbibliographies Modern, 300
Articles on Twentieth Century Literature, 300
Atlas of Discovery, 301
Atlas of Hawaii, 301
Australian Books in Print 1973, 302
Better Homes and Gardens Encyclopedia of Cooking, 302
A Bibliography of Finance and Investment, 302
A Bibliography of Noise 1965-1970, 303
Biographical Dictionary of the Comintern, 303
The Birds of America, 303
Black Africa, 304
The Book of Europe, 304
Books in Print 1973, 305
Books in Print Supplement, 1972-1973, 305
British Books in Print, 1973, 306
Business Books in Print 1973, 306
Canadian Reference Sources, 306
The Charles Dickens Encyclopedia, 307
Chicago Negro Almanac and Reference Book, 307
Chicano Bibliography 1973, 308
Children's Books in Print 1973, 308
Coins: An Investor's & Collector's Guide, 309
Collector's Guide to Antique Porcelain, 309

The Common Man Through the Centuries, 310
The Complete Book of Boating, 310
The Complete Book of Coin Collecting, 309
The Complete Encyclopedia of Motorcars 1885 to the Present, 310
Comprehensive Dissertation Index 1861-1972, 311
Compton's Encyclopedia Master Index, 312
Compton's Young Children's Precyclopedia, 312
Concise Encyclopedia of the Middle East, 314
Consultants and Consulting Organizations Directory, 315
Contemporary Games, 315
Dictionary of American Biography Supplement Three 1941-1945, 316
Dictionary of Black Culture, 316
The Dictionary of Foreign Terms in the English Language, 316
Dictionary of Gypsy Life and Lore, 317
A Dictionary of Modern Revolution, 317
A Dictionary of Non-Christian Religions, 317
Dictionary of Prehistoric Indian Artifacts of the American Southwest, 318
The Dictionary of Stamps in Color, 318
Directory of Consumer Protection and Environmental Agencies, 318
Directory of Counseling Services, 1973, 319
Directory of Publishing Opportunities, 319
Discover Historic America, 320
Ebony Pictorial History of Black America, 320
Education, U.S.A., 321
Education Yearbook 1973-74, 321
Eerdmans' Handbook to the Bible, 322
Encyclopaedia of Australia, 323
An Encyclopedia of Chinese Food and Cooking, 323
The Encyclopedia of Dogs, 324
The Encyclopedia of Floristry, 324
Encyclopedia of the Negro in Africa and America, 325
The Encyclopedia of Philosophy, 325
Encyclopedia of Southern Africa, 326
Environmental Atlas of the Greater Anchorage Area Borough, Alaska, 326
Esquire's Handbook for Hosts, 326
Film Literature Index, 327
Film Research, 327

Fine Arts Market Place 73-74, 327
Firearms Encyclopedia, 328
Foreign Affairs 50-Year Index, 328
The Foundation Grants Index 1972, 329
Frank Schoonmaker's Encyclopedia of Wine, 329
Funk & Wagnall's Standard Dictionary of Folklore, Mythology, and Legend, 329
The Gallup Poll: Public Opinion 1935-1971, 330
The Gardener's Basic Book of Trees and Shrubs, 330
A Gardener's Dictionary of Plant Names, 330
The Golden Book Encyclopedia, 331
The Good Housekeeping Illustrated Encyclopedia of Gardening, 331
Great Collectors' Cars, 331
The Great Ideas Today 1973, 332
The Grosset World Atlas, 332
Guide to Current British Journals, 332
Hammond Nature Atlas, 333
Handbook of Austrian Literature, 333
Handbook of English Costume in the Twentieth Century, 1900-1950, 334
Handbook of the World's Religions, 334
Harper's Bible Dictionary, 335
Illustrated Dictionary of Practical Pottery, 335
The Illustrated Library of Science, Nature & Man's Environment, 335
Index to the Contemporary Scene, 336
Index to Literature on the American Indian, 1971, 336
Index to Plays in Periodicals Supplement, 337
International Bibliography of Directories, 337
International Bibliography of the Book Trade and Librarianship, 337
International Bibliography, Information, Documentation, 338
International Bibliography to the Sociology and Psychology of Reading, 338
International Index to Film Periodicals 1972, 338
The International Jewish Encyclopedia, 338
International Organization, 339
International Wine and Food Society's Encyclopedia of Wines, 340
Investment Methods, 340
Latin America in the Nineteenth Century, 341
The Library Journal Book Review 1972, 341

The Life Cycle Library for Young People, 341
Literary and Library Prizes, 342
Literature By and About the American Indian, 342
Living Black American Authors, 342
Man and the Environment, 343
The Middle East and North Africa, 1973-74, 343
Military Aircraft of the World, 344
Military Dress of North America 1665-1970, 344
Motion Picture Directors, 344
Museum Media, 345
The National Directory for the Performing Arts and Civic Centers 1974, 345
National Security Affairs, 346
The Naturalists' Directory, 346
The New Dog Encyclopedia, 346
The New York Times Book Review (1896-1972), 347
The New York Times Book Review Index (1896-1970), 347
New York Times Everyday Reader's Dictionary of Misunderstood, Misused, Mispronounced Words, 347
Paperbound Books in Print with 114,500 Titles, November 1973, 348
Performing Arts Books in Print, 348
Periodicals for School Libraries, 348
Pest Control in Buildings: A Guide to the Meaning of Terms, 349
Pictorial Travel Atlas of Scenic America, 349
Plot Summary Index, 350
Publications of the United Nations System, 350
The Puerto Ricans: An Annotated Bibliography, 350
Ralph Nader Congress Project: Citizens Look at Congress, 351
Rand McNally Popular World Atlas, 351
Record and Tape Reviews Index 1972, 352
Records in Review, 1973 Edition, 352
The Scolma Directory of Libraries and Special Collections on Africa, 352
Selected Guide to Make-It, Fix-It, Do-It-Yourself Books, 353
The Statesman's Year-Book, 353
String Music in Print, 353
Subject Guide to Books in Print 1973, 354
Subject Guide to Children's Books in Print 1973, 308
Subject Guide to Microforms in Print, 1973, 354
Webster's Biographical Dictionary, 354
Webster's New Geographical Dictionary, 354
Webster's Seventh New Collegiate Dictionary, 354
Who Was Who in Florida, 355
Who's Who in Dickens, 355
Who's Who in Shakespeare (Morrow), 355
Who's Who in Shakespeare (Taplinger), 355
Women: Their Changing Roles, 356
Wood Preservation: A Guide to the Meaning of Terms, 349
World Communism: A Handbook, 1918-1965, 356
World Directory of Environmental Education Programs, 356
World Historical Fiction Guide, 357
World of Shakespeare: Animals & Monsters, 357
World of Shakespeare: Plants, 358
The World This Year 1973, 358
World's Great Men of Color, 358
Worldwide Directory of Computer Companies 1973-1974, 359
The Writers' and Artists' Year Book, 1973, 359
The Year Book of Social Policy in Britain 1972, 360
The Year Book of World Affairs 1973, 360
Yearbook of Higher Education 1973/74, 360
Yearbook on International Communist Affairs, 1973, 361
The Young Children's Encyclopedia, 312

BIOGRAPHICAL DICTIONARIES

Article on Biographical Dictionaries, 362

The Academic Who's Who, 365
American Architects Directory, 366
American Authors, 1600-1900, 366
American Men of Science, 366
American Men and Women of Science, 367

Asimov's Biographical Encyclopedia of Science and Technology, 367
Baker's Biographical Dictionary of Musicians, 367
Biographical Directory of the American Congress, 1774-1971, 368
Biographical Directory of Fellows & Members of the American Psychiatric Association as of October 1, 1967, 368
A Biographical Directory of Librarians in the United States and Canada, 368
Biographical Directory of the United States Executive Branch, 1774-1971, 369
The Biographical Encyclopaedia and Who's Who of the American Theatre, 369
The Blue Book, 369
British Authors Before 1800, 370
British Authors of the Nineteenth Century, 370
The Canadian Who's Who With Which is Incorporated Canadian Men & Women of the Time, 370
Celebrity Register, 370
Chambers's Biographical Dictionary, 371
Chambers's Dictionary of Scientists, 371
Composers Since 1900, 371
Concise Dictionary of American Biography, 372
Contemporary Authors, 372
Contemporary Dramatists, 372
Contemporary Novelists of the English Language, 373
Contemporary Poets of the English Language, 373
County Authors Today, 373
Current Biography Yearbook, 373
Dictionary of American Biography, 374
Dictionary of Canadian Biography, 374
A Dictionary of Contemporary American Artists, 375
Dictionary of International Biography, 375
Dictionary of National Biography, 375
Dictionary of Scandinavian Biography, 376
Dictionary of Scientific Biography, 376
Dictionary of South African Biography, 377
A Dictionary of Universal Biography of All Ages and of All People, 377
Directory of American Scholars, 377
Directory of Medical Specialists Holding Certification by American Specialty Boards, 378
Directory of Publishers Cited, 392
European Authors, 1000-1900, 378
Everyman's Dictionary of European Writers, 378
Everyman's Dictionary of Literary Biography, 379
Foremost Women in Communications, 379
Great Composers, 379
The International Who's Who, 380
International Who's Who in Poetry, 1972-1973, 380
The International Year Book and Statesman's Who's Who, 380
The Junior Book of Authors, 380
Leaders in Education, 381
McGraw-Hill Modern Men of Science, 381
More Junior Authors, 1963, 381
National Cyclopedia of American Biography, 382
New Century Cyclopedia of Names, 382
Notable American Women 1607-1950, 383
Popular American Composers, 383
Something About the Author, 383
Third Book of Junior Authors, 381
Twentieth Century Authors, 384
Webster's Biographical Dictionary, 384
Who Was Who, 384
Who Was Who in America, 385
Who Was Who in the USSR, 385
Who's Who, 1973-1974, 385
Who's Who in Advertising, 386
Who's Who in America, 386
Who's Who in American Art, 386
Who's Who in American Politics, 387
Who's Who in the East, 387
Who's Who in Finance and Industry, 388
Who's Who in Government, 388
Who's Who in the Midwest, 388
Who's Who in the South and Southwest, 389
Who's Who in the Theatre, 389
Who's Who in the West, 389
Who's Who in the World, 390
Who's Who of American Women, 390
Women Artists in America, 391
World Who's Who in Science, 391
The World Who's Who of Women, 1973, 391

Reference and Subscription Books Reviews Committee 1972-1974

MRS. JEANETTE SWICKARD, *Librarian, Washington Elementary School, School District 65, Evanston, Illinois (Chairman)*

RUTH E. AHL, *Science and Technology Librarian, University of Wyoming, Laramie, Wyoming*

MRS. ELIZABETH O. BEDIKIAN, *Librarian, Business and Science Division, New Orleans Public Library, New Orleans, Louisiana*

DR. MICHAEL J. BELICA, *Coordinator, Instructional Media Program, Northeastern Illinois University, Chicago, Illinois*

LYNNE M. BIRLEM, *Librarian, Quincy High and Vocational Technical Schools, Quincy, Massachusetts*

MRS. LESLIE BJORNCRANTZ, *Curriculum Librarian, Northwestern University Library, Evanston, Illinois*

DOROTHY L. BRISCOE, *Chief of User Service, Evergreen State College Library, Olympia, Washington*

WANDA Z. BROCKMAN, *Head, Literature, Language, Religion and Philosophy Department, Seattle Public Library, Seattle, Washington*

BARBARA J. BROWN, *Head of Reference and Public Service, Washington and Lee University Library, Lexington, Virginia*

BERNICE BRUNER, *Chief, Division of Work with Schools and Children, Evansville Public Library, Evansville, Indiana*

MARTHA A. BUCHER, *Head, Industry and Science Division, Dayton and Montgomery County Public Library, Dayton, Ohio*

ELEANOR BUIST, *90 LaSalle Street, New York, New York*

DR. LORENE S. BYRON, *Assistant Professor, School of Library Service, Atlanta University, Atlanta, Georgia*

DR. RAY L. CARPENTER, *Associate Professor, School of Library Science, University of North Carolina, Chapel Hill, North Carolina*

xi

DR. JACK A. CLARKE, *Professor, University of Wisconsin Library School, Madison, Wisconsin*

DR. TERENCE CROWLEY, *Associate Professor, Department of Library Science University of Toledo, Toledo, Ohio*

JACK DICKEY, *Physics Librarian, University of Iowa Libraries, Iowa City, Iowa*

DR. JOHN J. FARLEY, *Dean, School of Library Science, State University of New York, Albany, New York*

DOROTHY FIELD, *Reference Librarian, Science and Technology Department, Indianapolis Public Library, Indianapolis, Indiana*

CHARLES A. GARDNER, *Director of Libraries, Hastings College Library, Hastings, Nebraska*

HERMINE S. GOLDSMITH, *Librarian, Business and Science Department, St. Louis Public Library, St. Louis, Missouri*

RUTH M. HADLOW, *Coordinator, Work with Children, Cleveland Public Library, Cleveland, Ohio*

FRANCES H. HALL, *Librarian, Law Library, University of Illinois, Champaign, Illinois*

MRS. VERDA R. HANSBERRY, *Head, Circulation Services, Seattle Public Library, Seattle, Washington*

PATRICIA A. HENNING, *Research for Better Schools, Inc., Philadelphia, Pennsylvania*

PATRICIA HOGAN, *Head, Public Services, Schaumburg Township Public Library Schaumburg, Illinois*

D. RONALD JOHNSON, *Acquisitions Librarian, William Randall Library, Wilmington, North Carolina*

DR. ELLIOTT E. KANNER, *Resources Coordinator, North Suburban Library System, Morton Grove, Illinois*

MRS. ELIZABETH KRAKAUER, *Librarian, Goddard College Library, Plainfield, Vermont*

MARTHA LANDIS, *Reference Librarian, University of Illinois Library, Urbana, Illinois*

RACHEL S. MARTIN, *Reference and Serials Librarian, Furman University Library, Greenville, South Carolina*

GEORGE A. MASTERTON, *Humanities Division, Wayne State University Library, Detroit, Michigan*

MARGUERITE MURRAY, *Coordinator, Children's Services, Montgomery County Department of Public Libraries, Rockville, Maryland*

CHARLES H. NESS, *Assistant Director of Libraries, Pennsylvania State University, University Park, Pennsylvania*

B. JOSEPH O'NEILL, *Supervisor, Reader's Services, Boston Public Library, Boston, Massachusetts*

MRS. MARY Y. PARR, *Associate Professor, St. Johns University, Department of Library Science, Jamaica, New York*

JOYCE E. PECK, *Reference Librarian, Flint Public Library, Flint, Michigan*

CELIA PEPLOWSKI, *Supervisor, Library and Head, Adult Services, Mobile Public Library, Mobile, Alabama*

RICHARD H. PERRINE, *Assistant Librarian for Planning, Rice University, Fondren Library, Houston, Texas*

MRS. IONE PIERRON, *Associate Professor, University of Oregon, School of Librarianship, Eugene, Oregon*

GEORGE PITERNICK, *Professor, University of British Columbia, School of Librarianship, Vancouver, British Columbia, Canada*

EUGENE PRINGLE, *Director, Warner Library, Tarrytown, New York*

CLAIRE PYLE, *Head of Branch Services, Carnegie Library, Pittsburgh, Pennsylvania*

MRS. HELEN G. RENTHAL, *Associate Professor, University of Arizona, Graduate Library School, Tucson, Arizona*

RUTH ANN RICHARDSON, *Head, Adult Services, Cedar Rapids Public Library, Cedar Rapids, Iowa*

ELEANOR ROBINSON, *Head, General Information and Reference Department, Orlando Public Library, Orlando, Florida*

MRS. PAULINE ROBINSON, *Coordinator of Children's Services, Denver Public Library, Denver, Colorado*

MRS. BETSY A. ST. JULIEN, *Assistant Professor, Louisiana State University, Department of Education, Baton Rouge, Louisiana*

LELIA B. SAUNDERS, *Assistant Director, Arlington County Department of Libraries, Arlington, Virginia*

STEWART P. SCHNEIDER, *Associate Professor, Graduate Library School, University of Rhode Island, Kingston, Rhode Island*

VIRGINIA C. SCHWARTZ, *Librarian, Milwaukee Public Library, Milwaukee, Wisconsin*

CAROL E. SELBY, *Head, Humanities Division, Eastern Michigan University Library, Ypsilanti, Michigan*

MRS. ELIZABETH SILVESTER, *Head, Reference Department, McGill University, McLennan Library, Montreal, Quebec, Canada*

BARBARA ANN SIMONS, *Assistant Librarian for Reader Services, Goucher College Library, Towson, Maryland*

MARGARET SMART, *Documents Librarian, Colorado School of Mines Library, Golden Colorado*

MRS. JESSIE CARNEY SMITH, *Head Librarian, Fisk University Library, Nashville, Tennessee*

MRS. JANICE L. STEWART, *Assistant City Librarian, San Diego Public Library, San Diego, California*

RUBY WEAVER, *Coordinator, Adult Services, Houston Public Library, Houston, Texas*

DR. LUCILLE WHALEN, *Associate Dean, School of Library Science, State University of New York, Albany, New York*

MRS. JEAN E. WICHERS, *Associate Professor, California State University, San Jose, California*

DR. WILEY J. WILLIAMS, *Associate Professor, Peabody Library School, Nashville, Tennessee*

DR. RAYMUND F. WOOD, *Associate Professor, University of California, Graduate School of Library Service, Los Angeles, California*

DR. HERBERT C. ZAFREN, *Director of Libraries, Hebrew Union College, Cincinnati, Ohio*

Reference and Subscription Books Guest Reviewers 1972-1974

WILLIAM K. BEATTY, *Librarian, Northwestern University Medical Library, Chicago, Illinois*

MRS. HELEN L. BENNETT, *Reference Librarian, University of Missouri Libraries, Kansas City, Missouri*

MRS. FRANCES NEEL CHENEY, *Associate Director, George Peabody College, Peabody Library School, Nashville, Tennessee*

MRS. HELGA H. EASON, *Head, Community Relations, Miami-Dade Public Library System, Miami, Florida*

NORMAN FINKLER, *Director, Montgomery County Department of Public Libraries, Rockville, Maryland*

ROGER C. GREER, *Professor, Syracuse University, School of Library Science, Syracuse, New York*

DR. RICHARD S. HALSEY, *Associate Professor, State University of New York, School of Library Science, Albany, New York*

HENRY C. HASTINGS, *Head Reference Department, Gary Public Library, Gary, Indiana*

LUCILE HATCH, *Professor, University of Denver, Graduate School of Librarianship, Denver, Colorado*

MARY ANN HENEGHAN, *Regional Administrator, Eastern Massachusetts Regional Library System, Boston, Massachusetts*

MARJORIE E. KARLSON, *Reference Librarian, University of Massachusetts, Amherst, Massachusetts*

KENNETH F. KISTER, *Assistant Director, Palm Beach County Public Library System, West Palm Beach, Florida*

DONALD W. KRUMMEL, *Professor of Library Science, University of Illinois, Urbana, Illinois*

DR. STANLEY T. LEWIS, *Associate Professor, Library Science Department, Queens College, Flushing, New York*

JAY K. LUCKER, *Associate Librarian, Princeton University Library, Princeton, New Jersey*

ALBERT P. MARSHALL, *Dean of Academic Services, Eastern Michigan University, Ypsilanti, Michigan*

RUTH TARLETON POWER, *Librarian and Professor, University of Illinois, Chemistry Library, Urbana, Illinois*

HUGH PRITCHARD, *Reference Librarian, University of New Hampshire Library, Durham, New Hampshire*

MARJORIE L. ROGERS, *Retired Supervisor, Library Services, Cincinnati Public Schools, Cincinnati, Ohio*

†THOMAS S. SHAW, *Retired Professor of Library Science, Louisiana State University, Baton Rouge, Louisiana*

MARGARET R. SHEVIAK, *Associate Professor, Indiana University, Graduate Library School, Bloomington, Indiana*

DR. MARY E. STILLMAN, *Associate Professor, Albright College, Reading, Pennsylvania*

RUTH WALLING, *Associate Librarian, Emory University Library, Atlanta, Georgia*

†*Deceased*

Preface

The 137 reviews, 168 notes and the omnibus article covering 78 biographical tools in this eighth collection of materials originally appearing in *The Booklist,* September 1972-August 1974, are the work of the Reference and Subscription Books Review Committee and its alumni guest reviewers.

This committee of the American Library Association, established in 1926 by the Executive Board, has grown from its original six members to a high of fifty members in 1968. The committee is composed of librarians employed in many types and sizes of libraries in all parts of the United States and Canada. They represent all phases of the library profession, including library administrators, reference, technical service, adult service, children's and young adults' service, and rare-book department librarians, teachers of reference, book selectors, bibliographers, and librarians in schools, universities, and public libraries. Subject specialist librarians in the fields of art, music, science, the social sciences, humanities, and children's and young people's literature also contribute to the work of the Committee.

The Association has charged the Committee "to accumulate information about books sold on the subscription basis and about comparable publications; to prepare reviews and editorial comments about such books for *The Booklist;* to receive reports of questionable sales practices affecting such books and to transmit substantiated facts to such agencies as Better Business Bureaus and the Federal Trade Commission; to publish the findings of these agencies in *The Booklist* when authorized for release; and to act throughout only as an evaluating agency, not as an advisory group."

The Reference and Subscription Books Review Committee's work is confidential. All members participate in the reviewing process, and the reviews are published over the signature of the entire group. Every review represents a consensus, and no review is published until consensus is reached. Final conclusion of every review ends with a concise statement that the work is "recommended" or "not recommended."

Almost all books sold by the subscription method are candidates for the Reference and Subscription Books Review Committee's attention. The Committee also reviews reference works of general interest issued by trade publishers. In considering reference works the Committee defines a reference book as "a book designed by its arrangement and treatment to be consulted for definite items of information rather than to be read consecutively." An exception is multivolumed sets for children; these are often primarily anthologies which resemble young people's encyclopedias in format, method of distribution, and intended clientele.

In general, the Reference and Subscription Books Review Committee reviews books priced at $20 and over. Exceptions may be reviewed at the discretion of the Chairman. The priorities the Committee has adopted for review are based on such factors as general interest, importance of titles, and price to some extent. General English-language encyclopedias are given highest priority, and the Committee comments on every such encyclopedia in print at not longer than five-year intervals. As many as eight or ten members of the Committee may participate actively in the review of one major encyclopedia. When a full-length review is not necessary, as when there is a new edition with very little revision, or possible, in the case of a publisher who refuses to send materials for review, an informational note is published on the encyclopedia. A note may be published to inform prospective purchasers of plans for unusual revision or a new edition of an encyclopedia.

Next in priority are general fact-finding sources such as unabridged dictionaries, biographical reference works, atlases and gazetteers, directories, yearbooks and annuals, and statistical compendia. General bibliographical reference sources and periodical indexes follow in priority, and references confined to a single subject field are given least precedence in assigning reviews. The Committee does not review works so limited in scope or so technical in treatment as to be of use only to the specialist, and it does not review handbooks intended for use by the layman in the sensitive fields of law, health, and medicine. Reference works which except for price qualify for Committee reviews and which are needed by libraries or for home use are sometimes reviewed in an evaluative and descriptive note. These notes may cover almost any type of work. A new publishing house may be the subject of an informational note. In fact, notes may be used to give quick information on almost anything within the scope of the Reference and Subscription Books Review Committee.

After a reference or subscription work has been selected for review and comment, one Committee member is usually assigned primary responsibility for preparation of a review. This primary reviewer must frame his judgments within guidelines contained in *Subscription Books Committee Manual* of procedures. This *Manual* is available to the general public and may be ordered from ALA Publishing Services. It includes information on Committee policies, membership, and reviewing procedures plus a glossary of terms commonly encountered in the publishing industry. Other members who possess relevant subject competencies or who have had experience in the kind of library for which the work has been designed usually assist the primary reviewer in writing a preliminary draft which is submitted to all other members for comment and criticism. Committee policy requires that statements in reviews be documented with supporting evidence in addition to that included in the reviews themselves. Committee comments, dissenting views, and criticisms are carefully considered, and revisions of the preliminary draft are made until the review represents the combined judgment of the Committee. In effect Committee members accept coauthorship of every review which appears in Reference and Subscription Books Reviews. Some distinguished Committee alumni are now serving as guest reviewers whenever a specialized reference book comes up for review in an area where the guest reviewer has a special competence. These guest reviewers have done much to enable the Committee to enlarge its output. Occasionally alumni reviews are signed. All reviews, signed or unsigned, must go through the full Committee procedure and are therefore still consensus reviews.

Reference and Subscription Books Reviews cover as many of the following factors as apply to the particular work: general characteristics, history, scope and treatment, purpose, accuracy, devices for interpreting and making contents readily accessible, format, comparison, defects or points of special excellence, and summary evaluation.

The Committee has developed guidelines for reviewing particular types of references, e.g., atlases, bibliographies, children's sets, dictionaries, and encyclopedias. These guidelines are published in the Committee's *Manual*.

In the two-year period 1972-1974, the sixty-three members who served on the Committee, aided by the twenty-two guest reviewers, evaluated five times the number of titles evaluated in the preceding two-year period, during which the Committee had established the previous all-time high for number of titles reviewed. The Chairman is grateful to the Committee and the alumni guest reviewers for their patience, hard work and warm encouragement during these two very busy years.

MRS. JEANETTE SWICKARD
Chairman
ALA Reference and Subscription Books Review Committee, 1972-1974

Reference and Subscription Books Reviews Committee 1972-1974

Almanac of World Military Power. [By] T. N. Dupuy, Col., U.S. Army, Ret. and Wendell Blanchard, Col., U.S. Army, Ret. 2d ed. Dunn Loring, VA: T. N. Dupuy Associates, in association with R. R. Bowker Co., N.Y., 1972. xii, 373p. 28cm. fabrikoid. $22.50 net, ppd; no discounts.

The first edition of this work was published in 1970. Now, only two years later, a second, revised edition is being published which, as is stated in the Preface, "has been completely revised and updated." The Preface goes on to describe the work as "a compendium of all important information on the strategic situation and defense posture of every nation that exerts any significant military or politico-military influence on world or regional affairs."

The principal author of the work, Trevor Nevitt Dupuy, is well known in the field of military history. He was professor of military history at Harvard and Ohio State University, and is the author of a score of books on various aspects of military history and strategy, several of them in collaboration with Richard Ernest Dupuy, his father, also a retired army officer and military author. T. N. Dupuy's principal works are his *Military History of World War I*, in 12 volumes, and his *Military History of World War II*, in 19 volumes. No information was found on the second author, Wendell Blanchard, save what is given on the title page, that he also is a retired U.S. Army Colonel.

The work is organized geographically, in much the same manner as is *The Statesman's Yearbook* or the *Worldmark Encyclopedia of the Nations*. There are ten major regions (North America, Western Europe, Central and East Asia, etc.) and the pertinent countries are arranged alphabetically under each region. Under each country (the heading for which does not always appear at the top of a page), the nonmilitary information is minimal. A map of the country usually appears near the beginning; then a brief statistical summary entitled "Power Potential Statistics," which includes population, area, gross national product, total active armed forces, annual military expenditure, and some figures on the country's merchant marine and civil aviation.

1

This is followed by a series of paragraphs giving a detailed statistical account of the country's Defense Structure, Politico-Military Policy, Strategic Problems, Military Assistance, and Alliances, in that order. Information for each country concludes with a listing, usually detailed, of the number and organization of the personnel and the number of each type of weapon in the Army, Navy, Air Force, and paramilitary units of the country's defense system.

In addition to the information given for over 100 separate countries, each of the 10 regional divisions of the world is accompanied by an essay called a Regional Survey. These are uniformly divided into paragraphs dealing with Military Geography, Strategic Significance, and Regional Alliance, with a listing of Recent Intra- and Extra-Regional Conflicts. Each Regional Survey also has a full-page map of that region.

At the end of the volume is a 17-page, double-columned Glossary of military terms and acronyms, such as BAC-167 (a British light, ground-attack aircraft), or GOA (a Russian surface-to-air missile). Following this, and concluding the volume, is a three-page, double-columned Index of countries, regions, and international organizations—such as OAS and NATO, which are briefly discussed under the appropriate Regional Survey. This Index includes a few cross-references, such as Brunei (See Malaysia) and Congo (see Zaire); but there is no cross-reference from either England or Great Britain to United Kingdom, nor from Russia to U.S.S.R.

There is no bibliography in the volume; nor is the source given for any item of information. There are no illustrations aside from the maps.

Some potential users of the work might be students of current world affairs, news commentators and announcers, economists, military strategists, Foreign Service Officers, and other persons who have need for extremely detailed, and recent, figures on a specific country's military armament or strength. However, the information given is in many cases no better than that to be found in *The Statesman's Yearbook,* 1972/73 edition. For Ghana, for example, we learn from the book under review that the "Air Force operates over 50 aircraft, including about 10 helicopters." *The Statesman's Yearbook* devotes 7 lines to a detailed enumeration of 47 aircraft, including 15 helicopters—2 Wessex and 3 Whirlwind (British), and 3 Hughes 300 and 7 H-19 (American) models. This is surely more detailed and presumably more accurate than the *Almanac's* generalization. Likewise is information about the Ghanaian Navy. The *Almanac* says there is a force of 1,000 men, operating a total of 12 vessels, including a "maintenance craft." *The Statesman's Yearbook* specifies that in 1971 there were 180 officers and 2,000 ratings (which would be more than double the *Almanac's* figure), and lists 13 vessels, not including a maintenance craft. *The Statesman's Yearbook* also adds four lines of information about the Military Academy of Ghana, no mention of which appears in the *Almanac.*

In the case of a European country, the *Almanac* gives a strength figure of 5,000 troops for Belgium's Navy. *The Statesman's Yearbook* says that as of 1971 there were 335 officers and 4,800 ratings, which is at least 135 more men than the *Almanac's* round figure of 5,000. The listing of the ships in each volume is not quite the same. The *Almanac* lists "5 helicopters" omitted by the *Yearbook,* while the latter lists "13 tugs and harborcraft" omitted by the *Almanac.*

On the whole, the *Almanac* gives somewhat more detailed information as to specific types of military armament and equipment than does *The Statesman's Yearbook,* but minor variations between the figures given, both as to number and type, in the two volumes are fairly frequent.

The maps in the *Almanac* are not its best feature. They are primarily outline maps, usually showing no topography except rivers and islands, and very few place-names. Some maps show lines of human communication but do not indicate whether these are road or rail, and some show no lines of communication at all. The map accompanying the Regional Survey for North America is particularly unfortunate. Plotted on a Mercator projection, it shows only boundaries, omitting place-names. Canada appears as being about three times the size of the United States; and Greenland, if tipped on its side, would stretch from Cape Mendocino, in California, to Nova Scotia, and in width would cover North America from Lake of the Woods to Guatemala. In actuality, as may be seen by using an equal-area projection map, Greenland, if tipped on its side, would reach from Cape Mendocino to about the center of Missouri, and at its greatest width would reach only from Lake of the Woods to about the same point in Missouri.

The country maps are inconsistent in their coverage. Ireland shows all counties, but no railroads; England's map does the reverse. The map of the United States shows political capitals only, omitting major cities and railroads. Most other country maps show principal cities, whether capitals or not, and most show railroads.

The editing and proofreading of the book seem to be of a very high order. Only one minor spelling error was noticed—Commandante for Comandante. A sampling of index items revealed no errors. The type used is easy to read, and there is much white space on the double-columned pages. The volume lies flat when opened; the binding is attractively gold stamped, and appears sturdy.

The principal weakness of the volume seems to be the doubt which may be cast on the reliability of its statistics. No specific authority for any statement appears anywhere in the volume; nor is any statistic dated. The Preface states that the status of each item of information shown is accurate "to the best of our knowledge, as of early 1972." But the very next sentence reads "In those many instances in which up-to-date figures are not available, we have consulted all available sources and then made our own estimates on the basis of trends or projections." Unfortunately the text does not indicate whether the figures shown are verified statistics, rounded figures, or merely shrewd approximations, based on "trends or projections."

Although *Almanac of World Military Power* does contain considerable amounts of information as to specific types and numbers of aircraft, naval vessels, tanks, guns, and other military aspects of various countries, which might be of use to persons requiring such specific information, the deficiencies of the work as a whole seriously impair its value. These deficiencies are chiefly the lack of any citation to sources; the lack of dates for statistics given; the rather inadequate maps; and the fact that the information and the statistics given are frequently no better than, or not even as detailed as, those to be found in a well-established and well-reputed source, *The Statesman's Yearbook*. For these reasons the book cannot be recommended for general purchase by libraries.

(June 15, 1973, p.953)

The American Peoples Encyclopedia: A Modern Reference Work. 20v. New York, Excelsior Trading Corp., [c1973, c1962-1972]. illus. ports. maps. diagrs. 27cm. pyroxylin-coated tyvek $259.50; library discount available.
ISBN 0-7172-0304-2.

The American Peoples Encyclopedia has been reviewed four times in *Subscription Books Bulletin* and its successor, *The Booklist and Subscription Books Bulletin* (April 1949, Oct. 1953, July 15, 1961, and Jan. 1, 1965). The first review recommended the 1948 edition as a "moderate priced, useful although not exhaustive encyclopedia." In the second review, the 1952 edition was recommended "for public and school libraries with limited funds and for libraries desiring a supplementary reference set," but because of considerable price increases to individual purchasers, the review concluded that this edition could "no longer be recommended as a moderately priced set for home use."

The third review did not recommend the 1960 edition, because "revision effective during the first few years [had] decreased to the extent that the encyclopedia no longer [lived] up to the publisher's claim of continuous revision." The 1965 review noted that because of numerous improvements the 1964 edition was recommended for homes and libraries as a "moderately priced, useful, though not exhaustive encyclopedia." The present review will be based, to some extent, on a comparison of the 1973 and 1964 editions.

The American Peoples Encyclopedia was first published under its present title by Spencer Press in 1948. While based on *Nelson's Encyclopedia*, it was so thoroughly revised as to be essentially a new work. It was distributed by Sears, Roebuck and Company through catalog order. In August 1961 Grolier Incorporated acquired the encyclopedia from Spencer Press. In 1973 the copyright passed to the Excelsior Trading Corporation, a Grolier affiliate, which supplies books to independent jobbers and distributors. By arrangement with Excelsior, Grolier has responsibility for revision of the encyclopedia.

The new Introduction declares that *The American Peoples Encyclopedia* is revised annually, and it is a thoughtfully selected and carefully edited compendium of information designed to be helpful to the present-day nonspecialist. In a compilation of revision information submitted to the Reference and Subscription Books Review Committee, showing changes since the 1964 edition, the publishers claim the audience to be from advanced students in upper elementary years to those in high school and college and to the lay adult.

The set is characterized by numerous brief, general, biographical, and geographical articles; there are more than 34,500 articles on 11,125 pages. Nevertheless, the 18-page *South America* article, the 20-page one for *Anatomy*, and the 13-page coverage of *Brazil* are examples of lengthy treatment.

The editorial staff for *The American Peoples Encyclopedia* has been considerably changed from the one for the 1964 edition; yet the staff continues to reflect a variety of experience. Editor in chief since 1961, Edward Humphrey, holds a Ph.D. from Columbia University and is a former managing editor of the now defunct *Richards Topical Encyclopedia* and former executive editor of *The Book of Knowledge*. Managing editor Nicholas G. Demos is a former editor of the *Catholic Encyclopedia for School and Home*. Art director Robert K. Reddy studied commercial art and the fine arts at Ohio State University and designed both trade and textbooks at Holt, Rinehart and Winston. Lavinia P. Dudley, full-time consultant to the editors, formerly was editor in chief of *Encyclopedia Americana*, Grolier's major adult encyclopedia. The number of advisers in special areas has grown from six to ten. Among the advisers are Solomon Berson, Chief, Department of Medicine, Mt. Sinai School of Medicine, New York for medicine and Robert B. Downs, Dean Emeritus of Library Administration, University of Illinois-Urbana for library science. Some 1,700 signed contributors—about 450 more than in the 1964 edition—are represented. One hundred eighty-three contributors wrote more than one article; these specific articles, however, are not named in the Contributors' list. Among the new contributors are more than 100 persons from countries outside the United States and 25 Nobel prizewinners. Included are Thomas P. Abernethy *(Aaron Burr)*, John Bakeless *(Daniel Boone, Nathan Hale)*, Indira Gandhi *(Rabindranath Tagore)*, Allardyce Nicoll *(William Congreve)*, Mark Schorer *(Sinclair Lewis)*, and Seiji Yamaga *(Tokyo)*.

The 1973 edition has increased its type size slightly; this task required refilming and replating the entire encyclopedia. Page size has also been increased so that there is no loss in the amount of information on each page. Like the 1964 edition, this set is attractively bound; the green sturdite is embossed with gold lettering, and there is a simple gold design on the spine. The volumes are, however, tightly bound and do not lie flat when opened. The paper is of good quality.

Black-and-white illustrations, favorably commented upon in the 1965 review, are improved and are brighter, and more detail is visible than before. The total number of illustrations is reported by the publisher as 13,200 (15,444 in the 1964 edition), of which 11,875 (14,074 in 1964) are black and white and 1,325 (1,370 in 1964) are in color. Excellent new color illustrations have been added to some 20 articles including *Automobile, Canada, China, Chinese Art, Moon, South America,* and *Space Exploration.* Three detailed transparent sections have been added: *Human Body, Cell,* and *Rotary Cylinder Engine.* In spite of this, the decrease in the number of colored illustrations is regrettable when the trend in encyclopedias is toward more colored illustrative material.

Volume 20 contains the Atlas section of 420 pages (384 in 1964). The 139 maps are by Hammond. Many occupy two pages, and many are revised. One hundred seventeen are in full color; there are only two historical maps: U.S. and Canadian territorial growth, both in black and white. New topographic maps of the continents have been added. The other maps continue to be essentially political, showing international boundaries, internal administrative units, place-names (even very small places), and canals, railways, highways, scale and elevations. As before, the maps are bled to the edge of the page, with place-name index and up-to-date 1970 U.S. census population statistics on the reverse side. The maps are linked with the text through the Index and by references in the appropriate articles. The practice of referring the encyclopedia user to the atlas for most population statistics has been continued, the publisher states, as the most utilitarian solution to the problem of keeping up with thousands of population changes every year. Exceptions are the statistics for major geographical areas, states, and great cities.

In the Reference and Subscription Book Review Committee's 1965 review the addition of the Index in volume 20 received particular praise for increasing the reference value of the set. That review did, however, point out certain shortcomings. Among these were failure to list all pertinent articles under a major topic entry, such as geology, mathematics, and philosophy and insufficient citations to biographical articles of persons prominent in particular fields, such as American art and architecture. Examination of these and other Index entries shows that improvements have been made. The Index has about 126,000 page citations, an increase of some 26,000 since 1964 for some 34,500 articles. However, a spot check does reveal a few incorrect page citations.

According to the publisher, bibliographies accompany 2,736 articles—only about 8 percent—in the 1973 edition (1,974 in 1964). Inspection of the volumes points out many articles without bibliographies and others whose bibliographies are not up to date.

A sampling of articles was made, and comments will follow on some scientific and technical articles, some for language and literature, some in the social sciences, and some of a general nature. While the scientific and technical articles examined are often brief but accurate, they vary as to recency of information and the inclusion of bibliographies. They are the work of almost 600 contributors who are listed. Among them are two Nobel prizewinners: Irving Langmuir, who was awarded the prize in chemistry in 1932, and Francis H. C. Crick, Nobelist in physiology and medicine, 1962. Langmuir contributed the information on surface tension and Crick wrote on the genetic code. There are also advisers in special areas such as medicine, oceanography, and biochemistry.

There are six pages on human anatomy contributed by Dr. Albert I. Farbman, Associate Professor, Northwestern University School of Medicine. The article covers the systems of the human body in some detail. Included are the respiratory, cardiovascular, urinary, reproductive, and digestive systems. The material is well-written; the sentences are brief, and the vocabulary is intended for the intelligent layman. Preceding the article is a series of colored drawings showing the skin layers, the muscles (both anterior and posterior views), the bones, and the glands. Transparent sections are included on the respiratory, digestive, circulatory, and nervous systems.

The Index has 22 entries under *anatomy*. Eleven of the articles are signed. *See also* references direct the reader to *embryology* and its 5 entries and further to various organs of the body. There are, for instance, 33 entries under *eye* and 5 entries under the word *foot*.

The four-paragraph *Quasar* article is accurate. A second citation under *quasar* in the Index refers the reader to *Cosmology*, and quasars are mentioned briefly there.

Diesel Power is extensive, well-written, and accurate. It contains an insert showing detailed drawings on the design, construction, and operation of diesel engines. Also included are a brief glossary and a transparent section with cutaway views of a heavy-duty diesel engine. The article itself is not signed, but the insert is signed. A brief bibliography with only pre-1961 titles is appended.

Information on the Miami Conservancy District in the article on Dayton, Ohio is well presented. The district, built after the great flood of the Ohio River basin in 1913, is an example of effective flood control by local enterprise. This type of material illustrates the wide range of subject matter in *American Peoples*.

A useful insert under the heading *Comparative Anatomy* contains transparencies on the anatomy of the frog and the earthworm. These topics are often found in the high school science curriculum.

To test the coverage of *The American Peoples Encyclopedia* in literature and language, the articles *United States Literature* and *English Literature* were examined thoroughly; other literary subjects were examined more briefly. This examination revealed omissions in coverage, out-of-date material, and outdated critical judgments and bibliographies.

Random examples emphasizing social science and general topics suggest the need for greater consistency.

Commendably, the article *Nixon, Richard Milhous* is current to at least January 27, 1973, the date of the Vietnam cease-fire. The cease-fire is also mentioned in *Vietnam* and *Army, U.S.*, but neither article pinpoints the public's discouragement with the Vietnamese conflict. *Space Exploration* includes Apollo 17 (launched Dec. 1972) in a table. *Astronautics*, however, records only through Apollo 12 (Nov. 1969). *National Aeronautics and Space Administration (NASA)* is unchanged from the 1964 edition.

John Gardner, now active in Common Cause, the citizens' lobby, is included only in a list of Lyndon B. Johnson's cabinet, and there is no mention of Common Cause. The article on John V. Lindsay speaks of his first term as New York's mayor, but makes no reference to his re-election in 1969. In *Los Angeles* the Feb. 9, 1971 earthquake is mentioned. *Abortion*, now signed, refers to a 1970 New York statute, but not the U.S. Supreme Court decision on Jan. 22, 1973 nor the pros and cons of abortion. The text of *Abstract Art* is that of the 1964 edition; the bibliography has added a 1964 title and dropped a 1955 one. *Adoption* says nothing of unmarried parents. *National League* is current to 1962, although its Eastern and Western divisions and those of the American League are noted in *Baseball* up to 1969. There is no separate article on the American League. *Baseball Hall of Fame and Museum, National*, (the next article after *Baseball*), lists members only through 1970.

Still other examples of the inconsistency of updating social science and general articles may be cited. Ralph Nader, consumer protection, and snowmobile are not included in the 1973 edition of *The American Peoples Encyclopedia*. *Smoke Abatement* does not specifically cite any occurrence later than 1960, referring to the membership of the Air Pollution Control Association. *Sociology* is the 1964 article with a shorter bibliography. *Supreme Court of the United States* cites or refers to no case after 1964 (its bibliography has a 1963 imprint as the latest); yet the article *Censorship* refers to its 1970 cases. *Supreme Court* also includes photographs of the current court, but only four of the justices have separate articles. *Soilless Gardening* no longer includes a bibliography. While George S. McGovern's candidacy for president is included in his biography, Thomas F. Eagleton and Shirley Chisholm are not mentioned anywhere, and Sargent Shriver is represented only as author of the article *Peace Corps*. *Election* is silent on the 1972 elections and its map of electoral votes by state is incorrect.

The 1971 deaths of A. A. Berle, Jr., and Igor Stravinsky are recorded; those of Pitirim Sorokin in 1968 and Dean Acheson and Ralph Bunche in 1971 are not. The article *Bangladesh, People's Republic of* is not indexed, and the Atlas lists only Pakistan. The bibliography with *Adams, John Quincy* does not include Allan Nevins (ed.), *The Diary of John Quincy Adams* (1951).

Further instances of lack of currentness include the following: the chart on work stoppages in *Strike* covers 1940 to 1962. The tabulation of seating capacity of major stadiums in the United States is out of date. "World Production of Important Natural Resources" refers to 1961 or 1960 data. No table in *Accidents* is later than 1960, and *Advertising* shows average 1963 rates. *Air Transportation* makes a 1970 reference to skyjacking but its tables depict 1962 information. *Aluminum* tables are 1961 or 1962. The figures in *Social Security* are up to 1967. For most categories in *Disaster* the latest date is 1962 or 1963. *Crime* includes only one undated chart —"Crime Clocks" showing the average occurrences of property and violent crimes—and no other statistics.

The encyclopedia uses cross-references both in the body of the articles and immediately following them. For instance, *Diesel Power* contains cross-references to *Electric Power, Bus Transportation, Motor Truck, Motorboat, Motorship, Ship, Submarine,* and *Power*. A one-page article *DNA* refers the reader to *Amino Acids, Gene and Heredity*.

In summary, *The American Peoples Encyclopedia* only partially achieves its purpose of providing information that is helpful to the present-day nonspecialist from upper elementary level to lay adult. The encyclopedia may be satisfactory for coverage of historical topics and those where new interpretations have not been made, but it unevenly meets the needs of users for current up-to-date coverage of names, events, and statistics. Revision in page layout has been extremely scanty for the last eight years. Not recommended.
(July 15, 1974, p.1206)

American Reference Books Annual 1970- . 1st, 2d, 3d ed. Bohdan S. Wynar, ed. Littleton, Colorado, Libraries Unlimited, Inc., [c1970] 2v. 205, 210p., [c1971] xxi, 603p., [c1972] xxiv, 712p. 24cm. cloth $19.75 a volume; to libraries, 10 percent discount.

American Reference Books Annual is a classified guide intended to serve as an "annual inventory and evaluation of reference materials published in this country." It provides a complete bibliographic listing and, in most cases, a review of 1,476 titles in the first edition, 1,837 in the second, and 1,851 in the third. No criteria are given for selection, and some of the books are doubtful inclusions among reference materials, e.g., *Ann Ladbury's Book of Dressmaking* (South Brunswick, N. J.: Barnes, 1971) and *Sewing Children's Clothing Made Easy* (New York: Doubleday, 1971). The titles are primarily those of new books of publishers in the United States, but other types of publications are represented, e.g., annuals, new editions, reprints, and imports. Publications of the University of Toronto Press appear in the third edition, and some books from publishers in other countries are found in all editions when the foreign publisher has an exclusive distributor in the United States.

The editor, Bohdan S. Wynar, president of Libraries Unlimited, is the author or editor of a number of library publications, e.g., *Introduction to Bibli-*

ography and Reference Work and *Studies in Librarianship* (Graduate School of Librarianship, University of Denver). Wynar acknowledges the assistance of several subject specialists in the Introduction to the first edition, and shares credit with subject section editors in the second and third editions. These later editions also include a list of contributors (110 and 155 respectively) most of whom are identified as librarians or faculty members, mostly at library schools.

The first edition consists of two separately paged volumes. Title pages have as subtitles: volume 1, General Reference, Social Sciences, History, Economics, Business; volume 2, Fine Arts, Humanities, Science and Engineering. The Tables of Contents list 38 subject chapters, each of which is subdivided under more specific subjects or by type of reference work, i.e., bibliographies, dictionaries, handbooks, and indexes, for a total number of 704 subsections. The second and third editions, which are similarly arranged under subject chapters and numerous subdivisions, are each contained in one volume with the subtitle, "The single permanent record of reference books published in the United States January through December 1970 (1971 in the third edition)." This is not an entirely accurate statement since each edition includes some imprints from the previous years. It must be noted, however, that books of a previous year that arrive too late for inclusion in the current edition are reviewed in the subsequent edition.

Within the subsections of each subject chapter the books are arranged alphabetically by main entry. Information for each book includes, in addition to the full imprint, the price (with a very few exceptions when this was not available from the publisher), paging, and the following where applicable: illus. (col.), ports., maps, series note, bibliog., and index. The Library of Congress and International Standard Book Numbers are generally given, and the document number is included for United States and United Nations publications. This information is followed, in practically all entries, by an annotation and, in some entries, by a citation to one or more published reviews of the book. Reviews published as recently as three or four months after the first of each year covered by the *Annual* are cited. Reviews are cited in a notation headed by "R:" followed by the periodical title or its abbreviation, the date, and page. A table of abbreviations giving the full title of the periodicals represented by initials is in the first edition only. Citations are generally to reviews in library periodicals, but in a few instances there are references to other types of publications.

The annotations, which vary in length from one sentence to several pages, average about 150 words. Those in the first edition are unsigned, but many in the later editions are attributed to either the editors or one of the contributors. The annotations are very uneven in character and quality. Some are purely descriptive. Others are more or less critical and may include comments on the book's usefulness, or comparisons with similar publications, or a reference to other sources of information in the work under review or in Winchell, *Guide to Reference Books* and supplements (Chicago: Amer. Lib. Assoc., 1967-   ) or Walford, *Guide to Reference Material* and supplements (London: Lib. Assoc., 1959-   ). The statement, "Our reviews do not contain specific recommendations for purchase," appears in the Introduction to the first edition, but not in the second and third editions, in which some annotations conclude with a recommendation or a negative observation.

American Reference Books Annual has an author-title-subject Index. Each volume of the first edition has its separate Index referring to page numbers in the text. All text entries in the second and third editions are numbered consecutively, and their indexes refer to entry numbers. A check of 200 entries in the third edition Index reveals no errors. These indexes are made more compact than those of the first edition by use of smaller but still legible type, three columns to the page rather than two, abbreviations in titles, and initials instead of full first names of authors. Subject entries in the indexes of the second and third editions are emphasized by darker type. There are no cross-references. A cumulative index for the first five editions is planned for inclusion in the fifth edition. Volume 2 of the first edition includes a list of publishers and their addresses, but this does not appear in the later editions.

Coverage of *American Reference Books Annual* overlaps that of Winchell's *Guide to Reference Books*, 8th ed. 3d supp. (Chicago: Amer. Lib. Assoc., 1972) only to a limited extent. *American Reference Books Annual* excludes many foreign books which appear in *Winchell*. It includes many titles which are highly specialized and would be of marginal interest in most libraries, but might serve as unique reference sources in certain types of libraries, e.g., *Cut Glass Handbook and Price Guide, Export Directory of Portugal, Indexes to Irish Wills, Manual of Diseases of the Cornea, My First Picture Dictionary*, and *Servicing Electronic Organs.*

The typeface is clear; the paper is nonglare, and the margins are adequate in all editions. In the first and second editions the title in each entry is in boldface. That device is dropped in the third edition where the author's surname (or the title in title entries) is emphasized by printing in boldface caps. The cover, bound with Smyth sewing, appears to be sturdy, and pages stay flat when the book is open. The initials *ARBA* replace the title on the spine of the second and third editions.

Without a clear definition of the term "reference" the editorial claim that this work serves as an annual inventory of reference materials published in the United States may be accurate, since the number of entries constitutes the most complete single listing of such titles. It is almost 80 percent greater than the combined (overlapping) entries of reference books in a year's publication of *Choice, Library Journal, RQ*, and *Wilson Library Bulletin*, and some of the titles in *American Reference Books Annual* do not appear in *Winchell* or other listings of reference works. The claim for evaluation of these materials is not so well founded, since the annotations do not necessarily provide reliable appraisals. Nor are they free of editorializing. However, the extensive coverage of reference works with their complete bibliographic descriptions and the annotations, with or without a critical opinion, give *American Reference Books Annual* a unique usefulness as a selection tool. Since change seems to be a characteristic of the publication (as indicated by differences among the three editions), the usefulness of future editions may vary. Recommended. *(Jan. 15, 1973, p.453)*

The Barnhart Dictionary of New English Since 1963. Edited by Clarence L. Barnhart, Sol Steinmetz, and Robert K. Barnhart. Bronxville and New York, Barnhart/Harper & Row, [c1973]. 512p. 24cm. cloth $12.95; to schools and libraries, usual discount.
ISBN 0-06-010223-3.

The Barnhart Dictionary of New English Since 1963 is intended "to be a companion to standard English dictionaries and to bring them up to date." It provides detailed information on more than 5,000 new words and meanings "which have come into the common or working vocabulary of the English-speaking world during the period from 1963 to 1972."

Coeditors of the dictionary are the well-known lexicographer Clarence Barnhart; Sol Steinmetz, new words editor of *The World Book Dictionary* and biography editor of the first edition of *Who's Who in World Jewry;* and Robert K. Barnhart, coeditor of the revised edition of *The World Book Dictionary* and coauthor (with Clarence Barnhart) of the *Let's Read Series* of readers and workbooks. Under their direction the dictionary was "staff-produced by the professional and lexicographical department that produces the Thorndike-Barnhart school dictionaries and *The World Book Dictionary.*"

The editors were assisted by "an international advisory committee of distinguished linguistic scholars, librarians, and teachers."

Entries for the dictionary were selected from the quotation files maintained by Clarence Barnhart for the purposes of compiling and revising the Thorndike-Barnhart dictionaries and *The World Book Dictionary,* published in conjunction with *The World Book Encyclopedia.* For the years covered by the dictionary, these files contained over a million quotations collected from United States, British, and Canadian newspapers, periodicals, and books. The editors have attempted to include "the majority of new terms that are approaching the center of the language" and have based their selection on the criteria of "lexicality, frequency, topical interest, and similar properties." The selection includes new words, new meanings for older words, and older words which, since 1963, "have suddenly emerged from obscurity." The last named category consists largely of "technical terms of the sciences which have come to influence our technologically based modern society." "Highly technical or scientific terms used largely in professional work," have, however, been excluded along with "dialect and slang expressions of limited currency, and nonce or figurative terms created for ephemeral use."

Entries are arranged in letter-by-letter order, and all entries, including abbreviations, acronyms, and shortened words are included in a single alphabet. Definitions are followed by one or more quotations illustrating the usage of the word or meaning. Etymologies are provided for "those words whose forms or meanings call for some explanation . . ." The editors have availed themselves of the etymological brackets "to insert . . . information that concerns changes in the meaning and use of words that are already part of the language."

Footnotes (indicated by an arrow) are used "to separate editorial comment from definitions or to give ancillary information of interest about usage or other matters." Cross-references are provided to relate variant spellings and forms, to relate derived forms to their root forms, to relate scientific and technical terms to correlative terms, and to direct the user to entries providing supplementary information. The dictionary proper is preceded by 14 pages of explanatory notes which discuss the function and scope of the dictionary in considerable detail and provide guidance in its use.

The editors have sought "to shift the emphasis from the traditional dictionary definition to the quotation, which is . . . the basis of the definition," and have, accordingly, "tried to keep the definitions simple, generally relying on carefully selected quotations to supply details and complex explanations that in standard dictionaries would be covered in the definition."

A broad sampling of the entries in the dictionary appears to substantiate this claim. If the meaning of a word is adequately conveyed by the quotation, no definition is given and "the reader is instructed to 'See the quotation for the meaning.'" This practice is confined to a relatively small number of entries. The information supplied by the quotation is sometimes amplified by a note. In other instances, the user is directed to the quotation for additional facts which will help to clarify the definition.

Definitions for entries having more than one meaning are listed in the order of their greatest frequency. If the various definitions appear to be equally frequent, the meanings are given in chronological order. Chronological listing is also used when the editors wish to show the semantic development of a word.

The illustrative quotations are considerably longer than those usually found in standard dictionaries and range up to a paragraph in length. This method of bringing out the meaning of a word through its "environment" is especially helpful in the treatment of new words for which the reader may not be able to provide an enlarged context through previous association. The quotations have been selected to accomplish the following: to show the word's use in an actual context and a natural environment; to furnish additional details about meaning or connotation of the word that the definition cannot properly supply; to call attention to the range of use through several quotations from different sources, times, and places; to indicate the type of writing in which the word appears by the title and often the name of the author of the article, letter, poem, etc.

The citations which identify the sources of the quotations are sufficiently detailed to enable the user to locate the quotations in the works cited without consulting a bibliography. The names of publications are spelled out and dates are given in full; references to articles include titles and authors' names when these are likely to be helpful in understanding the context.

Pronunciation is given only for hard or unfamiliar words. In accordance with the recommendation of the Editorial Advisory Committee, a "broad transcription" of the symbols of the International Phonetic Association has been used to indicate pronunciation. While there may have been valid reasons for adopting this system (e.g., the editors' statement that it "should facilitate the use of this dictionary throughout the world"), the average American user will find it unfamiliar and will need to make frequent use of the pronunciation key. Unfortunately, the key is printed only on pages 27 and 28 and is not easily located.

Except for the label *slang* traditional usage labels are not employed in *The Barnhart Dictionary of New English*. Additional information on usage is, however, conveyed through the quotations and the sources from which they are drawn as well as through footnotes. The Speech Area Labels *U.S.* and *British* "are used to signal that the labeled term is associated primarily with the indicated region," and "wherever possible, equivalent or corresponding British and American terms are contrasted in definitions, as under *postcode* and *zip code*." Foreign words which are likely to be used intentionally for effect in place of their English equivalents are labeled with their country of origin.

One could no doubt assemble a list of new words and meanings which have been omitted from *The Barnhart Dictionary of New English,* but such an exercise would be pointless in view of the editors' admission that the dictionary is merely a sampling based on the selection criteria previously noted. The publishers' statement that "the record of new English, except for sporadic examples, in most general dictionaries now available to the public" terminated with the publication of *Webster's Third New International Dictionary* in 1963, cannot, however, go unchallenged. Such a statement ignores the special attention devoted to new words in the *Random House Dictionary* (New York: Random House, 1966) and *The American Heritage Dictionary* (Boston: Houghton Mifflin, 1969), both of which were entirely new works. The most recently revised of the standard desk dictionaries, *Webster's New Collegiate (The Booklist,* Nov. 1, 1973), includes more than 20,000 new words and meanings which have come into use since 1963. This is four times the number covered in *The Barnhart Dictionary of New English.* The unique contribution of *The Barnhart Dictionary* lies not in the number of new words which it includes but in the detailed information and extended quotations provided for the editors' selection of significant new vocabulary.

Occasional inaccuracies in the definitions were noted. One might question the definition of *intersex* as "another name for unisex" in spite of the fact that *Time* apparently does not distinguish between the two words in the quotation used to illustrate this definition. The prefixes "uni-" and "inter-" have different meanings and cannot be used interchangeably.

Similarly, defining *street theater* merely as another name for "guerilla theater" ("short antiwar or antiestablishment plays ... in any public place where an audience will gather") conveys a much too narrow conception of the former.

An attractive page layout and legible typeface facilitate use of the dictionary. Entries are printed in boldface, and the use of hanging indention makes them easy to locate. The reinforced binding in dark blue cloth should be able to withstand considerable use. Inner margins are three-quarters of an inch in width.

The Barnhart Dictionary of New English is a valuable source of information on some 5,000 new words and meanings profusely enlarged upon by fully documented quotations. It is recommended for purchase by individuals and by public, school, and academic libraries. *(May 15, 1974, p.1011)*

Bowker's Medical Books in Print, 1973; Subject Index, Author Index, Title Index. New York & London, R. R. Bowker Co., [c1973]. 806p. 28cm. Case-D $24.50 plus shipping and handling. ISBN 0-8352-0632-7.

Bowker's Medical Books in Print, 1973 is another addition to Bowker's in-print series of subject bibliographies reprinted from *Books in Print* and *Subject Guide to Books in Print*. The Committee reviewed the first in-print spin-off, *Scientific and Technical Books in Print* in the Nov. 1, 1973 issue of *The Booklist* and recommended it for libraries active in technology and the physical and biological sciences. *Business Books in Print, 1973* was covered in a note published in the Dec. 15, 1973 *Booklist,* and subsequent spin-offs will be reviewed as they come off the press.

Medical Books in Print lists some 24,500 titles available from about 950 publishers and is organized in four sections in this sequence: Subject Index, Author Index, Title Index, and Publisher Index. It was prepared by the R. R. Bowker Company's Department of Bibliography in collaboration with the Publication System Unit of the Xerox Education Group, and it was produced from records stored on magnetic tape, edited by computer programs, and set in type by computer-controlled photocomposition.

The publisher's general policy was to list books which are available in the United States in medicine, dentistry, veterinary medicine, nursing, psychiatry, psychology, sociological aspects of health, scientific and technical books directly related to these fields, and "some titles which are not scientific or technical but which might still be of interest to the professional in health sciences." Among the authorities used to help define the scope of the work were the National Library of Medicine Catalogs and Subject Headings, the New York Academy of Medicine Catalog, and the Catalog of the Columbia University Medical Library. The editors gave Dr. Vera Ortynsky, Head, Medical Cataloging Section, Columbia University Medical Library, special acknowledgement for her aid in determining the scope of the subject field as well as the inclusion of specific titles.

ALA Rules for Filing Catalog Cards (Chicago: American Library Assoc., 1969) was the guideline for the arrangement of entries. Entry information in each of the indexes includes author, coauthor, editor, coeditor, translator, title, price, imprint, and year of publication. If warranted and available, additional data may include publisher's order number, edition, number of volumes, series, illustration, type of binding if other than cloth over boards, International Standard Book Number, and distributor if different from publisher. Most prices are list prices; lack of uniformity among publishers' catalogs precluded indicating trade discounts. Tentative prices and short discounts are indicated.

According to the publisher, each title included was searched in the catalogs of the Library of Congress so that the Subject Index of this work might follow Library of Congress headings. The editors recognized that although the Library of Congress updates its subject headings constantly, it does not apply such updating retroactively to cards previously issued. So, for all books whose titles were indicative of specific content, the editors state that they updated headings and cross-references to conform with the latest supplement of the seventh edition of *Subject Headings Used in the Dictionary Catalogs of the Library of Congress*. Both *see* and *see also* references are included.

In the Author Index, cross references lead from joint authors, editors, etc., to the main entry. The Title Index includes nondistinctive titles, e.g., *Introduction to . . . , Proceedings of . . . ,* and *Principles of . . . .* The Publisher's Index includes publisher or distributor abbreviations used within the entries, name in full, complete address, and International Standard Book Numbers. The list of publishers includes not only the expected commercial publishers and associations like the American Hospital Association but also such associations as the National Council for the Social Studies and the American Philosophical Society, and such sources as City Light Books and Company & Sons (2940 Seventh St., Berkeley, CA). An adequate three-page statement preceding the Subject Index describes how to use the book.

The cross-references in the Subject Index and in the Title Index seem thorough and reliable. But the editors' use and updating of LC subject headings are less reliable and also point up the difficulties of defining boundaries of specialized indexes.

The format of *Medical Books in Print* is good. Each page has three columns, adequate margins and entry indentions, and running heads at the top. The print is small but clear; the paper is non-glare; and the volume is well bound and lies flat when opened.

Medical Books in Print, 1973, despite some weaknesses in its choice of subject headings, provides convenience and usefulness similar to other titles in Bowker's in-print series. It is recommended to those libraries needing this kind of specialized source. *(Jan. 1, 1974, p.451)*

Britannica Junior Encyclopaedia For Boys and Girls. Prepared under the supervision of the eds. of Encyclopaedia Britannica. 15v. Chicago, William Benton, Publisher, Encyclopaedia Britannica, Inc. [c1973, 1934, 1937-38, 1940-49, 1950-59, 1960-69, 1970-72]. illus. (part col.). maps. charts. diagrs. drawings. 25cm. Holliston special sturdite to schools and libraries, $109.50 plus shipping charge $3.50, total price $113; (two or more sets $99.50 each plus shipping charge $3.50, total price $103).

Britannica Junior is expressly designed "to provide an interesting, easily understood reference source for the elementary school student." Its 15 volumes contain over 4,100 main articles arranged alphabetically letter-by-letter and more than 24,000 brief entries in the Index volume. The coverage is broad, with notable emphasis on science and social studies.

Originally adapted from the 8-volume *Weedon's Modern Encyclopedia* (c1931) and expanded to 12 volumes, *Britannica Junior* reached 15 volumes in 1947, with content revision yearly since then.

Marvin Martin, a staff editor for the 1966 edition, is general editor of the 1973 edition. The Editorial Advisory Committee consists mainly of professors and teachers from the University of Chicago and the University Laboratory School, with representation also from Northeastern Illinois University, the Chicago Board of Education, and the Alessandro Volta School (Chicago). C. R. MacLeod is editorial advisor for Canada. Volume 1 contains an alphabetical list of the Editorial Consultants, Contributing Editors, and Writers, designating the areas or subjects for which each was responsible (articles are not signed), as well as indicating their professional and academic qualifications. Examples of experts who have contributed articles are William B. Baird, *Marionette*; Sonia E. Bleeker, *Mayas*; Mary K. Eakin, *Library*; Katherine B. Shippen, *Music*. The 1966 edition had some 700 Contributing Editors and Writers; the 1973 edition has about 780. Thirty-five names have been removed; 108 names have been added.

The 1958 edition of *Britannica Junior* was reviewed in the February 1, 1959 issue of *The Booklist and Subscription Books Bulletin;* the 1966 edition was reviewed in the July 15, 1967 issue. For purposes of this review the 1973 revision was compared with the 1966 edition.

Volume 1 consists of a *Ready Reference Index*, with the hope that it will be consulted first in searching for information in the set. In addition to the more than 24,000 entries in the Index, there are many cross-references and see-references. Each entry word or phrase is printed in capitals and is followed by a brief definition or description. Page references follow: the main reference given first in boldface type, then the supplementary references, with maps, charts, and illustrations indicated. Pronunciation is given where necessary; diacritical markings are explained at the bottom of each recto page. A spot check revealed no blind entries. The explanation for using the Index is clear with ample use of pictures and samples to facilitate an elementary grade child's use of the set.

The 1973 revision of *Britannica Junior* reflects the current trend of school curricula to relate to vital issues of today. Such areas as international affairs, minority groups, politics, economics, environment, science, and drugs were given special consideration in revision.

In the area of international affairs, a notable article is the excellent new one on China, written by Professor Jack Williams, China Specialist at Michigan State University. It is up to date, including Nixon's visit to China. The full-page four-color time line chart relates Chinese historical events with those of the western world. Almost every China-related article was reviewed and revised. Biographies of Chou En-Lai and Tzu Hsi An are new additions. Sixteen new fact entries were made, including *Acupuncture*. The new articles *Imperialism* and *Colonialism*, *Ho Chi Minh*, and *Hanoi*, with updating of the material on Vietnam and the Vietnam War, are further evidence of emphasis on international affairs. In fact, updating is noticeable in coverage of all areas of the world, including Africa, Bangladesh, and Ireland. Pierre E. Trudeau and Tito are covered in new biographies. Strangely there is no separate biography for Golda Meir; she is listed only in the Index with a brief note.

In the minority field Blacks (entered as *Negroes, United States*), and Mexican Americans are accorded wider coverage and updating.

Negro and *Negroes, United States* give the anthropological view of the race, historical background, slavery, law and government effects on American Negroes, social conditions, education, and military service, and cite prominent Negroes in various fields of endeavor. Evidence of updating on the accomplishments of Negroes in the United States are mention of Negro mayors in Cleveland and Gary; Brigadier General Daniel James, Jr. and Admiral Samuel L. Gravely, Jr. in military and naval affairs; Thurgood Marshall in law; Grace Bumbry in music; Bill Cosby, Godfrey Cambridge, and Flip Wilson in entertainment; and Roy Campanella in sports. Articles have been added on Dr. Ralph J. Bunche, Sojourner Truth, and Harriet Tubman.

Women's Liberation Movement is defined in the Index. In addition to the two women mentioned above, other women now having separate articles are Elizabeth Blackwell, Dorothea Dix, and Tzu Hsi An.

The history and problems of the Mexican American are covered in a new article by Dr. Julian Nava, Professor of History, California State University, Northridge, and author of *Mexican Americans, Past, Present and Future* (New York: American Book Co., 1969) and *Mexican Americans: An Anthology of Basic Readings* (New York: Van Nostrand Reinhold, 1971). *Chicano* is defined in the Index, and a biographical note for Cesar E. Chavez appears in the Index.

Census information on North American Indians and material on Indians today have been updated. A biographical article on James Thorpe has been added. There is some revision in the article on George A. Custer, lessening his role as an all-out hero and showing that his disobeying orders probably led to Custer's Last Stand.

In the political field, results of the 1972 presidential election are included. The articles the *Democratic Party* and the *Republican Party* are updated. Richard M. Nixon is now treated in a separate article. In the Index volume biographical notes are included for George McGovern and R. Sargent Shriver. Friedrich Engels and Norman Thomas are now treated in separate articles. Votes based on the 1970 census are listed under *Electoral College*. Current information on lobbying is apparent in the articles *Lawmaking* and *Lobbying*. Under *Ballot* information on the voting machine has been slightly enlarged and an illustration added (only partially successful because it is not too clear).

The article *Economics* has been rewritten with improvements in clarity; it is better related to consumerism and gives updated information on inflation and deflation. The article *Income Tax* reflects the latest changes to income tax laws in the United States and Canada.

The article *Environment* has been shortened and rewritten with see-references leading to more in-depth material. A brief article *Ecology* has been added. In the *Big Game Hunting* article more stress is put on the need for controlled hunting. The material *Ocean and Oceanography* has been rewritten and expanded with more information on the geography of the ocean, sea water and currents, waves and tides, and flora and fauna. Reference is made to food resources offered by the seas; however, aquaculture is not indicated by name; nor does it appear in the Index. There is good additional information on how the oceans are studied. The article *Panda* has been rewritten with note made of China's gift of pandas to the United States in 1972. *Space Travel* is now called *Space Exploration,* and the information has been updated.

The science articles are uniformly good. *Periodic Table of Elements* has been brought up to date. Masers and lasers, only defined in the 1966 edition, are now carefully considered in a separate article. Polaroid is discussed in the article *Photography,* but it is not listed in the Index.

Drugs and *Narcotics* are slightly rewritten with an improved definition of marijuana and a note that narcotic abuse increased greatly in the United States in the late 1960s.

Other examples of material added or updated: amnesty, Bangladesh, and United Arab emirates added to index; Barbados enlarged and updated; Sir Francis Charles Chichester, high rise, Nauru Island, pollution, UFO, and Wankel or rotary motor in Index; draft (conscription) updated to include draft protests; earthquake rewritten and updated; Mauritius updated; Tasaday Tribe index entry and added to *Philippines* article, and Tonga updated in Index.

The following subjects, important to children, are not covered: electronic music, methadone, Moshe Dayan, noise pollution, occult, population explosion, rock music, sickle cell anemia, snowmobile.

Coverage of each state is well done. Statistics and basic facts are concentrated on one page. There are subheadings for such facets as history, geography, government, people, industry, and economics. Maps, charts, and photographs add to the value of the state articles. The provinces of Canada are equally well handled.

The sports articles present history, rules, and records where pertinent, and give pointers on techniques. Terms are clearly explained.

As was noted in the review of the 1966 edition, there is a continuing trend toward a definitive, factual approach in writing. This is especially noted in the changes made in the first sentence of many articles. For example: *Cabinet:* a name for a group of men in government (1966); a group of governmental advisers (1973). *Hail:* hailstorms usually occur during the warm weather, when the conditions favorable for the formation of hail are most marked (1966); is falling lumps of frozen water that may have any one of a number of shapes (1973). *Sea Horse:* The sea horse is a fish which swims upright (1966); is a small marine fish of the genus Hippocampus, family Syngnathidae (1973).

No special yearbook is issued for *Britannica Junior.* There is, however, annual revision and updating, with a complete revision or in-depth cycle every five or six years.

Illustrative material is, on the whole, very good, many articles having new or better pictures replacing older ones. Patches or washes of color are still used as background for many drawings and charts. Photographic reproductions are clear and attractive. Color plates in the 1966 edition were printed on semiglossy paper; those in the 1973 edition are on matte finish paper. This does not seem to affect the colors. Many of the photographs of biographees have been replaced with drawings. The small marginal illustrations for *Children's Literature* and *Nursery Rhymes,* criticized unfavorably in the 1966 edition, have been eliminated and replaced with more attractive material. The Committee criticized the 1966 edition for the illustrations accompanying the articles *Japan* and the *Netherlands,* which tended to give " a false impression of backwardness." These pictures have been replaced with illustrations depicting modern dress and activities.

Volume 15 contains a world atlas, consisting of 143 maps, prepared by Encyclopaedia Britannica Cartography, C. S. Hammond, Inc., Jeppesen, Rand McNally, and Greco. For each of the continents both a relief and a political map are given. Most of the plates have insets, showing details of population, scale of miles, and location maps of specific areas. Generally the maps are clear and easy to use. Page layout is such that no details are lost on double-spread maps. Adequate directions are given for the use of the atlas, with reference made to the five-page article *Maps and Map Making.* Volume 15 also contains a 148-page Index to the atlas maps. The atlas maps are not listed in the *Ready Reference Index.*

In addition to the Atlas maps, there are 776 maps in the text. These include locator maps for articles on cities and specific geographical features (mountains and rivers), product maps, rainfall, population, etc. "Strato-View" maps for each state "designed to give a three-dimensional appearance in order to give a sense of terrain" supplement the maps in the Atlas. As was noted in the review of the 1966 edition, these maps are of varying success—often bright color wash tends to obscure some lines, and the wrinkle-effect for mountains and rivers is sometimes confusing.

Britannica Junior Encyclopaedia has an attractive orange and brown Holliston sturdite binding. The guide letters and volume numbers are placed at the top of the spine. The paper is good, non-glare quality. The type is clear and easy to read, set in an attractive format. An offset process was used for printing both text and illustrations. The volumes seem sturdy and lie reasonably flat when opened. Pagination is now placed at the top of the page, an easier to use arrangement than the bottom page position in the 1966 edition.

Britannica Junior Encyclopaedia should adequately fill the reference needs of elementary grade children. Its straightforward style and clear vocabulary are suitable for such grades. The set will have value also for older students who are reading at a lower level. *Britannica Junior* is recommended for home, school, and public libraries. Since the 1973 revision shows extensive rewriting and updating, libraries and homes having the 1966 or earlier editions will want to replace them with this revision. *(Sept. 1, 1973, p.1)*

Britten's Old Clocks and Watches and Their Makers: a Historical and Descriptive Account of the Different Styles of Clocks and Watches of the Past in England and Abroad Containing a List of Nearly Fourteen Thousand Makers. By Cecil Clutton and the late G. H. Baillie, and C. A. Ilbert. 8th ed. rev. and enl. by Cecil Clutton. New York, E. P. Dutton Co., Inc., 1973 [c1973, 1899, 1904, 1911, 1920, 1922, 1933, 1956]. 532p. illus. diagrs. plates. 28cm. cloth $40.
SBN 0-525-07150-4.

This is the standard general work on timepieces and horological history. First published in 1894 under the title *Former Clock and Watchmakers and Their Work, Britten's Old Clocks and Watches* is now in its eighth edition published in 1973. This is the first revision since 1956. Originally written by the late F. J. Britten, part of the seventh and eighth editions was revised by G. H. Baillie, Courtenay A. Ilbert, and Cecil Clutton; the final revision was completed by Cecil Clutton after the deaths of the other collaborators. Ilbert's collection of watches and clocks from which most of the illustrations for the book have been taken is now in the British Museum.

The greater part of the text is arranged chronologically as a history of time and the measurement of time from the beginning to 1830 and remains the same as in the seventh edition with "minor corrections." This is especially true in the section on Breguet in chapter IX. Here a long paragraph clarifying the chronology of numbers which Breguet used has been added, thus establishing a clear connection between dates and the numbers and facilitating the detection of fakes and forgeries.

Chapter I deals with time and its measurement: solar time, sidereal time, primitive timekeepers, and mechanical timekeepers. In succeeding chapters early clocks, early watchmaking in Germany, France and England, the guilds, the invention and inventors of the pendulum and balance spring are discussed. English clocks from 1660 to 1750 and French clocks from 1660 to 1830 each receive a chapter. Chapter V details a general history of clocks and watches from 1750 to 1830 and includes material on Turkish and Chinese market watches. Mechanisms (alarum, striking and repeating) and national styles comprise chapters VII and VIII. Chapter IX reproduces "notes collected by Mr. Britten concerning the lives and works of famous horologists and included in earlier editions" and is confined mainly to English clockmakers. The final chapter X, of 16 pages, is new to this edition and carries the history from 1830 to the present. Since developments of style and new mechanical inventions have been few since 1830, the new chapter deals for the most part with manufacturing and adds little to the reference value of the book.

The comprehensive Bibliography from previous editions is included and has been updated with an addendum citing reprints and new editions (5 titles), English translations (1 title), and new books since 1956 (18 titles) of which eight carry 1971 or later dates.

An Appendix on hallmarks and the useful Glossary of Technical Terms are unchanged from earlier editions. Accompanying the appropriate text are 192 black-and-white plates. Captions are clear and detailed. Four colorplates have been added. There were none in the seventh edition. Forty diagrams are used with the accompanying text; they are large and clear with detailed captions. The Index has been updated to include items from the new chapter X.

One of the most valuable sections of the book on "Former Clock and Watch Makers" remains unchanged from the seventh edition. As the subtitle says it is ". . . a list of nearly 14,000 makers" with dates, places of work and often a brief comment on their work. For example, *see* "Rousseau, Jean. A clever watchmaker; a crystal cased watch in the form of a cross by him in the Fellows collection, about 1590." This list should, however, be used with G. H. Baillie's more comprehensive but less detailed *Watchmakers and Clockmakers of the World* (London: A. G. Pr. Ltd., 1951) since it includes more than twice the number of names listed in Britten's list of "nearly fourteen thousand makers."

Binding for this new edition is very sturdy; heavy cloth is used for the cover. The paper is heavy and of good quality; the type is large, clear, and legible.

Britten's Old Clocks and Watches and Their Makers is an important reference book for the amateur collector, the professional dealer, and libraries. However, the library owning the seventh edition need not replace it with the eighth. Recommended.   *(Mar. 15, 1974, p.748)*

Butterflies of the World. By H. L. Lewis. Chicago, Follett Publishing Co., 1973. xvi, 312p. illus. colorplates. maps. 30cm. cloth $29.95. ISBN 695-80434-0.

There has long been a need for a general butterfly book with broad geographic coverage. Lewis's book fulfills the need as it includes all families of butterflies on a world-wide basis. The standard work in this field, *Macrolepidoptera of the World* by A. Seitz, is now out of print. Most of the other books pertaining to butterflies are limited in scope and deal only with a particular country.

The author, Brigadier H. L. Lewis C.B.E., retired from the Army in 1961. His lifetime hobbies, stamp and butterfly collecting, have resulted in two books on philately and this first butterfly publication. Many of his butterfly specimens can be found in museums both here and abroad. According to the author, the purpose of this book is "to provide a work which is as comprehensive as possible, to enable collectors and interested laymen to obtain ready identification of butterfly specimens which they encounter." There is a Foreword by J. M. Chalmers-Hunt F.R.E.S., President of the British Entomological and Natural History Society, and the illustrations are by Lionel Leventhal Ltd.

Following the Foreword and the Introduction are two pages of drawings containing Key to Life Sizes in the colorplate section. Next are two of General Identification Notes by genus. The rest of the volume is divided into three sections: Colored Plates, Text, and Index.

There are 208 pages of colorplates illustrating over 5,000 butterflies in full color. These color photographs make up the major part of the volume. The author has made the following geographic divisions: North America, South America including Mexico, Europe, Africa, Asia, and Indo-Australia. For each region he has illustrated representatives of each family including the Hesperioidea, which are all too often excluded from major works. Many of the uncommon species are portrayed along with the more common ones. Lewis is to be complimented on his choice of the species presented. Treatment is well balanced for each geographic region. He has not restricted the figures to "showy" species and the plates represent a good general coverage of fauna.

Every illustration is a picture of a specimen from the entomological collection in the British Museum's Department of Natural History in London. Pictures of small- and medium-sized butterflies are actual life-size, whereas certain families of large ones are shown according to reduced scales as indicated in the Key to the Life Sizes. Within each geographic area the colorplates are arranged by family, and the genera alphabetically within that family, followed by species.

All illustrations are numbered. At the bottom of each page the butterflies are identified by species and, where appropriate, male or female indicated, and notation as to whether the under or upper side of the butterfly is shown. The color reproduction of a few plates is not true to life. However, considering the number of colorplates and the relatively low cost of the book, the plates, as a whole, are of excellent quality. Each plate conveniently contains a small map of the geographic area represented.

The text portion of the work presents information about some, but not all, of the specimens shown in each of the plates. This includes scientific name, authority, common name, general geographic distribution, similar species, brood information, larval food plants and, in some cases, varieties and subspecies. Included is a complete Index which refers to the color illustrations of the butterflies. Not all species indexed are illustrated. Those not shown are indexed in italics, which are like slightly slanted numbers and are difficult to distinguish from those which refer to the colorplates.

As with any work of this magnitude, there are some negative comments to be made about this book. Had the author had the manuscript reviewed by collectors or authorities familiar with each of the geographic regions some problems with nomenclature and misidentification of species and genera might have been avoided. For example, European generic names have been applied to North American genera. It is not yet clear that these names correctly apply to North America.

In the treatment of North American families, the use of generic and subgeneric names, the use of species and subspecies names lack consistency. Examples are the use of Strymon without recognition of Chlorostrymon, Euristrymon, etc., while Icaricia, Agriades, etc., are used rather than Plebejus. There are several instances of this nature. In plate 15, for example, Speyeria calgariana and S. callippe are illustrated without any indication that two subspecies of the same species are involved. This is a common occurrence throughout the plates.

Although a Corrigenda sheet accompanies the book, a number of corrections are not included. For example, in the North American region, on plate 13, figure 3, Anartia amathea is not found in this region. The genus Metamorpha rather than Siproeta is used in plate 14. The butterfly illustrated in plate 17, figure 17, is identified as Colias hageni whereas it is Colias interior. The former is a subspecies of C. philodice. Figure 18 appears to depict the underside of Colias scudderi and not C. interior, and figure 19 is Colias eurytheme and not Colias pelidne.

Again on plate 20, figure 12, Glaucopsyche piasus daunia is shown as Phaedrotus (sic) sagittigera. The associated text restricts the butterfly to the Rocky Mountains without mention of the coastal races. In plate 22, figure 25, is identified as Pholisora mejicanus. The associated text cites Canada to Texas for the range. Obviously P. catullus and P. mejicanus have been confused. The former is found from Canada to Mexico. The latter occurs in Colorado, New Mexico, Texas, and Mexico.

In the text which accompanies plates 12-22, many of the listed geographic ranges are either incomplete or incorrect. A few examples have been noted above. These shortcomings of the book detract somewhat from its overall quality and utility.

The book is bound in cloth and is thread sewn. Margins are adequate and the book lies flat when open. The paper is woodfree glossy and adds to the attractiveness of the colorplates.

Butterflies of the World is in reality a pictorial encyclopedia of the world's butterflies and is valuable to the amateur and serious collector alike. Its major value is that it enables the easy identification of an unknown specimen as to family, and in most cases, genus, if the specimen itself is not illustrated. One can then refer to the existing regional works for in-depth study. Even with a few plates not true in color, the illustrations are beautiful and, despite some errors, the volume is a very useful reference work which museums, libraries, and many collectors will wish to own. Recommended.

(July 15, 1974, p.1208)

Cassell's Encyclopaedia of World Literature. Revised and enlarged edition in three volumes. General editor: J. Buchanan-Brown. New York, William Morrow, 1973. 3v. 24cm. cloth $47.95. ISBN 0-688-0022-5.

Cassell's Encyclopaedia of World Literature, which first appeared in England in 1953 and in the United States in 1954, was reviewed in *Subscription Books Bulletin* in Oct. 1954. The present review is concerned with the revised edition published in 1973.

The first volume is devoted to histories of the literatures of the world and to general articles; the two remaining volumes contain biographies of authors. The editors' aim has been to present "a work of reference to the literature not of any one language or of any one age, but of all periods and peoples." All articles are signed, and all except the shortest are followed by bibliographies which include titles of recent imprint. The contributors are primarily British scholars, and the writing is in the best British tradition: factual, clear, and concise. The phrase "world literature" properly belongs in the title, because not only are the literatures of Europe and the Americas discussed, but also those of Asia, Africa, and Oceana. The time span is equally generous, including the ancients as well as the moderns.

Volume I contains articles on the histories of individual literatures, definitions of literary terms, descriptions of literary genres, and other topics of literary interest. There are long articles on printing and publishing (16 pages), English literature (13 pages), the novel (9 pages), bibliography (5 pages), and shorter articles on such subjects as emblem books, futurism, and the Goliards. The articles on nonsense and the limerick have amusing examples. Some entries, definitions of obscure literary terms, are as short as four or five lines.

Volumes II and III contain biographical sketches of a dazzling array of literary figures. English and Continental writers predominate, but Americans are well represented. Writers in obscure languages such as Friulian and Raqusan are also included. An appreciation of the variety can be gained by noting that one page contains articles on William Henry Hudson, the author of *Green Mansions,* Langston Hughes, Hue de Rotelande, a twelfth-century Anglo-Norman poet, and Conrad Huet, a nineteenth-century Dutch critic. Nearby are biographical sketches of Hu Shih and a modern Chilean poet named Vincente Huidobro. In allocating space to each writer the editors betray no detectable bias. Hudson gets two-and-one-fourth column inches, Huet eight, Hu Shih five-and-one-half, and Huidobro three-and-one-fourth. The bibliographies, which are sometimes as long as the biographies themselves, include the major writings of the author as well as critical works about him.

A comparison of the revised edition with its predecessor of 1954 reveals that significant updating and changes have been made. The present editors have abandoned the awkward division of authors between those who died before 1914 and those who lived beyond that date. A comparison of the general articles in the letter *E* revealed that in the sample examined eight titles of literary works have been dropped as entries and twelve short definitions of rhetorical or literary terms have been added. Seven somewhat longer articles have been rewritten and have new or extended bibliographies. Minor changes were also found in seven long articles and most showed changes in the bibliography. There were also two completely new articles, and three others had new bibliographies. Eleven short definitions were unchanged.

The biography volumes have also been thoroughly reworked. A close examination of the first 55 entries in the letter *H* shows only 12 entries without some change. There were 11 new persons included and 10 others dropped.

Sixteen otherwise unchanged biographies had new or extended bibliographies, and six articles were completely rewritten with extensive changes in the bibliographies.

Sturdily bound, the volumes are businesslike in appearance. The typeface and page layout are unobtrusive and efficient.

Cassell's Encyclopedia of World Literature provides a current and comprehensive survey of its subject and is recommended for high school, public, and academic libraries.

Hugh Pritchard, Reference Librarian University of New Hampshire, Reference and Subscription Books Committee Member, 1960-1964.
(July 15, 1974, p.1209)

Chambers's Biographical Dictionary. Ed. by J. O. Thorne. Rev. ed. New York, St. Martin's Pr., 1969. v, 1432p. 25cm. buckram $17.50; to schools and libraries, 20 percent discount.

The original edition of *Chambers's Biographical Dictionary* was published in 1897; successive editions were issued in 1929 and 1946. The first Reference and Subscription Books Review Committee review was published November 1, 1962, in *The Booklist and Subscription Books Bulletin* following the appearance in 1961 of the "first fully revised, rewritten and expanded edition since its original appearance."

The editor, J. O. Thorne, is not listed in biographical dictionaries. Contributors are not identified by name; they are simply listed as the "combined editorial staffs of W. & R. Chambers of Edinburgh and St. Martin's Press of New York."

The Preface to the 1969 revised edition states that each entry has been reviewed, expanded or shortened, and possibly deleted, as required. Bibliographies have been rechecked and the Subject Index substantially revised. "In addition, there is a wealth of new entries."

Basically, the new edition follows the pattern of its predecessor. It includes over 15,000 persons "likely to be looked up," and covers all nations and all ages, as well as both living and deceased persons. The range of professions covered is broad: politicians and statesmen, authors, artists, jazz musicians, ballet dancers, film directors, even traitors (Donald MacLean) and double agents (Harold Philby).

Chambers's Biographical Dictionary includes a Preface, Key to Pronunciation, Supplement (formerly titled Addenda), 1,397 pages of biographical sketches in a single alphabet, and a 34-page Subject Index including such divisions as Art and Architecture, Cinema, Exploration and Geography, History, Literature, Music, Nicknames and Personalities, Philosophy and Theology, and Science and Industry.

Each entry contains the following information: surname (bold capitals), first and middle names and titles (lower case), pronunciation (of difficult names only), dates, biographical sketches, and bibliographical notes for further reading. *See* in lightface refers to bibliography; **see** in boldface is a cross-reference, in most cases leading to an alternate spelling. When more than one given name falls under a single surname, Arabic numerals in parentheses precede the given names.

Since it is the intent to produce a book that may be read as well as consulted, something more than a catalog of data, the biographical material is not abbreviated and compressed as in *Webster's Biographical Dictionary*. The style of writing is clear and informative. To illustrate: a 31-line entry under Marshall McLuhan includes this sentence: "He holds controversial views on the effect of the communication media on the development of civilization, claiming that it is the media *per se*, not the information and ideas which they disseminate, that influence society."

Bibliographies have been updated only minimally. They list recent, mostly popular works for further reading on the subject.

Changes in the new edition are relatively minor. An analysis of the entries under the letter *N* showed that these three names were added: Guilio NATTA, Italian chemist; Rudolf NUREYEV, Russian ballet-dancer; and Julius NYERERE, Tanzanian politician; all living persons. One name was deleted; one new cross-reference appeared; three entries were compressed; and ten entries were expanded. Expansions ranged from the brief addition of a death date to ten additional lines on Gamal NASSER and fifteen on Kwame NKRUMAH.

The only substantial amount of new material is in the Supplement, a section of eight unnumbered pages which precede the main alphabet. Of the 128 names, 46 are new; these include Spiro AGNEW, Neil ARMSTRONG, Christiaan BARNARD, Willy BRANDT, Alexander DUBCEK, and Benjamin SPOCK. Of the remaining 82 entries, 56 list the death date of persons in the main alphabet. No pronunciation is given for surnames in the Supplement. This is a frustrating omission to the reader encountering names such as Oistrakh, Sarraute, and Solzhenitsyn. From this analysis of the Supplement and from a sample of the main body of the work, it appears that about one percent of the names are new. This leads one to question the statement "a wealth of new material."

The format is good. The book is bound in an attractive blue-green buckram and seems sturdy. The print is exceptionally clear; margins are adequate; paper is matte finish without glare. Headwords and surnames are prominent and titles of books are italicized. There are no charts, tables, or illustrations.

Chambers's Biographical Dictionary is still a good reference book for home use and for the public, school, college and university library, because it gives biographical data in an interesting form for many persons likely to be researched. It is a recommended purchase for libraries needing a comprehensive source of biographical data on a wide range of persons. Those libraries with a good copy of the 1962 edition may not feel justified in making the $17.50 expenditure to acquire the new material which can be found in other sources.
(Feb. 1, 1974, p.550)

The Collectors' Encyclopedia of Antiques. Edited by Phoebe Phillips.

Associate editors: David Coombs [and] Joseph Butler. Drawings by Christopher Evans. New York, Crown Publishers [c1973]. 704p. 29cm. illus. (part col.) maps. $20. ISBN 0-517-504510.

The Random House Encyclopedia of Antiques. Editors: Ian Cameron and Elizabeth Kingsley-Rowe. [1st American ed.] New York, Random House [c1973]. 400p. 28cm. illus. (part col.) maps. $25. SBN 671-21506-X.

House and Garden's Antiques: Questions and Answers. [By] Louise Ade Boger. New York, Simon and Schuster [c1968-1973]. viii, 429p. 23cm. illus. $9.95. ISBN 0-394-48811-3.

Both *The Collectors' Encyclopedia of Antiques* and *The Random House Encyclopedia of Antiques* are American editions of works compiled in England and issued there under English imprints. (The English edition of *The Random House Encyclopedia* is entitled *Collins Encyclopedia of Antiques*).

The Random House Encyclopedia was edited by Ian Cameron and Elizabeth Kingsley-Rowe. Neither is further identified in the work; nor are identifications provided for the 11 staff members or the 14 editorial consultants listed on the first page of the volume. Although the latter are termed "specialists," their areas of specialization are not indicated. The only person associated with the work for whom identification is provided is John Pope-Hennessy, Director of the British Museum, who wrote the three-page Introduction.

Each of the 35 contributors to the *Collectors' Encyclopedia of Antiques* is identified except for the editor, Phoebe Phillips, who contributed the section on Roman and Venetian glass. Likewise unidentified is the Associate Editor for Great Britain, David Coombs. Coombs is deputy editor of *The Connoisseur*. The Associate Editor for the United States, Joseph Butler, is Curator of Sleepy Hollow Restoration, Tarrytown, New York; Adjunct Associate Professor of Architecture at Columbia University; and American Editor of *The Connoisseur*. Contributors range from collectors and dealers to professors and museum officials, the latter accounting for more than any other group. Ten of the contributors are Americans.

Both volumes have been compiled primarily for collectors, although the scope of the two works differs slightly. Coverage in *The Random House Encyclopedia* extends from the beginning of the Renaissance to 1875. Exceptions are made for Islamic areas and the Far East, for which treatment of important earlier periods was considered essential. *The Collectors' Encyclopedia* places its main emphasis on the eighteenth and nineteenth centuries, "where the examples illustrated will be of greatest value to collectors in identification." Earlier periods are represented, however, by "objects which show the historical background of each craft, since their traditional skills often extend into antiquity"; and in a few cases modern pieces have been included "where innovations have occurred which still use the old skills."

The Random House Encyclopedia omits coverage of coins and medals, dolls and children's playthings, needlework, militaria, and ethnographica, and provides only incidental coverage of several other areas (e.g., architects when they have influenced furniture styles.) *The Collectors' Encyclopedia* includes a number of the categories omitted from *Random House* (e.g., arms and armour, embroidery and needlework, toys and automata).

The Random House Encyclopedia is designed for ready reference and includes more than 5,000 entries arranged in alphabetical order. The entries range from two lines to about a page in length with entries of under 15 lines predominating. Entries run the gamut from generic terms (e.g., *Ceramics*) through types (*Earthenware, Stoneware, Porcelain*) to specific examples (*Staffordshire, Jasper ware, Meissen*). Other types of entries cover numerous objects; styles and stylistic details; designers, craftsmen, and manufacturers; and centers of production. The last named are also shown on a series of six black-and-white outline maps which precede the text. Appendixes include reproductions of some of the ceramic and silver marks mentioned in the encyclopedia and a bibliography.

The Collectors' Encyclopedia is divided into 16 sections, each of which is devoted to a single category of antiques (e.g., Clocks, Watches and Barometers; Furniture; Glass; Silver). Each section is intended to provide a survey of the category which it covers and includes a Table of Contents, an Introduction, and one or more articles by the specialist contributors previously mentioned. The articles are followed by a Glossary, information on maintenance and repair, a Bibliography, a listing of major museum collections in Great Britain and the United States, and an Index to the section. The sections covering ceramics, furniture, and glass are the longest, each being slightly over 100 pages in length. Other sections range from 66 pages (Silver) to 14 pages (Musical Instruments). The larger sections are divided geographically. The geographical divisions vary in accordance with the contributions made by different areas to the subjects covered in the encyclopedia. Thus, the section on ceramics includes separate articles on Chinese and Korean ceramics while the section on glass provides separate coverage of Roman and Venetian glass.

English and Continental antiques generally receive more attention than American antiques, but one would expect this to be the case in a work compiled in England. A reasonable balance is maintained in most sections of *Collectors'*, but there are some exceptions. American furniture is covered in 16 pages, while 45 pages are devoted to English furniture and 40 to Continental furniture (including the separate section on French furniture). The examples of American furniture which are included do not seem to be sufficiently representative of the history of the subject. American pottery and porcelain also seem to receive unduly brief treatment.

The Random House Encyclopedia depends on extensive cross-references to direct the user to entries related to the one which he has consulted. The 225-word article on American clocks, for example, contains 25 cross-references. If the user read each of these articles, he would be directed to eight additional articles relating to American clocks. Thus, information from a total of 34 articles is made accessible through the main article on the subject. Cross-references were, however, omitted for ogee and looking glass clocks, both of which are treated in separate entries.

The entry on Seth Thomas fails to note that an example of his workmanship is shown in the article on wall clocks; nor does the caption for this picture indicate that the encyclopedia includes an article on the maker of the Clock. The article on Seth Thomas includes a cross-reference to Eli Terry, with whom Thomas was associated, but the article on Terry does not include a reciprocal reference.

Similarly, the article on toleware concludes with the reference, *"See* tôle," but the tôle article lacks a similar reference to "toleware," the entry under which American examples of tôle are discussed. The article on the Boston and Sandwich Glass Company directs the user to a non-existent entry for Sandwich glass.

The Collectors' Encyclopedia, in which each section is organized as a virtually independent unit, contains relatively few cross-references. Only 18 cross-references were found in the 56-page section on clocks, watches, and barometers, and only five of these direct the user to information in other sections of the encyclopedia. Most of the cross-references direct the reader to illustrations.

Because of the specificity of entry utilized in *The Random House Encyclopedia,* the work does not include an index. As previously noted, each section of *The Collectors' Encyclopedia* concludes with its own index. The entries in the section indexes refer primarily to the illustrations and do not include proper names. Of the 278 references in the index to the section on clocks, watches, and barometers, all except two refer to illustrations.

Indexing appears to be incomplete and inconsistent. Of the 32 illustrations on the pages devoted to American clocks, only 13 were located in the section Index. (This figure does not include the entry under the broad term "wooden-cased clocks," under which 24 of the illustrations were listed.) No references were found to the illustrations of such distinctive types as the acorn clock and the beehive clock. While about half the illustrations depict shelf clocks, the index reference under that term refers only to the pillar and scroll shelf clock on page 244 (and there is no index entry for "pillar and scroll"). Although the term "gothic" is used in the descriptions of four of the American clocks illustrated (and applies to one other), the index references under "gothic clocks" refer only to Swiss and Dutch examples. The entry under "cottage style clock" refers only to the German imitation of this American style. The picture of the American prototype is not indexed; nor do cross-references link the two illustrations.

Similar inadequacies were noted in the Index to the section on furniture. Thirty-three of the 65 references under "*chairs*" are lumped under the uninformative subheading "Other." While there is a separate index entry for *candlestand*, lamp stand is included under "Tables—other." Highboys are sublisted under "Chests," with no cross-reference from the specific term. Two of the three index references under "*Chairs, Windsor*" are incorrect. The first leads the user to an illustration of a seventeenth-century elm chest and the second to a picture of a Chippendale settee. (In the first reference, two digits of the page number were transposed.)

What is described in the Introduction as a main index to the volume is actually an index of proper names only. Failure to indicate the limitations of this index is likely to cause difficulty for the user, especially since a few subject entries based on proper names have been included in the index (e.g., majolica, Staffordshire pottery).

While both *Random House* and *Collectors'* are profusely illustrated, *The Collectors' Encyclopedia* places greater emphasis on illustration. Illustrations in *Collectors'* occupy a larger portion of the volume and are generally larger in size. There are many full-page illustrations. While the proportion of colored to black-and-white illustrations is higher in *The Random House* volume, the 64 pages of colored illustrations in *The Collectors' Encyclopedia* are printed on glossy stock and are, therefore, much more effective. The quality of the colored and black-and-white illustrations is generally on a high level. Integration between the illustrations and the text is provided through the extensive captions which accompany the black-and-white photographs, by means of which much of the detailed information in the encyclopedia is conveyed.

About half of the 1,000 illustrations in *The Random House Encyclopedia* are in color. Most of the illustrations are small, ranging up to half a page in size. There are no full-page illustrations. Illustrations are, for the most part, sufficiently clear for identification purposes and usually large enough to show a fair amount of detail, but there is some variation in quality. Illustrations are well-integrated with the text and are adequately captioned.

The eight-page bibliography in *The Random House Encyclopedia* includes more than 550 books and is current through 1972. Books of English origin predominate, but there is a fair representation of American titles, and some English translations of works originally written in other languages are included. The Bibliography is not annotated.

Books are listed under very specific headings in many cases, and no mechanism for relating the various headings pertaining to a broad category of antiques is provided. The 57 books on clocks and watches are, for example, found under 17 different headings. A cross-reference under *watches* directs the user to look under *clocks* for titles covering both subjects, and a cross-reference under *chronometers* refers one to the name of a craftsman who contributed to their development. These were the only cross-references noted in the entire bibliography. Users must, therefore, scan the entire bibliography to be sure of locating all the headings pertaining to a subject or of finding the specific headings under which books treating particular aspects of the subject are listed.

Separate bibliographies are provided for each of the 16 sections of *The Collectors' Encyclopedia.* A total of about 665 books is listed, ranging from 78 in the bibliography for ceramics to 17 in the listing for jewellery. A good representation of recent items was noted along with several standard works in European languages other than English. Bibliographies are arranged in accordance with the main divisions of the text for each section. Entries are not annotated and publishers' names are not included in the citations.

House and Garden Antiques: Questions and Answers was compiled by Louise Ade Boger, coauthor with her husband H. Batterson Boger, of *The Dictionary of Antiques and the Decorative Arts* and author of *The Complete Guide to Furniture Styles, Furniture Past and Present,* and *The Dictionary of World Pottery and Porcelain.*

For the past several years Mrs. Boger has conducted a monthly column, "Antiques: Questions and Answers," in *House and Garden Magazine,* and the present work is a collection of the most interesting questions and answers which have appeared in her column. The book is addressed primarily to those readers of the column who expressed interest in obtaining previous installments, but the publishers stress the value of the work to others who are interested in antiques.

The column serves primarily as a means of identifying antiques and of conveying a variety of information concerning the items about which readers have inquired. Readers submit photographs along with their questions, and Mrs. Boger provides the required identification and comments on noteworthy features of the object.

The questions and answers have been divided into 17 categories. The 5 principal ones are Furniture (133 pages), Pottery and Porcelain (85 pages), Silver (43 pages), Glass (15 pages), and Clocks and Watches (34 pages). These main categories are subdivided geographically. The remaining categories, most of which are only a few pages in length, cover pewter, musical instruments, pictures, sculpture, lighting, heating equipment, toys and games, objects on wheels, weapons, food service, utility items, and decorative and useful objects.

Within each category or subdivision similar items are usually grouped together and arranged in approximate chronological order, but there are some exceptions to this practice. There seems to be no discernible pattern in the section on American clocks and watches, and the tables illustrated in the section on American furniture do not seem to be arranged in any particular order.

Each question and answer is accompanied by a small black-and-white photograph of the object to which the question relates. The photographs were supplied by the inquirers and the quality varies widely. Most are adequate for purposes of identification but not large enough to show much detail. In some cases, however, the photographs are so poor that they fail to convey an adequate idea of the objects which they depict (e.g., the Augustus Rogers teakettle on page 240 and the Victorian secretary on page 82).

While the question and answer format is no doubt appropriate for the author's monthly column, its effectiveness in the present instance is debatable. Does the reader really care that the English teapot illustrated on page 207 was given to the inquirer's mother 40 years ago by her great aunt, or that someone's mother bought the Davenport desk shown on page 144 at an auction in British Columbia? The space devoted to the questions might have been put to better use by giving more information about the objects pictured or by providing an index to the volume.

An unannotated Bibliography of 200 "interesting and standard reference books" follows the final section of the volume. The Bibliography is divided into nine parts and includes, in addition to general works on antiques, separate listings of books on furniture, pottery and porcelain, silver, pewter, glass, clocks and watches, and other subjects. Most of the works listed have been published within the past 25 years, but standard older works are also included.

While Mrs. Boger's replies to her readers' inquiries include much useful and interesting information, it is accessible only through reading or browsing in the text as the volume includes neither an index nor cross-references. The work is, therefore, recommended only for libraries requiring a volume devoted primarily to the identification of antiques.

Libraries looking for a ready reference volume on antiques may wish to consider *The Random House Encyclopedia* because of the ease with which the user can locate information on a wide variety of specific subjects. Any library considering the encyclopedia should, however, be aware of the manufacturing deficiencies of the volume. Owing largely to the very heavy stock on which the book is printed, the 400-page volume weighs over five pounds and is nearly as heavy as *The Collectors' Encyclopedia* which is 300 pages longer. More serious from the librarian's standpoint is the quality of the binding, which does not appear to be of sufficient strength for the weight of the volume. The bindings on all the copies received by the Reference and Subscription Books Review Committee were damaged in transit, and in one instance the pages became almost completely detached from the casing as a result of the use which the copy received in the course of preparing this review. Rebinding would be difficult owing to the narrow inner margins (approximately one-half inch). Because of these drawbacks, the volume cannot be given an unqualified recommendation.

Although the content is not so well arranged for reference purposes, *The Collector's Encyclopedia* is better suited for library purchase. The volume is attractive, and the binding is sufficiently strong to withstand heavy use. The inner margins are wide enough to permit rebinding. In spite of inadequacies of the cross-references and indexing, the encyclopedia is recommended as a useful survey of the principal fields of antiques' collecting. *(July 1, 1974, p.1158)*

The College Blue Book; U.S. Colleges: Narrative Descriptions; U.S. Colleges: **Tabular Data; Degrees Offered by Colleges and Subjects.** 3v. T. Allan Taylor, managing editor. 14th ed. New York, CCM Information Corporation, 1972. 29cm. cloth $59.85.

Published in various editions since 1923, *The College Blue Book* is "dedicated to providing detailed information regarding collegiate institutions throughout the United States." Previous editions were reviewed by the Reference and Subscription Books Review Committee in *Subscription Books Bulletin* January 1930, October 1936, October 1939, July 1941, October 1945, and April 1951. The fourteenth edition consists of three separate volumes: *U.S. Colleges: Narrative Descriptions; U.S. Colleges: Tabular Data;* and *Degrees Offered by Colleges and Subjects.* A fourth book in the series, *Supplemental Volume: Occupational Education* will not be reviewed here.

The data contained in the volumes were extracted from college and university catalogs and questionnaires supplied to the institutions. The types of institutions covered include universities, senior colleges, two-year colleges, technical institutions, nursing schools, vocational schools, and some nonaccredited schools.

T. Allan Taylor, the managing editor, was not identified through standard biographical tools. The Editorial Director for *The College Blue Book* is William E. Burgess, Vice President of CCM (Crowell Collier Macmillan) Information Corporation and a librarian. Burgess, a few other members of the Editorial Advisory Board who are librarians, and a former college dean were located in the reference sources checked.

All three volumes contain the same pattern of prefatory material, consisting of a Table of Contents for the volume, a brief Preface, and an Introduction with information about college selection: type of institution, costs of education, entrance exams, and admission policies. There are also statements on self-appraisal, referral centers, and dropouts.

The first volume, *U.S. Colleges: Narrative Descriptions,* provides a section explaining the specific content of its entries, a list of degrees and their abbreviations, and a discussion of the Federation of Regional Accrediting Commissions of Higher Education. The main text describes some 3,600 institutions of higher education, arranged alphabetically by state and by college within each state. At the beginning of each state section is a full-page black-and-white map of the state. The entries which follow are standardized to facilitate comparison of schools and contain these categories: name of institution in boldface with map location symbol in parentheses; address, description, entrance requirements; admission procedures; costs per term; collegiate environment and community enviroment. Within the description category is found information on type of support (public versus private), educational level, student body, subject fields, degrees granted, majors, term system, enrollment, size of faculty, accreditation, size of library, work-study programs, and availability of ROTC. While appearing consistently in entries, the amount of information on each of these items varies from school to school. The other categories are self-explanatory and provide adequate data on the type of college and major educational emphasis. The Community Environment sections are informative, giving climate ranges. When more than one school is located in the same area, a *see* reference is used for climate.

The usefulness of the statistics given is questionable. Recent changes in method of charging tuition are not always recorded; lack of public transportation to colleges is not cited sometimes; size of library collections is inaccurately recorded frequently; and other outdated figures, mostly for 1968-1969, are used. Without more accurate and current statistics, the use of this reference work is limited to providing only general information about institutions.

A valuable feature of this volume however, is the maps included for each state. Produced by the American Map Company of New York and clearly reproduced, each one indicates a scale of miles, state capitals, counties and county seats, cities, and population densities. The last is taken from the 1970 federal census. Map coordinates enable rapid location of the schools.

All three of the volumes of *The College Blue Book* are durably bound. They are eight-and-one-half by eleven inches and approximately one-and-one-fourth inches thick, containing between 700 and 800 pages. The pages lie flat when opened. Each volume is heavier than it appears. The first volume, just described, is arranged in a manner which is visually easy to use. Boldface type, paragraph indentation, and large spaces between entries are used. Occasionally entries run on to the next page, and there are no headwords at the top to facilitate location of entries.

The second volume, *U.S. Colleges: Tabular Data*, begins with a section describing organization and use of this volume. The approximately 3,600 institutions of the first volume are arranged alphabetically within each state. The information for each entry is in a table of 55 vertical columns extending across two pages. The first column identifies the institution by giving name of institution with city and zip code, name of college president and registrar or admissions officer, and the individual colleges or schools. These appear on the far left of every even-numbered page. The remaining columns contain letter or number codes representing the type of institution, sex of student body, entrance requirements, school affiliation, accreditation, degrees offered, costs per term for tuition and housing, scholarships, enrollment, faculty, dormitory capacity, size of library, ROTC availability, disadvantaged programs, percent of returning freshmen, percent of Blacks, and year of founding. Explanation of these categories includes editors' suggestion that the student check with the college for current information on costs, a deficiency which this review already has pointed out. A four-page list of abbreviations precedes the tabular presentation. Above the actual tables are boxes identifying the numbered columns. Broad subject headings, some encompassing several columns, appear at the top of the tables. In spite of these devices, the tables are difficult to use.

Though the type is clearly legible, the space allotted for the 55 columns necessitates the use of small symbols which are hard to read. By the time one is using column 55 on the far right of the two-page table, it is difficult to determine which school the information concerns. There are no horizontal lines to guide the reader. Unless the user is thoroughly familiar with this volume, he must constantly refer to the list of abbreviations to interpret the tables. Thus, it seems this volume may require more work for the user than sifting through the narrative descriptions of the schools presented in the first book of *The College Blue Book* set. In order to obtain best advantage in using the second volume, the user must also read the first volume. For example, names and telephone numbers as well as various percentages only appear in the tabular presentation, instead of being incorporated into the first book, which is easier to use. This second volume also lists many technical and vocational schools omitted from the first volume.

The third volume of *The College Blue Book, Degrees Offered by Colleges and Subjects,* is divided into two sections. Part I, Degrees Offered by Colleges, tabulates degree programs offered by over 3,000 vocational and technical schools, institutes, two-year colleges, colleges and universities in the United States. These programs are arranged by college in alphabetical order within states. Part II, Degrees Offered by Subjects, is arranged alphabetically by subject, incorporating those institutions within each state that offer the programs. A discussion of inclusions and omissions as well as organization of the material precedes the tables.

The physical layout for both parts is the same—columns for six types of degrees appear to the immediate left of the list of schools. An asterisk in the appropriate column shows the type of degree given for each subject for the institutions. Three such sets of columns and schools appear on each page. Again, subjects run on to the next page causing inconvenience to the user. Guide words are located awkwardly in the center of the page. The name of the state is printed at the top of the page, however. In accordance with the intent of this third volume, not all schools listed in the first two volumes are mentioned here.

The subjects used in Part II of this third volume range widely from Biblical Archaeology to Furniture Manufacturing and Management to Mortuary Science. In spite of the difficulty with its physical format, *Degrees Offered by Colleges and Subjects* is the most useful volume of *The College Blue Book* set.

When the fourteenth edition of *The College Blue Book* was compared with the eleventh edition of *American Universities and Colleges,* the lack of information and the outdated statistics of the former became more apparent. Although there is overlapping and duplication of information between the different publications, *American Universities and Colleges* has various appendixes providing data not found in *The College Blue Book.* The second part of *American Universities and Colleges* is similar to the third volume of *The College Blue Book* in that it lists colleges that offer professional degrees. However, it only includes 38 subject fields, fewer than found in *The Blue Book's* coverage.

The College Blue Book covers more subjects than *American Universities and Colleges.* Since it also includes various institutions not found in *American Universities,* which is limited to those offering a bachelor's or higher degree, it is recommended for purchase by public, school, and university libraries. Small libraries with limited budgets may not want to consider this purchase due to its price and the complexity of its use. *The College Blue Book* should be used in conjunction with current college catalogs or other sources such as *American Universities and Colleges* to aid the student in his selection of schools for higher education. *(April 15, 1974, p.886)*

Collier's Encyclopedia. William D. Halsey, editorial director; Louis Shores, ed. in chief; Robert N. Blackburn, consultant for Canada; Sir Frank Francis, consultant for Great Britain. 24v. [New

York], Crowell-Collier Educational Corp., [c1972]. illus. ports. maps. diagrs. tables. 28cm. buckram to schools and libraries, $307 for 1 set; 2 or more sets $278 per set.

During an era now spanning three decades, *Collier's* has come to be recognized as one of the foremost English-language general encyclopedias. *Collier's* was first published in 20 volumes in 1950 and was expanded to 24 volumes in 1962. The 1967 edition, which is used for comparative purposes in this review, was evaluated in *The Booklist and Subscription Books Bulletin*, November 15, 1968.

At its inception, *Collier's* was introduced as a completely new encyclopedia, designed to systematize all of the knowledge significant to English-speaking peoples, and undertaking to do this for the layman particularly rather than for the specialist. Prefaces to editions since 1959 describe the set as "a scholarly, systematic, continuously revised summary of the knowledge that is most significant to mankind . . . designed and built to fill the needs of the most exacting school and home users." Since 1959 there seems to have been somewhat more emphasis on scholarly quality in the work, particularly indicated in prefatory statements that while covering "the essential content of the curricula of colleges and secondary schools as well as the upper grades . . . included, too, is the important information desired by the professional in the field." The high school user is the encyclopedia's primary target.

The editorial director for more than a decade has been William D. Halsey, who was coauthor of *New Century Cyclopedia of Names* and managing editor of Thorndike-Barnhart Dictionaries before coming to *Collier's* in 1960. The 1972 set adds an international advisory board from ten nations (Australia, Canada, Denmark, France, England, Italy, Japan, Philippines, South Africa, and U.S.A.) with library and curriculum advisory boards retaining essentially the same membership from the 1967 edition. Senior Editors and Advisers include such authorities as Moses Hadas (Greek and Latin Literature), Hollis Alpert (Radio and Television), John Gassner (Theater), A. L. Rowse (British History and Literature), German Arciniegas (Latin America), and Ray Allen Billington and Allan Nevins (American History). Resident editors are responsible for five major areas of knowledge: *Biological Sciences, Humanities, Physical Sciences, Regional Studies,* and *Social Studies*. The list of "senior editors and advisers" for the five aforementioned fields is virtually unchanged since 1967 although in each case a new supervising senior editor is named.

Although the Preface states that there are 5,000 editors, advisers, and contributors to this edition, contributors alone number about 4,200. They are recognized authorities in their fields and include younger and newly productive scholars. This trend has increased since the 1967 edition. Information about a few contributors, however, regardless of the recency of their articles, was found to be outdated, e.g., Frank B. Sessa has not been director of the Miami Public Library since 1966, although this is the last entry for him; similarly, Joseph F. Schubert is still listed as Nevada State Librarian, a position which he has not held since 1961. While most contributors are from university faculties, a sizable number are from industrial research institutes, learned societies, libraries, museums, government, and the literary and publishing fields. A random sampling showed the same ratios as for the 1967 edition, with approximately 15 percent of the contributors residing outside the United States, mainly in Britain. About 10 percent who now reside in this country received academic degrees from foreign universities. About four-fifths of the articles are signed with full names of each author, while the unsigned ones are primarily brief biographies, classical terms, short entries covering small communities, flora and fauna, and the like.

The publishers state that the 1972 *Collier's* contains nearly 19,000 pages, 25,000 articles, 1,450 maps, hundreds of tables and charts, and 17,000 photographs and drawings of which 1,400 are in color. The final volume (24) contains a consolidated bibliography of 11,500 book titles, a 15-page Study Guide, and an analytical Index to the entire work containing approximately 500,000 entries. The contents of each volume are indicated on the spine by the full heading of the first and last entry, and articles are entered in a letter-by-letter sequence, e.g., *Newark* precedes *New York*. Articles vary from entries of a few lines, to those such as *Europe; Indians, American;* and *United States of America,* which cover up to 70 pages. The broad area approach is clearly favored, so that articles such as *Music, Christianity, City Planning,* or *American Literature* are quite comprehensive in covering as much information as possible, thus avoiding a proliferation of smaller articles. This feature does not, of course, restrict the often extensive coverage of subordinate fields, e.g., *American Revolution* and *Civil War, U.S.* are each given long articles in addition to the 74-page treatment of *United States of America*. This organization of subject matter is supplemented by an extensive number of *see* and *see also* references from smaller topics, though use of the index volume is mandatory for full access to related subject matter. For example, *Women's Liberation,* a new entry, is found only in the Index, and refers only to a small note in the section of the article *United States of America* which covers recent militant movements.

Continuous revision, emphasized by encyclopedia publishers, has been particularly stressed by *Collier's* throughout its history. In the case of the 1972 *Collier's*, it was found that all the fields in which recency of data is required for effectiveness included more current data than previously. Thus, articles in the areas of economics, labor, art, music, the sciences, religion, drama, sports, and recreation were updated to the early part of the present decade. The article *Negro,* for example, now includes a reference to the report of the U.S. Commission on Civil Rights issued in October, 1970, while *American Literature* includes references to black authors publishing in 1970. Records for major sports such as *Football, Basketball, Tennis,* or *Baseball* are current, but a 1949 professional record is the last given under *Bicycling,* though this record has changed annually. The article also omits coverage of the tremendous growth of Americans bicycling during the past five years. (Interestingly, the bibliography in volume 24 does include a major 1970 title in this field.)

Current data is emphasized in articles for foreign countries, with information on American states, cities, towns, and counties revised to include the 1970 census, as well as economic information from governmental sources.

The science and technology content of the encyclopedia provides perhaps the best sample for producing general conclusions about the extent of revision of *Collier's* 1972. The coverage of science and technology retains much of the basic 1967 text as far as general fields of biology, chemistry, engineering, mathematics, and physics are concerned, with only such minor changes as revised statistical tables or a new paragraph or two inserted or blended into the original text. There are a few exceptions to this such as the 48-page treatment of *Space Exploration* in which the 1967 article has been considerably altered.

New science and technology coverage is found mostly in new articles and some revised ones dealing with very specific subject areas. The authority and clarity of the articles continue to merit the praise earned previously, with authoritative and lengthy articles on all the major fields and concepts of the physical and life sciences and of the various applied sciences and technology updated to as recently as July 1971.

Illustrations are largely unchanged except in those articles on subjects where many developments have taken place during the last five years. The mixture of black-and-white and color photographs, diagrams, sketches, and maps continues to be a clear and attractive presentation, with a high quality of reproduction throughout. Black-and-white illustrations and halftones are of course more numerous than full-color plates, but good selection, placement, captions, and use of color, where necessary, enhance the effectiveness of the illustrations.

Most of the maps, again prepared by Rand McNally, are double page and very well delineated by color and shading to indicate physical features and geographical characteristics. Appended to each map are indexes with current population figures, physical features, and points of interest. Scale and projection are given for all maps, which are generally of sufficient size to include a great amount of detail.

The 200-page well-organized Bibliography in volume 24 is, in most respects, very similar to that in the 1967 edition, and the format remains essentially the same. A few new titles have been added to most categories. *Collier's* claims that grouping all bibliographic entries together as a separate unit in the index volume aids the reader. Some readers may wish that they would find the bibliographies, however brief, at the end of individual articles. The choice of approaches is undoubtedly debatable, and certainly *Collier's* bibliography is well treated in the single-volume form.

The bibliographies contain, for the most part, standard works by recognized authors and include many newer titles. The editors state that the books listed "begin at about the high school level and progress through college level and beyond." According to the editors, all books have been selected with a view to their availability. The Bibliography, then, has a refreshingly practical emphasis and in many areas could serve as a very basic buying guide. The annotations throughout are brief and helpful.

Examination of the *Plant and Animal Life* bibliography reveals that about 30 percent of the books listed are either new books or newer editions of old books. Books selected for inclusion will appeal to a large and varied group of readers.

The bibliography for *Camping* is sparse—only four titles. Two of these are new since the 1967 edition, but a 1964 guide to campgrounds which is included hardly seems useful. This list does not adequately cover the subject of one of America's fastest growing pastimes.

Bibliographic entries have been updated in the various science fields in a fairly regular and systematic way. One section of general science references in the 1967 edition carried imprint dates from 1950 to 1962. The same section in the new edition now has dates from 1967 to 1970.

A standard feature of *Collier's* is its 14-page Study Guide, located between the Bibliography and Index in the final volume. It is divided into sections "corresponding to the broad areas of study taught by most American colleges and universities." Under each subject heading are listed the articles in *Collier's Encyclopedia* which the editors consider fundamental to a thorough understanding of that subject. The articles are listed progressively in order of difficulty or complexity. For example, the *Guide* to the *Study of Physics* begins with the basic general article *Physics* and leads the student through the various branches of the science, ending with the detailed and highly specialized articles on particle physics. The ultimate value of this Study Guide remains somewhat questionable, however, since the articles referred to by Study Guide headings are replete with *see* and *see also* references, including related biographical entries.

The Index is accurate and adequate, with a format that is easy for the reader to use. Main entries in heavier type and subdivisions in lighter typeface aid clarity and increase the effectiveness of the volume as a quick access key to the entire set.

The pyroxylin-coated red and gold buckram binding is sturdily suited to heavy library use. The clear, readable print is on good quality opaque paper. Volumes are bound so that they open sufficiently flat.

Now recognized as a major general encyclopedia in the English language, the 1972 edition of *Collier's* further substantiates its appeal to the widest cross section of readers, with needs of high school and junior college students receiving greatest emphasis. *Collier's* eminently readable style and good overall organization and considerable revision justify a recommendation for home use, and for the full range of public, secondary school, and college and university libraries. *(June 1, 1973, p.913)*

The Compact Edition of the Oxford English Dictionary: Complete Text Reproduced Micrographically. 2v. Oxford, Clarendon Press, 1971. 4116p. boxed with magnifying glass. 32cm. $75.

The Oxford English Dictionary has been a standard reference source for the past century. Its history goes back to the summer of 1857 when the Philological Society appointed a committee to "collect unregistered words in English." After some 20 years the Society entered into an agreement with the Delegates of the Clarendon Press to publish their dictionary. The Society's aim was to include all words then in use or known to have been in use by 1150, giving for each word the history, différences in meaning, spelling, pronunciation, usage at different periods of the past, and using as a basis "a collection of some five millions of excerpts from English literature of every period amassed by an army of voluntary readers and the editorial staff." The publication of the dictionary extended over a period of 44 years: the 12-volume edition was begun in 1884 and completed in 1933 with publication of the supplement. (See *Subscription Books Bulletin* October 1934 for review.) It is still in print. Although it is costly ($300) and rather inconvenient to use because of the size and number of volumes, it is still basic for almost any library or for anyone interested in the history of words and development of the English language.

Now the complete dictionary has been published in only two volumes through the use of modern micrographic techniques. Four pages of the full-size edition are included on one page of the compact edition. The magnifier supplied (enclosed in a drawer of the box) enlarges approximately four times, so that entries can be read in their normal size.

Guide words and even · the entry words can be read without the magnifier, and a note across the bottom of each page gives the location of such sections as the supplement, corrigenda, spurious words, and the bibliography of most-used sources.

The dark blue binding with gold lettering is in the style of the full-size edition; the paper is thin but opaque. The print is quite clear when the magnifier is used. The margins are wide enough for rebinding, and the volumes lie flat when opened.

Readers may find it awkward and uncomfortable to use the magnifying glass for an extended period. There is some evidence of dissatisfaction with the magnifying glass enclosed. Judging from pictures and descriptions in advertisements and from actual examination, there have been three different glasses: one with an aluminum frame to prop on the page, one with a combination aluminum and wooden frame, also to prop on the page, and finally a regular Bausch and Lomb hand-held lens.

Whatever its design, the glass is not only awkward to use, but in any library other than a personal one keeping track of the magnifier would be difficult. There is the problem, too, of breakage or other damage to the glass. Some plan or system other than leaving the magnifier in the tray at the top of the case in which the two volumes are stored would have to be devised.

The case itself is not very sturdy, judging from the review copies, and even with the plastic strips in the case, removing and replacing volumes can be difficult.

However, the advantages of the compact edition outweigh the disadvantages. There are dictionaries modeled on or supplementing *Oxford English Dictionary* (Oxford: Clarendon Pr., 1933), as well as various shorter versions, but nothing has yet supplanted it.

For personal use, *The Compact Edition of the Oxford English Dictionary* is a bargain. For libraries which cannot afford either the money or the space for the 13-volume set, or for those libraries needing additional sets, it is now available at reasonable cost even if at some inconvenience. *The Compact Edition* is recommended. *(June 1, 1973, p.916)*

Constitutions of the Countries of the World: A Series of Updated Texts, Constitutional Chronologies and Annotated Bibliographies. permanent ed. v.1 Edited by Albert P. Blaustein and Gisbert H. Flanz. Dobbs Ferry, New York, Oceana Publications Inc., 1971. 27cm. (looseleaf) pyroxylin impregnate $69.

Hopefully, the beginning of this publication of national constitutions marks the introduction of an important special service. The primary importance of this set lies in providing current texts of national constitutions, a mission well underway in the first volumes presently available.

Constitutions of Countries of the World (hereinafter referred to as *CCW*) at this writing includes the texts of 48 national constitutions in English translation, each prefaced with a chronologically arranged analytical commentary on the political and legal history of the nation and followed by an annotated bibliography. The publisher intends to complete coverage of the world in some 10 volumes by March 1973. Designed for a loose-leaf set, constitutions (with commentary and bibliography) are issued individually on good heavy paper, spine-edge stapled. They are punched for easy insertion in the very well-constructed post and plate binder, which has a large and clear spine title. Arrangement of each issue can be made according to the subscriber's own plan (e.g., alphabetically, by continent, etc.).

The first volume includes a useful and interesting eight-page Introduction by the editors on the history and problems of publishing national constitutions. This scholarly review of the publication of constitutions makes a strong case for the need to provide *current* information.

Albert Blaustein, the senior editor, is Professor of Law, Rutgers University Law School, a distinguished lawyer, journalist, teacher, and law librarian with an extensive record of both scholarly and "popular" publications. Coeditor Gisbert Flanz is Professor of Political Theory and Comparative Politics, New York University and has served as consultant and advisor in the Near and Far East. In addition to serving as general editors of the entire set, both Blaustein and Flanz had a direct hand in writing the commentaries and bibliographies for about one half of the constitutions published to date.

Each of the first two binders (volumes) contains about 850 pages; 12 nations are represented in each volume. This review is based on the materials in these first two volumes. In volume I are Congo (Brazzaville), Congo (Kinshasa), Ecuador, Fiji, Gambia, Korea, Malawi, Paraguay, Turkey, Uruguay, Western Samoa, and Yugoslavia. In volume II are Ethiopia, Equitorial Guinea, Ghana, Kenya, Laos, Malta, Mauritius, Mongolian Peoples Republic, Democratic Republic of Vietnam, Sierra Leone, Somali Democratic Republic, and Republic of Vietnam.

All materials appear to be photocopies. In only one or two instances is this any disadvantage because of the small typeface, but those texts, fortunately, are very short. The format of the commentaries and bibliographies is uniformly easy to read. The commentaries present in chronological fashion quite concise statements of the political and legal developments leading up to the formation of the constitution. In volumes I and II they range in size from 3 pages each for Fiji and Mongolia to 20 pages for Turkey and 23 for the Republic of Vietnam—for an average of 7 to 8 pages. The credentials of 11 of the 14 writers of the commentaries in volume I are unknown. The three identified are either political scientists or lawyers. The commentaries are in general very helpful and quite judicious, but because of their brevity are hardly more than journalistic outlines. Readers will necessarily turn to other sources for more thorough and scholarly analyses of the respective histories. Six of the commentaries in volume I are authored or coauthored by coeditor Flanz, who was an advisor to the Constitution Deliberation Committee, Republic of Korea, 1962. These six commentaries seem somewhat less objective than the others. For instance, on page three of Korea (Republic of) we find the following entries: "1955-1959. Highly authoritarian course was taken by President Rhee and his supporters. Amended National Security Law was used extensively to quell opposition." "1960. Dr. Rhee 'reelected' for fourth consecutive term on March 15." At least one factual discrepancy appears: the commentators on the constitutions of the Democratic Republic of Vietnam and the Republic of Vietnam differ in identifying the dates of the Geneva Conference. The commentaries are, of course, a secondary feature of this set whose primary value lies in the texts of the constitutions.

The multilingual, annotated bibliographies range in length from two to six pages. They include primary as well as secondary sources, official and unofficial sources, and general or background literature. The annotations are concise and knowledgeable commentaries on the particular relevance of each item.

The texts of the constitutions proper range from 12 pages (Laos) to 156 (Ghana). Ethiopia's consists of 33 pages in English with the 33 parallel pages in Amharic, the official language. Pages in all of the issues are numbered except in the cases of the Somali Democratic Republic and Malta, which have 62 of English translation and 70 of the Maltese "original." Ironically, the constitution of the latter nation includes a Contents page with page reference numbers, although its 44 pages are unnumbered.

The significance of recency in the publication of constitutions can hardly be overemphasized, for during the past decade there has been widespread and comprehensive redrafting of constitutions. The process continues currently and gives indication of persisting in the foreseeable future. When compared with the third revised edition of the well-known *Constitutions of Nations* edited by the Peaslees (The Hague: Nijhoff, 1965-   ), this set demonstrates such changes quite dramatically. The current Peaslee edition appeared in the mid-1960s during a time of great change in constitutions throughout the world. The constitution of Yugoslavia, to select an example, appears in its 1963 version in *Peaslee*. This constitution, drastically revised in 1967, is presented in its current form with the appropriate analytical commentary in *CCW*. The revisions were far more than technical or legalistic; basic reforms which in effect reallocated much of the power previously held by the Communist Party were introduced. Anyone referring to the 1963 edition would be quite seriously misled in using it to interpret or understand present-day Yugoslavia.

Perhaps the constitutions of "emerging" nations alone would justify the need for current publication. Those for both the Congo (Brazzaville) and the Congo (Kinshasa) are not up to date in *Peaslee*, but do appear in current form in *CCW;* this is particularly important in that the old "Leopoldville" constitution was drastically revised in 1967 for "Kinshasa." (To clarify terminology about the Congos somewhat, it is worth noting that on October 27, 1971 a presidential decree changed the name of the Democratic Republic of the Congo (Kinshasa) to the Republic of Zaire.) In Peaslee's African volume the constitution for Malawi is out of date and that for Gambia does not appear at all; both are in *CCW*.

The Leslie Wolf-Phillips *Constitutions of Modern States* is another source often used for research on constitutions. It is much more compact by virtue of being selective—and consequently considerably less expensive than either *Peaslee* or *CCW*, but it does not carry complete text in many instances, many constitutions are not represented at all, and it does not provide bibliographies. Indeed, because of its lack of thorough coverage and its being out of date, in spite of bearing a 1968 imprint, *Wolf-Phillips* cannot be considered a satisfactory substitute for the materials in *CCW*.

Constitutions of the Countries of the World is available by subscription only. Each volume is priced at $69 for 12 issues, including the binder. The publisher plans to bill subscribers quarterly for $75 until the probably 10-volume set is completed. To keep the set up to date, the publisher will provide supplements included in the cost of the subscription beginning with volume v until the basic set of the 10 or so volumes is complete. Following the expected date of completion, March 1973, there will be a "small charge" for annual supplementation to keep the set up to date.

In accordance with Committee policy, no final evaluation is given when only a portion of a set is available for examination, and the customary recommendation paragraph is omitted.

(Nov. 15, 1972, p.249)

Cram Modern World Atlas. World Maps; Foreign Index; U.S. Maps: Political, Physical, Product; Color Photographs; 1970 U.S. Census and Zip Codes; World History Maps. 1971 ed. Indianapolis, Ind., George F. Cram Co., Inc., 1971. xvi, 358, 34p. illus. 31cm. linen $12.95.

George F. Cram Company, producer of atlases, maps, and globes since 1867, published an atlas with the same title in 1961. (See *The Booklist and Subscription Books Bulletin* October 15, 1962.) The present atlas is basically different from the 1961 *Cram Modern World Atlas* in that 352 of its pages, including the main series of maps (pages 1-320) and the approximately 25,000-entry Index of the World (pages 321-344) were produced by C. S. Hammond Company, and appear to be, plate for plate, a reprinting of pages 1-352 of *Hammond Citation Atlas* (Maplewood, N.J.: Hammond, Inc. 1971). *Citation* was reviewed by the Reference and Subscription Books Review Committee in an omnibus examination of seven Hammond atlases in *Booklist* May 1, 1972. *Citation* consists primarily of a basic set of maps of the world, separate maps for the United States arranged alphabetically by state, and maps of the provinces of Canada.

In addition to the material from *Citation, Cram Modern World Atlas* contains a three-page Detailed Index to Contents which has approximately 600 entries and cites maps by page number and latitude and longitude. At the front there is also a Condensed World Gazetteer listing some 175 countries with type of government, capital, area, and population. Other materials in *Cram* but not in *Citation* are 200 Largest Cities of the World listed both alphabetically and by rank, 206 Largest Cities of the United States listed alphabetically and by rank, an annotated list of United States National Parks, a narrative of the Polar Regions revised from the 1961 Cram atlas, but still inadequate when compared with standard encyclopedias, two pages of definitions of 145 map terms, and two pages of about 240 Definitions of Geographical Terms. These inclusions are surely not significant; nor are they unique to atlases.

The *Cram* volume concludes with World History, a section whose pages bear a duplicate set of numbers; pages H3 to H34 are also numbered 305 to 336. This latter numbering serves little purpose since it is nonsequential and, although the maps are included in the 600-entry Detailed Index to Contents, they are not in the 25,000-entry Index to the World. World History is exactly the same in both the *Cram* 1961 and 1971 atlases. The Reference and Subscription Books Review Committee's 1961 review noted that the 32 history maps are primarily concerned with Europe and only peripherally reflect American history in four maps displaying explorations and the campaigns of the two world wars of this century. This criticism is still valid. To this it must be added that these maps are printed in solid colors (as opposed to pastel colors around the boundaries of countries or states as appear in the Hammond portion of this atlas). These colors are of a more intense or vivid hue than is customary in modern-day cartography. All place-names are printed in black and are noticeably difficult to read because of the bright colors of the various geographical regions.

The volume is adequately bound in linen, but in copies examined by the Committee neither the signatures nor their pages were always carefully aligned before spine sewing.

In its survey of the new Hammond atlases published May 1, 1972 in *Booklist,* the Reference and Subscription Books Review Committee recommended the *Citation* atlas ($10.95), chiefly for its excellent map format, clarity of detail, good use of color, and adequate indexing. However, the Committee gave more favorable recommendation to the Hammond *Ambassador* atlas ($14.95), chiefly on the basis of a better index—110,000 entries, including U.S. ZIP codes, as against 25,000 entries in *Citation*. Since this new Cram atlas consists almost entirely (352 pages out of a total of 392) of the text of Hammond's *Citation* atlas and its price places it halfway between these two recommended Hammond atlases, it would appear that this atlas is little more than a third alternative. The purchaser may now obtain a good atlas of approximately 350 pages, with an index of approximately 25,000 entries, for $10.95 (*Citation*); or he may purchase the *Cram* atlas being reviewed, which is the same as *Citation* but with the addition of some minor geographical information and some brightly colored, unindexed historical maps, for $12.95; or he may purchase, for $14.95, the same basic atlas but with the addition of an index of approximately 110,000 entries, the U.S. entries being ZIP-coded. Whichever of these three possibilities is adopted, the purchaser will be buying a set of maps copyrighted by Hammond in 1971, and it is this set of maps which is recommended. *(Nov. 15, 1972, p.250)*

A Dictionary of Literature in the English Language, from Chaucer to 1940.
Compiled and edited by Robin Myers for the National Book League. 2v. Oxford, Pergamon Press, [1970.] xvii, 1,497p. illus. 26cm. buckram Redbridge Aberlave, set $40; to libraries, 10 percent discount.

Compiled and edited by Robin Myers for the National Book League, *A Dictionary of Literature in the English Language* is, according to the Preface, a bibliographical and biographical guide to "some 3500 authors who have used English as their medium of expression throughout the world over a period of 600 years."

Robin Myers, librarian of the National Book League, London, 1965-1969, has taught English in various English independent and grammar schools, and recently in the North London Collegiate School.

The compilation begins with Chaucer and his contemporaries because they were "the first to use a language that we can recognize as English." The editor admits the 1940 closing for those authors who began to write before that date is arbitrary, but "after that date adequate national bibliographies exist to which librarians and scholars can have easy access." According to the publisher, Miss Myers is now working on a sequel to this dictionary which will cover the period 1940-1970. One might query the need for such a sequent publication in view of the existence of national bibliographies.

The first volume is arranged alphabetically by author's last name. For each author the following information is given: a brief biographical note, indication of bibliographic sources used or recommended, and a list of first editions of the author's works in chronological order. Publisher and place of publication are omitted. Volume I also contains a Geographical and Chronological Index to Authors, arranged first by country (United States, Canada, England) and then chronologically by author's date of birth under each country. Volume II is a title-author index to the some 60,000 works cited in volume I.

This unique title index is a very helpful feature. This index is reasonably accurate and refers from the title to the author, but no page number is given, since volume I is alphabetically arranged by author. Cross-references are made from pseudonyms.

For the purpose of inclusion Miss Myers used a broad definition of literature. Therefore, she includes not only poets, dramatists, and novelists, but also authors of detective stories and romantic novels as well as scientists, historians, economists, lawyers, and statesmen "who have much influenced the thought of their day, or who have written excellently." Such persons as John James Audubon, Clarence Darrow, Albert Einstein, Isaac Newton, and Queen Victoria are included. English authors are represented in the greatest numbers, double the number of Americans. Canadians and Scots hold third and fourth place. The number of authors covered is closer to 2,700 than the 3,500 claimed in the Preface.

The dictionary also includes brief notes on major periodicals and newspapers, certain literary groups and movements, and literary prizes. These items, which are found in alphabetical order with the authors, are a minor part of the total coverage.

The publisher claims that "there is no other single volume reference work in which the user may find complete published works of literary authors writing in English in all countries, over so long a period, together with a biographical note and a reference to other bibliographical studies." To test this claim the dictionary was compared with other similar sources. The publisher's claim was borne out by this investigation.

Concise Cambridge Bibliography of English Literature 1600-1950 (Cambridge Univ. Pr., 1958) is the one-volume abridgement of the five-volume work with an added section on the early twentieth century. It covers only 400 writers from the British Isles writing in English while the dictionary under review includes authors writing in English from many countries. *Concise Cambridge Bibliography* lists works by and about the authors whereas the dictionary lists the authors' works by title and date.

A comparable source for American literature is Kunitz and Haycraft, *American Authors 1600-1900* (New York: Wilson, 1938) which includes approximately 1,300 authors, giving more complete biographical information than *Myers*. Here, again, there is a geographical limitation.

Burke and Howe, *American Authors and Books 1640 to the Present Day* (New York: Crown, 1962) is also limited to resident authors of the continental United States. Entries for the several hundred authors include brief biographical information plus the authors' works and dates of publication. Like *Myers*, *Burke and Howe* include brief descriptions of newspapers, periodicals, and literary societies.

Approximately 240 American authors are included in the bibliography volume and supplements of Spiller's *Literary History of the United States*. Extensive bibliographical information is given for each author, not only his works, but also biography and criticism, primary sources, and some evaluative comments on the editions listed. Kunitz and Haycraft, *Twentieth Century Authors* (New York: Wilson, 1942) and its supplement include about 2,550 authors who were active after 1900. Browning's *Everyman's Dictionary of Literary Biography, English and American* includes brief biographical and bibliographical sketches of approximately 2,300 authors. The biographical information given is a little more detailed than that in *Myers*. Comparing the number of English and American authors covered in *Browning* and *Myers*, one must note that the coverage is more inclusive in Browning.

The advantage of *Myers* in comparison with the titles mentioned above is its broad chronological and geographical coverage. It fills the gap when the nationality or time period of an English-writing author is unknown.

Fourteen black-and-white plates are distributed throughout volume I. They illustrate title pages of specific editions or depict pages of well-known periodicals.

The two volumes are sturdily bound, and pages lie flat when opened. The format is good, two columns of print on a page with broad outside margins.

Myers' *Dictionary of Literature in the English Language* is a useful addition to biographical-bibliographical reference works on English-language authors. Its unique features of broad geographical and chronological coverage plus its title Index make it a welcome reference source. Recommended. *(Jan. 1, 1973, p.409)*

Dictionary of Science and Technology.
Ed. by T. C. Collocott. New York, Barnes and Noble, [1972, c1971 by W. & R. Chambers Ltd.]. xvi, 1328p. 22cm. cloth $22.50. 20 percent discount to dealers.

Dictionary of Science and Technology (cover title: *Chambers Dictionary of Science and Technology*) is a direct successor to *Chambers's Technical Dic-*

tionary first published in 1940. Subsequent editions revised by adding supplementary pages were published in 1944 and 1958. By the late 1960s the publishers decided that the time had come for a complete revision of *Chambers Dictionary*. The rewriting was undertaken under the editorship of T. C. Collocott who had helped in the earlier revisions of the dictionary. Unlike the original work, this dictionary does not list the experts who contributed to it.

The first and second editions of *Chambers's Technical Dictionary* were reviewed unfavorably in *Subscription Books Bulletin*, January 1941 and January 1945 respectively. Due to its British bias and the fact that most of the words could be found with better definitions in an unabridged dictionary, the book was not recommended in either edition.

The aim of the compiler has been "to set on record the basic language of communication in the numerous branches of a scientific activity today." To do this he presents a work which follows much the pattern and format of its predecessors. The main body of the work consists of short definitions of some 60,000 terms arranged alphabetically letter by letter. Appendixes contain a miscellaneous collection of scientific tables, e.g., chemical elements, igneous rocks, and sedimentary rocks. The bibliography which appeared in the earlier work has been dropped.

In most cases each word is assigned to one of one hundred subject fields. The subjects and their abbreviations are listed in the preliminary pages. When a term relates to more than one field, definitions are arranged alphabetically under the classification term. For example, the building definition for area precedes the radio and surveying definitions. The complete listing for each work is presented in paragraph form, whereas the original work used separate indented entries for each definition of a word. The form now used may save space, but it is inferior to the earlier format because it is harder to find the separate meanings of a word. Pronunciation is not indicated.

While there are many dictionaries of terms from individual scientific fields

Dictionary of Science and Technology is the only up-to-date one-volume dictionary that attempts to cover all classes of science and technology. Its coverage can be compared, therefore, with an unabridged dictionary. A sample comparison of entries indicates that 33 percent of the definitions in *Dictionary of Science and Technology* are not in *Webster's Third New International Dictionary,* and 63 percent are not in *Random House Dictionary of the English Language* (New York: Random House, 1966).

Since this work was originally compiled in Great Britain it is not surprising that numerous examples of British usage and spelling diminish its value somewhat for use in this country. Examples range from the fairly well-known aerodrome and aeroplane to tyre and jink (a coupling between two mine tubs). The entries *aluminium* (with a note at the end of the definition "in U.S. aluminum") and *lift* (with a similar note "also called elevator") show some attempt to equate British and American usage. The entry *elevator* gives lift as one meaning, but among several definitions does not include its use as describing a storage building such as a grain elevator.

Good use has been made of cross-references not only for indicating the entry under which a term is defined but also for referring to entries for words used in the definitions. This latter is important since often words are defined in terms that themselves might be unfamiliar.

Updating of this work from the last edition of *Chambers's Technical Dictionary* has on the whole been successful. It has been expanded by 300 pages. Many new entries such as *codon, hologram, hovercraft, hythergraph, laser, mascons, Morgan's canon, operon, pulsar* and *quasar* can be found. While many entries have not been changed, numerous examples of rewritten and expanded articles could be cited. *Ecology* has been expanded from two lines to thirteen, and the number of entries starting with the word ecological has increased from one to seven. An updating of the entry **Greenwich Mean Time** reports the discarding of the use of British Standard Time in 1971. At least one error was found as a result of retaining an old entry intact. In the entry *time* it is stated that "the fundamental unit of measurement is supplied by the earth's rotation on its axis." The entry *second*, however, correctly defines the second in terms of the resonance vibration of the Caesium-133 atom. This work is not, however, without its omissions. Such terms as conodont, quark, magnetosphere and plate tectonics are not found here.

The definitions in this dictionary, although usually brief, are for the most part adequate. This brevity can produce definitions that in some instances are not particularly illuminating. For example, the definition of *molecular biology* as "the study of biological molecules" is merely a rearrangement of terms and gives no hint of the true extent of this field.

The material is presented in small but readable type, two columns to the page. Although there are no illustrations, these solid columns of type are occasionally broken by chemical structural formulas or mathematical equations. The volume lies flat when opened. The binding does not appear to be designed for heavy use, and the narrow inner margin would make rebinding difficult.

Dictionary of Science and Technology presents a large number of up-to-date, brief, but for the most part adequate, definitions of terms used in the whole area of science and technology in one easy to use volume. The British bias of this work and the brevity of many of its definitions may cause some problems for the layman. *Dictionary of Science and Technology* should be useful for ready reference and for placing a term in the field or fields in which it is used. Recommended. *(Dec. 1, 1972, p.305)*

Documents of American Theater History: v.1, Famous American Playhouses, 1716-1899; v.2, Famous American Playhouses, 1900-1971. By William C. Young. Chicago, American Library Association, 1973. 2v. illus. 26cm. cloth $50 the set. ISBN 0-8389-0136-0.

Famous American Playhouses is a two-volume set designed to be part of a series *Documents of American Theater History*. The series of seven volumes with no stated publication schedule, will include in addition *Famous Actors and Actresses on the American Stage, Playwrights of the American Stage, Major Events of American Theater History* and documents relating to directors and producers. The emphasis in the entire series will be on primary and secondary source materials to provide "a basic reference tool for librarians, scholars, students and others interested in the American theater." The author states that the series will offer "the first systematic documentary history of the theater in American society and culture." Primary source documents are used whenever their contents contribute to the history of a playhouse, but the author points out that primary sources often pay greater attention to the plays performed and less attention to the playhouse itself. Frequently, secondary sources give a more comprehensive picture.

The author is a contributing editor of *Educational Theatre Journal* and the author of *American Theatre Arts: A Guide to Manuscripts and Special Collections in the United States and Canada* (Chicago: American Library Association, 1971).

The author has clearly stated his purpose: "The focus of the first two volumes in this series is the American playhouse as a physical structure." He has used three criteria for selection of the theaters covered: historical, architectural, and social and cultural importance. Using these tests he has included 199 theaters out of more than 400 he investigated. The work does not claim to be comprehensive; many theaters described must be viewed as prototypes, with their importance being judged from a national viewpoint. In the Preface the author reminds that local theaters often are of importance only to local historians.

The entry for each theater is followed by the name of the city where it is located and the date of the theater's opening. Usually a short editorial introduction leads into the first source document. Each document is identified in a bibliographical footnote. The footnotes are adequate, except that newspaper citations do not give page references or titles of the news story. The source documents range in length from about 60 lines to over 1,000 lines. The earliest theater included is the First Williamsburg Theater (1716?), and the latest is the John F. Kennedy Center for the Performing Arts (1971).

Since the author's focus is supposedly on the playhouse as a physical structure, the documents he uses should be pertinent. However, the documents sometimes contain such material as human interest anecdotes, dramatic criticism, and theories of play selection in addition to plans of the theaters. This kind of material adds nothing to the reader's knowledge of a playhouse as a building; its inclusion leaves the author vulnerable to accusations of padding.

The arrangement of the documents is a combination of chronology, geography, and type of theater. It is confusing at first glance, but the scheme is workable. Each theater is assigned a code **number in numerical sequence;** all references to that theater throughout this set use this code number. The sequence of code numbers is separate for each volume. A theater may have more than one document to describe its building, and therefore each document pertaining to that theater also has a sub-number.

Each volume includes a Contents page and an Illustrations page. Volume 1 has two prefaces, the first, Preface to Documents of American Theater History for the whole projected series, and the second, Preface to volumes 1 and 2 for the set being considered in this review. Two pages of Acknowledgments follow the prefaces in volume 1.

The set includes 199 black-and-white illustrations. Each illustration carries the code number of the theater it pictures as well as the name of the theater. Not all theaters are illustrated, and most have only one illustration. The illustrations are near but not always opposite the related or appropriate text. They include pictures of exteriors, interiors, plans, models, and one of a drop curtain. The illustrations are reproductions of engravings, etchings, drawings, lithographs, watercolors, photographs, stereographs, and a mural. They are one, two, or three to a page and therefore often small. The plans and diagrams are floor plans, areas such as light bays, lobbies, and cross sections of the theater building. Of the 18 plans and diagrams all but two are in volume 2. The illustrations are generally clear, and the source of each is included in its caption.

Each volume has an Index of Theaters Arranged Alphabetically, an Index of Theaters Arranged Geographically, and an Index of Personal Names and Theatrical Specialties. The references in each Index are to entry number, not to page numbers.

Each volume has its own bibliography, Selected Bibliography of the American Theater, 1716-1899 (v.1), and Selected Bibliography of American Playhouses, 1900-1971 (v.2). Each follows the main text of its volume and opens with a brief statement concerning the location of theater subject collections, especially primary sources, in various American libraries. This information can be found in greater detail in Lee Ash's *Subject Collections,* 3d ed. (New York & London: Bowker, 1967) and Young's *American Theatrical Arts* (Chicago: Amer. Lib. Assoc., 1971).

In volume 1, the first part of the bibliography is a list of eight general histories of the American theater, followed by a selective bibliography of 70 titles related to American playhouses before 1900. Volume 2 refers the reader to volume 1 for the general bibliography, but adds a list of 36 books concerning twentieth century American theaters. In volume 1, the bibliographies list only books, with four exceptions. The exceptions include references to two manuscript collections, one in the University of Pennsylvania and one in the archives of the Maryland Historical Society, and two citations to the Columbia Historical Society Records. The manuscript collections are the only bibliographical listings giving location of materials. In volume 2 all items in the bibliography are books. All book items include author, title, and imprint.

The sources cited range in publication date from 1808 to 1971. Since the author indicates that his bibliographies are selective and in no way exhaustive, the books cited seem adequate to introduce researchers to additional sources. He also states that related bibliographies will appear in later volumes of the series.

The bibliography section in each volume also includes lists of newspapers, magazines, and journals consulted, but these lists include only titles, with no citations. The value of such lists is unclear, since full bibliographical citations have been given in the bibliographical footnotes of the main text.

The indexes are accurate and include not only references to the original name of each theater, but also cross-references to subsequent names.

The set is bound in brown cloth with gold lettering on the spine and cover. The series title appears on both spine and cover of each volume in larger letters than the subtitle of this set. The proper volume number and date covered for each volume is also on spine and cover. The text is legibly printed on opaque buff paper in two columns per page. The entry title for each theater is in boldface. The word "theater" in the entry titles is spelled "theatre"; in the text the spelling is "theater." The code number for each theater and the name of the theater appear as page heads. Each page also carries a consecutively arranged number in the middle of the bottom margin. Occasionally this pagination is very close to the lower edge of the page and could be lost in rebinding. The pages carrying illustrations are not numbered. Inner margins range from three-fourths inch to one inch. The volumes lie flat when opened.

The value of the set to scholars is minimal; the materials cited would be of use in brief preliminary research. For instance, the John F. Kennedy Center for the Performing Arts has only two documents, a brochure prepared by the Center and one periodical article for a total of 684 lines of text; yet the author of the set calls the opening of this theater "perhaps the single most important event in American theater history." The Lakewood Theater, Skowhegan, Maine, is covered by 1,013 lines of text. It is not clear why the author chose this imbalance.

Students, especially at the undergraduate or lower levels, would probably find enough materials conveniently assembled for their needs. Other users will undoubtedly find it convenient to have such materials gathered together, especially since many of the eighteenth- and nineteenth-century documents reproduced occur in newspapers and periodicals of the period. The scholar, however, will not find the in-depth analysis required for research.

The two volumes of *Famous American Playhouses* promise that the projected multi-volumed series *Documents of American Theater History*, of which they form a part, will become an important collection of source materials for the documentation of American theater history. In accordance with Committee policy, final evaluation of *Documents of American Theater History* is withheld until the complete set is available for examination.. *(Jan. 1, 1974, p.451)*

Dynamics of World Power: A Documentary History of United States Foreign Policy 1945-1973. General ed. Arthur M. Schlesinger, Jr. 5v. New York, Chelsea House Publishers and McGraw-Hill, Inc., 1973. 24cm. Roxite C grade pyroxylin cloth $169; to schools and libraries, $135.20. ISBN 0-07-079729-3. Western Europe, ed. by Robert Dallek, v.1; Eastern Europe and the Soviet Union, ed. by Walter LaFeber, v.2; Latin America, ed. by Robert Burr, v.3; The Far East, ed. by Russell D. Buhite, v.4; The United Nations, ed. by Richard C. Hottelet and Subsaharan Africa, ed. by Jean Herskovits, v.5.

For "the complex and anguished years" from the end of World War II to the Vietnam Agreement of January 1973 these volumes provide the texts, the "raw data of history," recording the essentials of United States foreign policy.

The words quoted are from the Introduction by the general editor, Arthur M. Schlesinger, Jr., who is the Albert M. Schweitzer Professor in the Humanities at the City University of New York. In addition to Professor Schlesinger's eminently readable essay, each volume or unit has a separate introduction by its specialist editor. The United Nations section, the first half of volume 5, was edited by Richard C. Hottelet, news correspondent of the Columbia Broadcasting System and its United Nations correspondent for many years. The other editors are identified on the title pages as "Professor of History:" Robert Dallek and Robert Burr at the University of California at Los Angeles; Walter LaFeber at Cornell University; Russell D. Buhite at the University of Oklahoma; and Jean Herskovits at the State University of New York at Purchase.

According to the general Introduction "A sixth volume, now in preparation, will cover United States policy toward Canada, Australia and New Zealand; it will also supply further documentation, in addition to that published in the United Nations section of volume 5, on United States policy in the Middle East and in Mediterranean Africa."

Within the regional volumes the treatment is topical, with the exception of the Latin American volume where all documents are chronologically arranged without subdivision for country or topic. In volumes 4 and 5 a major division such as "The United States and India and Pakistan" or "Disarmament and Outer Space" is introduced by historical Commentary of from one to five pages. In the first three volumes, commentary is confined to the Introduction.

As might be expected, official government publications of the United States are the source of most of the documents. Many of them are from the Department of State monthly or annual series, or retrospective volumes for a five- or ten-year period or for a special topic. The work under review differs from official collections in the extent to which speeches of foreign leaders responding to U.S. policy, as well as excerpts from documents of the legislative branch of government—Congressional hearings and committee reports—and occasional non-governmental sources, such as memoirs published at a later time, can be interspersed to round out the formal State Department record. The expertise in selection is, of course, the particular contribution of each editor.

Most frequently cited is the *Department of State Bulletin*, the source of approximately 90 percent of the documents in the Latin American volume. The volume on the Far East relies on that source for about 35 percent, citing also the State Department's *American Foreign Policy 1950-55: Basic Documents* (the successor to *A Decade of American Foreign Policy: Basic Documents 1941-49*) and the annual *American Foreign Policy, Current Documents*. Important additions to those records are the excerpts from Senate and House hearings, reports to Congressional committees, the reminiscences of a general (MacArthur) or a president (Truman) or a document published in *The New York Times* (President Ho Chi Minh to Pope Paul). The variety of sources used in volume 4 is representative for the work as a whole. The volume for Eastern Europe and the Soviet Union also draws on a wide range of sources, including the papers of Bernard Baruch and John Foster Dulles.

The contents pages of each volume provide a clear overview of its topical organization as well as the title and date of each document, for example: "Joint Statement of the United States and Korea on United States Troop Reduction and Korean Modernization, February 6, 1971."

A 25-page advertising brochure mentions "a number of texts never before published," but it is not possible to identify them easily. The wording in the Introduction that in a number of cases "texts appear for the first time between book covers" could refer as well to the considerable amount of material that appeared originally in government periodical and report form over many years.

No bibliography is included other than the footnote citations to the original text of each document and the short lists of acknowledgments for copyright material, at the end of volumes 2, 4 and 5.

Indexes at the end of each volume appear to be comprehensive for all major topics, political entities, authors of documents, and recipients when addressed to an individual, but are not exhaustive for all personal and geographical names mentioned in the text.

Beyond the usual forms of bibliography and volume indexing, however, the citations themselves serve as important access points to more detailed information in the larger series. This less obvious reference function is a valuable supplement to the work's primary function of supplying texts.

The volumes are heavy but appear to be durably bound and lie flat when open. There is sufficient inner margin for rebinding. Spines are clearly marked.

Dynamics of World Power illuminates the United States' role in world affairs since World War II by juxtaposing the texts of many historic documents, in a form for convenient reference according to world region and under specific topics. Recommended for academic, public, and government libraries. *(Feb. 15, 1974, p.606)*

The Earth and Man: a Rand McNally World Atlas. New York, Chicago, San Francisco, Rand McNally and Co., in association with Mitchell Beazly, Ltd., London, [1972]. 439p. col. illus. col. maps. 37cm. buckram over boards. $35.

Published in the fall of 1972 in Great Britain as *The Atlas of the Earth* and in the United States as *The Earth and Man, The Earth and Man* is a new addition to the family of atlases published by Rand McNally and reviewed in *The Booklist* December 1, 1972. Of its 439 pages, 290 are devoted to maps and Index. The first section of the volume (149 pages) is an encyclopedic presentation entitled "The Good Earth," a compendium of charts, photographs, drawings, and other graphic presentations accompanied by textual material on the structure, environments, and resources of the earth and man's history and relationship to the earth.

Although the atlas is intended to be "not merely a collection of maps, but an encyclopedia," as stated in the Foreword by Sir Julian Huxley, it is in reality two volumes in one rather than a single integrated work. While the pagination is continuous, each section is distinct and there are no cross-references or other referral devices between them. There are two tables of contents and two indexes. The first section, in fact, is separately copyrighted by Mitchell Beazly, Ltd. of Great Britain. Each section must therefore be considered on its own merits.

The first section, "The Good Earth," is divided into 5 chapters, each of which covers from 6 to 19 subtopics 2 or 3 pages in length. None of the entries is signed; however, the chief editorial consultants and advisers, together with their scholarly affiliations, are included at the beginning of the volume. The fact that only 2 of the 33 consultants listed are Americans and that nearly all the others are British scientists is further indication of the British origin of the first part of the atlas.

"The Good Earth" section presents a surprising variety of data for geology, meteorology, anthropology, astronomy, archaeology, nutrition, agriculture, mineralogy, and geography, largely in visual format, with just enough textual material to explain and amplify the graphic presentations. The publishers' claim of over 1,200 illustrations and photographs is not exaggerated. The photographs, all in color, are clear, well-reproduced, and closely related to the accompanying text. The drawings, graphs, artists' representations, and diagrams are presented in uncluttered fashion and are easy to read and interpret. A list of artists and photographic credits appears on page 358 before the Index.

Although sources for data used in tables and charts are not cited, the information is both accurate and recent. In anticipation of the universal adoption of the metric system, all figures used in the text and illustrations, both linear and quantitative, are followed in parentheses by their metric equivalent, a most useful device.

In scientific areas where there is still some disagreement among scholars, the editors are careful to state the most commonly accepted theories while offering alternative points of view as other possibilities. For example, in the presentation of the origin of the solar system, the accretion theory is given preferential attention, but other concepts (supernova explosion, tidal, and contracting nebula theories) are also explained.

While the textual material presented in "The Good Earth" contains many rather difficult scientific concepts, the accompanying graphic illustrations simplify these concepts greatly, so that this section can be used profitably by anyone of high school age or older who has only a minimum of scientific knowledge. Examples include the sections on geologic dating, plate tectonics, DNA and cell structure, and the structure and function of the human brain.

A unifying thread runs through the first section of this atlas: the abundant earth and the obligation of man to use it wisely. The final 13 pages of the last chapter (Man on Earth) are devoted to population and population problems and pollution and conservation. The final subchapter, Promises to Keep, is an editorial afterword extolling the riches of the earth and expressing an optimism for man's ability to preserve his planet. This common theme enlivens the many presentations and gives the work a sense of unity.

A very complete Index of over 1,800 entries supplements the pages of "The Good Earth" section. References are made to both illustrative and textual materials. The only weakness of the Index is its placement in the volume. Instead of appearing at the end of "The Good Earth" section, it is placed after the second section (Maps) and before the separate map Index making it both somewhat difficult to find and awkward to use. There are no bibliographies or suggested further readings to enhance the volume's usefulness.

The second section of *The Earth and Man*, entitled "Maps," consists of 151 pages of maps, a group of tables on world political information and population, and an 80-page map Index. This section exhibits most of the qualities of other atlases in the Rand McNally family of atlases (*Cosmopolitan World Atlas*; *World Atlas, Family ed.*; *Worldmaster Atlas*; *Premier World Atlas*) reviewed as a group in *The Booklist*, December 1, 1972. The same basic map plates, the publisher's "Cosmo" series, have apparently been used; U.S. information is presented in greater detail than world information, and The Ocean World unit, described in the previous review, appears again in the present volume. In contrast to the policy criticized in the earlier review, editorial responsibilities are stated. There is a single easily-found key to all map symbols used in the volume. This appears immediately preceding the maps as a section entitled "Legend to Maps" on the same pages with a clear guide to all maps used in the volume.

All maps are political-physical maps with the exception of the six pages of physical maps depicting the ocean floors in The Ocean World unit. With very few exceptions the maps are presented in one of four scales, from 1:12,000,000 to 1:1,000,000. While the smallest scale of 1:12,000,000, used for 12 maps, presents larger geographic relationships, it of necessity gives less detailed coverage of place-names and man-made features than do maps of larger scale. Thus, such detailed emphasis is not available for much of Canada, U.S.S.R., China, Western Australia, and central Africa, as maps of no larger scale for these areas are included.

The largest scale, 1:1,000,000, is used 30 times for some of the more heavily congested areas of the world such as west-central Europe and certain portions of North America. Unfortunately, large scale was not used for Eastern and Southeastern Asia for example, where it would have been equally useful.

Coloration of maps varies depending on scale. The maps of 1:1,000,000 use gradient shades of tan and contour shading to indicate elevation. The maps of other scales use contour shading and gradient shades of gray and blue. The colors selected in both cases allow for the readable overprinting of names and geographic features which are unobscured by the darker shades. All distances and distance scales are given in both kilometers and statute miles, but all elevations and depths are stated only in meters. Type of projection and scale are indicated on each map page. All maps are bordered except those in The Ocean World unit, which are bled to the edge of the page.

Although the editors claim that the 80-page Index contains "some 70,000 names appearing on the maps," a check indicates this figure may be closer to 66,000. Most map features are indexed to the largest scale map on which they appear. Names in the Index and on the maps are generally in the local language. For names in languages not written in the Roman alphabet, the locally official transliteration system has been used. For languages without an accepted translation system, "translation in general follows closely a system adopted by the United States Board on Geographic Names." Names in the Index are followed by a symbol if the name is other than a town or village. A key to symbols precedes the map Index. Because of the multitude of symbols used (75), it is necessary to refer to the key frequently when using the Index. Each entry in the Index is followed by a page reference to one or more maps and by the location on the map in coordinates of longitude and latitude.

The Index presents a reasonable number of place-names appearing on the maps and a sampling shows the Index to be 96 percent accurate.

Additional useful features of *The Earth and Man* are four tables on world political and population information appearing at the end of the map section. An examination of these tables shows them to be both comprehensive and up to date. Although a few minor errors were found, such recent political changes as the creation of Bangladesh, the federation of the Arab Trucial states into the United Arab Emirates, and the change of name of the Democratic Republic of the Congo to Zaire are all included. These changes appear also on the maps. The tables of population list all world cities with a population of 50,000 or more and all U.S. incorporated towns and cities of 600 or more.

Nineteen seventy census figures are used for U.S. locations. According to the editors, the population figures for foreign cities and towns are either from recent censuses or from official estimates with few exceptions. All population figures are labeled accordingly.

The volume is sturdily bound in buckram over binder's board with reinforced Smyth sewing. The pages are of heavy matte finish except for the Index and supplementary tables, which are of lighter weight blue paper. The volume lies flat when opened. The maps, which are not center-hinged, are carefully bound so that center registration is accurate in almost every case, and no map information is lost in the binding.

The Earth and Man offers both an extensive textual presentation on the earth and a reasonably comprehensive atlas section. The clear text and profuse graphics which illuminate and amplify the text, together with an emphasis throughout on the importance of man's responsibility for stewardship of his planet, commend this volume to a wide audience. The atlas section is comparable in size and coverage to Rand McNally's *Premier World Atlas* and maintains the same standard of quality as other atlases in the Rand McNally series reviewed in *The Booklist* December 1, 1972.

The Earth and Man, while not as comprehensive as other atlases in its price range, provides a unique reference resource for high school, public, and college libraries because of the variety of its features. For this reason it would also be a useful atlas for homes. Recommended.

(July 1, 1973, p.996)

Editorials on File. Twice-Monthly Newspaper Editorial Survey with Cumulative Index. v. 1, January 1970- . New York, Facts on File, Inc., 1970-   28cm. loose-leaf with buckram library binder $150 for one year or $250 for two years.

Facts on File, Inc. is the publisher of

Editorials on File, a semimonthly compilation of editorials on selected major topics in 120 United States newspapers. This firm is also responsible for the famous reference standby from which it takes its name. All areas of the continental United States as well as Hawaii and Puerto Rico are represented by the participating newspapers. The copyright statement in each issue notes that "Editorials are reprinted with the permission of the cooperating newspapers, which retain their copyrights." Only six states did not have newspapers whose editorials are used in this survey. The total daily circulation of the newspapers whose editorials appear in *Editorials on File* is over 27,000,000—one third of the total daily circulation in the United States. The circulation of the journals varies from *Sun Reporter*'s (San Francisco, California) 9,000 and *Emporia* (Kansas) *Gazette's* 10,000 to the *New York Times'* 846,000 and *New York Daily News'* 2,130,000.

Although a few states have no newspapers chosen for this survey, over 30 cities have more than one newspaper participating. Among those with two are Boston (*Globe* and *Herald Traveler and Record American*), Miami, Florida (*Herald* and *News*), Pittsburgh (*Post Gazette* and *Press*), Portland, Oregon (*Journal* and *Oregonian*). Baltimore has three newspapers represented (*Afro-American, News American,* and *Sun*). Chicago has five (*Daily Defender, Daily News, Sun Times, Today,* and *Tribune*) and New York has five (*Amsterdam News, Daily News, Post, Times,* and *Wall Street Journal*).

The editorials of the newspapers chosen reflect varying interests according to the size of the community, its region, and political leanings of the publication.

Each semimonthly issue averages 70 pages and treats about 7 topics, although the number of topics may vary from 5 to 9. "Each topic covered in these surveys is introduced by a brief summary of the events that stimulated the editorials. These introductions are written from material in the weekly *Facts on File* news reference service, where additional information on the subject can be found. The editorials in the survey are reprinted in full exactly as they appeared in the cooperating newspapers." Reproduction includes drawings, photographs, maps, other illustrations, and the typeface of the original text.

The number of editorials reprinted on a particular topic may vary from less than 10 to more than 50. The average number on each topic is about 25. Each editorial is identified by the title of the newspaper (reproduced from the masthead), city and state (district, territory) of publication, and date of issue.

Coverage of selected major topics in *Editorials on File* in the period January 1970-March 1972 included, under foreign affairs, 421 editorials on China, 128 on Latin America, 262 on India, Pakistan, and Bangla Desh, 433 on the Middle East, 2,340 on the Indochina War; under domestic affairs, 799 editorials on civil rights and black militants, 172 on draft and amnesty, 348 on Presidential campaign '72, 381 on environment, 289 on Supreme Court appointments, 275 on labor, 357 on crime and drugs, 426 on education and campus unrest, and 634 on the economy.

Indexes are published monthly and cumulated quarterly, semiannually, triquarterly, and annually. The monthly indexes are on green paper, the cumulative on yellow. "Because the indexes are cumulated a user of *Editorials on File* never has to keep more than three indexes in his binder to have full reference to all the issues of the current year." Each index gives instructions on which indexes should be retained and discarded.

In many respects the plan of the Index has not followed that of the specimen Index of the prospectus issue:

1. The specimen indexes contained references to "editorials which have not been reprinted" . . . and "are indexed in *italic type* entries ending with the date of the newspaper in which the editorial appeared. . . ." References to editorials not reprinted in *Editorials on File* do not appear in the subsequent indexes.

2. The specimen Index cited the names of the newspapers from which the editorials were reprinted and the

page numbers in *Editorials on File* where the respective editorials could be found. The subsequent indexes do not give the names of the newspapers, but under a main subject heading or subheading show only page references to *Editorials on File*.

3. The specimen Index employed an arrangement similar to *Reader's Guide to Periodical Literature*. The main subject headings were in boldface capitals. Subheadings in capital and lower case boldface letters were centered in the columns and were arranged alphabetically under each main heading. But in the subsequent indexes the subheadings of the type found in *Reader's Guide to Periodical Literature* are not used. Instead, the subheadings take one of several different forms such as (a) the full statement of the topic of the editorial as given in the introductory statement, (b) a paraphrase, or (c) abbreviation of this statement, (d) a related topic, or (e) a one-word passing reference. The subheadings are not arranged alphabetically but serially according to the lowest page reference following the entry. For example, under *Drugs* subheadings are arranged as follows:
G I drug abuse—7-11,655,656-667, 1263
Drug abuse bill—25,28,29,31
Tate-La Bianca killings—324
G I drug addictions in Vietnam reaching epidemic proportions—655,656
Addiction and crime—1195,1198,1246

4. Page entries in the specimen Index were preceded by the titles of a newspaper under specific subheadings. (Every main entry had at least one subheading.) The newspapers were arranged alphabetically under the subheadings. Thus the page entry is associated with a specific subheading and newspaper. In subsequent indexes the main entry may be followed simply by a series of page references (some single pages, others multiple consecutive pages). This type of reference does not give an indication of what aspect of the subject is being discussed such as would be provided by a subheading. One such entry, *Paris Peace Talks*, was followed simply by a block of page references, 29 single-page references and 5 consecutive-page references of 3 to 12 pages. Some other main entries which had no subheadings but which were followed by a block of page references are *AFL-CIO, Associated Press (AP), Burger, Chief Justice Warren E., Columbia Broadcasting System (CBS), Federal Bureau of Investigation (FBI), Nuremberg War Crimes Trials, Ping Pong Diplomacy, Supersonic Transport (SST), Ziegler, Ronald L.* The usefulness of these page references would be increased considerably if subheadings were included as they would provide clues to the phase of the main entry. Checking each one of the 13 page references following the entry *Kent State Killings* revealed only 3 substantial references to the incident; the other 10 were brief or passing references. Also the omission of the newspaper title from the index citation may require the scanning of several editorials reprinted on one page in order to find out which one contains the subject of the index reference.

5. The specimen Index was only about two and one half pages long; yet it used 102 *see* and *see also* references to cover a 32-page issue. The 1971 Semi-Annual Index about 11 pages long used only 76 such cross-references to cover 907 pages of text. A random check of these cross-references suggests that they are not being used in the most effective way. For example, in the Nine-Month Index 1971 there is a cross-reference "*Automobile Excise Tax —See Economy, U.S.*" Under *Economy, U.S* there are 46 subheadings, none of which includes "Automobile" or "Excise Tax" in its terms. One of these entries is "Nixon orders 90-way (sic) wage-price freeze"—1044-1095. This order did contain the announcement that the President was asking Congress to end the seven percent automobile excise tax. But in order to find references to the automobile excise tax it would be necessary first to select the proper heading out of the 46 under *Economy, U.S.* then scan 52 pages of reprinted editorials.

The *see* references from *Business Investment Tax Credit* to *Economy, U.S.;* and from *Import Tax* to *Economy, U.S.* lead to similar situations. Considering one more example, *"Libya—See Middle East,"* under *Middle East* there are a total of four subheadings none of which mentions Libya. To find references to Libya in the text requires scanning 30 pages in *Editorials on File*. A single reference was found to Libya in the sentence of one editorial.

Editorials on File is printed on good quality lightweight, off-white, nonglare paper. The reproductions of the editorials are excellent. The indexes are on heavier-weight yellow paper (except green for the monthly issues) of comparable quality. The entries in the Index are arranged in three columns. The main subject headings are in boldface with the initial word in capitals. The subheadings are in lightface type. The first words of the first and last entry on each page are printed in boldface capitals at the top left of the verso and top right of the recto. The arrangement and contrast facilitate rapid scanning of the index.

Each issue is center-stapled, and is punched with three holes so that the issues may be inserted in the sturdy binder provided. The loose-leaf binder resembles that used for *Facts on File*. Insertion of the issues in the binder is facilitated by a device which releases the issues or locks them in. The binder will hold a full year's issues. A table of contents is printed on the cover of each issue listing the title of each topic and the page on which it begins. Both the page number and brief running title of the topic are printed in boldface in the upper right-hand corner of each recto and upper left-hand corner of each verso.

Even when it is holding a full year's issues, the substantial binder opens wide enough to allow reading of material at the inner margins with no difficulty. This is true even after the issues are bound. The width of the inner margin varies, with a minimum of three quarters of an inch, but this includes the space in which the three holes are punched for the posts of the binder. Some users may prefer to keep the issues in the loose-leaf binder rather than binding them.

The publication provides a useful service bringing together, in a convenient easy-to-read format, editorials on the same subject from 120 United States newspapers of varying philosophy, region, and size of circulation. Even those relatively few institutions which could possibly have subscriptions to all these newspapers might nevertheless find it most useful to subscribe to this service. Surveying the newspapers, identifying the editorials, and bringing them together for comparison in a convenient format with a concise authoritative summary of well-chosen subjects make *Editorials on File* of considerable value to high school, college, and public libraries. The frequency of cumulation and ease of scanning are praiseworthy features. However, much more intensive indexing, using a system of subheadings as is done in the specimen Index, and citing the titles of the newspaper sources would make this tool much more useful. Lack of these features limits the reference value of the Index in locating editorials and editorial subjects rapidly and accurately. Recommended. *(Feb. 15, 1973, p.533)*

Encyclopaedia Britannica. 24v. Chicago, London, Toronto, Geneva, Sydney, Tokyo, Manila, Encyclopaedia Britannica, Inc., [c1929-1972]. illus. maps. plates. tables. 29cm. list price $498 up; Joanna Western A quality cloth to schools and libraries $299.50, $272.50 per set for two or more ordered at same time.

The long and distinguished history of the *Britannica*, now comprising over 200 years, needs no recounting here; it is included in past reviews in *Subscription Books Bulletin* (January 1930, October 1936, October 1939, July 1941, October 1945, April 1951) and *The Booklist and Subscription Books Bulletin* (February 1, 1957; December 15, 1961; December 1, 1967). Further, a thorough, scholarly account appears in *Britannica* itself in the article *Encyclopedia*.

The current edition follows the continuous revision policy established in 1932. It continues to be published by William Benton who marks his 29th anniversary in 1972 as head of the company. Under Benton's direction Encyclopaedia Britannica, Inc., acquired Encyclopaedia Britannica Films, published *Great Books of the Western World* and the Spanish-language *Enciclopedia Barsa*, and purchased *Compton's Pictured Encyclopedia*, G. & C. Merriam Company, and Frederick A. Praeger, Inc. His background as a former vice-president of the University of Chicago, assistant secretary of state, senator, and author makes him outstanding among publishers.

The present editor is Warren E. Preece, who has held the position since 1964, and has been an editorial executive since the late 1950s. He previously taught at the University of Chicago and served as a consultant to the Center for the Study of Democratic Institutions in California.

Continuing as Chairman of the Board of Editors and Director of Planning respectively are Robert M. Hutchins and Mortimer J. Adler, both of whom have been associated with *Britannica* for well over 20 years. The other three editors also have been on the editorial staff for over 20 years.

Assisting the editorial board are some 150 departmental editors and advisors. While this group is generally a stable one, each year there are members who, because of death or other reason, go off the board. A comparison of these names in the 1967 edition, (the last to be reviewed by the Reference and Subscription Books Review Committee), and those in the present edition, reveals that 27 members have been dropped from the board and 16 new members have been added. Among those added in the 1972 edition were Seiichi Izumi, Professor, Institute of Oriental Culture, Chairman, Graduate School Division of Sociology, University of Tokyo; Frank L. Kidner, Professor of Economics and Vice-President of Educational Relations, University of California, Berkeley; and Alfred Brian Pippard, John Humphrey Plummer Professor of Physics, University of Cambridge. Interestingly, almost all of the departmental editors appointed for the 1972 edition are also members of the Advisory Committee on *Britannica* either at the University of Chicago, the University of Tokyo, or for the United Kingdom. A comment was made in the Committee's review of the 1967 edition that only two of the Board members actually had any association with the *Britannica*.

While the number of contributors remains approximately the same as for the 1967 edition, the quality of expertness is sustained. The majority of contributors continues to represent universities throughout the world, almost all being recognized experts in their own field. However, there seems to be some tendency in the present edition to seek contributions from those more directly connected with the topic under discussion; for example, David Justice, Assistant Director of Research for Lever Brothers Company in New Jersey, wrote the article *Detergents and Detergency;* Edmond Levin, Engineer-in-Charge, Optics and Illumination Science, for Sylvania Electric Products Inc. in Massachusetts, the article *Photometry;* and Jerome Holtzman, a baseball writer for the *Chicago Sun-Times*, contributed to the article *Baseball*.

Signed articles—and they include approximately 90 percent of the total number—are signed with contributors' initials. The full name and identification of each contributor can be located in the introductory part of volume 1. As in the past, some articles are signed with two sets of initials usually indicating an updating by the second contributor, with the substance of the article remaining the work of the first named contributor.

The major objectives of a general encyclopedia would seem to be self-evident, and it is for this reason perhaps they are not precisely stated in each edition of *Britannica*. The objectives are, however, implied in the Editor's Preface in the statement "it is clear that encyclopedias will continue to be man's continuing and continuously updated record of what has happened to him, what he has learned, what he has done, what he thinks is important." This monumental task becomes more complex as each generation passes and, indeed, with each new edition of an encyclopedia. The extent to which *Britannica* has fulfilled these objectives depends in large measure on how much revision has taken place and where the emphasis of revision is. According to the publisher's own calculations, there are over 2,000 fewer entries in the 1972 edition than in the 1967 edition. However, during the same period the index, inserts, illustrations, and number of pages have all increased. While some entries were dropped and some consolidated into other topics, new articles on pertinent subjects were added, as, for example, those on information processing, space law, and snowmobiling.

Articles in *Britannica* are arranged alphabetically letter by letter with pages numbered consecutively throughout each of the 24 volumes. While many of the older, broad-subject type articles are still found, e.g., *Latin American Music, Architecture,* and *Biology.* the tendency seems to be toward the inclusion of more specific articles, e.g., *Tissue Culture, Landscape Architecture,* and *Electronic Music.* All major articles include bibliographies and a large number of cross-references, and many less important articles are followed by bibliographies.

It is perhaps best to evaluate these and other qualitative aspects of the set by examining the major subject areas covered.

The social sciences, very broadly understood and including history, geography, and certain biographies, continue to constitute the largest category of *Britannica's* contents—46.6 percent of the text and almost 18,000 entries, according to the editors.

A concern with the problems of war and peace is evident in many revisions and new articles. For instance, one innovation since 1967 is the impressive article *World Wars,* by 28 contributors, which is more than 290,000 words long. It is a thoroughgoing treatment not only of the military progress of the two world wars of this century but also of the complex combinations of events beginning in the nineteenth century that brought about World War I, and the ensuing developments during the twenties and thirties that evolved into World War II.

Disarmament, Conscientious Objector, and *Cold War* have been revised and expanded since the 1967 edition. *Guerrilla Warfare* has almost doubled in length, as has *North Atlantic Treaty Alliance.* A new, 14-page article, *Military Service,* subsumes several articles such as *Impressment. Militia, National Guard, Yeomanry,* and *Conscription,* that covered aspects of the subject in the 1967 printing. The article provides a concise history of the topic from earliest times to the thermonuclear age, with a distinction made between professional and nonprofessional military forces and with considerable attention to the relationships between soldier and citizen and the effect of those relationships upon society.

A great many historical articles have been extensively revised or rewritten in recent years. For example, the essay *Napoleon I* by the liberal historian Jacques Godechot replaces an older one by Jacques Bainville, a former editor of *Action Française,* who was active in right-wing movements. *Cardinal Wolsey* has also been completely rewritten and the bibliography brought up to date, incorporating the latest work on Wolsey's controversial career.

History has not been revised; this accounts, no doubt, for a reference to the Mississippi Valley Historical Association, now the Organization of American Historians. Other classic articles have been reprinted with only slight changes. *Huguenots,* for example, written by Frank Puaux (1844-1922), was slightly revised by his younger contemporary, Louis Mazoyer, but is badly out of date both in its interpretations of the Huguenot Wars and in its bibliography. The same can be said of *Renaissance* by Lynn Thorndike.

As was noted in the last Reference and Subscription Books Review Committee review, geographical entries showed a greater degree of revision than historical articles. This is perhaps understandable since it is relatively simple to change population and other statistics without substantially changing the content or length of the article. In an evaluation of some 200 geographical articles it was found that many did include only statistical and political changes with bibliographies sometimes failing to cite the latest literature on the area. *Indonesia,* for example, does not include Willard Hanna's American Universities Fieldstaff Reports, Simon Sheldon's *Broken Triangle: Peking, Djakarta, and the PKI* (Baltimore: Johns Hopkins, 1969), or Howard P. Jones' *Indonesia: The Possible Dream* (New York: Harcourt Brace, 1971). The bibliography for *New Zealand* contains many classic works, now mainly of historical interest, but omits such recent publications as *Encyclopedia of New Zealand* (Wellington: R. E. Owen, Govt. Printer, 1966) and *Modern Encyclopedia of Australia and New Zealand* (Sydney: Horwitz, 1964). *Uganda* has been rewritten and updated, but its bibliography is more evocative than well balanced.

Articles on war-threatened places, *Egypt, Iraq, Israel, Jordan, Lebanon, Libya, Sudan,* and *Syria,* have all been revised. *India* and *Pakistan,* although somewhat revised since 1967, unfortunately cannot be considered quite up to date, since they do not include (and could not have included) reference to the recent tragic events associated with Bangladesh. Similarly, *Ireland, Northern* has been slightly revised but gives only perfunctory treatment of the incidents of the late 1960s and early 1970s. Again, *Kenya,* while a well-written article, emphasizing the growth of African nationalism from the early colonial period up to the present rather than the "accomplishments" and developments of the white settlers, is somewhat out of date on certain statistical data. The population figures, for example, are from the 1962 census instead of the 1969 census, thus making Nairobi's population only about half of what it is in 1972. Also, in the section on politics an important 1969 development is not mentioned: the banning of the opposition party and the emergence of a *de facto* one-party political system. Although the bibliography is generally good, the 1962 edition of the *Kenya Atlas* by the Government Department of Survey is included instead of the 1970 revision which contains a considerable amount of new material.

There are articles for each of the United States and the District of Columbia, most of which were written some time ago by a prominent archivist, the state historian, or even a leading citizen. These articles have not been substantially rewritten or revised in recent years, although their statistics are regularly updated by the editorial staff. *Washington, D.C.* is about five years out of date in its chronology of cultural events and institutions—the Kennedy Center for the Performing Arts, for example, is not mentioned. Some of the state bibliographies are very much in need of revision, especially those for New Hampshire, New Jersey, Arkansas, Montana, and Kentucky. The bibliographic lists vary greatly in length, recency and comprehensiveness, ranging from a few items to 50 or more, depending on the importance or antiquity of the state. Occasionally, the original edition of a work is listed although it may have been reprinted many times.

There are also numerous articles on cities and provinces, many of which have been substantially revised. Notable among these are *Quebec,* which adds to the city's history, education, and health and welfare sections, covers budgets and departments in the government which had not been covered before, includes new headings for Tourism, Labor, and Trade and Commerce, and updates and doubles its bibliography; and *New York* which now includes under City Planning and Zoning some account of the "mile after mile of landlord-abandoned, health and fire hazardous, crumbling and vandalized tenements lacking service and maintenance." Earlier accounts of the city read more like a Convention Bureau release.

In the area of psychology the review of the 1967 edition pointed out that *Psychological Tests and Measurements* should have included material on recent work in testing for creativity, but the article in the 1972 edition remains unchanged except for minor updating in the bibliography.

There are over 200 items relating to

psychology in the Index, and the coverage of psychology seems generally to be thorough, especially in its historic treatments. However, the almost total absence of any revision in the articles *Psychology; Psychology, Abnormal; Psychology, Applied; Psychology, Comparative; Psychology, Experimental;* and *Psychiatry* is a serious omission for a major encyclopedia. There is no reference, for example, to the contemporary (and admittedly somewhat controversial) "humanistic" psychology, and the small number of Index references to Abraham Maslow and Carl Rogers relate only to insignificant parenthetical mentions in the text. Also, there is no reference to sensitivity or encounter groups.

Women may continue to feel somewhat slighted by *Encyclopaedia Britannica*. The standard articles *Legal Position of Women, Women's Suffrage,* and *Women's Education, History Of* (all with a somewhat archaic tone) appear, but nowhere in the encyclopedia could a single real reference be found to the modern women's liberation movement. Nor were there any bibliographic references to any of the recent books on the subject.

Again, the reader seeking information on the newly emerging "future studies" popularized by Alvin Toffler's *Future Shock* (New York: Random House, 1970) will find in the Index references only to futures in commodity markets, or futurities in horseracing, or futurism in art and literature.

However, a number of articles on social problems were considerably expanded. Among these are *Abortion*, which now covers social as well as medical aspects; *Drug Addiction* which now includes the incidence of drug dependence, the nature of addiction, treatment, and measures of international control; *Juvenile Delinquency; Prostitution; Venereal Diseases;* and *Pollution, Environmental*.

The coverage of science and technology, for the most part written by authorities in the field, continues to be extensive for a general encyclopedia. Many of the longer articles covering the major branches of science are preceded by short survey articles such as *Biology, (Articles On)* and *Mathematics, (Articles On)*. These contain *see* references which, with those in the main article, lead the reader to the various aspects of the subject. The admonition to use the Index to ensure finding all references to the subject is frequently added. The material on science and technology is presented in a style which is generally intelligible to the informed layman. There are numerous examples in the 1972 *Britannica* of updating information in the attempt to keep up with the rapid advances in science and technology. For example, the new 21-page article *Life* brings together material formerly found in scattered sections, along with much new material. After a discussion of the various definitions of, and mathematical and vital functions of, life, it proceeds to a section on the origin and evolution of life on earth. The last section is concerned with the possibility of, and search for, extraterrestrial life.

Gene and *Heredity* have been greatly expanded and cover the subjects much more thoroughly than in the 1967 edition. *Gene* now includes material on the development of the gene theory, molecular level analysis of the gene, gene ultrastructure, and the action of the genes. *Heredity* now deals with such topics as medico-legal applications, genetic counseling, and genetic improvements of animals, plants, and man. *Courtship, Animal* has been expanded by almost a page and several illustrations have been added. The article no longer simply describes courtship behavior but discusses experimental and theoretical work on the subject.

As might be expected, *Space Exploration* and *Moon* have been updated to include more recent information: Soyuz 10 and 11 flights in April and June 1971, and Apollo 14 and 15 flights in January and July-August 1971 are included in *Space Exploration;* results from Apollo flights 11 and 12 in 1969 have been incorporated in the new *Moon* article, written by Nobel prize winner Harold Urey. *Mars* and *Venus* have also been rewritten to include information gathered during various space explorations.

The new type of three-dimensional photography using coherent light produced by a laser is discussed in a new article *Holography*. The rewritten article *Catalysis* has been reduced from three to two pages by replacing the section on practical uses with a table of industrially important catalytic processes and by extensive use of chemical equations in explaining processes, thus making a more concise and readable presentation.

In *Science, History Of,* the section on Chinese science has been completely rewritten. The coverage has been changed from one by individual sciences to a chronological account extending into the late 1960s.

In the field of technology two major new articles are outstanding. *Technology, History Of* is a 40-page, well-illustrated account which traces the development of technology from prehistoric time to the twentieth century. The other, *Information Processing*, takes as its thesis the concept of information as a basic resource. It cuts across many technologies and disciplines in its discussion of the history of calculators, information media, storage and retrieval of information, and information processing systems.

There are, however, shortcomings to be found in *Britannica's* coverage of science and technology. The article *Particles, Elementary,* cited in the 1967 review, remains unchanged. There is no mention of the concept of quarks in particle physics, a term used in elementary particle theory for several years. In geology the theory of plate tectonics is not discussed in any of the articles *Geology, Geophysics, Continent,* or *Tectonophysics;* nor is it mentioned in the Index, and the scattered references to continental drift, a related theory, might leave the reader in some doubt as to the acceptability of this theory. Also, while *Microscope* contains a lengthy section on the electron microscope, only transmission electron microscopes are discussed; the newer scanning electron microscope is not mentioned; nor is it found in the Index.

The humanities, traditionally strong in *Britannica,* account for almost one fourth of the total text. In the area of language and literature, *Language* remains the same as in the 1967 edition; the latest item in the bibliography is for a 1956 publication. However, a check of that heading in the Index disclosed that there are six new entries listed. Fifteen new or revised language articles were examined closely and compared with the 1967 articles when they existed. Of these, *Clicks; Allegory; Mishima, Yukio; Children's Literature; Slang; Australian Languages;* and *Capek, Karel* were found to be new or completely revised.

In the articles examined, the scope and treatment of subject vary considerably from article to article. For example the mainly historical treatment of *Children's Literature* in the earlier edition has become a new article with numerous illustrations and is a much more useful and readable mixture of history and philosophy. Included in the 1972 entry is a 4½-page chart showing the development of children's literature by date, author and title, country, and significance of the title and event, covering the eleventh century through 1969.

Slang, on the other hand, was a rather generalized but interestingly written history with numerous examples; the subject has a more scholarly treatment in the 1972 edition. The six-column list of Mid-Twentieth Century slang terms arranged by country (United States, Great Britain, Canada, Australia, New Zealand), which was a quite useful feature of the earlier edition, has been omitted.

One of the original authors has revised the *Australian Languages* article to update such recent developments as the new breakdown of language groups. There is now no reference to *Pidgen* (still the same as the earlier entry) or to *Slang* (not now as useful since there is no list of Australian slang). Reference is made in the text to a book published in 1970; no book dated later than 1963 is in the bibliography, but several useful series are mentioned and a list of experts in the field is given.

Yiddish; Crane, Harold Hart; Tate, (John Orley) Allen; Wodehouse, Pelham Grenville; American Literature, and *English Literature* were found to be enlarged or changed to some degree.

American Literature and *English Literature* show most changes, naturally, in the twentieth-century sections. In both articles, incidentally, the double page of portraits in the 1967 edition has been omitted in 1972. The author of the complete 1967 article *American Literature* is responsible for the newer one only up to World War II and for the bibliography at the end. A new contributor and the editors are responsible for the remainder of the material in which the fiction section is redone; the poetry and drama sections have additions and elaborations (some of the sentences and phrases in the earlier edition are retained). A new section about literary and social criticism is added. There are few changes in the bibliography: one new edition, two new books, the latest 1967.

English Literature shows something of the same pattern, with some sections changed, some the same, and others enlarged, with most changes again in twentieth century coverage. The bibliography, however, has almost doubled and includes 1970 items.

African Literature, over eight pages long, is written by several well-qualified contributors, with many references and *see* references. Several well-chosen illustrations are included, as is a detailed bibliography listing material published as recently as 1969, arranged by type of literature and area.

In a check of language and literature omissions and inclusions, eight items out of seventy-one were in the 1967 edition but not the 1972; one article was new, and one was changed from a note in the 1967 Index to an entry in 1972. At least five have had changes of various kinds. Language and literature appear to have lost more than they gained in volume 17.

Some new fields of interest in which coverage in literature would be expected are Black, Oriental, or Eastern writers; for language, transformational-generative grammar. The 1972 *Britannica* treats transformational-generative grammar as part of the *Grammar* article in a section sufficiently detailed and with enough examples to be useful. Transformational-generative grammar is also part of the *Linguistics* entry, in which the subject is treated in even greater detail.

Six Black writers are subjects of new biographies in the 1972 *Britannica*. Four of these had either an article or a reference in the 1967 and 1972 *Britannica*.

Twenty-seven new biographical articles of Eastern writers, including philosophers and statesmen as well as those in the literary category, were added since 1967.

In order to assess the extent of revision and new material in the plastic arts in 1972, painting was chosen as the topic representative of the broader field. The article *Painting* is written from an entirely different viewpoint. Unlike the 1967 article, which was a history of the subject, the present article attempts to explain what the art of painting is in all its manifestations and techniques: realist, portrait, landscape, still life, abstraction. A new set of full-color illustrations covers 15 pages. The article also includes a lengthy bibliography. Much of the content of the 1967 article's subdivision Modern Painting is incorporated into a new article *Modern Art,* which deals with both contemporary painting and sculpture. Another new article on *Abstract Art* expands the treatment given this subject in 1967. Similarly, the new article *Art Nouveau* reflects the revival of this style in the fifties and sixties. On the other hand, such movements as Constructivism and Abstract Expressionism continue to be represented only by secondary references in the Index, the latter to be found under the heading *Action Painting*. A random check of twentieth-century painters revealed that Robert Motherwell and Hans Hoffman are not treated in separate articles in either the 1967 or 1972 editions; the articles *Jackson Pollock* and *William De Kooning* have been reprinted without change, but the 1972 edition does include new and expanded articles *Piet Mondrian* and *Pablo Picasso*.

On the basis of the articles examined it is clear that a reasonable amount of revision in the field of painting has taken place in the five-year period. The expansion and updating of the bibliographies is to be commended, and the quality of the illustrations is noteworthy.

The lengthy major articles on music history and theory in *Britannica* are classics, written by recognized authorities in the field and copiously illustrated with musical examples. An outstanding new article *Electronic Music* appears in the 1972 printing. It includes some fine illustrative material together with a discography and bibliography. A separate article for *Music, Twentieth Century* is another addition which provides an excellent summary. It must be pointed out, however, that articles on such major topics as *Jazz, Opera,* and *Symphony* have been reprinted without change and that the article on *Musical Comedy* gives no evidence of any real revision since the 1930s. The only change in the 1972 edition is a listing of titles of two musical comedies produced in the sixties. A new article *Popular Music* treats that subject historically, but the section on the twentieth century makes no real attempt to deal with contemporary developments. (The subject of rock 'n' roll is treated in one sentence in the article *Dance*.) The emerging field of Ethnomusicology has only a brief mention in *Music, Primitive*.

In order to determine the extent of revision of musical biographies, a group of late nineteenth- and early twentieth-century composers was selected at random. Articles *Dvorak; Bruckner; Vaughan Williams; Ives, Charles; Mahler;* and *Debussy* were reprinted without change in text or bibliography. Only one composer in the group, Brahms, had a new article, but with a considerably shorter bibliography than in the 1967 edition.

A sampling of contemporary composers and conductors was also checked. Articles on Karlheinz Stockhausen and John Cage are found, but no article on Edmund Rubbra was found in either printing. Igor Stravinsky, who died in 1971, is the subject of an entirely new article. *Varese, Edgard* and *Bernstein, Leonard* however, were reprinted without change, as was *Casals, Pablo*. Two eminent contemporary musicians absent from both text and Index are Eugene Ormandy and Yehudi Menuhin. In summary, it must be said that the music articles as a group give evidence of only a limited amount of revision and that relatively few new articles have been added or substituted.

The 1972 *Britannica's* illustrations, numbering nearly 23,000, continue to enhance the value of the text. These include black-and-white and full color illustrations, drawings, maps, photographs, and "trans-vision" illustrations which are full color "cutaway" drawings printed on transparent acetate overlays, especially helpful in studying anatomy.

The *Britannica* Index in volume 24 guides the reader to even fairly obscure facts. This is done either through direction to an article on the subject itself, to a related article, or possibly to an illustration or map. Index references indicate from the type—bold or light—whether the article is the major article on the subject or supplementary material in a related article. In the same manner, the location of the information is given: bold numerals indicate the volume; light numerals, the page number; and the letter *a, b, c,* or *d,* the quarter of the page on which the information may be found. In a check of some 200 entries in three different volumes, only one inaccuracy was found. Generally speaking, the Index is accurate and easy to use and indispensable for proper use of the set.

Included in the Index volume are the atlas and the atlas index. The maps for the atlas, comprising 153 up-to-date separate colored maps and 12 colored insets, were prepared by Rand McNally.

The 1972 edition of *Britannica* is attractively and durably bound, the Index volume having additional reinforcement in the Smyth-sewn binding. The volumes are clearly lettered on the spines and they lie flat when opened. The paper continues to be of excellent quality; the typeface is clear, and generally the page layout is attractive, providing good legibility.

Although there are minor inaccuracies and omissions in the 1972 edition of the *Britannica,* as in any encyclopedia, and the extent of revision is uneven, the tradition of authority and scholarship continues to maintain it as one of the major English-language encyclopedias in the world today. Because it includes almost all aspects of man's accomplishments and shortcomings today, and because its Index provides a relatively simple method of locating that material, and because its many excellent bibliographies give the reader further sources of information, *Britannica* is recommended for home and all public, academic, and secondary school libraries. Libraries with 1967 or older editions should replace them.

(Dec. 15, 1972, p.361)

Encyclopaedia Judaica. 16v. Jerusalem, [Keter Publishing House Ltd.] New York, The Macmillan Co., [c1971]. illus. maps. charts. diagrs. 31cm. cloth (Exfilin crash with plastic glue) $500 (introductory), $600 (after publication).

"The *Encyclopaedia Judaica* is the first Jewish encyclopedia on a major scale to be published for many decades (since the early 40's). It represents the culmination of years of intensive work by scholars from many parts of the world and provides a comprehensive picture of all aspects of Jewish life and knowledge up to the present day, intended for both the Jewish and non-Jewish reader."

The cataclysmic changes represented by the destruction of Jewish life in Europe in the Nazi period and by the establishment and development of the State of Israel are more than enough to justify a major new encyclopedia. In addition, these last decades have witnessed intensive research in all branches of Jewish studies, discoveries of significance (e.g., the Dead Sea Scrolls), broad changes in scholarly perspective, and radical realignment of the centers of Jewish life. To reflect this "new world," a new encyclopedia was developed. Where possible, the editors utilized still useful materials by translating and/or updating articles from two other encyclopedias. One, the German language *Encyclopaedia Judaica* (Berlin: Verlag Eschkol, 1928-34), is a monumental work, which suspended publication after volume 10 (completing the letter L) when the Nazis rose to power. The other is *Encyclopaedia Hebraica* (Tel-Aviv: Encyclopaedia Pub.), a general encyclopedia in Hebrew in process of publication in Israel since 1949 (and now about half finished), which contains a large amount of Judaic data. Nevertheless, *Encyclopaedia Judaica* is in no sense just a "remodeling and updating of the predecessors."

The comprehensiveness of the work can be seen from the list of categories presented in the publisher's prospectus: Bible, Hebrew and Semitic Languages, Second Temple Period, Rabbinical Literature, Talmud and Talmudic Period, Jewish Law, Jewish Philosophy, Mysticism, Medieval Hebrew Literature, Judaism, Jewish History, Zionism, Contemporary Jewry, Holocaust, Modern Hebrew Literature, Modern Jewish Scholarship, Participation of Jews in World Culture, Modern Yiddish Literature, Americana, and Erez ("Land of") Israel. The scope of the Jewish experience in time and place covered by *Encyclopaedia Judaica* is greater than even this list, and the task of recording it reliably and with balance is huge. It is natural to expect, therefore, that the decision on inclusion, the apportionment of space, and the point of view taken by particular contributors will not find unanimous acceptance.

The encyclopedia claims 25,000 entries, over 11,000,000 words, 8,887 black-and-white illustrations, 238 color illustrations, 424 black-and-white maps and one in color, 149 charts and diagrams, and 300 tables. It is very legibly printed, in 8 and 9 point type. The smaller size is used for bibliography and frequently to get more words into a given space. The illustrations are generally good to excellent, though a few are too small to be useful, some have poor contrast, and some are spotted. The pages are generally printed in two columns, and it is the columns that are numbered. The binding is attractive, but perhaps not so sturdy as it needs to be; the headband of the Index volume (volume 1) of one review set is separating after only moderate use.

There are four tables of abbreviations: general, abbreviations used in rabbinical literature, bibliographic abbreviations, and one for the Index. The general abbreviations and those used in the Index are not always the same; thus, for example, J generally means "Jahwist," but in the Index it means "Jew" or "Jewish." There is also a five-page glossary of recurring Hebrew and technical terms at the beginning of each text volume. To guide the reader in the difficult problem of transliteration, there are charts for Hebrew, Yiddish, Arabic, Greek, and Russian. In fact, there are two transliteration systems for Hebrew and no proper justification for either, for the "general" is not simplified enough, and the scientific is not that of the Academy of the Hebrew Language as the editors claim. Not only has a historic opportunity to bring order into the chaos of romanized Hebrew for English use been thoroughly missed, but the disunity of romanization is much greater than in previous major Jewish encyclopedias.

The centrality and importance of the Index are emphasized in that it constitutes volume 1. While there are frequent *see also* references at the ends of text entries and asterisked words within the text to signify that these words are the titles of entries, the 200,000 entries in the Index provide "the key which unlocks the *Encyclopaedia*." It is a very accurate index, revealing no blind or inaccurate references in a series of samplings. It is also quite comprehensive, including all illustrations except photographic portraits. Nonetheless, there are lacunae that remain inexplicable in the absence of any stated principles of exclusion. For example, references to Benjamin of Tudela in v.13, col. 1386 and v.15, col. 523 are not in the Index; nor is the one to Judah ibn Tibbon in v.3, col. 973.

Almost every article has references for further reading, entitled Bibliography. Long articles, broken into small sections, frequently have bibliographies for their separate sections. The bibliographies vary considerably in usefulness and quality; some are full and clearly related to the articles while others are skimpy or absent. The tendency is to be weak for minor subjects where the needs are probably greatest. In some cases, the bibliographies seem to have been provided by someone other than the author of the article, because key works that the expert would be sure to know are not listed.

Specialist reactions to selected subjects covered in the encyclopedia were sought. Summaries of their reports may be useful in gaining a cross-section view of the whole.

Hebrew Language covers 103 columns and is divided into six subentries by five authors, three of whom are established authorities. Two of the six subentries, "Dead Sea Scrolls" and "Medieval" are very good treatments. The "Mishnaic" section is almost as good, though it lacks a treatment of syntax and has only a short treatment of "vocabulary." The "Modern Period" is a convincing description of the problems and development in the areas of pronunciation, spelling, vocabulary, and grammar but contains a misrepresentation about the rules of unpointed Hebrew orthography. The "Pre-Biblical" section is fragmentized and does not present a coherent picture. Very adequate coverage of the *Hebrew Language* is gained by this long article and a series of other articles including a 99-column article on Hebrew grammar. The proofreading of both *Hebrew Language* and *Hebrew Grammar* is very poor.

Hebrew Literature, Modern, covering 39 columns, seems to have a disproportionately small allotment of space; but it and related articles give the subject excellent coverage and very good balance and objectivity, although treatment of the contemporary period is not so strong as that of the past, and prose is better treated than poetry. *Criticism, Hebrew Literary; Drama, Hebrew;* and

Prosody, Hebrew are also excellent articles. The articles on individual authors vary considerably in quality, and current writers are underrepresented.

The coverage in *Encyclopaedia Judaica* of the field of Yiddish is characterized by inconsistency, but the excellent far outweighs the questionable. The articles *Yiddish Language* and *Yiddish Literature* and most biographies are by contributors of recognized expertise; Yiddish theater, Yiddish press, and biographies of Isaac Leib Peretz, Shalom (should be Sholem) Aleichem, and Mendele Mokher Seforim, three of the most important Yiddish writers, are not as good. There are many transliteration errors in words of Hebrew origin used in Yiddish, like *likhvod* instead of *lekoved*. These reflect, undesirably, the Israel pronunciation of the originally Hebrew words rather than their Yiddish pronunciation.

Inconsistency also characterizes subjects like Talmud and Rabbinics, Kabbalah and Mysticism, Americana, Art, Bibliography and Libraries. In general, the longer articles and the specialized ones are well done while the shorter entries are less so. There are valuable articles like *Mishnah; Talmud, Babylonian;* and *Talmud, Jerusalem* even though these are not as "critical" in methodology as some might like. An innovative series of legalistic articles on such subjects as *Torts, Damages,* and *Hazakah* is commendable, but these are offset by pedestrian articles for *Sifra, Tosefta,* and *Midrash*. A major article of great value, *Kabbalah,* is not matched by the one on *Hasidism*. The general subject *Art* and the art aspect of various subjects (e.g., *Jerusalem, Temple, Moses*) are very good; articles on individual artists are less good. *New York; Pennsylvania; Brandeis, Louis D.; Zionism in the U.S.* are competently done. In certain treatments, for example, *United States Literature,* there is perhaps an overemphasis on works related to Israel, and one wonders whether 90 columns is sufficient treatment for *United States of America* compared with over 900 for *Israel*. In the treatment of books and libraries, *Incunabula* is a fine and full treatment of Hebrew incunabula. *Libraries, Bibliophiles,* and *Typography* are very slight.

The article *Bible* covers 155 columns subdivided by the headings "Canon, Text, and Editions," "Translations," "Exegesis and Study," "Religious Impact," and "In the Arts;" but nowhere is the reader told what the Bible is in its essence, intention, and manifestation. This is admittedly a difficult and controversial matter, but it should have been faced. While much of the material presented in this and related entries can be useful, the special danger of bias must be mentioned. The editors "solve" the problem of "radically opposing attitudes to the Bible and Bible scholarship" by allowing each contributor to go his own way. "A thorough reading of the entire Bible section will reveal the overall effort to present every aspect," but to best aid the reader it would have been better to juxtapose varying points of view rather than to require a total reading of many articles to find the variations.

What emerges from the survey of specialists is that there is considerable variation in quality. There are excellent people at the editorial level, from Cecil Roth as editor in chief during the most active period (1966-70), and Geoffrey Wigoder succeeding him (1970-71), through the divisional and department heads. There are 1,856 names listed among the contributors, and many are expert in their fields; but the competence of at least 20 percent cannot be ascertained even minimally by the data provided for them in the encyclopedia. Many are identified as rabbis, journalists, historians, or researchers without any further data. All articles are initialed, but initials are not as helpful as they might be when they so frequently lead only to an unknown name or the anonymity of "Editorial Staff."

Although there is a clear bias towards Israel throughout, the encyclopedia works hard at, and is more than acceptably successful in, presenting an objective position. *Apostasy, American Council for Judaism, Arab League, Christianity, Church, Catholic,* and *Spinoza* are very fairly presented. There is, however, an occasional Orthodox Jewish bias that is not easily recognized except by the expert.

Very unsettling are the many errors, both typographic and substantive. One's confidence is shaken by a Corrigenda section, 16 pages in length, inconspicuous at the end of volume 1, and by being informed that this huge list is not complete and does not include spelling and punctuation errors (unless they affect the meaning). No errors are listed for volumes 1 and 15, and a perusal of the set reveals many errors throughout that are not listed. The editors promise to publish a complete list of errata and corrigenda "at a later date." Overwhelmed by the factual errors, found and feared, one almost wishes to refrain from mentioning the simple misprints of which there are also many.

There is abundant evidence that *Encyclopaedia Judaica* was produced too hurriedly. The disturbing Corrigenda pages are not the only obvious clue. There are also six "Supplementary Lists" in volume 1 and 406 columns of "Supplementary Entries" in volume 16, the latter identified as late arrivals. Among the late arrivals are the essential articles *Economic History, Linguistic Literature, Hebrew, Masorah, Migrations,* and *Hebrew Language,* the last so late apparently that it stands alone at the end outside of even the supplementary alphabetical sequence. Of the "lists" in volume 1, including a 100-year Jewish calendar, a chart of Hasidic dynasties, an *Israel Place List, Newspapers and Periodicals, Hebrew, Pottery,* and a lonely page of the *Estimated Number of Synagogues According to Country (1971),* some, at least, would be better placed within the main alphabetical sequence.

The editors have done their best to correct errors and include whatever they could, and a positive result of their speed of publication is an up-to-date work including some population figures from reference works published in 1969. For further updating and provision of new results of research, they plan the *Encyclopaedia Judaica Yearbook* starting in 1973.

Subjects that are absent from *Encyclopaedia Judaica* or very inadequately covered include Criminals, English Language Press, Jew in American Folklore, Pornography, and Wit and Humor. Furthermore, a check of subjects listed in the prospectus indicates that important subjects like Hell, Hypocrisy, Image of the Jew, Philosemitism, Pseudonyms, and others were once considered but later omitted.

Encyclopaedia Judaica was conceived grandly to meet the needs of a vastly changed world, Jewish and general, and was motivated by "an awareness of the potential historic and cultural value of this work and the role it can play in Jewish education and culture, in the spread of Jewish knowledge . . . and in the closer linking of Israel with Jews as well as non-Jews the world over." It has, in fact, emerged as a monumental work of the broadest coverage, of the Jewish experience at all times and places, with particular emphasis on Israel. An innovator among Jewish encyclopedias, it has provided a useful index, excellent illustrative material, and an unusual treatment of Jewish law. It is regrettable that the work is not better coordinated and that more time and care were not taken to expand the excellent features and to produce a more nearly error-free work, because a specialized encyclopedia of this kind, with a relatively limited market, can be produced only very infrequently. Purchasers are advised to use the Corrigenda and actually to make, or at least to note, the corrections in the text.

There is much in *Encyclopaedia Judaica* that is useful and even excellent. There is, however, an inexcusably large amount of material written or edited at a less than satisfactory level of reliability. It is, therefore, not possible to recommend this encyclopedia without reservations; indeed, some of the specialists consulted would not recommend it at all. The question hinges on whether one prefers to be without the only current multivolume Jewish encyclopedia likely to be available for a long time rather than expose the reader to its many imperfections. In the absence of a competing work of any quality, let alone a better one, *Encyclopaedia Judaica* is recommended for purchase by libraries where there is substantial interest in Israel, Jewish history, and Jewish life. *(Nov. 1, 1972, p.209)*

Encyclopaedia of Occupational Health and Safety. International Labour Office. 2v. New York, McGraw-Hill, [1972, c1971]. 1621p. illus. 30cm. cloth $49.50; to schools and libraries, 10 percent

The Introduction states that the first edition of *Encyclopaedia of Occupational Health and Safety*, entitled *Occupation and Health*, was published between 1930 and 1934 in accordance with a resolution adopted by the First Session of the International Labour Conference in 1919. It contained 416 articles by 95 contributors in 16 different countries. "With the Second World War, however, there were so many changes in techniques as well as in living and working conditions that the need for a complete recasting became apparent. This edition is therefore designed for all who are concerned with the protection of workers' health."

The encyclopedia sets out, first, to provide industrial physicians and nurses with a compendium of the available practical knowledge in their field and to familiarize them with the technical features of prevention, and secondly, to make technicians aware of the more important biological and social aspects of their work. It is not intended exclusively for specialists.

The articles are classified in alphabetical order and arranged in a double column on each page. Article captions are in darker print and larger type to stand out readily on the page. When a caption consists of several words, the most significant of these is used as a heading. This is sometimes misleading. For example, protective creams are discussed under the title *Barrier Creams, Lotions* and indexed under *creams, protective, see*. . . . Because of their complexity, some subjects are dealt with in several articles which are usually grouped together. As an example, *Heat Acclimatisation; Heat Disorders; Heat, Hot Work;* and *Heat Protective Clothing* are grouped together.

Most articles are headed by a symbol referring to the faceted classification employed by the International Occupational Safety and Health Information Centre (CIS). The abstract service provided by CIS will make it possible for the user to update the information given in this encyclopedia.

The articles vary in length from less than a full column or approximately 500 words to more than four pages or over 4,000 words. However, the greater number of articles are about one full page.

More than 700 safety and health specialists have contributed articles to this encyclopedia. Each article is signed by the author, and a list of authors with their positions is given in the appendix. More than 60 nations and special organizations have representation among these authors. As might be expected, the largest number of contributors are from the United Kingdom and the United States.

The majority of the more than 700 authors contributed only one article to the work. A count of the contributors indicates that fewer than 10 percent of the specialists have contributed to three or more articles in the encyclopedia.

Although there are hundreds of contributors to the encyclopedia there is nonetheless uniformity of arrangement of content within the short articles. First a general definition and description of the term are given, followed by paragraphs on the hazards involved and safety and health measures to be taken. Each potential source of injury or occupational illness is examined on a practical basis of the risks involved in a particular job, equipment and the manner in which it is used, and the precautions that are necessary to prevent accidents or illnesses. A brief up-to-date bibliography is appended to most of the articles.

Data relating to the physical constants and chemical substances listed usually include specific gravity, melting point, boiling point, vapor density, vapor pressure, flash point, explosive limits, ignition temperature, and solubility.

There are 730 numbered black-and-white photographs, illustrations, diagrams, and charts in the two volumes, along with 150 numbered tables. In addition, each volume has two pages of illustrations in color; volume I has 20 illustrations, volume II has 10. Volume II also contains 22 black-and-white plates depicting pneumoconioses and other lung diseases.

The Appendixes include The Elements—(1) Symbols and Valencies, and (2) Periodic Table; Conversion Tables for Gases and Vapors; Threshold Limit Values of Airborne Contaminants and Physical Agents; Units of Measurement and Definitions; Conversion Factors; Abbreviations and Symbols of Units of Measurement; Definition of Pneumoconioses; ILO Conventions and Recommendations; and Select Bibliography of Material Published by International Organization. Following these is the List of Authors, an alphabetical listing of the contributors to the encyclopedia with pagination for locating their articles.

The Encyclopaedia of Occupational Health and Safety is bound in pyroxylin-coated cloth and is Smyth sewn. The two volumes open flat for easy use. The binding of volume II of several of the sets used by the Committee is broken. The paper is a matte finish with legible size type. There are ample margins on both sides of the page.

There is no other source that brings together the vast amount of information gathered in these two volumes relating to worker protection.

The Encyclopedia of Occupational Health and Safety provides public, academic, special libraries, and others with concise information on how to protect the worker from possible sickness, disease, and injury resulting from all types of employment. Recommended.

(July 1, 1974, p.1160)

Encyclopedia of Associations. 7th ed. 3v. Detroit, Gale Research Co., 1972- 29cm. Columbia Bradford pyroxylin impregnated buckram (grade D). v.1, $38.50; v.2, $25; v.3, $48.

The first edition (1956) of this directory, *Encyclopedia of American Associations: A Guide to the Trade, Business, Professional, Labor, Scientific, Educational, Fraternal, and Social Organizations of the United States*, was reviewed in *The Booklist and Subscription Books Bulletin* Oct. 1, 1957.

The title pages of volumes 1 and 2 and the cover title of the pamphlets of volume 3 list eleven persons with their positions. Among them are Margaret Fisk, editor, and Mary Wilson, Managing Editor.

Coverage from the first to the seventh editions has been expanded in several ways. First, the number of organizations included has grown from 6,000 to more than 16,000. Second, the 6 continuously paged sections in the first edition have now grown to 19, including 294 pages for Trade, Business and Commercial Organizations down to 9 pages for Horticultural Organizations. As before, within these sections, organizations are listed alphabetically by the underlined principal key word of the name of the organization. Third, the Introduction in volume 1 notes that in addition to national, nonprofit membership organizations which originally comprised the entire directory and still comprises the largest group by far, the scope now includes six more categories; e.g., non-membership groups (American River Touring Association, National Merit Scholarship Corporation, White House Historical Assn.), foreign groups of interest to Americans (Tennyson Society, Heraldry Society), and citizen action groups, projects and programs (Community Improvement Program, National Alliance on Shaping Safer Cities). Fourth, volume 1, National Organizations of the United States, has 1,452 pages as compared to the 306-page first edition, including a 186-page (64 pages in 1956) Alphabetical Index to Organization Names and Keywords. Fifth, this edition has a second bound volume, Geographic and Executive Index, and a binder for loose-leaf inter-edition quarterlies (volume 3, March 1972-   ) covering newly formed and newly found associations. These additional features go far to support the publisher's claim that the compilation, organization, and editing of the directory is a continuing program and that suggestions and revisions for future editions are welcomed.

Preceding the listings of associations in volumes 1 and 2 are detailed explanations of how to use the directory and a description of the type of information included in the entries. Volume 3 entries—alphabetical by association or project name, not by key word—have no such preliminary matter.

The following information, if it was available from the organization, is included for each association listed in volume 1: formal name; acronym; keyword arrangement; zip coded address of permanent headquarters or of chief official, secretary or president; founding date; number of members; number of permanent staff members; state and local groups; brief description of the activities, purpose and membership; committees, sections, divisions, publications; affiliated organizations; mergers and changes of name; convention data (frequency, date, location).

Running titles, absent in the 1956 edition, are now present throughout, but entry arrangement by underlined keyword or words still requires the ability to scan rapidly. Consider this partial sequence on two facing pages: AMERICAN INSTITUTE OF *LAUNDERING*, CHINESE *LAUNDRY* ASSOCIATION, KEX NATIONAL ASSOCIATION *(Laundry)*, *LAUNDRY* AND CLEANERS ALLIED TRADES ASSOCIATION, NATIONAL ASSOCIATION OF COIN *LAUNDRY* EQUIPMENT OPERATORS, NATIONAL ASSOCIATION OF INSTITUTIONAL *LAUNDRY* MANAGERS, NATIONAL AUTOMATIC *LAUNDRY* AND CLEANING COUNCIL, LAWYERS—See Index.

A spot check of associations in *National Trade and Professional Associations of the United States, 1972* (Washington, Columbia Books, 1972), a directory of some 4,300 organizations, revealed much duplication in coverage but also a few associations not in the Gale directory to the June 1972 issue of volume 3. Of the 67 higher education associations in *Education Directory, 1971-72—Higher Education* (Washington: Gov't. Print. Off., 1972) five, including New England Board of Higher Education and Western Interstate Commission for Higher Education, are not in *Gale*. Sixty-four national black organizations are cited in *The Negro Almanac* (New rev. ed.; New York: Bellwether Co., 1971); 24 of them are not in *Gale*. The 1971-72 *Manhattan Telephone Directory* was spot checked against Gale's Geographic Index in volume 2; very few differences were found. All in all these checks suggest that this edition of *Encyclopedia of Associations* is commendable for its accuracy and currentness.

The volumes are sturdily bound in green and black and stamped in gold and black. They are Smyth sewed and open flat for easy use. The paper is a white stock of good weight and quality. The type is readable, and the use of all capital letters for the names of associations (in all but the Executive Index of volume 2) makes them stand out from the body of the entry.

Encyclopedia of Associations is the largest directory of American associations currently available for library purchase. Listing more than 16,000 associations, it is accurate and reasonably current. Recommended.

(April 1, 1973, p.724)

Glenn G. Munn's Encyclopedia of Banking and Finance. Rev. and enl. by F. L. Garcia. 7th ed. Boston, Bankers Publishing Co., 1973. 953p. 27cm. buckram-vellum finish $49.75; discounts based on quantity only.
ISBN 0-87267-019-8.

Dating back to 1924, Munn's *Encyclopedia of Banking and Finance* has been a valuable reference tool for answers to everyday questions in the realm of business and finance. It goes far beyond basic definitions—discussing terms in detail. Illustrations are given with statistical tables and examples, current trends and recent developments are analyzed, and regulatory agencies and organizations are discussed. Older editions were reviewed in Oct. 1936 and Oct. 1938 *Subscription Books Bulletin*. Now, 11 years after the sixth edition, comes the newly revised and updated seventh edition.

Professor F. L. Garcia, Department of Finance, Fordham University, and editor since 1949, was in charge of this revision. Long recognized as an authority in his field, Professor Garcia holds B.S., M.A., J.D., and LL.M. degrees and has served as a bank analyst and investment advisor.

An introduction to this new edition explains some of the developments in the field which led to its publication. Professor Garcia mentions price and wage controls, two devaluations of the dollar, and the emergence of "consumerism" as examples of the changes necessitating the updating of this encyclopedia. In order to accomplish this task, nearly 4,000 terms are included in this edition, increasing the number of pages by 22 percent over the sixth edition, to 953 pages. Continued updating will be more frequent as the encyclopedia is now on computer tape.

Within the 4,000 entries, one may find information on virtually any subject within the scope of the title of this work. Coverage includes discussions of *Annuity, Bailee Receipt, Bear Market, Blue Sky Laws, Cambist, Double Liability, Dow Theory, Limping Standard, GATT, Trial of the Pix,* and *Women's Signatures.* The content of each entry is comprehensive and may take the form of a definition of a technical term—*Melon;* the essence of a business law—*McLean-Platt Act;* tabular information —the *New York Stock Exchange Abbreviations* list; statistical data—the *Number of Commercial Banks in Operation in December, 1971;* illustrative data—the application of *Distribution of Risk;* an analysis of trends—in *Market Times Earnings Ration;* citations of applicable regulations—in *Short-term Notes;* or various charts, lists, tables and sample forms to clarify the meaning of a term. Bibliographies are often used to aid in updating entries. *Cushion Bonds* refers the reader to a 1972 book for further information. The bibliographies vary in length according to the subject, with *Insurance* listing 26 items and *Federal Credit Unions* providing two titles. Another convenience is the use of cross-references found in the majority of entries. To enable the reader to do more research on a topic, sources of statistics are cited.

The entries vary in length from a short paragraph, e.g., *Intestacy,* to ten pages, e.g., *New York Stock Exchange.* Statistics cited generally are as current as 1970 to 1972. The tables and charts provide a wealth of information, including a list of Bank Holding Companies, Amortization Tables (an example only), Commodities Contracts Traded, Interest Tables, Volume of Trading on the NYSE, Evolution of Railroad Legislation, and an example of a bank statement.

Bound in buckram with a vellum finish, the volume is sturdy and should withstand heavy usage. The pages, made with a matte finish paper turn easily and lie flat when opened. Unfortunately, the margins are narrow, and rebinding may be a problem. The type is small but legible. Entry words are in boldface; running headings facilitate use. Tables, charts and sample forms are reproduced clearly in black and white.

Encyclopedia of Banking and Finance is highly recommended for use by businessmen, bankers, students, and anyone seeking an introduction to the world of finance. It is an indispensable reference tool for libraries serving this type of clientele. *(July 15, 1974, p.1209)*

The Encyclopedia of Education. Editor in chief, Lee C. Deighton. 10v. New York, the Macmillan Company and the Free Press, [c by Crowell-Collier Educational Corp., 1971]. illus. tables. 29cm. pyroxylin-impregnated buckram $395 plus $5 shipping and handling; no discounts.

The Encyclopedia of Education is designed to provide a "single reference source which describes the range of educational interests and practices." Its over 1,100 articles written by as many individual authors, arranged alphabetically word by word, deal with education in the broadest sense of the term. Lee Deighton, editor in chief of the encyclopedia, writes in the Preface: "Education is not limited locationally to the premises of an established school. It is not limited in time to a particular period of a learner's life." This point of view is reflected in the inclusion of many articles covering avenues of education outside the formal public and private school structure *(Museum as an Educational Institution, Industry Training Programs)* and articles dealing with the education and learning of individuals outside the traditional "school age" *(Adult Basic Education, Learning in Infancy.)* The Encyclopedia of Education was planned for use by "the generality of adults engaged one way or another in either educational practice or related educational decision-making," ranging from the elementary school teacher and the school superintendent or training director in industry to the scholar. Defined in an even more general fashion, the audience is mentioned in the Preface as "the adult concerned with educational practice." This definition could obviously include the interested parent as well as the specialist.

Most articles in the encyclopedia are fairly lengthy and present material under broad subjects; only 5 articles are 1 page or less and over 30 multipart articles cover 25 pages or more (for example, *Business Education*—52 pages, *English Language*—63 pages, *Mathematics Instruction*—57 pages.) Despite the broad coverage of the encyclopedia, its editors do not claim it to be a complete view of the subject since "education itself is necessarily and suitably in continuous change and can never be brought wholly into focus."

The Encyclopedia of Education is an entirely new work conceived five years ago to fill a long-felt need for a modern overview of education. Although neither the Preface nor other sections of the encyclopedia mention supplements or other plans for revision, Macmillan informs the Committee that *Education Yearbook,* the first of which covers 1972-1973, "will be released on about an annual basis to supplement and update the set."

Lee C. Deighton, editor in chief, has had a distinguished career in publishing. Presently retired, he most recently served as senior vice president of Crowell Collier and Macmillan, Inc. (1966-1970) and Chairman of the Board of the Macmillan Company (1965-1970), with prior experience in educational publishing as vice president in charge of the Educational Department at Macmillan (1957-1961) and as vice president of Science Research Associates (1954-1956). The Macmillan Company, publisher of *The Encyclopedia of Education,* has also published other well-known subject-oriented multivolume encyclopedias, such as *The Encyclopedia of Philosophy* (1967 *The Booklist and Subscription Books Bulletin* March 1, 1969), *International Encyclopedia of the Social Sciences* (1968 *The Booklist and Subscription Books Bulletin* June 1, 1969), and the one-volume *Encyclopedia of Educational Research* (1941-   *Subscription Books Bulletin* April 1941).

Deighton was assisted by an advisory board of 32 prominent educators, primarily affiliated with colleges and universities, who suggested essential topics and qualified writers to the editorial staff. Half of the members of the advisory board also contributed at least one article to the encyclopedia.

Sixty percent of the over 1,100 contributors from approximately 25 countries are scholars or administrators at colleges or universities; 16 percent are officers of educational associations, organizations, or councils; 8 percent hold positions with the United States government, and 16 percent fall into other categories. A Directory of Contributors in volume 10 lists under each name academic degrees, affiliations, publications, and the titles of the articles written in this encyclopedia. The wide diversity in contributors' experience is evidenced by a listing of some of the positions represented: project directors, librarians, executives of educational testing firms, directors of youth organizations, journal editors and educational publishers, physicians, engineers, officials in state departments of education, and teachers and administrators in public school systems. Many contributors are recognized authorities in their fields. For example, Edward T. Hall, author of *The Hidden Dimension,* is responsible for the article *Environmental Influences: Space,* Theodore M. Hesburgh for *Governance in Higher Education: Catholic Colleges and Universities,* and B. F. Skinner for *Operant Conditioning.* Other contributors are relative newcomers to their specialties.

Almost all of the articles in *The Encyclopedia of Education* appear over the signatures of their authors; a mere two to three percent are signed by validators only, who are indicated by asterisks. The editors claim that "all of the articles are original work, written expressly for *The Encyclopedia of Education.*"

The editor in chief states in the Preface that the encyclopedia was "planned as a source of information; its content was intended to be informative and descriptive. Its purpose was to describe things as they are, as they have been, and as they are trending." Although coverage of education is very broad, the editors have attempted to give structure to the work as a whole by concentrating on education as an institution, as a process, and as a product. Each of these three aspects of education is covered by many separate articles and index references. For example, education as an institution covers the wide variety of "institutions which carry on organized courses of instruction." *The Encyclopedia of Education* gives a balanced overview of educational institutions by including information about proprietary schools, correspondence schools, industry schools, schools affiliated with the federal government, health organizations, youth organizations, libraries, churches, and museums as well as formal public or private institutions from the preschool to graduate school levels. Education as a process "concerns not only the ends of instruction and the means by which they are attained but, quite properly, *what* is learned as well." Such diverse articles as *Learning; Area Studies, Teaching of; Social Control in Schools; Information; Attitude Change in the Classroom;* and *Peer Groups* fall under the category of education as process. Education as product is viewed as the outcome of the education process. For example, the articles *Sociology of Education, Instructional Objectives,* *Illiteracy, Efficiency in Education,* and many others deal with the results of "sufficient" or "insufficient" education and with attempts to improve the product.

A comparison between subject areas covered in the encyclopedia with the subject breakdown in Macmillan's one-volume *Encyclopedia of Educational Research* reveals balance and fullness of coverage in *The Encyclopedia of Education.* Twenty-four percent of *The Encyclopedia of Education's* major articles cover the foundation areas of developmental psychology, the psychology of learning, human behavior, and the social foundations (such as, the history, philosophy, sociology, and economics of education in addition to comparative education and religion and education). Sixteen percent deal with the function areas of curriculum, instruction, special education, educational measurement, and research. Twenty-two percent deal with individual subject areas taught, ten percent with student and teacher personnel plus teacher education and educational administration. Special breadth of coverage was noted for the social foundations of education, for vocational subject areas, and for topics related to school systems.

At the same time, no mention could be found in the Index in volume 10 to a number of details relevant to the daily operations of schools, such as secretarial assistance in schools, substitute teachers, teacher orientation, curriculum guides, rest periods for teachers, accidents in the school, and visitors to classrooms. *The Encyclopedia of Education,* therefore, cannot be considered a handbook or manual of operation for educators, but rather an authoritative source of background information in many areas of concern.

A few other gaps in coverage were noted. The encyclopedia includes the articles *Middle Schools* and *Public High School, United States,* but has no separate article on the elementary school in the United States. An entire article is devoted to *Infant Schools in England.* It would have been more convenient for the encyclopedia's users to be able to refer to a separate article about the elementary school in addition to the one and one-half pages of references in the Index to "elementary education" and "elementary school." The article *Theater, Children's* is good, but no coverage exists for creative dramatics in either full article form or index references.

As in any encyclopedia, the quality and scope of the articles and the tone and clarity of writing style vary. The editors had the added difficulty of defining education, a field which includes many disciplines which are constantly in a state of flux and which tend to offer two avenues of approach—the practical and the theoretical. In addition, the contributors, although offered guidelines for writing, were permitted to vary the structure and to incorporate unavoidably their "experiences and bias." This editorial flexibility coupled with a broadly-defined and ever-changing subject field results in an excellent encyclopedia viewed as a whole, but one which receives mixed reviews when individual articles or groups of related articles are examined.

For example, in the foundation areas of developmental psychology, psychology of learning, and the sociology of education, the articles examined were, for the most part, critical and scholarly. The article *Heredity, Environment, and Intelligence* is an excellent technical article and summary of research on general intelligence, special mental abilities, educability, and learning ability. The author, Arthur R. Jensen, has included equations and formulas in the article, yet directs many of his comments toward the nonspecialist through the expert use of examples. The article shows no obvious bias in favor of Jensen's controversial views on race and intelligence. The article *Child Development: Sex Differences in Development* is a critical and subtle survey of research on sex differences which emphasizes the natural difficulties of research in this area. *Learning Disabilities* is an excellent historical and current overview for the nonspecialist of learning disabilities and their treatment. The author succeeds in showing the complexities of the subject in a few pages of text and refers the reader to more technical items listed in the bibliography. *Mental Retardation* is a scholarly and critical overview of current research. It shows that identification procedures, educational assessment, and school programming are far from definitive but that findings in education and psychology are affecting the understanding of and the teaching of the mentally retarded. The article *Subcultures, Adolescent* might be more properly entitled "Subcultures, High School Student" since it emphasizes school environment over neighborhood groups or friendship cliques. The article is soundly based on research, but is more narrow in scope than the articles previously mentioned.

Approach in several of the encyclopedia articles dealing with curriculum subject areas and professional education was more descriptive than scholarly. *Anthropology in the Schools* is an example of an excellent descriptive article about the state of anthropology course content. The author achieves up-to-dateness by avoiding use of examples easily outmoded. The article is especially useful for its descriptions of curriculum projects and the background behind elementary and secondary curriculum development in anthropology. The author Malcolm Collier, director of the Anthropology Curriculum Study Project, does not give undue emphasis to his own work. In contrast, the article *Humanities in the Secondary Schools* is barely adequate. The author, a high school teacher, gives little attention to specific curriculum projects and generalizes for many paragraphs about "rationale and goals." However, his section on the four common approaches used—culture-epoch, great themes, multi-media, and major works—is informative. The article *Literature, Children's* lacks contemporaneity and scholarly backing. There is no treatment of creative drama, storytelling, use of paperbacks in the school or in libraries, or literary criticism of children's books. Coverage of the history of children's literature and of the various genres is sketchy. Little mention is made of modern trends, such as portrayal of minorities and use of realism in children's books. The statement "the old didactic literature moralized, as it was intended to do, but today's literature does no such thing" is certainly questionable. The section "Literature in the lives of children" is made up of undocumented cliches about understanding self, others, and the world. *Librarians, Education of* is seriously flawed by outdated statements. For example, the author, Lawrence A. Allen, states, "Estimates of the number of librarians needed in the United States alone have ranged from 20,000 to 120,000 and there is little doubt that the need is vastly beyond the present supply and will remain so for some time" and "the desperate shortage of librarians, especially school librarians, has created much of the need for the undergraduate programs." The author also discusses federal support of library training in the mid and late 1960s as if that high level of funding will always be available. Coverage of levels and history of professional training is adequate. The section on upgrading library programs is also adequate except for one confusing sentence which must have escaped editorial correction: "Answers were provided with the [library] quiz, and the new student was told how to become more at the university." *Business Education: Colleges* adequately describes the role, structure, and curriculum of business education on the college level. However, the article is marred by an overemphasis on the necessity of graduate education in business for those who aspire to high-level management positions. In addition, the author lists the "leading schools of business" and often refers to the "better" business schools without defining his criteria for evaluation.

Several articles dealing with the means of instruction vary greatly in quality. *Programmed Instruction* is an excellent, well-documented article about the possibilities and problems of programmed instruction. It considers the topic in light of current research and of the state of the American educational system today. *Audiovisual Instruction: Facilities* gives general guidelines for the planning of audiovisual facilities in schools with emphasis on equipment and building space requirements. It does not describe audiovisual facilities in specific settings, such as the instructional materials center in schools or the junior college media center; nor does it survey the variety of uses made of audiovisual facilities in the curriculum. In addition, the history of audiovisual facilities is neglected. Although the author covers space and equipment needs in detail, he has not written a comprehensive survey of the topic. In contrast, *Technology in Education* is a critical, descriptive article dealing with total education systems. The author covers both the drawbacks and advantages of different types of media and relates technology to learning objectives.

Contrasts in quality can also be seen in two articles dealing with libraries. *Libraries, Academic* is one of the few unsigned articles in the encyclopedia. The article is mediocre, because it misses many current and past developments. For example, Fremont Rider is not mentioned under "Growth of Collections." No mention is made of undergraduate libraries or cooperation between academic libraries. There is only one paragraph on automation and no separate section concerning technical services. The public service function of the academic library is mentioned in one simplistic paragraph about dealing with reference inquiries. The author states, "By introducing the student to varied sources of information, the librarian helps him to learn to select information." The article *Libraries, School,* written by a high school librarian, covers the topic well. It relates the changing nature of the school to the evolution of the school library into a media center. The author writes informatively about the effects of standards, the physical plant, data processing, federal aid, personnel, and the Knapp School Libraries Project on elementary and high school libraries.

The Encyclopedia of Education does not escape the unavoidable unevenness in quality found in any large encyclopedia with many contributors. All articles in the encyclopedia will give the reader some degree of authoritative information but will vary in character and fullness of treatment, up-to-dateness, and clearness of presentation. Most articles examined were adequate, and many were excellent. The style of writing is generally clear and understandable by the layman, the exception being technical articles directed toward scholars and graduate students (*Experimental Design; Test Scores and Norms; Readability, Measurement of; Sampling Procedures*).

The encyclopedia was prepared "without subvention by foundation or government." Treatment of controversial subjects is balanced, with no noticeable bias toward any one point of view. Controversy is handled with exceptional balance and attention to research in the articles *College Student: Student Protests; Urban Education: School Segregation, Desegregation, and Integration; Testing Special Groups: The Culturally Disadvantaged;* and *Church-State Relations in Education: Legal Aspects of Religion in the Schools.* Other articles, such as, *Transportation and School Busing; Drug Abuse Education;* and *Public Education, Criticism of* avoid bias but do not offer much detail about controversial topics.

The inquirer will find many articles on subjects of current interest, such as *Bilingual Children, Teaching of; Cluster Colleges; Computers: Computer-Aided Instruction; Head Start; Media, Instructional: Multi-Media Systems; Psycholinguistics;* and *Women, Education of: Continuing Education.*

Two bibliographical articles vary in usefulness. Sidney Forman's *Bibliography, Educational* gives excellent coverage of the literature of education, emphasizing American publications, and includes up-to-date comments about automation and bibliographic control. The article includes a bibliography of over 100 titles. In contrast, the article *Reference Books* can be faulted for a somewhat arbitrary selection of reference tools under different categories. For example, no mention is made of *Current Index to Journals in Education* or *Research in Education* under "Indexes." At the same time, *Union List of Serials* and *New Serial Titles* are discussed misleadingly under that same subheading. Some explanations are too simple to be of much use to the researcher, such as, "maps are found in atlases," or may even prove unsound advice: "To avoid this difficulty [in using a card catalog's subject approach], the reader should use general language or education dictionaries to determine the term synonymous with or related to the subject he is searching."

Although *The Encyclopedia of Education* deals primarily with American education, a number of articles concern international and comparative education and exchange programs. The encyclopedia also includes over 100 individual articles about the educational systems of specific countries or regions. Some political units, either small in size (Andorra, San Marino), remote (Nepal, Sikkim), in island form (Fiji, Malagasay Republic), or, in some cases, African (Chad, Sierra Leone) are not covered by articles or index references.

The editors decided arbitrarily to limit the number of biographical articles "because the detail of educators' lives is not consistently relevant to education. There is also the impossible problem of determining whom to include and whom to omit." Of the 18 influential persons treated, only Piaget was living at the time his biography was written. Each biography stresses the individual's contributions to education and holds to a minimum other biographical details. The encyclopedia gives ample index coverage to other important educators, both living and dead.

Another useful feature of the encyclopedia is the inclusion of over 140 articles concerning education-related associations and organizations. These articles usually give detailed information about the purpose, program, organizational structure, membership, and history of the organization. The contributors are often officers of the organizations they describe.

Approximately 60 career-related articles deal with professions (*Accounting, Librarianship*), training programs (*Management Training, Federal; Astronaut Training Programs*), specific careers (*Atomic Energy Careers, Engineering Careers*), educational programs for various fields (*Environmental Health Ser-*

vices, *Education for; Hospital Administration, Education for*), specialized schools (*Law Schools, Medical Schools*), and occupations (*Food Service Occupations*). The articles on specific careers usually contain definitions of the occupation or profession, educational requirements, and career opportunities. This type of information eventually will become of historical interest only, especially since no plans for revision or updating of the encyclopedia have been stated by the publishers. Therefore, the editors' claim that, "of all the school staff, the guidance counselors will make the widest and most frequent use of *The Encyclopedia of Education* not only in respect to guidance theory and vocational guidance but educational guidance as well" will not hold true for career information, which will continue to be updated in other sources, such as, the U.S. Department of Labor's *Occupational Outlook Handbook*.

Editorial recognition of the field of education's interdisciplinary nature is reflected in the inclusion of several articles drawing on two or more fields of study, such as, *Art Education Theories: Art, Experience, and Education—A Philosophic Inquiry; Moral Education, Philosophic View of;* and *Moral Education, Psychological View of*. The broad scope of education is also maintained by the 28 multipart articles which include an "Overview" of the topic. Some examples of topics with "Overviews" are *Business Education; Early Childhood Education; Foreign Languages, Teaching of; Independent Study;* and *Research, Educational*. A comparison of many pairs of articles with similar titles revealed little duplication of subject coverage. For instance, *Curriculum for Integration of Disciplines* shows how the fields of knowledge are structured within different curriculum organizations whereas *Curriculum Integration* deals with the attempts of educators to construct a curriculum which will best enable students to relate their school experiences to other life experiences and to their own needs and interests.

The editors state that they "have not tried for strict contemporaneity since the living moment does not survive encapsulation in print." They also claim that "the data and information in the articles were fresh at the moment of last editing; they provide a history and a standard against which later events may be considered." Since the date of last editing for individual articles is unknown, the Committee cannot challenge the editors' statements. However, as in many encyclopedias, the biographies and many historical articles will be of long-lasting value whereas some of the articles emphasizing current information are already dated.

Access to information included in *The Encyclopedia of Education*, for the most part, is easy. In volumes 1 through 9, the arrangement of the articles is alphabetical word by word, with the exception of the individually titled parts of multipart articles. Pages (an average of over 600 per volume) are numbered by volume. Volume 10, *Index*, includes the Directory of Contributors, the Guide to Articles, and the Index. The Guide to Articles is a word-by-word alphabetical listing of individual article titles which also provides *see also* references to related articles. Seventeen subject headings, such as, "Adult Education" and "High Schools" also serve to group related articles. Unfortunately, the reader must refer to 13 separate articles for information on the subject "Accountability" and can find no subject heading grouping articles on elementary schools or elementary education. However, the Guide to Articles is usually helpful, especially if used in conjunction with the Index. Instructions to the user of the Index state, "The Index includes cross references from subject headings to individual article titles and vice versa. It does not include cross references from individual article titles to other individual article titles; for such cross references see the Guide to Articles."

This excellent alphabetical Index of over 40,000 entries is arranged letter by letter in dictionary form. A check of 100 pages of the Index revealed three blind cross-references, but the general level of accuracy is high. The Index includes conceptual as well as topical references. Many publications mentioned by title in encyclopedia articles are listed by title in the Index. Important educational studies are listed by their popular names, such as, "Coleman Report" and "Plowden Report."

Approximately three-fourths of the more than 1,100 articles in the encyclopedia are followed by bibliographies of three or more titles. The bibliographies were compiled under the supervision of a Director of Bibliography, Paul B. Cumberland, for the purpose of aiding the general reader in further study. Over 30 articles conclude with bibliographies of 50 titles or more. Bibliographical information provided in each entry is adequate. Many forms of materials are included, from unpublished papers and journal articles to government documents. Materials listed are primarily American in origin, although publications from 46 other countries were counted. An unevenness in bibliographical coverage is apparent. Often articles on countries *(Austria, Brazil, United Arab Republic)* and associations *(National Education Association)* lack bibliographies. Other topics of major interest have little or no bibliographical coverage: *United States Office of Education* (none); *Universities, Intellectual Role of* (none); *Appropriations Process in Education, Federal* (two entries); *College Teaching: Collective Bargaining* (none); *Economics, Teaching of* (none). In contrast, some major articles have excellent and extensive bibliographies: *Art Education Theories: Scientific Inquiry* (70 entries), *Curriculum Building* (71 entries), *Heredity and Behavior Development* (97 entries). Some articles include specific citations to items in the appended bibliographies while others do not. Most bibliographies examined were up to date, except for a few glaring exceptions. For example, the only entry in the bibliography for *Transportation and School Busing* is a book entitled *Pupil Transportation*, published in 1965. The three books listed at the conclusion of *Vietnam: South Vietnam* are dated 1962, 1963, and 1967.

The set is attractively printed with two columns to a page. The typefaces are well chosen and the print is easy to read. Running heads on the top of each page aid the reader in location of articles. Over 150 halftone or line drawings, usually tables or figures, explain and clarify the text but are not consistently listed in the Index. The side-sewn buckram binding and fine quality of paper should stand up well under heavy use.

The Encyclopedia of Education, the work of a large and varied group of specialists, is the first comprehensive multivolume account of the field of education to be published since Monroe's *Cyclopedia of Education* appeared in 1911-1913. Despite variability in scope and treatment of its subject content, the encyclopedia can be considered a well-organized and useful reference set for educators, students, and nonprofessional users. Purchase is recommended to all libraries serving adult readers.

(April 15, 1973, p.769)

The Encyclopedia of the Horse. Edited by Lieutenant Colonel C. E. G. Hope and G. N. Jackson. Advisory editor: William Steinkraus. Picture editor: Diana R. Tuke. New York, Viking Pr., [1973]. 336p. illus. cloth 29cm. $22.50. SBN 670-29402-0.

The Encyclopedia of the Horse, "an illustrated encyclopedia designed for everyone interested in horses and horsemanship," is an attractive book arranged in a single alphabetical list. The book covers every recognized breed of horse and pony; evolution of the horse; history, training, and care; use in art, literature, and sport; and equestrian activities and competitions world wide.

The clear, concise articles are by acknowledged authorities from many countries. Each article is initialed by the author. An easy-to-use list of contributors has a short statement identifying each, noting his experience, profession, and published books in this field.

Articles vary in length from short paragraphs to several pages. Information is generally comprehensive and up to date. Bibliographies are given at the end of some articles. *See also* references to other entries containing related information are frequently given within the articles and also at the end. There are also many helpful *see* references usually from a specific term to a more general one. When words used in an article are also used as entry headings, they appear in the article in small capitals so that the reader may look for the entry if he wishes more information.

Each page has two columns of print, and many pages have one or more illustrations. Pictures are all well placed in relation to the subject matter. There are ten pages of excellent full-color plates of different breeds, and three hundred black-and-white pictures and drawings. A three-page list of notes gives page number, credit, and other information for each illustration or photograph.

It contains a useful list of Horse and Pony Societies divided into international and national groups, with the correct name and address given for each. A unique feature of the book is a series of maps, by continents, showing the types and breeds of horses and ponies to be found in each country. The only book comparable to *The Encyclopedia of the Horse* is *The Kingdom of the Horse* published by Time-Life, 1972. It, too, is a handsome, well-illustrated general book on the horse. More detailed, but less inclusive, it should be used with *The Encyclopedia of the Horse*.

The Encyclopedia of the Horse is printed on heavy, coated paper and is sturdy and well bound. The text will not be affected by rebinding, but some illustrations will be trimmed. The book lies flat when open.

In a field where there are many books on specific breeds, this book is a useful addition for reference, browsing, and circulation in school and public libraries and in homes. It brings together a wide variety of information which is well-organized and easy to locate. Recommended. *(Jan. 15, 1974, p.495)*

Encyclopedia of Psychology. 3v. Editors: Hans Jurgen Eysenck, W. Arnold and R. Meili. [New York,] Herder and Herder, [1972]; distributed in U.S. by Seabury Pr., 815 Second Avenue, New York 10017. 26cm. Columbia bayside linen, grade A pyroxylin impregnated $75; to schools and libraries, 20 percent discount.

Encyclopedia of Psychology was first published in 1971 by HKG Freiburg, Germany. The work under review is a translation from the German which was co-published in 1972 by Search Press (England) and Herder and Herder. Herder and Herder is now a part of Seabury Press. The set bears the Continuum Books imprint. The encyclopedia is also published in French, Spanish, Portuguese, and Italian.

Hans Jurgen Eysenck, Professor of Psychology, London University; W. Arnold of Wurzburg; and R. Meili of Berne edit the encyclopedia. Eysenck is an eminent psychologist who has taught at the University of London since 1955 and has been Director of the Psychological Department at Maudsley Hospital in London since 1946. He was educated in Germany, France and England, and has taught at the University of Pennsylvania and the University of California at Berkeley. He has written numerous articles for British, American, German, and French journals of psychology and many books. The other editors are well known particularly in German-speaking countries.

Encyclopedia of Psychology intends to be a comprehensive reference source covering all major phases of psychology presented in language that can be readily understood by the layman, yet useful to the professional. There are 5,000 entries from more than 300 contributors. Entries are of two kinds, definitions of one or two lines and essay articles written by authorities covering important terms and concepts, ranging in length up to 4,000 words, and containing bibliographies for further study. The encyclopedia is intended for professional psychologists, sociologists, educators, and anyone interested in modern psychology. For the most part the editors claim that subjects are presented as they are understood and accepted in the English-speaking world.

The international nature of this work is evidenced by the fact that the writing is by specialist authors from 20 different countries. There are 133 psychologists who are major contributors; of these 41 are from the United States, 37 from Great Britain, and 6 from the Soviet Union, while Japan, Switzerland, Canada, and South Africa are also represented. Among the American contributors are James E. Birren, whose field is the manifestations of aging, and Bernard Rimland, expert on childhood psychosis. Well-known contributors from other countries are Alexandr Luria, Soviet psychologist at Moscow State University, Philippe Malrieu of France, and Richard Pokorny of Israel.

The main articles are signed; briefer definitions are initialled. In general, each topic begins with a concise definition and then proceeds into fuller explanation. The wide range of subjects covered includes information on aphasia, ego-involvement, reflexes, depth perception, homeostasis, schizophrenia, and narcolepsy. The reader seeking information on behavior modification, causalgia, and transactional analysis must employ some ingenuity because index and cross-references are lacking. Depth of treatment varies. A lengthy article is provided on hormones along with a three-page chart listing the more important ones with their functions and associated disorders. The information on existential psychology is sketchy, but there is an interesting long analysis of Soviet psychology and its development in a distinct political and socioeconomic environment.

Brief biographies are provided for such eminent psychologists as William James, Lewis Terman, Arnold Gesell, and Robert Yerkes, but Karen Horney and Eric Berne are not mentioned.

The set, which is alphabetically arranged, is not indexed. Instead, volume 1 contains a list of the main articles, their contributors and their city and country for all three volumes. Unfortunately, this list is not repeated in volumes 2 and 3, but each of the three volumes contains a list of the authors of shorter articles with a key to their initials. Each volume also contains a list of the main abbreviations used in the set. According to the Prefatory Note, "short, unsigned definitions are the work of a group of psychologists and lexicographers in the Herder Lexicographical Institute."

Cross-references appear throughout, and are indicated usually by *see* references at the end of an article.

There are satisfactory short bibliographies after the more comprehensive articles, none after the shorter ones. They usually list from ten to twenty sources, and the authors are printed in dark type. The citations refer most frequently to British and American sources with occasional German, Russian, and Swiss publications.

Illustrations are not necessary in a work of this type, but there are a few charts and small drawings. There is an organogram for human information processing, and a small illustration of Helmholtz squares, the optical illusion whereby filled spaces look larger than empty ones.

The text is printed in a clear, modern typeface, two columns to a page, on antique stock. Subjects are printed in boldface, and key words are to be found at the top of each page at the outer margin, page numbers at the top inner margin. The three volumes are divided A to F, G to P, and Ph to Z. They are bound in linen. Adequate inner margins are provided. The volumes lie flat when opened. Each volume has separate pagination and contains approximately 400 pages.

Comparison should be made with Goldenson's *Encyclopedia of Human Behavior* (Garden City, NY: Doubleday, 1970), which in approximately the same number of pages also identifies terms, theories, and treatments in both psychology and psychiatry. *Goldenson* has 1,000 entries compared to 5,000 in the *Encyclopedia of Psychology*, but they are often substantially longer. Also provided are several hundred case studies illustrating various disorders.

There is no doubt that the contributions of psychologists from many countries lend a broad coverage from diverse viewpoints to the *Encyclopedia of Psychology*. It is probable that public libraries able to afford them should have both encyclopedias. Recommended.

(Mar. 15, 1974, p.748)

Encyclopedia of World Literature in the 20th Century. General ed., Wolfgang Bernard Fleishmann. 3v. New York,

Frederick Ungar Publishing Co., 1967-71. illus. 29cm. buckram $98; to schools and school libraries, 15 percent discount; to public libraries, 20 percent discount.

Encyclopedia of World Literature in the 20th Century is "an enlarged and updated edition of the Herder *Lexikon der Weltliteratur im 20. Jahrhundert* (Freiburg: 1960-61) created especially for the English-speaking world." Volume 1 was published in 1967 and was reviewed in *The Booklist and Subscription Books Bulletin*, December 15, 1968. Volumes 2 and 3 were published in 1969 and 1971 respectively. The encyclopedia attempts to cover, "in over 1,300 articles, the major aspects of literature in our century." Approximately half of the articles were written especially for this edition. The remainder are revised or updated translations of articles in the German edition. Most of the articles are signed; those which are not were written by the Herder staff for the original edition. A list of contributors and their articles is included at the front of each volume. The contributors are not identified by location, and no academic credentials are given. Approximately one sixth of a sample of contributors checked were located in standard biographical sources.

Most of the entries are biobibliographic in nature. These articles are organized in four parts: a headnote brief identification (Rumanian novelist and essayist); an article of critical appraisal of the author and his works in assessing his influence on world literature; "Further Works," listing titles not mentioned in the main article; and "Bibliography," a brief listing of articles and books about the author's works. Therefore, the amount of purely biographical information included varies considerably.

When the title of an author's work is mentioned in the body of the article or is listed in "Further Works," the only bibliographic information given is the date of publication. The editor claims also to have listed the English title of existing translations of works of major importance. An attempt has been made to include English language works in each "Bibliography" section, but material in other languages has not been excluded.

A fifth section consisting of a selection of critical quotations about the writer is appended to some entries for the best-known authors. Full bibliographic references are given for these quotations. When necessary, commentary from critics is translated into English.

The encyclopedia includes a number of survey articles covering genres, literary movements, and national literatures. However, the article *Science Fiction*, mentioned in the Introduction, has been omitted; no coverage of the subject could be located elsewhere either. A most useful feature is the presence of articles connecting literature with related subject areas, (e.g., *Cinema and Literature, Society and Literature, Psychology and Literature*). Most of the survey articles also include brief bibliographies. Whenever an author mentioned in a survey is the subject of a separate entry, this fact is noted by a cross-reference.

For this edition, the editors planned to expand the coverage of Asian and African literatures. Very little expansion is evident, however. The article *Indian Literature* is a bit longer than that in the Herder edition, but only two authors, Rabindranath Tagore and Dilip Kumar Roy, are subjects of individual articles. Only Tagore was treated separately in the Herder edition. The latest date in the *Indian Literature* bibliography is 1961. In the case of *Japanese Literature*, only four authors are treated individually, and the latest entry in the bibliography is dated 1963.

Each volume includes a list of periodical abbreviations used and a list of illustrations with page references. Approximately 100 halftone illustrations are included in each volume. They are of good quality and are placed close to the article concerning the author pictured.

A major deficiency is the lack of the index which was promised for volume 3. The many cross-references aid the user to some extent, but there is no easy way to locate authors who appear only in survey articles. This is especially true in the case of African authors because African literature is covered in 13 different entries.

The binding is sturdy, and the volumes are attractively printed on non-glare stock. The type is clear and the double column pages have ample margin for rebinding.

A comparable work, Cassell's *Encyclopedia of World Literature* (New York: Funk & Wagnalls, 1954), is now eighteen years old. Because it is not limited to twentieth-century literature, the treatment of individual authors of the period is necessarily brief. The currency of the title under review and the more comprehensive articles make it more valuable to all libraries. Although both encyclopedias contain survey articles, those in *Encyclopedia of World Literature in the 20th Century* dealing with the relationship of literature to other fields make it especially useful in today's world.

In spite of the absence of an index, *Encyclopedia of World Literature in the 20th Century* provides a useable and thorough coverage of twentieth-century world literature. Although the price may, of course, deter some buyers, this set does provide the broadest coverage of twentieth-century literature available in a current encyclopedia. Recommended. *(Feb. 15, 1973, p.535)*

The Environment Film Review; A Critical Guide to Ecology Films. New York, Environment Information Center, Inc., 1972-   (annual; v.1, Sept. 1972). 155p. illus. 28cm. paper $20.

The Environment Film Review provides descriptive and critical reviews of the coverage and content of 627 films arranged in 21 categories, e.g., air pollution, energy, land use and misuse, population planning and control, radiological contamination, solid waste, transportation, water pollution, and wildlife. The Introduction states that from several thousand possible unnamed candidates 800 unnamed films qualified as environmental cinema were screened, and from this pool, 627 were finally selected. *The Review* is characterized as "primarily a user-oriented publication, which identifies films according to broad and very specific subject terms, and provides a synopsis of contents, treatment, and ecological objectivity."

The publisher, Environment Information Center, is "an independent multiservice organization whose main goal is to facilitate access to environmental information and to increase the speed with which it can be assimilated; EIC maintains data banks which serve a variety of users, including governments, corporations, educational institutions, and environmental action groups." The firm's services revolve around *Environment Information ACCESS,* a twice-monthly multimedia clearinghouse for world-wide ecological information reviewed in *The Booklist* Feb. 15, 1973. A companion volume, *The Environment Index,* is an annual cumulation of important publications of the year. The Center is a part of Ecology Forum, Inc., a non-profit organization, founded in 1970, to improve national environmental communications in order to speed the problem-solving process. The Center's board of advisors includes Paul R. Ehrlich (Professor of Biology at Stanford University), ex-Senator Charles E. Goodell from New York, Senator Bob Packwood from Oregon, and Dr. Alan F. Guttmacher (President, Planned Parenthood Federation) —for whom biographical information is readily available. No biographical information, however, was located on the officers of the Center.

Films commented on in *The Environment Film Review* date from 1939 to 1972, though most are from the mid-1960s on. A star rating system is employed: 41 films which provided both superior cinematic treatment and subject coverage were awarded a two-star rating; 174 films which achieved either superior cinematic treatment or subject coverage, or a bit of both, received one star. The absence of stars, the publisher asserts, by no means discredits the other films.

Additional information on each film includes accession number (A72-00001 to A72-00627), title, length, color or black and white, purchase and rental price, release date, sponsor (when known), producer and/or distributor, director, writer, narrator (whenever significant), intended audience (from K-3 to College, Adult, General, Professional), text of the review, and cross-referencing to other reviews when appropriate.

To test the accuracy of the subtitle, "A Critical Guide to Ecology Films," a sampling of the reviews was read and compared with those in such sources as *American Film Review, The Booklist, Film Evaluation Guide* and EFLA cards (Educational Film Library Association), *Forecast for Home Economics, Journal of Geography, Landers Film Reviews, Media & Methods, Scholastic Teacher, School Library Journal, Science & Children, Science News, Science Teacher,* and *Social Education.* The subtitle is well supported.

The second major part of *The Environment Film Review* is the Index Section consisting of five indexes: (1) Alphabetical Index of film titles, (2) Keyword List (terms included in the next two indexes), (3) Subject, (4) Industry, and (5) Sponsor Index. The volume concludes with a page of standard abbreviations. The Alphabetical Index, as the headnote states, lists titles beginning with the word *A* under *A,* but those beginning with *The* are entered according to the word following. It is not explained why, for example, *Air: A First Film* follows three films titled *Air Pollution* or *The City of Necessity* precedes *The City Changes.* Four titles that begin with numerals are at the end of the alphabet.

Keyword List includes two alphabets —subject terms and industry terms.

The headnote of the Subject Index remarks that "all reviews are numbered sequentially in ascending order"; in actual practice this is not followed, e.g., the order under "Aquatic Communities" and "Colorado River."

Industry Index usually includes Standard Industrial Classification numbers, e.g., Agricultural Production 01, Copper SIC 3331, Pipeline Transmission 46, Water Supply 4941.

The Sponsor Index lists only sponsor's name and accession number or numbers of its film or films, e.g., Bureau of Reclamation 16-72-00430, Bureau of Reclamation 16-72-00433, Sierra Club 04-72-00066. No reason for this unique recording of the accession number and not as it is given in all other places in the volume (e.g., A72-00066) is given.

While the contents page says that *The Environment Film Review* is to be published annually (with the first volume dated September 1972), no second volume had appeared by December 1973.

In summary, *The Environment Film Review* is, as the publisher claims, a critical guide to 627 ecology films produced between 1939 and 1972 on a wide variety of topics and for audiences from kindergarten to professional levels. Recommended.

(July 15, 1974, p.1210)

Environment Information ACCESS. New York, Environment Information Center, Inc., 1970-   semimonthly, 28cm. $150.; to non-profit and government subscribers, $125. per year.

The Environment Index 71: a Guide to the Key Environment Literature of the Year. New York, Environment Information Center, Inc., c1972. annual 582p. 28cm. $75.

Environment Information Center, Inc., publisher of the two titles above, is part of a corporation known as Ecology Forum, Inc. The affiliate and its parent organization are described in a recent directory as follows: "The Environment Information Center (EIC) is a computer-assisted central data bank which gathers, indexes, abstracts, analyzes, and disseminates information on environmental matters. . . . EIC serves primarily those who make or influence environmental decisions. Ecology Forum, a nonprofit organization whose board of directors includes nationally recognized leaders serving as the core of an interdisciplinary effort to solve environmental problems, focuses on those professionally concerned with the environment. It attempts to fill information and communication gaps, to facilitate access to environmental data, and to increase the speed with which new information can be assimilated." The president of Ecology Forum, Inc. is James G. Kollegger.

The indexing, abstracting, and retrieval of information is performed by an EIC service referred to as "ACCESS." Information is selected from "more than 2,000 scientific, technical, trade, professional and general periodicals, . . . papers and proceedings from environment related conferences, . . . documents and research reports from private and federal agencies, . . . congressional hearing transcripts, . . . environmental project reports, . . . newspaper articles." Information so gathered, after being indexed and abstracted, is made known by means of the two Environment Information Center publications under review and, as of September 1972, through *Environment Science Citation Index* on magnetic tape. Items of information can be retrieved in microfiche or hard copy on a single item, subject category, or full subscription basis. Copy can be requested by mail or telephone.

The semimonthly abstract journal, *Environment Information ACCESS*, consists essentially of the "main entry section" which contains the bulk of the information abstracts, plus the *Federal Register* abstract section, the book review section, and the index section. Arrangement of the entries in the main entry, *Federal Register,* and book review sections is by accession number (not alphabetically) under 21 numbered subject categories which are defined at the beginning of the main entry section. These categories are Air Pollution, Chemical and Biological Contamination, Energy, Environment Education, Environment Design, Food and Drugs, General, International, Land Use and Misuse, Noise Pollution, Nonrenewable Resources, Oceans and Estuaries, Population Planning and Control, Radiological Contamination, Renewable Resources-Terrestrial, Renewable Resources-Water, Solid Waste, Transportation, Water Pollution, Weather Modification and Geophysical Change, and Wildlife. Cross-references under most of these headings lead users to related categories.

Entries under each category in the main entry section, following the accession number, include title, author, journal (or other medium), name, volume and number, date, pagination, the length of the article, the type of information (research report, news feature, hearing transcript, commentary, etc.), often an abstract, and a notation concerning illustrations. The abstracts, written by staff members, vary in length from one or two sentences to more than two hundred words. The editors claim the abstracts are "often cross-referenced with information that supports or contradicts the author's conclusions," but such supplementary data appears rarely in the review issue abstracts.

Entries under each category in the *Federal Register* section give, after the accession number, the name of the issuing agency (or its abbreviation), the title, volume, number, page, and a brief annotation. An asterisk before the accession number here and in the main entry section indicates that the original item is available in microfiche as well as in hard copy. In the review issue all of the 38 *Federal Register* and about half of the 400 main entries were so marked.

The books reviewed (38 in the review issue) cannot be ordered through EIC. The accession number of each book is followed by the title, author, imprint, number of pages, and price. The reviews average about 100 words and frequently conclude with a summarizing or critical comment.

The index section consists of a Subject Index, an Industry Index, an Author Index, and an Accession Number Index. The Subject Index includes geographical terms and organizational names (Conservation Commission, United Nations, etc.). The Industry Index contains names of industries with significant environmental involvements and gives the Standard Industrial Classification (SIC) code number for the industry.

Both the Subject and Industry Indexes are preceded by a "keyword list." Arrangement of the entries under each term is in their accession number order, and the entry gives the title, identification of its origin (volume, number, and page for a journal article; imprint for a book), and the number of pages. The name of the author does not appear in these index entries.

The Author Index consists of an alphabetical listing of authors' last names followed by first names or initials, and the accession number for the article abstract or book review. The accession number contains five digits, preceded by two digits to show the year of issue (by ACCESS), and by two digits to indicate the entry category in which the specific item can be found. In the Subject and Industry Indexes the letter "F" or "B" appears before an accession number which represents a *Federal Register* abstract or a book review. The Accession Number Index lists groups of accession numbers in ascending order and shows the entry category (by its number) in which the abstracts or reviews with those numbers are located.

All information in the indexes is given in three columns per page of upper-case print-out type with keyword entry headings emphasized by underlining. The abstracts and other sections are made more legible by printing which employs upper and lower case, different type sizes, and boldface for accession numbers and titles.

Introductory pages of *Environment Information ACCESS* give a description of the arrangement and use of the publication and of other services of EIC (literature searches, bibliography assemblies, etc.). They also include the Issue Alert, a brief guide to significant information in the issue; the Conference Guide, which lists meetings of environmental groups during the month of issue; and standard ACCESS abbreviations.

Environment Index 71 consists primarily of the cumulative indexes (Subject, Industry, Author, and Accession Number) from issues of *Environment Information ACCESS* published during 1971. Entries are in the same format as in the semimonthly abstract journal with the Subject and Industry Indexes, which comprise most of the publication, appearing under keyword entry terms in accession number order and with the name of the author not included. More than 1,000 keyword terms are used in the Subject and Industry Indexes, but many of these head several hundred entries. The more numerous groups of entries are particularly difficult to scan in these indexes because of the uniform uppercase print and the nonalphabetical arrangement.

The indexes occupy 514 pages of the review copy. Other pages contain introductory material similar to that in the semimonthly abstract journal, and 10 miscellaneous sections. Some of these sections provide information arranged under the 21 main entry categories, i.e., lists of pertinent books, films, patents, and current legislation. Other sections contain a directory of state environmental control agencies and brief articles.

An indication of the coverage of *Environment Index 71* may be gained from comparisons with entries under similar headings in the 1971 issue of other abstracting publications concerned with the same subject. Two such publications, *Air Pollution Abstracts*, (Raleigh, N.C.: U.S. Environmental Protection Agency Office of Air Programs, 1970), and *Pollution Abstracts*, (La Jolla, Calif.: Oceanic Library and Information Center, 1970), are of a more specialized nature than *Environment Index*, and they contain more entries under most of the headings used in common. However, *Environment Index 71* does have a few more entries than either of the other publications under certain headings, and it cites some articles which do not appear in either of the other two.

Environment Information ACCESS and *Environment Index* would be useful in libraries which do not subscribe to other indexes and abstracts that have overlapping coverage, or in libraries where depth of search in specific subjects is less essential than the broad environmental coverage shown in the 21 main entry categories of ACCESS. Recommended. *(Feb. 15, 1973, p.535)*

Exotica: Series 3: Pictorial Cyclopedia of Exotic Plants from Tropical and Near-Tropic Regions. By Alfred Byrd Graf. 6th ed. E. Rutherford, NJ, Roehrs Co., Inc., c1973. [c1957, 1959, 1963, 1968, 1970]. Distributed by Charles Scribner's Sons, New York 10017. 1834p. illus. 29cm. cloth $68. ISBN 0-911266-02-X.

Exotica first appeared in 1957 with the subtitle, *Pictorial Cyclopedia of Indoor Plants,* 643 pages and 4,000 photographs. Sidney Fay Blake took note of it in his *Geographical Guide to Floras of the World* (Washington, D.C.: U.S. Dept. of Agriculture, Misc. Pub. No. 797, 1961). His comment was that ". . . the most extensive series of illustrations of plants grown in greenhouses in temperate regions is contained in Graf's *Exotica.*" This comment could also tersely describe *Exotica*'s next five editions.

Author Alfred Byrd Graf, a vice-president of the Julius Roehrs Company Exotic Nurseries in Farmingdale, New Jersey had access to the Company's 145 greenhouses and to the New York Botanical Garden with its herbarium and library. His purpose is to provide for friends of horticulture a pictorial record of ornamental exotic plants which may be grown indoors or in sheltered outdoor areas in temperate climates. Some species which ordinarily are grown outdoors in temperate climates are included to round out a family or because they are sometimes forced or used for temporary indoor decoration.

The second edition, *Exotica: Series 2* was published in 1959. It listed 5,720 plants and included some 6,900 plant illustrations.

After extended travel, Graf prepared the greatly enlarged third edition for publication in 1963. Eight thousand eight hundred seventy species and cultivars were identified; total illustrations were 12,025. Revisions of this third series were published in 1968, 1970, and 1973. The last three editions enabled Graf to ". . . take care of necessary corrections and taxonomic updatings, in accordance with latest scientific literature, and the advice of dedicated specialists. . . ." Each correction usually means eight additions and deletions, as changes must be made in the running heads, the caption under the plant photograph, the Index, and the description of the species. Thus, just one hundred taxonomic changes may result in four hundred deletions and four hundred additions. In this process errors may and do creep in.

Revisions may become necessary whenever the International Code of Nomenclature for Cultivated Plants is revised by the International Commission for the Nomenclature for Cultivated Plants. This coordination is essential in view of the many existing systems of classifications. Old classifications are corrected to indicate new evidences of identification; new species have been identified. All flowering plants of the world have not been identified. In 1970 there were over 350,000 known species of plants. Thousands are discovered each year.

The sixth edition was issued principally to effect some 960 revisions and 190 corrections. As in previous editions of *Series 3* there is an introductory section which contains 12 brief treatments of such allied subjects as Decorating with Plants, Methods of Propagation, The Meaning of Botanical Terms, and Insect Enemies of Your House Plants.

The main section of the book consists of 1,456 pages of black-and-white photographs and 17 pages of colored photographs of the species specimens which are grouped under the proper family and genus arranged in alphabetical order with minor exceptions due to space requirements. One hundred eighty one families are represented; those represented by large numbers of species are Amaryllidaceae, Araceae, Begoniaceae, Bromeliaceae, Cactaceae, Liliaceae, Gesneriaceae, and Orchidaceae.

Each page usually carries from 2 to 10 photographs, which give identifying detail in most cases. Among the 204 plants pictured in color are popular species of Begoniaceae, Cactaceae, and Ericaceae. The photographs cannot be used to give comparative sizes as different enlargement ratios were necessary to produce the detailed prints for plants of different sizes.

The specimen photographs are followed by a section of auxiliary aids to plant identification, keys to plant care, a bibliography, and information on plant geography and the evolution of flowering plants. There are three auxiliary aids which are important to the person using the book. The first aid is entitled Descriptions of Plants Illustrated, Their

Family, Origin and Code to Care. Species with their descriptions are listed under the correct genera which are listed in alphabetical order. The family name is printed to the right of the genus in italics, and a code to the care of the genus is found at the extreme right of the family name. A key to the code has been provided by the author, who has also included an International Key to Care. There are cross-references from unused names to the prevailing ones and from one genus to another of the same family. Preceding this section is an appropriate page On Pronunciation of Botanical Names.

An alphabetical list of Common Names of House Plants is the second aid to the reader. It provides either the name of a genus or of a species for each common name. Only if the genus is given or is part of the species or hybrid name, may the reader use the Descriptive List and the Scientific Index, both arranged by genera. The first will provide a description, and the Index will provide the page number for the photograph.

The third aid is a Scientific Index to Plant Illustrations which gives page numbers to all pertinent photographs in the volume: the specimen photographs, the 17 pages of color photographs, and the pertinent identifying photographs in other sections of the volume. Genera are listed alphabetically in the Index with species then listed under the proper genus. There are no references to any information in the descriptive list or to the list of common names.

Earlier editions were well produced; the sixth is no exception. The type is clean and easy to read; the paper is suitable for the many photographic illustrations, and the volume is well bound. Adequate running heads are used throughout the book. There are minor errors such as page 1790 still being referred to as page 1821 in the Index to illustrations. It had appeared as page 1821 in the third edition. The inner margins are again too narrow. Since the book is heavy, rebinding may be required in a few years, depending on the extent of use.

Graf has produced other far less comprehensive works about tropical and subtropical plants. Those in print are: *Exotic Plant Manual* (2d ed., c1972) and *Exotic House Plants* (8th ed., c1973), both published by the Roehrs Company. The first edition of *Exotic Plant Manual* was reviewed in *The Booklist* (Nov. 15, 1971). Though based upon *Exotica,* it contains information on species and genera not included in *Exotica. Exotic House Plants* is labelled a "mini-cyclopedia of house and decorator plants" on its title page. Its 176 pages contain brief, practical plant care instructions, a 130-page core of photographs showing 1,200 plants from 87 families, and such aids as an Index which provides a description of each species and the page number of its photograph. This handbook is suitable for the circulating collection. The author has received many honors in recognition of his work. His latest, conferred by the Society of American Florists, came in 1972 when he was elected to Horticulture's Hall of Fame.

Although a genus or subgenus such as Azalea could be identified more easily if shown in color, the majority of the photographs and descriptions of tropical and subtropical plants are useful for identification. Decorators, florists, horticulturists, hobbyists, and botany students will find the volume useful and enjoyable. For these reasons, *Exotica 3* is recommended for purchase for all libraries serving such groups.
(Feb. 1, 1974, p.550)

Foundations of Colonial America: A Documentary History. v.I Northeastern Colonies, v.II Middle Atlantic Colonies, v.III Southern Colonies. Editor, W. Keith Kavenagh. 3v. New York, Chelsea House in association with R. R. Bowker Co., 1973. 2639p. 26cm. cloth $95 plus shipping and handling.
ISBN 0-8352-0624-6.

Foundations of Colonial America is a collection of more than 1,000 historic documents "designed to present a complete documentary picture of the thirteen original colonies in the 17th and 18th centuries," indicating a trend toward the use of primary materials for the study and teaching of American colonial history. The books are intended for the advanced undergraduate student.

Each volume contains documents relating to a specific geographical area of colonial America: v.I, *Northeastern Colonies;* v.II, *Middle Atlantic Colonies;* and v.III, *Southern Colonies.* The arrangement within each volume is topical, geographical, and chronological, allowing one to view the development of a particular subject colony by colony, comparatively or individually. Topics covered are Colonial Charters; Structure and Functions of Colonial Governments, including regulation of the status and activities of individuals, taxation, regulation of economic activity, and ecclesiastical affairs; Acts of Parliament and Royal Proclamations; Local Government; and Land Acquisition, including laws affecting property ownership and public and private records of land distribution. An Introduction written by the compiler, Dr. W. Keith Kavenagh of the Institute of Colonial Studies, State University of New York at Stony Brook, prefaces each major section, effectively placing the documents that follow in historical perspective. The Foreword is provided by Richard B. Morris, Gouverneur Morris Professor of American History at Columbia University.

The documents themselves, selected to portray examples of various aspects of colonial life or to allow comparison of changes in colonial society, are "reprinted in full, and, with the exception of the major chapters, translated into contemporary English." Citations for each document indicate the original was not always consulted; rather, many are reprints from such sources as F. N. Thorpe's *The Federal and State Constitutions,* W. J. River's *A Sketch of the History of South Carolina* and W. L. Saunders's *The Colonial Records of North Carolina. Foundations of Colonial America* simply draws together a selection of colonial papers for the researcher's convenience. Many scholars may be less than satisfied with the translations into contemporary English. Primary sources do not change; only our interpretations of them do. It follows that translations of documents, of necessity involving some degree of editing and subjective decisions regarding meanings, could hardly be regarded as primary source material. Fortunately source citations accompany each document so the user may verify the authenticity of the material presented.

Identical Glossaries and a Table of Regnal Years are appended to each volume. A Bibliography is included in each volume, and some identical sources appear in each. Although the Bibliographies are not annotated, an introduction to each discusses some of the major sources cited. The Bibliographies are arranged by form: "Guides and Bibliographies," "Documentary Collections," "English Public Records," and "Historical Societies Publications," the latter being subdivided by state.

The continuously paged set has a single subject Index in volume III, 21 pages in length and including both *see* and *see also* references. This seems too brief an Index to a work of over 2,600 pages containing more than 1,000 documents. The entries should be more detailed; for example, a *see also* reference leads one from "gambling" to "morals, regulation of," which, without further qualification of subject, lists 8 multi-page and 13 single-page references. One must consult each reference to discover which volumes contain material on gambling. Locating a specific document through the Index is also often difficult. For instance, "Form of Deed in North Carolina, 1735" appears on pages 2543-44, but searches of Index entries do not indicate its inclusion. One of the *see also* references from "land acquisition" is to "sales"; this descriptor does not appear in the Index. *Sale,* however, does appear, with the note: "for land sales *see* land acquisition," being both a blind and circular reference. Citations in the Index are to page numbers only, which is made practicable by the inclusion of pagination of each volume at the top of the Index pages.

The type font used in volume I is different from that used in volumes II and III, and, on the off-white paper used throughout, volume I's type is more aesthetically pleasing. Wide inside and

80

outside margins and judicious spacing of material combine to make a pleasant format. The binding is sturdy, and pages lie flat when opened.

No other single publication can be located which duplicates the material found in *Foundations of Colonial America*. This collection provides a wealth of documentary information on colonial American history. Therefore, despite its translating of primary forms into contemporary English and despite its less than satisfactory Index, it is recommended for academic and large public libraries. *(Mar. 1, 1974, p.700)*

Granger's Index to Poetry. Edited by William James Smith. 6th ed., completely revised and enlarged, indexing anthologies published through December 31, 1970. New York and London, Columbia University Pr., [c1973]. xxxvii, 2223p. 26cm. buckram $80; to schools and libraries, 10 percent discount. ISBN 0-231-036481-8.

Granger's Index to Poetry was first published in 1904 under the title *Index to Poetry and Recitations*. The index was edited by Edith Granger and was published by A. C. McClurg & Company in Chicago. Editing and publication was taken over by Columbia University Press in 1945 at which time several changes were made.

The purpose of the book is to assist the user in "identifying and locating poems or selections from poems which have appeared in the most generally accessible anthologies."

The 1973 edition edited by William James Smith, states that 514 volumes of anthologized poetry are indexed in this sixth edition, which "includes the bulk of those anthologies which appeared in the fifth edition copyright 1962, and the 1967 supplement. A number of out-of-print works and some titles whose popularity has waned have been eliminated from this edition. For some standard series of works, earlier editions are indexed along with the new editions, and a total of 114 new volumes have been indexed for the first time. The inclusion of a number of volumes of Negro poetry is welcome. Although the copyright date for the sixth edition of *Granger's* is 1973, the cut-off date for inclusion is 1970.

All volumes indexed, identified by a short alphabetical abbreviation (or symbol), are listed in the section Key to Symbols, which gives bibliographic information: title, editor, edition(s), date, and publisher. Earlier symbols used for indexed volumes have been retained, and no new symbol duplicates any used previously. The outside margins on each page in the sixth edition section on Key to Symbols are only slightly wider than in the fifth edition. Since individual libraries often write call numbers of holdings in the margin or between the symbol and title, it is unfortunate that more space is not provided.

In the Title and First Line Index the symbols listed after each entry identify each anthology in which the cited poem appears. The title and first line entries are alphabetical by word and include the name of the poet, and if pertinent, the translator. If the entry is a first line, the title of the poem is also given. This section comprises the bulk of *Granger's,* pages 1-1662. Entries are in double columns, in small but clear print with running heads on each page. Indented listings indicate selections from a work, or if doubly indented within the parentheses, a variant title used in the anthologies that follow.

The Author Index, arranged alphabetically in 3 columns per page, is easily used in connection with the Title and First Line Index. The authors' names are in boldface print with titles indented and listed alphabetically underneath. This section comprises 365 pages.

The Subject Index, according to the Preface, "itemizes poems under nearly 5,000 subject categories, including such timely topics as Ecology and Women's Liberation." This Index is arranged alphabetically by subject with an alphabetical list of individual titles under each, with the exception of such general subjects as Love, Children's Verse, Ballads and Folk Songs, Religious Verse and Parodies; instead, anthologies devoted to those subjects are listed in italicized print. Other subject entries list poems plus any relevant anthologies.

Authors are given after each title. This Index must be used in conjunction with the Title and First Line Index in order to find the anthology in which the poem appears. The two-column per page arrangement with running heads, boldface entries and indented titles makes for easy use. *See* and *see also* references are both used in this Index.

A sampling made to check accuracy of the three indexes found only one symbol listed that was not included in the Key to Symbols. All poems were found in the anthologies indicated.

Granger's is bound in heavy buckram. If rebinding becomes necessary, the inside margins are barely adequate. The thin paper used, as in previous editions, may crease with hard usage; this is especially true of the Key to Symbols section, which would be more durable if printed on heavier stock. The print is small, but legible, and the volume lies flat when open.

Libraries owning previous editions of *Granger's Index to Poetry* may want to keep and use them depending on their individual collections, since the sixth edition is a major revision and does not include some of the anthologies previously indexed. Despite its drawbacks in format, *Granger's* is still the best available general index to poetry and is therefore recommended.

(April 1, 1974, p.830)

Great Britain: Foreign Policy and the Span of Empire 1689-1971; a Documentary History. Edited by Joel H. Wiener; introd., J. H. Plumb. New York, Chelsea House Publishers in association with McGraw-Hill Book Co., [c1972]. 4v., liii, 3423p. 24cm. C grade pyroxylin $129; discount to schools and libraries.

The documents in this collection were selected from published sources, largely contemporary with events, and arranged by major topics in British diplomatic and imperial history.

A Preface and brief historical Commentary introducing five principal sections of the work are by the compiler Joel H. Wiener of the Department of History of the City College of New York. The Introduction by John Harold Plumb, Professor of Modern English History at Cambridge University assesses the "astonishing achievements" together with failures as Great Britain now "fades as a great power."

According to the Preface, the collection "is intended alike for the advanced research student, the undergraduate new to his discipline, and the general reader."

Foreign policy from the eighteenth century to the present is the chief subject of the first two volumes. An equal number of pages (approximately 1,500) in the last two volumes is given to documents on the Empire and Commonwealth, in three chronological divisions: Old Empire 1696-1851; the Age of Imperial Expansion 1852-1913; and Dissolution of the Empire 1914-present. Documents relating to Ireland, "in deference to its unique importance" and covering 1691-1922, are in a special 500-page section at the end of volume 2.

The selections are primarily from the vast store of official records. Approximately three fourths are from the various series of parliamentary debates, parliamentary papers, statutes, and treaties. The remainder are from collected speeches, contemporary accounts, and memoirs.

Policy of the London government is the predominant theme. There are few documents originating abroad or published in the colonies or Commonwealth. The dispatches from abroad and reports of local governors found in other document collections in this field are seldom included. Emphasis is on the range of opinion as expressed in debate in Parliament and other London sources. This is a legitimate limitation in scope in view of the time span and geographic area involved, but it should be made more explicit in the prefatory material.

The list of Principal Officials at the end, preceding the Bibliography, is useful and also indicative of the central government theme. They are the Lord Treasurers and First Lords of the Treasury, Prime Ministers, Principal Secretaries of State, Foreign Secretaries, and Colonial Secretaries, with the month and year they took office.

The complete texts of the documents

are reproduced in most cases. Omissions are indicated by three asterisks but have been used sparingly.

A few deficiencies in the format of the volumes lessen their usefulness. For example, the main structure of the work (Foreign Policy, Ireland, Empire) is not easily determined without going through 40 pages of Contents, because the title pages and the books' spines are all identical except for volume numbering. The Contents pages are, however, well designed to emphasize the shorter, topical divisions such as Commercial Ties with France or Colonization of Australia and New Zealand. Within each topic the individual documents are clearly identified and dated in concise form, for example: Attlee, Statement on Defence Policy, 1951, or Act for the Abolition of Slave Trade, 1807.

In the text, each document heading is footnoted with a brief citation of source. The complete bibliographic data appears only in volume 4, where the Bibliography appears to be limited to works used as the sources of the documents reproduced.

The one index to the set in volume 4 is made up chiefly of names of people and places, with a few subject terms such as Home Rule or Kaffir raids. For a work of this length the subject indexing is quite inadequate. The sample of the Index checked for accuracy, however, showed it to be reasonably correct. The running head at the top of each index page is a key to the pagination in the volumes. It compensates to some extent for the lack of volume numbering in the index items and lack of identification on the books' spines.

Although the Preface refers to brief "notes on each document" they do not appear. The compiler's Commentary, however, providing "interpretation" and "a basic narrative of events" consists of approximately three pages preceding each of the five major divisions: Foreign Policy, Ireland, and Span of Empire (in its three chronological sections).

The closing date of 1971 is slightly misleading in that there is only one document of that year (A White Paper recommending membership in the European Economic Community). Several documents of 1968 are included, but none for 1969 or 1970.

The volumes are heavy but sturdily bound and Smyth sewn.

Existing surveys and collections, other than official and unofficial multi-volume collections, deal primarily with British foreign policy or focus on Empire and Commonwealth history. The volumes under review differ by combining both subjects in one "set" but presenting them in separate, chronologically arranged units.

In the area of foreign policy the single volume collection in use for several decades is Harold Temperley and Lillian M. Penson's *Foundations of British Foreign Policy from Pitt (1752) to Salisbury (1902)* (Cambridge, Eng.: The University Press, 1938). More recent are Cedric James Lowe's *The Reluctant Imperialists: British Foreign Policy 1878-1902* (2v., London: Routledge and Kegan Paul Ltd., 1967) of which volume 2, or part II of the American edition, is a collection of documents, and Kenneth Bourne's *The Foreign Policy of Victorian England 1830-1902* (Oxford: Clarendon Press, 1970) which also includes as part II a selection of documents that have been checked against manuscripts wherever possible.

Twentieth-century foreign policy documents from the archives of the Foreign and Commonwealth Office are still being published in the three series of *Documents on British Foreign Policy 1919-1939* (London, H.M.S.O. 1946-). The fact that it is still in progress, with 35 volumes so far published, might account for the lack of a separate twentieth-century selection.

The documentary surveys and collections on the subject of Empire and Commonwealth corresponding to volumes 3 and 4 of the work under review include George Bennett's *The Concept of Empire, Burke to Attlee, 1774-1947* (2d ed., London: A. and C. Black, 1962) giving excerpts from numerous documents, interspersed with background and commentary. Various editions of the collections edited by Arthur Berriedale Keith are still in print as *Speeches and Documents on British Co-*

lonial Policy, 1763-1931 (2v., London: Oxford University Press, 1961). Collections edited by Frederick Madden and Vincent Todd Harlow are designated as supplements to the Keith volumes, giving additional documents from the eighteenth century through 1952. Two volumes extending the Keith collections chronologically are those edited by Nicholas Mansergh, *Documents and Speeches on British Commonwealth Affairs 1931-1952* (New York: Oxford University Press, 1953) and *Documents and Speeches on Commonwealth Affairs 1952-62* (London, New York: Oxford University Press, 1963).

Other text collections are for shorter periods or special subjects. Among them are Kenneth Norman Bell and William Parker Morell's *Select Documents on British Colonial Policy 1830-1860* (Oxford: Clarendon Press, 1968); Maurice Ollivier's *The Colonial and Imperial Conferences from 1887-1937* (3v., Ottawa: H.M.S.O., 1954) and Cyril Henry Philips, *The Evolution of India and Pakistan, Select Documents* (London, New York: Oxford University Press, 1962).

Thus the collection under review is more comprehensive in its subject matter and in chronological span than similar works. Although all the documents are from previously published sources and will duplicate much material in the larger libraries, the claim that some documents are made accessible for the first time is a reasonable one. Well over half of the documents are from eighteenth- and nineteenth-century publications, many of which would not be available in the average college or public library in the United States.

Great Britain: Foreign Policy and the Span of Empire 1689-1971 is a source book of selected documents from parliamentary debates and other published contemporary records, suitable for college-level history collections. Recommended. *(Mar. 1, 1973, p.601)*

Great Soviet Encyclopedia: A Translation of the Third Edition. v.1. A. M. Prokhorov, editor in chief. New York, Macmillan, Inc., London, Collier Macmillan Publishers, [c1973]. xxxvii, 678p. illus. 29cm. pyroxylin impregnated buckram. $1,100 for 30v. set if prepaid; $1,250 for set if volumes paid for as delivered; $50 per v. if ordered as single volumes.

This is the first volume of a projected volume-by-volume translation of the *Bol'shaia Sovetskaia Entsiklopediia*, the standard Soviet encyclopedia now being issued in its third edition and planned for completion in 30 volumes in 1977. The first volume of the Russian original was published in 1970, and at the time this review was written, the thirteenth volume, published in 1973, was available in American libraries. The publishers of this English version expect to issue five volumes per year until the set is completed, with the first five to be delivered by the end of 1974.

The Publisher's Foreword states that the "purpose of this translation is to convey the scope and point of view of the Great Soviet Encyclopedia and to bring to scholars and others with a serious professional interest in Soviet affairs a primary source through which they can gain a richer knowledge and understanding of the contemporary Soviet Union. The major value . . . lies in the wealth of information about the USSR and its peoples that has been previously unavailable in English. Although the Encyclopedia is general in scope, it naturally concentrates on the Soviet Union. . . . Another value . . . is its consistent statement of the Soviet point of view. . . . The Encyclopedia also reflects the state of the art in Soviet science and technology . . . and serves as a guide to current Soviet thinking and research."

Twenty-six Slavic scholars, most of them outstanding specialists in their respective fields, have acted as advisors to this English version. They include John Hazard, authority on Soviet law; Paul L. Horecky, of the Slavic and Central European Division of the Library of Congress; Alec Nove, British authority on the Soviet economy; Edward J. Brown, author of *Russian Literature Since the Revolution;* and John Turkevich, Professor of Chemistry at Princeton, and a specialist in Soviet science.

The work of translation is being done by teams of translators and bilingual editors, under the direction of Diana Nakeeb, who has a doctorate in Russian literature from Columbia. In cases of difficult problems in translation, the members of the Advisory Board have been consulted. To insure that the translation does not distort the meaning of the Russian text, it is verified by the Russian editors. The text reads smoothly and idiomatically. For readers who wish to compare the translation with the original text, a code number at the end of each article refers to the location of the article in the *Bol'shaia Sovetskaia Entsiklopediia*.

Because the *Great Soviet Encyclopedia* is a volume-by-volume translation of the original, this first volume contains entries from *A* to *Z*, although most of the entries begin with the letter A. Since the publisher chose to begin the publication of the English edition before the completion of the Russian set there was no alternative to this arrangement, but it will mean great inconvenience to users until the final index is published. Readers unfamiliar with the Cyrillic alphabet and the Russian system of transliteration will have difficulty even with proper names and cognate words; they probably would not expect to find, for example, entries for *Aqueduct; Asia; Aviation; Halphen, Louis; Idaho;* and *Iowa,* in a volume which covers a Russian original containing entries from *A* to *Angob*. As interim aids for finding articles, there is an alphabetical list of entries at the beginning of the volume and the publisher promises cumulative indexes (at extra cost) at the end of every five volumes. This solution is not a very satisfactory one; purchasers will not only have to pay for six volumes not included in the basic price, but users of the set are faced with the prospect of having to consult up to five different alphabets before the final index is published.

The publisher claims that except for the omission of "brief articles which are only dictionary definitions or which contain material found in all general Western encyclopedias," the entire contents of the Russian original will be available in the English translation. As far as the text is concerned, an examination of the first volume appears to support this claim for the most part. The Russian edition, however, contains a wealth of illustrative material, including many maps and photographs, which are of obvious importance, not only as information but also in expressing the official Soviet point of view. All of this material, with the exception of line drawings and charts, has been omitted.

Articles which have been omitted are included in the list of articles at the beginning of the volume and are indicated by an asterisk. No information is provided in the prospectus or in the introductory material in the first volume on who is responsible for making the decisions about omissions, and the application of the basic principle is not always clear. Presumably an interpretation concerning the Soviet Union's strategic interests might have dictated the omission of an article—a column in length—on the Adriatic Sea whereas a 6-line article on *Aden, Gulf of* is included. But why should an article on Amiens be omitted and the one on Amalfi included? And the reason for omitting an article on aluminum chloride (26 lines and a bibliography in the original) while including an 11-line article on aluminum fluoride is not obvious.

The Publisher's Foreword states that in the course of verification of the translation, the Soviet editors have updated facts such as statistics, dates, and name changes, and these have been incorporated in the article without notice and that where major updating has occured the word "updated" is inserted at the end of the article. There do not appear to be many such changes, minor or major, useful as this updating would be in view of the gap between the publication date of the original and the translation. The changes that have been made show no consistency; for example, the article on the Academy of Arts of the Union of Soviet Socialist Republics has information as recent as October 1, 1972, while the membership figures given for the Academy of Sciences of the USSR are dated 1969. The only 1970 census figure noted appeared in the articles on the Azerbaijan SSR and on the Azerbaijanis.

The bibliographies from the Russian edition are included in the English translation, and their entries are listed in the same order and in the same language as the original. They are interesting and useful not only for the usual reason that they indicate what are considered the standard references on various topics, but also because they are a handy source of information on what books have been translated into Russian.

This translation of the *Bol'shaia Sovetskaia Entsiklopediia* is a large-scale enterprise, the value of which is indicated by the support given to it by the specialists in Soviet and Russian studies who have lent their names as advisors. Librarians who serve readers with a serious interest in the Soviet Union but unable to read Russian will want to consider purchasing the set. They will need to take into consideration, however, the inconvenience which will be caused by the multiplicity of alphabets, which will not be overcome until the completion of the set, when the final cumulative index is published. The omission of all maps and practically all illustrations will detract from the informational value of the set. And the time lag between publication of the original Russian and English translation also needs to be borne in mind when a decision is made. In accordance with Reference and Subscription Books Committee policy, a final recommendation is postponed until the entire set is available for examination. *(July 15, 1974, p.1211)*

Grzimek's Animal Life Encyclopedia.
Editor in chief, Bernhard Grzimek. 2 of 13v. New York, Van Nostrand Reinhold Co., 1972. illus. 25cm. ballicron $29.95 per v. 13v. set $325.00; to. schools, 20 percent discount; to libraries, 10 percent discount.

Grzimek's Animal Life Encyclopedia was published originally in German in 1967, and has since been translated into French, Italian, and Dutch. In 1972 the first of the projected 13 volumes of this English translation were published. The publishing schedule calls for six volumes in 1972, four in 1973, and three in 1974. The volumes are not appearing in numerical order. This review is based on examination of volumes 10 and 13 which contain half of the material on mammals.

The editor in chief, Bernhard Grzimek, internationally known zoologist and conservationist, is director of the Frankfurt zoo, professor at Justus Liebig University of Giessen, author of numerous books on animals, and winner of an Academy Award Oscar for his film *Serengeti Shall Not Die*. Almost all of the 223 editors and contributors, who are listed in each volume, are affiliated with universities, museums, aquariums, or zoos from all over the world, although the majority are from Europe, predominantly from Germany. Seventeen are from the United States.

Rather than using a dictionary type of arrangement of individual articles, the editor has chosen a taxonomic approach with a narrative flow from subject to subject. When completed, the subject matter will be distributed as follows: v.1, *Lower Animals*; v.2, *Insects*; v.3, *Mollusks*; v.4, *Fishes*; v.5, *Fishes and Amphibians*; v.6, *Reptiles*; v.7-9, *Birds*; and v.10-13, *Mammals*. Since birds and mammals make up only a small percentage of the total number of species of animal life, it is evident that the editor, by devoting more than half the volumes to these two classes of animals, is concentrating on them.

Each volume is self contained. In addition to the main text, each has a complete list of contributors; a table of contents; a systematic classification table of the animals in the volumes; a cross-indexed lexicon in English, French, German, and Russian of the animals included; conversion table of metric to U.S. and British systems of measurement (all measurements in the text are given in metric units); supplementary readings; index; and a list of the symbols and abbreviations used in the text.

The main text of the work is divided into chapters usually covering an order, suborder, or family of animals following the systematic classification indicated in the volume. Each chapter is signed by the author or authors and in many cases the authors of individual sections are indicated. This identification is done in the wide inner margin which is also used to present a variety of other useful information. In addition to running heads, small but readable distribution maps, line drawings of individual species and parts of animals, and the bow and arrow symbol indicating endangered species can be found here.

In addition to the marginal drawings each volume is illustrated with approximately 100 full pages of colored illustrations. These colored illustrations are well chosen and the reproduction is good. They consist of either photographs or drawings of individual animals or groups of animals. Occasional phylogenic charts show the descent and relationship of present-day species. In volume 10 an acetate overlay of the anatomy of the dog represents the general anatomy of the mammal. Credits are given for all illustrations, including the line drawings.

Unless one is familiar with the systematic classification used in these volumes, entry into the text is best made with the help of the Index. If the work is to have much reference value, the Index takes on added importance. The indexes of the two volumes available for review do perform this function. A check of these two volumes reveals few omissions and no erroneous page references. The Index identifies not only references to the text but also to illustrations and distribution maps.

Supplementary Readings contained in each volume were prepared by John B. Brown. They contain only works in English and so give the impression of being prepared for this edition of this encyclopedia. The titles are about equally distributed between monographs and periodical articles. In some volumes the references are arranged under broad subject headings, although this is not always the case. These bibliographies are by no means exhaustive, being only a few pages in length. No claim to completeness is made for them. Many of the entries are for recent publications and should lead the reader to a good selection of easily obtainable material for further study.

The encyclopedia is intended for use by the high school student and the general public as well as the professional in the field. It is written in a clear, understandable and very readable style which is enhanced by the excellent translation from the German under the direction of Erich Klinghammer, the well-known Purdue University ethnologist. This readability has been achieved in part by a continuous narrative flow which omits footnotes or any indication of the source of the many quotations in the text. Suggested Readings, some of which are original sources, should be sufficient as a guide to further study for the high school student or general reader, but the lack of documentation diminishes the value of this work for the scholar.

In lieu of any foreword or preface an extensive quotation from the concluding paragraph of volume 13 best expresses the purpose and general tone of this work. "We hope that our encyclopedia on the animal kingdom may help to prevent more species from disappearing from earth. To help these animals, it is necessary to know what they need to exist and survive. It is only possible to help when one knows what is needed. Millions of people who are condemned to living in cities and large towns may be moved by the multitude and wonder of the animal kingdom. It may inspire them to know the real live animals of the wild and to ask their political leaders to establish national parks and protected areas for them. Hopefully, our efforts may contribute to the rescue and preservation of many other species of animals."

Grzimek is somewhat less concerned with the description, evolution, and taxonomy of animals, although these are well covered, than he is with animal behavior and conservation. Not only is behavior in the wild considered, but much attention is given to behavior in captivity and the care of animals in zoos. Special efforts to insure the survival of endangered species are given extensive coverage. A classic example is the Pere David's deer, which became extinct in its native China, but was saved from total extinction by the action of zoo directors in Europe in pooling their specimens into one breeding flock in England. The possibilities of further human use of other animals is not overlooked. Hans Fradrich, writing on hippopotamuses, proposes the raising of this animal on farms as a source of meat for the protein-starved peoples of Africa.

Only the coverage of mammals can be commented on since the volumes under review are devoted to mammals. This coverage is very good, although the amount of space devoted to individual species varies considerably. As has been pointed out, the coverage of birds and mammals is to be much more extensive than that for other classes of animals. These two classes of animals are the most interesting to man and more is known about their behavior, especially in zoos.

Grzimek's Animal Life Encyclopedia is the first major work of this type in years. It can best be compared with two older works that have been standards in the field, *Brehms Tierleben*, edited by Alfred E. Brehm (Leipzig, Wien: Bibliographische Institut) and *The Royal Natural History*, edited by Richard Lydekker (London: Frederick Warne & Co.). It most nearly resembles the fourth edition of *Brehms Tierleben* published from 1913 to 1920. *Brehms* also contains 13 volumes divided in much the same way, three volumes for birds, and four for mammals as is *Grzimek*. The opening section of the discussion on mammals of each uses the dog to show generalized mammalian anatomy. However, they do not use the same scheme for the distribution of materials in the individual volumes. *Lydekker* is arranged in much the same manner, but, being a shorter work, treatment of individual species is not as extensive. Comparison of content would be difficult considering the increase in knowledge in this field since these earlier works were published. *Grzimek* might also be compared with the older *Cambridge Natural History* (London: Macmillan), which is, however, devoted more to brief descriptions of animals, and to the detailed, scholarly, multi-volumed *Traite de Zoologie* (Paris: Masson) which is still in the process of publication. While the latter does contain some discussion of behavior, both these works are more concerned with describing anatomy, physiology, and taxonomy.

The *Grzimek* volumes are attractively bound in blue and red Ballicron with gold lettering. The type is pleasant and easy to read. The binding is Smyth sewn with no reinforcement. The thick volumes of thick heavy paper might not stand up under heavy use, and since the inner margins are used for informative material some problems with rebinding might arise.

Final evaluation will have to wait until the completion of this set. However, based on the volumes available for review at this time, *Grzimek's Animal Life Encyclopedia* promises to be a most useful work for both the student and the layman interested in the whole range of animal behavior.

(June 1, 1973, p.916)

Guide to Atlases: World, Regional, National, Thematic; an International Listing of Atlases Published Since 1950. By Gerard L. Alexander. Metuchen, N.J., The Scarecrow Press, Inc., 1971. 671p. 22cm. Arrestox B cloth $17.50.

Guide to Atlases "has been deliberately planned to fill a long felt need and to serve one specific purpose: namely, to list at a glance all atlases published since 1950, by whom and where, of what area, what type, in what language, and what size and date." The compiler is Chief, Map Division, Research Libraries, New York Public Library. The guide covers the period from 1950 to 1970; 14 world atlases are listed for 1970. In all, 5,556 atlases are listed. However, it must be noted that this total includes duplication of titles where there are new editions.

The *Guide* contains four groups of atlas entries (1) world atlases (2) regional atlases (3) national atlases (4) thematic atlases. The world atlas entries have been arranged chronologically by publication date, and, within each year, alphabetically by publisher. The regional atlases (continents or major regions) are alphabetically listed within each continent by publisher. The national atlases (single countries as a whole) are located by continent and country, then alphabetically by publisher; and finally the thematic atlases are divided by such subjects as economy, geology, history, and roads, and then arranged by publisher within each category. When atlases fit into two or more of the above classifications, the complete entry is repeated under each, thereby eliminating the need for cross-references. The entries are numbered consecutively throughout the work, and entries in the indexes refer to these numbers instead of the page numbers. Each atlas entry lists the publisher, title, edition, author, place and date of publication, number of pages, number of colored maps, and size of the atlas in centimeters. Prices are not given.

At the end of the *Guide* there is a List of Publishers by Country which is alphabetically arranged by continent, then by country, and, finally, by city, and a Publishers Index arranged alphabetically by name of publisher. This list gives the city and country of publication and the entry number for each atlas. Regrettably, street numbers are lacking. Following the index by publisher is a Language Index by country listing atlases in a language by entry number. An Authors, Cartographers, Editors Index completes the volume.

Entries have been transliterated for atlases in non-roman languages, and in some instances foreign titles have been translated into English. The author explains in the Preface that transliteration "was often problematic and made consistency difficult."

To test the publisher's claim that "Alexander's GUIDE is the only comprehensive searching tool for the vast uncontrolled reservoir of atlases published by virtually every country in the world over a twenty-year period," a sample from the *Guide* was compared with listings in *Library of Congress National Union Catalog: Books-Subjects*. The two works were found to contain almost the same listings, and entries in both works agree as to bibliographic data. The Library of Congress Catalog lists the atlases under the person or corporate body that is primarily responsible for the content. Libraries that since 1968 have cataloged their atlases according to this rule of entry as exemplified in *Anglo-American Cataloging Rules* (Chicago: American Library Association, 1967) may find it easier to use the Library of Congress catalog than the *Guide*, which enters atlases by publisher. However, there is much to be said for entry under publisher, not only because the practice was common prior to 1968, but also because the consistency of entry under publisher facilitates use of the book.

The binding is of sturdy cloth; the entries stand out clearly, and the print is easy to read. The work lies flat when opened and the paper is non-glare-acid-free paper.

Notwithstanding the fact that most of the atlases in *Guide to Atlases* may be located in Library of Congress printed catalogs, the *Guide* is an accurate, handy finding list in one volume and is recommended for all libraries with a major interest in atlases, maps, or geography. *(Sept. 15, 1972, p.49)*

A Guide to Critical Reviews. James M. Salem. 4 parts. Metuchen, N.J., The Scarecrow Press, Inc., c1966-1971. 25cm. $50.50 net. Part I, American Drama from O'Neill to Albee. 181p. $4.50 net; part II, The Musical from Rodgers-And-Hart to Lerner-And-Loewe. 353p. $9 net; part III, British and Continental Drama from Ibsen to Pinter. 309p. $7 net; part IV, The Screenplay from the Jazz Singer to Dr. Strangelove. 2v. 1420p. $30 net.

James M. Salem, Associate Professor of English, University of Alabama, has compiled a bibliography of critical reviews on drama in its many forms. Reviews are cited from some of the more popular American and Canadian periodicals and from the *New York Times,* and after 1940 from *New York Theatre Critics Reviews* which indexes other New York newspapers.

Part I, *American Drama from O'Neill to Albee,* cites reviews of the works of 52 playwrights from 1920 to 1965. Only plays produced during this period are listed even though the author may have been writing earlier. The Foreword suggests supplementing this bibliography with other critical bibliographies on well-known playwrights. The Table of Contents lists the names of the playwrights in alphabetical order, and the entries follow this arrangement. The date given after each play, except for plays with premier performances elsewhere, is usually the date of its first New York production. The date also helps to distinguish reviews of the first run of the play from reviews of subsequent performances.

There is no listing of periodicals indexed. A preliminary check of the first 25 pages revealed indexing from over 50 periodicals and that the most popular indexing source was the *New York Times* and after that *Catholic World, Commonweal, Nation, New Republic,* and *Theatre Arts.* The number of citations varied from one to as many as eighteen. Periodical entries give the volume, paging, and date, but do not include the title or author of the review. This is a drawback if the book is used for interlibrary loan citations, and more importantly it is a severe handicap for scholars seeking the reviewing output of certain reviewers. The index of titles which is at the end of the volume is accurate.

A Guide to Critical Reviews, Part I, can best be compared with a 1967 work *American Drama Criticism,* compiled by Helen H. Palmer and Jane Anne Dyson (Hamden, Conn.: The Shoestring Press, Inc. and its 1970 supplement). *American Drama Criticism* covers a longer period (1890-1968) and includes articles in books as well as periodicals. However, it does not include newspaper reviews. It lists 159 playwrights as opposed to *A Guide to Critical Reviews,* Part I, which covers only 52 playwrights between 1920 and 1965. However, Part I does include plays not listed in the other reference book. When a play is indexed in both, usually the same citations are in both, plus, of course, the additional references to more scholarly journals and books in *American Drama Criticism.* There is no pattern of listings in the *Guide to Critical Reviews,* Part I, when compared with *American Drama Criticism.* Such well-known playwrights as Rachel Crothers and T. S. Eliot are in the former, while Mary Chase, John Patrick, Dore Schary, and Archibald MacLeish are not. A library which has the latter book might not wish to purchase *American Drama from O'Neill to Albee.*

A library with a long run of *Reader's Guide to Periodical Literature* may decide not to buy *A Guide to Critical Reviews,* since most of the reviews are indexed in both, the major exception being the *New York Times* reviews which are not in *Reader's Guide.* However, *A Guide to Critical Reviews* is much more convenient to use since all reviews of a play or film are listed in one place.

Part II, *The Musical from Rodgers-And-Hart to Lerner-And-Loewe,* cites critical reviews of Broadway musicals from the 1920-1921 season to that of 1964-1965. The arrangement is chronological and alphabetical under title of production. Under each title are listed the number of performances, author and title of the book or sketch on which the musical is based as well as composers, lyricists, costume and set designers, choreographers, directors and opening date, followed by a listing of references to criticism by name of the periodical as in Part I.

The Foreword states that operettas have not been included, though "some works considered operas *(Porgy and Bess, The Consul, Regina*) have consciously been included." *The Red Mill,* a pre-1921 play is included, because it had a revival within the time span covered.

Much of the statistical information has been taken from *The Best Plays of the Year* and the *Yearbook of Drama in America.* A short bibliography of only nine titles which the author states are "valuable for statistical, historical, or general information" is included in the Foreword. The Table of Contents is arranged by the Broadway season. Cross-references are included from common names of musicals to the full names.

Indexes include Long Run Musicals, arranged in order of total performances given through May 31, 1966, beginning with *My Fair Lady* at 2,717 performances and ending at 200 performances with *Hooray for What*. An asterisk indicates that the play was still running as of May 31, 1966. This listing also includes the season date. New York Drama Critics' Circle Award Musicals are arranged by season beginning in 1945-1946. Pulitzer Prize Musicals are arranged by season listing the four musicals that received the prize. Authors, Composers, Lyricists are arranged alphabetically by name, listing the pages on which the names are found, but giving no indication in the Index as to which the person is—author, composer, or lyricist. Directors, Designers, Choreographers are arranged alphabetically by name listing pages on which the names are found. Index of Original Works and Authors is arranged in one alphabet with titles in capital letters. There is a cross-reference from one name to another. If the name of the musical is the same as the book from which it is taken, the book title is not listed. Index of Titles is arranged alphabetically with cross-references to the author in order to distinguish between musicals with the same name. In cases where a musical was presented for several seasons, each season date is included.

A check of the indexes of *A Guide to Critical Reviews*, Part II revealed very few inaccuracies. Other than *Reader's Guide to Periodical Literature*, no other reference work indexes reviews of musicals.

Part III, *British and Continental Drama from Ibsen to Pinter*, is a bibliography of critical reviews of modern British and Continental plays produced on the New York stage from the 1909-1910 to the 1965-1966 season. Beginning with the 1959-1960 season, selected Off Broadway productions have been included, and beginning with the 1961-1962 season, complete Off Broadway information is included. Plays by more than 140 dramatists are included. Mention is made in the Foreword of additional bibliographies. The Table of Contents lists the playwrights alphabetically and includes the indexes. Cross-references are used when pertinent.

The format for Part III is the same as for Part I in the main body of the volume, except that additional information is given, such as the dates the production opened, the translator and/or adaptor and the number of performances. However, Part III is not as easily used as Part I, because author headings are not carried over to the top of the verso, making it necessary to search for the playwright's name on previous pages. The spacing used also makes it more difficult to find a name.

Indexes in this volume include Dramatists, arranged alphabetically giving nationality and dates of birth and death; Successful Modern British and Continental Productions, arranged numerically by total number of performances, listing the play, year of production and author, and including in the total the Off Broadway productions with cross references to different runs of the same play; and Popular Modern British and Continental Dramatists (including some Off Broadway productions), arranged in order of popularity giving the name of the dramatist and productions and plays of more than 100 performances; New York Drama Critics' Awards (Best Foreign Play), arranged by season including the years when no award was given; Index of Authors, Adaptors, and Translators, arranged alphabetically; and Index of Titles, arranged alphabetically, with cross-references to the favored title. The indexes in *British and Continental Drama from Ibsen to Pinter* were found to be accurate.

Other than *Reader's Guide*, reference books with which Part I and Part III may be compared are *Drama Criticism* by Arthur Coleman and Gary Tyler, 2v. (Denver: Alan Swallow, c1966), *Modern Drama* by Irving Adelman and Rita Dworkin (Metuchen, N.J.: Scarecrow Pr., c1967) and *Dramatic Criticism Index*, compiled and edited by Paul F. Breed and Florence M. Sniderman (Detroit: Gale Research Company, c1972). Volume 1 of *Drama Criticism* is a checklist of interpretation since 1940 of English and American plays, while volume 2 covers classical and continental plays since 1940. The critical articles indexed in this work are in books and scholarly journals while *A Guide to Critical Reviews* indexes reviews in popular periodicals since 1909-1910.

Modern Drama is a selective survey of critical literature of Twentieth-century drama. Almost all references are to material in books, although some scholarly journals are cited. There is very little duplication between *A Guide to Critical Reviews* and *Modern Drama*.

Dramatic Criticism Index includes references both to drama as literature and to drama as theater and is a "bibliography of commentaries on playwrights from Ibsen to the Avant-Garde," which indexes 630 books and over 200 periodicals, mostly scholarly. A comparison of entries shows very little overlap between *A Guide to Critical Reviews* and *Dramatic Criticism Index*.

In summary, *A Guide to Critical Reviews* Part III indexes reviews from popular periodicals while the other three reference tools index more scholarly articles in both books and periodicals.

Part IV, *The Screenplay from the Jazz Singer to Dr. Strangelove*, volumes 1 and 2, is a bibliography of critical reviews of feature-length motion pictures released from October, 1927, through 1963. Screen titles were selected from Richard Dimmett's *Title Guide to the Talkies* (Metuchen, N.J.: Scarecrow Press, 1965) plus some additions by the author, and include 12,000 American and foreign screenplays.

Because *Dimmitt* includes copyright and release dates, producers and studio, screenplay author, and author and title of original works adapted to the screen, Salem does not provide this information here as was done in Part II, *The Musical*. These omissions detract from the volumes' usefulness as it makes it necessary to consult other sources for information one would expect to find here.

The main body of these two volumes is an alphabetical listing by title of the motion picture followed by the alphabetical listing of periodical review.

It is impossible to tell from the spine or title page of each volume which parts of the alphabet are included therein, although the numbering of pages is consecutive. Cross-references are few, referring to the main title listing.

Indexes include Academy Award Winning Screenplays, 1927/28 to 1962, arranged by year, listing the best actress and actor, film names; best supporting actress and actor, film names; best picture and best director, film names; and New York Film Critics' Award, arranged by year giving the best motion picture, best actor (and film), best actress (and film), best director (and film), best foreign language film (and indication of the language), special award, and best screenplay writer (and film).

Other than *Reader's Guide* no other reference book was found that indexes reviews of screenplays in popular periodicals, although *The New York Times Film Reviews, 1913-1968* (New York: New York Times and Arno Pr., 1970) does have the actual review as it appeared in the newspaper. For this reason, particularly, Part IV is recommended, even though it is limited by date to 1968.

A Guide to Critical Reviews is sturdily bound and should be able to withstand heavy usage. The printing is legible, but the author headings in Parts I and II do not stand out as they should for ease of use. The volumes do not lie flat when opened.

Because *A Guide to Critical Reviews* covers reviews of plays only up to 1963-1966, and because the reviews indexed are limited to popular and easily available periodicals, these listings would need to be supplemented by other and more recent reference books. *American Drama*, Part I, and *British and Continental Drama*, Part III, can be recommended for all libraries, but particularly to those with collections which are primarily popular. Despite the limitations of date and coverage, and since there are no comparable guides to reviews of the musical and the screenplay, other than *Reader's Guide*, Part II and Part IV are recommended for those secondary school, public, and academic libraries which have great demand for critical reviews.

(June 15, 1973, p.954)

Guide to Reference Material. Edited by A. J. Walford. 3d ed. v.1, Science and

Technology. [London], The Library Association, 1973; distributed in the U.S. by R. R. Bowker Co., P. O. Box 1807, Ann Arbor, MI 48106. 615p. cloth $17.95 plus shipping and handling.

When the first edition of this work was published, in one volume, in 1959, it could truly be called a British counterpart to the American *Guide to Reference Books*, then edited by Constance M. Winchell. Hereafter in this review the American *Guide* will be referred to as *Winchell*, the British *Guide* as *Walford*. *Walford* was expanded to three volumes in the second edition (1966-1970), and in its new, third edition, volume 1 *(Science and Technology)* alone is nearly as large as the eighth edition of *Winchell*, which still covers all fields of knowledge in one volume.

The Reference and Subscription Books Review Committee reviewed the 1959 edition of *Walford* in the June 1, 1960 *The Booklist and Subscription Books Bulletin* and recommended it for large public and university libraries and for special libraries in science and technology in the United States and Canada as a source of well-annotated current and British titles. The Committee will review and make recommendations on each volume of the third edition of *Walford* as it is published.

The intent of the editor is "to provide a signpost to reference books and bibliographies published mainly in recent years, international in scope, but with emphasis on items published in Britain." These words, taken from the Introduction to the third edition, are actually somewhat modest. The work provides more than a signpost. It also provides critical or descriptive annotations for about 5,000 reference works. The volume under review is limited to science and technology; the two other volumes will cover the social sciences, humanities, arts, and bibliography.

The arrangement is by the Universal Decimal Classification System, and this volume covers classes 5 and 6 of that system. Each entry provides the UDC number in the right-hand column, and where appropriate the related or auxiliary number for the type of material— 016 for bibliographies, 091 for histories of a subject, and so on. This has the advantage of grouping all works on a given subject, but since most Universal Decimal Classification numbers are quite precise, the editor had to face the question that confronts every subject bibliographer—where does one list a book that deals with more than one subject? Thus, there are 19 titles listed under "Hotels" (a subdivision of DOMESTIC SCIENCE), and four titles under "Restaurants," on adjoining pages. But three of the 19 titles in the first group include the words ". . . hotels and restaurants." These three titles are not listed under the heading "Restaurants"; nor is there a *see also* reference, and these three would probably not be found by a patron unless he were also thinking of hotels.

Each entry in the work gives author, title, and the usual bibliographical data, including pagination for monographic works. Price is generally given (in pounds) for British monographs, is frequently given (in dollars) for U.S. monographs, but is rarely given for books published elsewhere. Prices for serials, continuations, annuals, and the like are seldom given. After the bibliographical data comes a list of contents, or indication of what each part contains, such as, "Volume 1, . . . before 1641; Volume 2, 1641 to 1850," and so on. This is followed by an annotation, seldom less than three lines long, and often as long as twenty lines, with an average of about ten lines. These annotations often include quotations, either from the Preface of the work itself, or from a review in a journal, with full citation given. The annotations may be descriptive or critical, or both. Minor defects are sometimes pointed out; thus *Physician's Book Compendium* is criticized for having "slightly wordy annotations," and *Technical Abbreviations and Contractions in English* is disparaged because its bibliography is "unhelpfully arranged, A-Z, by authors."

Within any specific Universal Decimal Classification number, arrangement of titles is alphabetical by author. If the topic is large enough, for example,

"Patents," Universal Decimal Classification 608.3, there is further geographical breakdown—International, Great Britain, Eire, Germany, and France.

The user unfamiliar with the Universal Decimal Classification system must rely heavily on the double columned Index, pages 563-615. This is an author-subject-title Index, with titles given only when there is no author. Subjects in capital letters stand out clearly. However, the wording of the subject entries does not always agree with the subheads in the work itself. Thus, a person wanting a reference work on DIET or DIETING will find only the word *dietetics*, pages 263-64 in the Index. On these pages, however, the topics are "Health," "Nutrition," and "Occupational and Industrial Hygiene," and it would be necessary to read almost every title to discover even one work related to dieting. Another subject entry in the Index is *mapping*, pages 88-91, but on the pages cited, one finds only "Cartography." Since the running head at the top of the page reads ASTRONOMY, the reader might easily think he had turned to the wrong page.

Comparison between *Walford* and *Winchell* is perhaps inevitable. The basic difference between them is one of quantity rather than of quality. Volume 1 of *Walford* exclusive of the Index, contains 561 pages, covering science and technology. Eighty-four pages in *Winchell* make up the pure and applied sciences section; to these should be added the 55 pages in the three supplements issued to date (the latest covering to 1970). This makes a total of 139 pages for *Winchell,* or less than one-fourth the number of pages in *Walford.* Therefore, one may logically conclude that *Walford* will contain many more titles, and certainly more British titles, than *Winchell* on any given subject. In the Index to *Walford,* for example, 52 titles begin with the words "Advances in . . ." There are none in *Winchell. Walford* lists six titles under "Chemistry—History;" *Winchell* has only two. *Walford* lists such separate medical topics as *tuberculosis, cancer,* and *heart disease,* with one or two entries under each; *Winchell* lists them only under *medicine.*

Generally speaking, annotations are longer in *Walford*. The annotation for *Chemical Abstracts,* for example, is 39 lines long in Walford, eight lines in *Winchell.* A lesser-known work, Morrill's *Computers and Data Processing,* receives eight lines of comment in *Walford,* in contrast with three lines in *Winchell* (Supplement 3).

In general, *Walford* can be relied on to contain more titles, and certainly more British titles, than *Winchell,* and generally the annotations or comments will be longer—though not necessarily better. They may add information not mentioned by *Winchell* or they may refer the reader to an additional journal review.

A statistical comparison between *Winchell* and *Walford* was made, on the basis of the approximately 200 titles to be found in the Pure and Applied Sciences section of *Winchell,* 3rd Supplement (1969-1970). Of these, approximately two-thirds were published in the U.S., one-sixth in Great Britain, and the other one-sixth in other European countries. By contrast, a random count of 200 titles selected from *Walford* (taking one title from every third page) shows that less than one-fourth were published in the U.S., while close to one-half were of British origin (with a few published jointly in both countries). The remaining one-fourth were published in other European countries, with Germany, Holland, and France ranking highest, as they do also in *Winchell.* But *Walford* does include a small percentage (about 2 percent) of books published in India, Japan, and Israel, which do not appear in *Winchell*'s 3rd Supplement.

A second survey was then made to determine the amount of duplication between the two works. Of the 200 titles in *Winchell,* approximately 65 percent were duplicated in *Walford.* Of the remaining 35 percent, many were either psychological titles (a subject covered in another volume of *Walford*), or were somewhat localized American bibliographies. There still remained a residue of about 40 *Winchell* titles, mostly American works, which are not in *Walford.*

Working the same 200 titles in reverse produced about the same results.

Walford contained about 130 *Winchell* titles, the 65 percent mentioned above, in the same or almost the same edition. The remainder are for the most part British works, or works which relate to the sciences in areas of the world that were once part of the former British Commonwealth of Nations, such as Canada or India.

Aside from content a few other comparisons may be made between the two works. For example, the Index in *Winchel* refers to specifically numbered items in the text; *Walford* gives only page numbers, even for specific titles, so that the reader has to look up and down both columns of the page to locate the item. Furthermore, *Winchell's* Index gives both author and title entry, while *Walford,* as mentioned earlier, gives only the main entry (author or editor, and title only when no author is known). *Walford* gives initials only for first names, both in the Index and in the text, whereas *Winchell* gives full names, enabling a reader to identify authors exactly. One more point of difference is that *Winchell* provides introductory outlines at the beginning of each major topic and also some guidelines for evaluating reference books in most fields. None of this appears in *Walford.*

A random sampling of the index in *Walford* revealed no pagination errors, but did turn up a few trivial inaccuracies of another sort. One title uses the word *Handbook of* . . ., but it appears in the index as *Manual of* . . ., the former title being the correct one. Some minor discrepancies between *Walford's* and *Winchell's* spelling were also noted. In each case of discrepancy, reference to another source showed that *Winchell* was correct.

Present users of *Walford,* whether using volume 1 (Science and Technology) only, or all three of the volumes, will have to determine for themselves the importance of obtaining this new third edition. The publishers claim approximately 30 percent increase in the number of titles over the second edition. This claim appears to be substantiated by inspection of the two editions, since the type size (nine lines to the inch) and general page layout is the same in both. Pagination of the second edition was 426 pages excluding the Index; the third has 561 pages without the Index. Incidentally, the Index itself has been improved by substituting all capital letters for subject entries previously in boldface. Besides greater number of entries, new topics such as pollution, computers, astronautics, holography, oceanography, drugs, and containerism have been given prominence, the publishers say in their press release.

As already noted, volume 1 of *Walford,* in this third edition, is currently being distributed by Bowker. However, the third editions of volume 2 (Social and Historical Sciences, Philosophy, and Religion) and of volume 3 (Generalia, Language and Literature, and the Arts) will be distributed in this country by the American Library Association. Publication of these is promised for the spring of 1974 and the summer of 1974, respectively. In 1974 volume 2 will be replacing a volume which will then be six years old and a volume 3 which will then be four years old, with the cutoff dates in each case being over a year prior to publication. The cutoff date for volume 1 of the third edition was April 1972.

Volume 1 of the third edition of *Guide to Reference Material: Science and Technology* is recommended as an up-to-date bibliography for all science- and technology-oriented libraries, and for all large public, university, and research libraries because of the large number of entries, the fullness of coverage of the annotations, and the wide geographic spread.

(Dec. 15, 1973, p.393)

Harper's Dictionary of Music. By Christine Ammer. Drawings by Carmela M. Ciampa and Kenneth L. Donlon. New York, Harper & Row, [c1972]. xiv, 414p. illus. 24cm. cloth $10.

This new, one-volume dictionary of music is described by the publisher as straightforward in arrangement, readable in style, and intended for young persons and nonspecialist music lovers. The youthful author did editorial work and wrote for children before becoming editor of the second edition of Apel's *Harvard Dictionary of Music,* 1969, a respected reference tool on which Miss Ciampa, the illustrator, also was employed.

After a minimal introduction, list of abbreviations, and key to the pronunciation system, the dictionary begins with "a, à. For Italian and French musical terms beginning with *a* or *à*, such as *a cappella, à deux,* or *a due,* see under the next word (CAPPELLA; DEUX; DUE)." This is immediate evidence of a valuable characteristic of the work—that it requires no knowledge of foreign languages while providing, as the subject requires, definitions for words in Italian, French, German, Latin, and Spanish. Pronunciations are given by diacritical marks for all words and names, and when the title of a work appears in the original language in the body of an article, it is followed by a translation.

The arrangement is alphabetical letter-by-letter with entry words in boldface type. Cross-references throughout the text are in capital letters, and synonyms for which there are *see* references elsewhere are in italics. The double-column layout, on cream-toned paper, is easy to read and diversified by occasional clear line drawings of instruments and by simple musical illustrations.

There are about 2,800 entries including cross-references of which nearly half relate to the composition of music, about a third to its performance, and the balance to instruments, famous composers, abbreviations, etc. The forms of music are briefly defined and placed in history with the names of composers who signally employed them. Entries for other technical terms, describing writing or performing, are often broken into numbered sections which bring together related phrases, appearing elsewhere in the dictionary as *see* references; e.g., *score, 2 full score, 3 part score, 4 vocal score, 5 piano score.*

Current terms such as *moog* and *electronic music* appear and up-to-date editing is indicated by the 1971 death date for Stravinsky. The popular area of the art, in the 1960s and before, is not ignored, although a sentence on acid rock or soul is only a token.

The abbreviations explained are mostly performance directions, but they also include as well the "K" (Kochel opus numbers for Mozart compositions) as well as "R & B" (rhythm and blues), a term used in the recording business. There is no central gathering of signs and abbreviations, and for them one must look under such entries as *notes and rests, dynamics, ornaments,* and elsewhere. Instruments (not omitting the sweet potato) are described under their English names, with *see* references from their equivalents in other languages, and famous compositions written for them are mentioned so that the reader can augment his knowledge by listening to a recording. Examples of Oriental instruments are present as are various parts of instruments, e.g., fret, pick, stop.

Most of the important composers, living and dead, are included and a scattered representation of Broadway musical composers as well. Professional activity, not personal history, is recounted with the emphasis on the subject's characteristic works and place in music. Additional names are supplied in five lists of important composers, with dates, nationality and significance in a phrase, grouped by chronological period. More lists, to a total of 18, gather "Notable Song Cycles" adjacent to the entry *song cycle,* "Some Famous Violin Concertos" near *concerto,* etc. Noticeably lacking from the dictionary are bibliographies, lives of performers, entries for countries, and titles for operas and other works known by name.

The material is well written and organized for the intended audience. The youthful reader's attention is caught by interesting trivia such as the fact that the Japanese shamisen is covered with catskin, that the player of the double bass "perches on a high stool," and that the shanty is ". . . a work song sung by sailors (for example) 'Yeo, heave ho' used to hoist anchor which involved winding a heavy cable around a barrel." The remote complications of the medieval neumic notation receive half the space given them in the *Harvard Dictionary* (Cambridge, Mass.: Harvard Univ. Pr., 1969); the account of incidental music is enlarged by the logical addition of cinema backgrounds; and the write-up of the mandolin lists more composers than Scholes' *Oxford Companion* (Oxford Univ. Pr., 1970).

Presently available one-volume dictionaries of moderate price, with which *Ammer* might be compared, include the ultra-concise, often in pocket size, such as Apel's *Harvard Brief Dictionary of Music* (Cambridge, Mass.: Harvard Univ. Pr., 1960, $3.95; paperback, 95c), Blom's *Everyman's Dictionary of Music* (New York: Dutton, 1954, $6), and Scholes' *Concise Oxford Dictionary* (New York: Oxford Univ. Pr., 1964, $7; paperback, $2.95), all of which contain more entries and more advanced material than *Ammer* in less attractive form. Addressed to the same audience is Watson's *A Concise Dictionary of Music* (New York: Dodd, 1965, $6.95; Apollo paperback, $2.25) which has far fewer entries, less technical presentation of information, and more biographies of all kinds. Westrup and Harrison's *New College Encyclopedia of Music* (New York: Norton, 1960, $10) most resembles *Ammer*, but is more extensive, including performers' lives, some bibliographies, and titles of works. It is a British product with some national bias and a more traditional approach, excluding the recognition of hillbilly or hi-fi, and a bit more advanced in level of definitions. *Westrup* has no illustrations. It may be noted that Mrs. Ammer, born in Vienna, is lavish with German terms.

Harper's Dictionary of Music is a systematic presentation of musical facts at a fairly basic level, emphasizing the standard field and art rather than persons. It is considerate of the user who reads only English. Although some other dictionaries offer more information, the attractive appearance and readable style recommend it to students and the general public in both homes and libraries. *(Sept. 1, 1972, p.1)*

Harver Junior World Encyclopedia.
Editor in chief, Michael W. Dempsey. 16v. Freeport, NY, Harver Educational Services, Inc., [made and printed in Great Britain by Purnell and Sons, Ltd., 1971]. 1,344p. 27cm. illus. (part col.) maps. diagrs. tables. offset cloth $59.50 plus $5 shipping and handling charge.

Harver Junior World was first published in Britain in 1969 by Purnell and Sons as *Junior World Encyclopedia*. The volumes subsequently were "completely rewritten" for sale in the United States through supermarkets. The school and library edition under review is published by Harver Educational Services, Inc., Freeport, New York, is distributed by Purnell Library Service, New York, and bears a 1971 copyright. Harver Educational Services also publishes the 21-volume *Harver World Encyclopedia* which will be reviewed by this Committee in a future edition of *The Booklist*. Among the reference and subscription publications distributed by Purnell are *New Caxton Encyclopedia, Pergamon World Atlas*, and *Man, Myth, and Magic*. Each of these will be evaluated later by the Reference and Subscription Books Review Committee.

Michael W. Dempsey, publisher of McDonald and Company's London encyclopedic and reference division and author of over 150 nonfiction and scientific books for young readers, is editor in chief. No information has been located on any of the other 12 editors or members of the editorial or advisory boards. However, much is known about the four members of the consultant advisory board. The eminent Sir Bernard Lovell, who is director of Nuffield Radio Astronomy Laboratories in England and is author of many books and articles in physical and astronomical journals, heads the board. Other consultants are Asa Briggs, professor of history and vice-chancellor at University of Sussex; Yehudi Menuhin, the noted violinist; and Maurice Burton, zoologist and author of several books on animals, an officer of the British Museum, and editor of *International Wildlife Encyclopedia* also published by Purnell and reviewed in *The Booklist* October 15, 1972. Forty-one contributors, apparently all British, are listed at the beginning of each volume with no credentials other than college degrees. Information about only one, Jean Cooke, a British sculptor-artist, was found in a search of the usual biographical resources. Search was hampered because initials rather than first names of the contributors are given. No articles are signed; nor is there any evidence anywhere in the encyclopedia of what contributors were responsible for which materials.

A brief letter at the beginning of volume 1, written by the editors to "Our Readers and Their Families," explains that this encyclopedia is designed to help young people develop ability to use reference works at an early age. It describes the use of color illustration, explains the arrangement of topics, and use of cross references, and suggests that parents and children can "begin to read on almost any page and discover together that practically any subject can be fascinating when it is clearly and interestingly explained."

The pages are numbered continuously throughout the set, and there are exactly 84 pages in each volume. In order to maintain this pattern some arbitrary subject divisions were made, which result in volume 1 being labeled *aba-art;* volume 2 *art-bra.* A person looking up Arthur, King; Arthur, Chester; artist; or any other words beginning with *art* must look in two places. Other volumes that have conflicting letter combinations on the spines are volumes 3 and 4, 7 and 8, 12 and 13, 13 and 14, and 14 and 15. The Table of Contents or alphabetical breakdown of volumes 1-16 lists volume 14 as including *South Africa* through *Turks;* volume 15, *Turkey* through *Zoology.* In order to keep the letter by letter alphabetical arrangement intact, the concluding article in volume 14 is actually entitled *Turk,* although it discusses the nomadic tribe the *Turks.* The first article in volume 15 is *Turkey.*

Each volume averages 101 articles, most of which are brief in order to keep the volumes to the uniform 84 pages. Some items are no more than a dictionary definition, and the article for *Astronomy* is so abbreviated that there is room on the same page for the concluding three paragraphs of *Astronautics,* the article *Lake Athabasca,* the beginning of the article for *Athens,* plus a six-inch photograph of the Parthenon. Vague terms are often used in these brief definitions. The entire article for *Fuse* states: "Fuse contains a wire made from some metal which has a low melting point. If too large a current flows through the circuit, sufficient heat is generated to melt the fuse wire. This breaks the circuit and prevents more serious damage." An unlabeled drawing of a fused plug completes the article.

Another method of condensing many names or statistics into a small amount of space is the use of lists in a box column, as in *Inventions.* After a brief general statement about inventing, there follows a listing of names of inventors and their most notable invention, arranged chronologically, from movable type, 1450 to hovercraft, 1955. This device of box listing is also used for dramatists and examples of their plays, American literature, painters and painting, kings and queens of England, and famous names in Greek mythology.

Since space is an important consideration, one questions the inclusion of such articles as *Loess, Earwig, Servomechanisms,* and *Caisson* in an encyclopedia for ages eight to twelve. In this work caisson refers only to civil engineering use and omits any military association.

Geographical and scientific items received the most emphasis in the encyclopedia—about 58 percent of all entries are relegated to these 2 areas. Geographical items, which cover the usual continents, countries, states and Canadian provinces, include a rather hit-and-miss selection of lakes, rivers, cities, oceans, islands, mountains, and deserts. Position maps accompany each of the articles on states, countries, and provinces. These maps show the described area in black in relation to the surrounding territory but are miniscule (the map of Hawaii shows the islands as mere pinpoints with no shape or relative size). These are only outline maps giving no details and no source. Other small maps showing population density and rainfall are included in the articles on each continent, on Great Britain, and the United States, but not on France, Germany, or any other country.

A land use map—also extremely small—is sometimes included, but there is none for the United States. A "Facts and Figures" box for larger countries gives area, population, capitol, and sometimes money unit, labor force, exports, and imports. However, there is no consistency about including this information. Nineteen seventy census figures are used for the United States, but no source is indicated for population figures for other countries. A check with reliable sources reveals considerable variation between the figures in *Harver* and the other sources. Even within *Harver Encyclopedia*, population statistics for the states vary; the figures given in articles for the states do not agree with those listed in the box facts under United States.

The length of articles varies from nine pages of text and pictures for United States to one-fourth of a column for Haiti. A brief history of the geographical area is usually included. Sometimes this is condensed to a sentence or two as "Vikings reached Greenland in the 800's. The Danes began to colonize Greenland in the early 1700's. They held it against the Norwegian claims in the 1930's." Sometimes the history includes a listing of all rulers.

In the text, *see* references are used sparingly, and *see also* not at all, except in the index volume. There is an article for *Great Britain* with a *see* reference to *British Commonwealth*, but no reference to *British Commonwealth* or *Great Britain*. There is no article under *England*, just a *see* reference to *Great Britain*. There is also an article under *British Isles* with no reference anywhere to it or from it to similar articles. The term *United Kingdom* as used in other encyclopedias is not used in *Harver* for a main entry, although the term is mentioned in the text and the United Kingdom flag is pictured. Gathering these scattered articles under one head would be helpful. This policy of having several articles dealing with the same subject appearing in different parts of the alphabet with no *see also* reference is one of the most serious handicaps in the use of the encyclopedia.

Information on each state is scanty. Any reference to state bird, tree, flower, motto, seal, or flag is omitted. Statistics about population and area and meager facts about the beginnings of the state and its industrial development are presented. An incorrect date was noted in the article for *Indiana:* "In 1880 Indiana Territory was established." Since Indiana became a state in 1816, this date is obviously incorrect. However, more accurately, attention should be called to the fact that Indiana was a part of the Northwest Territory which was established in 1787.

National parks have been given incomplete treatment. The general article on national parks does not have a complete listing of parks. Yellowstone is mentioned, and there are pictures of Carlsbad Caverns and Banff National Park. All of these also have separate articles in their alphabetical places. There are no articles for Smoky Mountains, Mammoth Cave, Yosemite, Glacier, or any of the other parks. The article on national parks concludes with the statement; "Today most countries of the world have national parks." In the text only Kruger National Park is mentioned in South Africa. The Index omits this reference as well as an entry for the illustration of the Waukie Game Preserve, Rhodesia.

The encyclopedia title, *Junior World Encyclopedia,* suggests an international emphasis. This has been attempted in the inclusion of so many geographical references. Each of the independent countries of Africa rates a separate article. However, Congo (Kinshasa) is still used, and *Zaire* which it was renamed in 1960, is not mentioned in text or Index. A note gives this information, "Rhodesia declared itself a republic in 1970 but Britain did not recognize this act." Information about Iran is still found in the *Persia* article, although the article states that the country is now called Iran. There is an index reference both to *Iran* and *Persia*. There is an article on Pakistan but no mention of Bangladesh. Culture of countries other than the United States and Great Britain is not included; the article on schools has no information about education in other lands. The article on government contains only notes about the United States and Great Britain.

In addition to geography, a large part of the encyclopedia is devoted to science. More than half of the science articles are devoted to wildlife, wild and domesticated animals, and botany. These articles are the best written and the most useful in the entire encyclopedia, perhaps because of the influence of advisory board consultant, Maurice Burton. Entries are broad, e.g., *Crustaceans, Daisy Family, Deep-sea Fishes, Echinoderms, Rodents, Shells and Shellfish, Cattle, Poisonous Plants, Evergreens,* but there are also specific entries: *Jerboa, Hummingbirds, Hyena, Ferns, Lightning Bugs, Koalas, Jelly-Fish, Dragon-Fly, Elephant, Fox, Hogs, Hedge Hog, Roses, Sloth.* In contrast to the vague, general statements in most of the other articles, those on plants and animals are fact filled. The accompanying illustrations are drawings, not photographs, and are in sharp, bright colors with parts of the animal or plant clearly labelled. Scientific terms when used in the text are in italics with an explanation given. There is no pronunciation given anywhere. A clear distinction is made between the terms *species, genus, family, order, class,* and *phylum* in the animal kingdom, and a detailed family tree offers further explanation. However, all labels are the Latin scientific ones which require the user to check back into the text to identify the various phyla illustrated. Even then the reader will encounter difficulty. If he wants to identify "aves," he will read they are "warm blooded vertebrates that have feathers. Like most reptiles they lay eggs." Nowhere is the word "bird" used. Explanations are often more technical than they should be for the eight to twelve age group for which the encyclopedia is intended.

The allotment of space to the various items is puzzling. Four pages are devoted to *Flowers* and *Flowering Plants* (two separate entries). Then, in addition, there are allied articles in their alphabetical order for *Annual Plants, Biennial Plants, Climbing Plants, Perennial Plants, House Plants, Garden Flowers,* and numerous separate plants such as *Rose, Daisy Family, Grass,* and *Herb.* By contrast the article on astronomy as mentioned earlier fills only a quarter of a column—less, by far, than that given to the article on hogs or ferns. Separate articles are also allotted to such little-known animals as the *Slow Worm, Earwig, Pangolin,* and *Stick Insect* (praying mantis as it is generally known, but there is no mention of this).

There are noticeable omissions even in the science coverage, the best aspect of the encyclopedia. There are no articles on guinea pigs, gerbils, pigeons, parakeets, or any information on the care of pets. The article on cats has no illustrations and nothing about care or breeding.

Inconsistencies exist also in the pictured size of animals. A note on the illustration of the whale acknowledges that it is not drawn to scale. Drawings of birds have the note, "Birds vary in size so greatly that no attempt has been made to approximate them to a scale. Instead, the average length of the bird is given from the tip of the beak to the tip of the tail." However, in pictures of ants, an anteater, and an antelope on neighboring pages, everything depicted appears to be the same size, although size information is given in the text pertaining to the two animals but not in that for ants.

Moon exploration is covered under *Apollo Spacecraft, Moon,* and *Astronautics.* The latest developments described are the second walk on the moon in 1969 and the 1970 explosion in the service module of Apollo 13.

There is no article for engines nor any lead either in text or Index where such information could be located. However, a persistent searcher would find information and diagrams of various types of engines under the heading *Internal Combustion Engine.* There is even a picture of a Wankel or rotary engine with inadequate labelling, but no reference at all to it in the Index.

The intent of the editors to "match the interests and school work of young readers between the ages of 8 and 12 years" has not been entirely met. In fact there is little evidence that any attempt has been made to include current topics about which young people have a curiosity or interest. No information is included on flying saucers, UFOs, school busing, ESP, witchcraft, or venereal disease; and drug abuse is dismissed in the sentence, "Used otherwise they (drugs) can be very dangerous." Marijuana or amphetamines are not mentioned in the Index. Ecology is not in the Index, although it is introduced in the article for *Conservation*. No *see also* reference links this article to one for *Pollution*, although such a reference would be logical and helpful. There are no full articles on quasar, telstar, or women. Jazz is the latest musical development described. Rock and electronic music are not mentioned. History and rules for some sports are included, but biographies of athletes are limited to two—Jesse Owens and Mohammed Ali.

Biographies which constitute about 16 percent of the total entries consist mainly of presidents, former rulers, and statesmen. Some contemporaries such as Spiro Agnew, Richard M. Nixon, Haile Selassie, Mao Tse-Tung, Lester Pearson, and Fidel Castro are included, but not Queen Elizabeth.

Black leaders Martin Luther King, Jr., Malcolm X, Kwame Nkrumah, Jomo Kenyatta, Nat Turner, Marcus Garvey, Edward Brooke, and Ralph Bunche have full biographies in their alphabetical place. *Slavery, Negro History, Black Muslims,* and *Black Panthers* are also given articles. The five and a half-page *Negro History* article lists no development after 1968, and only a mention of the Civil Rights Movement. The Civil Rights Law is cited with brief comment in the biography of Lyndon Johnson. No cross-references link any of these articles together.

The whole field of entertainment is treated superficially in a two-page article for *Motion Pictures* and in even briefer summaries of *Theater* and *Television and Radio Broadcasting*. Black entertainers are represented by biographies of Louis Armstrong and Duke Ellington. Charlie Chaplin and Bing Crosby are the only others from the entertainment field to have biographies included. Although there is a biography of Walt Disney which credits him with being first to use individual drawings in a movie, the word "animation" is not used. However, animation is briefly explained in the article *Cartoon*. But again a cross-reference linking these two articles is lacking.

Literature is given very scanty treatment accounting for barely one percent of the total articles. Six pages are devoted to American literature and one page to English literature—but none to children's literature. There are articles for *Fairies, Mother Goose, Greek Myths,* and *Norse Myths* (no Roman), and biographies of some authors including Lewis Carroll, Mark Twain, and Robert L. Stevenson and legendary figures such as King Arthur, Robin Hood, and Paul Bunyan. Pearl Buck, John Dos Passos, and Zane Grey are the only twentieth-century authors mentioned. There are no references to any contemporary juvenile author, no selections from any literature, and no listing of Pulitzer, Newbery, Caldecott, or other literary awards.

The field of art is not covered under art or artists, but some information is included under *Painting and Painters, Mosaics,* and *Sculptors*. Biographies of such artists as Rembrandt, Renoir, Raphael, and Picasso are included, but there is no mention of recent pop art trends. Neither are there any articles on drawing, acrylics, finger painting, puppetry, or any kind of handcraft that children might expect to find.

Illustrations both in color and black and white are on every page. For the most part the colors of the drawings and diagrams are sharp and clear. However, photographs are badly reproduced, with the result that many of the photographs are a faded yellow-green color with obscure details. The black-and-white prints are generally of better quality.

Color contains a note under the chart of color triangle of pigments: "Because of limitation of the printing process used for this book, these colors may not be exactly correct." This note could well apply to other reproductions as well. Picture and text do not always correspond, and captions for two or more illustrations are usually printed together making it necessary for the reader to match pictures and label. Space is used unwisely; pictures need to be cropped. At the close of volume 16 a page of acknowledgments gives recognition to the assistance of various travel bureaus, airways, embassies, film studios, museums, and industries in assembling photographic material for the encyclopedia. No credit is given for individual pictures.

No bibliographies or even suggested readings are included anywhere in this set. The nearest approach to a bibliography is the statement, "There are many books that will tell you a great deal about growing house plants."

Volume 16 contains a geographical and historical atlas and an Index of approximately 8,000 entries. The maps bear a Hammond Incorporated copyright, but no date. In addition to the historical and geographical maps usually found in encyclopedias, there are world maps showing types of vegetation, average January and July temperature, rainfall, population distribution, world literacy pattern, rich versus poor nations, world nutrition, and products. Topography is incorporated in the geographic maps. Scale is given in miles. All maps are in vivid colors; boundaries are clearly marked, and place-names can be easily read. However, there are no individual maps for states, countries, or provinces; there is no gazetteer or any guide to locate a specific city, river, lake, or geographic area. In fact nothing in the 47-page atlas section is included in the Index; so information on these excellent maps is lost to all but the persistent browser.

The Index, which is alphabetically arranged in three columns on the remaining 34 pages of volume 16, is easy to use. A note at the beginning of the Index states that entries in bold type refer to main articles. Volume and page are given. Page numbers in italics refer to illustrations. There are *see* and *see also* references but not nearly enough. There seems to be no real pattern for the indexing. Some illustrations are included; many are not. Throughout the text words which need special defining are italicized. Some of these words are in the index; many are not. Broad subject entries such as chemistry, plant life, human body, and government are subdivided under topical subheads containing volume and page references. A random check shows that most of the entries are correct, but there are some blind leads.

The school and library edition of *Harver Junior World Encyclopedia* is bound in heavy board with a bright blue, soil resistant, matt grained, laminated cover. The binding on some of the review copies is splitting, and endpapers have become unglued from the board backs. The volume number and the letter sequence is on each spine in black. Insufficient contrast between the small black lettering and the blue binding makes it difficult to identify one volume from another. The 10½ by 7⅜ inch page size is easy to handle, and the slim volumes lie flat when opened. A different collage of pictures from the volume is arranged in the shape of a globe on the front cover of each of the 16 volumes. The text is set in easy-to-read type with generous leading, and the captions are set in a clear typeface. The type is larger than in many encyclopedias, and the two-column arrangement is pleasing. As there are no guide words or combination of letters either at the top or bottom of the page and the contrast of text and heading is not very pronounced, a careful search is required to find the beginning of an article. There are no subheads within the articles.

Sentences are short and lack variety, but they are not condescending. Their greatest fault is their vagueness. The article on glass includes this sentence: "This recipe produces the common soda lime glass that is used for windows, bottles, and so on." *Gold* concludes: "22 karat gold has 2/24 of alloying elements and so on."

There is some evidence that the original British publication has been altered for sale in United States. Spelling is in the American form. Few obvious British expressions are used, and there is no predominately British slant or emphasis in the choice of articles.

According to the editorial overview

provided by the publisher, "the specific aim of the editors and the editorial board has been to prepare an up-to-date, authoritative reference work which can be used by children in the primary grades themselves; will arouse young readers' interest and imagination; will lead to further study and reference work; and provides an essential link between learning at school and in the world at large."

These are worthy aims, but information is poorly organized and presented for the most part in generalities or vague sentences. The lack of bibliographies and cross-references will not encourage further study or research. Current interests of the young reader are largely ignored, and there is no evidence that the publishers plan to update the encyclopedia. *Harver Junior World Encyclopedia* is not recommended for purchase for home, school, or public libraries. *(Nov. 1, 1973, p.245)*

Harver World Encyclopedia. 21v. Editor in chief, Martin Self. Freeport, NY, Harver Educational Services, Inc., c1973. illus. ports. maps. diagrs. 28cm. deluxe binding $199; library ed. $169.
ISBN 0-88346-050-5.

Harver World Encyclopedia is an entirely new general encyclopedia, the culmination of four years of planning, writing, and production by a staff of 19 editors and 135 contributors. It is published by Harver Educational Services, Inc., of Freeport, New York, who also published the 16-volume *Harver Junior World Encyclopedia*, which was reviewed in *The Booklist* November 1, 1973. It is also copyrighted by Elsevier International Projects, Ltd. of London.

Martin Self, editor in chief, was formerly a senior editor on the staff of *Encyclopaedia Britannica*. In addition to the editorial and production staff, 135 contributors are named. However, no additional identification is given for these contributors; nor are subject areas or specific articles for which they are responsible indicated, except for the 7 advisory editors whose names are also listed among the contributors. Areas of editorial responsibility are given for these 7 persons. A search of standard biographical reference works failed to yield any information about the staff or contributors.

In the Preface the editors explain that this encyclopedia has attempted to do two things: "to provide the most up-to-date reference information that a family might require, lavishly illustrated, and to link that information together so that the entire set may serve as a kind of system of knowledge." They further state that particular emphasis has been placed on science and technology, history, geography, and contemporary movements and personalities. Their aim has been to provide "a really useful family encyclopedia."

The 4,112 pages are numbered continuously throughout the set; almost all volumes contain exactly 192 pages. In order to maintain this uniformity of volume size alphabetical breaks between volumes are arbitrary causing overlapping alphabetic labels from one volume to another in every case except one. Volume 1 is labelled *A-All*, volume 2 *All-Arg*, volume 3 *Arg-Ban*, etc. A person looking up a subject beginning with any of these three-letter combinations might have to handle two volumes.

The publishers claim that the set contains more than 4.5 million words in over 14,000 articles. Articles range in size from two or three sentences to as many as nineteen pages (*Africa*), although most articles are less than three paragraphs long. Few are longer than three pages, with the exception of articles on states of the United States and provinces of Canada, and articles on individual countries. These articles generally run four to eight pages in length. All articles are unsigned.

The text is arranged two columns to a page with wide outside margins which are used for small photographs, drawings, and other illustrative materials related to the adjacent text. An additional feature of *Harver World* is the frequent use of these outside margin areas for notes giving additional data on a subject discussed in the adjoining columns. These notes, each about 100 words in length and highlighted by being printed over a colored rectangle, are occasionally used to add interesting anecdotal material, but most often simply provide additional factual material on the subject under discussion. Although they make for a graphically pleasing layout, the material could have been very easily incorporated into the body of the articles to which they relate.

The text is in very readable type with bold headings and subheadings in suitable contrast. Running heads clearly identify the first entry on each page. Arrangement is alphabetical, letter by letter.

Cross-referencing is accomplished in **three ways**. Liberal use is made of direct *see* references from variant forms of entry to headings under which material is presented. A count of such direct cross-references in one volume revealed that approximately one of every 17 entries is a *see* reference. Within entries words are printed in small capitals for subjects for which articles appear elsewhere in the encyclopedia (although users must deduce this; no explanation of this device is given anywhere in the set), and references are made at the end of articles to other related articles.

At present, users of *Harver World* must rely on these devices alone to find their way through the encyclopedia as there is no index. According to the publishers an index volume is in preparation, but publication date has not yet been set.

In addition to the absence of an index, *Harver World* also lacks any other aids to guide or facilitate use of the set. There are no introductory materials explaining use of the encyclopedia, no study guides or outlines, no pronunciation keys, and no bibliographies either at the end of articles or in a separate section. The publishers do plan to include bibliographies in the index volume, but the nature and extent of these bibliographies is not known at this time.

The most striking feature of *Harver World Encyclopedia* is its illustrations. More than 12,000 illustrations, most of them in full color, are used throughout the set. Illustrations include photographs, drawings, diagrams, and charts. Although in many cases photographs and drawings are rather small because of space limitations, they are uniformly clear, easily understood, and sharply reproduced. Color reproduction is particularly outstanding in both photographs and color illustrations. Illustrations are well selected, related closely to the textual material and thoroughly up to date. Indeed, the high quality of the illustrative materials is perhaps the outstanding feature of *Harver World Encyclopedia*. Many of the photographs have been selected from the files of Elsevier, Amsterdam, and Elsevier International, London. Credits for photographs and other illustrative matter appear nowhere in the set, but are promised in the proposed index volume.

There is no atlas section in the encyclopedia, and maps generally appear only in articles on continents or major areas of the world and in articles on each of the states of the United States and provinces of Canada. There is an area map of Central America, but no maps accompany individual articles on Mexico, Guatemala, Honduras, Nicaragua, or other Central American countries. Likewise, there are maps of Africa and South America but not for countries of these two continents. The article on Brazil, for example, has no map of the country yet includes an almost full page sixteenth-century map of eastern Brazil used as an illustration. Individual maps are provided for most of the countries of western Europe (but not for Finland, Norway, or Sweden) and for China, Japan, Australia, and India (but not for Vietnam, Korea, or Bangladesh). There are no cross-references from articles on countries without maps to area or continent articles with maps.

Maps of countries, continents, and regions are physical-political maps with colors used to indicate various geographic regions. Major geographic features as well as cities, political subdivisions, man-made features (roads, railroads, airports) are depicted. Colors used are bright and tend occasionally to be garish. Because of page size limitations and the rare use of double-page maps, size and scale of most maps are small, making them somewhat difficult to read. Maps are bled to the edge of the page.

Maps of states and provinces, on the

other hand, are larger scale, less crowded, printed in light pastel shades with physical features shown by darker shading and are hence much easier to read. Major physical features are labelled, and major and minor highways are given, although railroads and airports are not.

Other maps appearing in *Harver World* are maps of some major world cities in articles on those cities and special maps of various kinds: exploration, bird and animal maps, ocean currents, etc. None of the maps appearing in the set give date, source, or other copyright information.

The writing style is clear, straightforward, and generally brief. Each entry begins with a one-sentence definition and proceeds in economical prose to an expansion of the subject in language which should be readily understandable by persons of high school age and above. Unfamiliar terms and words are defined or explained. A careful neutrality and an absence of value judgments is maintained throughout in such subject areas as religion, politics, and social issues.

An examination of *Harver World* tends to confirm that emphasis is given to subjects in science and technology and in geography, as stated in the Preface. Topics in the natural and physical sciences are treated at length, while topics in the areas of fine arts and humanities are generally given briefer treatment. Extensive and carefully written articles appear for such subjects as *Nuclear Energy, Astronomy, Earth, Brain, Television, Submarine, Water, Hydraulics, Horse, Computer,* and *Botany*. Articles on narrower subjects, such as *Refrigeration, Transpiration, Cacti, Interferometer, Conifers, Starch, Respiration, Nucleic Acids, Cryogenics, Dehydration,* and *Termites,* while briefer, are carefully written and well illustrated.

On the other hand, there are fewer articles in the fine arts, and they tend to receive briefer treatment. While such major subjects as *Architecture, Ballet,* and *Sculpture* receive major articles, other important subjects, *Painting, Dance, Music, Ceramics, Drama, Graphic Arts, Opera, Weaving,* and *Jazz,* for example, are given brief coverage and sometimes meager, if any, illustration. There are no articles on or cross-references from: printmaking; instruments, musical; makeup; composition; cinematography; design; chamber music; acting; or scenery.

As stated by the editors, geography is given major emphasis. Every nation of the world receives an article describing the land, people, economy, and history. Each article is accompanied by a shaded box listing basic facts (production, foreign trade, government, demographic data and education) and a small reproduction of the country's flag as well as a table giving area, population, language, monetary unit, etc. The articles are consistently up to date, in most cases discussing national developments and activities through 1972. Population figures conform to the latest available census figures. Recent name changes are acknowledged, but articles are placed under the older name in the cases of Zaire and Sri Lanka with cross-references from these new names to *Congo (Kinshasa)* and *Ceylon,* respectively. Apparent last minute editorial changes relating to the entries *Bangladesh* and *East Pakistan* result in some confusion. The Bangladesh article repeats verbatim most of the copy in the East Pakistan article with the addition of more recent developments to 1972. It concludes with the reference "see also East Pakistan" where no new information, in fact less, is given. The chief weakness in articles on nations of the world, as stated earlier, is the lack of individual maps for most countries.

Each state of the United States and each province of Canada is treated in a separate article. Each article is preceded by a pictorial representation of the state flag, bird, flower, and tree for states and by a table of basic facts for both states and provinces. The presentation format for each is the same, a discussion of land and climate, people, economy, education, government, and history. The articles are attractively illustrated and accompanied in each case by a good map as described above. As is true of articles on nations, articles on states and provinces appear up to date, in many cases giving information on events of 1972, such as the New Democratic Party sweep and the election of Dave Barrett in August 1972, in the article on British Columbia.

Literature is given brief treatment. While substantial articles appear for American and English literature, there is no entry for world literature; nor are there articles on other national literatures. There is no article on children's literature, and information on this subject can only be gleaned individually from such articles as *Mother Goose, Mythology, Fairy,* and *Folklore.* While genre articles for *Novel, Short Story, Poetry, Essay, Detective Story,* and *Drama* are present as well as very brief biographical entries for major world writers past and present, no lists of Nobel, Pulitzer, or other literary award winners are given; nor are there selections from any literature.

Religion and philosophy fare better. Substantial, well-illustrated articles are present for such major religions as Christianity, Judaism, Buddhism, and Islam, explaining belief systems, life styles, worship procedures, and history. Shorter supportive articles on such subjects as *Baptism, God, Papacy, Hasidism, Koran, Mohammed, Heaven, Heresy, Mishna, Nirvana,* and *Communion* expand and enhance the major articles. Clear, though succinct, articles are present for other religions as well as for Protestant denominations and Catholic orders. Philosophy receives broad treatment. In addition to a long article, *Philosophy,* short, separate biographical articles are provided for major philosophers as well as clearly written presentations on the various branches and schools such as *Logic, Neoplatonism, Empiricism, Metaphysics, Stoicism, Ethics,* and *Transcendentalism.*

The Preface states that in addition to emphasis on science, technology, history, religion, and geography, major attention has been devoted to "events, movements, and personalities of the modern world." An examination of six contemporary social concerns (the feminist movement, ecology, minorities, urban problems and housing, sex, and drugs) reveals for the most part adequate, if rather cursory, treatment of these subjects. The claim in the Preface is only partially substantiated.

Two rather short articles totaling less than two pages appear on the feminist movement: *Women's Liberation Movement* and *Women's Rights.* The first article presents the issues and development of this current social concern in a straightforward, objective manner. The article, *Women's Rights,* consists of eight short paragraphs tracing the history of the struggle for equal rights, chiefly in the United States. Mention is made of such contemporary personalities as Kate Millet, Gloria Steinem, Germaine Greer, and Betty Friedan, but no biographical entries appear elsewhere in the encyclopedia for these persons, although separate biographical entries for a number of historical personages are present (Stanton, Mott, Parkhurst, and Willard). NOW (National Organization for Women) is mentioned in the first article, but neither this organization nor other women's rights groups are treated separately. One rather obtuse nineteenth-century cartoon and one small photograph of Emmeline Parkhurst provide the only illustrative material for the two articles. In sum, the issue, while treated objectively, is given no special emphasis as might be expected by the statement in the Preface.

The subject of environment receives somewhat more emphasis. Substantial articles, well illustrated, are present for *Ecology, Conservation, Population,* and *Pollution.* Shorter articles appear for *Environment, Air Pollution, Recycling, Noise, Waste Disposal,* and *Land Reclamation.* Environmental concerns and dangers are included in the articles on *Nuclear Energy, Pesticides, Fuel,* and *Water.* The subject of world population increase and what it portends is particularly well done and graphically illustrated. The fuel and energy crisis is barely mentioned, however, and there is no separate article or mention in other articles of endangered species of birds and animals. The article, *Eagle,* for instance, does not tell of its endangered status.

The coverage of race problems and

minority concerns is spotty. No article is present which summarizes and consolidates information on contemporary ethnic awareness and current minority rights movements in the United States. *Civil Rights* gives only brief attention to minority rights and makes no mention of Chicano or native American struggles of recent years. In fact, nowhere in the encyclopedia is there an article on Mexican-Americans, their culture, contributions, and concerns or on movement leaders such as Cesar Chavez. *Indians, North American* concludes with a brief paragraph on the increasing self-awareness of American Indians. This is the only mention in the set of present-day Indian rights efforts. No articles appear on Indian organizations such as the American Indian Movement nor any mention anywhere of such personalities as Russell Means, Vine DeLoria, Jr., or LaDonna Harris. *Negroes, American,* on the other hand, is a rather complete and balanced presentation of the Black struggle for freedom and equality, including both a historical record and a discussion of current trends and problems. Separate short biographical entries appear for many Black Americans. These include such historical figures as W. E. B. DuBois, Frederick Douglass, Booker T. Washington, George Washington Carver, and Mary M. Bethune, as well as more recent and contemporary persons as Ralph Bunche, James Farmer, Malcolm X, Marian Anderson, Eldridge Cleaver, Robert C. Weaver, Thurgood Marshall, Gwendolyn Brooks, and Medgar Evers. There are, as well, separate articles on the Black Panthers, Black Muslims, NAACP, CORE, and other organizations related to the Black movement. In spite of adequate treatment given Black American history, the overall emphasis accorded minority and ethnic peoples and concerns is minimal.

Housing, City, and *Transportation* give adequate attention to the problems of urban sprawl, economic stress, governmental planning and coordination, slums, suburban out-migration, traffic control, and other complexities of urbanization as well as dealing with present efforts to confront these problems and possibilities for the future.

Subjects related to the general topic of sex are treated frankly and objectively. Articles appear for *Abortion, Birth Control, Prostitution,* and *Homosexuality* (although no mention is made of the Gay Liberation Movement). These articles are marked by carefully balanced presentations on issues about which there tends to be disagreement, such as public sentiment toward abortion and prostitution and promotion of birth control as governmental policy. *Sex* contains a particularly carefully written discussion of changing sexual mores. *Reproduction* presents human reproduction in a clear if somewhat clinical fashion with adequate drawings of male and female sex organs.

The articles on drugs, drug abuse, and drug treatment are especially informative and complete, though quite concise. Under *Drug Abuse* each category of drug misuse is described, including types of drugs and effects. A summary of current drug laws and the various efforts toward rehabilitation are presented. Separate short entries appear for *Amphetamines, Hallucinogenic Drugs, Barbituates,* and *Marijuana.*

Biographical entries both of contemporary persons and of historical figures appear frequently throughout the set. However, most of these entries are brief thumbnail identifications comprised merely of several sentences. Helpfully, most biographical sketches, despite their brevity, are accompanied by a small photograph, painting, or drawing of the biographee. A major biographical entry with several illustrations appears for each American president. These are especially well written and given full-dimensional accounts of the life and presidential records of each man. No other articles of such length appear for other persons, living or dead. Such contemporary world figures as Mao Tse-tung, Willy Brandt, Henry Kissinger, Golda Meir, and Fidel Castro, for example, receive disappointingly short entries of a few paragraphs each.

Sports, games, and hobbies are treated in a cursory fashion. There are no articles or cross reference entries for Sports, Hobbies, Games, or Recreation. Individual sports are treated but quite briefly. The short articles on *Baseball* and *Football,* for instance, present a brief history of each game and some of the basic rules, but do not discuss strategy or playing techniques. The article on *Badminton* consists of four sentences and the *Tennis* entry, while longer (four paragraphs), contains no discussion of professional tennis. The half-page article, *Olympic Games,* gives no lists of records or olympic sites.

In addition to the absence of a general entry for hobbies, individual popular hobbies are either not treated at all or given only the briefest of coverage. For example, there is no entry for models or model building, toys, gardening, needlework, rock collecting, sewing, or leather work. *Fishing* receives three paragraphs and *Hunting* less than a page. *Weaving* and *Photography* do not present material from a hobbyist's point of view, but rather emphasize the historical and commercial aspects of each. *Handicrafts* is a one-paragraph entry which contains cross-references to *Basket Weaving, Carpentry, Ceramics, Embroidery,* and *Knitting.* Each of these articles in turn is very short, unillustrated (except *Embroidery*), and contain little of help to the hobbyist. *Stamp Collecting* is given a half-column entry without illustration.

The library edition of *Harver World Encyclopedia* is bound in lightweight dark blue buckram with gold lettering on covers and spines. The volumes, though rather tightly bound, lie reasonably flat when opened. The volume number and letter sequence is on each spine; however, the letter sequence at the base of each spine is unnecessarily small in size and difficult to read from more than a foot away.

Harver World Encyclopedia is clearly written, carefully and abundantly illustrated, up to date, and accurate in its data. It is weakened, however, by lack of adequate map coverage, by absence of user aids such as explanatory material on use of the set, study guides, or pronunciation keys, by uncertainty of the authority and identification of its contributors, and by brevity of treatment of most subjects. It is uneven in its coverage, devoting less than adequate attention to literature, fine arts, and biography in particular. Its claim of emphasis on movements and personalities of the modern world is not uniformly verified upon examination, although the emphasis it claims for science and technology, religion, and social sciences is apparent. Above all, it is inadequate as a general encyclopedia because of its lack of an index and the absence of bibliographical references. Because of these shortcomings particularly, it cannot at present be recommended for homes or libraries. Final evaluation of *Harver World Encyclopedia* will have to await the promised publication of an index volume with bibliographies. *(April 1, 1974, p.830)*

Historic Documents 1972. Compiled by Editors of Congressional Quarterly and Editorial Research Reports. Washington, DC, Congressional Quarterly, Inc., 1973. xxv, 987p. 25cm. Roxite B (cloth) $25. ISBN 0-87187-043-6.

Congressional Quarterly Service and Editorial Research Reports have compiled the first of a planned annual compendium of speeches, government reports, treaties, and court decisions which the Foreword indicates is "intended to provide students, scholars, librarians, journalists and citizens with convenient access to the raw materials of contemporary history."

Historic Documents 1972 contains the texts or excerpts of more than 150 documents covering 97 events. The term "documents" is applied broadly since materials included are not restricted to official government publications. The editors state that the texts and the excerpts of excessively long documents follow the sequence, capitalization, and punctuation of the original sources. Omissions from the original texts are indicated by the traditional ellipsis marks.

Contents range from extensive documentation of foreign relations (Peking summit conference, meetings with Japanese Prime Ministers Sato and Tanaka, troop withdrawals from Vietnam, re-escalation of the Vietnam War, Vietcong peace plans, presidential addresses by South Vietnam's Thieu, Chile's Allende,

Mexico's Echeverria, and the World Bank's Robert S. McNamara) to education (U.S. District Court decision ordering a desegregation plan for the Richmond, Virginia metropolitan area, viewpoints on busing by President Nixon and Florida's Governor Askew, and the final report of the President's Commission on School Finance) to economic matters, environmental considerations, drugs, health, the political scene (platforms of the American, Democratic, and Republican parties, and the Eagleton affair), and security (highlighted by the Anderson and Ellsberg papers). Admiral Zumwalt's order directing that Navy women be prepared for assignments to warships and combat planes illustrates progress in attaining equal rights for women.

Each entry is preceded by a brief Introduction intended to place the document in perspective. Most of these introductory comments include a description of the reaction to or effects of the action. This feature should become increasingly useful in years to come as recall dims. Necessarily interpretive, the Introductions seem balanced and useful. The authority expected from this publisher is maintained.

The documents are arranged chronologically by date of event. Some exceptions to the chronological arrangement are made in order to keep together material pertaining to a single topic; for example, the SALT talks and the Moscow Summit reports dated May 22-30 have excerpts from June 15 briefings to Congress by Nixon and Kissinger.

Access to the contents is available by three separate methods: (1) a Summary Table of Contents for those who know in which month a report was released; (2) a Comprehensive Table of Contents for those who need more detailed descriptions to locate a particular document in the sequential arrangement; (3) a 15-page, double-column Subject Index with *see* and *see also* references. These aids provide more than adequate guides to the contents of the volume. The editors promise a five-year cumulative index to future volumes.

For some unexplained reason references to material in the section on the Eagleton affair are two pages off in the Table of Contents and in the Index; however, the overall quality of this publication is excellent, typographically and physically. Margins are wide and the book stays open at any page being used. *Historic Documents 1972* is an invaluable companion to the retrospective works of Henry Steele Commager. However, additional, easily noticeable bibliographic data similar to that offered in Commager's *Documents of American History* is needed.

All types of libraries will find *Historic Documents* most useful as a reference volume to search for authoritative materials. *(Feb. 15, 1974, p.607)*

History of American Presidential Elections, 1789-1968. Arthur M. Schlesinger, Jr., ed.; Fred L. Israel, associate ed.; William P. Hansen, managing ed. 4v. New York, Chelsea House Publishers in Association with McGraw-Hill Book Co., 1971. xxxvii, 3959p. 24cm. buckram $135; to schools and libraries, usual discount.

Since the last edition of E. M. Stanwood's *History of the Presidency* (Boston: Houghton Mifflin Co., 1928) which contained additions and revisions to 1928, no comprehensive history of American presidential elections has been published. Although Rosenbloom's *History of Presidential Elections* (New York: Macmillan, 1957) is more up to date, it does not supersede *Stanwood* as a convenient source of information. The four volumes under review now provide an analytical and narrative description of each presidential election through 1968. Each of these descriptive essays is followed by an appendix containing enriching and illuminating materials on the election discussed. In the Prefatory Note the editors state: "[These] volumes do not profess to be the definitive study of American presidential elections. . . . Our goal has been to provide a comprehensive history, written by prominent historians and political scientists." The editors further declare that they "have aimed at Edward Stanwood's goal—to record 'the circumstances of such elections, and of whatever had an appreciable influence upon the result.'"

The editor, Arthur M. Schlesinger, Jr., well-known American historian, had as his associate editor another American historian, Fred L. Israel. Forty-five outstanding historians and political scientists contributed the essays. Credentials for each writer are given at the bottom of the page facing the beginning of his essay. A check of the credentials shows that each has written about a period he is qualified to discuss. For example, Page Smith, who discusses the election of 1796, has written a two-volume biography of John Adams; Charles Sellers, who has written two volumes on James K. Polk, contributes the account of Polk's election to the presidency in 1844. In two instances two elections are covered in one essay: elections of 1789 and 1792 and elections of 1816 and 1820.

As related by the editors, the contributors had the assignment of both analyzing a particular election and selecting relevant documents to support their theses so that each essay is an entity. Since one essay does not actually build on the preceding one, perspectival or overall view of changes in the political processes, including influence of ethnic and religious groups, is lacking. Schlesinger's Introduction, "Presidential Elections and the Party System," is an attempt to survey the evolution of major political parties, but the brevity of the essay makes the comprehensive discussion one might expect in a work of this magnitude impossible. Schlesinger's account of the growth and influence of presidential primaries does, however, furnish interesting information.

The variety of style and analytical technique in the essays is due to the fact that each essay has a different author, and each author a unique style. Each essay is a factual and interestingly written account of the four years between presidential elections. In addition to the narrative analysis of the elections, many of the essays contain excerpts from letters, speeches, and newspaper articles. Tables, resolutions, slogans, verses, songs, or diaries are used effectively to illustrate and point up the issues of the campaigns. None of the essays has references or footnotes which would have been useful to a person engaged in research.

Appended to each essay is a series of documents selected by the author to illustrate and support his thesis and to present additional information on the election just analyzed. Contents and number of documents included vary greatly. For example, the Appendix to the Elections of 1789 and 1792 contains six letters, excerpts from three letters, Presidential Power as provided in the Constitution in 1787, 1804, 1969, and a Personal Memorandum. The Appendix to the Election of 1804 includes only three items: two platforms and a table showing electoral vote. Nine of the fifteen items in the Appendix to the Election of 1808 are newspaper articles or editorials, and 12 newspaper editorials are among the 20 documents appended to the Election of 1892. By contrast four platforms are included in the Appendix to the Election of 1860 plus nine statistical tables, and among the documents appended to the Election of 1900 are two telephone conversations. With two exceptions, electoral vote is the last item in each Appendix; it is included as part of the text of the essay on the elections of 1789 and 1792 and the election of 1840. Beginning with the Election of 1824, popular vote is also given, and from the Election of 1840 onward, party platforms are included in all appendixes. However, the documents to the Election of 1804 also include two party platforms.

Herbert E. Alexander contributed the concluding essay, "Financing Presidential Campaigns." Author of two books on financing elections, Alexander gives various methods used to raise money, tells how it is spent, and discusses the increasing costs of presidential campaigns. Among other tables included in the essay is one showing Costs of Presidential Elections, 1860-1968 for the two major political parties.

Following Alexander's essay is a presidential chronology arranged under the following topics: president and political party, date of birth and date of death, age at inauguration, native state,

state elected from, religion, service, and vice president.

An excellent Bibliography, "Selected Titles on Presidential Elections," gives first a list of 10 general books with a brief description of each. An annotated list in narrative form cites books on each presidential election. Included are basic older titles, definitive editions of presidents' papers, and imprints through 1969.

At the beginning of volume 1 there is a Table of Contents for the set; each of the other volumes contains only its own. All supporting documents are listed with the page on which they appear.

Concluding the set is a useful 40-page subject Index with a number of *see* and *see also* references. A check, which failed to reveal any blind references, did show a number of omissions. For example, the Index gives three page references for William C. Whitney, active in both of Cleveland's campaigns, but he is mentioned from one to six times on at least sixteen other pages. There is only one page reference for Matthew S. Quay, active in the election of 1888, and it is in the concluding essay in the set. Quay is named on numerous pages, and on one page two paragraphs are devoted entirely to him. No reference is made in the Index to the Sackville-West episode in the 1888 campaign, although this is discussed in the essay. Several helpful features of the Index should be noted: the inclusion under each presidential election of the issues in that election, specific references to presidential candidacy under the names of all those nominated for that office by the various parties, and across each double page of the Index a running heading of inclusive paging of each of the four volumes.

The set is attractively and sturdily bound in dark blue Ontario buckram. Type is used effectively on coated paper to provide optimum legibility. The volumes lie flat when open. Pagination is continuous through the four volumes.

While not intended to be definitive, *History of American Presidential Elections, 1789-1968* is a straightforward factual account of events, issues and campaigns in the elections, together with excerpts from reprints of the pertinent documents. Contributors of the essays are historians and political scientists highly qualified in their special areas of interest, and although the style and analytical technique of each are different, each essay presents important information in an interesting manner. Documents selected by each contributor are relevant and provide a good beginning for students researching the presidential elections. Recommended. *(Dec. 15, 1972, p.365)*

History of U.S. Political Parties. General ed., Arthur M. Schlesinger, Jr. 4v. New York, Chelsea House Publishers in association with R. R. Bowker, 1973. liv. 3544p. 25cm. cloth $135. ISBN 0-8352-0594-0.

History of U.S. Political Parties is a chronologically arranged collection of 26 essays, each accompanied by an appendix containing pertinent source material. The set is described in the publisher's release as detailing the history and contributions of political parties to American politics. The editor, Pulitzer Prizewinning historian Arthur M. Schlesinger, Jr., is currently the Albert Schweitzer Professor in the Humanities at City University of New York. Professor Schlesinger, in his 21-page introduction, surveys the evolution of the party system in this country and comments briefly on the essays which follow. He does not, however, enlighten the reader as to the scope or purpose of the set.

The essays are written by authorities, most of whom are professors of history. They include such well-known historians as Richard C. Wade, City University of New York; George B. Tindall, Kenan Professor of History, University of North Carolina; and David H. Donald, Charles Warren Professor of American History, Harvard.

The essays average some 30-odd pages in length. A few are documented with footnotes. Seven essays covering about 215 pages are devoted to the history of the Democratic Party. The Republican Party is covered in about the same number of pages, in six essays.

The histories of the Antimasonic and Know Nothing parties are combined in one essay as are the histories of the Liberty and Free Soil parties, the Greenback and Prohibition parties, and the Progressive and States' Rights parties of 1948. A single essay is devoted to each of the other parties.

Most of the set is comprised of documentary material gathered in the appendixes. These vary in length but average about 100 pages. They contain a variety of material such as party platforms, campaign and acceptance speeches, messages to Congress, reports of convention proceedings, letters, and excerpts from newspapers, magazines, books, and pamphlets. The content of the appendixes is not, however, consistent. These materials, while self-explanatory in most instances, are generally presented without comment.

A bibliographical note concludes each appendix. These are usually no more than half a page, although a few are longer. To a noticeable extent they reflect very recent scholarship.

Each volume has a table of contents; the table in volume I covers the entire set. The bibliographical notes, unfortunately, are not listed in the contents tables.

A 44-page Index appears at the end of volume IV. References in the Index are to page numbers only, although the volumes are continuously paged. The inclusive pagination of the volumes appears at the top of the pages, apparently to facilitate location. The Index contains some *see* and *see also* references. It appears to be reasonably accurate and to cover the contents of the essays satisfactorily, but it contains comparatively few references to the contents of the appendixes.

The essays are written with candor. In this regard, however, there may be those who will question the choice of Lee W. Huebner, a founder and former president of the Ripon Society and until recently a special assistant to President Nixon, to write "The Republican Party, 1952-1972" or the choice of Professor Wade, a state campaign manager for presidential candidates Kennedy and McGovern, to write "The Democratic Party, 1960-1972."

While these essays provide highly readable political history, they are much too brief to provide the "comprehensive," "definitive history" heralded in the publisher's release. Obviously party history on the national, state, and local level cannot be covered in essays of this brevity. It is disappointing that in a work of this size the history of any two parties, even minor ones, must be combined into one essay. It is regretted also that the bibliographical notes are not more comprehensive.

This set resembles the similarly arranged four-volume *History of American Presidential Elections, 1789-1968* (New York: Chelsea House, 1971) edited by Professor Schlesinger and F. L. Israel (see *The Booklist*, Dec. 15, 1972). There is some duplication in the appendix material contained in these two sets. As for that matter, much of the appendix material may be available in some libraries already. Nevertheless it is convenient to have this material together, and the set should be useful to libraries with less extensive United States history collections.

The format of the volumes is satisfactory. The print is clear and the paper glare free. The margins are wide enough to permit rebinding. The dates of the coverage of each volume are prominently marked on the spine. Some errors in typography were noted. The volumes are quite heavy, but the binding appears sturdy.

History of U.S. Political Parties provides a short, authoritative history which includes a large amount of primary source materials in convenient form. In view of the expense of the set, libraries with modest budgets should consider their need for the appendix materials, as well as the brevity of the histories, before purchase. Recommended. *(June 15, 1974, p. 1112)*

House and Garden's Antiques: Questions and Answers. [By] Louise Ade Boger. New York, Simon and Schuster [c1968-1973]. viii, 429p. 23cm. illus. $9.95. ISBN 0-394-48811-3.

Both *The Collectors' Encyclopedia of Antiques* and *The Random House Encyclopedia of Antiques* are American editions of works compiled in England and issued there under English imprints. (The English edition of *The Random House Encyclopedia* is entitled *Collins Encyclopedia of Antiques*).

The *Random House Encyclopedia* was edited by Ian Cameron and Elizabeth Kingsley-Rowe. Neither is further identified in the work; nor are identifications provided for the 11 staff members or the 14 editorial consultants listed on the first page of the volume. Although the latter are termed "specialists," their areas of specialization are not indicated. The only person associated with the work for whom identification is provided is John Pope-Hennessy, Director of the British Museum, who wrote the three-page Introduction.

Each of the 35 contributors to the *Collectors' Encyclopedia of Antiques* is identified except for the editor, Phoebe Phillips, who contributed the section on Roman and Venetian glass. Likewise unidentified is the Associate Editor for Great Britain, David Coombs. Coombs is deputy editor of *The Connoisseur*. The Associate Editor for the United States, Joseph Butler, is Curator of Sleepy Hollow Restoration, Tarrytown, New York; Adjunct Associate Professor of Architecture at Columbia University; and American Editor of *The Connoisseur*. Contributors range from collectors and dealers to professors and museum officials, the latter accounting for more than any other group. Ten of the contributors are Americans.

Both volumes have been compiled primarily for collectors, although the scope of the two works differs slightly. Coverage in *The Random House Encyclopedia* extends from the beginning of the Renaissance to 1875. Exceptions are made for Islamic areas and the Far East, for which treatment of important earlier periods was considered essential. *The Collectors' Encyclopedia* places its main emphasis on the eighteenth and nineteenth centuries, "where the examples illustrated will be of greatest value to collectors in identification." Earlier periods are represented, however, by "objects which show the historical background of each craft, since their traditional skills often extend into antiquity"; and in a few cases modern pieces have been included "where innovations have occurred which still use the old skills."

The Random House Encyclopedia omits coverage of coins and medals, dolls and children's playthings, needlework, militaria, and ethnographica, and provides only incidental coverage of several other areas (e.g., architects when they have influenced furniture styles.) *The Collectors' Encyclopedia* includes a number of the categories omitted from *Random House* (e.g., arms and armour, embroidery and needlework, toys and automata).

The Random House Encyclopedia is designed for ready reference and includes more than 5,000 entries arranged in alphabetical order. The entries range from two lines to about a page in length with entries of under 15 lines predominating. Entries run the gamut from generic terms (e.g., *Ceramics*) through types (*Earthenware, Stoneware, Porcelain*) to specific examples (*Staffordshire, Jasper ware, Meissen*). Other types of entries cover numerous objects; styles and stylistic details; designers, craftsmen, and manufacturers; and centers of production. The last named are also shown on a series of six black-and-white outline maps which precede the text. Appendixes include reproductions of some of the ceramic and silver marks mentioned in the encyclopedia and a bibliography.

The Collectors' Encyclopedia is divided into 16 sections, each of which is devoted to a single category of antiques (e.g., Clocks, Watches and Barometers; Furniture; Glass; Silver). Each section is intended to provide a survey of the category which it covers and includes a Table of Contents, an Introduction, and one or more articles by the specialist contributors previously mentioned. The articles are followed by a Glossary, information on maintenance and repair, a Bibliography, a listing of major museum collections in Great Britain and the United States, and an Index to the section. The sections covering ceramics, furniture, and glass are the longest, each being slightly over 100 pages in length. Other sections range from 66 pages (Silver) to 14 pages (Musical Instruments). The larger sections are divided geographically. The geographical divisions vary in accordance with the contributions made by different areas to the subjects covered in the encyclopedia. Thus, the section on ceramics includes separate articles on Chinese and Korean ceramics while the section on glass provides separate coverage of Roman and Venetian glass.

English and Continental antiques generally receive more attention than American antiques, but one would expect this to be the case in a work compiled in England. A reasonable balance is maintained in most sections of *Collectors'*, but there are some exceptions. American furniture is covered in 16 pages, while 45 pages are devoted to English furniture and 40 to Continental furniture (including the separate section on French furniture). The examples of American furniture which are included do not seem to be sufficiently representative of the history of the subject. American pottery and porcelain also seem to receive unduly brief treatment.

The Random House Encyclopedia depends on extensive cross-references to direct the user to entries related to the one which he has consulted. The 225-word article on American clocks, for example, contains 25 cross-references. If the user read each of these articles, he would be directed to eight additional articles relating to American clocks. Thus, information from a total of 34 articles is made accessible through the main article on the subject. Cross-references were, however, omitted for ogee and looking glass clocks, both of which are treated in separate entries.

The entry on Seth Thomas fails to note that an example of his workmanship is shown in the article on wall clocks; nor does the caption for this picture indicate that the encyclopedia includes an article on the maker of the Clock. The article on Seth Thomas includes a cross-reference to Eli Terry, with whom Thomas was associated, but the article on Terry does not include a reciprocal reference.

Similarly, the article on toleware concludes with the reference, *"See* tôle," but the tôle article lacks a similar reference to "toleware," the entry under which American examples of tôle are discussed. The article on the Boston and Sandwich Glass Company directs the user to a non-existent entry for Sandwich glass.

The Collectors' Encyclopedia, in which each section is organized as a virtually independent unit, contains relatively few cross-references. Only 18 cross-references were found in the 56-page section on clocks, watches, and barometers, and only five of these direct the user to information in other sections of the encyclopedia. Most of the cross-references direct the reader to illustrations.

Because of the specificity of entry utilized in *The Random House Encyclopedia,* the work does not include an index. As previously noted, each section of *The Collectors' Encyclopedia* concludes with its own index. The entries in the section indexes refer primarily to the illustrations and do not include proper names. Of the 278 references in the index to the section on clocks, watches, and barometers, all except two refer to illustrations.

Indexing appears to be incomplete and inconsistent. Of the 32 illustrations on the pages devoted to American clocks, only 13 were located in the section Index. (This figure does not include the entry under the broad term "wooden-cased clocks," under which 24 of the illustrations were listed.) No references were found to the illustrations of such distinctive types as the acorn clock and the beehive clock. While about half the illustrations depict shelf clocks, the index reference under that term refers only to the pillar and scroll shelf clock on page 244 (and there is no index entry for "pillar and scroll"). Although the term "gothic" is used in the descriptions of four of the American clocks illustrated (and applies to one other), the index references under "gothic clocks" refer only to Swiss and Dutch examples. The entry under "cottage style clock" refers only to the German imitation of this American style. The picture of the American prototype is not indexed; nor do cross-references link the two illustrations.

Similar inadequacies were noted in

the Index to the section on furniture. Thirty-three of the 65 references under "*chairs*" are lumped under the uninformative subheading "Other." While there is a separate index entry for *candlestand*, lamp stand is included under "Tables—other." Highboys are sublisted under "Chests," with no cross-reference from the specific term. Two of the three index references under "*Chairs, Windsor*" are incorrect. The first leads the user to an illustration of a seventeenth-century elm chest and the second to a picture of a Chippendale settee. (In the first reference, two digits of the page number were transposed.)

What is described in the Introduction as a main index to the volume is actually an index of proper names only. Failure to indicate the limitations of this index is likely to cause difficulty for the user, especially since a few subject entries based on proper names have been included in the index (e.g., majolica, Staffordshire pottery).

While both *Random House* and *Collectors'* are profusely illustrated, *The Collectors' Encyclopedia* places greater emphasis on illustration. Illustrations in *Collectors'* occupy a larger portion of the volume and are generally larger in size. There are many full-page illustrations. While the proportion of colored to black-and-white illustrations is higher in *The Random House* volume, the 64 pages of colored illustrations in *The Collectors' Encyclopedia* are printed on glossy stock and are, therefore, much more effective. The quality of the colored and black-and-white illustrations is generally on a high level. Integration between the illustrations and the text is provided through the extensive captions which accompany the black-and-white photographs, by means of which much of the detailed information in the encyclopedia is conveyed.

About half of the 1,000 illustrations in *The Random House Encyclopedia* are in color. Most of the illustrations are small, ranging up to half a page in size. There are no full-page illustrations. Illustrations are, for the most part, sufficiently clear for identification purposes and usually large enough to show a fair amount of detail, but there is some variation in quality. Illustrations are well-integrated with the text and are adequately captioned.

The eight-page bibliography in *The Random House Encyclopedia* includes more than 550 books and is current through 1972. Books of English origin predominate, but there is a fair representation of American titles, and some English translations of works originally written in other languages are included. The Bibliography is not annotated.

Books are listed under very specific headings in many cases, and no mechanism for relating the various headings pertaining to a broad category of antiques is provided. The 57 books on clocks and watches are, for example, found under 17 different headings. A cross-reference under *watches* directs the user to look under *clocks* for titles covering both subjects, and a cross-reference under *chronometers* refers one to the name of a craftsman who contributed to their development. These were the only cross-references noted in the entire bibliography. Users must, therefore, scan the entire bibliography to be sure of locating all the headings pertaining to a subject or of finding the specific headings under which books treating particular aspects of the subject are listed.

Separate bibliographies are provided for each of the 16 sections of *The Collectors' Encyclopedia*. A total of about 665 books is listed, ranging from 78 in the bibliography for ceramics to 17 in the listing for jewellery. A good representation of recent items was noted along with several standard works in European languages other than English. Bibliographies are arranged in accordance with the main divisions of the text for each section. Entries are not annotated and publishers' names are not included in the citations.

House and Garden Antiques: Questions and Answers was compiled by Louise Ade Boger, coauthor with her husband H. Batterson Boger, of *The Dictionary of Antiques and the Decorative Arts* and author of *The Complete Guide to Furniture Styles, Furniture Past and Present,* and *The Dictionary of World Pottery and Porcelain.*

For the past several years Mrs. Boger has conducted a monthly column, "Antiques: Questions and Answers," in *House and Garden Magazine,* and the present work is a collection of the most interesting questions and answers which have appeared in her column. The book is addressed primarily to those readers of the column who expressed interest in obtaining previous installments, but the publishers stress the value of the work to others who are interested in antiques.

The column serves primarily as a means of identifying antiques and of conveying a variety of information concerning the items about which readers have inquired. Readers submit photographs along with their questions, and Mrs. Boger provides the required identification and comments on noteworthy features of the object.

The questions and answers have been divided into 17 categories. The 5 principal ones are Furniture (133 pages), Pottery and Porcelain (85 pages), Silver (43 pages), Glass (15 pages), and Clocks and Watches (34 pages). These main categories are subdivided geographically. The remaining categories, most of which are only a few pages in length, cover pewter, musical instruments, pictures, sculpture, lighting, heating equipment, toys and games, objects on wheels, weapons, food service, utility items, and decorative and useful objects.

Within each category or subdivision similar items are usually grouped together and arranged in approximate chronological order, but there are some exceptions to this practice. There seems to be no discernible pattern in the section on American clocks and watches, and the tables illustrated in the section on American furniture do not seem to be arranged in any particular order.

Each question and answer is accompanied by a small black-and-white photograph of the object to which the question relates. The photographs were supplied by the inquirers and the quality varies widely. Most are adequate for purposes of identification but not large enough to show much detail. In some cases, however, the photographs are so poor that they fail to convey an adequate idea of the objects which they depict (e.g., the Augustus Rogers teakettle on page 240 and the Victorian secretary on page 82).

While the question and answer format is no doubt appropriate for the author's monthly column, its effectiveness in the present instance is debatable. Does the reader really care that the English teapot illustrated on page 207 was given to the inquirer's mother 40 years ago by her great aunt, or that someone's mother bought the Davenport desk shown on page 144 at an auction in British Columbia? The space devoted to the questions might have been put to better use by giving more information about the objects pictured or by providing an index to the volume.

An unannotated Bibliography of 200 "interesting and standard reference books" follows the final section of the volume. The Bibliography is divided into nine parts and includes, in addition to general works on antiques, separate listings of books on furniture, pottery and porcelain, silver, pewter, glass, clocks and watches, and other subjects. Most of the works listed have been published within the past 25 years, but standard older works are also included.

While Mrs. Boger's replies to her readers' inquiries include much useful and interesting information, it is accessible only through reading or browsing in the text as the volume includes neither an index nor cross-references. The work is, therefore, recommended only for libraries requiring a volume devoted primarily to the identification of antiques.

Libraries looking for a ready reference volume on antiques may wish to consider *The Random House Encyclopedia* because of the ease with which the user can locate information on a wide variety of specific subjects. Any library considering the encyclopedia should, however, be aware of the manufacturing deficiencies of the volume. Owing largely to the very heavy stock on which the book is printed, the 400-page volume weighs over five pounds and is nearly as heavy as *The Collectors' Encyclopedia* which is 300 pages longer. More serious from the librarian's standpoint is the quality of the binding, which does not appear to be of sufficient strength for the weight of the volume. The bindings on all the copies received by the Reference and Subscription Books Review Committee were damaged in transit, and in one instance the pages became almost completely detached from the casing as a result of the use which the copy received in the course of preparing this review. Rebinding would be difficult owing to the narrow inner margins (approximately one-half inch). Because of these drawbacks, the volume cannot be given an unqualified recommendation.

Although the content is not so well arranged for reference purposes, *The Collector's Encyclopedia* is better suited for library purchase. The volume is attractive, and the binding is sufficiently strong to withstand heavy use. The inner margins are wide enough to permit rebinding. In spite of inadequacies of the cross-references and indexing, the encyclopedia is recommended as a useful survey of the principal fields of antiques' collecting. *(July 1, 1974, p.1158)*

The Illustrated Encyclopedia of the Animal Kingdom. 20v. [Danbury, CT], Danbury Pr. (A Division of Grolier Enterprises, Inc.), 1972. 2,372p. illus. (part col.) col. maps. diagrs. tables. 28cm. Roxite cloth $99.50 (U.S.); $109.50 including shipping (Canada).

The Illustrated Encyclopedia of the Animal Kingdom is not so much an encyclopedia as it is a profusely illustrated descriptive text on zoology. It is intended for use by the elementary or secondary school student and the lay person not trained in science. *The Illustrated Encyclopedia of the Animal Kingdom* had its origin as an Italian publication entitled *Gli Animali e il Loro Mondo,* prepared under the editorial supervision of Antonio Valle, director of the Museum of Natural Sciences at Bergamo. A first English-language translation was edited by Percy Knauth; the present edition, referred to as "second English edition" by its publishers (but not in the work itself) was prepared by Herbert Kondo and Jenny Tesar, members of the Grolier staff. The text of the present edition has been checked for accuracy by a number of qualified zoologists at the American Museum of Natural History, including Dean Amadon (Ornithology), J.A.L. Cooke (Entomology), W. E. Old (Invertebrates), J. C. Pallister (Entomology), L. L. Short (Ornithology), C. Lavett Smith (Ichthyology), Richard G. Van Gelder (Mammalogy), and Richard G. Ziefel (Herpetology). A considerable number of the illustrations of the original Italian publication have been retained, with captions and general text freely revised and amended for an English-speaking readership. However, a large number of American illustrations are used.

The arrangement of *The Illustrated Encyclopedia of the Animal Kingdom* is unusual. Eschewing the conventional practice of starting with the one-celled "primitive" animalcules and working up to the mammals in a progression through the phyla based upon increasing complexity, *The Illustrated Encyclopedia of the Animal Kingdom* starts with the vertebrates and goes down the phyla to the lower invertebrates. The reason, related to the presumed readership, is "the desire to engage and hold the reader's interest by treating first the animals that are most familiar to him." The resulting order is as follows: *Introduction to Vertebrates* (v.1), *Mammals* (v.2-6), *Birds* (v.7-8), *Reptiles and Reptiles/Amphibians* (v.9-10), *Fishes* (v.11), *Arthropods* (v.12-13), *Arthropods: Insects* (v.14-16), *Mollusks* (v.17), *Lesser Invertebrates* (v.18-19), and *Endangered Species/Index* (v.20). "Endangered Species" consists of an essay of five pages and reproductions of full-page colored paintings of some 48 endangered species, executed by Helmut Diller.

Within each animal group the following topics are discussed: anatomy (including embryology and physiology), environment, behavior patterns, relation to man, and classification and description of specific groups. The description of specific groups may range from an individual species, with extended treatment of those most familiar, e.g., the domestic dog, cat, or horse, to whole phyla (the lower invertebrates).

The writing is simple, clear, and consciously directed toward children or those unfamiliar with biology. Scientific names and terms are avoided whenever possible in favor of common names and terms.

The illustrations are, of course, a main feature of *The Illustrated Encyclopedia of the Animal Kingdom;* there are approximately five thousand photographs, black-and-white drawings, maps, charts, and diagrams, of which over three thousand are four-color photographs. Altogether, the illustrations account for over 60 percent of the total page space of *The Illustrated Encyclopedia of the Animal Kingdom.* The general quality is very high; many are of spectacular beauty.

Each of the first 19 volumes has its own Index; these separate indexes are cumulated in an Index of larger typeface in volume 20. The indexing is not detailed. In general, common names of animals are indexed, as are the names of animal groups, illustrations, and topics mentioned. Scientific names of individual animals are indexed only when no common-name equivalent is mentioned. The cumulated Index appears to include all the single-volume index entries; their form may be altered however. For instance, names consisting of a noun and an adjective, e.g., *crested argus* and *collared hemipode,* appear in the individual volume Index in that form, but appear in inverted form, e.g., *argus, crested* and *hemipode, collared,* in the cumulated Index. No cross-reference from the unused form appear in either Index. The cumulated Index is illustrated with uncaptioned colored photographs to no apparent end. Index references to illustrations have page numbers cited in italics in both volume and cumulated indexes. The type font selected for the cumulated Index, however, has a very understated italic form—the difference between roman and italic is less striking than it should be for easy differentiation.

The 20 volumes of *The Illustrated Encyclopedia of the Animal Kingdom* are each about $9/16$ of an inch thick, and are bound in cloth with a sewed binding, headbands, and reinforced endpapers. The volumes open to an adequate flatness. A large colored illustration appears on the front cover of each volume. The volumes appear to be reasonably sturdy.

Some carelessness in editing is apparent. Although no specific search for errors and misprints was made, several were noted in the course of general examination. "Cornrake" is used in place of "corncrake" as a name for the common European rail; "Zoraptera" and "Zoroptera" are used interchangeably; and "Class Crustacean" is used for "Class Crustacea."

The Illustrated Encyclopedia of the Animal Kingdom will inevitably be compared with *International Wildlife Encyclopedia* (*The Booklist* October 15, 1972) if for no other reason than that they are almost identical in size (20 thin volumes) and have a wealth of pictorial illustration. Here the similarity ends. *The International Wildlife Encyclopedia* emphasizes specific animals and animal groups slighting to some extent general treatment of zoological principles, whereas *Illustrated Encyclopedia of the Animal Kingdom* emphasizes the latter and gives somewhat less emphasis to descriptions of individual species or groups. The two encyclopedias are thus basically quite different.

Illustrated Encyclopedia of the Animal Kingdom, a beautifully and profusely illustrated survey of zoology and natural history, is intended for children or lay adult readers. As such, it is a well-produced work for popular consumption. Its potential value lies chiefly in its illustrations—and these, as mentioned earlier, are superb. To the extent to which such illustrated books are needed in the library or home, *The Illustrated Encyclopedia of the Animal Kingdon* is recommended. *(Oct. 15, 1973, p.181)*

The Illustrated Libraries of Human Knowledge. 18v. Columbus, OH, Charles E. Merrill Pub. Co., [c by Aldus Books Ltd., London, 1968]. illus. 27cm. cloth $137.50. Man in His World Library: Life, v.1; Space, v.2; Races and Cultures, v.3; The Ancients, v.4; Ages of Discovery, v.5; Modern History, v.6. Creative Man Library: Technology, v.1; The Creative Spirit, v.2; Search for Truth, v.3; Societies, v.4; Communication, v.5; The

Arts, v.6. Man and Science Library: Natural History, v.1; Science Applied, v.2; Chemical Universe, v.3; Motion, Matter and Energy, v.4; Earth, v.5. Index to Libraries: Omni-Topika.

The 17 volumes that make up *The Illustrated Libraries of Human Knowledge* are divided into three groups, easily distinguishable by the different colors of their spine bindings—six volumes entitled *Man in His World Library,* six volumes entitled *Creative Man Library,* and five volumes entitled *Man and Science Library.* The eighteenth volume is an Index, entitled *Omni-Topika,* and its spine is a bright red color. Each volume is magnificently illustrated, mostly in color, and each contains exactly 160 pages of glossy paper illustrations and text, as well as a 32-page Appendix printed on dull-finish paper and illustrated only with line drawings in black and white. Each volume is sturdily and uniformly bound, except for the three different colored spines mentioned above. Colored illustrations on the front covers differ for each volume, and were evidently chosen as being both pictorial and relevant to the contents of the volume (a photograph of the U.N. Secretariat building for the *Modern History* volume; a photograph of the Temple of the Emerald Buddha for the *Races and Cultures* volume.)

The illustrations are the best feature of the set. They are generally in color and placed two or three to a page, with occasional full-page illustrations on two-page spreads. These pictures include historical events, places, persons, natural scenery, agriculture, wild animals, machinery, dams, flowers, highways, flags of countries—anything that can be illustrated with a colored photograph. The volumes, therefore, resemble *New Caxton Encyclopedia,* with the difference that *Caxton* is an alphabetical encyclopedia, while the arrangement of the work under review is topical.

The editorial director of *Illustrated Libraries* is Sir Julian Huxley, identified in the volumes only as a Fellow of the Royal Society, but whose extensive achievements in various fields of endeavor are well-documented in standard biographical works. On page 160 of each volume is a list of 21 Consulting Editors, 17 of whom are identifiable as Americans, and 15 of whom are entered with the honorific Dr. in front of their names, and whose affiliations, mostly university or other professional, are all indicative of good scholarship or expertise. No specific attribution of any article or chapter in the set is made to these scholars however; nor is any part of the set, with the exception of the Appendixes, signed or initialed in any way.

In addition to the list of Consulting Editors, there is also an alphabetical list on page 160 of each volume, different for each volume, of the picture and chart credits. However, since the list is alphabetical by the name of the copyright owner, it becomes a tedious task to ascertain the source of any given illustration.

Careful examination of the text of these 17 volumes shows that the intent of the editors is to produce a summary of information on these manifold topics which will appeal, primarily through lavish pictorial illustration accompanying the text, to students and lay adults without special training or knowledge. The textual content is therefore summary in form, but meaty in substance. The treatment of information may be demonstrated by examining a typical volume, *The Arts*. Chapters are entitled Music, Dance, Poetry, Storytelling, Drama, and Film. Selecting the chapter Poetry, pages 57-83 for analysis, one sees that it is divided into the following subheads, usually a page or two each: Sound and Sense, Rhythm Patterns, Rhyme Patterns, Shaped Poetry, Free and Blank Verse, Lyric Poems, and Poems that Tell a Story. Each of these is illustrated by beautiful color photographs (among them one of a surfer with the surf just about to break over him, to illustrate the notion of crashing sound); a reproduction of the Introduction page to Blake's "Songs of Innocence," with its repetitive sound of the word "pipe"; a cartoon of the poet Gautier, a writer of quatrains; some shaped poems by Dylan Thomas, E.E. Cummings, and others; portraits of Robert Burns, Carl Sandburg, Walther von der Vogelweide, and other poets; and finally an illustration from Stothard's "Canterbury Pilgrims," a Beardsley drawing for Malory's "Morte d'Arthur," and a Greek vase depicting a scene that could have illustrated Homer's "Iliad" or Vergil's "Aeneid," or both, for the section Poems that Tell a Story.

The text accompanying these illustrations, less than one half of the 27 pages allotted to Poetry, is admittedly sparse. Many great poets are omitted, and of many whose names are mentioned (Catullus, D'Annunzio, Villon), almost nothing is told except their dates of birth and death. However, these 27 pages communicate the "essence" of poetry quite adequately.

The same evaluation could be made of any other small section of any of the 17 volumes in the set. Each volume is divided into 5 to 12 chapters, and each chapter is further divided into subheads, which may vary from 2 to 12 depending on the complexity of the topic being discussed. Each chapter contains, in its double-columned pages, approximately 60 percent illustrative matter (with colored photographs predominating), and the balance explanatory text, as was shown in the example selected above, Poetry. The text, with unjustified right margins, is written at about the level of junior high school students. Some of the illustrations and their accompanying captions seem to oversimplify. A photograph of an American Express credit card is used as an illustration on the verso of a title page. Its text reads: "An American Express credit card. Such cards enable the holder to buy now and pay later."

In general the editors present a reasonably fair and unbiased picture of historical events and of present-day life. Despite the fact that the editorial director is British and that the copyright is held by Aldus Books, Ltd. of London, there is no noticeable slant towards British examples or citations. On the contrary, the work seems aimed at the American public, with the majority of the illustrations depicting scenes or events in the United States. Names such as Harrisburg, John D. Rockefeller, Berkeley (as the location of a university), and Billy Graham, are mentioned in the text without qualifying expressions such as "in the United States," or "the American." On the other hand, samples of posters illustrating the harmful effects of smoking and of forest fires are shown from both England and the U.S. There is no outstanding majority of pictures of countries other than the U.S. There are photographs of life in England, Russia, Japan, underdeveloped countries in Asia, Africa, and almost every other part of the world, in about equal proportion, though it is understandable that certain volumes, such as the ones for *Communication, The Creative Spirit,* and *Modern History,* emphasize the European/American tradition, and give prominence to writings and other communication achievements which are in the English language.

The Appendixes, each 32 pages in length, and printed on non-glossy paper, differ considerably one from another. They are written at a slightly more sophisticated level and are about 55 percent illustrated, with black-and-white line drawings only. Credit is given at the end of each Appendix to the author or authors. The purpose of the Appendixes seems to be to consider one of the topics of the pertinent volume at greater length, or with a greater degree of sophistication, or else to provide tabular or statistical data to support the topics discussed in the main part of the volume. These Appendixes offer valuable additional information; unfortunately their content is not included in the general index volume, the *Omni-Topika;* nor are they self-indexed.

There are no bibliographies or reading lists of any kind, either following the chapters or in the Appendixes. It is therefore impossible to ascertain the authorities for any statements; nor can a reader find lists of additional books on a topic in which he is interested.

Omni-Topika, the index volume, is bound with a red spine to make it easily distinguishable from the other volumes in the set. It has a one-page introductory "How to Use this Index," which starts with these words: "This volume is much more than a conventional index. Each entry is defined or has basic factual information." There are about 5,100 entries in the Index, the majority of them proper names. Each is defined in about four or five lines. A typical example reads: "Aphrodite. The Greek goddess of love, beauty and fertility, identified by the Romans with Venus. Eros was her son, AA, 74; AW, 37; LA, 90; RP, 16." There is no pronunciation given for any entry. The symbols following the definitions refer to the 17 volumes of the set, and an explanation or key to these letter-codes is printed at the foot of each odd-numbered page of the index. Unfortunately, the arrangement of these letter codes seems to have been made arbitrarily, without regard either to mnemonic aids or to volume numbering. Arranging the volumes in order by these letter-codes, AA to WO, produces a highly illogical and seemingly random arrangement of the volumes on a shelf, but it is nevertheless the most practical arrangement, since every entry in the Index that has more than one letter-code (for example, United Nations, which is followed by letter-code references to seven different volumes) arranges these codes in alphabetical order. Therefore, short of memorizing the exact order and position of each of the 17 titles, as well as its letter-code (which is not printed on the spine of the volumes), the easiest way of following up any complicated subject is to arrange the volumes in the order in which they are listed in the index, regardless of their jumbled appearance on a shelf.

Some of the definitions in the *Omni-Topika* are open to question. *Armenian* is defined as being "related to Georgian, written with a distinctive script derived from Aramaic." This definition would seem to be contrary to the common opinion of Armenian historians who state that their alphabet originally contained 36 letters and was devised about the year 404 by St. Mesrop, who used Greek, Syrian, and Phoenician alphabets as guides, so that it is not correct to say that Armenian is "derived from Aramaic." Another example of a poor, incomplete definition is that of the word *mercury*, which is given with two definitions, that of the liquid metal, and of the planet. But nothing is said about the Roman god Mercury or about the European plant of the same name.

The majority of the definitions, however, are accurate, although brief. The omissions are more serious, and they make one question the statement that the *Omni-Topika* is a "quick-reference encyclopedia." In the Index from letters Aa to Dz there are only 55 entries, including cross-references. Only names which are mentioned in the text, not those in the captions associated with the illustrations, are in the Index. Thus, on page 109 of AA *(The Creative Spirit)* is a picture of the Tacoma Narrows Bridge. A person having once noticed this picture in one of the volumes, and wishing to find it again, would have to search almost every page of all 17 volumes. The entry is not in the Index under Tacoma; nor is it under bridge, though some seven other named bridges are listed there. Nor is it in a likely volume, such as *Motion, Matter & Energy, Communication,* or *Technology;* it is, as mentioned already, in *The Creative Spirit.* There are several hundred such instances of specific names or places mentioned in the picture captions, but not in the text, almost none of which are to be found in the *Omni-Topika.* The index volume is further weakened by the fact that it fails to provide adequate cross-references. For example, there is no reference from *Catholic Church* to *Roman Catholic Church;* none from *lumber* to *timber;* none from "school" to *education* (there is no entry whatever under school); and none from *newspaper* to *journalism.* In some instances material may be found under more than one heading, not cross-referenced to the other. For example, there are entries for Great Britain and United Kingdom, each of which is cross-referenced to the other, but there are at least ten more entries under England which are not repeated in either of the other two, and which are not cross-referenced to either.

Comment should be made about the recency of the work. The copyright date of the set is 1968, but only a few volumes bring their subjects up to that year. Many volumes do not require recency of any kind—*The Ancients, Ages of Discovery, Races and Cultures* (which is largely geographical), *Earth* (which is largely topical, not chronological), and *Life* (which brings biogenetic theories as to the origins of life only up to 1952). Others, such as *Modern History* and *Communication,* refer to events that took place late in 1969, while the Appendixes generally include events up to 1969 (a Russian space flight in October 1969, in the Appendix to the *Space* volume), but diligent search could not discover any event dated in 1970. One may conclude then, that despite a copyright date of 1968, those volumes in which recency is of importance will take cognizance of events as late as the final months of 1969, but do not carry into the 1970s.

Comparisons can be made between this set and *LIFE Science Library* and its companion *LIFE Nature Library,* to which the volumes under review bear more than a superficial resemblance. The size and physical appearance of the volumes is much the same, and both are appealing to about the same audience. Specific comparisons are a little difficult to make, however. The volume of *LIFE Science Library* entitled *Man and Space* is concerned with man's conquest of space, from early dreams to the manned space flights of the 1960s just prior to that volume's publication. The pertinent volume in the set under review, entitled *Space,* is more concerned with the solar system, the earth, the stars, and so on; but these topics are fully covered in a corresponding volume of the other LIFE series, *The Universe,* one of the volumes in the *LIFE Nature Library.* The use of these two *LIFE* volumes, each with its own index, will give equal or better coverage of these topics than will be found in the volume *Space* in *The Illustrated Libraries of Human Knowledge.* Other similarities exist; editors of both series have made use of similar illustrations of such projectiles as Saturn V, and both have used artists' drawings of sunspots.

When the two series differ, the *LIFE* books are generally preferable. Each *LIFE* volume has its own index, and the general indexes for all the volumes of the *LIFE Science Library* and the *LIFE Nature Library* make use of a letter-code to designate the volumes that is not arbitrary, but is mnemonic in character—GM for *Giant Molecules,* ENG for *The Engineer,* MND for *The Mind,* MATH for *Mathematics,* and so on. In addition, the *LIFE* series volumes do have at least one page of bibliographies in each volume, while the set under review has no bibliographies at all.

The most logical purchasers of *The Illustrated Libraries of Human Knowledge* would be those families that wish to enrich their own or their children's knowledge. For this purpose the books are excellent, since they are well written, well illustrated, and informative. They might also serve to present a pictorial overview of some unfamiliar field of knowledge, for example, poetry, archaeology, or chemistry, for the college freshman, but they are not likely to provide enough substance for any in-depth study at the collegiate level. They may also serve as enrichment materials for high school students, and high school librarians may wish to purchase the set for this purpose.

However, the educational value of *The Illustrated Libraries of Human Knowledge* outside of a library is weakened by a lack of attribution to specific authority for each volume or chapter as well as by a complete lack of bibliographies or reading lists; in addition the reference value of the books in a library is limited, mainly because of a poor Index volume and difficulties occasioned by the use of a two-letter code in place of volume numbering. For these reasons the set cannot be recommended for purchase by libraries.

(Oct. 15, 1973, p.182)

Illustrated World Encyclopedia. 15v. Woodbury, N.Y., Illustrated World Encyclopedia, Inc., c1972. 5026, 249, L-1332, 16p. illus. diagrs. maps. fabrikoid $39.95; to schools and libraries, 25 percent discount.

Illustrated World Encyclopedia has two separate and distinct parts in each of its first 14 volumes. According to its Preface, the general encyclopedia part was "created to fulfill the educational demands of students on the elementary and secondary school levels—students who often have been found to be confused and disheartened by the complexity of information obtained in encyclopedias written for scholars far more advanced in the academic world than they." The other part, called *Literary Treasures,* contains a collection of book synopses of the " 'great books' including those that are standard on the required and recommended reading lists of schools and colleges." One of the purposes of the *Treasures* is "to give an adult the information he needs in social conversation about a book." Volume 15 contains the Study Guide, indexes, and Atlas.

The 1967 edition of *Illustrated World* was reviewed in *The Booklist and Subscription Books Bulletin,* July 1, 1968. *Illustrated World* was formerly titled *The Illustrated Encyclopedia of Knowledge,* and under that title was noted in *Subscription Books Bulletin,* January 1956. Roger Bobley, editor of the 1972 *Illustrated World Encyclopedia,* states that this encyclopedia "was compiled by a staff of several hundred editors under the direction of the late Albert H. Morehead, distinguished scholar, *New York Times* columnist, and author of more than 50 books."

In preparing this review the Committee examined all of the 1972 edition and part of the 1967 edition. Four prefatory pages of the 1972 edition list 105 Contributors and Consultants for the encyclopedia. The articles are unsigned, and the responsibilities of Contributors and Consultants are not specified. A search of biographical reference sources did not produce verification of the qualifications of many of them. As pointed out in the review of the 1967 edition, some of the Contributors and Consultants are not and have not been for some years in the positions attributed to them, and some have died. This raises a question about the nature and extent of their contributions to the latest edition.

In the 1972 edition there is no significant change in arrangement and scope of the encyclopedia. The letter by letter alphabetical arrangement of the encyclopedic and index entries and the total number of pages remain the same, although the 21 volumes of the 1967 edition have been condensed into 15 volumes. Such features as maps, a Study Guide, indexes, illustrations, and "Literary Treasures" are retained. There are no bibliographies.

Coverage is broad, encompassing the sciences, social sciences, the arts, biography, and even such less directly school-related topics as the Bible, sports, and games. Coverage occasionally is inconsistent. For instance there is an article on liberal but not on conservative. The articles range from one sentence in length to several pages. The adequacy with which they treat their subjects is not necessarily tied to their length. The style and treatment make the usefulness of the encyclopedia to children beyond the elementary grades questionable. Sentence structure and the general vocabulary are simple. The following excerpt typifies the elementary style and level of presentation: "The Congressional Record is a sort of newspaper published by the United States Government every day the Congress meets to do its work of making the laws of the country. The Record tells what laws Congress has talked about or passed each day and who has voted for or against each. It also prints every speech that any member of Congress makes. A member may also have printed in it a speech he has written but did not actually make." Occasionally ideas seem unnecessarily repeated, as in the article on ants: "Ants are called 'social insects'. . . . The ant and the bee are social insects." Oversimplifications occur. There are evidences of bias and value judgments.

Aside from some oversimplifications and omissions, inaccuracies occur. The range of temperature in Butte, Montana, does not typically reach 120 degrees. China is divided into 29 provinces, not 34 as stated in *Illustrated World.*

A prefatory claim that unfamiliar terms are always defined or explained when they are introduced usually sustains examination. However, "profilometer" is used undefined in the *Abrasives* entry, is not an index entry, and is not an entry in what would be its alphabetical place in the encyclopedia. The same is true of the term "anhydride," used in the *Acid* article.

The publisher's claim that "every volume is revised or brought up to date in every printing, sometimes two or three times in a single year" is only partially supported in the edition under review. Some entries reflect 1970 U.S. census figures and recent events; some new place-names are recognized with suitable entries, and some new emphases are included. However, many expected entries are missing. Examples, which are entries neither in the body of the encyclopedia nor in the Index, are DNA, organic gardening, cyclamates, consumer, thalidomide, quasar, transformational grammar, Morris Graves, pollution, recycling, Blacks, Chicanos, Mexican-Americans, poverty, and violence. Some population figures are from the 1960 census. Some articles refer to "today" or a "hundred years ago," or use similar vague phrases which can be misleading. For example, the article on Phoenix states that "Phoenix was once the home of several Indian tribes," giving no dates or internal cross-references to other possibly clarifying articles. The treatment of some topics is not contemporary. The *Ghetto* article discusses only Jewish ghettos, and racism in the Index refers only to the article *Nazism*, where the term is discussed entirely within that context. However, the article on Africa briefly mentions "apartheid," a term which appears in the Index. The labor force in the United States now numbers almost 90 million rather than the 60 million figure given in the encyclopedia. Shipbuilding is no longer a significant occupation in Oregon, and the long-existing influence of hydroelectric power on that state's economy should be mentioned.

The final 84 pages of each volume are assigned to *Literary Treasures*, subtitled "The novels, plays, poems, and other works of the most celebrated and historic writers of the English language in all lands and times." Adequate plot synopses for individual novels and plays and the principal themes and conclusions found in other works, following the structure of the original (chapters, acts, books), are provided as are the facts of publication. The historical background of the work, its impact on the culture of its time, and notations of derivative works and adaptations are also cited. The title page of each *Literary Treasures* section cites Albert H. Morehead as editor and lists the names of those who aided the editors in writing the outlines. A two-page statement on "How to Get the Most from 'Literary Treasures'" appears at the beginning of the *Treasures* section in volume 1.

The *Treasures* are paged consecutively but independently of the encyclopedic paging. In reducing the volumes from 21 to 15, 8 selections have been split between volumes, and in most volumes the alphabetical keys on the spine do not correspond to the included *Literary Treasures* selections, which are arranged by title.

The 520 synopses in the *Literary Treasures* section are directed to the mature reader. Of the total, approximately 7 percent might be found in a modern elementary school reading list. A check of the titles with three standard adult reading lists shows that 13 percent are not included in any of these lists. The typical work is a novel published between 1850 and 1900. Some works like *Lost Horizon, A Message to Garcia,* and *Forever Amber* do not represent enduring literary values but appear to have been included because of their popularity at the time of publication. Others may have been included because of their connection with a musical, opera, or motion picture, e.g., *Green Grow the Lilacs* by Lynn Riggs and *Thais* by Anatole France, or because the author (now obscure) was a Nobel prize winner, e.g., *The Mother* by Grazia Deledda and *Folly or Saintliness* by Jose Echegaray.

There are no books by Negro authors. The literary treatment of the black experience ranges from *Uncle Tom's Cabin* to Eugene O'Neill's plays and William Faulkner's novels. The user will look in vain for such current authors as Kingsley Amis, Samuel Beckett, Anthony Burgess, Lawrence Durrell, William Golding, C. P. Snow, J. D. Salinger, and J. R. R. Tolkien, all of whom might be considered to meet the qualifications of the *Treasures* subtitle ("The novels, plays, poems, and other works of the most celebrated and historic writers of the English language in all lands and times"), and whose works appear on recommended lists for high school or college reading. As in the 1967 edition, some of the selections are of works not first published in English; the subtitle has not been changed to recognize their inclusion. Critical notes in the *Literary Treasures* sections are minimal; there is no genuine analysis of plot, themes, or character development. The résumés are accurate and concise, without distortion of meaning.

Volume 15 contains the Study Guide, Index to All Volumes, Guide to Pronunciation of difficult words appearing throughout the encyclopedia, *Literary Treasures:* (a) Index of Authors; (b) Index to Titles; (c) Pronouncing Index of Proper Names (Characters and Places), and Atlas (maps in color).

The introduction to the Study Guide states that "many thousands" of the encyclopedia articles are listed in the Guide, but "less important subjects" are not and must be located through the Index. The Guide serves as a sort of classified index to what the editors apparently consider to be the articles of major importance to school children. The arrangement of the subtopics is alphabetical, but the arrangement of the major topics is in no apparent sequence. Finding them is aided somewhat by a two-page list of the major topics in the order in which they appear in the Guide, together with the pages on which they are listed.

The Guide's basic weakness is that topics are not described or classified in such a way as to make clear how one subject is related or subordinated to others. The examples of faulty classification cited in the Committee's 1967 review still remain. Others can be cited.

The quality of the Index to All Volumes is uneven. There are instances of inadequate indexing, inconsistencies, and omissions. For examples, there are no index entries for the articles on laser, Kosygin, and covenant. "Plateau" is defined in the article on mesa, but has no index entry. The entry for *escapement* refers to page 1258 of volume 4, but the term is used only on pages 1256 and 1260. Featherbedding is discussed in the article on labor and labor unions but is not indexed. The index references under *cloture* do not include its discussion in the article on Congress. There is a blind reference under Vietnam. The article *Ecology* contains, explains, and even emphasizes with italics the words "biosphere," "biome," "habitats," and "niche." However, only "biome" is indexed. Another weakness of the Index is that often the citations under a term are not subdivided. Some entries have a paragraph of undifferentiated citations to volumes and pages. The entry *diseases* (human) has 37; *Bible*—Old Testament persons and events has 33; and *Roman Catholic Church* has 45. It is unrealistic to expect users of any age to trace so many references in the hope of finding specific information desired. Of these three examples, only Roman Catholic Church states "see also Study Guide," although both Pathology—Human Diseases and their Treatment, and Bible are also major topics in that Guide. No other cross-references are made from any of the three terms.

In the Index to All Volumes, entries leading to articles carrying headings identical with the index entry are printed in boldface; this fact is not explained in the books. Index and Study Guide volume and page numbers are in boldface and italic type respectively. References to illustrations or maps are not distinguished typographically or otherwise.

The Guide to Pronunciation, which limits itself to proper nouns, shows pronunciation in two ways, first by using the diacritical marks of the National Lexicographic Board, and, second, phonetically. A brief, one-page explanation of the two methods precedes the Guide.

In the indexes to *Literary Treasures*, entries and volume numbers are in boldface type and page numbers are in normal type. The Pronouncing Index of Proper Names uses only a phonetic system. It is preceded by a one-paragraph explanation of problems in transliterating names from a non-Roman alphabet, anglicizing some foreign names, and alphabetizing the names.

There are a few *see* cross-references

in their alphabetical position in the body of the encyclopedia, see also references in the text of some articles, and both kinds of references in the Index to All Volumes. Those in the articles are typified by the one in the Onion article: "LEEKS, SHALLOTS, GARLIC, AND CHIVES are types of onion that you can read about in separate articles." This is an appropriate type of reference for elementary school children, but, unfortunately, is not widely employed in *Illustrated World*. This type of reference is sometimes inaccurately used, as in the article on grammar, which states that there are separate articles "on SYNTAX AND RHETORIC." There is no article on syntax; nor does the term appear in the Index. The article *Accent* refers to the "article on METER," which does not exist. The index entry *meter* (poetry) leads to the article on blank verse, which carries a *see also* reference to articles on poetry and meter (which is nonexistent). The *Abbey* article refers also to convent and to monastery, but there is no article on convent. The index entries under *convent* refer to the articles on abbey and on monastery. There are no cross-references between the various indexes except that a few entries in the Index to all Volumes refer also to entries in the Study Guide. It is necessary to use all the indexes, all cross-references, and the Study Guide to locate necessary information; yet using all of these aids still does not provide ready access to all the information available in the encyclopedia.

The illustrations are generally black and white. They are from many sources and are profuse. Although they are generally clear and helpful, they vary in quality and effectiveness. The unorganized scattering of the colorplates in the 1967 edition has been corrected. The few pages of colorplates that are used are good, credited to many different sources, usually grouped at the beginning of the related volumes, and carry a reference to specific articles. Small black-and-white outline maps are usefully adjacent to some of the geographic and economic articles; they give no scale, and are sometimes overlaid with one color as are some of the illustrations. At the end of volume 15 are 16 pages of Rand McNally Cosmo series colored maps. Scale is cited, but no dates are given. The maps are reduced to less than the page size of the encyclopedia making them cluttered and the print so fine that place-names are difficult to read.

The volumes are sturdily bound and lie fairly flat when opened. The pages are attractive and are printed in double columns with illustrations interspersed. Type is legible, and headings and running heads are in boldface. The paper is nonglare. An unexplained peculiarity is the occasional shifting of the page numbers from the upper margin to the lower margin.

Illustrated World Encyclopedia is physically sound. It contains much accurate and useful encyclopedic information suitably presented for elementary school children. However, the value of the set is limited by oversimplifications, inconsistent revision, and inadequate indexing and cross referencing. The *Literary Treasures* sections include works which only marginally merit the designation "treasure," omits others which logically might have been included, contribute little as literary criticism, and seem to be designed primarily for an older or more educationally advanced audience than is the rest of the set. The aims of the two parts of *Illustrated World* are dissimilar, and neither is entirely fulfilled. Not recommended. *(May 15, 1973, p.865)*

In Black America. Los Angeles, Presidential Publishers, c1970 by Books, Inc.; World-wide distribution by United Publishing Corp., Washington, D.C. xv, 560p. illus. charts. padded covers; to schools and libraries, $14.95 plus 42c postage.

In Black America is another source for locating little-known facts about black people and their contributions to American life. It relates how blacks fared socioeconomically during the 1960s. This book should not be confused with *In Black America—1968: The Year of Awakening*, edited by Patricia W. Romero and published in 1969 as a supplement to the ten-volume *International Library of Negro Life and History*. According to the publisher, the *In Black America* under review is also a yearbook to the basic set, *International Library*, and, "apart from its luxury binding, is essentially the same as the matching yearbooks which supplement the basic ten volumes except that in addition . . . it also contains a special 96-page excerpt which has been taken from a cross-section of the basic 10 volumes that appeared earlier." Both the books entitled *In Black America* are distributed by the United Publishing Corporation.

In Black America is a single-volume work divided into five broad areas in addition to an Introduction, a Picture Credits Section, and an Index. Section I is entitled A Pictorial Tour of Black America: Past and Present; Section II is untitled, but includes articles on politics, labor, education, welfare, urban development, media, sports, and police-black relationships. Section III gives biographical information, obituaries, two short bibliographies, information on the black press, and Greek letter societies. Section IV is devoted to the Civil Rights Act of 1964 and three other bills representing "a sampling of civil rights legislation introduced in the House of Representatives in 1969." Section V "contains brief statistical information in the areas of politics, education, labor, poverty, population, business, and sports."

Eight editors and writers, eight editorial assistants, eleven production staff members, three copy editors, and four researchers compiled the work. Descriptions of the editors' and writers' qualifications are not provided, and an attempt to identify them through such standard biographical sources as *Who's Who in America, Current Biography,* and *Biography Index* proved fruitless. With the exception of the article on the Black Panther Party, none of the articles is signed. None of those responsible for *In Black America* can be identified as scholars of the Afro-American experience. One editor, Dave Sendler, had served as editor of *Pageant* magazine and coauthored *Stars of Pro Basketball,* published in 1970.

The editors of *In Black America* attempt to go "beyond simple factual presentation . . . of data and events . . . to penetrate to the core of what these occurrences meant" for the purpose of improving understanding. The Foreword states that this work "evokes a whole gamut of emotions: it is exciting, upsetting, frustrating, inspiring, and to every American—black or white—intensely real."

The bulk of the information is devoted to the events of the decade from 1960 to 1970. However, earlier events and personalities are included. In the Introduction, opinions tend to be slanted toward separatism or undue pessimism.

The Pictorial Tour begins with a very short review of the "Black African background and then shifts swiftly to this continent," where a chronological review of facts is revealed mainly through thumbnail biographical sketches beginning with Estevanico in 1539. Included in this section are "churchmen, abolitionists, businessmen . . . writers and poets, physicians and inventors as well as entertainers" and sportsmen. Much of the information is mainly factual listings. The text lacks sufficient narration on the effect and significance of black accomplishments which would add to the overall usefulness of this section. For example, the Negro church, of great significance to the black experience, is not dealt with as such. Famous churchmen are listed with brief mention of achievements. Nor is information organized so as to give maximum continuity and a clear picture of the various aspects of black American life.

Section II is the largest part of the book, covering approximately 174 pages of text with 70 pages of pictures. The overall coverage in this section is generally good although written in a popular rather than a scholarly style. Most of the information is drawn from a number of sources. Direct quotations are used frequently, although the documentation is not sufficient and would be difficult to trace. For example, the article on the "Poor" under "Urban Development" is 17 paragraphs long and quotes

11 sources, but fails to give full documentation.

This section begins with the "Police —Black Panther Conflict," written by Andrew B. Haynes, Jr. Containing nine pages of text with an additional six pages of pictures, it is included because the "violence-prone rhetoric, as expressed by the Black Panthers and others, has taken the place of . . . non-violent integrated protest groups." The article proper is preceded by a one-page introduction by Haynes who outlines the events leading to his acceptance of the assignment. The article is said to be based on "an investigation of police relations with the Black Panthers and with the Black Community." The editors acknowledge the controversial nature of the article, but included it because it is "thought-provoking . . . and might lead to further research."

Section III is devoted to personalities from all walks of life. The list is not very inclusive and many personalities are conspicuous by their absence. For example, James Brown who is known as the "King of Soul" is listed, but Aretha Franklin who is the "Queen of Soul" was omitted. Other omissions include Barbara Jordan and Yvonne Braithwaite in politics, poetess Nikki Giovanni, writer Margaret Alexander Walker, and civil rights activists Angela Davis, Fannie Lou Hamer, and Rosa Parks. One could rationalize the omission of these persons from this section if they were noted elsewhere in the book. A check of the Index, however, reveals that this is not the case. Andrew Brimmer, the only Negro member of the Federal Reserve Board and Arthur Fletcher, Assistant Secretary of Labor, are included in another part of the text.

The section "Military Personalities" consists of four pages containing seven pictures of military personnel with a brief caption under each picture. Two of the pictures are of unidentified men. In all, the total text of this section consists of ten lines.

There are two bibliographies: "A Selected Annotated Bibliography of Articles," and a "Bibliography of Recently Published Titles." The bibliography of articles consists of 41 articles dealing "with various aspects of the black experience in nine major areas." The list is not "meant to be definitive, but only . . . representative of the types and quality of articles published." Nevertheless, more articles from more scholarly journals would have increased the usefulness of this section. For example, under "Black Politics" there is one article from the *New Republic* while other superior articles on the same subject appeared during the same period of time in *Journal of Conflict Resolution, Massachusetts Review, Western Political Quarterly, Social Forces, Phylon, Public Opinion Quarterly,* and the *Economist.* Under "Black Capitalism and Business" there are two articles, one from *Saturday Review* and the other from *Journal of Negro Education.* Other journals publishing articles on the same subject included the *Economist, Social Casework,* and *American Journal of Economics and Sociology.* Under "Black Religion" three articles are taken from *Church in Metropolis* and *Journal of Religious Thought* while *Catholic Historical Review* and *Religion in Life* also published articles of relevance.

The topically arranged "Bibliography of Recently Published Titles" lists over 250 books. Included are recent biographies and other books relating to blacks, both American and African, published either during 1968 or 1969. Twelve of the titles are juvenile books. "Textbooks and reprints were omitted unless of particular significance to the general reader." Also, since the book itself purports to cover the events of the 1960s, the bibliography does not include works earlier than 1968 and 1969.

In Black America lists only 85 of the 158 black newspapers with the names and addresses of publishers. The circulation and frequency of publication are not given. Journals and religious publications are excluded.

The list of "Greek Social and Professional Organizations" is one page long and includes only 15 Greek letter societies; the list gives only the society, national presidents, and number of members. The purpose, major projects, the changing role of such societies on black college campuses, and national addresses are not included.

Section IV, "Summary of the Civil Rights Act of 1964" and "Civil Rights Legislation," is 97 pages long. The summary of the 1964 legislation is accompanied by a list, by states, of housing discrimination and school desegregation cases. The bulk of this section is devoted to the text of three bills without any commentary on the effectiveness or ineffectiveness of each. The bills are introduced by a paragraph pointing out that the bills "represent only a portion of the extensive efforts being expended in this vital area." They are printed in large type with a great deal of leading, whereas the main text is set in smaller type with less leading. The margins are slightly over an inch and a half wide.

The last section contains a useful variety of political, economic, and social statistics that are not easily available in other sources. However, most of the information given is earlier than 1970. The book has up-to-date statistical coverage only for the sports section and notes, "Since the most up-to-date figures are not always available in all areas [of politics, education, labor, poverty, population, business and sports], those materials included here (with the exception of sports information) have been chosen to illustrate trends." Sources are cited for information in each category.

In Black America is written in a popular style and is not purely as objective or as scholarly as might be desired, resulting in interpretive opinion in many instances, and causing one to doubt its authentic reference value.

The format is good. The stitching, nonglare paper, pictures, and charts are good. However, covers are padded and of a leatherized material which has a tendency to warp and bulge if exposed to heat.

In spite of the generally good pictorial tour in Part I and the useful statistics in the last section, *In Black America* falls short of providing in depth, complete reference material on the accomplishments of the black man in America. Personalities who were prominent in local, state, and national politics, literary figures, and others who made definite contributions during the 1960s were omitted or referred to only slightly. Blacks in the military are not adequately covered. Medal of Honor and Spingarn Medal winners are not cited. Contrary to its stated purpose, Section I simply recounts occurrences with narration too brief to make the reader aware of the significance of the events. The arrangement of the book does not provide for easy access to information. For these reasons, *In Black America* is not recommended.

(April 1, 1973, p.721)

Index to Fairy Tales, 1949-1972: Including Folklore, Legends and Myths, In Collections. By Norma Olin Ireland. Westwood, MA, F. W. Faxon Co., Inc., 1973. (Useful Reference Series No. 101.) xxxviii, 741p. 23cm. cloth $18. ISBN 0-87305-101-7.

Index to Fairy Tales, 1949-1972; Including Folklore, Legends and Myths, In Collections is designed to continue *Index to Fairy Tales, Myths and Legends,* second supplement, by Mary Huse Eastman (Boston: F. W. Faxon, 1952). The scope of the volume under review is stated in the Foreword. Eastman's second supplement indexed fairy tales through 1948; so the present compilation begins with the year 1949 and brings the *Index to Fairy Tales* to 1972. The compiler notes that a few older titles which are now in new editions or were simply not included in the earlier indexes have been listed. Only collections of stories are indexed, no single stories. All the collections indexed are in English, but all continents are represented in the collections analyzed. The compiler makes no claim for inclusiveness, stating only that all collections available to her were analyzed.

Ireland states clearly that the *Index to Fairy Tales* does not pretend to use a scholarly approach: "We hope this index will be helpful to all types of libraries: Public, school, college and university—the latter for use in their classes in folklore. It is a 'popular' type of index, however, and we have made no scholarly break-down of folkmotifs in stories."—*Foreword.*

The second supplement to Eastman's *Index to Fairy Tales* indexed 280 books, whereas *Ireland* covers 406 books. There is no indication of the criteria used in selecting the books to be indexed within the chosen subject areas other than their availability to the compiler.

The compiler is a librarian, indexer, and researcher who has produced many similar indexes for Faxon, but these published works and her activities as a librarian are not in juvenile areas of knowledge or interest. In the Foreword however she acknowledges assistance from other librarians and libraries, including at least one children's librarian. The Useful Reference Series, of which this *Index to Fairy Tales* is a part, is a well-known and established series.

Preceding the Index proper is the List of Collections Analyzed in This Work and Key to Symbols Used. This list is arranged alphabetically by the so-called symbols, which are one or two words serving as code phrases for the collections analyzed. Under each symbol, which is printed in capitals, is the bibliographical listing consisting of author, title, imprint, and pagination for the analyzed collection.

The Index proper is arranged alphabetically by the first word of the title of the fairy tale, myth, or legend, and by subject. Title and subject entries are in one alphabet. Title entries are in lower case, except for the first word, and the subject entries are in boldface. The title is the main entry, with citations to the proper symbol of the preceding List of Collections Analyzed and Key to Symbols Used. Inclusive pagination is included for each tale, myth, or legend in the title entry. Variant titles are listed if the indexed collection mentions them; the Foreword indicates that if necessary *Eastman* should be consulted for variants.

Ireland has used subject indexing to facilitate location of tales the exact titles of which are unknown. The subject headings in this *Index to Fairy Tales* are correlated with those in the *Eastman* indexes, but many hundreds have been added, according to the compiler. Subject headings used are not based on any standard of such headings; the compiler states: "We have tried to choose subject headings which would be simple and easy to use and yet enable users to locate special, unusual subjects as well." Many of the subject headings used in the more recent *Index* have only one entry, but the heading *Kings and Queens* has 342 entries. There are 286 entries under *Ireland*, but only one under *Ireland—History;* many of the entries under the former subject heading could have been put more exactly under the latter. There are fairly numerous *see* and *see also* references used in the subject headings.

This edition is printed on opaque paper. The margins are adequate, and the book lies flat when opened.

Index to Fairy Tales, 1949-1972: Including Folklore, Legends and Myths, In Collections is recommended for libraries, because of the easy access it provides to a large group of recent popular collections of fairy tales, folklore, legends, and myths through its title and subject approaches.

(Feb. 15, 1974, p.607)

The International Encyclopedia of Dogs. Ed. by Stanley Dangerfield and Elsworth Howell. New York, Howell Book House, 1971. Distributed to schools and libraries by Franklin Watts. 480p. illus. 26cm. cloth $19.95.

The World Encyclopedia of Dogs. Ed. by Ferelith Hamilton. New York, The World Publishing Co., 1971, 672p. 29cm. buckram $20; to schools and libraries, 25 percent discount.

Dog lovers, exhibitors, and breeders are always anxious to read any new materials on their favorite subject, regardless of the form of presentation. In fact, they are especially pleased if this material happens to be cataloged in some semblance of order so that quick reference is possible. These new encyclopedias should meet this requirement and much more.

In keeping with their titles, both of these books are international in scope. *The World Encyclopedia of Dogs* presents information on "over 280 breeds from all over the world," and *The International Encyclopedia of Dogs* gives coverage to over 190 breeds that are "recognized by kennel clubs of America, the United Kingdom, Canada, Australia, and New Zealand."

The World Encyclopedia of Dogs is edited by Ferelith Hamilton, with Arthur F. Jones as the Associate Editor in America. Hamilton is the editor in chief of *Dog World*, one of Great Britain's dog magazines, and Arthur Jones is a former editor of *American Kennel Gazette*, the official publication of the American Kennel Club. Most of the articles and information in *The World Encyclopedia of Dogs* was contributed by 120 of "the world's leading authorities on the individual breeds and supplementary canine matters." The Notes on Contributors detail the work or accomplishment of each contributor. The list of photograph and illustration credits is given in Acknowledgments. Many of the illustrations were done by famous dog photographers such as the Englishman C. M. Cooke, who contributed photographs for both encyclopedias, and Barbara Burrows, who is also English.

The International Encyclopedia of Dogs has 16 contributors; all are associated with various kennel clubs, are canine specialists, or are veterinarians. The editing was done by Stanley Dangerfield, who edited the international contributions, and Elsworth Howell, who edited the American contributions. Special American articles were written by Maxwell Riddle. All three editors have written extensively for dog lovers and are noted international judges. There are 12 major photographers contributing pictures to this encyclopedia.

Both encyclopedias give information on dogs that are most popular in Great Britain and the United States, but breeds which have their origins in other countries are also listed. However, *The World Encyclopedia of Dogs* covers more worldwide breeds than *The International Encyclopedia of Dogs* which gives greater coverage to canine-related topics.

The format of the two encyclopedias is quite different. *The International Encyclopedia of Dogs* is arranged alphabetically by subject and has two columns of rather small print to a page with two-inch inside margins in which some illustrations with captions are found. It includes approximately 194 entries on breeds per se, and over 500 entries of supplementary canine material such as registration in various countries, *Communicable Diseases, Insurance for Dogs, Transportation of Dogs, Viciousness, Chromosomes, Nursing Sick Dogs,* and *Whelping*. It has over 600 illustrations in halftone and line throughout the text, and over 126 color illustrations. Color illustrations are placed in four different sections of the book in the following groupings: Gun Dogs, Hounds, Working Dogs, and Terriers. Color picture location is possible through an alphabetical list of colorplates preceding the text. Line illustrations are used near appropriate topics where words alone will not suffice to describe a subject in sufficient detail, e.g., *Digestion, Hock, Pulse,* and *Scaling Teeth*. This encyclopedia has no table of contents or index. Many cross-references are used throughout the text, primarily in the *see* reference form.

The World Encyclopedia of Dogs, unlike *The International Encyclopedia of Dogs,* is arranged by "breeds in sections according to the standard groupings adopted by most countries—gundogs, working dogs, other working and utility dogs, toy dogs, terriers, hounds and Spitz or Nordic dogs. Within these groups the breeds appear in alphabetical order." The editor acknowledges that the manner of grouping follows the British method and may not be to all users' liking, since each country has different ideas about grouping.

Preceding and following the main text are approximately 97 pages of complementary information: *Dog Evolution, Basic Canine Anatomy, The Dog in the Home, Nutrition, Diseases, Showing and Championship Systems, The Dog in Use and in Sport, National Canine Authorities, Notes on Contributors,* and a *Glossary of Words and Terms*. There is also an excellent bibliography and an Index. The bibliography is a selected list "concentrating on breed origin, history and show points," arranged alphabetically by breeds with a five-page introduction on early and general works. "The Index gives the page number of all breeds, whether" they are "of the articles concerning them or of reference to them in other articles." Full indexing is said to be given to the complementary articles; although a check in the Index under "parasitic infestation," "hepatitis," "leptospirosis," "thorax," "hounds," "spinal column," and "training," all of which are discussed in the supplementary articles, showed these terms omitted. Because of the arrangement of the book, the Index is a necessity, since the use of the Table of Contents presupposes some knowledge of canine vernacular and grouping, especially the British method of grouping. Helpful cross-references are indicated in the Index by placing subjects referred to or from in parentheses.

"The chapters on breeds are presented in the same sequence throughout —history and development, color, care, character, standards and other forms of the basic breed." Having these aspects as subheads in bold print makes for easy use.

Style of writing is admittedly inconsistent, because each contributor was allowed to present material in his or her own manner. This, however, does not detract from the usefulness of the book; it is readable and informative.

Throughout the text there are 1,100 black-and-white illustrations—most of which are photographs. These show the development of each breed with many head studies, and front and side views of the leading pedigree dogs. With the exception of the frontispiece, there are no color illustrations; nevertheless, the black-and-white illustrations provided adequately cover the subjects. This encyclopedia has one column to the page. Outside margins are three and one half inches, and many of them contain captioned photographs.

These two books are for different users. *The World Encyclopedia of Dogs* seems geared to the novice and readers desiring a guide to general knowledge of dogs. It is devoted mainly to more complete discussions on the various breeds of dogs, and, in general, has less complementary canine information. For example, someone desiring to buy a pet would find the information on the care and character of individual breeds helpful, and someone looking for a guide to the various breeds might be interested in the inclusion of such less-known breeds as "Leonberger," "Hovawart," "Mudi," "Alentejo Herder," "Armant," and "Wetterhoun." The special sections on diseases, anatomy, and the dog in the home will prove helpful to those unfamiliar with dogs. The information given is concise and conveniently located. Coverage of these topics is given in *The International Encyclopedia of Dogs,* but under specific diseases and the various parts of the dog's anatomy. Various aspects of dog care are given under separate headings such as *Behavior Pattern in Puppies* and *Puppy Shots.*

On the other hand, *The International Encyclopedia of Dogs* has greater appeal to the serious breeder of dogs. It devotes much less space to the various breeds, and incorporates much more information on all canine-related subjects in an encyclopedic fashion. Its arrangement makes for easy reference; although, for best use, one must be aware of its scope. Both encyclopedias include breed standards of the English Kennel Club and the American Kennel Club, but where the standards of the two clubs differ, as in the case of *Papilon, Elkhound,* and *Borzoi, The World Encyclopedia of Dogs* states the differences whereas *The International Encyclopedia of Dogs* gives the English standards with no mention of the variations. Where there is a difference in the breed names, both encyclopedias use the British name instead of the American, i.e., "King Charles Spaniel" rather than "English Toy Spaniel."

The International Encyclopedia of Dogs and *The World Encyclopedia of Dogs* are designed for different readers. *The International Encyclopedia of Dogs* is a true encyclopedia in that all information is arranged alphabetically, and all subjects regarding the canine are discussed. *The World Encyclopedia of Dogs* is more general in its approach to the various topics discussed, with its primary emphasis on the various breeds of dogs. Readers desirous of a general knowledge of dogs and a guide to a particular breed of dog will find *The World Encyclopedia of Dogs* especially useful. This volume is recommended for the novice as its style of writing makes it easy for the newcomer to be introduced to the world of dogs. Those readers desiring more detailed information on a variety of topics will enjoy browsing through *The International Encyclopedia of Dogs*. This volume is a requirement for the serious dog breeder. Its excellent color photographs are one of its outstanding features. Both are recommended. *(Dec. 1, 1972, p.306)*

The International Encyclopedia of Film.
Roger Manvell, general editor; Lewis Jacobs, American advisory ed.; John Gillett, Margaret Hinxman, David Robinson, assoc. eds. New York, Crown Publishers, Inc., [1972]. 574p. illus. cloth 28cm. $17.95; to schools and libraries, 25 percent discount.

The World Encyclopedia of the Film.
John M. Smith and Tim Cawkwell, assoc. eds. New York, World Pub. Co., [1972]. 444p. illus. cloth 27cm. $25.

The publication of two reference works on film in the same year, both claiming to be unique as international encyclopedias, poses a problem in selection for many librarians. While *The International Encyclopedia of Film* and *The World Encyclopedia of the Film* are similar in many aspects and overlapping in content, to be sure, there are unique features in both volumes. Both, it should be noted, are British publications, these being the first American editions of each. World Publishing reports that *The World Encyclopedia of the Film* is out of print.

The International Encyclopedia of Film, edited by Roger Manvell, a well-known author who holds a doctorate from London University and is head of the Department of Film History at the London Film School, was designed and produced by Rainbird Reference Books Limited in London. Lewis Jacobs, an American filmmaker and critic who has published and edited works on film, is the American advisory editor. A number of other contributors who have specialties related to the film industry are listed, as for example, Margaret Hinxman, a film critic for the *Sunday Telegraph,* and Jay Leyda a film historian specializing in Soviet cinema.

Although the work does not attempt to cover the complexities of film or sound recording technologies, some general terms relating to the technology are included. Its purpose is "to cover the international history of the film, mainly as an art, but also as an industry which forms a significant part of the social development of our century."

The general arrangement of the work is alphabetical by subject. However, preceding the alphabetical listing are (1) Manvell's excellent 18-page Introduction on the history of film; (2) a section on The Development of Colour Cinematography including 16 colorplates showing the use of color from the 1898 hand-colored slides to the use of Cinerama/Eastman color of the 1950s and 60s; and (3) a list of important events in the history of film by year. Following the main body of the work is a 14-page bibliography, including works on filmmaking, film criticism, national histories of film by country, and individual studies listed alphabetically by person; an index of title changes which is mainly a list of American or British films having different titles in the other country, such as the American *The Children's Hour* whose title was changed to *The Loudest Whisper* in Great Britain; an index of film titles; and an index of names for persons mentioned in an article but who are not subjects of a separate entry.

The encyclopedic part of the work contains a large number of entries on people connected with films or the film industry, a lesser number for techniques or genres such as "trucking shot" and "puppet film," and also articles on countries. Entries range from two lines to a twenty-two page article *United States of America.* Entries, particularly those on actors, directors, and producers, contain frequent references to film titles, but no attempt was made to include every film in which the person acted, or which he directed or produced. For each person, the birth date, birthplace, and death date (if deceased) are given. Other information on the person's life and contributions since he or she entered the film world are included. The material is up to date including references to some 1972 films.

References to foreign films do not always seem consistent in the matter of translation; however, in general, film titles in French, Italian, and Spanish are usually left in the original language, as for example, *L'Année Derniére á Marienbad, Divorzio all' Italiana,* and *La Caza.* Film titles in other languages, especially those in non-Roman alphabets, are given in translation. While this is understandable for films in Russian, Japanese, and the Scandinavian languages, it seems strange to treat many German films in the same manner. The 1966 prizewinning film *Abschied von Gestern,* for example, is referred to only by its English title *Yesterday Girl;* there is no mention of the German title even in the Index.

The articles on major figures and countries are signed with initials as for example, the article *France* was written by Roy Armes, an author of three books on French cinema. Names and terms within the article for which there are separate entries are indicated by use of capital letters.

Numerous black-and-white photographs are interspersed throughout the volume. These average about three or four per page and refer to the nearby text if on the same page; if not, they refer to preceding or following page. While these vary somewhat in quality, most are surprisingly clear. In addition, there are 21 full-colorplates found throughout the volume. Most are scenes from well-known films of different countries. These plates, however, are not related to the text where they are placed. Thus, one finds a beautifully-executed colorplate of a scene from *Dr. Zhivago* in the middle of the article on Latin America.

The indexes must be used to locate much information contained in the volume. Since there are no entries for films as such, the Index of Films is particularly useful. The Index of Names indicates, in bold type, the pages of the main entry and, in regular type, other pages on which appear further information or photographs. In addition, one can find references to names for which there is no separate article.

The World Encyclopedia of the Film would seem at first glance to be quite similar to *The International Encyclopedia of Film*. There are, however, differences which tend to make one more suitable for finding certain kinds of information than the other.

The World Encyclopedia of the Film is edited by John M. Smith and Tim Cawkwell, who are cited on the book's jacket as "two London film experts." With the exception of George W. Smith, an art director, neither the two editors, nor any of the 34 contributors, are listed in standard biographical directories. The editors state that the volume was in preparation continuously since 1964 in order "to ensure a balanced selection of entries and to respect the enormously different kind of cinema which they represent." Further, they note that the silent period of film is less well-covered than the sound period, that there is an imbalance in favor of American cinema (which they feel is simply a reflection of the medium's historical development), and that there is some emphasis given to actors, choreographers, and directors. The Introduction includes certain criteria for selection, information on the dating of films, and the method of treating the translation of foreign films.

The main 303-page text is an alphabetical listing of biographical entries for writers, producers, actors, directors, designers, and others connected with the film industry. Each entry includes the occupation of the biographee, e.g., director, composer, or actress, the place and date of birth, and place and date of death, if deceased. The entries themselves, unlike those in *The International Encyclopedia*, is a who's who type of entry, giving dates for every aspect of the person's career. Following that is a list of films the person directed, acted in, or was in some way associated with. The editors claim completeness of listing only under the director's entry and even this was not always possible, but is so indicated. The listing of films, however, is much more extensive than in the *International Encyclopedia* which makes no claim to include all films with which a biographee was associated. The British director, Humphrey Jennings, for example, has a listing of some 24 films in the *World Encyclopedia*, but only 13 in the *International*.

On each right-hand page in *The World Encyclopedia* there are three small (2½" x 2½") photographs relating to the text on that page or the one facing it. While some are not quite as clear as those in *The International Encyclopedia of the Film*, they are easily identifiable and, for the most part, good selections.

Following the biographical section is a 138-page Index in which films cited in the biographical entries are listed with cross-references to alternative titles. The main entry for each film in the Index is given under the original title with a cross-reference from the English version. The main entry for *Wild Strawberries,* for example, is found under *Smultronstallet,* the original Swedish title, just as the main entry for *Knife in the Water* is found under *Noz W Wodzie*, its original Polish title. Each entry gives complete credits for the film, even the literary source if it is noteworthy *(Dr. Zhivago*, for instance), the date of completion or first showing, the production company, the length, and whether it was in color or wide-screen process. The bold capitals used for the main entries make this Index considerably easier to use than the very small print indexes in *The International Encyclopedia*.

The Index of *The World Encyclopedia* undoubtedly enhances the work as a reference tool. One can find specific information on a film and go from there to the biographical section for further information. Although the work contains no entries for terms related to film and only biographical entries, it does contain more biographies than *The International Encyclopedia*. If one wants a brief who's who type of account for a lesser-known actor or director, *The World Encyclopedia* would probably be the better choice. If one is interested in a critical commentary on the work of a certain director or an overview of the film in a given country, *The International Encyclopedia* is the likelier choice.

Neither volume claims to be totally complete in world coverage of films, and perhaps this would be impossible in a one-volume work. Most of the notable figures are covered in both volumes. More of the lesser ones are covered in *The World Encyclopedia*. There are some names, however, found in *The International* and not in *World*. A few are omitted from both. It is perhaps surprising not to find an entry for an actor such as Don Ameche, especially when his films so frequently rerun on television.

While there are a few minor inaccuracies in both volumes—and these may be typographical errors since they are usually one number in a date or minor word in a film title—both works are generally of high caliber in content and form. They are approximately the same size, are sturdily bound, and lie flat when open. *The International Encyclopedia* has a slightly larger inside margin and glossier paper.

To recommend one over the other would be not only difficult but also unfair. The choice would depend on the primary use one would make of the encyclopedia. For extensive factual information on directors, actors, producers and others connected with the film industry and for specific information regarding film credits on a particular title, *The World Encyclopedia of the Film* is recommended as a first choice; for critical comments on people related to the film industry and their major works, and an overview of a country's film production, *The International Encyclopedia of the Film* is superior. Both, therefore, are recommended.
(Oct. 1, 1973, p.129)

International Library of Negro Life and History. Charles H. Wesley, editor in chief. 10v. New York, Publishers

Company, Inc., under the auspices of the Association for the Study of Negro Life and History, c1967, 1968, 1969, 1970. illus. 28cm. c-1 textbook cloth, pyroxylin impregnated $185; individual volumes $13.88 each; to schools and libraries, 25 percent discount. The Negro in Music and Art. Lindsay Patterson, ed. xvi, 304p. illus.; Anthology of the American Negro in the Theatre: A Critical Approach. Lindsay Patterson, ed. xiv, 306p. illus.; Negro Americans in the Civil War: From Slavery to Citizenship, by Charles H. Wesley and Patricia W. Romero. xi, 291p. illus.; The History of the Negro in Medicine, 3d ed. by Herbert M. Morais. xiv, 322p. illus.; Historical Negro Biographies, by Wilhelmena S. Robinson. xii, 291p. illus.; In Freedom's Footsteps: From the African Background to the Civil War, by Charles H. Wesley. xii, 307p. illus.; The Quest for Equality: From Civil War to Civil Rights, by Charles H. Wesley. xii, 307p. illus.; I Too Am America: Documents from 1619 to the Present, by Patricia W. Romero. xv, 304p. illus.; The Black Athlete: Emergence and Arrival, by Edwin B. Henderson. xiii, 306p. illus.; An Introduction to Black Literature in America: From 1746 to the Present, by Lindsay Patterson. xvii, 302p. illus.; (yearbooks) In Black America 1968: The Year of Awakening, by Patricia W. Romero. xvii, 445p. illus. $11.25; 1970 Year Book: Events of 1969, xv, 455p. illus. $11.25.

The multivolumed *International Library of Negro Life and History* and its two yearbooks are designed to form a comprehensive picture of the black experience in the United States; the set presents a record of a people from their African beginnings through slavery and ends in present-day struggles "to cast off the last vestiges of the bonds." The set includes coverage of achievement in sports and medicine, selected biographies, documentary history, and anthologies treating music, art, the theater, and literature.

The two yearbooks and each of the ten volumes are designed as independent units. Each volume has an author or compiler who interprets the material presented in his area of speciality, and each book contains a Preface, Introduction, Bibliography, Index, and a list of picture credits where appropriate. The volumes are not numbered, and each bears a distinctive title as indicated in the heading of this review. There is no general index to the series; nor are there cross-references to related materials in the various volumes.

Three of the volumes (*In Freedom's Footsteps, Negro Americans in the Civil War,* and *The Quest for Equality*) are concerned with the history of the black man. They present background information which provides a perspective for the material in the remaining volumes. Three of the books deal with humanities and the black man (*An Introduction to Black Literature in America, The Negro in Music and Art,* and *Anthology of the American Negro in the Theatre. The Black Athlete* covers sports; *The History of the Negro in Medicine* is devoted to the black man in medicine; short biographies are given in *Historical Negro Biographies,* and *I Too Am America* presents documents from 1619 to the present in "the words of those who participated in or witnessed" this drama of human events.

International Library of Negro Life and History is sponsored by the Association for the Study of Negro Life and History, a pioneer in Negro history. Since it was founded in 1915, the Association has supported many publications concerned with the contributions of black people to the growth and development of the United States. Under the direction of its founder, the late Dr. Carter G. Woodson, the Association disseminated factual studies designed to place the black man in true perspective in American history. Publishers Company, Inc. publishes a number of subscription sets and reference books.

Dr. Charles H. Wesley is editor in chief of the ten-volume basic set and also contributed substantially to writing materials included in each volume. He was executive director for the Association for the Study of Negro Life and History from 1965 until his retirement in 1972. His writings include: coauthor, *The Story of the Negro Retold* (Washington, D.C.: Associated Pub., 1959) and *Negro Makers of History* (Washington, D.C.: Associated Pub., 1959), and *The Negro in Our History* (Washington, D.C. Associated Pub., 1962); editor, *The Negro in the Americas* (Washington, D.C.: Howard Univ. Grad. Sch., 1940) and *Neglected History: Essays in Negro American History by a College President* (Washington, D.C.: Chas. H. Wesley Res. Fund, 1965); and contributor to *What The Negro Wants* (Chapel Hill, N.C.: Univ. of North Carolina Pr., 1944). Patricia Romero served as research editor for the present series and also wrote one volume and the 1969 yearbook and coauthored another volume. She holds a doctorate in history.

The first five volumes covering medicine, the theater, Civil War, music and art, and biographies were reviewed in *The Booklist and Subscription Books Bulletin* November 1,1968. At that time the Committee characterized the books as covering their subjects with varying degrees of comprehensiveness in clear and concise language. The present review will be devoted primarily to the last five volumes. The books will be discussed in the order in which they are listed in the review heading.

In Freedom's Footsteps written by Dr. Wesley, consists of 17 chapters covering the period from the earliest exploration and discovery of both Africa and America, with a brief account of the Spanish, Portuguese, and New England slave trade, and a longer account of the situation in the Southern states. There are chapters on the free Negro in the Colonial era, the Negro and the War of 1812, Negro participation in the abolition movement, early Negro crusaders, and plantation life and southern labor.

The material covered is adequate for use by nonspecialist adults and by students at the high school and junior high school levels. The information is presented fairly in an unbiased manner covering the controversial facts of slavery in the United States prior to the Civil War. However, information on specific subjects is scattered and difficult to locate. For example, there is no entry in the Index under churches. It is necessary to look under specific entries to locate information on the African Methodist Episcopal Church, Baptists, and Methodist Episcopal Church. The volume is profusely illustrated, mostly with contemporary line drawings or engravings, reproductions of title pages of books, newspapers, bills of sale, and advertisements for runaway slaves. The Index differentiates between text and illustrations, and also between titles of books and subjects. *In Freedom's Footsteps* contains a very good bibliography subdivided by topic. Most books cited are secondary, not primary sources. They are intended to provide additional readings and are chosen for readability at the adult level, not for research value.

Quest for Equality, also written by Dr. Wesley, is a continuation of *In Freedom's Footsteps*. It relates the story of the Negro from the Reconstruction period to the April 1968 slaying of Dr. Martin Luther King Jr. This volume is also well illustrated, most frequently with reproductions of engravings. There is also a generous sprinkling of reproductions of newspaper front pages, title pages of books, and similar documents. *Quest for Equality* treats black Reconstruction, Negro participation in politics and labor, first movements toward black unity, depression and New Deal, World War II, Korea and Vietnam, and Black Power in the establishment. The vague titles of some chapters are somewhat offset by the more exact running heads on text pages. The sequence of chapters is generally chronological, and use of the Index is required to locate information on a specific subject.

The text of the 17 chapters, like that of *In Freedom's Footsteps*, covers the history of a century rather superficially. A single chapter, for example, suffices to cover the achievements of Negroes in World War II, the Korean War, and Vietnam, but the facts presented are generally correct and unadorned, and are presented in an unimpassioned manner. A typical passage reads "Hard-boiled General Patton generously praised the work of the all-Negro 514th Quartermaster's Corps Company attached to the Third Army in Europe." This plain, straightforward sentence is typical of Dr. Wesley's style of writing.

The volume concludes with a group of miscellaneous pictures of Negro life, Negroes in action in civil rights demonstrations, and photographs of riots and arrests during recent civil disturbances, particularly those of 1968. This volume treats many controversial subjects such as education, equality, black inferiority, and the Negro and labor in a factual manner, and the illustrations are well chosen and clearly reproduced.

I Too Am America: Documents from 1619 to the Present is compiled and edited with an Introduction by Patricia W. Romero, who is also the research editor for the entire set of ten volumes. According to the Introduction "The purpose of the volume is to relate the history of the black people in America through the words of those who participated in or witnessed this great drama of human events." A broad interpretation is given to the term "document" as poetry, cartoons, periodical articles, and addresses are included as well as original documentary papers. These are well selected to illustrate the issues.

I Too Am America has three sections. The first portion begins with the arrival of the first Negroes in the United States and covers slavery in all of its aspects. The period from the Civil War to *Plessy v. Ferguson* is treated in the second part, and Booker T. Washington's era to the present is covered in the last section. The major shortcomings of this volume are the lack of comprehensive text and of exact and complete entries in the Index. An example of the seriousness of the lack of complete text to accompany the documents is the coverage of Detroit Race Riot of 1943 where the only document furnished is the article in *Detroit Free Press* for June 30, 1943 and text which states that the violence that lasted 24 hours occurred on June 20, 1943, that there was destruction and loss of life, and the cause. This information is inadequate for most users who would like to know what followed and what the final results were.

The lack of exactness for some Index entries is illustrated by the entry for "executions" which is followed only by the page numbers 34, 36-37, 58, 123, 227-229. An analytical index reference which indicates that Abraham Johnstone is on page 34, the Prosser Insurrection on pages 36-37, Nat Turner on page 58, John A. Copeland on page 123, and Rainey Bethea on pages 227-229 would have been more useful.

The Black Athlete, by Edwin B. Henderson and editors of *Sport Magazine*, has an Introduction by the late Jackie Robinson and is comprised of ten chapters, Bibliography, picture credits, and Index. This volume covers all sports in which Negroes have participated. Coverage is adequate and useful to supplement other publications on the Negro in sports. The book is profusely illustrated with 344 black-and-white photographs to 274 pages of text. The Bibliography at the end is valuable both for its size (over 900 items) and for its recency, since most items are dated from 1960 to 1966. The Bibliography is divided into 11 topics: General Sources, Baseball, Football, etc., then Olympics, Other Sports, Integration in Sports, Education, Recreation and School Sports. The Bibliography is followed by an Index of approximately 1,200 entries, most of them names of athletes or of teams, making it, together with the extensive Bibliography just mentioned, a valuable contribution to the reference literature on Negro athletics.

The final volume to be considered, *An Introduction to Black Literature in America*, is an anthology of selections from black writers from the eighteenth century to the present. Included are such popular authors as Charles Waddell Chestnutt, Frederick Douglass, James Weldon Johnson, and Jean Toomer, but a number of the emerging and modern writers such as Lorraine Hansberry, Ann Petry, Chester Himes, E. J. Gaines, and Ed Bullins are omitted. Selections are arranged chronologically by century—eighteenth, nineteenth, and twentieth. Following the literary selections, there are four critical articles on black literature by black writers, and a Bibliography which includes lengthier works by the authors in the anthology as well as additional material by others. Each section has a short introduction which traces the main developments of the period.

The eighteenth century section contains five very interesting selections, narratives of the life of the black man in colonial America, and a section of poetry. These pieces show Negroes in a light that will be new to most Americans: Benjamin Banneker planning a "Peace Office" for the government of the United States; Gustavus Vassa describing his capture as an eleven-year-old in the forests of Africa; Briton Hammon's tale of his shipwreck in 1760. The nineteenth century section has selections from the work of 15 writers and a group of spirituals. The selections center around slave life, the Civil War, and Reconstruction. Many of them were published in the first black literary magazine, *Anglo-African.*

The twentieth century section is much broader in content. Fifty-three writers are included, 18 of whom are writers from the 1960s. There is also a small collection of blues, work songs, ballads, and street cries.

The selection is generally good and quite representative. As is true of the other volumes, this book does not claim complete coverage, and some important authors are omitted. Since political aspects of black writing are not represented in this anthology, LeRoi Jones is represented only by his poetry and one prose piece.

The ten basic volumes of *International Library of Negro Life and History* are supplemented by two yearbooks. The 1969 yearbook bears the title *In Black America, 1968: The Year of Awakening,* and is compiled and edited with an Introduction by Patricia W. Romero. The 1970 yearbook is entitled *Events of 1969.* These two books are separate entities and are independent of the other volumes in the set. They present the new awakenings of the Negro race in 1968 and 1969, the black woman, blacks in the mass media, business and economy, literature of the year, education, rural and urban problems, statistical information on numerous subjects, and similar information. Inconsistent with most of the other volumes, they contain no bibliography; references to sources are given only in a list of publications. Where titles are given, no publishers are included. The volumes present a kaleidoscopic approach to black history in 1968 and 1969 and may serve uniquely but in a limited capacity, without the addition of the other volumes. Unfortunately, there are no cross-references to the other volumes, and some of the materials included, for example, in 1968, *Public, University and Private American Library Holdings on the Negro,* by Ernest Kaiser, pages 271-279, are not peculiar to the year 1968.

The entire set is profusely illustrated with facsimiles, portraits, plans, and maps in black and white. The illustrations are usually good, though some, due to the nature of the historical originals, do not show up as well as others. It is regrettable that the art reproductions lack color.

International Library of Negro Life and History is handsomely bound in tan buckram with black trim and black and silver lettering. The text is arranged in two columns; margins are adequate. Various typefaces are used in the text as well as in the headings. Running heads are supplied throughout. Both texture and quality of the off-white paper are adequate. The pages of text are clear and easy to read and lie flat as the volumes are opened.

International Library of Negro Life and History presents interesting reading for students and adults. The title is misleading, however, because coverage is more American than international. The major limitation of the set is its lack of a general cumulative index to the text and illustrations. For example, to obtain references to statesman Blanche K. Bruce, a comparatively narrow subject, one must use the indexes in three volumes, but for material on civil rights, a broad subject, five indexes must be consulted. Furthermore, the individual volume indexes are not sufficiently comprehensive and analytical to provide maximum access to the material.

Repetition and overlapping seems inevitable in a series written by a number of people and containing individual volumes intended to stand as independent units. Marian Anderson, for instance, has a one-page biography in *Historical Negro Biographies* while a long article by David Ewen in *The Negro in Music and Art* contains more information about her art, including also some biographical facts. Even within the same volume repetition occurs. Thus, one reads about the fate of the American Negro theater several times in the *Anthology of the American Negro in the Theatre*.

International Library avoids references to and information on the more radical members of the black world. A search of the indexes of all volumes revealed only a one-line reference to LeRoi Jones and his anarchistic leaning, a photograph of H. Rap Brown, five references to Stokely Carmichael, and no mention of Eldridge Cleaver. There is also no index entry for the Black Panthers.

Some volumes will be more useful as reference tools than others. Those that contain biographical sections or well-organized historical accounts will be the most useful.

Despite the absence of a general index, the lack of color illustrations particularly in the art volume, limited use of cross-references, and occasional omission of pertinent information that would present a full picture of the cultural and historical experience of the Negro in the United States, *International Library of Negro Life and History* brings together a wealth of information in convenient form. With the warning that a substantial amount of information on the Negro is missing, the set is recommended for homes, public, and school libraries.

(July 15, 1973, p.1025)

International Visual Dictionary. Editor, Leo F. Daniels. Los Angeles 90017, Clute International Institute; Distributor, Carroll Book Service, North Tarrytown, NY. 1973. ix, 710p. illus. 29cm. cloth $19.95; to schools and libraries, $9.95. ISBN 0-88217-001-5.

International Visual Dictionary is published by the Clute International Institute, Los Angeles and distributed by Carroll Book Service, North Tarrytown, New York. The writer and editor of the dictionary is Leo F. Daniels listed as a lexicographer. Daniels coauthored *The International Dictionary of Thoughts* (Chicago: J. G. Ferguson, 1969) reviewed by the Committee April 15, 1970 in *The Booklist*. An impressive "Advisory Board" includes librarians, teachers, authors, and editors including John Carroll, bookman John Clute, and William J. Roehrenbeck, Director, Jersey Free Public Library, who wrote the Foreword.

The dictionary claims to be a "tool for learning the English language" and "designed for children in the early grades of elementary school and for adults learning English," including those who are "foreign born." It contains a word list of approximately 3,000 entries based on published word lists, on consultations with "many elementary school teachers, teachers of the English language, and school librarians," and from an examination of children's textbooks and language arts books.

Words follow in typical letter by letter dictionary arrangement, but it is doubtful that the designation of "dictionary" for this publication is a correct one. Since the stated policy is to provide for large type and "fresh and clear" uncrowded pages, no accent or diacritical marks, hyphenated symbols, syllable divisions, or foreign language roots or derivatives are given. At times a statement of definition is given. At other times the word is described through usage within a sentence, or several uses within several sentences. A further departure from the dictionary approach comes with the frequent inclusion of Mother Goose or original rhymes and, at times, the inclusion of arithmetic problems and posed questions. The volume might better be described, as the advertising copy does, as an "English language learning and reading tool."

The listing of approximately 3,000 selected words may well increase the vocabulary of the child using the volume. The explanation of words and their usage could certainly aid such development and carry out one purpose of the dictionary: "to express oneself more easily and confidently in English" and "find one's way in the informative and fascinating world of words." Though these stated purposes have been, in general, successfully carried out, they have failed in many instances by causing confusion and by not giving clear direction. Such failure is especially true if this publication is to be considered as an "international" dictionary directed toward those who are schooled in another language, with a different cultural background, and desirous of learning English usage.

When definitions are simple as in the case of *woods*—"a place where many trees grow close together"—an understanding of the word can be grasped. The same can be true when simple explanatory sentences are used, e.g., *a* followed by the statement, "John has *a* ball," which is, in turn, followed by another explanation, "John has *one* ball;" or for the word *able* the statement, "I am *able* to read," followed by "I *can* read." In each case, and in all explanations, comparable words are in bold type.

In too many instances, however, the definitions or usage explanations are less simple and lead to confusion, or they are too general in explanation, leading to a wrong concept. To define a *witch* as an "ugly old woman," is certainly questionable even though witch is further defined by the statements: "In fairy tales, *witches* ride on brooms. *Witches* are not real." A more serious generalization is given for *"jail"* as: "People who do not obey the law are put into *jail*. . . . Jail is a place where bad men are locked behind walls made of bars." Several students from foreign countries who aided in the evaluation of the dictionary took strong opposition to this definition, feeling that many prisoners are not "bad men." Certainly there have been miscarriages of justice in the United States, and it would be wrong to classify some youthful first offenders who are placed behind bars as "bad men."

Any number of examples can be given in which definitions provide little in the way of explanation or are confusing in the concepts given or in any additional explanation found in the definition of an unfamiliar word used in the initial definition. Examples: *Ouch,* explained by "when Sarah hurt her finger she said, ouch;" *library* is a "place where many books are kept . . . ;" *blackberry* is called "a purple fruit" while all standard dictionaries define this berry as being black or dark purple; *hog* is defined as "a large pig," with *pig* defined as "a young hog" and *pork* as "meat from pigs."

Further confusion is found in such a word as *aboard*. The first explanatory sentences are reasonable, "Peter is getting *aboard* the ship," explained by "Peter is getting *on* the ship." Then we learn that since Peter likes to travel he has also "been *aboard* a train, a bus, and an airplane." The added sentence may require the user to turn to an explanation of train, bus, and airplane which can provide an additional learning experience. However, the explanation of an airplane is very long and involved, introducing a number of new words. One of these words, *wings* when checked for meaning begins with a five-line explanation of wings as "a part of an animal that flies," an explanation that is dubious in itself, but it is only after one gets through this explanation that one learns that "an airplane has two wings."

Not only does the reader have this problem of referring from one explanation to another because of the length of the original definition with its possible new terms, but the word *aboard* also includes a two-stanza verse. Why? Is this a dictionary or a textbook? Poetry is the most difficult form of literature for a beginning reader to master. Further, in this case as in many of the rhymes included with the definitions, additional and often difficult words are introduced which would cause a child to look up word after word only to become more confused.

The poem included with *aboard*, for example, has as its first two lines: "Aboard the boat, aboard the ship,

"The whistle whistles, 'Pip! Pip! Pip!'" The definition for *whistle,* one of the possible new words, has an illustration of three varieties of mouth whistles and reads: "These are whistles. A whistle makes a noise when you blow through it," and then further defines it as "a sound made with the mouth." These definitions have no relation to the boat whistle, and certainly the use of the word "pip" does nothing to help the concept of a ship's whistle. The word was evidently chosen to rhyme with ship and is indicative of the inanity of some of the original verses.

Illustrations by Fernando Burgos Perez are included as part of the majority of the definitions and often help in understanding the definitions, e.g., those of line, squirrel, cup, rose, lily, acorn. However, the lack of size relationships may cause confusion. The acorn size is out of proportion to other figures which appear on the same page, and the two lovely illustrations for the lily are twice the size of that of the lion adjacent to them on the following pages.

Choice of illustration can also be questioned at times such as the one using a postcard to demonstrate the meaning of *address.* The illustration includes a written message as well as the address with no indication that one side of the card only is the address. The use of an addressed envelope would have provided a more explicit example. *Cottage,* defined as "a small house," has a large home depicted with certainly more than the three rooms described in the definition. The definitions for *quarter* are illustrated by a pie divided into quarters, while a depiction of the piece of money, also a part of the definition, would have been most helpful for one from another country.

Poor color reproduction is another failure in aiding comprehension. Color is defined by: "Alice likes to color eggs for Easter. She likes to make the white eggs different colors." The accompanying illustration depicts a row of labeled colored circles with a girl coloring Easter eggs; a good idea except that the reproductions of the colors purple, black, and brown are not true. Under the definition of *ribbon* is the statement "Nancy has two pink ribbons in her hair" but an illustration of Nancy shows her with red hair and with red, not pink, ribbons. Because of this faulty reproduction the ribbons are virtually indistinguishable.

Illustration does little to enhance the definition of *add* which begins with an abstract instead of a concept idea. Such abstract explanations are true of other mathematical terms, and mathematical questions are constantly being posed within definitions which have little relation to modern teaching methods. Zero is a concept not a number, and does not always come before one as stated in the definition. Further explanations, dealing with the place of zero in counting by tens, ends with the question: "How many tens are in one hundred and twenty?" Is this volume a dictionary or a mathematical workbook? Under *eleventh,* where the reader learns that "K" is the eleventh letter of the alphabet, is the question: "Do you know what the seventeenth letter of the alphabet is?" Why ask this question when the child has not yet been introduced to the word "seventeenth?" If it is to send him to seek the definition of this new word he will find that with "seventeen people standing in line, Barbara is seventeenth." This is hardly a satisfying explanation.

Perhaps one of the more serious criticisms that can be aimed at the dictionary is its lack of concern with international views and backgrounds. Why use snow as an explanation for "white" when something more people in the world know, such as milk, would offer a clearer understanding? The picture of a three layer cake to illustrate "whole" and "half," especially since the layers are pink, yellow, and red in color, is perhaps not the clearest way to demonstrate these terms. "In the morning I have bacon and eggs" can be questioned as the most fitting way to explain "bacon" for a child outside the United States. Why not a more natural explanation for *absent* such as absent from school rather than the more unusual one of being "absent from the table?" It would seem more reasonable to refer to many Indian "tribes," since the definition of this word refers to Indians rather than to talk of many "kinds" of Indians. It would seem reasonable that a child from East India might question the exclusion of East Indians from the definition. The explanation of *Japanese* includes a picture of "Kazuko wearing Japanese clothes," the traditional Japanese costume. There is no indication that this is no longer the only or usual attire of these people. Most questionable is the original rhyme included in the definition with its generalizations: The Japanese are very nice/So kind and gentle and polite/A people known for liking rice/and clothes that are a pretty sight.

The international picture is further disregarded in the overabundance of white blond or red-headed children and adults which people the illustrations. Of 40 illustrations of "father" appearing in the definitions, 25 show a definitely white father, and the color of five of the remaining 15 is indistinguishable because of poor color reproduction. Of the 31 mothers depicted, 22 are white; the 2 grandfathers shown are white, as are six out of the seven grandmothers.

The word *black* is illustrated by a white father wearing a black tie and holding a piece of black coal in his hand, items which appear in the definition. Persons depicting various careers are white: queen, king, aviator, doctor, dentist, radio announcer, teacher, band leader, fireman. Are there no third world peoples in such professions? The illustration accompanying "nurse" could depict a dark skinned person; a dark skinned soldier is used in the definition of "medal;" both illustrations of men selling balloons are shown as dark skinned.

The dictionary has a useful Word-Usage Finder "designed to help location of a particular word within entries different from its own main entry." A following section is headed "The Sentence and Eight Parts of Speech." Though a clarification of grammatical terms can be useful to one new to the English language, the opening explanation of the section, defining a sentence, fails to recognize the latest methods of teaching English. A sentence is not necessarily "a group of words that tells us, or expresses, a complete thought." One word can be a sentence.

International Visual Dictionary is attractively and quite sturdily bound and stays open well for ease of use. Certainly through illustration, simple explanation, and examples of usage, a child could gain an understanding of the English language. However, because of the lack of regular features of a dictionary, and the often irregular, involved and confusing definitions and explanations, the value of this volume as a dictionary is in question. The inclusion of posed questions, mathematical problems, and rhymes and jingles give it a textbook-workbook context. The price of $19.95 ($9.95 to schools) makes this a very expensive learning tool. Lastly, the dictionary fails to be fully aware of its stated purpose to aid non-English speaking children and adults to a better comprehension and understanding of the English language. *International Visual Dictionary* is not recommended for purchase by libraries, schools or homes.

Margaret R. Sheviak
Associate Professor
Graduate Library School
Indiana University
Bloomington, IN 47401
(Feb. 15, 1974, p.608)

The International Wildlife Encyclopedia.
General editors: Dr. Maurice Burton [and] Robert Burton. 20v. New York, Marshall Cavendish Corp. (Exclusive school and library distribution by Purnell Library Service, 850 Seventh Avenue, New York, 10019) [1971, c1969]. 2,800p. illus. (part col.) col. maps. diagrs. tables. kivar kidskin grain. $185.50 net, ($155.50 each when more than one purchased.) Available to homes on subscription from Marshall Cavendish, 6 Commercial St., Hicksville, NY 11801, v.1 free, v.2-20 for $4.39 a volume or $83.41 a set.

International Wildlife Encyclopedia originally appeared in the United Kingdom in 1968 as a weekly continuation entitled *Animal Life*. The present edition is a revised and updated version of these 96 weekly issues.

The senior editor, Maurice Burton, is a zoologist of international reputation.

An officer of the British Museum (Natural History) for over 30 years, he is a world authority on invertebrates in general and sponges in particular; he has also written or edited a large number of popular works on animals, and has been nature correspondent for the *Daily Telegraph* since 1949. The individual articles which make up the bulk of the encyclopedia are not signed, and no indication is given any place in the books as to authority or responsibility for the writing. However, authors are indicated for the general essays in the last volume. These are, in the main, well-known zoologists, such as Miriam Rothschild and Peter Scott.

International Wildlife Encyclopedia lacks any introduction, foreword, or preface identifying its objectives and readership. It is, however, fairly obvious from the style of writing, selection of topics, and the profusion of illustrative material that this is a publication for the youngster interested in animals or the nonspecialist adult of general interests.

"Wildlife" is here used as directly synonymous with "animal life" without any connotation of wildlife from a resource or ecological viewpoint. The British title, *Animal Life*, seems more appropriate. Coverage of the animal kingdom is of necessity uneven in a work of this type; emphasis is placed on those animals most likely read about or seen in backyard, park, zoo, or aquarium. That is, concentration is on animals or groups of animals which have acquired some specific and general identity by virtue of size, color, song, intrinsic interest, or impact on our daily lives. Within these limitations coverage is very good. No animal or animal group likely to be encountered, read about, or heard about by the average nonzoologist is missing from the encyclopedia, and many appear about which the reader is doubtless entirely ignorant. Nonetheless, the birds and mammals clearly have the best of it, and that is perhaps only natural.

Throughout the alphabetically arranged sections the overemphasis in coverage of mammals and birds displays this type of bias. There are separate entries for specific birds, mammals, and even insects, e.g., *Atlas Moth*, but the single article *Starfish* must suffice for an order of invertebrates which contains over 2,000 species.

The first 19 volumes consist of alphabetically arranged articles on 1,229 animals or animal groups. The entry word or phrase is the vernacular term or common name, where one exists; otherwise a scientific name is used. An individual article may cover a single species ("Apus," "Archerfish"), a single genus ("Apollo butterfly"), a single family ("Armadillo"), a group of families ("Backswimmer"), or even an order ("Starfish"). Articles range in length from one to four pages (mean length 2.2 pages), with very few exceeding this number. The actual length of each entry in words, however, varies considerably depending on the amount of illustrative material.

Articles are typically in the following form: (a) a brief diagnosis and description of the animal or group, appearing at the beginning of the article in italic type, (b) the text of the entry, giving details of the biology, feeding, life history, reproduction, relationships, appearance, and special features of the subject, (c) one or more illustrations, including distributional maps, tables, etc., where appropriate and (d) a brief tabular representation of the scientific nomenclature of the subject, usually with three or four levels of classification given. These may be phylum, class, order, family, or genus and species as appropriate.

The specificity of entries should be emphasized. There is, for example, no entry for "Seals." There are, however, separate articles for *Common Seal, Crabeater Seal, Elephant Seal, Fur Seal, Grey Seal, Harp Seal, Hooded Seal, Leopard Seal, Monk Seal, Ringed Seal, Ross Seal, Sea Lion,* and *Weddell Seal,* with mention within these several entries of the Baikal seal, Caspian seal, Greenland seal, harbor seal, saddleback seal, and white seal.

Following the last of the articles, *Wryneck* to *Zorro,* volume 20 is in two parts. First, a "Special Contents" section of 80 pages presents short, general essays on selected topics dealing with animal life, e.g., evolution, behavior, ecology. These are the essays mentioned earlier whose authors are identified at the end of the "Special Contents" section. Three indexes comprise the final part of volume 20.

The first, an "Animal Index," is an alphabetical list of common and scientific names of animals used in the encyclopedia. The second is a "Subject Index," and the third a "Systematic Index," which arranges all the scientific names used in the encyclopedia in hierarchial order. All indexes feature page references; there are no cross-references. All indexes indicate, by appropriate symbols and typography, the type of entry and the presence or absence of illustrative material.

The "Animal Index" is by far the largest. It contains approximately 11,650 terms in reference to the 1,229 entries comprising the main part of the encyclopedia, a mean of 9.5 index terms per entry. A random sample of 20 encyclopedia pages revealed that 42 of 44 scientific names and 22 of 27 common names mentioned on these pages appeared in the Index. The indexing thus seems to be adequate. The "Systematic Index" shows comparable adequacy.

The "Subject Index," however, does not rate very well. First, it is extremely short—one page in length, with only about 460 headings and subdivisions. It is evident that many general subjects discussed in the pages of the encyclopedia are not brought out in the "Subject Index." For instance: the entry *Butcher-bird* includes a good 300-word essay entitled "What is a songbird?" in which the mechanism and taxonomic significance of bird song is discussed. The "Subject Index" does not list this section; in fact, there is nothing in the "Subject Index" under "Bird" or "Song." Similarly, a paragraph "Riding the Thermals" in the *Vulture* article is listed under neither "Soaring" nor "Thermals," although a reference is found under "Flight—Soaring."

International Wildlife Encyclopedia is profusely illustrated; its 2,800 pages contain more than 2,500 full-color illustrations. Most of these are photographs; the remainder are colored distributional maps, provided where helpful. There is a lesser number of black-and-white illustrations, including some portraits. The selection of the colored photographs is good, and the quality of reproduction excellent. Only rarely are the colored photographs fuzzy, out-of-register, or off-color; the great majority of them are striking, instructive, and beautiful.

The encyclopedia's 2,800 pages are distributed among 20 volumes, paged continuously, each with 140 pages. Each index page has, at its foot, a colored diagram indicating volumes and their corresponding page numbers. The inclusive pagination of each volume, as well as its alphabetical spread, is also stamped, but almost illegibly, on its narrow and quite crowded spine. The volumes are very thin, 9/16-inch by actual measurement.

The binding is sturdy enough, with Smyth sewing and cambric-reinforced hinges. The pages lie flat when the volumes are opened, but the inner margins are very narrow. In some cases the adhesive has evidently penetrated between gatherings and glued them together to the extent that some inner columns are not fully legible. The binding is a red soil-resistant material which shows marks of wear in the review sets.

There is no other publication to which *Encyclopedia of Wildlife* can be readily compared in scope and treatment. The arrangement of entries under common-name, direct headings tends to separate related material, as the treatment of "Seals," previously described, indicates. The "Animal Index" brings these related entries together in an adequate fashion, but it still requires much effort on the part of the reader whose interests transcend the contents of a single entry to find all relevant data.

The content and style of writing are very good. The North American reader may find some few Briticisms still unexpunged from the first compilation, but these are neither many nor serious. "Hyaena," for example, is used where "hyena" is the more customary American form, and "carcase" for "carcass." The writing itself is simple, direct, and not condescending. Only in the illustration captions does a note of archness or anthropomorphism occasionally appear.

Mating earthworms are called "the *happy* couple;" we are told that female earwigs are *"model* mothers" and that they watch over "earwig *toddlers;"* and that octopuses are *"cruel* but beautiful."

By and large, however, *The International Wildlife Encyclopedia* should prove fascinating and instructive to anyone, especially the young person, interested in animals and seeking general well-presented and well-illustrated information. It is recommended.

(Oct. 15, 1972, p.153)

Irregular Serials and Annuals: an International Directory. [Edited by Emery Koltay, director of Bowker Serials Bibliography Department.] 2d ed., 1972. New York, R. R. Bowker Co., c1972. xxxv, 2017-3382p. 29cm. cloth $38.50.

Users of the earlier edition of *Irregular Serials and Annuals,* first published in 1967, will find some surprising changes in this new edition. First of all, the work is no longer merely a supplement to the well-known *Ulrich's International Periodicals Directory,* but is an integral part of a combined work, referred to in the Preface of the present work as "Bowker Serials Bibliography," consisting of *Ulrich's Directory* and *Irregular Serials* (by which briefer titles these two will henceforth be cited), the database for both having been combined and converted to magnetic tape. The Preface to the present volume states that it is "a companion volume" to *Ulrich's Directory,* but a statement appearing at the end of the same Preface, signed by Emery Koltay, Director, Serials Bibliography, reads: "We intend to publish new editions of this directory biennially, with quarterly supplements appearing between the editions. A supplement for serials, covering both *Ulrich's* and *Irregular Serials,* is planned for the end of 1972, while the quarterly updating service will begin in March 1973."

The second point to notice is that although the words "volume III" do not appear anywhere on the spine, cover, or title page, it is evident that the editors are considering this to be the third part of the Bowker Serials Bibliography. The pagination of the present work begins at page 2017; the highest numbered page in volume II of the 14th edition of *Ulrich's* was page 2016.

Another factor indicating that *Irregular Serials* is henceforth to be considered an integral, rather than a supplemental, part of the Bowker Serials Bibliography is the inclusion of the new "Title Index for Bowker Serials Bibliography," running from page 2781 to page 3382 of the present work, and therefore constituting almost half of the work under review. This Index includes the International Standard Serial Numbers (ISSN) for every item in the Index, a total of approximately 70,000 publications. The Index is a combined Index for all parts of the Bowker Serials Bibliography, and therefore indexes, by title only, the two volumes of the 14th edition of *Ulrich's* as well as the present volume under review. The explanatory text at the beginning of the Index states that pages 1-1006 refer to *Ulrich's,* volume I; pages 1007-1658 refer to *Ulrich's,* volume II; while pages 2017-2780 refer to "this volume," once again carefully avoiding the use of "volume III," though such designation would be completely logical in view of the continuous pagination, and in fact the term "volume III" is actually used in the article on International Standard Serial Numbering which Koltay wrote for *Bowker Annual,* 1972, which essay is reprinted in part on pages xi to xiii of the present work.

The content of this second edition of *Irregular Serials and Annuals* has been updated and increased approximately 40 percent, but not radically changed. The arrangement is still alphabetical by subject, from Abstracting and Indexing Services to Water Economics. Large subjects, such as Biology or Chemistry are subdivided—Botany, Entomology, etc. Not counting such subdivisions, there are 128 subjects; the subdivisions add about 100 more. In addition to the list of subjects there is a 12-page Cross Index to Subjects, enabling the user to discover, for example, whether PHILATELY is a subject in itself or, as it turns out, is to be found as a subdivision of HOBBIES. The Cross Index also has many *see also* type entries, and includes some specific topics, such as "Esperanto See LINGUISTICS."

Criteria for inclusion in the body of the work remain about the same as in the first edition, and are spelled out as follows: "Titles issued annually or less frequently than once a year, or irregularly; serials published at least twice under the same title, and those first publications which plan to have subsequent numbered issues; current materials whose last issue was published no earlier than January 1, 1963." Criteria for exclusion are also spelled out: "National, state, and municipal documents, with the exception of selected serials which are generally regarded as part of the conventional literature of scientific, technical, or medical research; and publications which are essentially administrative in content, such as membership directories, annual reports, house organs, or local interest publications." With regard to the exclusion of "annual reports," the editors appear to have been somewhat broad in their interpretation. The Preface states that in many cases "information was gathered . . . from sample copies of serials." This, together with the fact that many entries with the words "Annual Report" or its equivalent are to be found, would indicate that only those annual reports are excluded which are internal in nature, and not of interest to outsiders. Koltay confirms this criterion for selection, and notes that "only those reports which have substantial outside circulation were considered eligible for listing . . . in *Irregular Serials and Annuals.*" For example, Alaska, Department of Fish and Game, Annual Report, is included because upon inspection it was deemed to be of importance to outsiders.

As in the previous edition every serial or annual is assigned a classification number according to the 17th edition of the Dewey Decimal System. Sometimes alternate Dewey numbers are suggested, when an item covers more than one topic.

Coverage is worldwide, as in the better-known series of *Ulrich's* directories, with emphasis on American serials and annuals, and with the majority of non-American titles being from British, Canadian, Latin American, and Western European countries.

Specific information given includes at the minimum, title, frequency, price if available, publisher, address, and Dewey classification number. In addition to this minimum information the following items are sometimes also to be found: translation of title in the case of bi- or trilingual titles; former title, if any; statement as to language of content —for example, "Text in Rumanian; summaries in French, English, or Russian"; series statement; name and address of U.S. distributor; and occasionally other facts which may be of use in ordering.

The total number of entries is stated by the editor in the Preface to be "some 20,000." However, a news release dated July 7, 1972, says that the figure is "more than 19,500." A page count reveals that this latter figure is probably more accurate.

The Title Index for Bowker Serials Bibliography, which, as stated earlier, occupies the latter half of this bulky volume (pages 2781 to 3382, with four columns to the page), is an alphabetical listing of all periodical titles appearing in the 14th (1971/72) edition of *Ulrich's International Periodicals Directory* as well as the irregular serials appearing in the volume under review. Each of the approximately 70,000 serials so listed in one alphabet gives the page number (or numbers if the item also appears on another page as a cross-reference) on which it appears in either *Ulrich's* or *Irregular Serials,* followed by a two-letter code for the country of origin (US, UK, SW—Sweden), and finally the eight-digit International Standard Serial Number (ISSN).

The chief limitation for the user of this massive Index is the fact that it is only a title index, not a subject index. For example, let us assume that one wishes to know if there exists a directory for Singapore. There are in the title index 17 entries (both periodicals and annuals) beginning with the word Singapore, but no directory is listed. A search under the word *directory* discloses a title, *Directory of Singapore Manufacturers,* too specialized to be very helpful in a search for the name of a college, museum, or dentist. A further search discloses that there is indeed a complete directory, entitled *Directory of the State of Singapore*, separated by circumstances of alphabetizing from the other entry by as many as 17 items— and had it been entitled *New Directory of the State of Singapore*, it would have been separated by some 160 pages. To the question "Are there any periodicals or serials concerned with dominoes?" there is no adequate answer. The mere fact that no title beginning with that word is to be found in the Index is not certain proof that none exists. Or, to take another example, suppose a patron wants a camping guide to Italy. There are 17 titles beginning with the word "camping," but none refer to Italy. Nevertheless, an item-by-item perusal of the section Sports and Games (consisting of 114 entries) will turn up an annual entitled *Guida Camping d'Italia*.

Another deficiency, though perhaps less important, is the fact that the title index does not list titles by the first word of their second language, if any. For example, there is published in New York an annual entitled (in English) *Nobel Prizes*, and it is no doubt known to Americans under that title. However, it is a bilingual publication, and it happens that its French title, *Prix Nobel*, appears first on the title page or cover title. Consequently it is listed in the Title Index only under *Prix*. . . .

Another point to consider is the inconsistency of the cross-references from subject not used to subject used that appear in the Cross Index to Subjects in the front of the book, as well as, in some cases, in the Index itself. Taking the letters *N* and *O* as examples, there are 38 cross-references in the Cross Index to Subjects; of these 14 are to be found in the same format in the Index, while 24 of them are not in the Index. There appears to be no logical reason for inclusion or exclusion.

The type chosen for *Irregular Serials and Annuals* and the page layout make the volume similar to, if not almost identical to, the well-known *Ulrich's International Periodicals Directory*. A minor difference is the inclusion, in *Irregular Serials*, of a Dewey classification number below each entry, in the left margin. (The first edition of *Irregular Serials* also included this, but it was in the right margin). The paper is nonreflective white, printed with ample margins; the pages lie flat, and the binding is of good quality, matching in color and spine lettering the two volumes of *Ulrich's*. A spot check of the Index revealed no inaccuracies or blind references, and typographical errors in both text and Index are almost nonexistent.

Despite some deficiencies in the indexing of *Irregular Serials and Annuals*, the present volume is a welcome updating of an already useful work, *Ulrich's International Periodicals Directory*. For those libraries that have need for an international bibliography of elusive, infrequently or irregularly published serials, or annuals and biennials, this work is recommended.

(May 15, 1973, p.868)

Kobbe's Complete Opera Book, edited and revised by the Earl of Harewood. New York, G. P. Putnam's Sons, [1972]. xii, 1262p. music. 22cm. cloth $12.50; to schools and libraries, 25 percent discount.

When last reviewed in *The Booklist and Subscription Books Bulletin* (October, 15, 1964), *Kobbe's Complete Opera Book* was characterized as "an indispensable tool in libraries and a valuable home reference book for lovers of music." The appearance of a "new, revised edition" calls for a fresh examination of this respected work in its most recent version.

Readers who were hoping that the new edition might provide expanded coverage of contemporary opera will be disappointed as no new operas have been added to the 237 included in the previous edition. Thus, the most recent work covered is still Benjamin Britten's *Gloriana*, which had its premiere on June 8, 1953. American opera continues to be represented by only three composers: Thomson, Gershwin, and Menotti, and by no work of later date than Menotti's *The Consul* (1950).

The book jacket of the new edition

mentions a projected supplement by the Earl of Harewood, currently director of the Sadler's Wells Opera. Although contracted for in 1958, this supplement is still in preparation. The author states, however, that he plans to have it finished "well before the operas he is writing about are forgotten," thereby implying that he does not expect these contemporary works to remain in the permanent repertory.

As there has been no significant change in the scope and character of the work since the publication of the 1963 edition, there is no need to repeat the detailed analysis provided by the last Reference and Subscription Books Review Committee review. The volume provides for the 237 operas included detailed plot summaries with musical examples of the principal arias and motifs, brief stage histories, notes on the composers, and occasional passages of analysis and commentary. The present review will be confined to a comparison of the new edition with the last printing (April 1969) of the previous edition in order to determine the nature and extent of the revisions in the new edition.

New material in the revised edition consists almost entirely of additions to the stage histories which comprise the opening paragraph of the article for each opera. These histories have been updated to include revivals and noteworthy performances through 1969 for approximately 125 of the 237 operas in the book. (Extensive stage histories are not always provided for works which have remained continuously in the repertories of the major opera companies. The stage history of *Aida*, for example, is carried only as far as the first performance in English in 1880).

These additions to the stage histories sometimes include revivals or performances which antedate the most recent ones recorded in the previous edition. The additions for Beethoven's *Fidelio*, for example, date from 1927 through 1950 and antedate the 1961 revival at Covent Garden which concluded the stage history in the 1963 edition. In order to avoid extensive resetting of type, however, the new material has not been inserted in its proper chronological position but has merely been tacked on to the stage history as found in the previous edition. Thus, the 1961 revival noted above is now followed by an entry for the 1927-1936 performances in Salzburg, and the stage history of *Fidelio* concludes with the 1948-1950 Salzburg performances under Furtwangler. This departure from the normal chronological order of listing performances is regrettable and may actually be misleading to the user who does not scan the complete stage history but merely consults the final entry under the assumption that the most recent revival or noteworthy performance will be listed in that position.

The names of singers who have in recent years become noted for their performances of major roles have been added to the rosters of famous performers included in many of the stage histories. Names have sometimes been added even when there have been no additional listings of revivals or performances (e.g., Tebaldi and Vishnevskaya are added to the list of famous Aidas even though there are no additions to the opera's stage history).

In order to provide space for the expanded stage histories and still keep the articles within the pagination of the previous edition (the pagination in both editions is identical), some minor changes have been made in the textual matter which precedes and follows the stage histories. Most of these deletions and condensations are of an inconsequential nature (e.g., the deletion on page 37 of the statement that "Gluck retired to Vienna, where he died, November 25, 1787"); but occasionally the editors have deleted material which is of somewhat greater value (e.g., Professor Westrup's comment on Monteverdi on page 6 of the previous edition, or the concluding lines of the analysis of Verdi's *Nabucco* on page 423).

While the copy on the jacket flap states that the revised edition "adds valuable details to the plot descriptions," the evidence does not appear to support this claim. The only instance in which a significant addition was noted was in the treatment of Janacek's *Jenufa*, the plot summary of which is now preceded by an introductory paragraph explaining what has taken place prior to the opening of the first act.

A number of minor corrections and additions have been made in the portions of text devoted to analysis and commentary. The statement on page 448 of the previous edition that the aria "Possente amor mi chiama" from Act II of *Rigoletto* is usually omitted in performance has been corrected to read, "the cabaletta [i.e., the final section of the aria] is usually omitted in performance." The statement that Berlioz's complete *Les Troyens* "was too exacting for most managements to tackle, and so it has proved to the present day" has been modified to read, "and so it has proved until most recent times," since a number of complete performances have been staged in recent years.

Additions include such items as the footnote on page 643 pointing out that the tenor role of Prunier in *La Rondine* was originally composed for a baritone, and that early performances of *Fidelio* at the Metropolitan included "recitatives composed by the conductor Bodanzky to replace most of the spoken dialogue."

Some of the omissions noted in the review of the 1963 edition have still, however, not been rectified. While death dates have been added for Vaughan Williams and Charpentier, neither birth nor death dates are given for Goldmark, Johann Strauss, or Lortzing. The previous review noted that these omissions had been carried over from the 1954 edition. Their perpetuation over such a long period of time seems inexcusable. Dates for Cornelius and Nicolai are still buried in the text instead of appearing beneath the composers' names at the beginning of the articles which cover their works. Nicolai's date of birth must, as a matter of fact, be inferred from two statements which are separated by approximately a half page of text (viz., that his death occurred in May, 1849, and that he was not yet 39 years of age when he died). Four composers who died between 1962 and 1972 (Hindemith, Weinberger, Kodaly, and Stravinsky) are still shown as living.

Changes in the Index are minimal, consisting of one or two additions or deletions. In one instance a cross-reference has been changed to a main entry and the previous entry has become a cross-reference.

The format of the new edition is identical to that of the preceding one although the boards used for the covers do not appear to be quite as sturdy as those provided in the past. The text has been garbled at the bottom of page 899, where two lines have inadvertently been dropped, and also at the top of pages 901 and 905, where the last two lines of the preceding pages have been repeated.

The 40 halftone illustrations originally included in the 1963 edition were dropped in later printings of that edition and have not been restored. Their absence does not detract seriously from the usefulness of the work and probably is in part responsible for holding the price increase on the new edition to a modest $1.55.

In 1963 the publishers termed *Kobbe* "the standard reference book for all who enjoy opera . . ." With the present edition they elevate the status of the work to "*the* standard reference book on opera." This claim hardly seems justified in view of the many other "standard" reference books on the subject, each of which usually has its own special emphasis. The special value of *Kobbe* lies in its inclusion of detailed plot summaries for more operas than are covered in any other comparable work. *Victor Book of the Opera* (New York: Simon & Schuster, 1968), perhaps the work which most closely resembles *Kobbe*, provides less detailed plot summaries and covers only about half as many operas. (The latest edition does, however, include a number of contemporary works not covered by *Kobbe*).

While *Kobbe's Complete Opera Book* is still "an indispensable tool in libraries and a valuable home reference book for lovers of music," the work has remained essentially unchanged since 1954. Libraries owning editions published from that date on will probably find their present copies satisfactory. The additions and changes made in the

new, revised edition do not seem extensive enough to warrant replacement of previous editions except those published prior to 1954. The new edition is recommended for libraries not owning an edition published since that date and for those libraries where updated information on the stage histories of the operas is considered important.
(July 15, 1973, p.1027)

Lands and Peoples. 7v. New York, Grolier, Inc., c1972. illus. maps. 26cm. Holliston's Roxite C with Sparatone no. 61 finish, $89.50; to schools and libraries, $69.50.

Lands and Peoples is an entirely new reference set. According to the publisher, "it retains the title of a reference source which Grolier published for many years, but every word and every illustration is new."

Its stated purpose is to help young people prepare for a world where modern means of communication and transportation have made all men neighbors rather than "strangers in far off lands." The set, too, is designed to take into account the new ways in which young people are learning geography—the interaction between man and his environment.

The senior editorial staff is the same one that produced *The New Book of Knowledge*. Articles in *Lands and Peoples* were written and signed by authorities in the fields of social studies, by encyclopedists, by authors of books about geography, sociology, history, and language, and by people native to the country or region considered. For articles not written by a person native to the area, "a national was often used as a reviewer." In some instances heads of government or leading members of government wrote introductions to the articles about their countries.

Coverage is worldwide: v.1 *Africa*; v.2 *Asia, Australia, New Zealand, Oceania*; v.3 and v.4 *Europe*; v.5 *North America*; v.6 *South and Central America*. Each volume opens with an overview of the whole continent, followed by articles about individual countries arranged alphabetically, and occasional articles on some cities, mountain ranges, and key rivers. For example, the *Africa* volume has articles on the Congo, Niger, and Nile rivers; the volume on *North America* covers the Appalachian and Rocky Mountains; the *South and Central America* volume contains separate pieces on the Amazon and Orinoco Rivers.

The 40-page section on Spain in volume 4 is an example of a typical longer article. First, Spain is described in its geographical and historical context showing how history and geography have contributed to Spain's greatness and its tragedies. The article then goes on to The Land—geography, climate, mineral resources, the islands of Spain, and overseas territories. The country's economy is then treated in some detail. This section is followed by a view of The People—their language, religion, problems of regionalism, characteristics, customs. Specific cities—Madrid, Avila, Toledo, Barcelona, Seville—are considered. Finally Spain's history is discussed and predictions are made concerning the future. The article was reviewed by Jose Ignacio Jimenez, Public Relations Officer, Permanent Mission of Spain to the United Nations.

Each volume has a table of contents. The organization within the articles is logical and easy to follow. Cross-references are used where needed. Fact boxes contain useful quick reference statistical information and other basic data on government, language, and religion.

The material seems to be free of bias, prejudice, and stereotypes. If a country has had or is having problems, these are stated and handled objectively.

Checking the statistical information against *The World Book* and *The Merit Students Encyclopedia* revealed only minor differences. Area figures are given in both miles and kilometers.

The states of the United States of America are not considered individually, but are treated as parts of regions. More extensive material can be found on some countries in *The World Book*, *The Merit Students Encyclopedia*, and *Worldmark Encyclopedia of the Nations*. However, *Lands and Peoples* carries out successfully its stated purpose of presenting "an integrated approach to the peoples and lands of the world."

Volume 7 *The World Facts and Figures Index* is a rich source of thought-provoking articles and valuable tables, guides, and charts. The articles presented are Peoples of the World, Folklore, Man's Environment, Man's Food Supply, Forms of Government, Industrialization and Technology, International Monetary System, and the United Nations. Sections on Antarctica and the Arctic follow these articles. Examples of the tables and charts included are Continental Extremes, Largest Cities of the World, Some of the Great Mountain Peaks of the World, A Glossary of Geographic Terms, World Leaders, and Rulers and Leaders of Major Countries, Past and Present. Sufficiently large and detailed flags of the world are shown in color. There is a Reading Guide, arranged by country, which includes over 1,600 books and audiovisual items. Where a title does not give a clue to contents there is a very brief line of identification. The book titles include reference, general informational reading, fiction, folklore, and a few scholarly works. Except for a few outstanding publications, most of the works listed have been published since 1965. There are a few titles in languages other than English. Some maps are included, for example, International Time Zones, Vegetation, and Population Density. The final major section of volume 7 is devoted to the general Index for the set. Instructions are given on how to use the Index, noting a letter-by-letter alphabetical arrangement. The Index is both analytical (bringing out material contained within longer articles) and supplementary (very brief or minimal factual information such as identification of people, places). A spot check of the index entries revealed only a few minor errors in page references. Some entries lead to only a sentence or two in the set.

The level of readership for the set is upper elementary and above. While the publisher states that the staff is "thoroughly trained in the use of the Dale-Chall readability formula," there is no monotony of style in writing and expression.

Over 1,400 clearly reproduced color photographs appear in the set. These were selected from authoritative sources, and many represent the work of well-recognized photographers and journalists. Although the photographs at times resemble those on postcards and calendars, in general they not only enhance the set visually, but also increase empathy for the countries and their peoples. There seems to be a good balance of subject coverage—urban and rural areas, cultural aspects, topography, industry, occupations, and people. Generally the photograph size ranges from 3½ inches by 3¼ inches to 5¼ inches by 5½ inches and 4½ inches by 6¼ inches, with the majority of the illustrations being the larger sizes.

Maps used in *Lands and Peoples* are in four colors and were prepared by professional cartographers. Each continent and the Polar Regions have either a full-page or a double-spread map, including perspective maps. Smaller maps show population density and precipitation for each continent and the Polar Regions. Maps for each country, average size 3½ inches by 4 inches or 5 inches by 7 inches, show the relationship to the continent and pictorially depict a feature or two characteristic of the country. For example, the Rhodesia map pictures a lion and the Kariba Dam; the map of Swaziland shows the Havelock Mine and native huts; the map of Colombia, the Sun Gate at Cartagena, Bogota, jungle, and an oil well; Malta, boats. A few historical maps have been included, such as one showing Early African Kingdoms and another the Ottoman Empire in 1566.

Each volume is individually paged, with the number of pages ranging from 314 in volume 3 *Europe* to 538 in volume 2 *Asia, Australia, New Zealand, Oceania*. The page layout is pleasing and easy to use. The print is clear with text type and picture captions of good size for legibility. The Index uses good size type with italics and boldface. The pages lie flat when opened. The binding, in a light-colored cloth, seems sturdy, and may be cleaned with a damp cloth. Each volume has the title and volume number printed in gold color on the spine. A two-color picture, representative of the area considered, is on the cover of each volume. For example, volume 1 *Africa* has lions on the veld, with a modern city in the distance; volume 5 *North America* has the New York skyline.

Grolier promises continuous revision for *Lands and Peoples.*

Lands and Peoples is recommended for students in grade five and up, especially to give them an understanding of the world's people and their varying ways of life. It is also recommended for adults who need a nonspecialized introduction to countries and people of the world. *(Feb. 1, 1973, p.497)*

Larousse Illustrated International Encyclopedia and Dictionary. [Edited by O. C. Watson.] New York, World Pub., [c1972]. 527, [3], 1,023p. illus. maps. diagrs. 29cm. buckram $19.95; deluxe ed. $49.50.

"*Larousse International* is an English-language reference book of a new conception, in which access to language and general knowledge are taken as one" —Preface. Pierre Larousse initiated the encyclopedic dictionary method in France in 1865. *Larousse International* is the first American edition and is equivalent to *Petit Larousse Illustré,* published in 1923 (1968 edition entitled *Nouveau Petit Larousse*).

The work consists of two parts, Part 1, encyclopedia, which comprises one-third of the book's 1,550 pages and Part 2, dictionary, which makes up the remaining 1,023 pages. The parts are to be used together. While the book purports to be international in scope and point of view, it also claims to give special attention to American topics. For example, all the United States are covered. *Larousse* is geared to a general audience from the mature youngster of ten to the lay adult.

The three preliminary pages contain a Preface by O. C. Watson, editor, a list of editorial abbreviations and phonetic symbols, and a brief explanation of the use of cross-references.

Larousse Illustrated International Encyclopedia and Dictionary is designed in the same format as *Nouveau Petit Larousse.* Each page consists of three columns of entries, arranged alphabetically letter by letter. Entries also follow a consistent form—indented entry word in boldface, phonetic spelling with diacritical marks, and explanation or definition of entry word. At the bottom of each odd-numbered page is a pronunciation key, and the first entry word is repeated at the top of each page. The entries are not signed; the only mention of contributors appears in the editor's Preface. Like *Nouveau Petit Larousse, Larousse International* is profusely illustrated with photographs, reproductions, diagrams, and maps. The only full-color illustrations in *Nouveau Petit Larousse* are 48 full-page illustrations, while most of the 3,000 illustrations are in color in *Larousse Illustrated International Encyclopedia and Dictionary.*

Dr. David Wingate Pike wrote the great majority of the entries dealing with North and South American history and civilization in Part 1, the encyclopedia. Coverage includes personalities, movements, and institutions prominent in recent social history. Entries consist primarily of explanations of proper names—geographical and historical place-names; famous people in the physical and social sciences and fine arts; and mythical, religious, and historical personages. Interspersed within the text are maps and photographs of individuals, famous paintings, and architecture. Photographs resembling picture postcards show places of interest in the United States. For example, under *Wisconsin* appears a picture of the state capitol and a cheese factory. The entries vary in length from 10 words under *List, Friedrich* to some 2,000 words under *Thailand.* The pages average 30 entries. The 30 entries to a page are concise and brief, about the length of a fact-index entry in a children's encyclopedia, and they provide only an introduction to the entry word.

For each geographical entry, standard information is presented—area, population, capital, and agricultural and industrial facts. Sources are not given for statistics. Brief histories and notable features conclude this type of entry. **The information provided for individuals is also standardized—birth and death dates, accomplishments, and examples of the person's work. Special features of the encyclopedia include a table of U.S. Presidents and a list of Nobel prizewinners from 1901 through 1971.

Part 2, the dictionary, contains the vocabulary of the living language, without slang or cant terms and without archaisms. It includes many scientific and technical terms, as well as compound words and proper names. Where British spelling or usage differs from American, the reader's attention has been drawn to the British variants. Most entries contain a phonetic spelling of the word with diacritical marks in parentheses and the part of speech listed. The amount and type of other information varies. In addition to a simple definition, one may find word derivations, examples of usage and idioms, definitions according to various parts of speech, and some historical background for a word. Two vertical lines are used to separate definitions within each entry. Word derivations are given in brackets at the end of the entry. Synonyms, but no antonyms, are used in definitions. Variant spellings are given. The definitions are fairly accurate, clear, concise, and comprehensible. Illustrations are used to clarify meanings of words in the dictionary.

Cross-references are indicated by an asterisk and small capital letters. They have been kept to a minimum, according to the editor. Proper names mentioned incidentally in the dictionary are all main entries in the encyclopedia, and all scientific and technical terms used in the encyclopedia articles can be found in the dictionary. All of the cross-references checked, direct and implied, lead to the proper entry in the other section of the volume. Cross-references also are used for variant spellings and synonyms of entry words. They adequately perform their function.

There are some omissions in the book: no entry for Henry Kissinger, even though the editor claims a slant towards an American readership, and no modern terms like "lunar module," "consumerism," and "organic food." "Ms" does appear in the dictionary section.

A comparison with the third edition of *Columbia Encyclopedia* (New York: Columbia University, 1968), another one-volume encyclopedia, points out the more popular appeal of *Larousse Illustrated International Encyclopedia and Dictionary* versus the scholarly *Columbia*. The latter asserts that it is an encyclopedia and not a dictionary, and should be used in conjunction with a dictionary. A comparison between *Larousse Illustrated International Encyclopedia and Dictionary* and *Columbia* under the entry, *Constitution of the United States,* illustrates the difference in treatment between the two volumes. In *Columbia,* history and bibliography appear in the entry, while neither is found in *Larousse Illustrated International Encyclopedia and Dictionary.* The latter provides only the year of adoption, omitting the month and date as is found in *Columbia.* The information found in the *Larousse Illustrated International Encyclopedia and Dictionary* consists of the text, without mention of the Articles of Confederation or dates for the Amendments. Footnotes are added for amended or repealed sections of the Constitution. *Columbia* provides all of the above information. The physical appearance of *Larousse Illustrated International Encyclopedia and Dictionary*'s entry, however, is compact and clear with indentations, boldface type and numbering; while *Columbia* entry is in one long paragraph.

The physical arrangement of the *Larousse Illustrated International Encyclopedia and Dictionary* is most satisfactory. In spite of its bulk, nine inches by eleven inches and almost three inches thick, the pages lie flat when the book is opened. With its one-inch margins, clear type and boldfaced entry words, the volume is easy to read and use. The illustrations are attractive and useful. Color reproduction is sharp and realistic. Credits for the photographs used in the book are given at the bottom of the pages. Good quality maps, providing scale, are plentiful. They range in size from 2¾ inches by 1½ inches to two pages for the United States.

Larousse Illustrated International Encyclopedia and Dictionary is a good source of general information on a wide range of subjects. Its attractive appearance, compact one-volume form, concentration on social sciences and fine arts, and brief definitions recommend *Larousse Illustrated* for use by young people and adults, primarily as a supplement to more comprehensive encyclopedias and dictionaries currently available. *(Nov. 15, 1973, p.297)*

The Law of War: A Documentary History. Ed. by Leon Friedman; with a foreword by Telford Taylor. 2v. New York, Random House, 1972. xxv, 1764p. 25cm. buckram $65.

The Law of War is a collection of materials on the origin, development, and enforcement of the laws of war for the use of lawyers and historical scholars, as well as the general reader. The editor, Leon Friedman, is an attorney on the staff of the Association of the Bar of the City of New York and the coeditor of and a contributor to *The Justices of the United States Supreme Court: 1789-1969*, which won the 1970 Scribes Award. See *Booklist* July 15, 1970 for review of *Justices*.

Telford Taylor, Professor of Law, Columbia University and the chief counsel for the Nuremberg war crimes trials, is the author of the Foreword. Here, Professor Taylor points out that "the publication of these volumes is especially timely, in view of the pervasive and deepening concern aroused by military excesses and atrocities in recent years." He then goes on to present a brief history of the problems confronted by the United States in defining and applying the laws of war.

The collection is arranged in three sections, each preceded by an Introduction. The first section is entitled "Hugo Grotius and the Law of War." The Introduction to this section contains a brief review of the limitations on the conduct of warfare from early times to Grotius' day (1583-1645) and contains citation to the early writers on the subject. This is followed by 131 pages of selections from Book III of Grotius' *The Law of War and Peace*, the work which is considered the "starting point for the study and development of the modern law of war" and "the most comprehensive attempt to bring together both classical and medieval thought on war." Book III is concerned with what is permissible in warfare and considers the treatment of prisoners, civilians, hostages, and enemy property, as well as the rights of neutrals.

The next section, "Treaties, Conventions and Agreements," includes the texts of 52 documents in which the attempt has been made "to establish rules of war as binding enactments of international law." The first document is the Declaration of Paris (1856) in which seven European states defined a binding blockade and agreed to recognize certain neutral rights and the abolition of privateering. This is followed by the Lieber Code (Instructions for the Government of Armies of the United States in the Field, 1863), adopted in part by many European states and the basis for subsequent army manuals in this country.

Among other documents included are the Red Cross Conventions of 1864, 1906, and 1929 for the amelioration of the condition of the wounded and sick of the armies in the field and the 1971 draft protocols on the same subject; the Hague Conventions of 1899, 1904, and 1907 pertaining to the pacific settlement of international disputes, the laws of land, maritime, and air warfare, the rights and duties of neutrals, the use of gases, the laying of mines, and the launching of projectiles; the London Naval Conference of 1909 Declaration on the subject of blockades, neutral rights, convoys, searches, and compensation; the Treaty of Versailles, containing the Covenant of the League of Nations; the Geneva Convention of 1949 concerning the treatment of the wounded and sick in the armed forces, the treatment of prisoners of war, and the protection of civilians; the Genocide Convention; and the United Nations resolutions and reports on nuclear weapons, human rights in armed conflicts, the protection of civilians, and war criminals. The final document contains the text of the 1972 convention prohibiting the development, production, and stockpiling of biological and toxic weapons.

The third section of *The Law of War*

"deals with the application of the rules established by international law: the actual trial of war crimes." The first of these is the 1865 trial by a military commission of Captain Henry Wirz, the Swiss doctor in charge of the Andersonville prison during the American Civil War. This is followed by excerpts from United States Senate documents containing the report of the court-martial of three army officers for atrocities committed during the Philippine insurrection of 1899-1902. Also contained in this section is the report of the Commission on the Responsibility of the Authors of the War and on Enforcement of Penalties created by the Allies after World War I and the judgment of the German Supreme Court in the 1921 *Llandovery Castle* case involving U-boat officers who were tried for their part in the sinking of a British hospital ship.

Almost the entire second volume of *The Law of War* consists of documents from the World War II war crime trial reports. These include samples of the different types of cases and show the manner in which the courts operated and the kinds of crimes found to violate the laws of war. Among these documents are the Judgment at Nuremberg by the International Military Tribunal, reports of trials by United States and British military courts in Germany and courts of Poland, France, and the Netherlands. Japanese war crimes documents include the report of the Tokyo trial by the International Military Tribunal for the Far East, trials by Australian, Dutch, and United States military courts, and the decisions on appeal to the United States Supreme Court in the Yamashita, Hirota, and Homma cases.

Questions of international law are examined in the decisions of the Israeli District and Supreme Courts in the Eichmann case, which are also included. The final documents are the instructions from the Military Judge to the members of the court in the trials of Lieutenant William L. Calley Jr. and Captain Ernest L. Medina.

Both volumes of the set have a Table of Contents. The Table in the first volume lists all the documents in the set; that in the second volume lists only those in volume II. A detailed 26-page Index covering both volumes appears in volume II. This Index includes *see* and *see also* references. Some minor discrepancies were noted in the indexing.

The format of the volume is satisfactory, but the running heads are inadequate. From page 775 to page 1737 the running head is "War Crimes Trials," a completely inadequate indication of the page content. The print is clear, and variations in type size have been used where appropriate. The volumes are quite heavy, however, and the binding may not withstand heavy use, although the first and last signatures have been reinforced.

While many libraries will already have the text of the treaties and many of the reports of war crime trials contained in *The Law of War*, as well as the complete text of Grotius' work (about ⅔ of Book III is included in the set), small libraries may not. The convenience of having this material together is obvious, and there is no similar collection. There are other collections of international law materials available such as *Basic Documents in International Law* (Oxford: Clarendon Press, 1972), compiled by Ian Brownlie, and Edward Collins' *International Law in a Changing World: Cases, Documents, and Readings* (New York: Random House, 1970). These, however, are concerned with international law in general and do not concentrate on the law of war. The collection of treaties and conventions on this subject in this set is quite comprehensive. The editor has been careful to give the source of the documents contained in the collection, and this information will be useful if the official publications are needed for consultation.

In view of the timeliness of the subject of this collection, its value for reference and research, and the convenience of such a compilation, *The Law of War* is recommended for academic and public libraries.

(Sept. 15, 1973, p.57)

The McGraw-Hill Encyclopedia of World Biography: An International Reference

Work in Twelve Volumes Including an Index. New York, McGraw-Hill Book Co., [c1973]. 12v. 29cm. c-1 grade pyroxylin $275; to schools and libraries, $250. ISBN 07-079633-5.

According to the introduction, this new work, *Encyclopedia of World Biography,* is "designed to meet a growing need in school and college libraries as well as in public libraries. . . . Its 5,000 articles discuss the lives of representative men and women whose achievements are important to the understanding of social and cultural history." It consists of eleven volumes of text and a twelfth volume which contains lists of contributors and consultants, Study Guides, and an Index. Because it is very up to date in its coverage of persons of significance in the twentieth century, many living persons such as John Lennon, Harold Pinter, Golda Meier, Margaret Mead, Ralph Nader, and Henry Moore are included.

In order to be sure that contemporary persons were not overlooked, a panel of 29 subject area consultants which included such well-known authorities as David Daiches, Morton A. Kaplan, and John Horace Parry reviewed the planning outlines and selected names for inclusion in this work. These planning outlines then went to an "International Advisory Panel of 36 distinguished statesmen, educators, scholars and authors around the world." These persons (such as Alan Paton, Chinua Achebe, Charles Malik, and Santha Rama Rau) looked at the outlines from the points of view of their own countries in order to give fresh perspective to coverage of such areas as Africa and Asia.

A National Advisory Committee composed of teachers, librarians, and specialists who reviewed the work in progress was also involved in the making of this encyclopedia. Titles and present positions are given for all contributors, including the advisory panel.

The actual writing of the biographies was done by 884 specialists, most of whom are affiliated with institutions of higher learning in the United States and abroad. Each article is signed and varies in length from 500 to 3,500 words, averaging around 800. The many contributors make for diverse coverage of so many persons' lives, since some of the articles go into considerable personal detail while others concentrate mostly on the subject's contributions to society. Since this set is designed for high school as well as college use, the articles are very readable and curriculum oriented, rather than scholarly. The surname of the biographee (unless usage dictates using the forename, as for kings and saints) is in large type followed by the contributor's name. A short opening paragraph, printed in color, "provides a capsule identification and statement of the person's significance" and gives the complete name and life dates. Usually the first sentence of the main article contains the pronunciation of non-American or British names. This is very useful as pronunciation of foreign names is sometimes difficult to find. The Pronunciation Key is printed only in volume 1.

Arrangement is alphabetical word by word; if the name is hyphenated, all parts are treated as separate words. Names with prefixes such as De Gaulle are treated as single words. There are no *see* references such as from William H. Bonney to Billy the Kid or from Canute to Cnut in the main body.

Each biography includes a Further Reading statement telling where the name is listed in the Study Guide, references to other biographies, if pertinent, and a short bibliography (sometimes only one book) which may include books discussing the biographee's achievements as well as his life. The books listed in these bibliographies or suggestions for additional reading are all in English and are fairly current. The books are likely to be in print or available from the average library either on direct or interlibrary loan.

Most articles have at least one illustration, usually a portrait, but where none are available, as with ancient leaders, likenesses from coins, sculpture, and monuments are used. Other illustrations also are used in longer biographies —these may be pictures of tools, weapons, houses or manuscripts. "There are 5,500 halftone and 32 full color illustrations" in this encyclopedia, which also has 200 historical maps illustrating routes of explorations, spread of religions, battle lines, territorial growth, etc. A list of the colorplates is given in volume 1. The pictures and photographs used are quite clear and very useful, since such illustrations are sometimes difficult to find.

The Study Guides, in volume 12, are divided into 17 general subjects: Africa; American History; Ancient History; Art; Asia; Australia and New Zealand; Canada; European History; Geography and Exploration; International Law and Organization; Latin America; Literature; Music; Philosophy; Religion; Science; Social Science, History and Education. Here the user who is unfamiliar with the names of persons prominent in various subject fields, can find suggestions in his field of interest. These Guides, in outline form, are arranged chronologically with subheadings by topic and/or country, under which are listings of pertinent names. A name may be listed under more than one heading.

The 100,000 entry Index, also in volume 12, is a comprehensive aid to locating "persons, places, battles, treaties, institutions, buildings, inventions, books, pictures, ideas, philosophies, styles and movements." Personal entries include life dates and brief identification; all entries include the title of the article, volume, and page number. The Index also lists persons by occupation: astronomers, philosophers, etc., as well as by such categories as "child prodigies, the blind, conspirators, immigrants, [and] assassination victims." Entries for articles are in boldface capital letters. Other entries are in boldface, using initial capitals and lowercase letters. These include *see* and *see also* references and subjects. Indented under entries are the listings of names of articles, volume (in boldface), and page. Colorplates are indexed by title as well as by subject and artist; their index entries are in italic type, as are those for illustrations and maps. Books, plays, operas, paintings, and literary characters are indexed. The listing under nicknames is both interesting and useful in identifying such persons as big asparagus—Charles De Gaulle; Gigger—Rudyard Kipling; light haired boy—Crazy Horse; lion of the Punjab—Ranjit Singh; and the Sphinx—H. Ibsen. Under main subject entries are subentries with pinpoint specific groupings, i.e., Military Leaders, British has subheads under Army-Captains, Colonels, Commanders, and Generals, Navy—Admirals, Commanders. The abbreviations used in the Index are listed preceding it. This Index is quite complete, useful, and accurate.

In general the coverage is fairly good, especially of contemporary black leaders such as Carl Stokes, Eldridge Cleaver, Malcolm X, Martin Luther King, Jr., and Thurgood Marshall. Lacking are biographies of women such as Eva Peron, the Duchess of Windsor, Gloria Steinem, Germain Greer, Gwendolyn Brooks, and Jacqueline Kennedy Onassis. There is an article on Cesar Chavez, but none on Vine Deloria, Jr. or Russell Means.

The McGraw-Hill Enycyclopedia of World Biography is unique in its coverage and cannot easily be compared with other sets such as *Dictionary of American Biography* (New York: Scribners, c1928-73), *National Cyclopedia of American Biography* (New York: White, c1891-1971), *Dictionary of National Biography* (New York: Macmillan, c1885-1960) or *Current Biography* (New York: H. W. Wilson, c1940-   ). The first two cover only Americans; the *Dictionary of National Biography* includes only British and Colonials; and *Current Biography* has articles only on living, newsworthy persons.

This set is sturdily bound in bone-colored pyroxylin with attractive maroon line drawings of faces on its covers. The hinges are reinforced. Volume numbers and inclusive alphabetical symbols are well marked on each spine. Endpapers are printed with reproductions of signatures. Margins are adequate, the print is very readable, and volumes lie flat when open. The set seems very durable.

The McGraw-Hill Encyclopedia of World Biography, with its world-wide coverage of both the living and the dead, its readable articles, and its quality Index is a welcome new reference set that is geared to secondary school and college curriculum. It is recommended. *(July 1, 1974, p.1161)*

McGraw-Hill Encyclopedia of World Drama: an International Reference Work in Four Volumes. 4v. New York, McGraw-Hill Book Co., [1972]. illus. 29cm. buckram $119.50; to schools and libraries, "usual" discount.

Essentially, *McGraw-Hill Encyclopedia of World Drama* is a biographical dictionary of dramatists from those literatures most likely to be of interest: Greek, Roman, Italian, French, Spanish, German, Slavic, English, and American. Although the editors claim that "scattered among the biographical entries in the text are some hundred abbreviated non-biographical entries—dramatic terms, theatre movements and styles, anonymous plays," the non-biographical entries are inadequate in number. Despite its title, this is not an encyclopedia of *world* drama.

The large editorial staff is comprised of a General Adviser, Bernard Dukore, professor of theatre at Hunter College, an Editorial Advisory Board of 13 scholars, including Allardyce Nicoll, dean of drama historians, a McGraw-Hill editorial staff of 45, and 68 Contributing Editors, with Ruby Cohn and Gerald Weales among them.

Within the limits set for it, the encyclopedia does its work well enough and even provides a liberal representation of contemporary playwrights from the most popular literatures, including those whose works are few and whose reputations are uncertain. The drama of other languages and cultures, however, is given scant attention and even the post-World War II interest in Japanese drama is scarcely satisfied. There are no survey essays for national literatures, and there are comparatively few non-biographical entries defining terms or characterizing movements.

In an introductory statement, the editors make this disclaimer: "The editors eschewed lengthy discussions of these topics, or of the history of drama in specific areas or countries, in the knowledge that other sources readily available to any reader provide this material." Thus, somewhat less than ten percent of the entries are terms taken from literature or drama. One-third of the entries are longer biographies and include synopses of all or some of the author's plays, a chronological listing of first production and publication, and bibliographies both of the author's works and criticisms of those works. Another five percent lack only the bibliographies, and an additional twelve percent include synopses, but have neither the chronologies nor the bibliographies. Approximately forty percent are brief biographical entries, ranging from two to fifty lines in these double-columned pages. In short, about 900 dramatists from the English-speaking and European cultures are included, and the biographies of half of them are accompanied by at least one plot summary. None of the articles are signed, and they generally maintain a neutrality of tone and a style appropriate to an encyclopedia whose readership is expected to include the secondary school student and whose editorship is so large as to be communal. Examination bears out the claim in the Introduction that major playwrights receive longer treatment, and lesser ones are treated more briefly. However, some of the shorter articles are too brief to be useful.

The longest non-biographical entry, *Musical Comedy,* has more than 175 short plot descriptions, together with the titles of the principal songs. Operettas are included, but the Gilbert and Sullivan operettas are not; they are independently synopsized under Gilbert's name.

Musical Comedy is illustrated with more than 65 photographs, and the encyclopedia includes 2,000 illustrations, selected from the collections of the Theater Collection, New York Public Library, regional theater companies, and foreign sources. However, none are from the Stratford, Ontario productions, although the high quality of their costumes and settings is well known and photographs abound. Photographs—and hence depictions of twentieth-century productions—predominate. More than 60 of the 70 illustrations accompanying the Shakespeare entry are of twentieth-century productions and more than half of these come from productions of the past decade. Although the encyclopedia's illustrations both enliven the page and instruct the reader, they occasionally appear to have been selected for their photographic quality or for the fame of those photographed. Unfortunately, many famous thespians go unrecorded, since there is no index to the illustrations, and one must come upon Judith Anderson as a sultry-eyed temptress only by accident.

The chronologies of performance included for almost 40 percent of the biographies are uniquely useful, since they provide easy access to the dating orders of first performance, a matter often difficult to ascertain.

The multilingual bibliographies are prudently described as "selective." Although they contain much of value, both the listings of plays in anthologies and the bibliographies of critical works vary greatly in quality and comprehensiveness.

An Index of Play Titles of 25,000 entries concludes the final volume. For foreign plays, both the original title and the title of any English translation are given. Initial articles are disregarded for English titles, but the foreign titles are indexed by the first word, article or not. The Title Index accurately identifies the playwrights of all plays included in the text, whether they are synopsized, barely mentioned, or listed only in the author's chronology.

The Reader's Encyclopedia of World Drama by Gassner and Quinn (New York: Crowell, 1969) covers world drama more comprehensively, and is an excellent compendium of biographies, literary terms, synopses, and national surveys.

The volumes of *Encyclopedia of World Drama* are attractively bound in a sturdy blue buckram; the paper is an excellent weight in a coated, dull finish. However, the positioning of the illustrations and their captions frequently leaves edge margins of only three-eighths of an inch. The volumes lie flat when opened.

Although less global than its title suggests, *McGraw-Hill Encyclopedia of World Drama* provides a good biographical overview of the dramatists writing in English or in the major continental languages. Although brief in identification and description, the play synopses and the Title Index are the largest multinational listings available in English. The encyclopedia is recommended. *(Oct. 15, 1973, p.184)*

Magazines for Libraries: for the General Reader and School, Junior College, and College, and Public Libraries. [By] Bill Katz and Berry Gargal, science editor. 2d ed. New York & London, R. R. Bowker Co., 1972. xviii, 822p. 29cm. cloth $23.50 net postpaid. ISBN 0-8352-0554-1.

The second edition of *Magazines for Libraries* expands and updates the contents of the first edition, which was reviewed in *The Booklist* April 1, 1970, and recommended as "valuable in any library where questions are asked about contents, scope, and treatment of magazines."

Bill Katz, journalist and librarian, continues as editor. He has served as editor of a column of magazine annotations in *Library Journal* since 1967. Katz is assisted, once again, by Berry Gargal, as science editor. Gargal is qualified by experience as a science librarian and technical editor. Seventy-nine contributors and advisers, mainly employed at college and university libraries or library schools, are, for the most part, acquainted with the subject fields assigned to them but could not always be identified as "all experts in their fields," as claimed in the Preface. In the second edition contributors' and advisers' contributions are acknowledged by their initials appearing after almost all annotations of magazines in this work. Many annotations are written by the co-editors, and these are not initialed. The section Contributors and Advisers, under Abbreviations, lists initials of each contributor along with full name, affiliation, and assigned subject areas. Unfortunately, identical sets of initials hamper identification of the work of 16 contributors. No list of contributors appeared in the first edition.

The Preface of the second edition states that the purpose remains identical to that of the first edition, "to help guide the librarian, teacher, and layman through the mass of magazines." To emphasize the continuity of purpose the Preface to the first edition is partially reprinted along with the Preface to the second edition. The reprinted purpose is "to suggest to the general reader and librarian the titles best suited for his individual needs" with the exception of the specialist in his particular field.

Over 4,500 titles are annotated in the second edition, an increase of 2,100 over the number covered in the first edition. The over 100 subject areas in the edition under review are conveniently listed in the Contents. They include 41 new headings, among which are topics of current interest such as Computers and Automation, Environment and Conservation, Latin American and Chicano, Occult and Witchcraft. Some headings of the first edition have been modified, dropped, or merged into broader headings.

As in the first edition, most of the titles included are American, with some treatment given to Canadian and British publications. Some of the other countries represented, largely by multilingual or English-language magazines, are Switzerland, Denmark, Austria, and West Germany.

Many recently published titles have been added. Most of these began publication in 1970, but 1971 and 1972 are also well represented.

Each subject section begins with a list of Basic Periodicals, divided by audience and type of library. This feature was located in the back of the volume in the first edition but was moved to a more convenient position at the suggestion of librarians. Other features are Basic Abstracts and Indexes, Cessations, and an Introduction, where appropriate, within each subject. Subject headings are based on *Ulrich's International Periodicals Directory*. Titles are listed alphabetically under each subject. Some large subjects have subdivisions.

The editors claim that "each and every annotation from the first edition has been carefully examined. Some, although not all were rewritten." This claim was substantiated by a full comparison of all titles listed in both editions under ten subjects. Out of a total of 164 titles, almost all bibliographical information and annotations were slightly to totally revised.

As in the first edition, standard bibliographical information is included. New features especially useful to librarians, include "Sample" to indicate that a publisher will send a free sample, the date when the publisher ends a volume, and "Refereed" which tells the reader that articles have been evaluated by specialists before publication. Ranking symbols have been reduced to two: "V" for exceptional magazines and "C" for unexceptional or below average. Availability of microfilm files and their publisher is also indicated.

Cross-references within the body of the book facilitate use. *See* references guide the reader to the subject heading where a title is annotated and to former or alternate titles.

The Bibliography, which follows the 762 pages of magazine annotations in the second edition, has been revised, updated, and enlarged. Grant T. Skelley, from the School of Librarianship, University of Washington, compiled this selective annotated bibliography of materials dealing with magazines in general and with other lists of magazines which can be used to supplement the contents of *Magazines for Libraries*. In the second edition, 93 percent of the entries are for publications dated 1968 or later. Many annotations have been revised and new subject areas such as Africa, Consumer Services, and Spanish Language have been added. The addition of a Table of Contents and the numbering of entries in the second edition's Bibliography make it easier to use.

In any work of this kind, even though extensively revised, there will be some omissions and errors. For some magazines, indexed elsewhere, the bibliographical information does not include where the periodical is indexed.

The Index, with over 5,000 entries of magazine titles, subject headings, and cross references, is almost twice the size of the Index in the first edition. The Index includes titles which have ceased. Entries are arranged alphabetically word by word, but often inconveniently disregarding the words "of," "to," and "and" in the alphabetical sequence. Page numbers are listed for all maga-

161

zine titles, except cessations, and for the beginning page of each subject section. Useful *see* references guide the reader to places where a title not annotated is mentioned within an annotation; to former titles; to titles incorporated into other titles; or to subject headings used. The Index is largely accurate.

The second edition of *Magazines for Libraries* is more up to date than Evan Farber's *Classified List of Periodicals for the College Library* (5th ed. Westwood, MA: Faxon, 1972), since *Farber* is limited to journals that began publication before 1969. *Magazines for Libraries* also annotates over 4,500 titles as opposed to *Farber's* more selective listing of 1,050 for a smaller audience, the college library. A comparison between the Africa sections in both works revealed one title listed in *Farber* only and 37 titles listed in *Magazines for Libraries* only. Some sections, such as Home Economics, show more similarities in coverage.

The binding of the second edition of *Magazines for Libraries* may not withstand heavy use, since it separated from the casing on several review copies used by the Committee. The print, on good quality paper, is clear and easy to read.

The second edition of *Magazines for Libraries* has been enlarged, updated, and extensively revised. Modifications and additions to the arrangement of the book and to devices for interpreting its contents make the second edition easier to use than the first. Recommended.

(June 1, 1974, p.1062)

Makers of America. 10v. Editor: Wayne Moquin. Chicago, Encyclopaedia Britannica Educational Corporation, 1971. illus. 28cm. sturdite $83.50 plus $2.50 handling and shipping; to schools and libraries, $83.50 plus $2.50 handling and shipping. ISBN 0-87827-000-0.

Described as a "documentary history of the ethnic pluralism of America," the set consists of ten volumes arranged in chronological order with thematic titles as follows: v.1, *The First Comers*, 1536-1800; v.2, *Builders of a New Nation*, 1801-1848; v.3, *Seekers After Freedom*, 1849-1870; v.4, *Seekers After Wealth*, 1871-1890; v.5, *Natives and Aliens*, 1891-1903; v.6, *The New Immigrants*, 1904-1913; v.7, *Hyphenated Americans*, 1914-1924; v.8, *Children of the Melting Pot*, 1925-1938; v.9, *Refugees and Victims*, 1939-1954; v.10, *Emergent Minorities*, 1955-1970. There is no indication in the books or the publisher's promotional material that the set will be updated. The tenth volume contains five indexes and a Bibliography of recommended reading. Each volume contains a table of contents and an interpretive essay for each section of text and headnotes for each selection used. The size of the volumes, eight-and-one-half by eleven inches, the typeface, 11 point, and the colorful blue and orange-red binding facilitate use by young people, although no age level is mentioned in the promotional material issued by the publisher.

The arrangement of *Makers of America* is similar to that of Encyclopaedia Britannica's earlier publication, *The Annals of America* reviewed by the Reference and Subscription Books Review Committee in the July 15, 1972 *Booklist*, but the publisher's claim that "it is not a distillation from that work," that fewer than 10 percent of the selections in *The Makers of America* are found in *The Annals*, that 90 percent have been newly researched. Mortimer J. Adler and Charles Van Doren are general editors of both sets. Both editors are well known, Mortimer Adler as co-editor of *Great Books of the Western World* and Director of Planning and Chairman, Editorial Executive Committee for the new edition of *Britannica*, and Charles Van Doren as historian and author of numerous books in the fields of history and philosophy.

Wayne Moquin, editor, and academic consultants Theodore C. Blegen (1891-1969), University of Minnesota; Nathan Glazer, noted sociologist and historian, Harvard University; and Feliciano Rivera, head of the only Department of Mexican-American History in the country at San Jose State College are listed. Moquin is described as a scholar of immigrant history.

The intent of *Makers of America* is to document the ethnic history of the United States. There is no other reference work on the present market that collects so much source material on minorities into a single production. Its content and the easy-to-read, attractive format of the set should make *Makers of America* useful for school assignments in the secondary grades, but its broad coverage of material will extend its use to a much wider audience. According to the publisher, 731 selections of source material such as letters, readings, diaries, newspaper editorials, congressional debates contemporary with the periods described are included. These selections pertain to or are drawn from the writings of more than 50 separate ethnic, national or religious minorities that "regardless of origin, call the United States their home." Subgroups of the 50 ethnic minorities include more than 100 Indian tribes and "several different" Eskimo tribes. The publishers make a point of the representation of the many cultures and subcultures including "three currently very interesting and important minorities— that were here . . . 'before the *Mayflower:*' the Indians, the blacks or African Americans, and the Mexican Americans." It is pointed out that these groups do not speak with one voice, and in the case of the Indians, "the majority of selections dealing with the various Indian tribes consists of speeches, letters, articles and books by whites."

The selections are not limited to writings of well-known persons, although many famous names are included, but the emphasis is rather on the extent to which the particular document contributes to the theme of the section in which it is included. For instance, in volume 8, *Children of the Melting Pot*, one section is entitled "Assimilation and the Second Generation." Selections include a personal narrative describing the attempts of a Polish immigrant to find work in America in 1907, an editorial from the *Bulletin* of the Italian American National Union offering advice to the Italian community on adjusting to American mores, two articles on Jewish separatism, one on the second generation Polish, an article from the Croatian-language newspaper *Novi Svijet* on the cultural-linguistic heritage of immigrants, etc. An attempt is made to trace, through these writings, the feelings of various minority groups at various periods of history, to show their contributions as groups and to illustrate the growth, often through turbulence and violence, of the cultural pluralism apparent in our society today. Because many of the selections are taken from letters written home to the old country, an intimate and unrehearsed view of America emerges. The various volumes deal, through source material, and through the interpretive essay and headnotes of the editor, with many timely and thought-provoking topics such as the span of immigration movements from melting pot to cultural pluralism, nativism and racism, and the history of immigration legislation.

The Introduction notes that the quiet, contented voice is heard less often than the more strident or passionate voice speaking out in the cause of justice or freedom. Certainly the general tone of the set reflects violence and bitterness in both selection and illustration. It is inevitable that, in trying to cover such a large span of history and to represent so many different minorities, some simplistic statements are made, or that occasionally only one voice from a particular group may be heard. The last volume, entitled *Emergent Minorities*, is already outdated and ends with a rather negative note, a particularly vitriolic selection from Peter Schrag's *Decline of the WASP*. Nevertheless, the selections included show the set as a whole to be quite free from bias and very fair in trying to present representative viewpoints on a single subject.

The thematic and chronological arrangement of the set is interesting and useful. Each volume is typically organized into four to six chapter sections, each with its theme and grouping of materials. The tenth volume contains a series of five indexes, Ethnic, Proper Name, Topical, Illustration and Author/Sources. These are somewhat difficult to use; tracing immigration laws is a case in point. There is a listing for the McCarran-Walter Immigration Act in the Proper Name Index, but no mention of immigration legislation in the Topical Index. The subject can be located only in the Proper Name Index under the names of the various Immigration Acts. The Proper Name Index does analyze the listings by content, but the Topical Index is too broad, and it is virtually useless, since a long list of volume and page numbers is entered under each very general topic with no clue whatever as to content. For example, under Assimilation and Americanization there are three inches of closely crowded, unanalyzed page numbers. A straight alphabetical index comprised of the five indexes would have been much easier to use. The tenth volume includes a Bibliography of Recommended Readings, which needs updating. Novels on the Anglo-Saxon in America, for instance, include six authors, Clemens, Dreiser, Lewis, London, Frank Norris, and Owen Wister, hardly a contemporary offering. Although the contributions of an ethnic group are implicit in the selections chosen by the editors, it would take searching on the part of the student to identify them and to track them down through ten volumes.

The Makers of America is a sturdy, attractive, easy to handle and to read set. Its double-columned pages lie flat, the black-and-white halftone illustrations are clear, informative and illustrative of the text. The selections are produced with modern spelling. However, the original writing style apparently is unaltered. The modernized spelling detracts somewhat from the flavor of the original documents, but it makes the set undeniably easier to use. Perhaps some facsimile representations could have been included. When selections are abridged, the heading typically makes clear that a fragment or portion of the whole is being reproduced.

Libraries and schools which have a need for source material in this area will find *The Makers of America* a useful tool. It should be stressed, however, that this publication is not an encyclopedia in intent or form and will not readily answer such specific questions as may be found in a general encyclopedia. A stimulating and accessible collection of historical materials which develops the theme of cultural pluralism in our society and which lends understanding and dignity to the many ethnic groups in America, *Makers of America* is recommended.

(May 15, 1974, p.1012)

Man, Myth & Magic: An Illustrated Encyclopedia of the Supernatural. Ed., Richard Cavendish. 24v. New York, Marshall Cavendish Corp.; [1970]. Distributed by Purnell Library Services, 850 Seventh Avenue, New York 10019. 3376p. illus. 31cm. permalin $109.50.

Published originally in Great Britain in 112 weekly newsstand installments, this profusely and colorfully illustrated encyclopedic set intends a comprehensive exploration of the nature, magnitude, significance, and validity of occult superstition and parapsychological phenomena, both ancient and modern. The over one thousand entries range from *Africa; Extra-Sensory Perception; Sex;* and *Witchcraft* to the narrower *Cayce, Edgar; Hunting Magic; Riddles;* and *Thracian Rider God.*

The initial volume contains an introduction to the supernatural by editor Cavendish, an adaptation of an article published in the (London) *Observer Magazine* (November 24, 1968), in which he states that, "The last hundred years have been the most flourishing period in the history of magic and occultism in the West since the 17th century. They have also seen the rise of the modern study of comparative religion, the modern interpretation of mythology, the attempt to test objectively such phenomena as ghosts and telepathy, and the application of modern psychology to beliefs about the supernatural. These new lights in the darkness provide the basis of our approach in *Man, Myth and Magic.*"

In the same article Cavendish disavows any intention to proselytize: "We have not set out to convert you, to or from anything, but to explain the structures of ideas which men have built in the past, and which they continue to build now. You must decide for yourself where truth and value lie." Promotional material for the set, however, is much less restrained, asking "Can you see into the future? Do the stars determine your fate? Are Witchcraft, Black Magic and Voodoo real forces in your life?" and promising that "the answers will truly amaze you."

The final volume includes a classified Contents Guide with accompanying bibliographies, a feature entitled "Cast Your Own Horoscope," a list of contributors and their qualifications, and an alphabetical index to the set. Volumes 23 and 24 also contain a supplementary section called "Frontiers of Belief"—about 70 two-page articles arranged in no discernible order on such diverse subjects as *Ku Klux Klan, Are Popes Doomed?, Folk Medicine, Jayne Mansfield—Satanist,* and *Do It Yourself Astral Travel.* Some of these articles are signed, some are not, and, when signed, the authors are not always included in the aforementioned contributors' list; nor are these articles indexed. The "Frontiers of Belief" section gives every appearance of being a hasty addendum.

In addition to editor Cavendish, identified as the author of the book *The Black Arts* (London: Routledge & Kegan Paul, Ltd., 1942), there is an editorial advisory board of eight scholars and writers, none of whom will be familiar to the general American public but who all possess solid reputations in their areas of specialization. For instance, Glyn Daniel, E. R. Dodds, William Sargant, and R. C. Zaehner (all British academics) are listed in *Who's Who;* John Symonds, author of novels and children's books, is well-known to British readers; and the board's only American, University of Chicago Professor Mircea Eliade, is a recognized authority on the history of religions. Advisory board members are not merely editorial figureheads as is sometimes the case but active contributors to the planning and writing of the set. Moreover, five special consultants (also contributors) are noted, including the English painter and art critic William Gaunt, anthropologist Francis Huxley, and Katharine Briggs of the British Folk-Lore Society.

Like the editorial staff, the 195 contributors are predominantly British and bring good credentials to the work. Among the many recognizable names from multifarious disciplines—Ivor Brown, critic; Sir Cyril Burt, psychologist; E. E. Evans-Pritchard, social anthropologist; Robert Graves, poet; Christopher Isherwood, writer; J. B. Rhine and wife Louisa, parapsychologists—are found numerous lesser-known albeit respectable scholars and members of various societies and institutes involved in psychical or related research.

The articles, all signed except for the very brief, run in length from a paragraph (*Asafoetida, Succubus*) to 12 or 13 pages *(Head, Mediums, Spring).* Most, however, tend to be 4 to 6 pages long, with extensive space devoted to illustrative matter. The arrangement is A-Z, although early volumes contain "Special Features" not in alphabetical sequence; for instance, in volume 2 *Psychical Research Today* is sandwiched between *Bells* and *Beowulf.* While these special articles are accessible through the index (unlike those in the supplementary "Frontiers of Belief" discussed above), this procedure is likely to disconcert if not bewilder the reader. Likewise, most but not all articles append "further reading" suggestions, but these are uncorrelated with the bibliographies found in the final volume. Cross-references appear throughout.

Given the sometimes sensational nature of the subject matter, the overall tone of the articles is conspicuously discreet and the style usually straightforward and informational, similar to that characteristic of the leading general encyclopedias. S. G. F. Brandon's article on *Book of the Dead,* for example, simply relates the pertinent facts without embellishment, concluding that "This lengthy tradition bears witness to the enduring strength of the Egyptian belief that the ancient Osirian mortuary ritual effectively provides the means of defeating the dread consequences of death and attaining a state of eternal bliss." The same prudent, academic approach also characterizes articles on even the most bizarre ceremonies (*Black Mass*) and metamorphoses (*Werewolf*).

By contrast, the illustrations—over six thousand, many full-page, and "nearly every one in blazing full color" —are striking, extravagant, and at times lurid or horrific, suggestive of "creature feature" fare. There are numerous vivid reproductions of paintings, drawings, posters, artifacts, etc. (often attributed to the British Museum, the National Gallery in London, the Louvre, and other prominent collections) as well as many photographs from various sources, some identified, some not. The illustrations range from Goya's rendering of Saturn devouring his son to demons reproduced from Collin de Plancy's illustrated *Dictionnaire Infernal* and depictions of skulls, death's-heads, mummified corpses, poltergeists, and cult rituals. In like manner, nudity (classical paintings and contemporary photographs) and other aspects of sexuality such as fertility totems and phallic symbolism are graphically represented. None of this material is, in the Committee's judgment, salacious or obscene; moreover, where opportunities for potential exploitation occur (in such articles as *Nudity* and *Godiva*), the editors have exercised considerable constraint. Nonetheless, in view of the recent Supreme Court ruling on community standards, the encyclopedia should if possible be examined prior to purchase, particularly for use in school and public libraries.

Ultimately, however, the illustrative matter notwithstanding, *Man, Myth & Magic* must be judged by its efforts—averred by Cavendish—to eschew the proselytizing bias so common in the genre, and concomitantly to distinguish clearly between information which is factual and responsible in the light of current scientific knowledge and that which is pseudoscientific in nature. As Dr. Edward U. Condon, a highly regarded scientist, has written, students "are educationally harmed by absorbing unsound and erroneous material as if it were scientifically well founded. Such study is harmful not merely because of the erroneous nature of the material itself, but also because such study retards the development of a critical faculty with regard to scientific evidence." In this very important respect, the encyclopedia scores high marks; it makes genuine and usually successful efforts to be as objective and discerning as possible in what is admittedly an imprecise and often polemical area of human knowledge. For instance, the article *Abominable Snowman* notes that people have reported "what were thought to be its footprints in the snow, but research has revealed that these tracks were made by other animals. Anthropologists have shown that the Sherpas' stories are questionable, and the view that the snowman is a legend is now widely accepted." The article *Vampire* relates the creature's origins in folktales, describes its mythic characteristics and so forth, and ends with a modern psychosexual theory about the traditional appeal of vampire stories. The article *Flying Saucers*, citing the 1969 University of Colorado report (the most thorough investigation of the UFO phenomenon to date), asserts that while "It is always dangerous to be too dogmatic, and one certainly cannot deny the possibility that the earth might be visited by extraterrestrial beings . . . it seems as certain as anything can be that there is no intelligent life in our solar system, except on the Earth." The article *Extra-Sensory Perception*, although written by an advocate (Professor J. B. Rhine), makes no claims except for research which "has followed the course that has been taken by all the basic sciences."

Likewise, the articles *Faith Healing, Miracles, Necromancy, Psychokinesis, Spontaneous Psi Superstitions, Reincarnation, Sorcery, Witchcraft,* and *Zombies*—all topics open to biased suasion —carefully attempt to differentiate between folk and scientific information; nor is there an overt effort to promote occult practices or validate untested or unproved psychical experience. Pleas for tolerance toward the unknown, however, are not uncommon, and occasionally overly serious enthusiasm is exhibited for such parlor games as ouija boards and tea leaf reading. Also, instances of parapsychological fraud are generally avoided (for example, Ted Serios and his "thoughtographic" hoax of a few years ago are nowhere to be found in the encyclopedia), and some subjects are inadequately covered (e.g., *Dolls, Hypnotism, Plants and Flowers*), being either disappointingly cursory or short on current developments. In addition, there is an unmistakable British emphasis in the selection of topics, a criticism which also extends to the bibliographies (both the "further readings" accompanying individual articles and those found in the final volume). But considering the broad scope of the work, the rapid accretion of research data in certain areas, and the generally controversial nature of the subject matter, *Man, Myth & Magic* provides reasonably sufficient, up-to-date, reliable, and objective coverage of the supernatural from both the contemporary and historical points of view.

The Index, which indicates articles in bold type and illustrations in italic type, is satisfactory except in one respect: volume numbers are not included with the page references; a colored box noting inclusive pages for each volume is reproduced on every other page of the Index, but this procedure adds an otherwise unnecessary and at times tedious step to the reference process, particularly in the case of multiple entries.

The physical format also presents some problems. The individual volumes are attractive, with bright lettering and illustrations on each cover; they are, however, too slim (this easily could have been a 10 or 12 volume set) and they tend to be difficult to handle physically, easily slipping out of hand or off the shelf as a result of their slick varnished surface.

Man, Myth & Magic is an imperfect reference work in many respects. Its idiosyncratic arrangement, its sometimes gruesome illustrations, its less than full treatment of some subjects, and its inferior physical format all impair its usefulness. The Committee, however, believes that its strengths—the high caliber of contributors and editorial staff, the erudite tone, the general reliability and currency of the articles, and the largely successful effort to distinguish between the scientific and the pseudoscientific—are sufficient to recommend it with the proviso that if possible prior to purchase the set be examined.

 Kenneth F. Kister
 Formerly Non-Fiction Editor
 Kirkus Reviews
 Reference and Subscription
 Books Review Committee Member
 1966-1970

(Dec. 15, 1973, p.395)

Masterpieces of Chinese Art:
Masterworks of Chinese Painting in the National Palace Museum, Masterpieces of Chinese Portrait Painting in the National Palace Museum, Masterpieces of Chinese Album Painting . . ., Masterworks of Chinese Porcelain . . ., Masterworks of Chinese Bronze . . ., Masterpieces of Chinese Bronze Mirrors . . ., Masterworks of Chinese Jade . . ., Masterpieces of Chinese Carved Lacquer Ware . . ., Masterpieces of Chinese Silk Tapestry and Embroidery . . ., Masterpieces of Chinese Enamel Ware . . ., Masterpieces of Chinese Miniature Crafts . . ., Masterpieces of Chinese Writing Materials . . ., Masterpieces of Chinese Calligraphy . . ., Masterpieces of Chinese Tibetan Buddhist Altar Fittings . . ., Select Chinese Rare Books and Historical Documents . . . . 15 unnumbered v. Taipei, Taiwan, National Palace Museum, 1969-73. illus. 28cm. cloth $187.50; individual volumes, $14.95 each.

Art collecting in China has been going on for one thousand years. There are historical records of royal collections as far back as the T'ang dynasty. In spite of the fact that these collections were sacked again and again by barbarian invaders and by native rebels, by the time the Ch'ing dynasty arrived (1644-1912) there was a large collection of ancient works of art distributed through the various royal palaces. The Ch'ing dynasty produced several connoisseur-collectors among the various emperors, and the royal collections became exceedingly rich. In 1925 the National Palace Museum was created in Peiping to house the collection of the Imperial Palace. This museum survived many vicissitudes, and in 1937, just before the outbreak of hostilities with Japan, the choicest items of the collections were spirited out of China and, after incredible wanderings, were finally gathered together in Formosa, where once again, they became available to the public. This was no small collection; 875 crates containing 17,934 pieces of porcelain alone were shipped to Taiwan via anything but direct route. There were, in addition, thousands of paintings, tapestries, jewels, carvings, and rare books. The total present collection numbers 40,940 objects and 178,464 books and documents.

When the Reference and Subscription Books Review Committee first began its examination of these books, they were available in the United States from Gakken Corporation of America, Irvine, California. Three months ago the company, which was an affiliate of Gakken Company, Ltd. of Tokyo, notified that its U.S. operation was discontinued. The project for the series, complete in 15 volumes, was begun in the mid-1960s with the National Palace Museum of Taipei approving production by Gakken. In 1969, five volumes were completed, and in 1970-71 the ten remaining were completed. Complete sets were not released in the United States until January 1973.

The beautiful volumes show only a small and extremely select sample of the main types of objects in the collection. Each volume is edited by the curators responsible for the museum department that it represents. The Preface in each volume is signed by Dr. Chiang Fu-tsung, director of the museum, and identifies the curators responsible for the selection of items and for the text and catalog which accompany them. Each volume then presents 50 full-page illustrations of works of art in full color. Sometimes there are two views of an object or a detail, and sometimes there are more than fifty works represented, when, as in the volume on jades, more than one can be shown in a photograph. There are also occasional small black-and-white pictures and drawings which relate to the works—a set of rubbings from the bronze and lacquer pieces, for example. Following the plates, there is a very good short essay on the history and techniques of the craft and then a catalog of the works in the illustrations giving full descriptions. The complete text, including the Preface and table of contents, is given first in Chinese, repeated in Japanese, then finally in English. Names of the translators are not given. The English is fairly smooth, but in a few cases there are awkward phrases which suggest that English was not the native language of the translator.

The volumes are not numbered, but the distinctive titles of the volumes, which are listed at the head of this review, are on the spine. The period covered runs from Shang (1550-1030 B.C.) to Ch'ing (A.D. 1644-1912), and each volume represents the most important period of the craft under discussion. Thus the bronzes are mainly from Shang to Warring States (1500-222 B.C.), while porcelain is mainly Sung and Yuan dynasties (A.D. 960-1368), and the enamels are Ming or Ch'ing dynasties (A.D. 1368-1912).

The percentage of works in the collection represented in the books is, of course, minute; 50 out of 17,934 pieces of porcelain can hardly be representative and even 50 out of 421 pieces of lacquer is only about 11 percent. The selections were made by the curators and may represent their preferences to a degree.

The volumes are attractively bound in a linen-like cloth binding and are a convenient size to handle. They have wide margins and lie fairly flat. They are glued rather than sewn. The print is clear on heavy white opaque paper in the English section. The oriental section is particularly attractive. The volumes open as a normal occidental book does rather than in the back-to-front oriental fashion.

Masterpieces of Chinese Art represent a summary or overview of the main areas of Chinese art. There are no indexes, no cross-references, and no particular reference application except perhaps in a very large research library. The volumes would be best in the art section of a public library or university library, and they should be considered for such libraries. For a small library, the series is a bit too specialized, although the text could be understood by anyone with a high school education and some background. The volumes are too specific for ordinary reference.

(July 15, 1973, p.1029)

Merit Students Encyclopedia. Emanuel Friedman, editor; William D. Halsey, editorial director; Louis Shores, senior library advisor. 20v. [New York], Crowell-Collier Educational Corp., [c1967-1972]. illus. ports. maps. diagrs.

27cm. buckram $224.50; to schools and libraries, $165 delivered.

Merit Students Encyclopedia, first published in 1967 as a new 20-volume reference tool for students of the fifth grade and up, was reviewed in *The Booklist and Subscription Books Bulletin,* July 15, 1969. The set is revised continuously. From 1967 to 1969 Bernard S. Cayne was editor, and since 1970 Emanuel Friedman has been editor. The Resident Editorial Staff and Advisory Editorial Board have been decreased in membership (by 67 percent) and altered in composition to include Departments of Bibliography and Reference Service and a Board of International Advisors.

The Board of Special Editors, however, has not changed. This Board is accorded much credit by *Merit Students Encyclopedia* since it selected, reviewed, and/or wrote the articles initially comprising the set. A random sample confirms that these special editors have verified a majority of the articles checked, in accordance with the Preface which claims that each article was written or reviewed by an acknowledged authority. The fact that few articles in the set were actually written by the authorities whose names are appended to the text is not immediately apparent to the reader because of the methods used to attribute credit. "When a signature is preceded by an asterisk, it indicates that the person signing the article vouches for the accuracy and completeness of the article, but did not write it. Such articles were in general written by the members of the editorial staff." An extensive random sample shows the majority of articles (85 percent) have signatures preceded by an asterisk; the remainder divided among articles signed by both author and reviewer (7 percent), articles signed by the author alone (4 percent), and short unsigned definitions (4 percent). Thus a small number of editors (17) initially writes or revises a preponderance of the articles.

In spite of its impressive appearance, the list of over 2,300 Contributors and Reviewers, volume 20, does not represent a broad responsibility for articles in the set. Nearly half (47 percent) of those named are persons who have verified short descriptive articles about colleges and universities. Alterations in this list since 1967 are primarily the result of changing those who verified these college articles. The list also repeats the names of the Board of Special Editors listed in volume 1. It does not indicate the titles of articles which the person wrote or reviewed; it does provide brief biographical information.

Merit Students Encyclopedia continues to emphasize topics common to the upper elementary, junior high, and high school curricula: science, geography, history and allied social sciences, biography, national literatures, mathematics, fine arts, and religion. As delineated by two samples cited in the review of the 1967 edition, approximately one-third of the articles were concerned with science, one-fourth with biography, one-fifth with geography, and one-tenth with history and allied social sciences. General scientific, historical, and geographical articles are designed to give the intended audience an overview; they are longer and often contain cross-references and study aids such as mathematics examples, line diagrams, photographs, or outline charts. Biographical articles span the disciplines. Great movements, specific achievements, national traditions, and general developments in art and literature are treated extensively. Articles about religions, their institutions, doctrines, practices, and terminologies are numerous and often are signed by two authorities when controversy may exist. In essence the coverage and range of subjects are both suitable and adequate for the intended audience.

The system of updating the encyclopedia is uneven. Some areas have received consistent attention. Each article about states in the United States has been rewritten to include information on elections held between 1967 and 1971, pertinent recent events, and information made available by the 1970 census. City articles reflect the same census. In addition, the tables included in all state articles have been updated uniformly. Tables of Farm Production—1968, Mineral Production—1967, and Manufacturing Production—1967 include the latest figures available to the staff at the time of compilation and replace tables of Crop Production, Livestock Receipts, Mineral Production, and Value Added by Manufacture, all of which cited average annual production for a three-year period. Similarly, international geographical-political articles throughout the set have been updated generally over the past five years—*Northern Ireland* through March 1972, *Indonesia* through 1969, *Germany* (East and West in one general article) through 1969, *China* through 1971, *Vietnam* (North and South in one general article) through 1969. However, most changes are minor, amounting to a few words or lines changed on a page.

Although some major rewriting is evident in such articles as *Vietnam War*, current through May 1972, and *Space Flight*, current through February 1972, and while a few articles such as *Environmental Pollution* have appeared, many subjects have received little or no attention. The list of Academy Award Winners is current only to 1969; less than half of the biographical articles were updated to show deaths recorded by *Current Biography, 1971;* the table of Prime Ministers of Great Britain does not list Edward Heath, but the text of the article does. Histories of the U.S. Coast Guard and Navy are current through World War II, of the U.S. Air Force and Army through the Korean War, and only the U.S. Marine Corps article chronicles involvement in the Vietnam War. Some topics such as Black Panthers and consumerism, which have become important to many students now, have received no treatment. *Popular Music* devotes three lines each to the Beatles and Bob Dylan as the most recent figures—neither is the subject of a separate article. *Drug Abuse* takes three columns, *Heroin* 10 lines, *Marijuana* 18 lines; none of the aforementioned is supplemented by a bibliography. Finally, a majority (84 percent) of the articles and pages (74 percent) checked in a random sample showed no revision at all.

Merit Students Encyclopedia's Preface emphasizes the use of full-color, two-color, and black-and-white illustrations as an aid for its intended audience. Fortunately the policy has continued. Some illustrations were deleted to make space for new material. Four illustrations in *England, History of* were dropped in providing space for *Environmental Pollution*, a new article. Sometimes revised or new text has new illustrations. This edition, for example, carries a picture of "New Scotland Yard."

Throughout the encyclopedia, the indexes which accompany the maps cite the latest available population statistics, and maps prepared by the Crowell-Collier cartographic staff and Rand McNally show alterations wherever necessary. However, black-and-white photographs often lack definition; color photographs are frequently muddy, and both kinds of photographs provide many examples of fading and/or darkening.

As with the original *Merit Students*, the set is organized into 20 volumes with each page headed by guide words. Cross-references in the text have been increased slightly and are divided almost equally among *see, see also,* and *see under*. Since this is a specific entry encyclopedia, and since many students cannot, or do not, utilize an index volume, additional cross-references might help the student. For instance, *Russia, History of* covers up to 1917 but contains no cross-reference citation to *U.S.S.R., History of*.

As indicated by the publisher, shorter articles are often followed by citations to at least one additional source of information, and longer articles sometimes carry graded bibliographies. Although the Preface states that each major article is followed by a bibliography, bibliographies were found with only 19 percent of the articles checked in an extensive sample. Most of these were short bibliographies of fewer than six items intended for further study. Of these approximately one-third have been revised since 1967. Bibliographies for *Army, U.S.* (newest item 1959), *Astronomy* (newest item 1959), *Automotive Industry* (newest item 1957), and *Indian, American* (newest item 1965), are not updated to reflect changes. in all fields and the newer books for students on these subjects. Broad articles such as *Central America; Europe, History of; Flowering Plants; Radio; World, History of; Greece, Ancient*—all "major" articles of two or more pages—have no bibliographies, a fact not consistent with the publisher's stated policy of providing a bibliography for every major article.

Merit Students Encyclopedia is a well-illustrated, attractive comprehensive set which will be useful to students in homes and libraries. Although the continuous revision given the books since the first edition of 1972 is slight, statistical changes are present throughout the set, and new articles reflecting the informational needs of students have been added during the period between 1967 and 1972. Recommended. *(Dec. 15, 1973, p.396)*

Modern Century Illustrated Encyclopedia.
(Scholastic Book Services Ed.). 24v. Modern Century Illustrated Encyclopedia, Inc. Publishers. McGraw-Hill Far Eastern Publishers (S) Ltd. [c1972]; distributed by Scholastic Book Services, New York. illus. maps. charts. diagrs. drawings. 21cm. paperback $39.93.

Although copyright information indicated that *Modern Century Illustrated Encyclopedia* was first published in Australia, there is no discernable remnant of an Australian slant. The publishers, McGraw-Hill and Scholastic Book Services, did not answer the Reference and Subscription Books Review Committee's request for information on the history of the publication. Perhaps the set was always as it is now. The encyclopedia has a two-fold purpose: "to provide a wide range of information that is concise, accurate, up to date, and easily accessible; and to give that information maximum visual appeal." It is presented as a "first encyclopedia to encourage further exploration into the . . . world of knowledge" and to stimulate the use of a reference source and lead on to more complex material. The Editorial Board consists of 22 persons, who are listed with only their degrees after their names. No background information could be located on them. The 12 members of the Board of Consultants are identified. Included are Ralph Backlund, an editor of *The Smithsonian Magazine,* Arthur C. Croft, founder of *Business Week,* and Dr. Roy Hill, chairman, Department of Black Studies, Rutgers (Newark Campus). There is no indication of who is responsible for certain subjects or for the writing of specific articles.

The claim that the encyclopedia covers a wide range of information seems to be borne out. Topics cover the sciences, fine arts, social sciences, economics, literature, history, geography, and sports. The articles range in length from a few lines to several pages. Each volume contains between 60 and 100 articles. The articles are not signed and are arranged alphabetically word by word.

There are entries for every country of the world and every state in the United States, and all Canadian provinces and territories are covered. No inaccuracies were noted in the entries. The information is up to date to the time of publication. Population figures are those of the latest census year.

Historical and contemporary personalities are covered. There are brief entries for such individuals as David Ben-Gurion, Pablo Casals, Fidel Castro, Charlie Chaplin, Chou En-Lai, Pierre Elliot Trudeau, Margaret Mead, Arthur Miller, Richard Nixon, Benjamin Spock, and Andy Warhol.

Basic coverage is given for such current topics as Democratic Party, drugs, civil rights, ecology, elections, microfilm and microfiche, pollution, Republican Party, space travel, Spanish-speaking Americans, and Women's Liberation. For the most part, controversial subjects such as birth control, marijuana, the Nuremberg trials, and the Oscar awards are treated objectively, with various positions mentioned.

Blacks, an eight-and-a-half-page article, is unbiased and gives adequate consideration to opposing views with an historical survey from early history to the 1970s. Prominent Blacks of the twentieth century mentioned in this article include Marian Anderson, H. Rap Brown, Stokely Carmichael, Shirley Chisholm, Eldridge Cleaver, Countee

Cullen, Langston Hughes, Martin Luther King, Jr., and Robert Weaver. Of these, only Hughes and King are covered in separate articles.

The science articles, though brief, are uniformly adequate for basic information. The periodic table of elements is up to date. *Kidneys* mentions transplants, and there is an article on transplants.

Sports articles give some history of the games, brief facts about the rules and records, and a few pointers on playing.

Children's Literature has a short survey of the subject. Note is made of the popularity of Dr. Seuss and the *Peanuts* books, and the fact that "recent stories for teenagers . . . reflect trends in adult life . . ." and that juvenile books are beginning to deal more with minority groups.

Measurements are given in both English and metric units. There are no bibliographies and no pronunciation guides. Difficult words are explained in parentheses following the word's use in the articles. For example: boycotted (refused to use), caricature (humorously exaggerate), demoralized (without spirit), hallucinations (insane visions), luminous (glowing), and salvage (save).

While the text is geared to upper elementary and junior high school reading levels, the interest level goes beyond. The style is factual and straightforward. The most common spelling of proper names is used, and the Merriam-Webster dictionaries are the authority.

The encyclopedia is comprised of short, specific entries. Volume 24 has a detailed Index for quick reference giving volume and page numbers. Main entries are in bold type; lighter typeface is used to indicate entries which refer to subjects discussed as part of a major article. Titles of books, works of art, and names of ships are in italics. A spot check revealed few inaccuracies.

Cross-references are used in the body of the set, listed at the end of articles, or indicated in the text with small capitals. A spot check revealed no blind entries.

Illustrations are used generously, with only a few two-color pictures. Most illustrations consist of photographs in color, and maps, diagrams, and flags are also shown in color. The illustrations range in size from one-and-three-fourths inches square to about five inches by seven-and-one-half inches. Most are in the smaller size range. In general, color and clarity are only fair; however, some pictures are quite clear.

There are 2,249 continuously-paged pages of text and 49 pages of Index entries. The print is small but legible. The pagination is at the center bottom of each page. The lead subject heading also appears at the bottom of the page. The text is arranged in two columns on good quality, non-glare paper. The illustrations and format fulfill the set's stated goal of "maximum visual appeal."

Each volume is bound in black glossy coated heavy paper, with white lettering and an assortment of color photographs on the covers. The volumes lie flat when opened. While the binding will not allow for the prolonged wear of a hard-bound book, the set held up remarkably well under examination for this review.

Portions of the *Modern Century* were compared with similar portions in the *Young People's Illustrated Encyclopedia* (Chicago: Children's Press; McGraw-Hill Far Eastern Publishers (S) Ltd. first published in Australia copyright 1972), because of similar copyright information and because the general editorial staff of the *Young People's* lists the names of three individuals who also are editors of *Modern Century*. These comparisons revealed that little of the same wording is used in the two sets. *Modern Century* has a much broader and better coverage of subjects. Some of the illustrative material is similar, with the *Modern Century* having some cropped portions of larger pictures appearing in *Young People's*. Except for biographical article pictures and the maps, the illustrative materials in general are not duplicated. An exception for the maps is that the one for the United States in *Modern Century* shows the state lines; the one in *Young People's* does not.

Modern Century Encyclopedia cannot compare in scope, coverage, and depth with such standard children's reference sets and encyclopedias as *Britannica Junior Encyclopedia, Compton's Encyclopedia, Merit Students Encyclopedia, New Book of Knowledge,* and *The World Book Encyclopedia.* The publisher's purpose is valid and has been met for the most part; the use of *Modern Century* fosters the development of research skills and saves the process of digesting a great deal of information especially for students in the second, third, and fourth grades. Even though the coverage is brief and basic, the set would meet the interest and informational needs of elementary school students and could be used with reluctant readers. *Modern Century Encyclopedia* is recommended for supplementary use in homes and with the libraries' standard, more comprehensive encyclopedias for children.

(April 1, 1974, p.835)

Music of the Middle Ages to the Renaissance. Edited by F. W. Sternfeld. New York, Washington, Praeger Publishers, [c1973]. Praeger History of Music Series v.I. 524p. illus. cloth $20; to schools, 5 or more copies, 25 percent off.

Music in the Modern Age: A History of Western Music. Edited by F. W. Sternfeld. New York, Washington, Praeger Publishers, [c1973]. Praeger History of Music Series, v.V. 524p. illus. cloth $20; to schools, 5 or more copies, 25 percent off.

The volumes at hand are the first and last of the planned five volumes. They are entitled respectively *Music from the Middle Ages to the Renaissance* and *Music in the Modern Age.* Each volume has a separate staff of from 17 to 20 contributors under the editorship of Frederick W. Sternfeld who is a Reader in the History of Music at Oxford and author of several books on the subject. He has also served as editor of the *Renaissance Quarterly* and, curiously, is also on the staff of *New Oxford History of Music.* Each of the contributors is identified at the beginning of each volume by a paragraph detailing his credentials. Most of the contributors are connected with English universities, but several Americans are also included.

The author of each chapter in the volumes is identified. The books are being published simultaneously in England, by Wedenfeld & Nicholson and in the United States by Praeger.

The first volume is a history of music beginning with the Greeks and organized more or less chronologically with growing emphasis on individual countries and composers as it progresses. The closing date is about 1601, and a short chapter on music in the western hemisphere completes the volume. Volume v, on the other hand, is divided by country to include the twentieth-century musical movements and the leading composers who contributed to each development. The accounts are clear and very interesting, but they are by no means simple reading. While not as complicated as Gustave Reese's *Music in the Middle Ages* (New York: Norton, 1940), the discussion of medieval music in volume I of this set requires at least a working acquaintance with musicological terms. A glossary in each volume would have been a useful addition, as many terms are not clearly defined, though there are some helpful footnotes. The reader may want to keep Apel's *Harvard Dictionary of Music* (Harvard, 1969, 2d ed.) at his elbow.

The plentiful illustrations in both volumes are musical illustrations, and they explain the subject or composer under discussion. The writing is generally excellent, although occasionally the writer's personal view may appear unobtrusively, but the writers are experts. Thus one may respect their opinions. Accounts of twentieth-century composers in volume v are particularly impressive and contain many fine points, such as the comparison of Schonberg's and Berg's attitudes toward the 12-tone row. The study of their works is excellent—a formal analysis of Berg's *Wozzeck* on page 159 is a case in point. The American chapter also contains an interesting section on Jazz.

An impressive feature in both volumes is the bibliography section and even a discography is included. Bibliographies are arranged by chapter, and in volume I a long "general alphabetical bibliography" follows the subject section. Each Bibliography contains a section of reference tools, congresses, Festschriften, and a list of periodicals. Books are in many languages, and the latest publication date is 1972.

The discographies are also arranged by country and include general anthologies and recordings of individual composers. Each volume is indexed in two ways—by proper names which may include some individual works in volume I, and by subjects. In volume V, one has to look under the composer's name to find the works. The indexes seem to be accurate.

"Yet another history of music?" says Sternfeld in the opening sentence of his preface to the first volume of the new *Praeger History of Western Music* of which he is editor. He recognizes *Praeger History's* nearest rivals, *Norton History of Music Series* (New York: Norton, 1940-) which is a series of independent books by such authorities as Curt Sachs, Gustave Reese, and Alfred Einstein, each treating a separate era of music history from the ancient world to Stravinsky, and *New Oxford History of Music* (London: Oxford Univ. Pr., 1954-) which more closely resembles *Praeger*. The Oxford set is a connected set of volumes each covering an era in music history with writings by a group of contributors. As yet the *New Oxford* has reached only volume four to the year 1630 of the ten planned volumes. Further comparison is not possible at this time, since only two volumes of *Praeger History* have been published.

The other volumes in the series will be volume II, *Music in the Baroque Age*, volume III, *Music in the Classical Age*, and volume IV, *Music in the Romantic Age*. In accordance with Committee policy no recommendations can be made for the set until these volumes complete the series.

(*July 1, 1974, p.1162*)

The Musician's Guide: The Directory of the World of Music. 1972 ed.
Editor-in-chief, Gladys S. Field. [New York, Music Information Service, Inc., 1972]. 1013p. 27cm. buckram $39.50.

This is the fifth edition of a work first published in 1955. The third edition, 1957, was reviewed in *The Booklist and Subscription Books Bulletin,* December 15, 1958, and was recommended as "a welcome addition as a reference yearbook, and as a trade and professional directory for both the music library and the general public, school, or university library." A fourth edition was published in 1968. Although no longer an annual publication, its purpose remains the same: "a reference guide directed primarily to the commercial side of music which also covers music education, the music industry, and the profession."

The new edition lists an Editorial Advisory Board of 10 persons prominent in American and Canadian music circles, but their contributions to the work are not indicated. All entries in the *Guide* are unsigned with the exception of one discography.

The arrangement of the *Guide* remains basically the same: more than 50 lists and rosters of persons, organizations, activities, and businesses concerned with the profession and performance of music in the United States and Canada, gathered into seven sections. These seven sections include 23 new lists and rosters added since the 1968 edition. Three lists have been dropped. Also missing is the series of brief essays on various aspects of the music profession which served little reference purpose.

Important among the additions to the new edition is a group of listings of significant performance and industry awards. Other new entries include lists of record companies, recording companies, concert and personal managers, magazine music editors and critics, national music centers of the world, and summer music camps for young musicians.

The section entitled Libraries, Publications, and Recordings includes two new bibliographic essays and three discographies of basic collections of classical, jazz, and rock recordings. The discographies were compiled by the editorial staff in consultation with authorities in each field. Similar discographies appear frequently in library and music journals. The inclusion of yet another "basic" library of recordings seems peripheral to the central purpose of the *Guide* and adds little to its value as a reference work.

Another questionable inclusion is a bibliography in this section entitled "Recent Books on Music (1967-1971)." This unannotated listing covers the years since the last list, which appeared in the 1968 edition. This compilation in two parts, a subject arrangement followed by a title list, is not a comprehensive bibliography even of works published in English during these years. Other readily available and more comprehensive tools, including the *Cumulative Book Index,* will better serve the person seeking a mere listing of music books published from 1967-1971.

In spite of these few extraneous additions, the work has been greatly strengthened both by the many new lists, rosters, and organization entries and by the enlargement and updating of many of the retained lists, such as those on colleges and conservatories, music libraries (a much more meaningful and helpful chapter than the former "Libraries with Music Collections"), music festivals, music competitions and musical instrument manufacturers.

Most of the weaknesses pointed out in the review of the 1957 edition have been eliminated. There is now a directory of symphony orchestras and conductors; the two tables of contents have been replaced by one; the Index, still brief but adequate, now includes both *see* and *see also* references; clear geographic running heads appear on every appropriate page; all schools of music appear in one geographic arrangement. The binding is now of buckram with reinforced spine and endpapers and will withstand heavy usage. The volume lies flat when opened, has adequate margins and good print quality.

Musician's Guide, 1972 edition, gives evidence of extensive editorial revision and expansion since the 1968 edition. Most of the weaknesses pointed out in *The Booklist and Subscription Books Bulletin* review of the 1957 edition have been corrected and a significant number of useful additions have been made. The *Guide* contains much information difficult or impossible to find in other sources, and is again recommended as a welcome trade and professional directory for school, public, and academic libraries.

(Dec. 1, 1972, p.307)

National Geographic Atlas of the World.

Melville Bell Grosvenor, ed. in chief; Wellman Chamberlin, chief cartographer; Frederick G. Voxburgh, ed. Rev. 3d ed. Washington, D.C., National Geographic Society, 1970. 331p. col. illus. col. maps. 49cm. standard binding $18.75; deluxe, $24.50.

Although the National Geographic Society has built a reputation for high-quality map making since 1899, its first world atlas was not published until 1963. (See *The Booklist and Subscription Books Bulletin,* July 15, 1964). An enlarged second edition was published in 1966, and the third edition, examined in this review, appeared in 1970. The editor in chief states in his Introduction that the Society's aim has been to produce a "volume of such quality and detail that it would rank among geography's truly great atlases." He stresses that the atlas was planned to provide the "maximum" facts for which people consult maps, and in that connection points out that the folio page size permits presentation of "large-scale maps found only in the truly fine atlases." An implied objective is to supply maps and other information useful to travelers.

Basically the arrangement of the 1970 edition is that of the preceding editions. Portions of the world are treated by continents or regions. An overview is provided by a series of world maps followed by the continental areas, beginning with North America, followed by South America, Europe, Asia, Africa, the Oceans, Australia, and ending with Antarctica. There are few maps of individual countries; exceptions are those of the United States and Canada, the Soviet Union, China, Germany, Ireland, Italy, Scotland, and Australia. Instead, related countries such as the Scandinavian countries; India, Pakistan, Ceylon; France, Belgium, and the Netherlands are mapped together. The mapping of these sections within a continent was planned so as to avoid separating economically and culturally linked areas. If a political area extends over part of a continent, overlapping in successive maps assures that the divided portions are adequately represented. Omission of state and country maps was deliberate. In the view of the editor in chief, "Techniques that give a page-size map to each country—the same for Switzerland as for sprawling Brazil—can lead an atlas user into confused concepts of geography."

Physical and political maps predominate, although there are some historical and specialized maps. Most of the maps are two-page spreads. Six physical maps have been added since the first edition, one each for North America, South America, Europe, Asia, Africa, and Australia. The Global View of the World which precedes the rest is also a physical map. Topographic land features on the physical maps are displayed by means of the shaded relief system without contour lines, but spot elevations are given in feet. For water areas some layer tinting in blue, combined with contour lines shows depth curves; spot soundings are indicated in fathoms. Small insert maps accompanying the physical maps show above-sea-level heights by layer tints. There is a color scale, and height is given both in feet and meters.

There is a matching political map for each geographical area and additional ones for key parts of each area. The use of white backgrounds, clear typeface, and of light gray shading on the political maps to show mountainous areas makes these maps easy to consult.

Since this is an American atlas, it is not surprising that the largest number of maps is devoted to the United States and Canada. However, good coverage of Europe and Asia is provided. It should be noted that a number of the European maps are one-page maps whereas all the maps for the United States and Canada and Asia are double-page ones.

There is no one ideal universal projection for maps. Many different ones are required to give adequate two-dimensional representation of the three-dimensional globe and its parts. The several types of projection used in the *National Geographic Atlas* in all three editions reflect the new techniques of mapping, and the ones selected for given areas have been designed to minimize distortions and to keep in reasonable balance the four basic properties of distance, direction, area, and shape. According to the editor, several of the projections employed were developed by the Society's cartographers. They give a reasonably close flat representation of global form or shape over fairly large areas, the most difficult aspect of map making. The oblique cylindrical projection was devised to map an area like Hawaii which is stretched out over a wide area. The two-point equidistant projection was developed for the continental Asia maps. For the triangular land areas of Africa and South America, the Chamberlin Trimetric Projection was evolved. However, it should be noted that the same projection is used for maps forming smaller areas of a region to facilitate comparisons. For example, Albers conical equal area projection is used for the maps of the United States, Canada and parts of Europe. Other currently recognized projections used in the atlas include Polyconic and Transverse Mercator. The projection is clearly specified on each map. However, the atlas lacks an adequate explanatory section on map projection, the brief explanation on the inside of the back cover being more pictorial than explanatory.

The varying scales used are determined by the area mapped, but in all cases the scale is indicated. On the large maps scale is specified in the professional decimal manner with two scale bars, one in statute miles and the other in kilometers. In the case of the many insert maps, showing metropolitan areas, islands, etc., the scale is less precise and is merely stated in terms of one inch to a given number of miles. The continent maps have scales, ranging from 1:9,504,000 for Europe to 1:21,225,600 for Asia. The scales for smaller areas within a region are naturally larger but vary considerably, depending upon the surface mapped.

Some maps present statistical data,

but no section in the atlas is devoted to socioeconomic maps. At the head of the text preceding each of the continental maps, there is a small map of the region which not only serves as an Index key, but also, by means of small dots, shows population concentration. Each dot represents 20,000 persons, except for Asia where the dots each stand for 100,000 persons. A world map of vegetation and land use accompanies the text essay "The Earth We Live On." A similar map limited to Alaska, Western Canada, and Siberia is an insert for the map of Alaska. The Moslem World map shows the percentage of Moslems to the total population in Africa, the Middle East, Southern Asia, including China, and the Southeast Pacific as far as the Philippines, and appears as an insert on the map for Southwest Asia.

The Introduction concludes with a section explaining "Map Symbols and What They Mean." Selected appropriate symbols are repeated on individual maps, usually below the scale bars. On the same page with the explanation of the map symbols is a chronology of Great Moments in Geography which in the 1970 edition covers events down to 1969, the year astronauts Armstrong and Aldrin made man's first walk on the moon.

"A Glossary of Foreign Terms Used in This Atlas" is given on the second and third pages of the Index. There are approximately 700 terms with English equivalents; however the language of the foreign terms is not indicated. Abbreviations adopted for the Index to identify country, state or province, and geographical features, such as P.E.I. for Prince Edward Island or W. for Wadi, follow the Glossary and number nearly 300.

The historical maps are interesting features of the atlas and combine scaled maps with textual explanations. Especially useful are maps of the Nile Valley and the Holy Land Today, trouble spots in post-World War II years. Those of the Battlefields of the Civil War reflect the American public interest in the centennial celebration which ended in 1965, and are a convenient source for students and the general public when a Civil War atlas is not available. Battles shown on these maps are indexed but other place-names are not, since the maps are based on the United States as of 1863.

The map showing the location of National Parks of the United States and Canada and those of the individual state parks are designed for travelers and vacationers and will have a popular appeal. "Pointers about National Park Vacations" accompanies the descriptive text.

Of special interest to travelers is a tabular presentation of "Temperature and Rainfall Each Month for Selected Places Around the World." Useful for settling geographic arguments although available in many standard reference sources, is the page entitled "Geographic Extremes and Comparisons: Vital Statistics of Our Sprawling Earth."

The flyleaves and endpapers are attractive and informative. The front endpaper is devoted to a word and picture account of the "Earth In Space" and the back endpaper to a history of cartography, entitled "The Round Earth on Flat Paper."

The editor in chief claims more than 139,000 entries in the Index. For the first edition the figure claimed was 127,000 and for the second, 138,000 entries. In the 1970 edition 149 pages of the total 331 pages are devoted to the Index, with 7 columns to a page. Each entry is located by country or, for the United States and Canada, by state or province. Entries for names other than cities or towns are identified as to geographical feature if this is not indicated in the name. The alphabetical arrangement is essentially letter-by-letter, but place-names beginning with the same word are grouped into three subgroupings. In the first group are the cities and towns by location, as Adams, *Mass.;* in the second group the place-names are arranged by a descriptive geographical feature, either added by the editors, in lower case, or inverted, as Adams, Cape, *Antarctica* and Adams, river, B.C. In the third group are the names with an added word as a part of the official name, and these are subalphabetized by the second word as Adams Bay, *La.;* Adam's Rock, *Pitcairn I.*, with places like *Adamson, Okla.* inserted before Adam's Peak, *Ceylon.* The headnotes regarding the use of the Index make no mention of this arrangement, which may be confusing to users, or of the practice of inverting place-names when the first element is nondistinctive as Cape, Mount.

The map references in the Index are clear and accurate. They consist of two elements: the map reference figure in boldface followed by a standard letter-number coordinate in light type. The exact latitude and longitude, however, is lacking. If a place appears on several maps, only the best display is indexed. Reference to an insert map is indicated by a capital letter enclosed in parentheses, following the map reference.

A convenient feature of the index is inclusion of the complete map reference under both the vernacular name and the English or alternate name. Thus, although conventional "see" references are provided, it is not necessary to turn to the name adopted by the editors to locate the place through the Index.

There have been considerable changes in the content of *National Geographic Atlas* since the first edition. Most of these changes were made when the 1966 edition was issued. The changes from the 1966 to 1970 edition are relatively minor and represent mainly updating and corrections. Probably the most significant change was the addition of physical maps in the 1966 edition. In the 1970 edition these physical maps cover the same area, although there have been changes in the number of colors and tints used. As a result the land topographic features are more sharply delineated than they were in the 1966 edition, but the place-names in the mountainous areas cannot be read as easily as in the 1966 edition. In the case of the political maps, a number were added in the 1966 edition which have been continued in the 1970 edition. For example, maps were added for England and Wales, Ireland, Scotland, the Low Countries, and Denmark.

Corrections, name changes, and new cities and towns are reflected in the 1970 maps. Examples are the additions of new entries on the map of Antarctica which reflect continuing explorations in that area, changes in place-names in Outer Mongolia, substitution of latest names on the political map of Africa and the delineation of the areas occupied by Israel during the 1967 Six-Day War on the map "Holy Land Today."

Population figures are given at the end of the state, province, and country text summaries. In addition there are two population tables: "Major Cities of the World" (over 500,000) and "U.S. Cities" (over 25,000) as well as the boxed table in the text on Europe called "The Face of Western Europe" with population of 11 leading cities. The exact source of these and other statistical figures is not indicated. In the Introduction there is a statement that the figures are the "latest . . . from the most authoritative source." Also in the explanatory note accompanying the table of "Major Cities of the World" it is stated that "statistics in this tabulation come from the most recent national census or from official government estimates." The edition under review was apparently in the press before the preliminary 1970 U.S. Census figures were released. Accordingly, the U.S. population figures are out of date, varying considerably from the 1970 Census data.

The text accompanying the continents, etc., shows some evidence of updating and correction of previous inaccuracies but not of substantial revision. For example, in the case of individual state sketches of the United States, the descriptions of economy, social factors, and addresses for information, have been changed where appropriate. An example of a correction of an inaccuracy is the change in the Maryland sketch of a date for the bombardment of Fort McHenry by the British fleet in the War of 1812 from 1812 as contained in the 1963 and 1966 editions, to the correct year, 1814, in the 1970 edition.

The maps of *National Geographic Atlas* were compared with those in *The Times Atlas of the World* (Comprehensive ed., 1967) which was reviewed in

The Booklist and Subscription Books Bulletin, July 15, 1968, and the maps in Rand McNally's *The International Atlas* (1969) which was reviewed in *The Booklist* October 1, 1970. Both of these atlases contain many more maps at a larger scale than does *National Geographic Atlas.* In general, however, *National Geographic Atlas'* political maps of broadly comparable areas and scale are as readable and detailed as those in the other two atlases. Since *The Times* and *Rand McNally* atlases are the works of English and an international board of cartographers, respectively, there are expected differences in the scales and projections used. The mapping of smaller areas at larger scales than is true for *National Geographic Atlas* means that the indexes of both *The Times* and *Rand McNally* atlases include more place-names. The *Times Atlas* Index consists of about 200,000 entries and the *Rand McNally,* of about 160,000, whereas *National Geographic* has about 139,000.

The Times Atlas uses the more sophisticated layer tints to indicate elevation, and all its maps are in fact physical-political maps. The variation in the size of the typefaces used on the maps is an outstanding feature, and for cities and towns the size indicates their relative population. The *Rand McNally Atlas* employs hill shading and altitude tints on some maps. Thus, the land areas on these maps have a colored background and as a result place-names do not show up as sharply as on the *National Geographic* maps whose land masses have a white background with contrasting color tints to mark boundaries. This same readability difference applies also to the *Rand McNally* maps other than politico-physical maps.

While the atlas is available in two editions, the difference in the two is solely in the covers. The regular edition has a maroon flexible cover, and the deluxe edition has boards covered in two tones of blue buckram. Both are bound by the method called perfect binding. As a result the pages do not lie flat and under heavy use the sheets tend to come loose since they are not sewed. Also, it is difficult to use a few maps in the center, not merely because the pages do not lie flat, but because in some cases the center of the map is in the binding. No cases of inability to read place-names due to this faulty method of binding were discovered, because in drafting the maps, proper allowance was made. In other cases the two pages of a map were found not to register exactly at the center, at least in a review copy. This latter defect seems to be a printing problem.

National Geographic Atlas of the World does not take the place of the more comprehensive and scholarly *Times Atlas of the World* (New York: Houghton, Mifflin, 1971). Nevertheless, it is based on sound mapping principles and techniques. The maps, especially the political ones, are easy to consult and are attractive and readable. The general accuracy of the Index and the use of latitude and longitude as the locating device make it possible to find the desired locations on the maps readily. The supplementary material and accompanying text add information and comparative data not on maps. It is true that in many cases this information is available in other sources, and in the case of some population statistics, is more up to date in those sources, but not always in such convenient form. The pages do not lie flat, and under heavy use the pages tend to come loose. There have been substantial changes and an enlargement of the atlas since the first edition. Revisions, updating, and corrections are evident throughout the atlas.

The 1970 *National Geographic Atlas of the World* will be useful in both homes and libraries. Especially libraries holding the first edition should replace with this one. Recommended.

(*Dec. 1, 1972, p.308*)

The Negro in American History. Mortimer J. Adler, general editor; Charles Van Doren, editor; George Ducas, executive editor. 3v. Chicago, Encyclopaedia Britannica Educational Corp., c1969, 1972. illus. 26cm. C-grade pyroxylin impregnated cloth $24.50. v.I Black Americans 1928-1971 with an Introduction by Saunders Redding. xxxiv, 468p. v.II A

Taste of Freedom 1854-1927 with an Introduction by Earl E. Thorpe. xxviii, 452p. v.III Slaves and Masters 1567-1854 with an Introduction by Charles H. Wesley. xxi, 466p. ISBN 0-87827-007-8.

The 1972 revision of *The Negro in American History* is an anthology of 195 selections of primary source materials which relate to the experience of blacks in the Americas, primarily the United States. Except for 20 selections in the 1969 edition and 9 additional ones in the 1972 edition, all appear in the 20-volume *The Annals of America* (Chicago: Encyclopaedia Britannica, 1971) reviewed and recommended by the Reference and Subscription Books Review Committee in *The Booklist*, July 15, 1972. Some minor editorial changes are acknowledged, but most selections appear to be exact duplicates of those appearing in *The Annals*.

An Editors' Preface in volume I points out that "the headnotes are the same" (as in *The Annals*) and that "many of the biographical sketches are carried over verbatim." *The Negro in American History* is "the first in a series of books that will be drawn from *The Annals* . . . . The subject chosen was of great importance for contemporary Americans." The editors believe that the "reprinting of over 400,000 words of writing by Americans all on the same subject serves to isolate that subject, to illuminate it, and to identify those aspects of it that require either thought or action at the present time."

A highlight of the set is that each volume is introduced with an essay by an outstanding writer on black subjects. In volume I, J. Saunders Redding traces the gradual awakening of the black man to his political, social, and economic potential in the United States during the years 1928 to 1968, in 17 pages. In volume II, Earl E. Thorpe provides a 20-page overview of the period between 1854 and 1928. Charles W. Wesley's essay in volume III covers the years before 1854 in 13 pages.

Some selections are repetitious and now very well known: the Emancipation Proclamation (v.II, p.318-320); the *Brown v. Board of Education of Topeka et al* decision (v.I, p.334-358); the Nat Turner Confession (v.III, p.279-306); Martin Luther King's "Letter from a Birmingham Jail" (v.I, p.238-247); William John Grayson's "Hireling and the Slave" (v.III, p.13-20); and the Greeley-Lincoln letters on slavery and union (v.II, p.341-346). They are not the less important for that, however, nor the less needed in an adequate anthology purporting to treat the black experience in America. However, they are readily available in many other anthologies. Other selections are less readily available, for instance: Judge Baker's decision in the case of Mrs. Douglass (v.III, p.42-46); "Flournoy's Protest" (v.III, p.189-190); and the dialog between Julian Bond and Roy V. Harris (v.I, p.39-48).

The selections are arranged without any regard for topical considerations. The organization is strictly chronological, although the uncommon practice of reversing chronology is followed. Beginning with the present and moving into the past seems to have brought the editor to an illogical extreme, as the present receives disproportionate attention. For the period 1966 to 1968, volume I provides 117 pages of text. But for the period 1567 to 1819 (a period 84 times longer than that of 1966 to 1968) the third volume provides a disappointing 101 pages of text. The rule that as one recedes into the past one has less to say, or needs to say, is not followed precisely, however. For the period 1941 to 1953, for example, volume I provides a scant 33 pages of text, while for the earlier and much shorter period of 1862 to 1865, there are 63 pages of text in volume I. Thus, during the period 1966 to 1968 and 1862 to 1865 a good deal was happening. On the other hand, between 1941 and 1953 and 1567 and 1819 not much was happening. If this is the suggestion being made, then what happens with the period 1759 to 1776, which is inexplicably excluded from this anthology?

The organization of material by reverse chronology is less satisfactory than a topical approach would be. However, the editors seem to have solved this difficulty by giving topical names to each of the periodic divisions. The period 1850 to 1854, for example, is called the period of "The Great Compromise," and the period between 1866 and 1883 is called "Civil Rights and Reconstruction." All other chronological breakdowns are similarly titled. The result is that the topics are too general and often misleading. The period of 1832 to 1839 is titled "The Abolitionists" (volume I); yet included in this section are William Harper (p.193-202), John C. Calhoun (p.202-208), George McDuffie (p.230-234), and Thomas R. Dew (p.269-276). The first issue of *The Liberator* (p.311-313) is not in the section on "The Abolitionists," but in another section entitled "A Firebell in the Night."

An analytic topical arrangement would likely have pinpointed the need for more treatments of slave protests and insurrections, in terms of both primary and secondary sources. As it is, Nat Turner (v.III, p.279-306) is the only representative of this class covered. The New York rebellion of 1712, the Stono Insurrection of 1739, the Gabriel Prosser Revolt of 1800, the Vesey Conspiracy of 1822, and the numerous other abortive insurrections of the ante-bellum and colonial periods are entirely overlooked. Inadequate also is the treatment of African origins and the Atlantic slave trade, lacking such selections as Vassa's narrative and the Germantown Petition, which would have enhanced this coverage. Accounts of the Indians' attitudes toward blacks and the daily routine of slave life and work in cities and on plantations are missing from the compilation.

Blacks speaking for themselves are represented by William Johnson's "Diary of a Free Negro" (v.III, p.209-218); Nat Turner speaking through his white "interlocutor" (v.III, p.279-306); Frederick Douglass (v.II, p.208-212); Charlotte Forten (v.III, p.3-6); John S. Rock (v.II, p.350-366); and a few others. David Walker, H. H. Garnett, and a host of black abolitionists are missing, as well as the scores upon scores of blacks interviewed during the New Deal about slavery times and who testify in their own eloquent and moving responses to the questions asked of them by the WPA workers.

The illustrations inserted within each volume are judiciously selected, although some lose their effectiveness when limited to black and white.

The 1972 edition contains an Index of Authors and a General Index of proper names and important themes at the end of volume III, but since the General Index omits the useful introductory essays, a part of its effectiveness is lost.

The binding is reinforced to present sturdy volumes which lie flat when opened. The paper is of a smooth white finish which provides a good basis for the offset printing. The type size has been selected to provide readable print.

In summary, the 1972 edition of *The Negro in American History* is a collection of source materials depicting the history of black people in the United States and North America from 1619 through 1971. Though many of the selections are readily available in other sources, there are some which are not so accessible to the average reader. Except for the insertion of biographical information and cumulative index in volume III, volume I is the only volume which contains new materials not in the original 1969 edition. Libraries which have the *Annals* in their collections should decide whether they have a need for the duplication of materials extracted from that publication. Even if libraries have the 1969 edition of *The Negro in American History,* it would be well to determine whether the new material in the 1972 edition covering such persons as Shirley Chisholm, the Reverend Jesse Jackson, Whitney Young, Jr., and Julian Bond are available in the library. Despite the omission of several items which would illuminate the history of blacks in America more fully, and in spite of the unevenness of coverage of various periods of history, *The Negro in American History* is recommended as a useful resource for high school, public, and college libraries.

(Mar. 15, 1974, p.749)

The New Book of Knowledge. New York, Grolier, Inc., 1972. 20v. plus index. illus. ports. maps. charts. 26cm. sturdite. $200; to schools and libraries, $149.62.

When *The New Book of Knowledge* first appeared in 1966 (reviewed in *The Booklist and Subscription Books Bulletin,* December 15, 1967), the publisher announced that two distinctive features marked it "as an innovation in reference book publishing." 1.) It "is designed explicitly as a children's encyclopedia; it is *not* a modified or simplified general encyclopedia expected to be suitable for children, young adults, and adults." 2.) It "is based on the underlying principle of individualized and partially self-directed education which emerged in the 1960's and which has significantly affected elementary education in the United States and elsewhere. *The New Book of Knowledge* no longer has the subtitle: 'The Children's Encyclopedia.'"

In order to maintain this philosophy in the 1972 edition, Grolier, Inc., a publishing firm well-known for its reference works, retained most of the former members of the Curriculum and Library Advisory Board, the consultants in Special Fields, the Editorial Staff, and the contributors and reviewers. To the Curriculum Advisory Board, composed of such authorities as Jeanne Chall, John Jarolimek, and J. Harlan Shores, have been added Robert J. Havighurst, Professor of Education and Human Development, University of Chicago, and Herman Schneider, author, Heath Science series. Richard Darling, Dean, School of Library Service, Columbia University has been added to the Library Advisory Board.

Martha Glauber Shapp continues as editor in chief with Lowell Martin, editorial consultant. Credentials of these staff members and advisers are listed at the beginning of volume 1, and a full list of the 1,303 contributors and 81 artists appears in volume 20. Forty-three percent of the consultants listed and 50 percent of the editorial staff are included in standard biographical references. A spot-check of the names confirmed the accuracy of their credentials as listed.

As was reported in the earlier review of *The New Book of Knowledge,* the set is intended to be useful to a wide range of users starting with preschool children and including students in school up to the age when they are ready for an adult encyclopedia. The chief purpose of *The New Book of Knowledge* is "to provide accurate information. But the editors make every effort to present this factual information in a style of writing that will capture the interest and imagination of readers." To accomplish this, a number of authors of juvenile books contributed articles, among them Millicent Selsam, Robert McClung, Marchette Chute, Arna Bontemps, and Leonard Cottrell. Since they are accustomed to writing for children the level of readability is maintained. Every article is also tested against the Dale-Chall readability formula. Large, clear print with boldface for words being introduced within each article for the first time also contributes to the attractiveness and readability of the text. Sentence length and vocabulary of many articles are determined by the grade level at which subjects are normally introduced into the school curriculum. Even within an article, the style may change. The beginning paragraphs may give information in simplified sentences and vocabulary, and the remaining paragraphs may add more elaborate concepts.

As in the previous edition, most of the articles (about 85 percent) are signed in one of two ways—the full name of the author and/or the name and credentials of the person who reviewed the article. The few not signed are brief biographies of half a page or less, or descriptions of craft techniques such as etching and enameling.

Long articles like *Environment* are broken by headings in capital letters and further subdivided with headings in boldface. While articles tend to be many pages long and comprehensive rather than short and specific, the abundant use in the main text and in the Index of both *see* and *see also* references utilizing wording familiar to young readers makes the full resources of the encyclopedia readily available.

Continuous revision has been the basic policy for *The New Book of Knowledge.* In addition to changing population figures to conform to the

1970 census, revision includes the addition of 49 new articles and 18 expanded ones. Changing interests or curriculum demands necessitated the inclusion of new articles, e.g., *African Literature; Air Pollution; Civil Liberties and Civil Rights; Consumerism; Drugs, Abuse of; Electronic Communications; Food and Population; Paperback Books; Rock Music; Snowmobiles; Vietnam War;* and *Women, Role of.*

Political changes caused new articles to be written on Barbados, Mauritius, Nauru, Tonga, Bangladesh, Yemen, and the Union of Arab Emirates. President Nixon's trip to China, and new material on the school busing controversy were added to the second printing of the 1972 *New Book of Knowledge.*

The 1972 revision while still maintaining the general, broad subject headings, breaks down some of the subjects into more specific articles. One such major change is in the articles on the provinces of Canada. Earlier editions included information under the general headings *Maritime Provinces* and *Prairie Provinces*. The 1972 edition has separate articles for Prince Edward Island, Manitoba, Alberta, and each of the other provinces. A new three-page article *Prehistoric Animals* and a four-page one on vitamins bring together information previously scattered in various places.

Many minor corrections have also been made. In other instances changes in drawings or diagrams have been made to correspond with the text. Factual errors have also been corrected. Some inconsistencies have been remedied. Spellings of place-names have been changed so that names on the maps and in the text are alike; the word "colored" is deleted and "Negro" or "black" substituted. In a few instances strong, positive statements have been toned down.

The greatest number of changes have come about through the process of updating the information. Dates and statistics have been updated to conform to 1970 United States census figures or to other available reports from foreign countries. Name changes, Botswana from Bechuanaland, and the creation of new nations, Mauritius, Nauru, and Tonga have been noted in this revision. Numerous biographies of current notables have been updated because of new honors, new books written, or because of other accomplishments. In the case of persons who have died since the first edition, the date of death has been added.

New space explorations have been fully reported; *Earthquakes* has been revised to mention computerized handling of earthquake data; new text added to the *Sanitation* article includes "recycling" among the methods of garbage disposal; up-to-date information on the lottery system has been added to the article *Draft or Conscription;* new developments such as the Moog Synthesizer have been explained in *Electronic Music.* The article *Soviet Union* has been expanded to 25 pages to allow for detailed descriptions of each of the republics.

Some articles have been rewritten for clarity. An example is the article *Ice Ages* which has been changed to present a simpler explanation of the Ewing-Donn theory of the Ice Age and for a clearer explanation of the method of determining the ocean temperature. *Football* includes clarified references to the Heisman trophy and a better description of how the ball may be advanced.

In a few instances new authors have been commissioned to rewrite entire articles with a new emphasis. For example, Julian Villarreal, M.D. and Ph.D., Associate Professor of Pharmacology, University of Michigan Medical School, discusses the therapeutic use and the abuse of drugs called narcotics as defined by the medical profession in a revised article on that subject. He discusses the life of a narcotic addict and describes methods of treatment and legal measures taken to control narcotics.

The editors claim that "cumulatively all these specific changes and revisions constitute more than 2,000 pages changed or up-dated—often with multiple changes on a single page."

The New Book of Knowledge is more than a curriculum-oriented set. It also encourages individualized or self-directed education, mainly through how-to-do-it instructions for crafts.

Indoor Activities for Rainy Days covers many handicraft activities—making gift wrapping paper, silhouettes, spool knitting and giving directions for group or guessing games. Recipes for fudge, heavenly hash, television nibbles, and cupcakes are included under *Recipes*. How to make barbecue sauce and shishkebabs is explained in *Outdoor Cooking*. For some musical instruments there are instructions for playing and music to play.

The Emperor's New Clothes by Hans Christian Andersen, *The Elephant's Child* by Rudyard Kipling, *The Gift of the Magi* by O. Henry, are examples of stories told in their entirety along with biographical information about the authors. Excerpts from longer stories as *Alice in Wonderland, Gulliver's Travels, Little Women,* and *Charlotte's Web* are also included. In addition there are articles for *Children's Literature, Fables, Fairy Tales, Fiction, Folklore, Mystery, Detective and Suspense Stories, Novels, Science Fiction, Greek Mythology, Legends,* and *Storytelling*. Many of these articles also contain illustrative stories. Although some repetition exists in these various articles, e.g., much of the information found under *Fables* and *Legends* is repeated under *Fiction*, these and other literature articles appeal to different age groups ranging from the preschooler to the high school student. Selections illustrating the various types of literature have been chosen obviously with these age interests in mind, and thus provide an introduction to children's and young adult literature. *African Literature, American Literature,* and other similar articles present a broad background of world literature.

In the article *National Anthems and Patriotic Songs* music and words (in the language of origin and in English) of the national anthems of eight countries are given in full, and a brief summary without music is included for 26 other national anthems.

The 1967 Reference and Subscription Books Committee review reported that "adequate coverage is provided in the subject fields within the intended scope of the encyclopedia—the curricular and interest reference needs of children. The information is up to date with recent events and contemporary figures given adequate coverage. No evidence was found of national, political, or religious bias. Although the encyclopedia is international in scope, greater emphasis is placed upon the United States." These statements remain true for the 1972 edition of *The New Book of Knowledge*. Social studies continue to be the best covered of the curriculum subjects with 39 of the 67 entirely new or expanded articles dealing with some phase of the social sciences. Geographic materials are given the most emphasis; 19 of these 39 new articles concern a state, province, country, or geographical area.

Science and technology account for 13 entirely new articles on such subjects as *Botany, Heart, Electronic Communications, Environment, Medicine, Tools and Techniques of,* and *Noise*. New developments have been added to numerous other articles in an effort to maintain a contemporary emphasis. One of the new developments added is the Wankel engine which although now mentioned in articles *Automobile* and *Internal-combustion Engines* is inadequately covered.

Coverage of art is improved with a new nine-page discussion of what art is and how it has functioned as a record and reflection of man's ideals in all cultures. With this article are eight four-color illustrations. *Modern Art* has also been expanded to include contemporary trends. *Illustration and Illustrators* has some reproductions of illustrations from juvenile books, but the text devotes only two sentences to the subject.

The four-page addition *Rock Music* recognizes the acceptance of this genre and its influence on other kinds of music.

Although designed as a children's encyclopedia and although the material is obviously written and organized with this purpose in mind, there are also articles of interest to parents and teachers. *Tests and Test Taking, Handicapped, Rehabilitation of, Parent-Teacher Asso-*

ciation, and *Kindergartens and Nursery Schools* are some of the subjects which seem to have been included for the older reader.

Modern, clearly detailed photographs and diagrams with appropriate, pertinent captions were chosen or developed especially for the first publication and reevaluated for the annual revisions. Photographs have been substituted to show a changed city skyline, newer dress styles, a less stereotyped view, or for better color quality. Diagrams have been clarified, and color contrast in the maps has been improved. Place-name changes have also been freely made on maps whenever necessary. Fact boxes, a device originating in the 1966 edition to highlight statistics, chronology, or to set apart brief facts, have also been carefully reviewed, and in almost every instance added to and updated. Fact boxes are used effectively to break up paragraphs of text and to provide a pleasing ratio of print, color, illustration, and summarized facts on the two-column page.

Paging is separate for each volume. No artificial attempt has been made to keep volumes uniform in length, since they vary from 572 pages in the *S* volume to 348 pages in the *H* volume. When new articles have been added, letters have been added to the page numbers.

Appropriate changes, such as indexing new articles, have been made in the 1972 Index. The general plan of indexing both at the end of each volume and in a cumulated index volume has been maintained. Blue pages easily identify the index portion of the individual volumes. According to the publishers the Index now has 90,000 entries—an increase of more than 4,000 entries since the first appearance of the set.

While the Index is accurate, and an examination of random entries found no errors, items are mentioned in the text that are not in the Index. Most of these omissions were illustrations—art reproductions and titles which would be useful if located. The painting *Sunrise* by Claude Monet shown in the article *Modern Art* is not mentioned in the Index either by title or artist, although *Beach at Sainte-Alresse* and *Water-Lilies* are listed under Monet in the Index. Similar inconsistencies are found in the illustrative paintings in the article *Design and Color*. The story of the origin of the Alaskan flag is not mentioned in the Index, although the story has a prominent place in the text about *Alaska*. Two movie titles, *Patton* and *Love Story,* referred to in the article *Motion Picture Industry* are not in the Index, although *Hair,* mentioned in *Musical Comedy,* is indexed.

The Index not only provides access to the text, but is also a fact index. There are some 5,000 such short-entry articles —about 600 more than in the first printing. This feature of the Index provides ready reference on a variety of subjects and reflects the names, places, things, and events seen and heard by children in the course of their day-to-day lives and their exposure to the media.

This fact-index gives brief biographies of authors of children's books as Carol Ryrie Brink, William Lipkind, Astrid Lindgren; of sports heroes— Bobby Orr, Kareem Abdul Jabbar (Lew Alcindor), Gordie Howe; of entertainers Elvis Presley, Arlo and Woody Guthrie, Paul Newman, Flip Wilson; of political figures—Robert Sargent Shriver, John Tunney, Ronald Reagan; of news items—Amtrak, Ralph Nadar, Black Panthers, Lobbying; new abbreviations such as NOW, SALT talks, as well as KP and PX have been added. Everyday terms as *bugging, jelly and jam, Ivy League, hippie,* and *Sesame Street* are included in the fact-index. *Gerbil, fungicide, macrame, tie-dyeing, transplant of body organs, Lippizaner horse,* and *recycling,* now in the fact-index, require fuller treatment.

The revision and expansion of the *see also* references in a part of the editors' continuous revision policy. The frequent use of direct cross-references in the text plus *see also* references at the close of most articles and in the Index makes readily available the details not located in their alphabetical listing.

The Index provides the only aid to pronunciation in the set. Instructions in the use of the Index located at the beginning of the separate index volume are reprinted from volume *A* and describe the Index arrangement in addition to providing the pronunciation guide. The Index is easy to use.

The New Book of Knowledge maintains its attractive appearance with its ivory washable sturdite binding. The blue panels on the cover have been replaced with bright red ones on which the gold lettering shows up to a greater advantage than on the blue. Although the pages, particularly of the larger volumes, do not lie entirely flat when opened, there are ample inner margins, so no words or pictures are lost.

Bibliographies are found only in a paperbacked supplement, *Home and School Study and Reading Guide*. This, too, has been constantly revised since 1966 resulting in the addition of 300 new books to the bibliographies. The purpose of the study guide is to organize and relate the wide scope of content in *The New Book of Knowledge* to curriculum areas in present-day schools and to study interests of present-day children. It is included in the purchase price of the encyclopedia.

The editors of *The New Book of Knowledge* have achieved their purpose of providing an encyclopedia for the elementary school child based on his curriculum needs and interests. Rewriting, expansion, and updating are evident throughout. The reliability, attractiveness, and readability that characterized the 1966 edition have been maintained and improved. Because of the thoroughness of the revisions, those libraries with the 1966 edition will want to replace that edition. *The New Book of Knowledge* is recommended for homes, elementary school libraries, and children's departments of public libraries.

(*April 15, 1973, p.773*)

The New Century Handbook of Classical Geography. Edited by Catherine B. Avery. New York, Appleton-Century-Crofts, [1972]. v, 362p. maps. 21cm. Roxite, $7.95.

The New Century Handbook of Classical Geography "presents concise discussions of the major geographical locations, incorporating the facts and legends drawn from such diverse sources as modern archaeology and ancient poetry."—*Preface*. It is intended for use by students and travelers to the Mediterranean region. The handbook like the other four in New Century's series of handbooks of Greek culture and history (*The New Century Handbook of Greek Mythology and Legend* $7.95, *The New Century Handbook of Greek Literature* $5.95, *The New Century Hankbook of Greek Art and Architecture* $7.95, and *The New Century Handbook of Leaders of the Classical World* $6.95) is based on *The New Century Classical Handbook* (New York: Appleton-Century-Crofts, 1962, $18.90) which was reviewed in *The Booklist and Subscription Books Bulletin*, July 1, 1962, and is still in print.

The articles in *The New Century Handbook of Classical Geography* are arranged in alphabetical order; most are unsigned. Those bearing the initials JJ were written by the late Jotham Johnson, Chairman of the Department of Classics, New York University. The other two contributors are Abraham Holtz and Philip Mayerson, identified as professors at New York University. The entries range in length from one-sentence identifications (e.g., *Baetica, Salerno*) to over five pages (e.g., *Athens, Mycenae*). Each place is geographically located as precisely as possible. The more extensive articles describe the historical and/or mythological significance of the locale. In many cases, the modern name of an ancient place is included. Most entries include a guide to pronunciation; a key to the symbols used runs along the bottom of the page. Often, variant names and spellings are included (e.g., Lemnos. also: Limni, Limno, Limnos). There are no bibliographies and no index.

The Preface states that most of the entries are "derived from *The Classical Handbook*" but that "in a number of cases, information on finds that have been made since 1962 has been added. . . ." In a comparison of the two volumes, little added information was found. Although there are many cross-references, use of *The New Century Handbook of Classical Geography* will be limited by the lack of needed references. Nimes and Arles are described in the article *Narbonensis,* but there is no cross-reference from either name. Selinunte is listed only under *Selinus* with no reference to the modern name; Merida is not mentioned at all. The one new article mentioned in the Preface (Akrotiri) does not appear.

The only illustrations in this volume are three maps of Italy, showing cities of Magna Graecia and the early Roman Republic, and the Greek World of the 5th Century B.C. There is no map of the rest of the classical world. The volume is attractively printed on antique stock. The binding seems sturdy, but there is very little binding margin.

The New Century Handbook of Classical Geography is not and does not claim to be scholarly. It is, however, a source of quick, readable information for the student or layman. Recommended for all types of libraries.

(Dec. 15, 1973, p.397)

The New Century Italian Renaissance Encyclopedia. Ed. by Catherine B. Avery. New York, Appleton-Century-Crofts, Educational Division, Meredith Corporation, [1972]. illus. 25cm. cloth $29.95.

This new handbook to the civilization of the Renaissance is unique, not even the *Oxford Companions* having, as yet, entered this field. It is not, however, a first for the editor, Catherine B. Avery, who produced *The New Century Classical Handbook* in 1962 (reviewed in *The Booklist and Subscription Books Bulletin* July 1, 1962). Those familiar with *Classical Handbook* will find that Avery follows much the same plan and format in *The Italian Renaissance Encyclopedia.* Editorial consultants for the new work are Marvin B. Becker, professor of medieval and Renaissance history at the University of Rochester and Ludovico Borgo, associate professor of fine arts at Brandeis University. Also mentioned in the Preface as assisting in reviewing material are Professor Charles Trinkaus, a member of the history department at the University of Michigan and Professor Pearl Kibre of the history faculty at Hunter College. Except for these four persons, no contributors are listed for the thousands of entries in the book. Some long articles are signed by Professors Borgo and Kibre, but they are few.

The book covers the period from "the time of Dante (1265-1321) and Giotto (c1267-1337) to about the death of Michelangelo (1565)" thus continuing through the High Renaissance and up to the second generation of the Mannerists. There are over 3,700 entries including a great many biographies, some definitions of literary, political, and art terms, characters from literature, and résumés of important literary works, together with some longer essays on such subjects as painting, architecture, humanism, astrology, and music. As indicated in the title, and as is to be expected, since the Renaissance was concentrated in Italy and reached its highest development there, emphasis is mainly on Italy and the Italians. However, there are articles on people from outside Italy who were active during the Renaissance, and a few articles on persons of earlier times who influenced the period.

The articles are arranged alphabetically and vary in length from short identifying or defining paragraphs to essays of several pages.

Most of the material is biographical, covering a wide variety of people active in many fields, e.g., lawyers, statesmen, explorers, humanists, scientists, philosophers, scholars, churchmen, and craftsmen. There is information on many Spaniards, Britons, Frenchmen, and Greeks. Other nationalities represented in a sample are German and Portuguese. Women are not slighted. Artists and writers predominate.

The array of artists is impressive. Comparison of coverage of artists in *New Century, McGraw-Hill Dictionary of Art* (New York: McGraw-Hill, 1969), and *Praeger Encyclopedia of Art* (New York: Praeger Publishers, 1971) revealed that in a check of the "A" sections of all three publications, *New Century* compared quite well with *Praeger* having 31 artists listed which are not in *Praeger. McGraw-Hill Dictionary* has 35 artists which are not in *New Century,* but *New Century* lists 16 which are not in either of the other dictionaries. Biographies of artists range in length from a short identifying paragraph to several pages. Each entry mentions the artist's best-known works and the museums and collections to which they belong. In addition to biographies there are long essays on architecture, painting, and sculpture, and definitions of some technical terms.

Ranking second in number of articles in the Committee's sample are persons known primarily as writers. There are also articles on individuals who are principally famous in other fields, but who also wrote, e.g., Michelangelo and Francesco Landino. In addition to life histories, the entries include details about style and list the main works of the authors. Entries by title, which give very brief synopses of individual works, are a useful feature of the encyclopedia. Included are both Italian and non-Italian literature. Most of the *Canterbury Tales* are included, so that one can look up Chaucer's *The Nun's Priest's Tale* or *The Pardoner's Tale* as well as *Orlando*, *Orlando Furioso* or *Orlando Innamorato*. Less familiar works such as Boccaccio's *Amorosa Visione* or Jorge de Montemayor's *Diana Enamorada* are also included. In view of the presence of the latter, one is surprised to find no entry for *Amadis de Gaula* and no definition of the pastoral and chivalric romances, literary forms which matured in the Renaissance and remained overwhelmingly popular until *Don Quixote* finally ridiculed them out of existence. This points up one of the weaknesses of the *Renaissance Encyclopedia*—it is occasionally inconsistent in coverage and also in length of treatment.

In comparison with the emphasis on the other arts, musicians and music are rather neglected. In a sample of 277 articles only 4 are devoted to musicians. Although music in Renaissance Italy was largely in the hands of the imported Flemings, and the great flowering which ended in the creation of the opera came about after 1565, still, the madrigal developed and flourished at this time, and there is no definition of it in the text. Of the 28 madrigalists whose works appear in Alfred Einstein's *The Italian Madrigal* (Princeton, N.J.: Princeton University Press, 1949) volume 3, and who belong to the time period in question, only seven are in the *Renaissance Encyclopedia*. Articles on most musicians are very brief as compared with those on even minor painters. Palestrina rates the longest article, Josquin des Pres is identified in two sentences, and Orlando di Lasso in three. Few terms are defined, and there is no article on music, though there are essays on painting, sculpture, and architecture.

There is a good survey article on Humanism, but none on Renaissance literature or theater, on politics or religion.

Politics can be approached only through long essays about some outstanding event such as the Pazzi Conspiracy, the Black Death, or the Inquisition, or through the very careful and extensive treatment of the great Renaissance families—the Medicis, Estes, Gonzagas. Each of the family survey essays is followed by individual treatment for the important members of the family. Royalty of other countries, such as the various Maximilians of the Holy Roman Empire, the Ferdinands and Philips of Spain, and the Charleses, Louises, and Francises of France are also quite generously treated.

Religion is approached in the same way through the treatment of specific events. There are also articles on the popes, some saints, and many churchmen. St. Ignatius of Loyola, St. Carlo Borromeo, and St. Catherine of Siena are to be found—St. Catherine in a three-page essay. Luther is dealt with in a page and a half, but the Reformation is discussed in only about half a page. The Council of Constance can be found, the Great Schism, also (under Great and not cross-referenced from Schism), but the Council of Trent is not mentioned. Admittedly, the Council happened late in the time scheme of the book, but it climaxes the Renaissance and is a turning point as well as a natural follow-up of the Reformation, and so might have been included.

The style of writing is vivid and readable though occasionally there is a bit of hyperbole. In general the facts are accurate, and though the articles are written for adults, they can easily be comprehended by high school or even advanced elementary school students.

Any variation of the name used as an entry is given in brackets, and a phonetically spelled pronunciation is included, the symbols of which can be identified at the bottom of each page. There are cross-references from names not used. When first names have been used as entry words, however, the cross-references are less dependable. For such entries as Giasone del Maino, there are rarely cross-references from the last name (Maino in this case), unless the person was of considerable fame. Paolo Veronese, Domenico Veneziano, and Leonardo da Vinci are cross-referenced, but not Paolo Veneto.

There are three types of pictorial illustrations all drawn from the fine arts. The first type accompanies the entries for individual artists, with the reproduction of drawings varying in size from a quarter to a full page. These illustrations enhance the format, but where they are the only reproduction to represent the artist, the choice of a drawing rather than a more important work might be questioned. In the center of the book, there are 10 colorplates which "reproduce paintings that were executed over a span of about 250 years." The subject of the first seven plates is the same, with the dual purpose of illustrating the developments that took place in the art and techniques of painting and of illustrating the changes that took place in the painters' approach to the subject. The plates are well chosen to represent the high point of each style from Giotto to Tintoretto, and are well enough reproduced although the Botticelli and the Leonardo are a bit on the red side.

At the back of the book are 175 black-and-white reproductions "arranged to give a chronological survey of the arts of painting, sculpture and architecture in the period covered." They are captioned, but not numbered in any way; nor are the pages numbered. The emphasis is firmly on the arts—some portraits are included, but nothing in the text refers to them, so that the reader does not know by reading about Pope Julius II that there is a portrait of him by Raphael in the section. These photographs are listed in the front of the volume in the order of their appearance, but there is no other index to locate them by artist, title, or subject. Thus, they exist as a sort of separate comment on Renaissance art, unconnected with the text. The interest of the user would be better served if he were informed in the applicable text that reproductions exist elsewhere in the book. Since the *Renaissance Encyclopedia* is so biographically oriented, portraits scattered through the book would perhaps have done more to illuminate Renaissance life. There are no maps except for the map of Italy reproduced on the endpapers.

The *Italian Renaissance Encyclopedia* contains no bibliographies either with the entries or in any other part of the volume. There are occasional quotations and references to statements of contemporaries (for instance, Vasari for the artists), but no direct quotations giving the exact source were found.

The format is attractive. Each page is divided into two columns. The type is clear and easily read, each entry being captioned in bold type extended by the width of a letter into the margin. The volume is sturdily bound in cloth and opens well.

In spite of its occasional inconsistency and unevenness and of the general lack of exact attribution for quotations and of bibliographies, *The New Century Italian Renaissance Encyclopedia* is unique and useful. Its chief virtue lies in the broad scope and the many minor Renaissance figures that can be identified along with the great and famous, and in the fact that it brings considerable information into a compact, systematically arranged volume, directed at the general reader. The ready reference section of almost any library will no doubt find use for it. The encyclopedia is, therefore, recommended.

(Oct. 1, 1972, p.105)

New International Illustrated Encyclopedia of Art. 24v. Sir John Rothenstein, general editorial director. New York, Toronto, London, Greystone Press, [c1967-1972]. illus. 29cm. mail order ed., pyroxylin-coated paper v.1 free; v.2-24, $5.89 per vol. B-grade printed offset cloth library ed. available from Educational Marketing and Research Inc., 1020 Prospect St., La Jolla, CA. $169.50 for the set.

The first nine volumes of *New International Illustrated Encyclopedia of Art* were reviewed in *The Booklist* December 15, 1969. At that time, the encyclopedia was rated as "a well-written, straightforward encyclopedia of the visual arts excluding theater and dance. . . . Its value will be to the average layman or student seeking a good, basic survey—not necessarily in depth—or to those pinpointing information on a wide range of subjects." Examination of the remaining 15 volumes now available confirms the statement. The encyclopedia continues the same consistently conscientious coverage of definitions, techniques, biography, and history of the arts in the same useful and readable style.

In the earlier review the desirability of an index was noted. Volume 24 supplies this need with an 80-page Index which includes illustrations by title and artist and many artistic terms. A sample survey of the Index reveals that it efficiently and accurately facilitates access to the text. However, there are still no bibliographies either with the articles or in a separate section.

The type and tone of the articles are consistent with that of the first nine volumes. There are many biographies, some definitions, some long articles on historical styles and national developments. These are written in clear language and style suitable for the non-expert student or layman. Many of the long articles are excellent; since they do not assume previous knowledge on the part of the reader, they usually provide full coverage in nontechnical language. The article *United States Art and Architecture,* for instance, is 150 pages long and covers the subject into the 1970s, including the various recent styles (op, pop, kinetic, and minimal). It provides a readable as well as informative survey. Closely following this article is a comparable treatment of *Urban Planning and Industrial Design.* This article is about 40 pages long and contains many city plans, aerial views, and old engravings of historic cities. Regrettably, the articles are unsigned.

The quality of the illustrations varies, ranging from excellent to merely satisfactory. All are well chosen and relate closely to the text.

The typography of *New International* is large and clear with bold black headings. The format, as was pointed out in the earlier review, is acceptable, the only drawback being the fact that each volume consists of exactly 211 pages which may cause an article to fall into two consecutive volumes.

The two dictionary-encyclopedias most closely resembling *New International Illustrated Encyclopedia of Art* are *McGraw-Hill Dictionary of Art* (New York: McGraw-Hill, 1969), reviewed in *The Booklist* June 1, 1970 and *Praeger Encyclopedia of Art* (New York: Praeger, 1971), reviewed in *The Booklist* November 1, 1971.

A comparison of *New International* with *McGraw-Hill Dictionary* reveals the difference in the purpose of the two publications. As a dictionary, *McGraw-Hill* has nearly four times as many entries (including many short definitions) in the section *Baroque* to *Braque* (volume 3 of *New International*). There is some duplication. Sixteen technical terms, a lesser number of historical and other terms, and 141 biographies appear in both. However, *McGraw-Hill* has 288 biographies which do not appear in *New International,* and also covers museums, identification of specific works of art, archaeological sites, etc., which are not included in *New International.* *McGraw-Hill* is the most complete art reference dictionary of its kind.

The same section (*Baroque* to *Braque*) was compared with *Praeger Encyclopedia of Art,* and here the difference was less apparent. Both encyclopedias have about 200 entries. They overlapped in 106 biographies, but *Praeger* had 78 biographies not found in *New International* while the latter had 46 biographies not in the former. *New International* is stronger in the number of definitions of technical terms, especially in the areas of decorative arts and porcelain, and also in its coverage of specific cities connected with the arts. Both are good on national arts and historical styles.

The contents, language and style, and organization of *New International Illustrated Encyclopedia of Art* are well selected to meet the needs of the nonspecialist audience for which the encyclopedia is intended. It is recommended for school and small public libraries.
(May 1, 1973, p.817)

New Scribner Music Library. Howard Hanson editor in chief. New York, Charles Scribner's Sons, c1972-73. 11v. piano scores. 30cm. buckram available from the publisher by direct subscription; not available to the trade. $175; to schools and libraries, $150.
SBN 684-13100-5.

In the 1950s and earlier, many of us who "studied piano" as children stumbled onto those multivolumned publications which had "pieces"—dozens of them in all grades of difficulty. Such was the old *Century Library*, the *International Library of Music* (said to have been edited by Paderewski) and the *World's Best Music*, editorially attributed to Victor Herbert. Happy hours could be spent choosing pieces by Cécile Chaminade or Ethelbert Nevin, and one could also find easier things by Tchaikovsky, Beethoven's "Fur Elise," and sometimes even Rachmaninoff's "Prelude in C# Minor," which was usually a bit beyond most of us.

One of these favorite sets, *Scribner Music Library*, has now been revised and reedited into an updated collection of 11 volumes; Howard Hanson, dean of American composers with fame as a conductor, composer, and editor is its editor in chief. For many years, he was Director of the Eastman School of Music and he has won many awards, including the Prix de Rome and the Pulitzer Prize. There is an advisory committee with excellent credentials, each with a particular field of specialization; Philip L. Miller, one-time head of the Music Division of the New York Public Library Reference Department, specialist in all forms of vocal music; Dr. Peter Mennin, composer and Head of the Julliard School; Eugene List, concert pianist of distinction; Risë Stevens, who has charmed Metropolitan Opera fans for years; Walter Kramer, Nicolas Slonimsky, and Kurt Stone, known for their writings on music; and Douglas Moore and Sister John Joseph, well-known educators. Dr. Moore is also an important composer and conductor.

With this array of talent and taste, it is not surprising that *New Scribner Music Library* is a most interesting collection of piano music and a first-class teaching tool. The introductory pamphlet mentions "nearly 1,000 pieces," and a spot check of the complete Title Index at the end of volume 11 indicates that there are probably more than 1,000. The set includes music of all periods, from the Renaissance to the present. There are pieces from the Fitzwilliam Virginal Book, and dances from Pierre Attaignant's fifteenth-century collections, and also works from Prokofief, Schönberg, Stravinsky, Bartok, and Kodaly. Included are works by a good number of Americans, many Europeans, and several Japanese.

Each volume, covering a particular field of music, has its own editor and an individual title. Within each volume, the music is subtly graded, but not obviously, and only the first volume, *Easy Piano Music by American Composers*, edited by Dr. Merle Montgomery (theorist and educator, President of the National Federation of Music Clubs), is specifically directed toward the beginner. Most of these 201 little pieces were commissioned especially for the volume. They teach particular piano techniques during the first year of study, present useful material for sight-reading and musical analysis, as the Introduction states. A separate, paperback *Teacher's Guide* by Joseph Rezits, professor of piano at Indiana University, is especially useful for this volume, though it also analyzes the other volumes in the set. The *Guide* has an Index to the contents of volume 1 arranged by the technical skill to be studied.

From volume 2 on, the grading is of less importance than the type of music presented. Volumes 2 and 3, called respectively *Keyboard Panorama* and

Piano Classics, are edited by Blanche Winogron, well known for her performances of early keyboard music on the virginals and harpsichord. There are 180 items which contribute to a "comprehensive view of forms, styles and idioms in keyboard music, as they have evolved over the centuries. The compositions in these volumes, therefore, have neither been arranged according to technical difficulty nor in strict chronological order, but rather according to certain structural, stylistic and expressive aspects, as these have been developed historically." In volume 2, one finds "instrumental settings of songs and dances" which date back as far as 1350, jigs by John Bull, tunes from Couperin, pieces from the Notebooks of Anna Magdalena Bach, as well as short pieces by Mozart, Beethoven, Schumann, and Prokofief. They are all smaller forms—dances, fugues, and preclassical sonatas.

Volume 3 supplements volume 2 with the larger forms, beginning with Bach's period and again ending with Prokofief. This volume contains three complete sonatas, one by Mozart, one by Beethoven, and one by Haydn; a sonatina by Clemente, familiar Chopin, Schumann pieces, and some music by Brahms, Scriabin, and others. In general, they are longer "recital" pieces. The table of contents in the Teacher's Guide shows the grading level of both volumes as running between grades two and seven in each volume, though no indication is made within the volumes.

Volume 4, *A Century of Piano Music,* consists of works written between 1867 and 1967, from Liszt to Villa Lobos and Aaron Copland with emphasis on American writers. According to the publishers' Preface, there are "30 new compositions by 21 of America's most distinguished composers, from Douglas Moore and Charles T. Griffes to Aaron Copland, Morton Gould, and Virgil Thomson" including Emma Lou Diemei, Mary Howe, Julia Perry, and Louise Talma. The grade levels are given as from three to eight, and the volume is again edited by Dr. Merle Montgomery. At the front of the volume, there are three pages of short biographical sketches of the American composers.

Volume 5, *All-Time Favorites,* contains the salon pieces that charmed our youth—"Love's Dream after the Ball" and "Stephanie (Gavotte)," by Czibulka, "La Paloma" by Vradier, "Under the Leaves" and "Simple Aveu" of Thome, "Kamennoi-Ostrow" of Anton Rubenstein as well as short works by Tchaikovsky, Gounod, and Delibes. The volume is edited by Ruth Watanabe, musician, musicologist and head of the Sibley Music Library at the University of Rochester, New York. She also edits volume 6, *Piano for Two,* which consists of duets from grades 1 to 8 including Mozart's *Sonata* K358 and Beethoven's *Sonata* op.6 and his *Sonatina in F Major.*

Volume 7, *At the Opera,* consists of highlights of 12 operas, ranging from Monteverdi to Debussy, including arrangements of the most important arias for singing with piano accompaniment and also piano arrangements of instrumental intermezzi, introductions to acts and passages which, as the editor David Russell Williams (member of the Department of Theory and Counterpoint at the Eastman School of Music and operatic coach in their Opera department) says, "convey most vividly the plot and the mood and color characteristics of that opera." Each score is preceded by a short synopsis of the opera. The piano arrangements seem particularly well adapted to the abilities of the ordinary pianist.

Music for the Dance, again edited by Ruth Watanabe, refers to dance forms and rhythms rather than folk dance. Thus the collection contains dance movements from larger works by Bach, Haydn, and Lully; waltzes by Strauss, Waldteufel, and Lehar; marches by Sousa; less-familiar selections from Schonberg and Bartok; and even two dances by Japanese composers. This is as close as the volume comes to national dances.

Volumes 9 and 10 are devoted to vocal music. Both are edited by Philip L. Miller, who is an authority on Lieder in particular and song in general. Volume 9 is called *Home Songs,* and here are the folksongs of various nations, some patriotic songs, nursery songs, carols, hymns, spirituals, ballads, and Stephen Foster favorites. Words in the original language are included as well as the translations.

Volume 10, *Art Songs,* must have been incredibly difficult to edit. The adherence to a limit of four Schubert songs, three Brahms, one Faure, and three Hugo Wolf in order to make space for beautiful things from the baroque and unexpected things from moderns like Copland and Alban Berg, must have set Miller a major problem. There are 64 songs by 45 composers, and one would hate to see any of them eliminated however much one regrets missing a favorite. In connection with this volume, the *Teacher's Manual* has a very good short analysis on the art of accompaniment, including examples of scores edited to demonstrate the techniques of reading three staves at a time, omitting occasional doubled notes to thin out textures, fingering, dividing large chords between two hands, and other good hints for the amateur.

Volume 11, *Reference Volume,* contains much useful textual material, a complete index by composer and one by title, and a pictorial history of keyboard instruments which begins, however, with the spinet and clavichord of the Renaissance and does not mention organ forms, and which includes some facsimiles of music from various periods. This is followed by a biographical dictionary of the composers included in the set and a dictionary of musical terms edited by Nicolas Slonimsky. No bibliographies are included in the set. The inclusion of some book lists and perhaps a discography would have been helpful to users. The separate *Teacher's Guide* is certainly useful for its graded index which does not appear in volume 11, and also for its tips to the casual performer concerning various techniques. The volumes are attractively bound in blue buckram with clear, legible typography on spacious pages. The volumes lie fairly flat, but rebinding would make it difficult to play from them.

New Scribner Music Library is useful on two levels: for the casual pianist and for the teacher. Advanced piano students will undoubtedly find good things to play, but for study they would be more likely to require the whole of an opus rather than one or two numbers from it. It is the sight reader and the pianist who is not performance bound who will enjoy the variety and find challenge in the range of difficulties in each volume. As teaching material, the presence of Renaissance and Baroque music gives a teacher an opportunity to present rhythmic and harmonic characteristics of those periods to younger children. Volumes 2 and 3 have been edited carefully with barlines introduced and time signatures simplified for easier reading by the person who has not been introduced to the complicated rhythms of earlier times. Volume 3 has a good short essay on the use of ornament in preclassic music and both volumes include a table of examples of ornaments. In volume 2, some of the ornaments are footnoted at the bottom of the page and there written out for the student.

The set is expensive, and one regrets perhaps that the individual volumes cannot be bought separately. The best place for this delightful set is in homes where people can amuse themselves with it as well as learn from it, and in the hands of teachers, who can use it to find new material for students. Libraries will have to decide how closely the set relates to the musical life of their patrons. In a public library, it would seem the volumes should circulate—they are not particularly useful for reference. Rather, they are for piano lovers to take home and browse through blissfully. With these reservations, *New Scribner Music Library* is recommended.

(June 1, 1974, p.1063)

The New York Times Atlas of the World: in collaboration with The Times of London. London, Times Newspapers Ltd. and John Bartholomew & Son, [New York, Quadrangle Books, 1972]. 40, 143, 1, 84p. col. maps. 38cm. cloth $35.

The Times of London, long known for its *Atlas of the World,* has now issued a new atlas designed for use in the home. Many of the maps from the *Comprehensive* edition have been adapted to a smaller format, and 15 pages of new maps, along with a preliminary section, have been added to create a new work, not merely an abridgment, of the parent atlas. The atlas "has been designed for those who wish to understand something of the physical nature of the earth and man's life on it, as well as to find their way over its surface." In Great Britain the atlas is published under the title *Times Concise Atlas,* and this name is used frequently in the Introduction, and also appears at the top of most even-numbered pages.

Most of the maps are by John Bartholomew & Son, Ltd., eminent British map publishers. The conurbation maps (for metropolitan areas), however, are compiled and drawn by Fairey Aviation and A. W. Gattrell Ltd. The members of the editorial board for this atlas are primarily educators and journalists.

The Introduction is followed by 35 pages of text, illustrations, and thematic maps which focus on the geological and atmospheric aspects of earth, water resources, vegetation, and human phenomena such as food and nutrition, population and settlement, fuel and energy, manufacturing, world trade, and tourism. This section also includes a discussion of human ecology, navigation, and outer space, with lunar charts and a presentation of the several theories on the origin of the universe. Most of the paragraphs reflect recent, rather than classical points of view in geological research.

A table of symbols and abbreviations precedes the 142 pages of maps. Although most of the maps are primarily political maps, elevation is indicated by brightly-colored layer tints in conjunction with contour lines. A key to the tints accompanies each map. The maps indicate the projections used, but the predominant one is conic. Scales are given in metric and English units, and the projection used is specified with each map. Interspersed with the country maps are the conurbation maps, showing close-up views of major urban areas. These maps include such details as the location of airports, parks, zoos, universities, and monuments. The amount of detail varies, however. The conurbation maps range in scale from 1:24,000 for Rome to 1:720,000 for Fort Worth-Dallas, but most of them have a scale of 1:300,000.

In general, the place-names throughout the atlas were chosen in agreement with the U.S. Board on Geographic Names and the Permanent Committee on Geographical Names for British Official Use. The modified Wade Giles system is used for China and Mongolia.

Following the maps, a three-page section lists data for the world's lakes, rivers, oceans, seas, and mountains, and gives the size and population of the largest and most populous countries. The estimated populations of the 65 largest metropolitan areas and an alphabetical list of the countries of the world, with the area and population of each, are also given. The data appear to be recent.

Eighty-three pages of Index complete the work. The publisher's claim of 90,000 entries appears correct. A sample check of the Index showed it to be generally accurate, though it does not index all the names on the maps, omitting some of the smaller towns and physical features. Each index entry is followed by the name of its country, a page number, and grid reference. Longitude and latitude are not shown in the Index. Each name is entered only once. There are some cross-references.

Endpapers facilitate locating a map of a given area. The front ones are key maps of the world which show the plate numbers for the various mapped areas; the back endpapers are key maps to the larger scale mapping of North America and Europe. This valuable location device would be lost in rebinding.

The paper is opaque, the colors clear and the lettering legible. The volume lies flat when open. The maps are sometimes bled to the inner margins, and margins often have arrows indicating the plate numbers of the maps of adjoining areas. These would make rebinding undesirable; the original binding however, is sturdy.

In size, price and coverage, *The New York Times Atlas* is quite comparable to *International Atlas* published by Rand McNally in 1969 and reviewed in *The Booklist* October 1, 1970. The

Rand McNally atlas has an Index of 160,000 place-names, but *The Times Atlas* has only 90,000 in its Index. Both atlases show metropolitan areas, though the Rand McNally atlas has 28 pages of them and *The Times* has only 15 pages. The statistics in *The Times Atlas* are more recent. Both atlases devote approximately two thirds of their maps to Anglo-America, Europe and Asia, with the remaining portion for Africa, Oceania, Latin America, and the Soviet Union, thus giving well-balanced world coverage. A sample check showed that both atlases treat the same countries at similar scales. For instance, both atlases map Iran at a scale of 1:6,000,000 and Germany at 1:1,000,000. Chile is shown at 1:6,000,000 and Canada at 1:3,000,000 in both. The United States is mapped at 1:300,000, with insets of some cities at 1:500,000. The colors in *The Times Atlas* are brighter than those in Rand McNally. The lettering in *The Times Atlas* is easier to read when trying to locate a specific place.

The New York Times Atlas is attractive and easy to use. It covers the world thoroughly but in much less detail than the *Comprehensive Edition* of *The London Times Atlas of the World* (reviewed in this same issue of *The Booklist*). For this reason large libraries may prefer the *Comprehensive Edition*. Individuals, however, will find this atlas sufficient for home reference use. The defective inner margins noted in the *Comprehensive Edition* have been corrected in this edition. It is recommended.

(Dec. 1, 1973, p.345)

The New York Times Book of Antiques.
By Marvin D. Schwartz and Betsy Wade. New York, Quadrangle Books, [c1972]. [8], 344p. 28cm. illus. (part col.). cloth $25.

The New York Times Book of Antiques attempts to cover the history of antiques from the ceramics of ancient Egypt through the Art Deco style of the 1920s. Author Marvin D. Schwartz, antiques columnist of *The New York Times,* was for 14 years Curator of Decorative Arts at the Brooklyn Museum and was a Fellow at the Henry Francis du Pont Winterthur Museum, "the major collection of American decorative arts. . . ." His previous writings include *Collector's Guide to Antique American Glass, Collector's Guide to Antique American Ceramics,* and (with Richard Wolfe) *History of American Porcelain.*

Coauthor Betsy Wade is head of the foreign copy desk of *The New York Times* and author of *The Encyclopedia of Clothes Care* and a children's book. The Committee could not verify that she has special qualifications for serving as coauthor of a book on antiques.

Following an introductory chapter, "The Joys of Collecting," the text is divided into six main sections, each covering a broad category of antiques: furniture, textiles, ceramics, pictures, metals, and glass. A concluding chapter discusses collecting "bargains." The longest sections are those covering ceramics (70 pages) and furniture (68 pages), while the shortest is on pictures (22 pages).

Treatment within each section varies according to the requirements of the subject matter but is basically chronological with special consideration by geographical area when appropriate. In addition to providing historical background on the development of styles, the text includes useful information for the collector on availability and prices and, when germane, on reproductions, imitations, and fakes.

Unfamiliar terms are usually explained, although one cannot always count on finding the complete explanation in a single place. By looking up the various references to Art Deco, for example, one can learn (p. 6) that it was an experimental style of the 1920s named for l'Exposition International des Arts Decoratives, an exhibition held in Paris in 1925 (p. 184). One can also learn from pages 80, 234, and 251 that the style was characterized by simple lines and innovative, angular shapes "resembling the simplified forms found in the work of Leger and Picasso." Page 9 reveals that Art Deco is an exception to the rule that "the serious dealers are most interested in work that was done before 1850," while the information that the best pieces in this style "now command prices above those for simple eighteenth-century pieces" is found on page 6.

The reader would have been better served had these various bits of information been presented in one place with cross-references from other parts of the text where the style is mentioned. As there is considerable interrelationship between the subjects treated in various sections of the text, the absence of cross-references is unfortunate.

Even though the text contains much valuable information, the fact that it constitutes less than half of the volume seems to place *The New York Times Book of Antiques* primarily in the "picture book" category. Of the 324 pages in the text section of the volume, 108 have no textual matter other than captions while less than half the space is devoted to text on an additional 134 pages. Many of the remaining 82 pages contain less than a full page of text. By even the most liberal measure, the text totals only about 125 double-column pages, hardly enough to provide the "painstakingly detailed survey of the fields of collecting" claimed by the publishers. Duncan Phyfe, for example, "the most famous American cabinetmaker," is treated in two short paragraphs. The four references to Josiah Wedgwood and his influence add up to less than a page of text while Currier and Ives are covered in less than a column.

Of the approximately 275 illustrations in the volume, 60 are in color. Approximately 90 of the illustrations are full-page and most of the others are in the half-page range. The generous size of the photographs permits easy observation of detail, and the reproduction is, for the most part, outstanding.

An unannotated bibliography of 74 books published during the past 20 years follows the text. The bibliography is divided into sections corresponding to those in the text, and the entries range from 16 under Ceramics to 3 under Pictures. The compilers suggest that persons with access to a large library "would do better to begin . . . [their] search for books in the card catalogue."

The volume concludes with an eight-page Index which provides entries under the names of objects (chairs, plates), distinctive materials or techniques (stoneware, tole), styles (Georgian, rococo), historical periods, countries, personal names, names of manufacturers, and under several other categories. There are no cross-references in the Index. A person looking up bentwood chairs would find no listing under the word "bentwood" directing him to look under "chairs, bentwood." When a proper adjective is involved, on the other hand, as in the case of Windsor chairs, entry is made under both the direct and inverted forms. Similarly, a person looking for information on Sandwich glass would need to know enough to look under "glass, pressed," or under the name of the manufacturer, the Boston and Sandwich Glass Company.

The volume is attractively designed and is printed on coated stock which enhances the quality of the photographs. A clear, modern typeface and ample leading contribute to easy legibility. The light-brown cloth binding seems designed to withstand extensive use. Although the inner margins are ample on the text pages, some of the illustrations come too close to the gutter to permit rebinding, and a few illustrations extend partway across the facing page. The volume lies flat when open.

The New York Times Book of Antiques is recommended for libraries and readers who want a concise survey of the field accompanied by numerous illustrations of superior quality. Readers who are looking for in-depth treatment of the subjects covered in the volume will need to consult works which treat these subjects in greater detail.

(Dec. 15, 1973, p.398)

The New York Times Directory of the Film. Introduction by Arthur Knight. New York, Arno Pr./Random House, 1971. vi, 1243p. illus. 32cm. buckram $25.

The New York Times Directory of the Film, a one-volume abridgment of the six-volume *The New York Times Film Reviews, 1913-1968* (reviewed in *The Booklist* December 15, 1971), is essentially an enlargement of the original index volume with some updating. It is a comprehensive directory of performers, directors, producers, cinematographers, screenwriters, and major motion picture companies and the pictures they made between 1913 and 1970. The introduction is by Arthur Knight, a prominent figure in the field of films and reviewing.

The main body of the work is divided into four parts: Part I (Listing of Awards) lists *The New York Times'* choice of the ten best films (by title only) for each year from 1924-1970; the New York Critics Circle awards from 1935-1970; and the Academy Award winners from 1927-1970.

Part II (Reprints of Reviews) reprints over five hundred *New York Times* reviews for all of the movies mentioned in part I, arranged chronologically and then alphabetically by title. The reviews are signed and are printed four columns across the page in very fine print.

Part III (Portrait Gallery reprinted exactly from the $100 index to *The New York Times Film Reviews*), contains 1,831 small black-and-white photographs (42 photographs per page) of movie stars. Actors and actresses are grouped by sex and within each group alphabetically by surname. To qualify for inclusion a performer must have been included in at least 15 reviews, although exceptions were made in cases of unusual public interest. Many supporting actors such as Hattie McDaniel and Edward Arnold are included. The portrait section is especially useful to those who wish to reminisce. However, those who want a current photograph will find this section of limited value.

The last section, part IV (Index), the largest portion of the book (998 pages) is in two parts: Personal Name Index and Corporate Name Index.

The Personal Name Index is an extensive index covering all personal names (actors, directors, producers, or animals) cited in the 18,000 films reviewed by *The Times* during the period 1913-1968. Under each name, a chronological listing of films is given with a complete citation to the date, page and column where the review appeared in *The New York Times*. An adequate system of cross-references leads the user to variant spellings of the artist's name, different surnames, nicknames, and middle initials.

The separate 70-page Corporate Index lists all companies that produced, distributed, or were otherwise associated with the films reviewed during the period. Their films are listed chronologically and with detailed citations to *The New York Times* reviews. The main defect in this Index is the lack of cross-references to variation in company names causing the user to rely on his imagination for possible variations.

Unfortunately this abridged volume does not contain either the title index to films found in the original work or an index to the 500 films in this book itself.

The volume is buckram bound and lies flat when opened. However, loose stitching and insufficient spine reinforcement will necessitate rebinding after limited use, since the book is large and heavy. The photographs, paper, and printing are good except for reprints of reviews where the print varies from very light to excessively dark.

The lack of a film title index and the absence of cross-references in the corporate index decrease the usefulness of *The New York Times Directory of the Film*. However, the book is a useful library reference tool for tracing an artist's career and viewing the changes that have occurred between 1913 and 1970. Recommended for the libraries which do not own or cannot afford the multi-volume set or its separately available index, this abridgment will serve as a partial and useful substitute.

(Dec. 1, 1973, p.346)

The New York Times Directory of the Theater. Introduction by Clive Barnes. New York, Arno Press, published in cooperation with Quadrangle/The New York Times Book Company, c1972-1973. [112], 50, 1009p. 31cm. cloth $25. ISBN 0-8129-0371-4.

The New York Times Directory of the Theater, according to its Introduction, is a separate issue of volumes 9 and 10, the Appendix and Index volumes, of *The New York Times Theater Reviews*,

1920-1970 (New York: The New York Times and Arno Press, 1971). The Reference and Subscription Books Review Committee will review the larger 11-volume set in a forthcoming issue of *The Booklist*. What this one-volume issue "gives you is simply the clear facts of 50 years of the American theater. Who did what, and when did they do it. As a supplement, did they win any prizes for it?" If the user of the directory is willing to accept the term "American theater" as a synonym for New York City theater, the directory does provide access to 50 years of theater activity. Both the multivolumed set and the directory cite only articles and reviews in *The New York Times*. However this directory is not only an exact reprint of volumes 9 and 10 of the larger set but also includes material from volume 1 as well as some new text.

The directory contains an Introduction, Theater Critics of the New York Times 1920-1970, Listing of Theater Awards, Reprints of *Times* Articles on Awards, and Indexes by title and personal name. Titles of these sections differ slightly in the main body of the work.

An Introduction by Clive Barnes is new to the directory and it does not appear in volumes 9 and 10 of the set. The section Theater Critics of *The Times* in the directory is an exact reprint of the same section in the set, where it occurs in volume 1. It consists of brief biographies of the critics with portraits.

The Awards section arranged chronologically and then by award, is the same as the set's Awards section in its volume 9, but the directory's listings update the original to 1972. Articles in the Awards section are presumably reprinted from *The New York Times,* but there no citations are included. The directory's Awards section lists the Nobel prize winners in literature, Pulitzer prizes for drama, the New York Drama Critics Circle awards, the Antoinette Perry (Tony) awards, and the Obie (off-Broadway) awards, from their respective beginnings. In the directory these are updated to 1972. The news articles are also reprinted from *The New York Times* and are updated to 1972 in the directory.

The Indexes section of the *Directory* contains only two of the indexes present in the larger set, those by titles of the plays and by personal name. The indexes cite articles in *The New York Times* by date, page, and column. However, the Index citations do not go beyond 1970 and thus do not cover the updated material in the Awards section of the directory.

The Personal Name Index includes not only actors and actresses but also playwrights, producers, translators, directors, composers, and costume designers. Again this Index covers the 50-year period 1920 to 1970 only. One must use volume 11 of the larger set *The New York Times Theater Reviews* 1971-1972 for more up-to-date coverage.

The directory does not reprint the actual reviews from *The New York Times* which are reprinted in the multivolumed set. The pagination of the directory presents a serious problem. The first 112 pages, which contain the sections entitled Introduction, Theater Critics of *The New York Times* 1920-1970, Listing of Theater Awards, and Reprints of *Times* Articles on Awards, are unpaged. The Title Index and the Personal Name Index are paged in two separate sequences. Thus the lack of numbering in one area and the duplication of numbers in another makes citation difficult.

The directory is well bound in maroon cloth and lies flat when opened. Margins are generous. Some of the Awards articles reprinted from *The New York Times* apparently by a photocopying process are not clear, and the portraits in these articles are often poor.

Since there is considerable difference in price between the multivolumed set ($850 plus $45 for volume 11) and the directory, it is possible that some public and academic libraries may prefer to purchase the latter. Since the principal part of the volume, the indexes in the directory, are almost useless without files of *The New York Times, The New York Times Directory of the Theater* is recommended only for those libraries with files of *The New York Times* who

need limited, less expensive indexing of that newspaper's drama reviews.
(April 15, 1974, p.887)

The New York Times Film Reviews: A One-Volume Selection, 1913-1970; Chosen from the 7-Volume Set with an Introd. and Six Original Essays. By George Amberg. [New York], Arno Pr. in cooperation with Quadrangle Books, [1971]. 495p. ports. 22cm. cloth $12.50.

This one-volume selection of 400 of the 18,835 film reviews which appeared in *The New York Times* from 1913-1970 was chosen from the seven-volume set of complete reviews: *The New York Times Film Reviews*. This condensation is divided into six periods, each covering a decade. According to the compiler, "The samples ... have been chosen not so much for their individual merit or the artistic significance of a particular film as for their function in the continued flow of cinematic events." The reviews are reproduced in their entirety; none has been cut or condensed in any way.

There is an introduction by George Amberg, and his six original essays serving as introductions to each period are "intended to put the reviews printed in this collection into the larger context of the critical profession."

When *The Times* decided to review motion pictures in 1913 the new medium had existed for 15 years. The volume begins with a review reporting the opening of *Quo Vadis* on April 22, 1913, aptly posing the question, "whither art thou going?" The entire work seeks to provide some insight into the answer to that question. Fittingly, the last review is Vincent Canby's critique of *The Confession*, which title captures the essence of the preceding revelations about the film industry.

The history of movies as perceived through the medium of reviews commences with a chapter entitled "From the Birth of Movies to the *Birth of a Nation.*" Through the reprint of original reviews one can follow the development of Chaplin's screen character and witness the invention of the Keystone cops by Mark Sennett. On March 4, 1915 a review described the key event of the period: David Wark Griffith's *Birth of a Nation.*

The history of films continues as the roaring twenties glorified the colossal production which found its master in Cecil B. De Mille. The December 22, 1923 *Times* account of the opening of the *Ten Commandments* records the acclaim which was accorded to this production.

This continuing narrative records that in the thirties "sound arrived with shocking suddenness, throwing the whole movie industry into total disarray." The report of the premiere of *Jazz Singer* in 1927 signifies the event that established sound in the history of cinema.

The tendency toward greater realism and less romantic escape which characterized the forties is highlighted in the section entitled "Hollywood: The Beginning of the End." The climate of fear and suspicion which swept the country at large during this period is revealed through Hollywood's reaction. *Of Mice and Men,* which reflects the temper of the times, was reviewed on February 17, 1940. Another milestone in this journey through history is Bosley Crowther's exhortation not to miss *The Maltese Falcon* which was the first endeavor of a young film director named John Huston. Progressing to 1941, *Citizen Kane* came "close to being the most sensational film ever made in Hollywood." The reader's attention is next brought to the fact that television made its appearance at the end of this decade.

Eventually film and television producers arrived at mutually beneficial agreements. A. W. Weiler hailed *On the Waterfront* as "movie making of a rare and high order." As foreign films began to make their appearance they received critical attention. One of the first attempts was Bosley Crowther's encounter with Ingmar Bergman's *Seventh Seal.*

Finally, the sixties are depicted as an era when television liberated the cinema to experiment with art films as well as conventional films and documentaries. The new cinema ranges from *Masculine Feminine* by Jean-Luc Godard to *Easy Rider,* to *They Shoot Horses Don't*

They? to *Zabriski Point,* all of which contribute to the story of film as told through critical commentary.

The volume has only a Title Index. There is no listing of actors and directors as they relate to specific films, and there are no cross-references.

The binding is adequate for the volume; however, the paper is of poor quality and the quality of the photo-offset printing is poor. Some reviews are almost totally illegible.

However, eight pages of 128 good quality photographs of stars at a memorabie time of their careers are included. The pictures are from the 1,831 that appear in *The New York Times Directory of the Film,* reviewed above. Many of the well-known faces of the earlier years of the industry are shown, but Jeanette MacDonald and Nelson Eddy are conspicuously absent. Well-known contemporaries such as Dustin Hoffman, Jon Voight, Peter O'Toole and Jane Fonda, all of whom appear in films reviewed in this work are also missing.

The New York Times Film Reviews presents not only the history of the development of the art of criticism in *The New York Times,* but also gives a balanced overview of the development of the cinema. These positive features outweigh the poor quality reproduction and paper. The work is recommended for those unable to afford either the $25 *New York Times Directory of the Film* or the complete $395 set of the six-volume *New York Times Film Reviews 1913-1968.* *(Dec. 1, 1973, p.346)*

The New York Times Guide to Continuing Education in America. Prepared by the College Entrance Examination Board. Frances Coombs Thomson, ed. New York, Quadrangle Books, [c1972]. 816p. 24cm. paperbound volume $4.95; previously published (1972; 811p.) in hardcover $12.50.

This paperbound edition of *The New York Times Guide to Continuing Education in America* describes in one volume the opportunities available to adults at the nation's accredited educational institutions. The softbound and hardcover editions are identical except for four extra pages of text in the paper volume.

Established in 1900, the College Entrance Examination Board (CEEB) holds a unique position in American education, occupying the middle ground between secondary schools and colleges, dominated by neither, yet responsive to both. The Board is a federation of colleges, universities, and schools working cooperatively toward the goal of helping students make the transition from secondary school to college. While its basic function is to provide a series of uniform entrance examinations on a national scale, CEEB also operates extensive programs of research in the fields of measurement, admissions, and financing of higher education. Its publication program is likewise an extensive one and includes *College Board Review* (quarterly, 1947-), *College Handbook* (frequency varies; 1941-), and *College Board Publications* (annual). *Publications* lists a number of books in the fields of secondary and post-secondary guidance, curriculum, admissions and placement, research, and financial aid, and the *Guide* under review is one of the books included in this 1973 catalog.

The *Guide* consists of two major portions. The first part describes more than 2,100 institutions—two- and four-year colleges, hospitals, trade and technical schools, etc.—offering classroom courses for adults. These entries are arranged alphabetically by state and then alphabetically by institution. In the second section, 184 institutions offering correspondence courses are listed alphabetically and described. The separation was made in the expectation that the two groups of entries would be used differently by prospective students.

The information generally listed for each institution includes address, telephone number(s), size of student body, class meeting hours, acceptance of transfer students, and general admissions requirements. The entries were prepared by the individual institutions during the summer and fall of 1970 in response to a questionnaire sent from CEEB. The *Guide* appropriately reminds readers (1) that while some of the details included in the entries may change rather quickly, the usefulness of the entries as introductory glimpses of the institutions and the opportunities they offer is not thereby significantly affected and (2) to write or call individual institutions for additional and current information.

Preceding the descriptions of the institutions is a variety of prefatory material: (1) the credentials of the editor, Mrs. Frances Coombs Thomson, and a suggestion that other editions of the *Guide* may follow; (2) an essay, "Education for Fun and Profit," by Harold Howe II, vice-president of the Ford Foundation and former United States Commissioner of Education; (3) "New Ways to New Worlds," information on how adults can earn a high school equivalency certificate or college credits by taking certain tests, how they can study by correspondence, and how to acquire new learning habits; (4) "Other Books of Interest to Adult Students," an annotated, selected bibliography of 31 diverse titles, e.g., Harold J. Alford, *Continuing Education in America* (1968), Dorothy Whyte Cotton, *The Case for the Working Mother* (1970), Simon Marcson, ed., *Automation, Alienation and Anomie* (1970), William Strunk, Jr. and E. B. White, *The Elements of Style* (1962); (5) a glossary of 30 terms ranging from anomie and community college to open-door admissions policy; (6) "Organizations Active in Continuing Education," which briefly describes 18 organizations such as Adult Education Association of the United States, Corporation for Public Broadcasting, and National University Extension Association of the National Center for Higher Education, whose primary purpose is to serve professionals who work in one of the many specialized areas of adult or continuing education; (7) "How Accreditation Works," an explanation of how institutions become accredited and what this means to students (the list of accrediting associations and agencies, however, is near the back of the book); and finally (8) "How to Use This Book."

Within the two sections of institutional descriptions comprising more than 80 percent of the book, entries are arranged letter by letter, not word by word, so that Northern Reception Center, Sacramento, Calif. precedes North Orange County Community College District, and Western College of Medical and Dental Assistants, Van Nuys, Calif. precedes West Hills College, Coalinga.

The volume concludes with (1) addresses and telephone numbers of the regional offices of CEEB, from which information about its College-Level Examination Program (CLEP) is available on request; (2) a list of about 900 institutions that award credit on the basis of CLEP examination scores; (3) the 6 accrediting associations and 33 agencies recognized by the U.S. Office of Education in April 1970; (4) the Index of Institutional Descriptions (which is letter by letter and with almost no errors); and (5) 9 schools of New York University. These are cross-referenced from the New York text on classroom courses and account for the extra pages in this edition that are not found in the hardcover edition of the *Guide*.

The New York Times Guide to Continuing Education in America, prepared by the College Entrance Examination Board, brings together in a single-volume reference book descriptions of adult classroom and correspondence programs of more than 2,300 accredited institutions as well as supplementary information about the academic process. The fact that the information was gathered in 1970 emphasizes the validity of the *Guide's* suggestion that readers should recognize the dynamic state of continuing education and should contact individual institutions for further and current information. Recommended. *(Oct. 1, 1973, p.131)*

The New York Times Guide to Federal Aid for Cities and Towns. [By] Howard S. Rowland. New York, Quadrangle Books, [1972, c1971]. xxxii, 1243p. 26cm. cloth $65. ISBN 0-8129-0267-X.

Guide to Federal Aid for Cities and Towns was published to meet the long-felt need for a guide to the myriad federal grants and funds available to the municipalities. The author of this work is Howard S. Rowland of Glassboro

State College. He states that his major sources of information were the documents prepared for Senate and House Committee hearings on each of the major U.S. departments and agencies. He used the detailed budget justifications, the questioning of officials, and testimony of special witnesses.

The book includes an Introduction; the main text, divided into three parts; Appendixes; and an Index. The introductory material includes two pages entitled "How to use this Book," which describe the contents of each section. Part One, "City in Action-Peekskill," details the beginning of the successful regeneration of what Rowland calls a "dirty, backwater town bypassed and surrounded by the expanding suburbs of New York City." This section presents a picture of a city with seemingly insurmountable problems which organizes to get effective federal and state aid. It then shows how that city obtained aid and began to revitalize itself completely. Part One is intended as an example of what can be done by identifying and procuring federal aid.

Part Two, "How to Write a Proposal," with a section on how to obtain federal aid, includes a checklist of information needed before applying, such as assessing needs and identifying the approving agency. It also includes a section on how to write the proposal itself, with tips on selection of a project director, coordination with other programs, and the details of the written proposal. Other inclusions are tables of the most common shortcomings of proposals and the suggested procedure to follow after the proposal is accepted.

Part Three, the bulk of the volume, is a detailed explanation by chapter of the 420 federal programs. Grant programs have been analyzed and regrouped according to city departments and special constituent group headings. Included under each program are current priorities, criteria for awards, deadlines, allocations, application procedures, recent developments, and similar pertinent details. The chapters in this section cover city planning; community relations and civil rights; consumer affairs; cultural activities; economic development; education; emergencies (flood, riot, and disaster); employment and training; fire; health and hospitals; housing and renewal; mayor's office (miscellaneous programs); police and justice; pollution (air and water); public safety; public utilities; public works; transportation; welfare and social services; disadvantaged; handicapped; senior citizens; veterans; youth and juvenile delinquency; and programs for the Indians, migrant workers, women, the Appalachians, and the Tennessee Valley Authority. Each chapter discusses the various programs, federal acts, and executive orders which make funds available. For each the purpose, financing, eligibility, activities, and sources of additional information are presented.

The 21 appendixes which follow include tables of dollar amounts allotted to communities for various programs, many statistical summaries of people and funds for fiscal years up to 1970, and organizational charts of the programs. There is a 45-page directory of the addresses of the field offices of the federal departments and agencies which administer the grants and, finally, a 28-page Index which provides page references to the many programs and to the various subjects, including individuals, in a single alphabet. It has cross-references, and a random check showed the page citations to be generally accurate.

Although the *Guide* is a very thick volume, it lies flat when open. The inner margins are ample and the sewing appears sturdy enough to last a long time. There are many statistical tables, charts, and diagrams. There is one map which shows which counties in the United States qualified for financial assistance and for grants as of June 30, 1969. This small scale black-and-white map is legible.

There are no bibliographies, though there are occasional bibliographical references.

In spite of its thoroughness, this catalog is not as up to date or as easy to use as *Catalog of Domestic Assistance,* a publication of the federal government. First published in 1965, it is now in its seventh edition, 1973. Issued by the Executive Office of the President, Office of Management and the Budget, the government catalog is a comprehensive listing and description of 868 programs and activities which provide assistance or benefits to the American public. It sells for $7 plus $2.50 for binder. A subject index and a functional index provide access to the program descriptions. The 1973 edition describes the programs and gives information on the nature of the grants, who is eligible, where, when, how, and to whom to apply, and other special information. The program descriptions are arranged by agency, but there is also an agency index. Local contacts are listed, so that one may easily get in touch with the proper authority for more information. The work includes only those programs which are active and for which funding is currently available.

In view of the fact that the federal *Catalog of Domestic Assistance* is more up to date, and realizing that currency is extremely important in this field, the Committee cannot recommend *The New York Times Guide to Federal Aid for Cities and Towns.* (Jan. 15, 1974, p.496)

Notable Names in American History: A Tabulated Register. Third Edition of White's Conspectus of American Biography. [Clifton, NJ.] James T. White & Co., 1973. 725p. 29cm. buckram grade C $44.95; 20 percent discount on order for two or more copies. ISBN 0-88371-002-1.

Notable Names in American History is a revised edition of *White's Conspectus of American Biography,* published in 1937 and reviewed in *Subscription Books Bulletin* April 1938. This book was, in turn, a revision of *The Conspectus of American Biography* of 1906. These earlier editions served as quick reference tools with their listings of the names of noteworthy persons of achievement in the United States and were designed to be used with *National Cyclopedia of American Biography,* since entries indicated the volume and page of the *Cyclopedia* on which a biography might be found.

The editors, who are not identified, state in the Preface that "the current edition has been completely revised and brought up to date and that its scope has been enhanced by the addition of new listings." No mention is made in the Preface or elsewhere of *Notable Names'* connection in earlier editions with *National Cyclopedia of American Biography;* nor are there any volume and page references to pertinent biographies therein. The Preface also states that "the current volume is designed as a primary handbook for students, research workers, editors and writers, public officials, teachers, librarians, and others seeking data concerning this nation's prominent citizens, past and present."

The subtitle, *A Tabulated Register,* "perhaps describes most accurately its contents: a chronological compendium in a multitude of categories of the persons who have shaped this country's history." The tables of names listed under many subjects confirm this description.

The book is divided into the following chapters: The Colonial Era, The United States Government (Executive Branch), Cabinets, The United States Government (Legislative Branch), The United States Government (Judicial Branch), States of the Union, The Confederacy, The Military, The Foreign Service, The Federal Services, Local Government, Higher Education, American Foundations, Art and Science Collections, Religion in America, Commerce and Industry, Organized Labor, National Associations, and Laureates. It concludes with a comprehensive Index.

As an example of inclusiveness, the chapter on Cabinets first lists members of the Cabinet by Presidential term (with inclusive dates) and office held; then comes a listing of members of the Cabinet by Department arranged chronologically and giving years in office, State, and Presidential Term(s).

The chapter on the Legislative Branch lists members of Congresses, identifying Presidents of the Senate and Speakers of the House; under an alphabetical listing by state, the Senators and Representatives are given along with their party affiliations. Much of the same information is included in the chapter on States of the Union, but there it is in chronological order under each state with the addition of Governors and Chief Justices.

The chapter on Local Government lists the mayors or chief executives of 75 cities which are state capitals or which have populations in excess of 500,000. This chapter was included in the 1906 edition, but was dropped in the 1937 revision.

The presidents of 100 leading foundations, trusts, or funds are tabulated in the chapter on American Foundations, as are the directors of the principal museums and art galleries in the chapter Art and Science collections.

Religion in America lists the various denominations in the United States and their religious leaders in chronological order and then by diocese, district, or state, ending with the founders of religious sects, societies, and movements and the year founded. In this last table, there is no entry for Joseph Smith of the Church of Jesus Christ of the Latter-Day Saints, although that church is listed on another page.

The Commerce and Industry Section lists presidents, board chairmen and officers of "160 corporations, banks, companies, and utilities with assets or sales over $1 billion."

Some chapters are less useful than others: National Associations, for instance, includes the presidents of national learned, scientific, technical, professional, and fraternal organizations. These organizations are not indexed, so a user would have to know that they were listed in order to find out the names of the officers. The same dilemma exists with the chapter on Laureates which has the names of Pulitzer prizewinners (alphabetically by year) and a listing of many other prize and medal winners. There is no way of knowing that the Capezio Dance Award winners are included, as well as the winners of Holley Medal and the Isaac Ray Award winners. Also, only the American winners of the Nobel Prize are cited. These tables are not particularly up to date, nor inclusive. The Joseph Lippincott Award goes through 1969, but the John Fitz Medal has a 1973 entry.

Omitted in *Notable Names,* included in the 1937 edition are: directors of astronomical observatories in the U.S.; principal treaties and conventions with the names of the American signers; public statues in the U.S.; Americans in fiction, poetry, and drama; pseudonyms and sobriquets; Americans preeminent in literature, the arts and sciences, and the professions; and the anniversary calendar (newsworthy events and birthdays in American history and biography).

The Index, printed four columns to a page, is an alphabetical listing of all the names of individuals throughout the book. Surnames are in capital letters, with indented first names listed underneath. In cases where names are identical, an identifying term is used in parentheses; e.g., Adams, John (Mass.), John (N.Y.), John (Va.); John C. (Educator), John C. (Mayor). An asterisk following a page number indicates that the name is listed more than once on that page. Unfortunately the names of organizations, cities, awards, museums, and churches are not indexed, a handicap in locating the directors, presidents, and recipients, of such institutions and awards. The publisher states that this Index contains over 51,000 names; this claim is not substantiated by count. No errors were found in the Index.

Notable Names in American History is bound in buckram, lies flat when open, and has legible, clear print. The book is fairly heavy and would probably have to be rebound if it received hard usage, in which case some of the outer margins are barely adequate.

Even though some of the material in *Notable Names in American History* can be found in other books, the many compilations of names to which access is provided make this book a worthy reference purchase for libraries. Recommended.   *(June 1, 1974, p.1066)*

Oxford Economic Atlas of the World.
Prepared by the Cartographic Department of the Clarendon Press. Advisory ed., D. B. Jones. 4th ed. London, Oxford Univ. Pr., 1972. viii, 239p. maps. 38cm. cloth $25, paper $7.95; to schools and libraries, 20 percent discount.

Oxford University Press, known for its excellent atlases, has now issued the fourth edition of its unique *Economic Atlas of the World*. The first edition, published in 1953, was reviewed in *Subscription Books Bulletin* April 1955. The third edition, published in 1965, was reviewed in *The Booklist* July 1966. The present fourth edition is almost an entirely new work. More detail concerning specific areas is found in companion volumes of *Oxford Regional Economic Atlases*.

The advisory editor to the fourth edition is D. B. Jones, Institute of Economics and Statistics, Oxford University. No other editors are credited in the atlas, although acknowledgements are made to "numerous government bodies and statistical agencies, national trade associations and private companies." One hundred eight individuals and organizations are specifically listed.

No specific purpose or objective is stated, either in the atlas itself or in the publisher's announcement. Like the earlier editions, it appears to be designed for geographers, economists, and students. It should be useful also to businessmen as well as the general public, since it provides a clear picture of world economic conditions and trade flow.

The fourth edition is twice the size of the earlier works. Both the hardbound and spiral-bound paper editions open easily and lie flat for use. The maps, index, and tables are printed lengthwise so that the top of each map or table is at the left margin of each page. The volume is therefore to be rotated 90 degrees from the normal position when in use. This allows the world maps to be printed on one page avoiding breaks at the binding which become necessary in two-page spreads.

The atlas is arranged in two parts: a section of maps, including a gazetteer, and a section of statistical information. Following the title page, Acknowledgements, and table of contents, there is a Subject Index of 299 entries, referring to the maps. There are no cross-references in this Index, but page references are provided under both direct and inverted headings, e.g., *aid, foreign* and *foreign aid*.

The Subject Index is followed by an introductory statement and 91 pages of maps. The maps show world distribution patterns for all the more important commodities, industries, and resources. The maps have all been redrawn for this edition, using the modified Gall projection. Scales are indicated on all maps, including the numerous inset maps which provide greater detail for many areas. Data used are 1963-1965, although more recent data were used when available for the whole world. English versions of country names are used. Spelling and locations of most place-names are taken from the U.S. Board on Geographic Names. Lettering is black and legible, the paper pearl opaque. Oceans are a gray or tan color and the continents white. This gives the double benefit of reducing glare and making the symbols easy to distinguish.

The general design and use of color are excellent. The increased size of this edition has permitted larger scale maps with more detail. An especially helpful addition is the use of trade flow arrows. These lines are drawn schematically and show the value of flow in millions of U.S. dollars between countries. Data were obtained from the United Nations Statistical Office Data Bank, International Trade Statistics Centre and cover over 90 percent of total world trade in each commodity since 1966.

A two-page list of sources, between the maps and the gazetteer, is the only section approximating a bibliography. Entries are arranged under subject headings such as *crops* and *disease* and list author, title, and date of publication. Works included range from such general sources as *Goode's World Atlas,* 1964 to the more specialized *International Journal of Leprosy*.

One of the most helpful innovations in this edition is the inclusion of a gazetteer, listing 8,000 names, including physical features, mines, dams, and specific sites. Each entry provides latitude, longitude, and page number of the map or maps on which it appears. *See* references are used and alphabetization is letter by letter, putting *Westbury* before *West Carrollton*. The names of countries and some administrative districts are not indexed. A sample check revealed a few errors in the Index. Occasional errors, however, do not seriously detract from the general usefulness of an excellent addition.

The statistical section provides a short textual description of each country's government followed by such pertinent facts as land area, population, employment, communications, finance, trading, and then statistics in 11 categories of statistics covering production, exports, and imports. The countries are arranged alphabetically within the section with the data for each country occupying about a single page. Preceding this section a one-page *Country Index* refers users to the page on which each country's data begins. *See* references are used to locate nations not in alphabetical sequence such as *Azores see Portugal.*

The statistical section facilitates comparisons by providing figures for the 1963-5 average in boldface and for the 1953-5 average in lightface type. This edition has expanded the third edition's 10 categories by the addition of *Chemicals and Fertilizers,* which includes commodities under the subheadings *organic chemicals, inorganic chemicals, plastics,* and *fertilizers.* Data are given in metric units and where data were insignificant or unavailable these circumstances are so noted. The statistics in this section are new, and the textual information has been rewritten for this edition.

Making up the last pages of the volume is an appendix which defines each commodity and specifies the standardized units used for each.

The bindings of both the cloth and the paper editions are sturdy and may be expected to wear well.

The atlas is attractive. Text and insets in the map section are neatly arranged. The statistical section has been redesigned with all category headings at the left edge of each column and each country's entries uniformly presented. Not only has this improved the atlas's appearance, but it also will greatly facilitate use.

The fourth edition of *Oxford Economic Atlas of the World* presents a wealth of new economic, demographic, and social information. The additions of a gazetteer and of trade flow arrows, plus new statistics and totally redrawn maps make this, in fact, a new work. Material is presented attractively so that comparisons may be easily made and so the book is enjoyable to use. The atlas is an excellent reference tool. It is recommended for all public, academic and secondary school libraries, including those already owning the third edition.
(March 15, 1973, p.653)

Patterson's American Education [1973].
Editor and publisher, Norman F. Elliott; assoc. ed., Gertrude Woods. v. LXIX. Mount Prospect, IL, Educational Directories Inc., P.O. Box 199, c1972. 772p. 29cm. linen cloth grade C $27.50; to schools and libraries, $21.50 plus postage; three-year paid-up subscription $67.50. ISBN 0-910536-13-9.

Patterson's American Education, reviewed in *Subscription Books Bulletin,* January 1948 and October 1951, was published by the American Educational Company from 1904-1949, by Field Enterprises, Inc., 1950-51, and by Educational Directories, Inc., 1952-1962. The present publisher acquired the property in 1962, and he claims a listing of "more than 10,000 school systems . . . more than 7,000 universities, colleges, professional schools, private, preparatory, business, military, technical and vocational schools arranged under more than 50 classifications." This claim is substantiated by a sample count. Norman F. Elliott, the editor and publisher, has a background and education in journalism.

Prefatory material includes instructions on how to use the book, a table of contents, and a page of abbreviations. Part I, School Systems, is arranged alphabetically first by state, and then by town or community. Under each state are listed the name and address of the State Superintendent of Public Instruction or his equivalent title and the names and titles of the principal department heads in the state office, as well as **boards of education, and education as**sociations. This section is followed by a listing of county or district superintendents of schools.

Under each town or community are entered the county, population of town, school district and number, number of enrollees in the school district, the superintendent's name and address, the name of each high school, address, principal and then the name of each junior high school, address, and principal. Any academic or private educational institutions in that location are listed, giving the date established and the names of schools within that institution, with a cross-reference to Part II, Schools Classified, for additional information. No public elementary schools are listed, but private elementary schools sometimes are listed, particularly when the school includes secondary grades.

Following the entries by states are the listings of schools in U.S. territories —Canal Zone, Guam, Puerto Rico, Samoa, and the Virgin Islands.

Diocesan Superintendents of Roman Catholic schools are listed by state and territory in the next section giving the name and address of the supervising officer followed by a listing of superintendents of Lutheran schools, arranged by district and state giving the supervising officer and address. The General Conference of Seventh Day Adventists is listed alphabetically by the names of the Unions, giving the secretary's name and address and then an alphabetical listing under each union of the various state and regional conferences each with its own superintendent's name and address. The next index is of Education Associations and Societies which are listed alphabetically by subject such as administration, communications, libraries, and sciences. At least two of the addresses given in the section on library associations are incorrect, and several are omitted.

A comparison between the 1973 and 1972 editions reveals considerable updating—some deletions, some changes, and some additions.

Schools Classified is aimed at helping the guidance counselor, parent, or student find schools offering courses in specific subjects in which the student is primarily interested. For the most part, the information listed is supplied by the educational institution. The 55 subjects under which schools are classified range from agriculture through home study to veterinary schools. Cross-references are used to other classifications in which the user might be interested. Under each classification, entries are arranged alphabetically by state, and then by the name of the school, giving the name of the dean or administrator, if known. Curiously, some of the college names are in boldface, and such entries contain considerably more information than others on the same page. The publisher informs that these prominently displayed entries are paid for by the inch by some 15,000 institutions. An alphabetical finding Index of private schools, colleges, and universities is included at the end of the volume. This gives the city and state for each school listed so that a user can turn to the School Systems section and find the information needed under the state and then the city. No pages are cited in the Index.

In spite of the fact that all the information supplied in this reference tool is brought up to date by annual questionnaires, and although there are new entries, *Patterson's* is not as current as it ought to be.

Schools Classified, Part II, with a 1973 copyright is also available as a separate paperback for $4. This edition has been updated from the 1973 hardback edition (copyright 1972) with some changes and additions. Libraries owning the hardback edition will not need to purchase the paper edition. The Home Study and Correspondence Schools section in Schools Classified is similar to a section in *New York Times Guide to Continuing Education in America.*

Sturdily bound in linen and printed legibly in three columns on opaque paper, the volume should stand up well with hard use. It lies flat when open.

Patterson's greatest value is in its Schools Systems which makes it possible for the user to find schools by geographical locations. Its coverage in this area is excellent, and the yearly updating keeps the information relatively current. The Index, too, is valuable for finding rather obscure schools by the name of the institution. The Schools Classified section is also useful in locating little known colleges or schools, particularly those with a religious orientation. However, other publications are preferable for identifying subject classifications more specifically and more thoroughly, especially for colleges and universities. *Patterson's American Education,* 1973, is recommended. *(Jan. 1, 1974, p.453)*

The Penguin Dictionary of Science. By E. B. Uvarov and D. R. Chapman. rev. for the 3rd and 4th eds. by Alan Isaacs. [1st Schocken ed.] New York, Schocken Books, [1972]. 443p. diagrs. tables. 24cm. cloth $11.95; to schools and libraries, 15 percent discount.

The Penguin Dictionary of Science was originally published in Great Britain in 1944 by Penguin Books under the title, *The Dictionary of Science.* Under this title it has been through four editions (1944, 1959, 1964, and 1971), all in paperback. *The Penguin Dictionary* under review is a hard-bound edition and is also called "first Schocken edition 1972." It is identical in content with the fourth British edition, published by Penguin Books in 1971. The Schocken edition has an enlarged text page, heavier paper, and wider margins, and appears to be one of those rare cases in which a paperback book has been converted into a hardcover book instead of vice versa. None of the earlier editions has been reviewed by the Reference and Subscription Books Committee.

The authorities associated with the production of *Penguin Dictionary of Science* have appropriate qualifications. E. B. Uvarov graduated in chemistry and, before becoming a scientific literature consultant and translator, was head of a technical information bureau in a large industrial organization. D. R. Chapman, a physicist, is engaged in textile research. The reviser of the present edition, Alan Isaacs, holds a doctorate and has taught mathematics and conducted research in rocket propulsion. He is the author of *Introducing Science* (Harmondsworth: Penguin, 1962) and *The Survival of God in the Scientific Age* (Harmondsworth: Penguin, 1966).

Penguin Dictionary is a relatively small one. The American publisher's claim of "nearly five thousand entries" appears to be accurate. It has grown from 192 pages to 443 pages during its successive editions. The major changes in this edition are the addition of new words in science and the revision and conversion of all quantitative data into SI units (i.e., Système Internationale d'Unités). This conversion has necessitated the provision of tables for converting SI units into CGS (centimeter-gram-second) and FPS (foot-pound-second) units, along with other useful tables. The names of 600 new chemical compounds have been added as entries. When one realizes that there are only 5,000 entries in toto it is readily seen that names of specific substances account for a significant percentage of all entries.

All branches of science are not covered in the same depth, and the dust jacket and the Foreword are at odds in this respect. The former declares that "Astronomy, biology, biochemistry, cosmology, mathematics, physics, the space sciences—all are covered in this comprehensive scientific dictionary." The Foreword, with more candor, states that "Fuller and wider treatment of words used in computers, electronics, biology, and astronomy will be found in the Penguin dictionaries covering these subjects."

Inadequacy and unevenness of coverage are especially striking in the biological sciences. No entries are provided for even such prominent animal groups as "vertebrates," "annelids," "anthropods," and "insects" (although *insecticide* is defined). *Embryology* is defined, as is *blastula,* but no definitions are provided for such comparable terms as "gastrula," "blastopore," and "notochord." Terms used in physiology, molecular biology, genetics, cellular physiology, etc., are defined in greater number, but this volume cannot accurately be termed a "comprehensive scientific dictionary."

The British orientation of *Penguin Dictionary of Science* may occasionally cause some difficulty to North American users. Names of chemical compounds constitute a sizeable number of entries, as mentioned earlier, and many entries and cross-references are trade names. Names and trade names are in the form recommended by the British Standards Institution and will not always be identical with the accepted North American forms. For example, the entry for *polymethyl methacrylate* mentions its British trade name "Perspex," and there is a reference from the latter. There is no equivalent treatment for "plexiglas," the comparable North American term.

In all cases analyzed the definitions are generally concise, accurate, and unambiguous. Entries are alphabetized letter-by-letter, and consistently. The binding appears to be relatively sturdy, but is definitely not a "reference" binding; the cover cloth is light and the dictionary does not lie flat when opened.

The Penguin Dictionary of Science is not nearly so comprehensive or so useful a one-volume dictionary of science as is *Chambers's Dictionary of Science and Technology,* published in the same year and reviewed by the Committee in *The Booklist* December 1, 1972. *Chambers's* has approximately 50,000 entries, as compared to the 5,000 of *Penguin Dictionary of Science. Chambers's* also a British publication, but available from Barnes & Noble at $22.50, costs more. Libraries considering purchase of only one science dictionary and for which initial cost is the major or sole determinant, might well consider purchase of the paperback *Penguin Dictionary* (Baltimore: Penguin Books, Inc., 1971, $1.25). Its text is identical with that of the Schocken edition.

(Nov. 15, 1973, p.298)

Pergamon World Atlas. [Prepared by the Polish Army Topographical Service.] Oxford, London, New York, Pergamon Pr.; Warsaw, Polish Scientific Publishers, 1968. viii, 525p. col. maps. (part fol.) illus. 42cm. plastic looseleaf $59.50.

Pergamon World Atlas was produced as a translation of *Atlas Swiata,* prepared by the Polish Army Topographical Service. The Pergamon edition has added extra maps of the United Kingdom and Canada and has provided scales in the English system of measurement in addition to the metric units given in the original. According to the Preface, this translation was undertaken because the atlas' large-scale maps and details of the Soviet Union and Eastern Europe provide information not readily available in the West. This claim is substantiated because the West has little or no access to maps of Eastern Europe and the Soviet Union.

The introductory material lists the individuals responsible for both the Polish and English editions and their titles or academic positions. In addition to the Polish Army officers, the individuals are primarily academics or professional scientists.

The atlas begins with an Index of sovereign states and dependencies listing page numbers for the maps of each nation. *See* references from old to new names are included. Following this index are a table of contents, a key to signs and symbols, reproductions of some early world maps, photographs of the planets and the moon, charts of the atmosphere, and 44 pages of thematic maps of the world. Most of these employ many colors and are dated 1967. Their scales range from 1:90,000,000 for geology, population density, and water economics to 1:240,000,000 for atmospheric pressure.

The main section of the atlas (maps of the continents and countries) occupies 317 pages. Like most atlases, it features the continents first, with both political and physical maps, then more detailed maps of the most populous areas. Europe has 105 pages, Asia 49, North America 45, USSR 39, Africa 27, South America 23, and Oceana 5. Asian coverage is especially good. A sample check of a southern China map showed that it included more than twice as many place-names as did the map of the same scale in the United States Central Intelligence Agency's 1971 *People's Republic of China Atlas.* Almost every map is dated and most of the dates are 1967, with an occasional 1964. Many of the maps cover several connected sheets, so the reader must unfold the page to see the entire map. Single and even double-folded pages make it possible to view sizable areas at a fairly large scale. This is especially useful for countries the size of the USSR. However, the page edges become worn from constant folding and unfolding and the edges wear thin at the folds from recreasing. This is a common problem with any folded page with printed information on the folded surface. Unfortunately, the map numbers are not all at the outer margin, and some are not visible when the pages are folded. At times this makes it difficult to locate the desired map.

The maps as a whole are pleasing to the eye; the colors are muted but are effectively used to show elevation. Lettering is clear and the typeface well chosen so that it is easily read. The use of color is not consistent, however. Some of the larger scale maps have brighter hues than the smaller scale maps for the same elevations. The ocean colors are inverted in relation to depths, with the deepest areas being lightest in color. This places the darkest blues nearest the coastlines and makes it difficult to distinguish between land and water. Elevation is shown in layer tints.

Perhaps the weakest feature of this atlas is the thematic maps. The political maps of the various countries are accompanied by a variety of maps which illustrate different themes, such as economics, population, and climate. The quality of these maps is not always consistent. The maps seem designed for each country with no thought of comparing the thematic maps from one country to the next. For instance, the population density maps of Spain and France use two different color ranges, Spain's ranging from orange to yellow to brown, France's from red to cream. It is very difficult to compare the population densities of the two countries by comparing the two maps. The population maps in the introductory section (p.37) are of such a small scale that comparison is difficult there, too. Also, population maps vary in their choice of class interval, that is, the difference between the numbers of people shown by each color. On the U.S. population map only seven different colors are used, and the darkest color is used for all areas with more than 100 inhabitants per square kilometer. This causes the western shore of Lake Michigan to appear as populous as the New York metropolitan area. The economic maps use pictograms, and some of the symbols, such as the cattle, pigs, and sheep are very similar in appearance. The mineral resources and industry maps do not assign values and merely indicate the presence of some of that activity in each area, regardless of its importance. The thematic maps are not the most important feature of this atlas, and their defects should not be considered a major detriment. In general, they contribute to the value of the work by giving the reader some idea of elements of geography other than political boundaries and physical features.

Between the maps and the Index are an extensive guide to pronunciation and a glossary of geographical names and terms. The Index is reasonably accurate and includes cross-references from conventional English forms to the forms of names used on the maps. Index entries provide page numbers and grid references, but do not give latitude and longitude. The publisher's claim of 140,000 entries is accurate. The entries are in very small size brown-colored type on cream-colored pages and are difficult to read without magnification.

The paper is opaque, but of a soft texture that may not wear well. The 12-pound atlas is bound in a soft cover plastic looseleaf binder. The weight of the volume and the many folds make it difficult to avoid recreasing the pages in several places and the inner corners of the folded pages become dogeared easily.

Pergamon World Atlas provides much valuable information on Russia, eastern Europe, and Asia. It is generally attractive, and its folding maps enable one to view large areas all on one sheet. The thematic maps are inconsistent in quality and may be confusing. The index entries are difficult to read, because of poor choice of type size and color of paper. The paper in the atlas itself is of a soft texture that may not wear well. The many folded pages make it difficult to avoid recreasing. Pages may be unfolded unnecessarily, because map numbers are not all visible when the maps are folded. The detailed mapping of the eastern hemisphere, however, is enough to recommend this atlas to large library collections. Though its material is now becoming dated, much of the atlas is still useful as it provides detailed coverage of the entire world. Recommended. *(Feb. 15, 1974, p.609)*

Phaidon Dictionary of Twentieth-Century Art. London and New York, Phaidon Pr. Ltd. 1973. (Distributed in U.S. by Praeger, New York). [6], 420, [48] p. illus. 26cm. A-grade starch cloth $15; 25 percent discount for 5 or more copies. ISBN 0-7148-1557-8.

This small dictionary is one of those useful tools whose restrictions of scope contribute to its effectiveness. It is confined to twentieth-century "artists whose major creative phases fall within this century, including those active at the present time. There are no entries on young painters and sculptors who are only now beginning to gain recognition, since it is not yet possible to say whether they will live up to their promise or whether, like many an acclaimed newcomer before them, they will sink rapidly into obscurity." However, the editors also felt that "the giants of the late nineteenth century have, properly speaking, no place in a dictionary of twentieth-century art; yet it was felt that without mention of the innovators who gave a new direction to art, any discussion of the style and development of their successors would be meaningless."—*Foreword*. Thus one can find "the most influential figures from the great decades at the end of the last century"—Cezanne, Monet, Renoir, Rodin, the most important representatives of the Impressionist and Post-Impressionist movements, but not representatives from the earlier nineteenth-century movements.

No editor is listed, and the short Foreword is neither signed nor initialed. It must be noted however, that Phaidon ranks very high as a publisher of art books. Forty contributors are listed, representing, as the Foreword points out, "many nationalities." Twenty are cited in *Art Index, Books in Print,* or art biographies. Several have written authoritative books on their subject, and at least two are well known in the museum world. Contributors are not identified; nor are the articles signed in any way. The Foreword says that "much of the material here presented was originally written in German" and gives credit to Gerald Onn for the translation.

Phaidon Dictionary gives important coverage in three main areas: biography of artists, art movements and groups, and stylistic trends and schools.

The artists selected are mainly North American, British, and European with a few from Latin America and the Orient. The book is particularly valuable for its coverage of artists from smaller European countries such as Finland and the Slavic nations. However, very few Soviet artists are included, and those represented are the ones who were accepted at the beginning of the Soviet regime and who have been fairly unproductive since about 1925. The biographies, varying in length from a short paragraph to almost a page, outline the life of the artist, including a good account of his work and stylistic tendencies. Though subjective, the biographies seem generally accurate in judgment, based on standards of current art criticism.

Almost all twentieth-century movements and groups are represented, from the well-known Brucke and Blauer Reiter to the less well-known Blaue Vier. The history of the group, its members and exhibitions are covered in the account.

The many styles which have developed in these changeable times are examined from Abstract Art, which began at the start of the century, to Pop Art and Op Art of the 1960s. There is no article on Impressionism, in spite of biographies of some Impressionists. The coverage really begins with Expressionism and ends with a discussion of computer art through 1965, which seems to be the cutoff date for the text. Recent movements such as Funk Art, Found Art, Conceptual Art, Art Povera, color fields, and earth works are not included, and neither are their practitioners. Realism in twentieth-century art is given no separate treatment as a style. The Eight, or Ash Can group (c1910), the Social Realism group of the American 1930s WPA days, and the European New Realism group of the 1960s are treated, but there is no mention of Magic Realism, an American solution which fell midway between European surrealism and naturalism. The Precisionists, Americans who applied the European cubist principles to realism, are represented. Accounts of art under the names of countries do not appear, because there is no national coverage.

Many paragraphs, even short ones, end with a bibliography of one or more items. These include periodical articles, books, and exhibition catalogs. There are also cross-references to preferred terms, but not from prefixes of names, for instance, Van Gogh, though there is one from Segonzac to its compound form, Dunoyer de Segonzac.

The dictionary does not include technical terms or descriptions of processes. Its approach seems to be purely historical. This is emphasized by the illustrations collected in a group at the end of the volume. The first is a Van Gogh painting from 1889 and the latest is one by David Hockney dated 1970. Between the extremes, the 66 paintings and sculptures represent the main trends of twentieth-century art. They are quite well selected and well printed usually two to a page in black and white. The captions give dates, size, and location, but no hint of the stylistic trend which they supposedly illustrate. There is nothing in the text that indicates the existence of the illustrations, so that one would not know from the articles on Gaudier-Brzeska and David Smith that their work is illustrated. Nor is there a list of illustrations in the book. They exist as a separate section which could easily be overlooked.

The format is pleasant—pages are divided into two columns with subjects in bold type and a key word at the top of each page. The print is clear and legible. The book is sewn and bound in a linen-like dark brown material, which is only moderately strong. One review copy is breaking along the back hinge. Inner margins are narrow, but the book is flexible and lies flat when opened.

There is really no art tool with which to compare *Phaidon Dictionary*. Other dictionaries like the *McGraw-Hill Dictionary of Art* (New York: McGraw-Hill, 1969) are much more comprehensive. The little *Dictionary of Modern Painting* (New York: Tudor, n.d.) and the *Dictionary of Abstract Painting* (New York: Paris Book Center, 1957) are limited to painting. *Phaidon Dictionary* makes a fine complement to *Oxford Companion to Art* (Oxford: Clarendon Pr., 1970, ed. by Harold Osborne) supplementing *Oxford Companion* where it is weakest. These two titles would be excellent for a small library reference shelf and certainly for art students. By itself, *Phaidon Dictionary of Twentieth Century Art* will be useful for ready reference on twentieth-century art in any library. Recommended. *(Jan. 1, 1974, p.453)*

The Practical Encyclopedia of Good Decorating and Home Improvement. 18v. [New York, Greystone Press, c1970, 1971, 1972 by the Meredith Corp.] illus. 26cm. permalin $3.98 plus shipping and postage per v.

The Practical Encyclopedia of Good Decorating and Home Improvement provides a wealth of information on almost every aspect of home decorating. The set includes the basic subjects one would expect to find in a decorating, home building, and repair guide. The 18 volumes were produced as a joint venture: the pictures were supplied by the Meredith Corporation and the editorial work done by the Greystone staff. Free-lance writers supplied the manuscripts, which were edited in house. Design and layout were by the Greystone staff and free-lancers.

Henry W. Engel and Donald J. Dooley are respectively executive editor and editor for the encyclopedia. Neither is listed in major biographical references. In addition, eight editorial consultants are identified in the first volume. They are all active in the world of design. Two pages of designers, decorators, architects, artists, photographers, museums, institutes, and private industries are listed as important contributors.

The editors' claim that this is "the most comprehensive and complete encyclopedia on home decorating and improvement ever assembled" for the homemaker or amateur decorator is achieved reasonably well, within the limitations set forth for the set. That the set is designed for the homemaker or amateur decorator is apparent from the Introduction and the text itself.

Articles in the encyclopedia are in alphabetical order, beginning with *ABC's of Decorating* and ending with *Workshops, Benches, and Tools*. There is no master list of topics. The pages are numbered consecutively, and each volume's spine indicates the letters covered. However, some of the articles are split between two volumes, resulting in confusing duplicate lettering on adjacent volumes.

The text in each volume is followed by a section called *Master/Guide*, an alphabetical listing of decorating terms and styles and briefer treatments of the subjects in the main text, to which the reader is referred. The last volume includes a 46-page Index to the entire set.

The style of the prose is breezy, with an occasional touch of humor. Coverage is comprehensive and generally up to date. However, the set does not specifically discuss two popular decorating styles: the use of graphics and the multiple-pattern room. The three pages devoted to avant-garde as well as the illustration of a supergraphic on page 3154 seem the closest to graphics. There is no index entry for graphic or supergraphic. Some modern trends, such as the use of beads as room dividers, are included; other new trends like beanbag chairs or inflatable furniture, both popularized in recent years, are omitted.

The encyclopedia gives the reader an overview of each field and presents some of the basics, but it is not a substitute for detailed information on specific subjects; nor can it be considered "all you will ever want to know" on a specific subject, though its advertising claims this. For instance, the articles on heating, air conditioning, and mobile homes are weak. The article on security and safety in *Consumer Reports,* Feb. 1971 pages 93-103, is much better than the brief treatment of that subject in this set. Also, some of the how-to-do-it articles are less detailed than they should be. Nevertheless, despite various omissions, the encyclopedia contains an enormous quantity of information on widely diverse subjects.

The most outstanding feature of the set is the striking illustrative material. Each article in the text sections is profusely illustrated with photographs and drawings, well chosen to illustrate the subject under discussion and excellently reproduced. The colors are sharp and clear, the settings appealing to the eye. The black-and-white photographs and drawings are just as clear. The illustrations include "before" and "after" views of floor plans and room design with detailed explanations of what was wrong and how it has been corrected. This is very helpful for the novice.

The Practical Encyclopedia of Good Decorating is ideal for browsing, but the arrangement makes it difficult to locate all of its information on one subject, thus restricting its usefulness as a reference work. The material on any one subject may be scattered among several articles. For instance, there is a separate section *Carpets and Rugs* in volume 4, but there are also 13 pages on this topic in the article *Floors and Floor Coverings* in volume 8. Furthermore, the material in the *Master/Guide* is sometimes repetitive of material in the text section, and it is not indexed.

The *Master/Guide* follows the text section in each volume. The Introduction claims that this section provides complete listings and identifications of decorating and home improvement terms, but it is not clear why the publishers chose to divide the work in this way. In the *Master/Guide,* entries are arranged alphabetically and are provided with *see* references to longer articles. The *Guide* articles themselves are descriptive and illustrated, as are those in the main text. All of the articles in the main text are treated again, briefly, in the *Guide* and this section also gives short descriptions of terms, names of specific pieces of furniture, styles and individuals important in the history of design. For example, in the Index *fingerbowls* refers the reader to page 1762 in volume 10, *Glassware*. The only information on this page is that fingerbowls may be used for desserts, cold soups, or floral arrangements. The definition and explanation of what a fingerbowl looks like and what it was originally intended for appears in the *Guide* section in volume 8 where the topic is listed in its alphabetic place between *Fine Wool* and *Finger Joint*. There is nothing to indicate to the Index user that he should also check the *Guide* under the name of the item for which he is searching. This lack of ready access to every item of information is serious.

One must try both the alphabetical text itself or the Index, as well as the *Guide* to locate material. The Index is generally accurate and cites volume number as well as page reference. Although the paging throughout the set is continuous, the cited volume number facilitates finding the desired page.

However, the Index is neither sufficiently analytical to provide ready access to material in the text; nor is it consistent. For example, the Index entry *furniture, French design, history of* has four subtopics, but the Louis XIII, XIV, XV, and XVI styles are listed directly under *furniture*, not under *French*. The American styles under *furniture* are not grouped. The section on bedrooms in the unit on additions is indexed under *bedrooms-remodeling,* but not under *remodeling-bedrooms* or *additions-bedrooms*. Therefore, the reader must try both approaches.

Although the Index makes a considerable effort to bring together references to various sections of the encyclopedia dealing with the Index topic, it does not attempt to list illustrations. For instance, there are many illustrations of rooms with beamed ceilings, but the Index refers only to those text sections designed to focus on them. It would be useful to a home planner or carpenter to be able to scan all of the pictures showing beamed ceilings. There is, for example, an unusual beamed ceiling in an illustration on page 149. This is not indexed under beams or ceilings; nor would it be otherwise located through the Index, because it is included in an illustration of an add-on kitchen.

There are very few cross-references in either the text or the Index. There are no bibliographies.

The meaning of a statement in the Introduction is not clear: ". . . whenever possible, instructions are provided as to where you can get a specific Project Plan or Home Plan that is illustrated in an article (see Index)." Since none of these references appear in the Index, the Committee queried the publisher. In response Greystone states that accurate instructions for obtaining plans are on the copyright pages of all volumes except volume 1 and that the next printing of the encyclopedia will correct the error.

The volumes are glued rather than sewn. They do not lie flat when open.

The Practical Encyclopedia of Good Decorating is an attractive set that offers many decorating ideas and includes much informative material. It gathers information on a wide range of subjects into one work, though it scatters the information throughout its volumes. Its lack of adequate cross-references and its incomplete indexing, however, limit its value as a reference work. The colorful illustrations and smooth prose make it ideal for the home library and browsing collections in public libraries with a demand for material on decorating. Recommended.

(Nov. 15, 1973, p.299)

Profiles of Involvement. 3v. Philadelphia, Human Resources Corporation, [1972].
v.1, Perspectives, Corporate Profiles; v.2, Organizations, Government Agencies; v.3, Biblio-view, Glossaries, Indexes. illus. 21cm. paper $59 the set, plus $2 shipping per book. ISBN 0-913272-00-0.

"Human Resources Network is a nonprofit educational corporation whose charter purpose is to collect and disseminate important information about pressing social issues. It is an urban clearing house of information and a catalyst for communications."—page I-15.

Profiles of Involvement, the first result of the corporation's effort to fulfill the purpose for which it was created, seeks to provide a compendium of business and organizational involvement in today's social problems and programs. The editors say, "Frankly, it is a $300,000 experiment in communications."

With Stephen E. Nowlan as Publisher and Chairman and Diane Russell Shayon, Executive Vice President, the Corporate Group is composed of seven persons; the Print Communications Group has Suzanne R. Tiernan as vice president and senior editor assisted by ten others in various capacities. Information on backgrounds of these individuals is not available in standard biographical dictionaries.

Volume 1 subtitled "Perspectives, Corporate Profiles," gives an introductory description of the history and purposes of the book and a statement of the responsibilities of large corporations. "Pragmatics of Involvement" by Muffet Russell Shayon explains the methods used to obtain corporate profiles, reactions of some corporation officials to the questionnaire used, how replies were analyzed, the effects of the communications revolution brought about by television, and case studies of three corporations which have become deeply involved in rebuilding human resources. Following this are copies of four speeches made by major executives, Hazel Henderson, Robert D. Lilley, Ian H. Wilson and Robert Theobald, dealing with corporate social responsibility; and four original articles by Theresa Abbott, Saul Alinsky, Wayne Owens, and Elmer Young, on corporate social involvement. Included in this section are pictures and biographical sketches of these eight contributors.

The major portion of volume 1 is devoted to corporate profiles ". . . brief case studies of those programs which corporations have implemented in an effort to fulfill their role as responsible corporate citizens." There are 16 topic areas, General Community Affairs, Consumer Programs, Drug Abuse, Education, Environment, Housing, Employment Opportunities, Job Training, Health, Minority Enterprise, Urban Development, Consumer Safety, Youth, Volunteerism, The Arts, and Miscellaneous. Companies are listed in alphabetical order within each topic; and when programs are applicable to more than one topic area, they are printed under all appropriate areas.

The following information is included in the industry profiles: name, address, business, sales, CEO, employees (number), contact, address, telephone, number of persons program reaches, when started, budget, program outline, company personnel involved, measure of success. Two profiles are included on most pages. No effort was made by the editors to evaluate the projects; profiles consist only of information submitted by the company.

Volume 2 has the subtitle, "Organizations, Government Agencies." The editors state that "Organizations and government agencies are included . . . to help complete the picture of social action in America today . . ." and to provide ". . . a diverse information bank of organizations, trade associations and various civic groups: their composition, goals, and activities," which may in turn encourage interaction.

Organization profiles are arranged in alphabetical order and include, in addition to name, address, contact, etc., identification as to the type of organization, up to six principal office locations for organizations having several, overall purpose, and one or more of the following: main divisions, programs, projects underway, methods of operation, functions and services, and a maximum of ten board members. Organizations included vary from Southern Christian Leadership Conference, Synanon Foundation, U.S. National Student Association, Jewish Board of Guardians to Just One Break, Inc., Keep America Beautiful, Inc., Zero Population Growth. One hundred fifty-nine organizations are listed.

The last part of volume 2 is devoted to government agencies in order to show ". . . how our government is applying its resources to the solution of our nation's problems." Information given is similar to that for organizations.

Biblio-view in volume 3 provides sources of published information in areas of social concern. The editors state that it is neither extensive, complete nor even selective. Nine items are reviewed briefly, including *The Federal Register, Federal Civil Rights Enforcement Effort, A Report of the United States Commission on Civil Rights, 1971,* and *The States and the Urban Crisis,* edited by Alan K. Campbell (Englewood Cliffs: Prentice-Hall, 1970). A bibliography compiled by Human Resources Network lists 14 books with publication dates from 1959 to 1972. Nine of these have brief statements of contents. Eight titles are listed under the caption, "Special Reports/Articles." This is followed by a portion of a bibliography compiled by the Bank of America N. T. and S. A. of San Francisco, California. This includes 16 books, 63 magazine articles, 33 special studies/papers/reports. These are very uneven in treatment. Bibliographic information is given for each book, but no annotations are given. However, brief statements of contents are given for 17 of the articles. No page references are given for 10 of the articles.

Three glossaries are included in volume 3: Noise Pollution, adapted from *Glossary of Terms Frequently Used Concerning Noise Pollution* and *Glossary of Terms Frequently Used in Acoustics* (American Institute of Physics); Water Pollution; compiled by Human Resources Network; and Drug Glossary (United Systems Quarterly, v.9, Winter, 1970-71, no. 4).

Three indexes to volume 1 give first a list of corporations included and the areas in which their programs are involved with page references; the second index is corporations listed by topic; the third, corporations listed by state. Use of hanging indention, three sizes of print and only two columns per page make the indexes easy to use. A check showed the indexes to be accurate.

The Index to volume 2 is on green paper in clear legible print with topics in heavier type. Asterisks are used to show those organizations which have materials available to the public. Random checking showed this Index to be accurate also. Indexes to both volumes are followed by blank pages for notes.

Volume 1 has a variety of illustrations: colored photographs of plants and insects, black-and-white pictures as well as drawings at the beginning of each topic area. There are also several illustrations in vivid colors that might be classified as pop art. Volume 2 contains a number of advertisements that illustrate information given by various organizations. The illustrations in both volumes effectively point up the message these volumes were intended to convey.

The volumes are bound in board, and glossy paper is used. Use of different shades of print makes a clear cut and very legible format. Volumes lie flat when open, and inside margins are ample should rebinding be necessary. Pagination is continuous. There is no guide to abbreviations used in the volumes, and for some users this may present a problem.

The editors of *Profiles of Involvement* have succeeded in presenting a diverse information bank of the efforts of some corporations and organizations in the conservation of human resources. Although less than 25 percent of the corporations queried responded to the questionnaire, 186 did respond with information on 535 social action programs that will serve as examples for other corporations and perhaps emphasize the need for more involvement in similar programs. Information is presented in a clear and concise manner, and the indexes in volume 3 made it easy to locate. Recommended.

(March 1, 1974, p.700)

Purnell's History of the 20th Century.
10v. A. J. P. Taylor, editor in chief. New York, London, Purnell, c1971, 1972. J. M. Roberts, general editor. illus. 30cm. vinyl $149.50 multiple order; $179.50 single order.

Purnell's History of the 20th Century is a ten-volume set edited and published in Great Britain but "neither conceived, written, nor illustrated from any one nation's point of view," according to the Introduction. A. J. P. Taylor, editor in chief and Fellow of Magdalen College, Oxford, is a well-known and prolific historian, an expert on German history and the history of the two World Wars and author of the volume dealing with the twentieth century in *Oxford History of England.*

John M. Roberts, general editor, a former member of the Institute for Advanced Study at Princeton, is Tutor in Modern History, Merton College, Oxford, former visiting professor at the University of South Carolina, author of the Longman's *History of Europe, 1880-1945* and joint editor of the *English Historical Review.*

Purnell's History of the 20th Century purports to be no less than a "history of *all* the world in the 20th century" and "a history of the world in all its important aspects." "Subjects like the revolution in the home caused by detergents and refrigerators or the changes in sexual morality brought about by cheap and efficient contraceptives must have a place alongside the great battles and political events." Great emphasis is placed upon illustrations for, as the editors state, "no other century possesses such an abundant visual record of history in the making."

Purnell's is a history, not an encyclopedia. Its continuously paged ten volumes are divided into a total of ninety-six chapters, and each chapter typically includes from four to eight signed articles. The arrangement is roughly chronological in the sense that one moves from the world at the turn of the century in volume 1 to such contemporary events as space exploration, the Vietnam war, the environmental crisis, and modern psychology in volume 10. Actually, the plan of the history is not strictly chronological since it ranges geographically across the entire world and attempts to cover social, economic, cultural, political, military, and technological life in this century.

Purnell's is a lavish pictorial treasure. At least one-half of its page space is devoted to illustrations, a large percentage of them in full color and all of them contemporaneous with the events, trends, or movements they illustrate. The pictures represent a triumph of thoroughgoing research and intelligent selection. The hundreds of picture credits reflect a truly international search for the apt photograph, painting, poster, cartoon, headline, chart, advertisement, magazine cover or other graphic object to clarify or complement an article or a chapter. The choice of illustrations seems almost always to have been made with a view to combining technical pictorial excellence with a kind of summarizing iconographic revelation of an event, while avoiding the obvious or the expected.

The 477 articles in *Purnell's* were written by 242 contributors. Alphabetically arranged photographs and very brief capsule biographies of the authors are provided in volume 1.

As might be expected, the largest number of contributors is British. In addition to English journalists, writers, and government officials, 101 persons are listed as having an active or retired connection with a British university, and there are 5 contributors from Australian universities and 2 from universities in Canada. Twelve authors are identifiably American and, interestingly, 13 are Russian. France, West Germany, Italy, Spain, Czechoslovakia, Mexico, Chile, Japan, and several other nations are represented.

Among the better known contributors are Denis Brogan of Cambridge; Alan Bullock, biographer of Hitler; American historian Foster Rhea Dulles; novelist Constantine Fitzgibbon; physicist Denis Gabor; John Kenneth Galbraith; Christopher Hollis; Princeton historian Arthur S. Link; Lord Mountbatten; Roger Manvell, the film expert; and Arnold Toynbee.

At the end of the brief biography of each contributor the titles of the articles he wrote are conveniently listed, together with their page references. The contributors seem to be an eminently qualified and expert group. Without exception there is coincidence between the contributor's academic specialization, his record of authorship, his experience, or his listed position and the topics on which he writes for *Purnell's.*

There is, however, no Black African contributor; there are only two contributors from all of South America (both from the University of Chile), none from mainland China, none from Indonesia, and no native of India or Pakistan. The editors' claim that "never have so many of the world's distinguished historians, journalists, and writers cooperated on such a scale" may be something of an exaggeration, but there is no glaring racial bias evident in the treatment (typically by British experts) of the countries of Africa or Southeast Asia. The article on Rhodesia, for example, by the late Frank Clements, British-born former mayor of Salisbury, Rhodesia, a journalist, broadcaster, and author of five books about Africa, is almost painfully balanced and fair. The same can be said about the articles *China under Mao* and *The Cultural Revolution* (in *China*) by Jack Gray, specialist in modern Chinese history and Chinese communism at the University of Glasgow.

Purnell's History of the 20th Century also lists the names and positions of an "International Panel of Consultants." They are referred to in the Introduction as a "distinguished panel of consultants from all over the world," but their specific functions are not mentioned. One each is listed from West Germany, Australia, France, Russia, Czechoslovakia, Japan, Italy, Chile, and England. The remaining three are from the United States. Curiously, the three Americans are Allan Angoff, director of public relations at the Teaneck, New Jersey, Public Library, William J. Roehrenback, director of the Jersey City Public Library, and Robert Ochs, who is identified as "Professor of Modern History at South Carolina University." Of the three Americans only Ochs is also the author of an article *(Theodore Roosevelt* in volume 1).

The format of *Purnell's* is designed to provide maximum convenience of access to the contents. At the beginning of volume 1 the Contents of the Work appear. This lists the table of contents of each of the ten volumes, chapter by chapter, including each article and its author and page. At the beginning of each volume the appropriate table of contents for that volume is reprinted.

There are three indexes at the end of volume 10: a Thematic Index, an Illustrations Index, and a General Index. All index references are to pages, not volumes, but the inclusive pages of each of the ten volumes are conveniently given across the top of each of the index pages.

The Thematic Index arranges every article under 17 topical headings with a view to enabling the reader to identify and locate all of the articles dealing with a given theme. Examples of the headings are Art and Architecture, Communications, Economics, Entertainment, Cinema and Sport, Imperialism, Literature, Political Theory, Politics and Society, and Science and Technology. There are some chronological subdivisions. Politics and Society, in addition, is subdivided by countries and geographical areas. There are no cross-references in the Thematic Index.

If one approaches *Purnell's* by way of one of the thematic headings he is given a list of all of the articles in the set that fall under that heading. A specific article may be listed under more than one theme. "The Boer War," for example, appears under *Imperialism, Africa,* and *Warfare.*

The 27-page Illustrations Index is a locator for every illustration in *Purnell's* ten volumes. Drawings and paintings are indexed both by their title and the name of the artist. Each illustration is indexed by the name of a person, place, object, or idea illustrated, and a given illustration may be listed in several places.

In the Thematic Index and the Illustrations Index no errors or blind references were found and, with allowances for some subjective latitude in deciding precisely what a picture is "about," the Illustrations Index seems to serve its purpose quite well.

The third index is the General Index containing "entries on all people, places, objects and ideas discussed." While this index is useful for locating a specific reference in the text, it shows some indications of having been done by untrained indexers.

Apparently there has been an attempt to list in the General Index every person mentioned in the ten volumes, even if there is no real information provided about the person. For example, the name of gangster Dion O'Banion appears only in a picture caption, and his name therefore appears in the General Index, yet there are places in the text where crime is treated or mentioned but there is no heading "crime" in the General Index. One might locate the subject crime by going to the Thematic Index, except that there is no such heading there either. One has to know to look under *"politics and society,"* go to a subdivision, *United States of America,* and then run through the titles of some 30 articles to come upon one called *Crime and Prohibition.* (There is, incidentally, no treatment of crime anywhere else in the world but the United States in *Purnell's*).

There are peculiar inconsistencies in the General Index. Sometimes, when a person is mentioned in the text without his first name being given, he is listed in the Index without his first name, but this isn't always the case. Sometimes titles are given and sometimes not. Thus, *Fulbright, Senator* and *Morse, Senator* appear while *McCarthy, Joseph* gets a first name but no title. *Spellman, Cardinal* is listed with *Muller, Bishop Ludwig,* and *Radford, Adm.* with *Pershing, General John Joseph,* and *Tedder, Air Chief Marshal Sir Arthur* (later *Lord Tedder*). There is a listing of *McLuhan, Marshall* next to a *McLeod, Prof.* Max Weber is referred to in the Index in one place as *Webber, Max* and in another as *Webber, Prof.* A passing reference to psychologist Kurt Lewin in the text as "Lewin" shows up in the Index as exactly that—*Lewin.*

There are no bibliographies in the main body of *Purnell's.* A 16-page Bibliography is provided in the final volume. It is divided according to the 96 chapters in the set, and there are between one and five, rarely more, bibliographic references for each article. An editorial note states that the bibliography "is invaluable to the reader who wishes to study in greater depth the topic dealt with in any article in *Purnell's History of the 20th Century."* In each case the bibliography was compiled by the author of the article.

Actually the 477 bibliographies (1 for each article), are an uneven conglomeration, and the whole bibliographic section would seem to be of very limited use to the average reader. Author, title, and publisher are provided for each entry, but there are no dates and no annotations. The user has, therefore, no information on suitability for his purposes, or up-to-dateness, or likelihood of a book's availability. No periodical articles are listed. There are some examples of careless proofreading in the bibliographies. Jacques Barzun's *Race; a Study in Superstition,* for example, has its title listed incorrectly. Theodore White's *The Making of the President 1960* is listed in one place without the date, which is part of the title, and in another place with the date. Isabel Leighton, editor of *The Aspirin Age* is listed as Isabel Deighton.

Since *Purnell's* articles were written by more than two hundred contributors, one might expect that there would be considerable variety of writing style throughout the ten volumes. There are some stylistic differences but actually much less variety than one would expect. The editors have managed somehow to have their authors maintain a kind of straightforward, generally readable, somewhat long-winded but high-level journalistic style, the kind of writing that one thinks of as appropriate for the intelligent reader or the well-informed layman.

Purnell's claim to be a history of "all of the world" in "all its important aspects" during the twentieth century is, of course, a bit of poetic license of the dust jacket variety. Any such history must be a selective affair, and one can argue interminably, especially in dealing with recent history, about what is proper to include and exclude.

Generally speaking, *Purnell's* inclusions can be said to be fair, reasonable, and interesting. The total text presents a thoroughly respectable social and political history of the twentieth century with due regard for both the Eastern and Western worlds. The emphasis is heavily political-military-social-economic with a generally successful attempt to juxtapose and integrate those four aspects of history rather than artificially to separate them.

The cultural is not neglected but is a distinctly secondary facet of the work. Literature, for example, during a period of ·complex and interesting developments world-wide, is slighted or treated superficially, as is music. They are dealt with in a total of 7 out of the 477 articles; fewer than 10 are devoted to art and architecture, while entertainment, cinema and sport receive a total of 7, and even these totals are arrived at only if one counts some general articles like *Men and Movements* and *Expressionism* which treat broadly of several cultural topics more than once.

Religion, despite one article by Arnold Toynbee entitled *Religion: A Personal View,* comes off rather poorly. There is a total of five articles, and four of them are concerned with politics rather than religion, dealing principally as they do with the accommodations made by the churches, particularly the Roman Catholic Church, with Hitler. The Toynbee article is in no sense a survey or summary of religious thought or religious history in this century.

Psychology, one of the twentieth century's serious preoccupations, is dealt with in only three articles: a very brief and somewhat perfunctory one on Sigmund Freud, plus two others, both by H. J. Eysenck of the University of London whose reputation, at least in the United States, is based upon his anti-Freudianism. The articles are very much behaviorist-oriented (though without any mention of B. F. Skinner) and condescending toward Freud and psychoanalysis.

Science and technology are covered, in more than 30 articles, including fine, readable treatments of electricity, scientific agriculture, the new physics, the electronics revolution, medicine, automation, nuclear energy, space and genetics, with strong emphasis on their social context.

The tone of *Purnell's* is distinctly British, and many of the inclusions and exclusions reflect, not so much British nationalism or conscious bias, as a British (rather than an American) view of things. This is not necessarily a criticism of the work but merely a descriptive note. The word "emigration," for example, is used for what Americans call "immigration." There is an index reference to (British) football but none to baseball or basketball. There is very extensive treatment of labor and employment problems and the rise of organized labor but no mention of Samuel Gompers, William Green, John L. Lewis, Philip Murray, or Walter Reuther. The work of Lincoln Steffens, Ida Tarbell, and Burton Hendrick receive mention, but the familiar Americanism, "muckrakers," does not appear.

Purnell's is large in page size, but the volumes are relatively slim. Page size is 9 by 11¾ inches, but the volumes average only about 250 pages. The volumes lie flat when open, and there is an adequate although not generous inside margin. The binding is not particularly sturdy, especially for books which, because of their lavish and unusual illustrations, will be much leafed through by library patrons. The set will probably need rebinding.

In summary, *Purnell's* is a selective, readable, and profusely illustrated history of the twentieth century in ten volumes, done by more than two hundred highly qualified contributors apparently for a British readership and with a strong emphasis on political and social developments. It is convenient to use, but its General Index needs improvement. While *Purnell's* is an excellent and broad-ranging work of collective history, its principal achievement is as a collection of illustrations, and these will constitute its major value to the typical reference collection. They provide a unique, indexed pictorial view of the world since 1900 and are well worth the price of the volumes. *Purnell's History of the 20th Century* is recommended for all high school, college, and public libraries. *(Jan. 1, 1974, p.454)*

Rand McNally Cosmopolitan World Atlas. [Enlarged "Planet Earth" ed.] Chicago, Rand McNally and Co., [1971]. lvi, 252, 100Xp. col. illus. col. maps. 37cm. regular ed. buckram over boards $19.95; deluxe ed. padded covers $25.

Rand McNally Premier World Atlas. [New Census ed.] Chicago, Rand McNally and Co., [1971]. xvi, 220, 100Xp. col. illus. col. maps. 37cm. buckram over boards $14.95.

Rand McNally World Atlas. [Family ed.] Chicago, Rand McNally and Co., [1971]. xl, 288p. col. illus. col. maps. 32cm. regular ed. roxite $9.95; deluxe "Imperial" ed. padded covers $12.95.

Rand McNally Worldmaster Atlas. [Reference ed.] Chicago, Rand McNally and Co., [1971]. xl, 207p. col. illus. col. maps. 32cm. clothbound, roxite $6.95; paperback, patent bound $4.95. Price to schools and libraries subject to "sliding discount based on quantity." Regular editions were submitted for review.

Rand McNally and Company continues as one of the two major publishers of atlases in the United States, in addition to publishing children's books and adult nonfiction. The other "atlas giant" is Hammond, Incorporated, whose seven 1971 atlases were reviewed in *The Booklist* May 1, 1972, pp.729-333. Both companies incorporate results of the 1970 United States census in their 1971 atlases.

The four atlases listed above and in the tables on page 311 are general world atlases in the medium size and medium price range. They are referred to in advertising and in this review by the brief titles *Cosmopolitan, Premier, Family,* and *Worldmaster.*

None of the four atlases is new, and all are built around a basic set of map plates, the publisher's "Cosmo" series, designed originally for *Cosmopolitan* when it was first published in 1949. In 1971 the four had essentially two formats. The first format is employed in *Cosmopolitan* and its "less expensive counterpart," *Premier,* each approximately 15 inches high and having the same 125 pages of political-physical maps and an Index keyed to those maps which locates "over 82,000 places." *Premier,* however, has 72 fewer pages of supplementary features.

The other format appears in *Family* and *Worldmaster,* which are both approximately 13 inches high and have as their core 89 pages of maps from the same "Cosmo" series and an Index of some 30,000 names accompanied by population figures. *Worldmaster* is a reprint of the first 207 pages of *Family,* omitting the last 80 pages of historical maps and illustrated geographical survey.

All are intended as general reference atlases, but *Family* is planned for use by children of elementary school age as well as by older students and adults.

All but the *Worldmaster* have been reviewed previously by the Committee: *Premier*—July 1956; *Cosmopolitan*—April 1950, July 1956, November 1, 1963, and under the title *New Cosmopolitan,* October 15, 1966; *Family*—September 15, 1966.

New features in the 1971 atlases, including some new maps, are independent units which may be added to or subtracted from the basic set of maps and index. That set is substantially of the same plan as in earlier editions, but some information printed on the maps and in the Index has been updated.

None of the four atlases names the editor, editorial group, or consultant list for the volume as a whole. The user is, in effect, asked to rely on the authority of the publishing house and the fact that its name has long been associated with map and atlas publishing in the United States. Under today's conditions of frequent mergers and change of personnel the more academically oriented adult and student users may question the authoritative character of such atlases.

Two higher priced atlases: *The International Atlas* (1969, $35, *The Booklist,* October 1, 1970) and Patrick Moore's *Atlas of the Universe* (1970, $35, *The Booklist,* May 15, 1971) are also published in the United States by Rand McNally. Both provide the names of consultants or editor for the work as a whole. The four atlases under review represent a more popularly priced line in a highly competitive market. Part of their updating consists of reprinting some pages from the two more recently developed atlases in making up the package of supplementary units.

A general acknowledgment of sources appears in the one-page Introduction to the *Cosmopolitan* where the U.S.

TABLE I

FOUR 1971 RAND McNALLY ATLASES

TITLE	PRICE	SIZE	PAGES	INDEX PAGES	MAP PAGES	HISTORY
Rand McNally Worldmaster Atlas. Reference ed.	$ 6.95	12½ x 10	247	96	107	Rev. ed. of Worldmaster Atlas, first published in 1961.
Rand McNally World Atlas. Family ed.	$ 9.95	12½ x 10	328	96	133	Rev. ed. of World Atlas, Family ed., first published in 1964.
Rand McNally Premier World Atlas. New Census ed.	$14.95	14½ x 11½	336	143	175	Rev. ed. of various atlases published under Premier title.
Rand McNally Cosmopolitan World Atlas. Enlarged "Planet Earth" ed.	$19.95	14½ x 11½	408	153	201	Rev. ed. of Cosmopolitan Atlas, first published in 1949; published in 1965, 1966 and 1967 under title: Rand McNally New Cosmopolitan World Atlas.

TABLE II

1971 RAND McNALLY ATLASES ANALYZED

	Cosmopolitan		Premier		Family		Worldmaster	
	Pages	%	Pages	%	Pages	%	Pages	%
MAPS								
Political-physical maps ("Cosmo" series)	125		125		89		89	
Map explication	6		6		4		4	
Global Views (Physical)	21		21		14		14	
Physical maps	13		13					
Ocean World (Physical)	8							
U.S. Metropolitan Area maps	10		10					
World Metropolitan Area maps	18							
World History maps					26			
Total no. of pages of maps	201		175		133		107	
INDEXES								
Index to political-physical maps	99		99					
Index to political-physical maps with population					96		96	
Index to U.S. Metropolitan Area maps	6		6					
Index to World Metropolitan Area maps	10							
Populations of U.S. cities etc.	32		32					
Populations of Foreign cities etc.	16		16					
Total no. of pages of indexing	153		143		96		96	
Subtotal for MAPS and INDEXES	354	88	318	95	229	70	203	82
SUPPLEMENTARY (Photographs, text, tabular data etc.)	54	12	18	5	99	30	44	18
TOTALS	408	100	336	100	328	100	247	100

Geological Survey and NASA are cited as the source of "much material." The other three atlases have no general introduction.

Throughout the four atlases specific bibliographic citations with dates have been avoided. References are given in general terms to "the 1970 census" of the United States in *Cosmopolitan* and *Premier* or to the "final 1970 census figures" in *Family* and *Worldmaster*. For foreign population no sources of information are mentioned in *Cosmopolitan* and *Premier* other than "recent censuses (designated C) or estimates (designated E) . . ." and the year of the census for the country as a whole.

Throughout the series, United States information is presented in its separate units and in greater detail than world information. As a result, the tables of contents are particularly important for rapid location of individual maps in the main series and for finding other topical sections where United States data and the equivalent for the rest of the world or for the world as a whole may be widely separated. The fact that the atlases are composed of sections which are essentially self-sufficient has the disadvantage for the user that the volume as a whole lacks organic unity. In the pagination the use of roman numerals up to lvi, arabic for the major maps and several supplementary series and some indexes, and arabic plus suffix "X" for the largest index in *Cosmopolitan* and *Premier* is not unusual but tends to detract from ease of use. Frequently the title of a major heading used in the table of contents is not given, or not repeated exactly, in the body of the atlas. Running heads that would help to differentiate three adjacent indexes at the end of *Cosmopolitan,* for example, are not used.

In *Cosmopolitan* the main series of maps, as in previous editions, emphasizes North America and Europe. Maps for Asia, Africa, Australia and South America occupy only 28 pages or approximately one fifth of the 125 pages devoted to political maps. The scale used for maps of the United States and European countries is, similarly, larger than that used for other areas. Scale for Switzerland (1 inch=17 miles), Quebec (1 inch=30.5 miles) and Ireland (1 inch=32 miles) contrasts with Ecuador (1 inch=126 miles), Nigeria (1 inch=252 miles). There is relative consistency of scale for maps of regions or countries within a given continent, but considerable variation in scale for maps of the states of the United States, with a range from Connecticut (1 inch=11.5 miles) to Alaska (1 inch=189 miles).

The "Cosmo" maps were designed as general purpose maps combining political and some physical information. Nations or states are given visual emphasis by solid color over the entire area. Physical features such as mountains are shown by shading. The combination of color and gray shading tends to obscure place-names in black in the smallest type size. The light blue print for hydrographic features is somewhat less visible than black print against the solid colors, but it is useful in decreasing the effect of crowded printing. Railroad lines are shown in red, but no road communications.

Maps in the "Cosmo" series carry a publisher's code number but are not dated in any way to which the user can refer. With some exceptions names of countries are indexed in accord with recent changes, but in most cases the traditional English variant of the country's name continues to be used on the map, with or without the official name in parentheses. In some cases political status is incorrect in the Index. For example, of four countries achieving independence in 1968 two are correctly identified as countries (Equatorial Guinea and Nauru), but two are still identified as British dependencies (Mauritius and Swaziland). Disputed areas are identified by devices such as printing in red type or cross-hatching. Information about the United States appears to be the most accurate and up to date. A lag may be found for features such as man-made lakes and dams if one compares the maps with lists of such information available in inexpensive annual reference books. For example, two of the world's largest man-made lakes completed in 1968 are not found in

Cosmopolitan (Daniel Johnson, Canada; W.A.C. Bennett, Canada).

Type of projection and scale are indicated on each map page in the bottom margin. Maps are frequently printed at right angles to the bottom margin, necessitating turning of the atlas.

Four other map series in *Cosmopolitan* supplement the basic political-physical maps. They are designated as the Ocean World, Global Views, the Physical World in Maps, and Metropolitan Area Maps. Of these the ones for oceans and for large cities are new to *Cosmopolitan*. The Metropolitan Area maps were first published in *International Atlas* (1969).

The Global Views are raised relief maps photographed in color, depicting continental landmasses. They are impressionistic maps intended to show "how the land might appear in its summer mantle of vegetation if viewed from far out in space." They are attractive as illustrations on a two-page spread accompanied by a small outline map showing the countries of the continent and by some paragraphs of text sketching the physical geography of the continent or region as a whole. In *Cosmopolitan* the Global Views are interspersed with the main series of maps, paged as inserts (7A-7B) and serve as an introduction to the conventional political maps of a particular continent.

For the Ocean World unit, with a type of physical map based on relatively new information, Dr. H. W. Menard of the Scripps Institute of Oceanography is listed as Consultant, Dr. Bruce C. Heezen of the Lamont-Doherty Geological Observatory and the U.S. Naval Oceanographic Office assisted in preparing the section. The introductory text is presented with graphs and illustrations on two pages, followed by six pages of maps. Projections are those which "maximize water areas relative to land areas," and the "colors used are those thought to exist on the seafloors." Maps are bled to the edge of the page, unlike all other maps in the atlas. Although the scale used is small, one inch representing 500 miles or 660 miles, the result is informative for the nonspecialist.

The Physical World in Maps is a series of the more traditional physical maps emphasizing major landforms. There are 13 pages of maps for the world, the continents, and in larger scale for the United States and Canada (1 inch=152 miles). Gradient tints enclosed by generalized contour lines show elevation zones and depths in offshore waters. Major political divisions and transportation lines are shown. An introduction, a list of physical map symbols used, and the relief legend on each map complete the section.

Among the supplementary maps in *Cosmopolitan* the Metropolitan Area maps offer the most detail, with a scale of one centimeter to three kilometers, or one inch representing 4.7 miles. Thirty-six of the world's largest cities and their immediate environs make up one group of maps with its own Index, and 12 United States cities another, separately indexed. Unfortunately no legend or list of symbols is included; nor is there any reference to the fact that an explanation could be found in *International Atlas*'s three-page "Legend to Maps." Although most interpretation is clear, there is the possibility of confusion when used in conjunction with the main series of "Cosmo" maps which the Metropolitan Area maps supplement. For example, a red line represents a road or a street in the Metropolitan Area maps, whereas it represents a railroad in the "Cosmo" maps which show no road communication lines.

Cosmopolitan's general alphabetical index is keyed to the main series of maps and their inserts. Separate alphabetic indexes are provided for the two groups of Metropolitan Area maps, and there is no cross referencing from either type of index to locations that appear in both. In the Index to the U.S. Metropolitan Area maps "neighborhoods and local area names that occur within cities are shown in *italic* type." These appear to be place-names found only in that Index and not in the main alphabetical Index. The Index for the World Metropolitan Area maps, however, does not use the same device. There are also two population indexes subdivided first by state of the United States, or by foreign country. Centers with a population of 1,000 or more inhabitants (some centers of 500 or more) are included for the United States, and cities of 50,000 or more for cities abroad.

As a result of the five units of indexing, the names of several thousand towns, cities, and countries are listed in three different indexes in the same volume. The separate treatment makes some types of comparison easier, particularly in the subdivision by country in the population Index, but there are disadvantages from the point of view of rapid reference. For example, when using one of the two population indexes, it is difficult to locate the other elsewhere in the volume without first turning to the table of contents. There is also the juxtaposition of three lists at the end of the volume, two of them straight alphabetical and one alphabetical first by country, all without distinguishing running heads at the top of the page.

According to the publisher's sales catalog "the 100-page index locates over 82,000 places." A sampling indicates approximately 77,000 terms in the main Index. The U.S. Metropolitan Area map Index, however, showing local names in italics, and the Index to the World Metropolitan Area maps with an additional number unique to that index, would bring the total for the volume to a higher figure.

The introduction to *Cosmopolitan*'s main Index states that all "important" names on maps are indexed. This appears to be a reasonable claim, in that in a sample 90 percent of the place-names, political divisions and physical features printed on the maps are found in the Index.

In the main Index an asterisk is used to designate the places which are not printed on maps for lack of space but may be located approximately by the letter and number combination. The device could be used more extensively to increase the total number of names indexed while avoiding overcrowded printing.

Index accuracy is about 93 percent judging from a sample.

Policy on place-name spelling is stated in the Introduction to *Cosmopoli-* *tan*: The United States Postal Guide is the authority for this country, and recommendations of the United States Board on Geographic Names for foreign areas and languages are generally followed but with more anglicized names "for some areas and languages." There are some omissions and inconsistencies in cross referencing from official or native forms of important place-names. For example, the city of Bangkok appears in that form on one map, as Bangkok (Krung Thep) on another, and as Krung Thep (Bangkok) on a third; in the general Index it may be found under Bangkok but not under Krung Thep; in the Index to Metropolitan Area maps it is found under both forms, and in the population Index first under Thailand, in its alphabetic list as Bangkok (Krung Thep).

Supplementary material in *Cosmopolitan* other than maps consists of color photographs and text at the beginning of the volume, and tables and charts of miscellaneous geographical information in the latter part.

In the two introductory sections, the Planet Earth and the Moon, there are some spectacular panoramic color photographs of the earth taken from space vehicles. Pictures, diagrams, captions, and brief text present a survey of the solar system, earth's phases and atmosphere, weather systems, continents, geology, human geography, and moon exploration. Most of the section is a reproduction of selected pages from *Atlas of the Universe*. The color photography and layout are of good quality, and the text is simple and clear. The two introductory sections are generally a good example of maximum use of visually attractive material and more limited use of the printed word in educational and reference material directed to a wide audience.

Geographical and political "facts and figures" in the form of tables and charts make up two other supplements. For the world as a whole, principal mountains, oceans, lakes and rivers, and air and steamship distances are examples of the type of information included. For states of the United States a general information table gives capital, largest city, highest point, state flower, state bird, and state nickname. Most of the information is of the type which may be found in inexpensive almanacs or reference books other than atlases.

The binding of *Cosmopolitan* appears to be strong, and the stitching permits the volume to lie flat when open. Double-page maps have divided printing at the seam rather than hinged plates so that some printed information would be lost if the volume were rebound.

Premier differs from previous atlases issued under that title. The 1971 *Premier* is described by the publisher as "an economical alternative to the *Cosmopolitan*, containing the same features as the *Cosmopolitan*, but fewer of them, with 72 fewer pages and a uniform paper stock throughout." An advantage of *Premier* other than the price is that it has the larger percentage of the total content allocated to the atlas essentials of maps and indexes (95 percent as compared with *Cosmopolitan*'s 88 percent).

Premier is identical with *Cosmopolitan* in the sections entitled: Maps and Map Projections, World Reference Maps (the heading used in the table of contents for the political maps of the publisher's "Cosmo" series), the Physical World in Maps, and Geographical Facts, Figures and Information about the World and the United States, including under this heading the U.S. Metropolitan Area Maps and Index to Political-Physical Maps. It differs by substituting a briefer introductory section of six pages entitled Space for *Cosmopolitan*'s extensively illustrated opening sections designated in the table of contents as the Planet Earth and the Moon, and by omitting the oceanographic section, the Ocean World, and also the World Metropolitan Area maps and their Index.

Family atlas is planned for use by children of elementary school age as well as by adults. There is no introduction. The table of contents makes good use of simple color contrasts to indicate the major sections of the atlas and facilitates quick location of a particular map of the largest countries on most continents, although Africa is subdivided only by region ("Northwestern Africa, Northeastern Africa, Central and Southern Africa"). The Index is bound in the center of the volume, but not immediately following its maps.

The political-physical maps are a selection from the publisher's "Cosmo" series. Of the 89 map pages almost two thirds are devoted to maps of North America. Maps of the world and of Europe, Asia, Africa, Australia and New Zealand, and South America make up the remaining third.

The maps are printed in slightly reduced size as compared with *Cosmopolitan*, to fit a volume just over 12 inches high. The paper is not glossy, and the solid colors of the political-physical maps are bright. Black letter printing of most names on the maps is legible in spite of the reduction in size, but blue ink used for names of counties, regions, and hydrographic features is less visible.

Family atlas has one Index of approximately 30,000 items keyed to the main series of maps. It includes some physical features in addition to place-names and political divisions. Population figures for the United States are "from the final U.S. census for 1970;" for foreign countries the figures are estimates for January 1, 1970 "from the latest available official census figures and estimates." A typical index entry is: "Iwo, Nig. 158,583 G5 22." The Index is printed in a legible type on an uncrowded page of four columns.

Many more names appear on the maps than are found in the Index. For example a sample quadrate of the map for Yugoslavia showed 17 out of 34, or 50 percent indexed. A sample from the Manitoba map showed only five places listed in the Index compared with 46 on the map, or about 10 percent.

Of the supplementary sections in *Family* atlas the opening section, the Universe, includes a page on the history of astronomy, followed by brief text and photographs for planets and other solar system bodies, a moon map, the sun, stars, and galaxies, followed by a space glossary. According to information printed on the back of the title page above the copyright statement "This section was written in cooperation with the Office of Public Information of the University of Chicago by Stuart M. Kaminsky and Charles E. Yoder."

The charts and tables of Selected United States Information follow the maps for that country, but that arrangement separates the main maps from their Index. Selected World Information follows the Index. Completing the volume are two sections, the first of which is a series of 48 historical maps, including insets, on 27 pages. Its introductory page of text explains that "Since this book is mainly for American use the treatment of North American and European history is given better coverage."

As a part of the final section designated in the table of contents as the World in Focus, there are seven double-page spread maps of the world illustrating the topics of world population, transportation, languages, religions, vegetation, climates, and landforms. Color photographs and brief text make up the balance of an attractively designed survey of physical and cultural geography.

Family atlas has a sturdy binding and heavy paper, but as a result of tight stitching the volume does not lie flat when opened. However, there are no political maps on two-page spreads where it would be difficult to read printed information at the inner margin.

Worldmaster as issued in 1971 duplicates the first 207 pages of *Family*, omitting the last 80 pages, as stated above. Of the two it has the higher proportion of pages given to the main maps and Index: 82 percent as compared with 70 percent of the *Family* atlas. Other sections are those on astronomy and space, raised relief maps of continents, and charts and tables of selected information for the United States and for the world as a whole. The two sections of *Family* omitted from *Worldmaster* are the historical maps and the illustrated geographical and cultural survey.

The higher prices for deluxe editions of the *Cosmopolitan* and *Family* atlases are for padded bindings. *Worldmaster* is available in a flexible cover "paperback," but the patent binding does not permit the volume to lie flat when open.

In summary, merits of the four Rand McNally atlases under review are the reasonable degree of accuracy and legibility of the maps, and, for the supplementary sections, the well-selected and reproduced color photographs and clear and simple text. Among the less creditable features shared by the four are the lack of identifiable authority for the editors, use of very few, generalized, and scattered references to sources, and the avoidance of dates for map and bibliographic information. There is no single, easily found key to all map symbols used within a given volume. Furthermore, indexing is not sufficiently comprehensive. Purchasers will also need to consider that the emphasis continues to be on United States maps and data in comparison with those for other parts of the world.

Of the four atlases under review the *Cosmopolitan* is an acceptable choice for small and medium-size public libraries. *Family* is suitable for homes with children of elementary school age. Purchasers of the economy versions of each, *Premier* and *Worldmaster,* would receive the same atlas with somewhat fewer extras beyond the essentials of maps and index. Subject to the qualifications summarized in the preceding paragraph, the atlases are recommended. *(Dec. 1, 1972, p.310)*

The Realm of Science. 21v. Stanley B. Brown, editor in chief. L. Barbara Brown, associate editor. Louisville, KY, Touchstone Pub. Co. [c1972]. Distributed by Carroll Book Service, Inc., P.O. Box 1776, North Tarrytown, NY 10591. illus. 26cm. buckram $150. The History and Spirit of Science, v.1; Tradition of Scientific Inquiry, v.2; Fundamentals of Mathematics, v.3; The Language of Science: Mathematics and the Physical Sciences, v.4; Discovering the Nature of Matter, v.5; The Dynamics of Being: Matter and Carbon Chemistry, v.6; Foundations of Physics: Mechanics and Optics in Classical Physics, v.7; The Evolving Knowledge: Further Developments in Classical Physics, v.8; Revolution in Science: Relativity, Quantum and Nuclear Physics, v.9; The New Science: Recent Advances in Physics, v.10; Atoms, Stars and Nebulae, v.11; Many Worlds: The Discovery of Galactic Systems, v.12; The Nature of the Universe: Modern Cosmology, v.13; Man and the Conquest of Space, v.14; The

Earth and its Origin, v.15; The Substance of Our World: Earth, Water and Air, v.16; The Living World: Cells, Molecules and Metabolism, v.17; The Code of Life: Genetics and Development, v.18; The Continuum of Life: Structure, Classification and Evolution, v.19; Directions and Dimensions of Life: Ecology, Man and Nature, v.20; Scienthesis: Science Concept Index and Cumulative Index for Volumes 1-20, v.21.

Several years in preparation, *The Realm of Science* has been compiled as "A Library of Selected Readings Exploring Great Concepts of Science." The editor, Stanley B. Brown, formerly Dean of Instruction and Professor of Science Education, Southwestern Oregon Community College, has been assisted in his task by a Scientific Advisory Board made up of seven popularizers of science including Ashley Montagu, Isaac Asimov, and George Gamow. An additional list of 26 consultants and contributors of whom 17 are listed in standard biographical sources, is given in the front of each volume. The final authority of this work rests, however, with the authors of the selections included: among the authorities are Isaac Asimov, George Gamow, Martin Gardener, Marston Bates, Theodosius Dobzhansky, James D. Watson, C. P. Snow, Fred Hoyle, Gregor Mendel, Charles Darwin, Henry Cavendish, and Michael Faraday.

In its 4,140 pages the work contains 324 readings from both monographic and periodical works, ranging in length from one-page excerpts to complete articles of several pages. Each reading is preceded by a short unsigned introduction of less than one page, establishing its historical context, summarizing the ideas it presents, or making other comments about the selection or its author. These introductory comments provide continuity for the selections in each volume.

Designed to provide a broad, general picture of the evolution and current status of specific areas of scientific inquiry, as well as the philosophical and sociological implications of science, *The Realm of Science* is divided into five parts each covering a broad concept of science. The range of the set can best be indicated by considering the titles of the individual volumes as listed in the heading of this review: Part I, *The Nature of Science*, is treated in volumes 1-4. Part II, *The Nature of Matter and Energy*, is covered by volumes 5-10. Part III, *The Nature of Space*, is dealt with in volumes 11-14. Part IV, *The Nature of the Earth: Environment*, is handled in volumes 15 and 16, and Part V, *The Nature of Life*, is treated in the four remaining volumes. Volume 21, *Scienthesis*, contains the indexes.

There are numerous collections of readings in the various fields of science which cover specific fields more completely than this set, and at considerably less cost. Yet, none attempt to cover the entire field of scientific inquiry as this set does. However, this coverage tends to be uneven. The physical sciences are covered more extensively than the biological sciences. The development and current state of the fields of physics and astronomy have been given eight volumes, while only five volumes have been devoted to the biological sciences.

The readings range chronologically from a selection from Lucretius' *De Rerum Natura* of the first century B.C. to the excellent review article *Introducing the Black Hole* by Remo Ruffini and John A. Wheeler published in 1971. While there are numerous papers from earlier dates, the majority of the selections are from the past 25 years. They have been for the most part well selected. With the possible exception of the mathematics in some of the readings they should all be readily understandable to the readers for whom they are intended, that is, high school and college students and the layman. In the first two volumes the editors have been particularly successful in their presentation of a good summation of the nature, history, and methodology of science as well as its role in modern society.

A primary aim of this set is to demonstrate the basic unity of science. Although the material has been organized in such a manner as to cut across the lines of the various scientific disciplines, there is still a compartmental design.

Volume 21, *Scienthesis*, has been designed to help overcome this compartmentalization. It contains in addition to the Cumulative Index a special Science Concept Index.

Each volume has its own Index, but the usefulness of the set has been considerably enhanced by the inclusion of a cumulated index where all references to a person, place, thing, or idea can be found in one place. This Index covers 133 pages and contains approximately 8,000 entries. Since some entries contain more than one reference, the number of total references is considerably higher. The indexing is fairly comprehensive but not always accurate. Illustrations are identified in the Index.

The 41-page Science Concept Index is a special index designed to bring together concepts from the various scientific fields. Entries are arranged under 87 subjects or concepts, several of which are broken down into numerous subheadings. The number of entries ranges from 252 under *mathematics*, with 14 subheadings, to only 2 under *serendipity*. How this Index complements the regular Index can be seen by considering the headings under the concept *time*. In the Concept Index under 28 entries can be found a total of 46 page references. The regular Index of 133 pages contains only 8 references. There are not this many different references, however, since references to the same page numbers are often given under more than one entry. *African, early lunar calendars*, for example, refers to the same volume and page numbers as *lunar calendars*. That this indexing has not been done as comprehensively as originally planned can be seen by comparing the actual entries under *relativity* with the sample page from the prospectus for the set. The sample page shows a detailed analytical index of the subject containing 233 references, with an additional list of 31 scientists and philosophers to be consulted in the General Index. The actual Index, however, does not refer to these scientists and philosophers and contains only 47 references under subject. In the Cumulative Index also there is evidence of lack of editorial care. *Circadian rhythms* is listed as v.14, p.104-105. The correct reference should be v.18, p.104-105. Although there are no cross-references in the text proper, both indexes contain a number of cross-references which are substantially accurate.

With the special attention to indexing the editors have somewhat enhanced the reference value of this set. A collection of readings such as this is, by its very nature, not particularly effective as a reference source. The material has been written originally with other purposes in mind. Also a collection of readings, however extensive, tends to be spotty in its coverage. Nevertheless valuable information on a limited number of subjects is available in this set and the Index does provide access to it.

Basically, the primary use of this set will be as a source of collateral readings for the intended users: the student and teacher at the high school and college freshman level as well as the interested layman. For these groups *The Realm of Science* will provide a broad general picture of the evolution and current status of specific areas of scientific inquiry.

The set does not contain a general bibliography. Some of the readings, however, include their original bibliographies, which may range from a single item to as many as 20 references. They can be of use to the reader seeking additional information on a subject, although some will prove too technical for the typical user of this set.

The Realm of Science is an attractive set of books. The entire work has been reset in a readable type. Unlike many collections of readings, which contain few illustrations, in most cases the original illustrations accompany the selections in the set. Most of the photographs are in black and white. However, color limited to greens and yellows is often used as a background to accent charts, graphs, and other line drawings as well as some of the photographs. Original one- or two-color illustrations sprinkled liberally through the text and as frontispieces add much to the attractiveness of the volumes. Credits are given for many but not all of the photographs. The art staff is listed in the front of each volume, but individual efforts are not credited. The volumes are Smyth sewn and sturdily bound with bright buckram covers. They will lie flat when opened.

The Realm of Science is an attractively packaged collection of readings which present a broad overview of the evolution of scientific thought and methodology. It is primarily useful as collateral reading not only for the student and teacher, but also for the interested layman. Recommended as a set of science readings.   *(Sept. 15, 1973, p.58)*

The Romantic Movement Bibliography, 1936-1970: A Master Cumulation from ELH, Philological Quarterly and English Language Notes. Edited and with a Preface by A. C. Elkin, Jr. and L. J. Forstner. With a Foreword by David V. Erdman. 7v. [Ann Arbor, MI] The Pierian Pr. in association with The R. R. Bowker Co., 1973. xiii, 3289p. 24cm. (Cumulated Bibliography Series, no.3). buckram $160. ISBN 87650-025-4.

This set is a cumulation in chronological order of the annual bibliographies entitled "The Romantic Movement: A Selective and Critical Bibliography," sponsored by groups General Topics II and English IX of the Modern Language Association and appearing successively throughout the years in three different journals. The intent, as has been stated in the introduction to each annual bibliography for many years, has been "to include, with descriptive and, at times, critical annotation, all books and articles of substantial interest to scholars of English and Continental Romanticism, and critical reviews of such books." Although coverage is of a movement, not a period, for English literature it has been limited to writers active during the period 1800-1837 (later 1789-1837) in order to avoid duplication with two other annual bibliographies previously established—"English Literature, 1660-1800: A Current Bibliography" and "Victorian Bibliography," (1837-1900).

Literatures covered most regularly through the years have been English, French, German, Italian, Portuguese, and Spanish, while sections devoted to such literatures as Slavonic, Scandinavian, and Spanish American have appeared and disappeared. The annual bibliographies are arranged in sections designated by these literatures, with listings under such subheadings as General, Bibliography, and Studies of Authors.

The bibliography for the years 1936-1948 was originally published in the March issue of ELH; for 1949-1960 in the April issue of *Philological Quarterly* and for 1961-1963 in its October issue; and for the year 1964 and thereafter to the present as a supplement to the September issue of *English Language Notes*. Its editors have been Walter Graham for the bibliographies covering the years 1936-43; Charles F. Harrold, 1944-1945; J. Raymond Derby, 1946-1955; Martin K. Nurmi, 1956-1960; and the present editor, David V. Erdman, Professor of English, State University of New York at Stony Brook, who began with the issue for 1961.

The cumulation is edited by A. C. Elkins, Jr. and L. J. Forstner, both Assistant Professors in the Department of English Language and Literature, University of Michigan. The reprinting in chronological order of the 35 annual bibliographies for 1936-1970 constitutes volumes I-VI. They are preceded in each volume by the title page and the Contents for all seven volumes; and in volume I by a Foreword by David V. Erdman which gives a succinct history of the compilation of the bibliography through the years, carefully tracing the changes in its scope and coverage. These changes may be followed in greater detail by reading the introductions to the individual annual bibliographies, all of which are included in the reprinting. There is also a brief preface by the editors of the cumulation. Volume VII consists of the indexes.

According to the Foreword the advantage of reprinting the annual issues in sequence over consolidation into a single alphabetical file is that users are enabled "to single out the scholarship of a given year . . . or to make a chronological survey of scholarship on a given author." It would be possible to argue that the advantages of consolidation could outweigh these considerations (surely economics must also have been a factor in the decision), but there is ample precedent for the sequential arrangement. The cumulations of "English Literature, 1660-1800" and of "Victorian Bibliography" follow the same plan. An example of a cumulation which does utilize an alphabetical sequence is *Articles on Twentieth Century Literatures: An Annotated Bibliography 1954-1970,* based on the quarterly listings in the periodical *Twentieth Century Literature.*

The indexes in volume VII are a great contribution and will bring to light much scholarship now buried. The two major ones are the Author/Main Entry/Reviewer Index and the Subject Index: Personal Names. The first has names of individual and joint authors of the works listed in the bibliographies, titles used as main entries, and the names of reviewers, editors, contributors, translators, etc., appearing within entries, approximately 45,000 citations according to the editors. The second lists the authors that are subjects of the bibliographical items and the "names, nicknames, aliases and pseudonyms of authors, poets and other individuals, fictional characters, folk heroes and mythological figures alluded to in the titles and annotations within the bibliographies," approximately 38,000 citations. The use of both indexes is facilitated by coding systems which indicate, for example, whether the reference is to the name appearing in the body of the text rather than in the alphabetical sequence, whether the reference is to the name in the role of reviewer, whether there are multiple references to the name on the page. The third index is a Subject Index: Categories, which is made up of the "headings used to denote national literatures, language groupings, subcategories, and other sections which make up the classified scheme of the bibliographies." Volume VII also contains a Cross Reference Conversion Table, which lists the reference for the original publication of each of the bibliographies and gives the corresponding volume and page in the cumulation; and a list of Periodical Title Abbreviations, indicating the years a particular abbreviation was used for each periodical. A Note on the Indexes at the beginning of the volume explains their use, points out the reasons for some inconsistencies such as variant forms of names in the text, and delineates measures taken to minimize these inconsistencies. However, some omissions were noted in the first two indexes.

The devices employed to facilitate the location of any single year's bibliography are well planned and effective. Pagination running continuously through the set is given at the bottom of the page. The inclusive pages and the years of the bibliographies included are printed on the spine of each volume. Running heads on the verso of each page give the source of original publication of the bibliography and on the recto the title and year of the bibliography.

The bibliographies are excellently reproduced on good quality paper with wide margins. The volumes lie flat when opened, but binding is not sturdy enough for a reference set. The edges of the spines of the review sets already show signs of wear.

The Romantic Movement Bibliography, 1936-1970 brings together in convenient form the separate issues of a valuable scholarly bibliography which has been published serially over a long period in three different journals and provides indexes to it which will facilitate research by Romanticists. The set is recommended for academic and research libraries and for any other library where there is interest in literary research.

Ruth Walling
Associate University Librarian
Reference Dept., Emory University
Reference and Subscription Books Committee Member 1958-1962
(July 15, 1974, p.1212)

St. Martin's Dictionary of Twentieth-Century Composers (1911-1971). By Kenneth Thompson. New York, St. Martin's Pr., [1973]. 666p. 25cm. cloth $30.

Thompson's *Dictionary of Twentieth Century Composers* consists of extended lists of facts relating to 32 major composers, now deceased, who did their most important work between 1900 and 1920. Such being the case, the title of the book is most unfortunate, although a better one is hard to suggest. It is unexpected, in any event, to find a dictionary with as few as 32 entries. Nor does the book cover more than the early part of the twentieth century, and thus the title's dates of "1911-1971" can hardly be more than an irritating attempt to appear up to date. Admittedly, the composers' death dates do indeed range from 1911 to 1971 (Mahler to Stravinsky); but as a result their birth dates range from 1845 to 1899 (Fauré to Poulenc). Some, like Fauré, Elgar, and Janáček, did their best work before 1900, while others, like Busoni, Holst, Puccini, Rachmaninov, Sibelius, Strauss, and Vaughan Williams, belong in spirit mainly to the late nineteenth century although they did a good deal of their work after 1900. Most of the major composers associated with the distinctive music of the years after 1920 are excluded, since happily they are still alive. One thinks of Boulanger, Britten, Copland, Dallapiccola, Orff, and Shostakovich, among others.

What we have for each composer is a biographical sketch, catalog of works, and general bibliography. The sketches run to around 500 words and are the factual kind which users will especially appreciate. The catalog presents the major works in chronological sequence by date of composition. Here one finds the English as well as the original title; the date of composition and of any major revisions; the duration and the specific medium; the date of various first performances (not only the first anywhere, but often the first in other countries as well as the first broadcast); the author of the texts and often the names of any descriptive subdivisions of the work; the date and publisher of the first edition; and a list of writings about the particular work. Such writings about one work will appear under the work in this rubric, but writings about the composer in general or about groups of his works come in the general bibliography which follows. The bibliographies include materials in many languages, although British material is probably covered better than that from other nations. The biographical entries range from 40 pages or more (Strauss, Stravinsky) to 10 or fewer (Bloch, Satie, Varèse), in double columns, with small type and large octavo format. Coverage extends into 1972 (for such a work as the Kirkpatrick edition of Ives' *Memos*), and the level of accuracy appears to be reasonably high, if not perfect. A brief list of "Addenda" appears at the end (pages 659-66). In all, this is a most impressive reference work.

Thompson's *Dictionary of Twentieth Century Composers* will be most useful to those users of a library, scholars and serious laymen alike, who need more recent and more ample information than one finds in *Baker's* or *Grove's*, or in a more serious presentation than one finds in Ewen's *Composers Since 1900*. The book belongs in libraries which serve serious students of early twentieth-century concert music.

D. W. Krummel
Professor of Library Science &
 of Music
University of Illinois
Urbana
Reference and Subscription Books
Review Committee Member
1964-1969
(*July 1, 1974, p.1163*)

Science and Technology Research in Progress, 1972-1973. 12v. v.1, Engineering Sciences, $95, ISBN 0-87876-017-2; v.2, Chemistry and Chemical Engineering, $75, ISBN 0-87876-018-0; v.3, Earth and Space Sciences, $60, ISBN 0-87876-019-9; v.4, Electrical Engineering, $60, ISBN 0-87876-020-2; v.5, Materials, $60, ISBN 0-87876-021-0; v.6, Mathematics, $65, ISBN 0-87876-022-9; v.7, Physics, $65, ISBN 0-87876-023-7; v.8, Medical Sciences (2 pts.), $185, ISBN 0-87876-024-5; v.9, Biological Sciences (2 pts.), $145, ISBN 0-87876-025-3; v.10, Agricultural Sciences (2 pts.), $165, ISBN 0-87876-026-1; v.11, Behavioral Sciences, $95, ISBN 0-87876-027-X; v.12, Social Sciences, $95,

ISBN 0-87876-028-8; v.1-12, $895, ISBN 0-87876-016-4; v.1-7, $432; v.8-10, $445; v.11 & 12, $169. Orange, NJ, Academic Media, 1973. 29cm. cloth.

The first edition of *Science and Technology Research in Progress* is published by Academic Media "in cooperation with the Smithsonian Science Information Exchange, Inc.," hereafter referred to as SSIE. The data base of the SSIE, located in Washington, DC, is the source of information for this publication.

Since around 1951 SSIE has become a central repository for most federally-funded research projects. Currently the file "consists of approximately 140,000 research projects in twelve major disciplines." Included are federal and non-federal projects both foreign and domestic. The information registered here is furnished by supporting agencies and/or investigators.

The aim of this series of publications is "to provide the research community with the most comprehensive listing of current research projects ever available." The Introduction to volume 2 indicates that this published work contains a listing of over 125,000 current investigations. An estimate based on an examination of the volumes would indicate a list of over 135,000. This edition covers the fiscal year of 1972 (July 1971 through June 1972) and the first part of 1973. A few projects from June 1970 through July 1971 are occasionally included to give further information for current projects.

Besides providing information on current research in progress, this series can be a means of identifying individuals working in an investigator's area of concentration. It is also a source for determining the level of funding for various fields and the organizations involved in supporting the research.

The information is divided into volumes according to the major disciplines as given in the heading of this review. The Tables of Contents, basically the same for each volume, list the following: Foreword, Introduction, Table of Abbreviations, Research Project Section and Indexes.

The one part of the Table of Contents which is treated in detail is the Research Project Section. It lists broad numbered subject headings. Under each is either (1) a statement of the types of projects assigned under this discipline term or (2) subheadings indicating coverage. An example of the latter are the subdivisions Aeronautics, Aircraft and Helicopter, Aircraft Equipment and Components, and Aviation and Flights under the broad category of Aeronautical Engineering.

Each volume's Foreword of one or two pages is written by a subject specialist in that particular field. All but one of these specialists are listed in standard biographical directories. Each Foreword concludes with a short paragraph giving the author's present and, in most cases, previous positions.

Each volume contains an Introduction by Dr. David F. Hersey, President of SSIE since 1972 and previously its Vice President. There are three variations of the Introduction with minor insertions to correspond to the subject matter contained within that particular volume (e.g., v.3, Earth and Space Sciences).

Abbreviations of federal agencies used in the Research Project Section are printed in the Table of Abbreviations and are arranged according to the federal agency to which they belong. The full name of the organization follows the abbreviation. For example, A.S.R. is the Animal Science Research Division and is found under the heading U.S. Department of Agriculture. Again, only those abbreviations used in the particular volume are noted, not those in the whole series.

The Research Project Section which follows is also referred to as the title section. The projects under each heading are preceded by the chapter and subchapter number of the project. Both the title and the project's principal investigator are listed in dark type. After the initials and last name of the researcher, the organization with which he is associated is given. The organization's location and address, including zip code, are printed in smaller, lighter type. In some instances the investigator may be "a program manager not working at the stated research organization location."

Next the supporting agency is named. To the right of the entry is a letter indicating the funding code for each project. An explanation of the code is found at the bottom of each recto throughout the title section. It should be noted that each research project is listed only once even though it may be relevant to more than one subject area.

To some researchers the inclusion of foreign research projects in these volumes might be of special interest. Two examples of foreign research contained in the Research Project Section are a project on "Subsurface Geological Mapping" being conducted at the Hong Kong Public Works Department and supported by the Hong Kong Government and one on "Automatic Cartography" by M. Ledru of the Roads & Motorways Dept., Bogneux, France and supported by the French government.

The titles of grant proposals which have been funded are very general, therefore they yield little or no information on the specific research in progress. No abstract or annotation of the project indicating the projected direction of the research is given. In volume 9, *Biological Sciences,* the classification of research into genetics, invertebrate physiology, etc., is not as useful as using topics such as specific diseases or citing problems being investigated would be.

Next comes the Investigator Index which consists of an alphabetical listing of all researchers cited on the source document followed by the project entry number. An asterisk following the entry number indicates a principal investigator. Knowing any one of the researchers on a particular project one can use this index to find the project number and thus gain entry to the title section. However, the title section, as noted earlier, cannot be used to determine all the individuals working on a specific project.

The Research Organization Index consists of an alphabetical listing "of the recipient organizations and their locations." The Funding Organization Index is an alphabetical listing of both federal and non-federal supporting agencies.

The last Index is the Subject Index with an alphabetical listing by subjects. "Each project is indexed in hierarchies indicating relationships between broader and narrower concepts." Hierarchy is indicated by bold type descending to smaller type and then project entry numbers. Subject headings are very broad as compared to *Index Medicus* for medical projects. The term carotid arteries is found as a subject heading in the latter, but in volume 8, *Medical Sciences,* this heading is found under the larger term "Cardiovascular System" and under the lesser term "arteries." No *see* references are provided from one term to another. One must think in terms of the largest concept in order to find the appropriate project. Another example is that ampicillin, lincomycin, penicillin, and tetracycline do not have separate headings as in *Index Medicus* but are listed under "Antibiotics." Yet phenobarbital and secobarbital have separate listings rather than being a subheading under "Barbiturates." This seems to be an inconsistency.

Globulins (blood), collagen, and keratin are found under "Proteins." Leukemia was found under the large term "Cancer-Body Sites" and the subheading "blood cancers." *See* references from leukemia would have been most helpful.

It is important to read the Introduction in each volume in order to understand the subject grouping for that field. In the Subject Index section the same project may be listed under several applicable headings. In spite of the broad classifications by subject, the use of the various indexes described does facilitate the location of information by a number of specialized approaches.

Each volume states that "all information contained herein has been drawn from sources and using procedures believed to be reliable and current as of the date of publication, but the accuracy of such information cannot be guaranteed." A statement in the Introduction asks that errors and omissions be reported to SSIE. A user feedback card is provided in the back of each volume for this purpose and for notification of additions for non-federally-funded programs; government agencies are expected routinely to supply information on their projects.

To test accuracy, the federally-funded research projects of the physics and mathematics departments at one university were compared with the information given in volume 7, *Physics*. The listing of four projects contains either misinformation, the grants have expired, or the listings are misleading as given. Only two are accurate. The projects of eleven investigators are missing entirely. Since all are federally funded, either the supporting agency neglected to report the research or the information was not included in the data base. If other organizations find this same percentage of inaccuracy, accuracy of this publication is in question. One would also conclude that missing federally-funded projects should also be reported on the cards supplied.

All the indexes are produced by computer. Type is clear but small; margins are wide, and the volumes lie flat when opened. Volume numbers are on the title page but omitted from the spine. Pagination is inclusive for each volume. The smallest volume is *Materials* with 307 pages and the largest is *Medical Sciences* with 1,519 pages. The set is bound in cloth over binders board, and first and last signatures are reinforced.

Science and Technology Research in Progress is a very specialized reference work produced for persons involved in research with the hope that duplication may be avoided and communication furthered. While this work makes it possible to correspond with investigators it must be remembered that they are under no obligation to respond since the research is in progress and not yet published.

Information in these volumes will become outdated rapidly. Recognizing this and the fact that not enough information is given in the present set, Academic Media plans a quarterly current awareness service in microform. The new updating service will provide a descriptive abstract of each research project, and Academic Media plans to publish everything currently in Smithsonian files current to within 45 days. The first microfiche will be available in late 1974.

Considering the cost, the fact that it will become outdated, and its value to a limited number of users, *Science and Technology Research in Progress, 1972-1973* can be recommended only for large university, research, and special libraries. Individual researchers might wish to purchase single volumes which relate to their particular projects or interests. *(June 1, 1974, p.1067)*

Scientific and Technical Books in Print 1972; Subject Index, Author Index, Title Index. New York, R. R. Bowker Co., [c1972]. 1575p. cloth $28.50.

Prepared by R. R. Bowker Company's Department of Bibliography in collaboration with the Publications Systems Unit of the Xerox Education Group, *Scientific and Technical Books in Print* is a new addition to Bowker's "in-print" series, being a reprint of information in *Books in Print* and *Subject Guide to Books in Print*. Its distinctive feature lies in the selection of subjects by Ellis Mount, Science and Engineering Librarian for Columbia University Libraries. This first edition was produced from records stored on magnetic tape, edited by computer programs, and set in type by computer-controlled photocomposition. This is the same method used for *Books in Print*, and it permits spin-off publications such as this. Acknowledgment is given to the Senior Staffs of both Bowker and Xerox involved in the production of *Scientific and Technical Books in Print*, as well as special recognition to Ellis Mount, whose Foreword follows the title page. The book's limitation to English-language books and primarily U.S. publishers is not mentioned in the introduction to this book.

Intended to meet the needs of professionals in scientific and technical fields as well as laymen and young adults with interests in these areas, it lists titles for all aspects of the physical and biological sciences and their applications, as well as engineering and technology. Titles in the field of industry are selected for their treatment of technological problems rather than for their economic, marketing, or managerial aspects. In architecture, the emphasis is on materials and structure rather than on design and social considerations. Material pertaining to hobbies covers technical rather than artistic pastimes. Business and economics, included in *Business Books in Print 1973*, are excluded from *Scientific and Technical Books*. Medicine and psychology are accounted for in Bowker's *Medical Books in Print 1972*, which will be reviewed by the Committee in a forthcoming issue of *The Booklist*. Relevant biographies, philosophical works, and histories of technologies are included as background to contemporary science and technology.

Scientific and Technical Books in Print combines indexes to subjects, authors, and titles in one volume. An alphabetical list of publishers and their addresses concludes this edition. Over 52,000 titles from 1,200 publishers are included.

The entry information is uniform in each of the indexes. Bibliographic data consist of author, coauthor, editor, coeditor, translator, title, price, imprint, and year of publication. Additional information such as number of volumes, illustrations, series, and type of binding may also be given. International Standard Book Numbers are also supplied in most cases.

The Subject Index appears first. Duplicating the physical format of other Bowker "in-print" volumes, the arrangement of titles is alphabetical by author under the appropriate subject headings. The subject headings, in capitalized boldface type, have been selected from Library of Congress headings and are in alphabetical order. Accurate *see* and *see also* references appear throughout the book. Since some titles appear under more than one subject heading, some 52,000 titles can be seen about 65,000 times under 12,000 headings with 7,500 cross-references. In comparing subject entries with those in *Subject Guide to Books in Print, 1972* entries were almost the same. No new subject headings could be found in the new volume, but some in the 1972 *Subject Guide* were omitted. New titles put in Bowker's database during November after publication of *Books in Print* and *Subject Guide* in October are in future editions of *Scientific and Technical Books in Print*.

The Author Index immediately follows the Subject Index and is arranged alphabetically by the author's last name or the corporate body responsible for authorship. Full bibliographic information is again supplied. *See* references are employed to direct the user from a joint author to the author under which the bibliographic citation appears.

The Title Index repeats the bibliographic information under titles arranged alphabetically. A Key to Publishers' Abbreviations is the last section of the volume. This is an alphabetical list of publisher or distributor abbreviations which are used within entries. When an abbreviation is listed, the name of the publisher is then given in full with the complete address, and the International Standard Book Numbers in parentheses.

Each page in *Scientific and Technical Books in Print* has a uniform physical format—three columns per page, indentations between entries, and the first word on the page repeated at the top for easy access. The print is small but legible, and the margins are adequate. The volume lies flat when opened. The binding is sturdy.

Although *Scientific and Technical Books in Print, 1972* duplicates sections of *Books in Print 1972*, its existence is justified for the convenience it will provide for those libraries involved in science and technology fields. Recommended for special libraries active in these areas, as well as large public libraries and academic libraries with science or technology oriented curricula. Smaller libraries could manage with *Books in Print* and *Subject Guide* only. *(Nov. 1, 1973, p.249)*

Selective Guide to Materials for Mental Health and Family Life Education. 1973 ed. Compiled by the Mental Health Materials Center. Northfield, IL, Perennial Education, Inc., P. O. Box 236, 1825 Willow Road, [c1972]. xiii, 841p. softbound volume, $35; previously and until June 30, 1973 available in two-volume loose-leaf binders, $150, from Mental Health Materials Center, 419 Park Ave. South, N.Y. 10016.

This is a review of the new one-volume

edition of *Selective Guide to Materials for Mental Health and Family Life Education.* The work is also available in a two-volume loose-leaf edition.

Established in New York City in 1953, the Mental Health Materials Center (MHMC), a nonprofit educational agency headed by Alex Sareyan, is committed to promoting the effective dissemination and utilization of educational materials based on soundly conceived accepted mental health principles. This objective is achieved through searching and screening educational and training aids in the form of films, tapes, plays, filmstrips, government documents, pamphlets, and other ephemeral materials by Information Resources Center, a division of MHMC. Approximately 52 specialists in subject areas related to mental health scrutinized the materials according to established criteria. Those which met their standards are listed as "IRC Recommends" in the *Selective Guide to Materials.*

The new one-volume *Selective Guide* consists of over 400 recommendations in 4 major subject areas with 21 subdivisions. Preceding the actual entries is prefatory material defining the scope and use, guidelines for ordering the items, as well as methods of utilizing the pamphlets and films in mental health and family life education programs.

The first section, "Child Growth and Development," covers childhood, infancy, early and middle childhood, preadolescence, and adolescence. The second section, "Adults," spans the young adult and college student, marriage and family, sex education, maturity, and aging. The third division, "Problem Areas," encompasses alcohol and drug abuse, crime, mental illness and retardation, physical handicaps, and suicide prevention. The final subject area, "Community Mental Health Programs and Resources," provides materials concerning philosophy, education, and techniques for those involved in mental health and family education programs. The second half of the last section covers community resources and services. Each section of entries is preceded by a page captioned with the subject of that section. *See also* references are provided to relevant subject areas and the individual entries by page and title.

Within each of the subject areas, the recommendations are arranged alphabetically by title. The recommended items have been selected from over 1,000 educational materials evaluated annually. The criteria used in assessing the materials include authoritativeness, balance of presentation, use in education program, bias, appropriateness for intended audience, worthiness of subject matter, and currency and accuracy of information.

The information provided for each recommended title follows a uniform outline throughout the *Selective Guide.* A bulletin number and date appear in the upper right hand corner of each entry. The number and date refer to an MHMC identification symbol and the date when reviewed or published. Below the heading "IRC Recommends," the title appears in boldface in the center of the page. Neatly arranged in two columns per page, the review then repeats the title with full bibliographic information, varying according to type of material, e.g., film—running time, color, size, date, and producer. The next information is a Summary, usually an abstract, indicating the principal points developed and the primary purpose of the item. Thirdly, the "Evaluation" aims at pointing out assets and limitations, as well as unusual features of the material. A brief statement as to audience and use is the next feature. "Ordering Information" provides detailed data on how to obtain the item, including addresses, price, and special discount offers. At the bottom of each page is the "Primary Audience," the specific group for which the producer intended the item. Beneath this appears "Readily Understood By," referring to the comprehensibility of the item. This statement usually consists of a level of educational attainment and is based solely on the reviewer's judgment. "Category" is the last standard designation on each review. It is here that the IRC subject heading(s) are assigned. All of the above data are printed on one page, facilitating instant scanning.

The second page of each recommended title, the verso, contains added information. This may consist of a reproduction of the table of contents, a summary of the item's theme, questions for discussion, notes on the author, or short bibliographies.

Ample information is provided for the careful selecting of materials to serve all types of groups with special interests in the fields of mental health and family life. The ordering directions are adequate and easy to follow, and most items are of minimal cost.

The number of materials recommended amounts to more than 240 booklets, pamphlets, handbooks, and other printed matter, with the remaining 150 or so being films, plays, tapes, and slides. The materials range in date from 1948 to 1971. The majority of items appear to have been produced in the mid-1960s. This new edition of the *Selective Guide* adds over 60 previously unlisted titles and deletes items no longer readily available. Replacements of more recent materials have also been included. Over 200 of the items retained from earlier loose-leaf editions have been revised and updated. Mention has been made of plans for periodical revisions in the future.

Selections reflect trends of current interest in health topics and sociological problems. The largest number of entries occurs under "Drug use and abuse"-48, while the fewest items are under "Middle childhood (7 to 9 years)"-4.

The volume concludes with a title index arranged alphabetically. After each title, the page on which the review appears is listed. Reviews which cover more than one title are indexed under each individual title.

While other sources to educational materials exist, such as *Educator's Guide to Free Health, Physical Education and Recreation Materials*, none goes into as much depth in coverage as does the *Selective Guide*. *Educator's Guide* is comprised merely of short annotations as compared with the more extensive reviews of the latter. The same subject coverage was not found in any other comprehensive one-volume other than in the *Selective Guide*.

While *Educator's Guide* provides a greater quantity of materials, the brief annotations (10 to 70 words) are merely descriptive as compared to the more comprehensive and critical entries of the *Selective Guide*. The materials provided in the former are exclusively free items, while *Selective Guide* chooses its entries without monetary limitation. Thus, *Selective Guide* selects items from a number of available materials.

The softbound volume is bound in heavy coated stock. The pages lie flat when open. However, the durability of the volume is questionable due to its bulk and weight. The paper is offset uncoated finish. The appearance is neat, and the text is legible.

Intended for health educators, teachers, and social workers, *Selective Guide to Materials for Mental Health and Family Life Education* adequately fulfills its function. With its uniformity of entry, concise presentation of information, and depth of subject coverage, it is a handy tool for finding and using recommended, available publications and other educational materials in the mental health and family living fields. Libraries serving clientele interested in community education, as well as public libraries with audiovisual collections, will find it useful. Recommended to be used with other tools such as *Educator's Guide*. *(May 15, 1973, p.870)*

Sources and Documents of United States Constitutions. v.1 of 10v. Edited and annotated by William F. Swindler, Dobbs Ferry, NY, Oceana Publications, 1973- . buckram $35. ISBN 0-379-16175-3 (Series); 0-379-16176-1 (v.1).

The first collection of American state constitutions was published in French in 1778 for a European public. Other collections of fundamental sources in English or French soon followed; several of these were sponsored by the American Congress. Almost a century later, in 1877, the Library of Congress published Benjamin Perly Poore's standard two-

.volume edition of historical documents, entitled *Federal and State Constitutions, Colonial Charters and Other Organic Laws of the United States.* Poore's collection was superseded in 1909 by a seven-volume set prepared for Congress by Professor Francis Newton Thorpe of the University of Pennsylvania. His edition remains the standard reference in this field, although it is now sadly out of date and out of print.

The editor of *Sources and Documents,* a projected ten-volume set, is William Finley Swindler, a Professor of Law at the College of William and Mary, who has written extensively on law and journalism. Professor Swindler points out in his Preface that all of these documents have been reproduced from the best available primary sources although some of them were originally published under "primitive frontier conditions." His commentary has been based on his own legal research as well as the advice and judgments of numerous archivists, historians, scholars, and public officials. Occasional gaps between his collection and the Columbia University collection which is supposed to contain the latest only, will occur, Professor Swindler concedes, whenever a state adopts a new constitution but "it is believed that on the whole these two collections will complement each other by this editorial plan."

The Preface to *Sources and Documents* indicates that the present collection has been planned to correlate with the three loose-leaf volumes of contemporary state constitutions and their amendments, *Constitutions of the United States, National and State* (see *The Booklist and Subscription Books Bulletin,* March 1, 1963), compiled by the Legislative Drafting Research Fund of Columbia University and published by Oceana. Edited by Professor Shirly Abrahamson of the University of Wisconsin, this latter work consists of the latest texts of each state constitution with all the amendments to date.

For each state covered in this volume the editors of *Sources and Documents* have included in this order (1) one or more tables summarizing the historical development of its present constitution (2) a brief note on the early legal history of the state (3) a brief introduction to each of the documents that are reproduced here (4) editorial comments intended to clarify the meaning of a given document (5) the typographic treatment of each item (6) a selected bibliography of both primary and secondary sources on the constitutional history of each state, and (7) an index digest of the constitutions which covers such diverse topics as courts, education, militia, and miscegenation.

The first of the ten volumes projected in the *Sources and Documents* series covers five states—Alabama, Alaska, Arizona, Arkansas, and California. The number of fundamental sources reprinted here ranges from 14 for Alabama to 5 for California. They retain the typography of the original documents including foreign language texts of treaties such as for Alaska the Treaty of Cession, March 30, 1867 which is printed in French and English. References are frequently made to previous editions of American state constitutions, to the *Territorial Papers of the United States,* and to microfilms of Early State Records in the Library of Congress.

The format of this set is excellent. The margins are sufficiently wide to permit rebinding, the print is clear, and the paper is acid free antique vellum. The binding is red library buckram with the first and last signatures strongly reinforced. The volume title is printed in gold letters on a blue background.

Sources and Documents of United States Constitutions has been prepared with careful, meticulous scholarship. Incorporating all these important documents in one place is highly commendable. In keeping with the Committee's policy, final evaluation of the set is withheld until all volumes are complete.

(June 15, 1974, p.1112)

The Standard Directory of Newsletters. 1st ed. New York, Oxbridge Publishing Co., Inc., 150 E. 52 St., 1972. 210p. 26cm. buckram $20.

This directory identifies almost 4,300 newsletters current at the time of its publication. Information is grouped in over 200 subject categories and includes for each newsletter: title of the newsletter, publishing house with address and telephone number, editor's name, frequency, publisher's name, name of the advertising director, description of editorial content and scope, year founded, subscription rates, single copy price, qualifications for receiving publication, circulation, advertising rates, auditing organization, and publication address. A descriptive annotation indicating the scope, purpose, and content is supplied for most of the newsletters listed. A 14-page Cross-Index to Subjects is a useful section of the directory.

A news release from the publisher announces that for "the first time there is a comprehensive reference source available for newsletter information." *The Standard Directory* may be comprehensive by its own definition, but it certainly is not the first source.

A special feature of *The Standard Directory* is the 31-page section excerpted from *The Newsletter on Newsletters* (New York: Hudson Associates, 1968-   ) which details the value of newsletters, outlines results which can benefit newsletter publishers, discusses format, printing, distribution techniques, and editorial practices. This section is excellent and should be of special interest to present and potential newsletter editors and publishers.

For the purposes of this book, the editors have qualified the definition of newsletter ("an 8½ x 11 four-page folder") to include "those services that sell by subscription and usually by mail" and those periodic publications in which advertising is notably absent. Since information was compiled from questionnaires sent to newsletter publishers, fullness of the bibliographic entries varies according to the data received. There is no indication that the compilers collected or reviewed the newsletters included. The basis for inclusion is not stated.

House organs and newsletters published by businesses, associations, educational institutions (including elementary and secondary schools), foundations, trade organizations, government agencies, libraries, and other professional groups are shown. Sample subjects listed are accounting, advertising and marketing, atomic and nuclear energy, botany, dance, ecology, engineering, golf, home economics, law, management, mining and minerals, music and music trades, packaging, printing, produce, skiing, snowmobiling, taxes, traffic and transportation, vending machines, unidentified flying objects, waste and scrap, women's liberation, youth, and zoology. There is some discrepancy between the plan for subjects and their execution, since snowmobiling, vending machines, and unidentified flying objects are listed with an asterisk meaning "subject is not in the directory."

Although Gale Research Company published *National Directory of Newsletters and Reporting Services* in 1966, the directory under review is the only publication providing information about newsletters during the early 1970s. *The Standard Directory* is more comprehensive also.

Coverage of *The Standard Directory* is almost entirely limited to English-language newsletters published in the United States and Canada. Six staff members for the directory are listed on the verso of the title page.

The double-column Cross-Index to Subjects employs both *see* and *see also* references. The effectiveness of the main portion of the work, Listings by Subject Classifications, is diminished by format. Newsletters are listed alphabetically by title under subject categories. A three-digit code is assigned to the subjects which are arranged alphabetically. *See also* references to subjects and their codes follow immediately after the main subject entry. Placement of the main subject entries makes it difficult to use the Cross-Index. Entries are indented (not necessarily centered) in the double-column listings. No special typeface or underlining is used to set off the subject guides. More difficulty arises from the fact that the subject headings are listed one time only. There are no running heads to indicate continued listings under subject or category. For example, the entries for 018, Banking & Finance, run for 18 pages. The inconspicuous placement of the main subjects requires constant referral to the Table of Contents to determine the beginning page for a particular subject.

Further frustration occurs when using the Index, an alphabetical listing by title of newsletters. A careful reading of On the Use of This Directory is necessary to realize that reference is to the number (186, 002, 098A) subject code rather than to a page; the Index gives no explanation for its use. Lack of running heads in the main section requires a "flip-the-pages" approach to locating the coded subject shown in the Index. Newsletters which qualify under more than one subject are given repeated entries in the Index. There is no way of judging multiple listings for the same title—they may represent various placements of a single newsletter or they may be newsletters with identical titles published by different agencies. A unique identifier or an entry number is needed to facilitate use of this directory.

The directory is uneven in the treatment of individual titles. A newsletter which appears under several subjects may be described differently under each heading. The user might get one impression from one entry and another description from another entry. Of the five titles appearing in the Unclassified Section, four are listed and classified in the Index or Addendum.

Use of this important work is marred by poor format. Introductory sections use different type styles (two-column, offset copy, unjustified right margins followed by type-set material in very small size followed by full-column excerpts from *The Newsletter on Newsletters*). The two-page section On the Use of This Directory is presented clearly. Aesthetic considerations are less important than the difficult-to-use format in the body of the work. Format used throughout the book requires unnecessary persistence to find the desired information. The book is well bound and has good quality paper. It lies flat when open and has the full title on the spine.

The overall usefulness and comprehensiveness of *The Standard Directory of Newsletters* outweighs its confusing format and other faults. The directory is recommended as a useful reference tool for locating information on the constantly changing field of newsletters.

(Dec. 1, 1973, p.348)

Statutory History of the United States.
Bernard Schwartz, ed. 3v. in 4. New York, Chelsea House Publishers in association with McGraw-Hill Book Co., [c1970]. 24cm. buckram $120; sold separately: v.1, *Civil Rights,* ed. by Bernard Schwartz (in two parts), $55; v.2, *Labor Organization,* ed. by Robert F. Koretz, $40; v.3, *Income Security,* ed. by Roger B. Stevens, $40.

Statutory History of the United States is the first edition of what the publishers hope will become an open-end series covering the principal subjects of federal legislation. The Preface announces that each volume will present with commentary, the text and legislative history of the important statutes on the subject covered. The legislative history will include extracts from Presidential messages, congressional debates, and committee hearings and reports. Major U.S. Supreme Court decisions which bear upon the history of the statutes will also be given. The series will thus provide legislative materials which are not available in many libraries.

The editor of the series is Bernard Schwartz, Webb Professor of Law at New York University, who is well-known for his treatise on administrative law and his commentaries on the Supreme Court. Professor Schwartz points out in his Preface that it was not until modern times that legislation began to play the positive role in ordering society to which we are accustomed today. Now, however, it is the essential government instrument used to regulate the economic, social, and political system. "The primary place of legislation in the governmental system has made it appropriate to publish the *Statutory History."*

Civil Rights, the first of the three volumes of the series now published, is edited by Professor Schwartz. Part I begins with an introductory essay entitled "Equality and the Constitution." This is followed by a commentary on the Thirteenth Amendment, the text of the amendment, and its legislative history.

The Civil Rights Act of 1865, the Fourteenth and Fifteenth Amendments, the civil rights legislation of the Reconstruction era, and the 1894 act repealing the voting rights legislation are presented in a similar manner. Part II, bound separately, covers the legislative history of the civil rights legislation of the 1950s and 60s ending with the Civil Rights Act of 1968. Judicial decisions interpreting the legislation are included where appropriate. The legislative history of the older statutes is made up almost entirely of extracts from congressional debates. In the last century, Professor Schwartz says, the speeches in Congress gave a better understanding of the issues, but since that time the caliber of congressional debate has declined drastically. For the more recent legislation, committee reports are given greater emphasis, because of the ever-increasing resort by courts to legislative history as an aid in interpreting legislation. As a result, congressional committees now prepare reports which explain in detail the provisions of bills they report.

The second volume of the series, *Labor Organization,* is edited by Robert F. Koretz, professor of law at Syracuse University, who teaches courses in labor law. This volume concerns the principal statutes involving trade unionism and collective bargaining, and covers the Railway Labor Act of 1926, the Norris-La Guardia Anti-Injunction Act, the Wagner Act, the Fair Labor Standards Act, the Taft-Hartley Act, and the Landrum-Griffin Act. Commentary, text, legislative history, and court decisions are presented for each.

Roger B. Stevens of the Yale Law School faculty edited the third volume in the series, *Income Security.* Among the courses which Professor Stevens teaches is one entitled Social Legislation. He explains in his Preface that he has narrowed the scope of his subject, income security, to legislation which provides cash benefits, i.e., social security. As a result this volume is concerned almost entirely with the various titles of the much amended Social Security Act, including those providing for old-age, survivors, disability, and health insurance; grants-in-aid under public assistance; and unemployment compensation.

This presentation is to some extent in narrative style. The editor has "let documents speak for themselves," and a running commentary has been used for linkage. The first section, "Pre-New Deal Developments," gives the background for the legislative history of the Social Security Act of 1935, which follows. The legislative history of the amendments to the Act is arranged by Presidential administrations with a section for each President from Franklin D. Roosevelt through Lyndon B. Johnson. The volume ends with a brief section entitled "Appendix: The Nixon Program 1969" which documents developments concerning income security during that year.

These three volumes provide legislative histories which will be useful, particularly, to high school and college students who need primary materials for the history and interpretation of legislation. Libraries with large collections of U.S. government documents will already have the complete text of many of the documents cited. But the accessibility of the most significant parts of these documents which appear in these volumes makes the set useful even in these libraries.

The editors have had to select from a mass of material and, as Professor Schwartz points out, there is danger of arbitrary inclusion and exclusion in such a process, and all will not agree with the editors' choice. While the editors see legislation as an instrument of advance, they have been careful to include selections which present opposing views.

Each volume of *Statutory History* series has a detailed Table of Contents and an Index containing the names of individuals, agencies, and acts, as well as topics. Some *see* and *see also* references are included. The sample of the indexes checked for accuracy revealed no errors. Unfortunately, in the *Civil Rights* and *Labor Organization* volumes, neither the page number nor the report number has been included in the citations to the congressional material excerpted. Complete citations would be useful for those interested in locating the complete texts in the original documents.

There is no legislative history series comparable to *Statutory History*. Union lists of legislative histories compiled by librarians in the Washington area have been published by the Law Librarians' Society of the District of Columbia since 1950. Most of these legislative histories are available in microform beginning with selected legislation of the 82d Congress (1951-52), but are sold only on an annual basis. A few printed legislative histories have been published by government agencies and commercial publishers. Legislative histories of this type are unedited and are intended for attorneys, government officials, and others who require the complete text of the relevant documents for exhaustive research. The *Statutory History* series would not, of course, suffice for such an audience.

The format of the set is satisfactory. The binding and paper are sturdy enough to withstand considerable use. The margins are wide enough to permit rebinding. The print is clear, and variations in typeface are used to good effect. The volumes are easily distinguished. Each is bound in a different color of buckram with the volume title as well as the series title printed on the spine in large letters.

Statutory History of the United States has been prepared by scholars who have presented the background and purpose of certain significant legislation by the use of congressional and judicial documents not available in many libraries. The convenience of having this well selected documentary material brought together makes the set especially useful. Purchase is recommended to high school, college, and public libraries.

(May 15, 1973, p.871)

Studio Dictionary of Design & Decoration. [Editor: Robert Harling]. New York, The Viking Pr., [c1973]. 539p. illus. 29cm. $28.50; to schools and libraries, 25 percent discount. SBN 67-68011-7.

A prefatory statement to *Studio Dictionary of Design and Decoration* calls it essentially a journalistic enterprise growing out of the post World War II popular interest in subjects which prior to the war had been considered the realm of "specialists and dilettantes." The dictionary defines, illustrates, and discusses terminology and styles of architecture, interior design, furniture, and decorative and applied art. Biographical entries give concise information about the work of major architects and designers. Editor Robert Harling is a prolific author and is editor of the British *House and Garden*, in which much of the dictionary under review appeared in serial form between 1962 and 1971. The dictionary claims to represent a "vastly revised and extended" publication of the periodical material.

The dictionary emphasizes the architecture, design, and decorative arts of Europe and the United States, ranging in time from ancient Egypt to modern times, industrial buildings, and plastic furniture and including articles on Japanese architecture, garden design, and interior design. It combines in one volume information which is available, sometimes in more detail, in encyclopedias and dictionaries of architecture, antiques, interior design, furniture, and crafts. The more than 2,000 alphabetically arranged entries vary from brief ones of 16 words like *overstuffed furniture* to relatively long ones of 7 pages on such subjects as German architecture. No clear editorial statement on scope is made, but such arts as aquatint, lithography, painting, and engraving fall outside the compass of the dictionary.

The material is accurate; it is summarized concisely in a very readable style. Only one serious spelling error was noted: Sir John Vanbrugh's name is spelled correctly in the text, but is misspelled in each of the five picture captions. Some questions, as the following, can be raised, but are minor to the overall coverage. The entry *Oak* might well mention the prevalence in the United States of oak furniture in the late nineteenth and early twentieth century. It is debatable that Italy leads the field in contemporary lamp design. The definition of *crochet* should mention thread as well as yarn. The logic of the *see* reference from doorstops to paperweights is not entirely evident. Only the cheap Parson's tables are made of plastic; the early ones and the fine ones today are of good woods and sometimes painted or otherwise decoratively finished.

Although there is no editorial statement about choice or structure of cross-references, four types are provided: *see* references, *see also* references, *q.v.* references, and *see* references in the body of articles. The cross-references are often used inconsistently.

The editors claim to have avoided conventional photographs and frequently-seen drawings. Three to twelve illustrations are positioned to a page; they are black-and-white photographs or drawings and are straightforward and large enough generally to be clear in detail. They are well-integrated with the text except that the full-page photographs which introduce each letter of the alphabet sometimes create strange juxtapositions. The page of acknowledgments for the illustrations gives special thanks to the Victoria & Albert Museum, The National Monuments Record, Christies, Sothebys, and Spinks.

Both the general articles and the specific entries are illustrated. For instance, *Clock* has six illustrations (a long-case clock, a box watch movement, a Louis XIV clock, a chronometer, a modern battery clock, and an iron mantel clock). Where there are separate entries for particular types of clocks, each type is illustrated, e.g., *Act of Parliament Clock, Cartel Clock,* and *Bracket Clock.* Another clock picture illustrates the article *Victorian,* and the face of a clock is shown with the article *Dial.* There is no cross-reference between the entries. The practice of illustrating both types of entries is helpful to the user but also has its drawbacks. For example, it results in the scattering of illustrations of Wedgwood pottery among *Black Basalt Ware*; *Wedgwood, Josiah*; *English Pottery; Cup; Earthenware;* and *Jasperware.* No cross-references link these illustrations. This is similarly true of those of all works, e.g., chairs, desks, bridges, and their designers. The editors have usually been quite successful in avoiding depicting the same work twice, although the Thonet rocker, the Clifton Suspension Bridge, and Robert Heritage's Oregon chair each appear twice under different entries.

The volume is sturdily bound in cloth and lies flat when opened. The inner margins are each about one-half inch wide, and many of the illustrations bleed to the edges of the pages. The print is small but readable; the illustrations are clearly reproduced; the paper is nonglare.

Studio Dictionary of Design and Decoration is an accurate, well-illustrated single volume source of information on European and United States design and architecture. Despite its cross-reference shortcomings it will be useful to public library reference departments needing an additional source of such information.   *(May 15, 1974, p.1013)*

A Supplement to the Oxford English Dictionary. v.1, A-G. Edited by R. W. Burchfield. Oxford, Clarendon Press, 1972. xxiii, 1331p. 31cm. buckram $50.

A Supplement to the Oxford English Dictionary, Volume I, A-G contains over 17,000 main entries and is the first of three supplements planned to treat the vocabulary which came into use during the publication of *Oxford English Dictionary,* 1884-1928, together with accessions to the English language in Britain and abroad from 1928 to the present day. The remaining two volumes, H-P and Q-Z, are planned for publication at intervals of not more than three years. The three together will replace the one-volume *1933 Supplement to Oxford English Dictionary.*

Revision of the *1933 Supplement* was planned by Oxford Press immediately following World War II and R. W. Burchfield was appointed editor for the new work in July 1957. Burchfield, a graduate of Oxford University, assisted the late C. T. Onions and G. W. S. Friedrichsen with the preparation of *Oxford Dictionary of English Etymology* and is currently in charge of the lexicographical side of the various Oxford dictionaries at the Clarendon Press. Among the lexicographers and linguists making valuable contributions to the present work are Dr. Onions and Dr. Friedrichsen, both of the original *Oxford English Dictionary* staff; Raven I. McDavid, Jr., American linguist at the University of Chicago and editor of the *Linguistic Atlas of the U.S. and Canada;* Norman Davis, Merton Professor of English Language and Literature, Oxford; Clarence Barnhart, American lexicographer; and Philip B. Gove and his associates at G. C. Merriam Co. A total of 87 contributors of quotations upon which *Supplement . . . A-G* is based, and 74 outside consultants for specialized words and subjects are noted in the introductory pages. The editorial staff includes graduates in scientific subjects.

Basically, the aim of the parent *Oxford English Dictionary,* or as it was originally known, *A New English Dictionary on Historical Principles,* is continued in the current revision: "to present in alphabetical series the words that have formed the English vocabulary from the time of the earliest records down to the present day, with all the relevant facts concerning their form, sense-history, pronunciation, and etymology. It embraces not only the standard language of literature and conversation, whether current at the moment, or obsolete, or archaic, but also the main technical vocabulary, and a large measure of dialectal usage and slang."

Preparation of a dictionary on historical principles involves reading and collecting quotations from many sources: since 1957 about 1½ million quotations have been assembled for the 50,000 main words to be included in the projected three-volume supplement. Although conversational English, slang, and even formerly unprintable sexually-oriented words are discussed with supporting evidence, this evidence is supplied only by written language sources, whether they be novels, letters, newspapers, or "underground" periodicals; consequently, currency of usage is to some extent sacrificed in this kind of descriptive dictionary. In spite of this limitation, numerous illustrative quotations from the late 1960s and the 1970s are found in *Supplement . . . A-G*. The publisher states that copy for the present volume was sent to press in installments, and that one result of this method of sending copy "is that the earlier letters of the Supplement are not quite as up to date as the later ones." First copy went to press May 1965, and the final installment of the letter "G" was sent in May 1971.

Supplement . . . A-G, in preparation for 15 years, evidences scholarly research and good editing. Nearly all the material in the *1933 Supplement* has been retained, though in revised form. For the present volume "The sources included all important literary works (in both prose and verse) of the period, a wide range of scientific books and journals, and large numbers of newspapers and periodicals, ranging from *The Times* to those publications that emanate from the so-called 'underground.' Numerous works containing multiple lexicographical information, for example, articles in *American Speech* and in *Notes and Queries* and the whole of Eric Partridge's *Dictionary of Slang,* were also converted into the form of dictionary slips." Central vocabulary of the major academic subjects has been gathered from textbooks and journals. The written English of regions such as Australia, South Africa, and India has been treated along with that of Britain, the United States, and Canada.

Main words are alphabetized letter by letter. For new words information includes pronunciations; syllabication; variant current spellings; form history —changes in languages, spellings, inflection, etc.; part of speech identification; subject, regional, or stylistic labels if pertinent; meanings in order of historical development; and illustrative quotations in chronological order for each meaning. Differing word senses with their accompanying illustrative quotations are both outlined and paragraphed on the page to aid clarity. Each quotation's source is indicated in abbreviated form; an extensive Bibliography of works cited is planned for the Q-Z volume.

Combination words when truly related to main words are treated in their proper grammatical categories at the end of main entries; when combinations have their own specialized development, they appear as main words themselves in proper alphabetical order. *Breaststroke, crash-helmet, door-casing* are examples of the former, and *breastwork, crashworthiness,* and *dooryard* are examples of the latter.

Pronunciation for new words is indicated by a rather elaborate system of diacritical marks. A Key to Pronunciation appears on page xi and is found nowhere else in the volume. Pronunciations follow those used in the *Oxford English Dictionary* and are labeled in this supplement as those found in the educated speech of southern England.

Spelling is British-oriented as evidenced by *colour* and *day labour,* but *see* references to variant spellings and forms are common. *Supplement . . . A-G,* in contrast to *Oxford English Dictionary,* capitalizes only words commonly capitalized, i.e., those derived from names of persons or places. The many *see* references and *variant of* references to related main words broaden the dictionary's use considerably.

Since the work under consideration is a revision as well as a supplement, the amount of information for particular entries varies greatly—from a single line to six to twelve columns for common words like *air, come, fly,* and *go.* Occasionally, there is a brief correction to be noted in the original *Oxford English Dictionary.* Frequently, older words have new uses; these are always entered with the same outline pattern so that a clear relationship to the total word history is insured. Meanings reaching obsolescence or obsolete words revived are also indicated. Illustrative citations follow for each word use. Sometimes earlier examples or later examples for previously researched uses are inserted. Occasionally quotations appear where none were available for the *Oxford English Dictionary.*

The range of vocabulary described in *Supplement . . . A-G* may be illustrated in several ways. Enrichment of the English language by the adoption of words from various countries and cultures can be seen by such new words as *bonsai, daiquiri, dashiki, denuclearize, boing, corgi, fuzz* (for police), and *golem.*

Supplement . . . A-G's coverage of the central vocabulary of the academic world and individual scientific disciplines can be shown by a sampling. Counting the broad subject labels assigned to word uses on 24 pages scattered throughout the volume revealed 56 labels, of which 64 percent were for various fields of science and technology. Also, just two pages illustrate such diverse sources of quotations as the following: *Globe Magazine,* 1958; *Inorganic Chemistry,* 1965; Dylan Thomas, *Letters,* (1966); A. Koestler, *Encounter,* 1953; *Chambers' Techn. Dict.,* 1940; A. Nisbett, *Technique Sound Studio,* 1962; A. C. English, *Dict. of Psychological Terms,* 1958; *Times,* 1970; C. F. Hockett, *Internat. Jrnl. Amer. Linguistics,* 1947; *Economist,* 1964; *Jazz Scene,* 1959; *Encycl. Canadiana,* 1958; E. Chambers, *Photolitho-Offset,* 1967; *Nature,* 1970; *Aeroplane,* 1947; I. M. Copi, *Introd. Logic,* 1953; and W. Faulkner, *Fable* 1954.

First appearance of word uses is another indicator of broad coverage: older uses added to this supplement include *ground,* 1400; *abbe,* 1530; *feud,* 1673; *backwoods,* 1709; and *crossroad,* 1795. Examples of new words are *go-kart,* 1959; *biogenesis,* 1960; *cartridge* (cassette), 1960; *decoupage,* 1960; *condominium,* 1962; *grand tour* (for planetary travel), 1970; and *frag,* 1971.

Although name words and place words are not treated separately in this dictionary, their numbers and importance in modern English should be mentioned since nearly every page has at least one word with this origin. The editors provide clear precise definitions often with real reference value. Some easily-found examples are the *Argyll Robertson* eye condition, *Benelux* customs union, *Dewar* flask, *Darjeeling* tea, *Chien Lung* art, *Chipsham* limestone, *Fermi* surface, *Coriolis* effect, *Biafran, expo,* and *Goldwaterism.* None of the above are found in the *1933 Supplement.*

Supplement . . . A-G contains 23 pages of preparatory material. In addition to listing the Editorial Staff, Contributors, Outside Consultants, Key to Abbreviations, Signs, etc., the introductory section explains basic editorial policy, including practices for identifying sources and the handling of scientific terms and proprietary names.

The volume is sturdily bound in dark blue Buckram with easily-read gold lettering on the spine. Apparently the completed three-volume supplement will match the *Oxford English Dictionary* 1961 reprint in size and appearance. The volume lies flat when open. The text is printed three columns per page in eight and six point type with boldface and italics used judiciously to aid readability. All main words and dates for citations are in boldface. Alphabetical guide words are found at the top of each page. The paper is white with a dull finish and is heavy enough to avoid show-through and to prevent easily torn pages. Inner margins measure ¾-inch, so that rebinding after heavy use is possible.

Etymologists, linguists, and grammarians particularly, and also scholars and students in other major fields of knowledge, will find important information in this revised *Oxford English Dictionary*. It provides an adequate record of English vocabulary, whenever, wherever, or however used. In accordance with Committee policy, final evaluation is withheld until the entire set is available for examination. *(May 1, 1973, p.818)*

Tapestry and Embroidery in the Collection of the National Palace Museum. 2v. text and 2v. plates, boxed. Tokyo, Gakken Co., Ltd. 1973; distributed in U.S. by Takahasi and Associates, Inc., 971 Sonora Road, Costa Mesa, CA 92626. 14"x18" and 10"x18". cloth $275.

These are the first two volumes of a projected fifteen-volume set, each volume of which will treat one aspect of the collection of the National Palace Museum in Taipeh, Taiwan. The present set consists of two large volumes of plates, measuring 14 by 18 inches each accompanied by a smaller volume of descriptive text in Chinese containing Japanese and English translation and also small black-and-white photographs. Between each of the two parts which make up a unit, a complete catalog is presented of the holdings of the National Palace Museum in each of the two art forms. The large volume on tapestry contains 95 colored plates representing 66 items, while the small text volume supplements these with additional black-and-white photographs bringing the total to 175 tapestries, which are, according to the introductory essay, the total tapestry holdings. Likewise, the Museum's two volumes on embroidery present 39 embroideries in color and the remaining 140 in the collection in black and white. The volumes are not numbered, but evidently the pair on tapestry may be considered volume I as it contains a more complete title page which says that the editing is done by the National Palace Museum. Also in this volume are a table of Chinese ruling dynasties and their dates, a preface signed by Wang Yun-wu, Chairman of the board of the National Palace Museum, and a foreword signed by Dr. Chiang Futsung, Director of the Museum.

Each of the smaller volumes contains an unsigned essay on the history of the art form represented followed by a list and detailed descriptive notes on each of the colored plates. The section of small but very clear black-and-white plates follows to complete the collection, but these photographs do not have descriptive notes, only titles and sizes being given. The English title page and texts are at the front of the volume by Occidental standards, but this is actually the back of the volume to an Oriental. Numbers accompanying the photographs run backward in oriental fashion as they do in the large volumes also.

The colored plates are so beautiful they defy description. For many of them, there are additional detail views which are the actual size of the original so that stitches can easily be identified in the embroideries and the size of the weave measured in the tapestries. The delicacy of color is particularly delightful in the Sung dynasty tapestries which often have landscape subjects resembling those of Sung painting. These paintings are usually monochromatic and it comes as a particularly charming surprise to see them blossom into elegant and delicate color in the tapestries. A few of the colored plates are duplicated in the small black-and-white photographs, usually because the whole work is not shown in the colorplate, or perhaps because some calligraphy has been left off. No reference to the black-and-white copy is made in the detailed note on the colored plate in the text volume. Except for the list of colored plates in each text volume, there is no index of any kind in English, so that individual plates can only be found by searching.

The books are well bound in a linen-like textile, the tapestry volumes in orange and the embroidery set in plum. The large volumes are difficult to handle. All four are boxed together in a strong and handsome Oriental box covered with the orange linen.

These beautiful volumes are extremely expensive—$275 for the first two of the projected set, and for all their visual appeal, their use is certainly limited to experts. Museum libraries or public and university libraries having very large art departments may want them, or perhaps special oriental collections and collectors may be interested. Since this is the first part of a large set, no recommendation for *Tapestry and Embroidery in the Collection of the National Palace Museum* can be made at this time. *(June 15, 1974, p.1113)*

Taylor's Encyclopedia of Government Officials: Federal and State. By John Clements. v.IV, 1973-1974, 2d ed. Dallas, Political Research, Inc., 1973. 213p. illus. 31cm. sturdite fabric C grade $90 for two-year subscription, including biennial volume, supplements, magazines, and research service; to schools and non-profit libraries, $75.

Beginning with instructions for addressing lawmakers and ending with information on the Federal judiciary, *Taylor's Encyclopedia of Government Officials* provides a wealth of federal and state political facts and statistics and information on personalities.

In 1967 Political Research published the first volume (1967-1968) of the encyclopedia in response to a need for a consolidated presentation of facts on American federal and state government. The quarterly cumulative supplements to the encyclopedia led Political Research to claim to be the only publisher of its kind capable of making subscribers aware of every consequential change in federal or state government. Concurrent with publication of volume II, 1969-1970, a toll-free telephone reference service became a part of the subscription. With the next volume, a periodical, *World of Politics*, was added to the subscription program. Currently, a subscription includes the bound biennial volume, quarterly supplements, phone service, *World of Politics*, and a chart of state officials.

Taylor's covers federal officials, state officials, and delegates to the 1972 Democratic and Republican Conventions.

Each branch of the federal government is covered. The section on the Executive includes U.S. emblems, the current and former presidents and vice-presidents, current cabinet members, and lists of executive department officials and their titles.

An organization chart of the 93d Congress highlights its leaders. Senate and House standing committees and members of each, the Supreme Court justices, U.S. ambassadors and ambassadors to the U.S., a list of the independent agencies, political party officials, and an explanation of the American flag complete the federal section.

The "Roll Call of States," prefaced by color pictures of state flags, contains political summaries for each state: Governor, Lieutenant Governor, U.S. Senators and Congressmen, a list of state senators and representatives, minimal national election statistics, and a map of congressional and state representative districts keyed to elected officials. Other miscellaneous information, e.g., capitol, number of electoral votes, and state supreme court members, is also included.

A page devoted to an historical view of Presidential Elections provides the party affiliation and names of all presidential and vice-presidential candidates since 1788.

A list of delegates to the 1972 National Conventions by party and state contributes to the stated purpose of providing "a treasure of voting history presenting facts and faces on the state and federal level that would otherwise be unbelievably difficult to find."

Realizing that the government, being dynamic, is constantly changing, each biennial bound volume is updated quarterly by supplements containing corrections, additions, and adjustments to the text of *Taylor's Encyclopedia of Government Officials*. Each supplement is cumulative; only the most current need be retained. Data, arranged by page number of the bound volume, should always be consulted for possible changes. To obtain the most current information available, however, one may utilize what is perhaps the most valuable part of the subscription: Political Research guarantees "to accept [telephone] toll charges for anywhere in the continental U.S. when brief instant answers are needed involving the material found in" the work. The publisher offers to provide an answer "to any factual, substantive, non-editorial question concerning U.S. federal or state government, free of charge (with the exception of at cost charges for extensive photocopying)."

Although containing neither a bibliography nor sources of its information, the data presented in the work seem accurate.

Taylor's contains more than 20,000 names and 850 photographs of federal and state officials. The information provided is not nearly as detailed or comprehensive as that found in more established reference works of this genre. Virtually all the information *Taylor's* presents on federal officials can be found in *Congressional Directory, World Almanac*, or the *U.S. Government Organization Manual*, except for the pictures. Similarly, most of the data *Taylor's* provides on states can be located in *The Book of the States* and its supplements, excluding photographs and maps. No other single source, however, could be found which so succinctly presented this much data about both state and federal governmental officials. Further, straightforward presentation makes retrieving data from *Taylor's* uncomplicated. The encyclopedia would be most useful for those seeking non-detailed data about government personalities.

The Index includes subjects but no cross-references, and is composed mostly of names of individuals. The names of national convention delegates and state judicial officials do not appear in the Index.

The thematic state maps of counties and voter districts are of good quality, but are not drawn to the same scale. They are repeated when needed for user convenience. Both black-and-white and color photographs are clear, with only a few being less than sharply reproduced. The layout is pleasing. Inner margins are too narrow for rebinding, but rebinding should be unnecessary since the original seems very sturdy and will be heavily used for only two years. Statistics are current—1970 population and 1972 election figures are used.

Taylor's Encyclopedia of Government Officials is a unique subscription service. It is recommended as an additional source which consolidates and compresses current information on officials in both the federal and state governments. *(July 1, 1974, p.1163)*

Time-Life Encyclopedia of Gardening. By James Underwood Crockett and the editors of Time-Life Books. 7 of 19v. v.1, Annuals; v.2, Roses; v.3, Landscape Gardening; v.4, Lawns and Ground Covers; v.5, Flowering House Plants; v.6, Bulbs; v.7, Evergreens. New York; Time-Life Books, 1971- . library and school ed. dist. by Silver Burdett Co., Morristown, N.J. illus. 29cm. kivar, $6.60 per v.; cloth, $7.60 per v., less 25 percent discount to libraries.

Basic information on gardening is available in a wide variety of sources ranging from inexpensive pamphlets published by the United States Department of Agriculture, through such single-volume encyclopedias as *Wyman's Gardening Encyclopedia* (*Booklist*, Sept. 15, 1971) and *Taylor's Encyclopedia of Gardening* (*Booklist*, July 15, 1961), to multivolume sets. Although designated as an "encyclopedia" the *Time-Life Encyclopedia of Gardening* is actually a series of volumes on gardening, each of which is devoted to a specific group of plants (annuals, bulbs, etc.) or an aspect of gardening (e.g., landscape gardening). Each volume is complete in itself and is entirely independent of the other volumes in the series. The independent character of the individual volumes is further suggested by the omission of volume numbering on the copies distributed by Time-Life Books. Numbers have been added to the spines of volumes in the library and school edition, but these numbers are not printed anywhere within the volumes themselves. Volumes may be purchased separately, and subscribers to the encyclopedia have the privilege of returning volumes which they do not wish to keep.

James Underwood Crockett, a columnist for garden periodicals and author of the monthly bulletin *Flowery Talks*, which is widely distributed through retail florists, is listed as the primary author for each volume. Most of the volumes include a note identifying by name only other individuals who have written portions of the text. Since this note always appears at the beginning of the paragraph which acknowledges the assistance rendered by various individuals and departments of Time, Inc., there is reason to conclude that these persons are probably staff writers for that organization.

General consultants are listed at the beginning of each volume and include such recognized names as Donald Wyman, Horticulturist Emeritus, Arnold Arboretum at Harvard University and author of *Wyman's Gardening Encyclopedia;* Carlton B. Lees, Executive Director, Massachusetts Horticultural Society; and various members of the staff of the Brooklyn Botanic Garden, which publishes a widely known series of booklets on gardening. The volume on annuals also includes a list of regional consultants. While the extent of the consultants' involvement in the project is not indicated in the encyclopedia itself, promotional material distributed by the publisher claims that the text has been checked "with authorities in every state and section of the country to be sure that the information is accurate, up-to-date and keyed to local needs."

Each volume is 160 or 176 pages in length and is organized into three main divisions: the text, an illustrated encyclopedia, and an appendix. The number of pages devoted to each division varies from volume to volume, depending in part on the nature of the subject covered by the volume. The volume *Landscape Gardening* contains only 36 pages of text (not including the "Picture Essays") while the text in the volume *Flowering House Plants* covers 73 pages. (These comparisons are only approximate as they disregard illustrative material included on the text pages). The "Illustrated Encyclopedias" range from 38 pages *(Lawns and Ground Covers)* to 75 pages *(Annuals)*, and the appendixes vary from 7 to 25 pages in length.

The textual portion of each volume is devoted primarily to basic information and covers such topics as planning, selecting plants, soil preparation and planting, basic care (feeding, watering, pruning, mulching), controlling diseases and pests, and propagation. Most volumes also cover additional subjects appropriate to the type of plant treated in the volume; e.g., the chapter "Bringing Oudoor Beauty Indoors" in the volume on annuals and the section on bonsai in the volume on evergreens. Information is presented in a clear, concise style easily comprehended by the nonspecialist and is supplemented by numerous charts and instructional drawings closely related to the text. When a subject is covered briefly in one part of the text but treated in greater detail elsewhere, cross-references direct the reader to the pages providing fuller information.

Interspersed among the chapters in the text sections are "Picture Essays" (two to four per volume) which expand on topics treated in the text (e.g., "A Timetable for Year-Round Bloom" in the volume on bulbs) or present background information related to the subject of the volume (e.g., "The Romance of the Rose" in the volume for *Roses*). While material of the latter type extends the scope of the encyclopedia beyond the limits of "gardening" in the usual sense, its inclusion enhances the appeal of the volumes to gardeners whose interests include the history and lore of plants. The outstanding color photographs, which constitute the principal feature of the "Picture Essays," are accompanied by detailed captions and concise textual introductions. While the selection of photographs for the volume on *Landscape Gardening* tends to convey the impression that landscaping is primarily for the affluent, the textual sections of the volume are oriented toward a somewhat more representative readership.

The "Illustrated Encyclopedia" section of each volume is arranged by botanical name with cross-references from the common English names of the plants covered. (An exception is made in the "Illustrated Encyclopedia of Roses" which, because it is concerned with a single genus, lists the roses under their English names within the nine broad classes into which roses are usually divided). Entries include a description of the plant, information on its range and uses, and instructions for growing. Each entry is accompanied by a watercolor illustration portraying one or more varieties of the species described in the text.

The watercolor illustrations for five of the seven volumes under consideration are the work of Allianora Rosse, identified by the publishers as a specialist in flower painting and staff artist for 16 years for *Flower Grower* magazine. These watercolors are, on the whole, skillfully executed and constitute one of the most attractive features of the volumes in which they appear. With few exceptions the colors are reasonably true to nature, although subtle hues are often lacking. Moreover, the white flowers sometimes do not show up well against the white background on which they are reproduced.

The watercolors in the encyclopedia sections of volume 3 *(Landscape Gardening)* are by Rebecca A. Merrilees and Barbara Wolff, and those in volume 7 *(Evergreens)* are by Rebecca A. Merrilees and John Murphy. While these illustrations usually give a satisfactory visual impression of the trees, shrubs, and plants which they portray, they do not possess the aesthetic interest of the flower paintings previously described. Since the subjects portrayed in these volumes range from groundcovers to trees, the amount of detail included in the illustrations depends largely on the size of the subject. The volume on evergreens provides more satisfactory coverage of detail by including an enlarged picture of an individual spray or blossom as part of the illustration in most cases. Unfortunately, this practice was not followed in the volume on landscape gardening.

The material included in the appendixes varies slightly from volume to volume according to the nature of the subject covered. All volumes except the one on flowering house plants include one or more maps which provide information on climatic conditions in various parts of the United States and Canada. The information included on the maps and in the accompanying text relates especially to the type of plant covered by the particular volume.

The appendixes in all except volume 3 *(Landscape Gardening)* include a chart detailing the salient characteristics of plants included within the scope of the volume. These charts are essentially a rearrangement in tabular form of information included in the "Illustrated Encyclopedia" sections of the respective volumes and cover only the plants and varieties found there. The charts are especially useful for comparing the characteristics of individual plants or for finding plants with a specific characteristic (e.g., shade tolerance). Regrettably, these charts are not easy to read owing to the crowded format utilized in order to fit the material to the width of the page. Location of information on the charts would have been facilitated by allowing for some separation between the vertical columns covering plant characteristics and by the use of a heavy horizontal rule after every fifth or sixth entry in the lists of plants.

The appendixes in the volumes on

bulbs and evergreens include illustrated charts on pests and diseases similar to those found in the text sections of other volumes. The appendix in the volume on roses includes a list of 97 rose gardens in the United States and Canada which are open to the public.

Bibliographies are included in all the volumes under consideration except those for *Annuals* and *Landscape Gardening*. Entries range from 16 to 26 items and are limited to monographic works, many of which are recognized as standard treatments of the subjects which they cover. The bibliographies include an adequate number of items with recent imprints, the most recent being the 1971 edition of *Wyman's Gardening Encyclopedia*.

Each volume of the encyclopedia includes an Index which does not, however, include references to information in other volumes of the series. Nor does the publisher's promotional material give any indication of plans for a general index. However, in view of the essentially independent character of each volume, the lack of a general index is not a serious drawback. Nevertheless, it is necessary to consult two or more indexes in order to locate all the information given on plants covered in more than one volume of the encyclopedia (e.g., plants grown both indoors and outdoors are treated in the volume for *Flowering House Plants* as well as in the appropriate volume on outdoor gardening; many of the plants discussed in the volume for *Landscape Gardening* are also included in the volume for *Evergreens*).

Plants are entered in the indexes under both their botanical and common names, with cross-references from one to the other. Entries under common names refer to the textual sections of the volumes (where common names are employed) while entries under botanical names refer to the "Illustrated Encyclopedia" sections. Consequently, one must usually look in two places in the Index in order to find all the references to a single plant. This method of indexing is somewhat inconvenient; providing complete references under both names, or under one name (preferably the botanical) with a cross-reference from the other, would have been more satisfactory. Entries include plant names appearing on charts except for the charts in the appendixes covering the characteristics of plants. Italicized numerals are used for entries which refer to illustrations.

The arrangement of the text into chapters necessitates frequent use of the Index for locating information on specific topics. Subject entries, while less numerous than those for names of plants, are sufficiently detailed to serve the needs of most users. *See* and *see also* references are provided, although there is some inconsistency in their use. The Index in the volume for *Roses*, for instance, includes an entry for *powdery mildew*, but no entry or cross-reference under the less exact but more commonly used term "mildew." The volume for *Annuals*, on the other hand, has full entries for both *powdery mildew* and *mildew, powdery*.

The volumes are attractively printed on glossy white stock which enhances the effectiveness of the numerous color photographs. Extra-wide outer margins have been provided in the textual sections of each volume to allow space for section titles, instructional drawings, and sidelights on the text (such as the recipes for cowslip wine and marigold chowder in the volume on annuals). Consequently, inner margins are usually too narrow to permit rebinding, which would be impracticable in any case owing to the double-page photographs and charts included in the volumes. The sturdy cloth binding of the library and school edition should, however, last for the life of the book under normal use. Cover illustrations in color add eye appeal to the outward appearance of the volumes.

While the *Time-Life Encyclopedia of Gardening*, when complete, will provide reliable basic information on all major forms of gardening, and on many minor aspects as well, its principal advantage over other works with similar coverage lies in the abundance of illustrative material which supplements the text. If not the "most superbly illustrated set of horticultural books ever published," it comes within reasonable distance of achieving this aim by virtue of its wealth of color photographs, watercolor illustrations, instructional drawings, and illustrated charts. Although the volumes are not overpriced by comparison with other works having similar pictorial emphasis, the total cost of the projected 19 volumes for the encyclopedia ($95.48 for the kivar binding; $109.73 for the cloth binding) may place the encyclopedia in the luxury category for some libraries. However, libraries that cannot afford the entire series may find it possible to purchase individual volumes of particular interest to their clientele. Since the encyclopedia has been planned with browsing and sustained reading, as well as reference use, in mind, some libraries may wish to place these volumes in their circulating collection. Following Committee policy, no final evaluation is given until the complete set is available for examination.

(Nov. 15, 1972, p. 251)

The Times Atlas of the World.
Comprehensive ed. 2d rev. ed. Produced and Published by The Times of London in collaboration with John Bartholomew & Son, Ltd., Edinburgh. Boston, Houghton Mifflin Co., 1971, [c1968]. xliii, 272p. illus. (part col.) 128 col. maps. 46cm. buckram $65.

The first *Times Atlas* was printed in Germany in 1895. The second, *The Times Survey Atlas of the World* (1920-1922), was edited and printed by John G. Bartholomew of the Edinburgh Geographical Institute. The third, *The Times Atlas of the World,* mid-century edition, was published in five volumes between 1955-1960 under the direction of the Bartholomew firm in Edinburgh. The five-volume set was reviewed in *The Booklist and Subscription Books Bulletin,* September 1, 1961. The comprehensive edition of this famous atlas, published in one volume in 1967, was reviewed in *The Booklist and Subscription Books Bulletin,* July 15, 1968.

The edition under review is the second revised edition of the comprehensive edition. A third revision of the comprehensive edition was published in 1972, and a concise version was also put out by Quadrangle Books, a *New York Times* company, in 1972. The shorter version is entitled *The New York Times Atlas of the World*. It sells for $35, and it is reviewed above in this issue of *The Booklist*. The four-page Foreword containing a brief historical background of the atlas is the same in the 1967 and 1971 single-volume editions. Acknowledgements are identical also, except that Professor A. André, Rabat, Morocco has been added and Instituto Geografico Militar, Buenos Aires, Argentina has been deleted in the 1971 edition being reviewed here.

Prepared by the Edinburgh firm of John Bartholomew & Son, arrangement of the atlas is the same as it was in 1967. Following the Foreword and Contents are: (1) a list of states, territories, and principal islands of the world, followed by a page of geographical comparisons; (2) resources of the world in relation to man's needs, depicted by maps and charts on minerals, energy, food, climate and food potential; (3) maps and charts relating to the earth and its atmosphere, the universe, stars, the solar system, sunrise and sunset, artificial satellites and space flight, and the moon; (4) table of symbols and abbreviations; (5) the main section of 122 double-page physical-political maps of the regions and countries of the earth including seven plates entitled World Physiography, World Oceanography, World Climatology, World Vegetation, World Mankind, World Political, and World Air Routes; (6) an international glossary, terms used in geography, and abbreviations; and (7) an index-gazetteer.

For each place in the list of states, territories, and principal islands of the world the name, location, area in square miles, population with year of census used, and plate number are given. Population Data for Australia and France are as of 1968. For all other countries the data are as of 1967 or earlier. Some revisions are recorded on the maps depicting world minerals and world energy.

The 122 map plates are based on those in the 1967 comprehensive edition and are in the same order in both editions. Some revisions reflecting changes are noted on many of the maps, however. Additional air routes are indicated; many road changes are shown, and political name changes are recorded.

The maps are conic projections, simple conic or secant conic projections predominantly. The Lambert Zenithal Equal-Area projection is also used. Few Mercator projections are utilized. For plates showing the world as a whole, Winkel's "Tripel" projection is usually employed. Since, as noted in the Foreword "no map can be absolutely precise, because an approximately spherical body cannot be accurately applied to a flat surface," the *Times* has attempted to employ the projection most suitable for each particular map. The scales of the maps vary depending upon the size of the area to be depicted. Most of the maps of the United States, for example, range from 1:250,000 to 1:12,500,000. However, for the most part, there is a reasonable consistency in the scales used. Both the type of projection and the scale used are printed on each page. A line scale showing distance in both kilometers and statute miles is found at the bottom of the page for each map also. Altitude is shown by the use of shading or layer tints. A color scale depicting heights in both meters and feet is shown on each map.

In this revised edition, the Index Gazetteer has been increased by approximately three-fourths a page, from 261 to 262 pages, thereby adding an estimated 500 new place-names to the 200,000 names listed in 1968.

Printed by the offset process on fine quality paper—antique finish for the text and English finish for the maps—the atlas is sturdily bound in buckram. The volume is smythe sewn. Libraries should be aware of the fact that the map plates are bound too closely at the spine. Several plates have no margin, or less margin than those in the 1967 edition, and some instances of letters disappearing in the margins causing distortion of place-names were noted. Some libraries have reported problems with broken binding.

The maps in the second revised edition of the comprehensive edition of *The Times Atlas of the World* are comprehensive, well organized, accurate, and clear. However, the usefulness of this edition is gravely impaired by outdated population figures, meager revision, and faulty binding and defective inner margins that deter use of all double spreads. The atlas only partially maintains the high standards of previous editions. Recommended only to libraries not owning an earlier edition of *The Times Atlas of the World* or a good atlas published within the past two years. *(Dec. 1, 1973, p.349)*

The Times in Review: 1960-1969: A New York Times Decade Book. Introd. by Clifton Daniel. New York, Arno Press/Random House, 1970. xii, 852p. illus. 43cm. buckram $25.

The Times in Review: 1960-1969 is a collection of 207 headline news stories from the decade of the sixties, selected from the pages of *The New York Times* by the editors and reprinted in reduced size. Clifton Daniel, Assistant Managing Editor, Managing Editor, and Associate Editor during the decade provides a brief Introduction.

Each item includes a reproduction of the full front page and related inside pages of the edition of *The Times* printed the day the event appeared as headline news. As the preface states, "In almost every case, the event chosen is one in a chain or sequence of events. No attempt is made here to present a full story; quite the contrary. An event is reported with no more background information than the reporter was able to incorporate in his story or the editors decided to present in an accompanying 'sidebar;' and, of course, no story presents the consequences of an event that were not visible and reportable that day."

The arrangement of the collection is chronological, beginning with the settlement on January 5, 1960 of the record-breaking steel strike of 1959-1960, and ending with the news of the indictment of Newark Mayor Hugh J. Addonizio, December 18, 1969. A Table of Contents indicating date, headline, and page number precedes the text. A topical index provides subject entry into the text. The Introduction by Clifton Daniel consists primarily of personal reminiscences of the sixties and does not include useful data for the reference librarian.

This collection of front-page stories provides not only a reasonably complete panorama of national and world events during one of the more turbulent decades of history, but also an opportunity to examine how the editorial staff of one of the world's distinguished newspapers responded in print to those events as they occurred. The major strengths of this work are those of *The New York Times* itself: the thoroughness of treatment of each event, the clear journalistic style, and the authority of presentation.

The editors acknowledge that "This is history hot off the presses. It is not warmed over, recreated, retold, reinterpreted or revised." This is at once both a strength and a weakness. While the presentation of news events just as they were originally recorded provides a dramatic sense of contemporaneity and also a fascinating study in editorial selectivity, it does not permit that retrospective evaluation which would provide balance and seasoned editorial judgment. The editors recognize this in the preface: "we . . . tried to stay with the contemporaneous editorial judgment of the times. Thus this book presents what seemed most important at the time, not what may be judged most important in retrospect."

This policy explains the failure to cover certain events historically important to an understanding of the 1960s which unfolded gradually over a period of weeks or months, rather than coming to a clear focus on a given day. The escalation of the Vietnam War in 1965, the McCarthy presidential quest of 1968, the student unrest and campus disorders of 1969, and the growing tragedy of the Biafran War of 1968-69 are examples of these omissions.

The subjects most frequently reappearing as headline events are space travel (32 items), civil rights (23 items), and U.S. elections (21 items). In general, national events receive more coverage than international events, and news of New York (City and State) receives somewhat disproportionate coverage (19 items). Robert Wagner's refusal to run for re-election as mayor is included in the 1965 events; the Cooper-Conrad record-setting eight-day space flight is not. For 1967, the stories of the New York electorate's rejection of a proposed new constitution and the scandal concerning the taking of kickbacks by New York City official, James Marcus, are included; the news of the seizure of power in Greece by a military junta and of the first successful heart transplant are not. In sum, however, the coverage is broad and presents the very comprehensive view of the decade one would expect from this country's major newspaper of record.

The Index, consisting of 70 topics, provides adequate subject access to the 207 items. The headings are generally broad rather than specific, and occasionally some small amount of searching is necessary to pinpoint the proper heading. Names are not indexed.

The quality of the binding is poor for a volume of this size and weight and is likely to break at the hinges under normal library usage. The quality of the off-white, nonglare opaque paper is good. However, the printing quality varies. Some pages received noticeably too much ink, and many others too little, and there are occasional variations of such print quality on the same page. Photographic reduction in page size from the original 22 inches by 14 inches to 16 inches by 11 inches necessarily reduces the type size from the traditional 9 and 10 point to the equivalent of 5 and 6 point making sustained reading hard on the eyes. The quality of the photographs suffers in the reprinting process, generally appearing too dark and frequently indistinct. This is a minor point in terms of the overall value of the book, however.

The Times in Review: 1960-1969 provides a comprehensive overview of the major events which shaped the 1960s, and fulfills its stated purpose, "to convey to students of recent history a sense of that history in-the-making." For libraries whose holdings include

The New York Times and *The New York Times Index* it will be of minimal reference value. However, for small libraries and libraries which lack *The New York Times* and *Index* for this period, it is a handy reference to the major news-making events of the 1960s and is recommended.

(*Nov. 1, 1972, p.212*)

Treasury of American Design; a Pictorial Survey of Popular Folk Arts Based Upon Watercolor Renderings in the Index of American Design, at the National Gallery of Art. By Clarence P. Hornung. New York, Harry N. Abrams, 1972. 2v. illus. col. plates. 20cm. linen $50; 25 percent discount to schools and libraries and for cash.

In the midst of the Depression in the 1930s, when there seemed no place at all for artists, the U.S. government hired a large number of them to record the folk arts and crafts of America in precise renderings in watercolor of an enormous number of objects ranging from ships' figureheads to quilts. In all, over 17,000 renderings were made which are now permanently housed in the National Gallery of Art in Washington, DC, the collection being called the Index of American Design.

For many years, the collection went unpublished, but in 1950, a volume called *The Index of American Design* was created by Erwin O. Christensen, who was then Curator of the collection. However, less than three percent of the entire collection was represented in that volume. Holgar Cahill, who was the National Director of the Index of American Design collection, wrote the introduction for this volume, including the history of the Works Progress Administration project.

Now, a two-volume set called *Treasury of American Design* has been issued under the authorship of Clarence P. Hornung. He is a designer who has been particularly interested in the history of such objects as automobiles, fire engines, and carriages, and who has published many prints of them. Probably his best-known set is *Gallery of the American Automobile*, a limited edition of 100 prints in portfolio which has been much exhibited in the United States and abroad. He has also produced a number of books on trademarks, lettering, and advertising, and since he has an avid interest in the useful products of the American imagination, he is well qualified to write about the contents of the Index of American Design collection. Not only did he write the text for the *Treasury*, but he also designed the volumes and hand-set the chapter headings.

Treasury of American Design reproduces 2,900 objects most of which are from the Index collection. The selection is catholic, ranging from dolls and dainty embroidery to fittings for Conestoga wagons and cattle brands. The items, representing every part of the United States, date from about 1700 to the early twentieth century. The two volumes are divided into six books, each of which is subdivided into many chapters which illustrate the types of objects more closely. The books run as follows: Book 1, "On Land and Sea" contains figureheads, cigar store figures, and tavern signs; Book 2, "In the Home" contains complete coverage of household equipment—dishes, glassware, furniture, including a special chapter on the Windsor chair; Book 3, "Around House and Garden" contains garden figures, wrought iron, lighting equipment, weather vanes; Book 4, "Woman's World" includes cooking equipment, quilts, woven pieces, samplers; Book 5, "The Children's World" has the circus, toys, banks; Book 6, "Across the Nation" includes crafts from the Shakers, Pennsylvania Germans, the Spanish Southwest, cowboys and pioneers, George Washington and Mount Vernon, and finally a chapter on the use of the eagle as a symbol.

Each chapter begins with a several-page account of the craft with information on the history and developments of the particular genre and its relation to the society that used it. There is also information about the craftsmen whose names are known as well as those who worked anonymously. These accounts are well written in narrative, nontechnical style for the use of the general public and for collectors and hobbyists as well as students. Following the account, there are several double pages in color alternating with double pages in black and white. Each double page contains good-sized reproductions of from six to eight objects, harmoniously arranged in relation to each other without borders or other barriers. At the end of many chapters, there are double pages of small black-and-white reproductions which often contain 50 or more additional objects in the genre. Each item is numbered, and captions with corresponding numbers are printed on most of the pages. In addition, most chapters begin with a full-page illustration. Many of these are from the Index of American Design collection, but there are some which are actual photographs of paintings and interiors of famous houses and of objects which belong to important public and private collections. Sometimes there are illustrations from other sources. All of the illustrations are well reproduced. Even the small ones are clear and readable. Arrangement on the page is faulty. The pictures are bled toward the center of the page as well as toward the outer margins, and some items partially disappear into the gutter, particularly since the volumes are so tightly sewn that they do not lie absolutely flat.

Because of the difference in arrangement, it is difficult to compare the illustrations in the *Treasury* with those of the book *The Index of American Design* as far as duplication goes. It seems likely that many of the reproductions in the latter are repeated in the new book. The *Index* contains 378 objects, the *Treasury* 2,900. The texts are similar in content and style.

One feature of the *Index of American Design* which would have improved the use of the *Treasury* as a reference tool is a catalog of the illustrations giving the name of the renderer and the location of the object at the time the rendering was made. This catalog is arranged by the number of the illustration. *Treasury of American Design* has an Index at the end of volume 2, which is useful in locating various types of items, and some of the better known ones which have proper names (the names of ships for which figureheads are reproduced, for instance), as well as whole classes such as "kitchen equipment," "tin," "glass," etc. The reference is to page rather than item number, and there is no information in the volume as to the illustrator or the location of the item.

In addition, the *Treasury* has a list of the cities in which the state Works Progress Administration design projects were located and a list by state of the artists who worked on the Index of American Design project. No attempt is made to connect any of the artists with the illustrations in the book. Finally, Holgar Cahill's splendid Introduction to the volume *The Index of American Design* is reproduced at the beginning of the *Treasury* and provides an interesting and informative account of the Works Progress Administration.

The two volumes are bound in dark blue linen which seems fairly sturdy. The book is Smyth sewn but does not lie flat when opened. The offset print and layout are beautiful and clear.

Most libraries should own this book. As a source history of our ancestors' ingenuity in making and decorating the objects needed for carrying on life in sometimes very difficult situations, *Treasury of American Design* is unique. Collectors, art students and designers as well as the general student will find the book informative. Recommended.

(May 1, 1973, p.820)

Ulrich's International Periodicals Directory: A Classified Guide to Current Periodicals, Foreign and Domestic. A Bowker Serials Bibliography. 15th ed., 1973-1974. New York & London, R. R. Bowker Co., 1973. 2706p. 28cm. $46.50 plus shipping and handling.
ISBN 0-8352-0659-5. ISSN 0000-0175.

First published in 1932, issued for a time triennially, more recently biennially with an updating supplement on alternate years, *Ulrich's International Periodicals Directory* supplies information on approximately 55,000 periodicals published throughout the world. Now in one volume, the new edition expands the fourteenth edition by an additional 5,000 journals. *Ulrich's* was last reviewed and recommended by the Reference and Subscription Books Review Committee in the October 1951 *Subscription Books Bulletin.*

The most significant new feature is the inclusion in the main entry of the assigned International Standard Serial Number (ISSN). The ISSN, an identification number for serial publications and an international standard, is intended to expedite the development of an international data base on serials. It will provide the "publisher, subscription agency and the librarian with a tool for communicating basic information with a minimum of error." The use of ISSN will be valuable in acquisition control, cataloging, circulation, retrieval, interlibrary loan, and development of regional holdings lists.

All of the introductory material appearing in the fourteenth edition is contained in the fifteenth: the Preface and those sections headed Abbreviations, Abstracting and Indexing Services, Money Symbols, Country of Publication Code, and a Key to Subjects in English, French, German, and Spanish. The new sections are those giving a description of the background and the use of the ISSN.

As in the fourteenth edition, a User's Guide following the Preface tells the reader that the book consists of these sections: (1) the Main Text, (2) the Index to New Periodicals, 1971-1973, (3) Cessations, and (4) Index. In the 2,105-page main text, entries are arranged under 249 headings and subheadings and then alphabetically. Main entries include as much of the following as applicable: full title; former title; editor's name; circulation figures; subscription rates; frequency of issue; year first published; name and address of publisher; languages used in the text; names of services which abstract or index the periodical; special features as advertising, book reviews, bibliographies, illustrations; availablity of microfilm or back issues; Dewey decimal classification number; and the International Standard Serial Number with country code. A sample entry in the User's Guide clarifies all this information.

The Index to New Periodicals is an alphabetical listing of 3,500 periodicals published since 1971. Full entries appear under appropriate subject headings in the main text, with page references to this entry in the title index. The Cessations Section lists over 1,800 periodicals which have ceased or suspended publication since the last edition, with full information in each entry. For the most part, no date of cessation is given; however, in a few instances, the year of cessation is supplied. Finally, the Index by title and subject in one alphabet includes the title, country code and ISSN for main entries, title cross-references, subject headings with cross-references from related categories to main headings, and cessations.

Classifications have been updated since the last edition. Ten new subjects have been added; 10 others expanded with additional subheadings, and 20 have been dropped or incorporated with others. Housing and Urban Planning is a new section with 380 entries, and Women's Interests is another with 207. The number of environmental journals has been increased by 25 percent; ethnic interests which includes black interests and American Indian interests, by 50 percent; communications, by 10 percent. For the first time, the main entry indicates sources of microfilm, but in a spotty fashion. According to a large sample checked, only a third of those periodicals listed as available in *Guide to Microforms in Print, 1973* are actually shown in *Ulrich* as so available. This, however, is not an important deficiency, as one is more likely to consult *Guide to Microforms in Print, 1973* for this particular information.

On tests run for accuracy, the new *Ulrich's Directory* scores high. All Index listings which were verified proved to be accurate, as did all cross-references checked.

The book is bound in gold buckram, and the format is quite satisfactory. Clear type on opaque paper makes the text easy to read. The paper weight has been considerably reduced to permit binding into one volume instead of two. Heavier stock, however, has been used for the gatherings at the beginning and end to prevent pages from curling.

A comparison with *The Standard Periodical Directory* (Leon Garry, editor, New York: Oxbridge Publishing Co., 4th ed., 1973, $60), also in common use, shows a difference in scope between the two publications. *The Standard Periodical Directory* is limited to the United States and Canada, while over half of *Ulrich's* entries are publications from 165 other countries of the world. The former includes publications with a regular frequency of at least once every two years; the latter, those issued more frequently than once a year. Since the Oxbridge publication has less comprehensive geographic coverage, it can be more inclusive and incorporate such items as organization newsletters, house organs, student newspapers and alumni bulletins, and even comic magazines. It can also supply a longer entry; for many titles it gives such information as the telephone number of the publisher, the name of the advertising director, a description of editorial content, the types of material used, the name of the auditing organization, the advertising rate, the magazine size and method of printing, and the average number of pages in an issue. For the first time, the latest edition includes a limited indication of where a magazine is indexed—but without the thoroughness found in *Ulrich's*.

Ulrich's International Periodical Directory is the standard periodical directory and a basic reference source. Libraries will require it as a selection aid, a buying guide, and a reference tool. Traditionally, the most valuable feature has been the indication of which service abstracts or indexes the periodical. Ulrich's directory still performs this function along with many others. It is recommended for purchase by school, public, academic, and special libraries. *(July 15, 1974, p.1213)*

United Nations Resolutions. Series I, Resolutions Adopted by the General Assembly, v.I (1946-1948) of projected 12-15v. set. Compiled and edited by Dusan J. Djonovich. Dobbs Ferry, NY, Oceana Publications, Inc., 1973, [c1972]. 505p. tables. 26cm. buckram $40 per volume; to libraries, discounts with multi-volume series.

Dusan J. Djonovich, Foreign Law Librarian at New York University Law Library, has undertaken the preparation of a comprehensive compilation of the resolutions of the four major deliberative bodies of the United Nations: the General Assembly, the Security Council, the Economic and Social Council, and the Trusteeship Council. Publication began with volume I of the first and largest of the planned four subseries, *Resolutions Adopted by the General Assembly,* covering that body's two regular and two special sessions, 1946-1948. This review is based on examination of that volume. The publisher plans that the completed series will contain 12 to 15 volumes.

While United Nations resolutions do not carry the weight of international law and are only persuasive in their authority, they do represent the definite expression of opinion and intent of the four major organs of the United Nations. They are the principal source of guidance to the international community in the promotion of friendly relations among states and the promotion of peace in the world. Until recently access to these resolutions has been a very cumbersome process, since they are scattered through many United Nations publications. To retrieve them one had to consult the *Official Records Supplement* for each year or search *United Nations Documents Index* and its predecessor, *Checklist of United Nations Documents, 1946-1949.*

The publisher states that when complete this set will consist of four subseries, each presenting the full text of all resolutions in numerical order by resolution number of the four principal organs of the United Nations. Each volume in each subseries will contain a table of contents, the voting record on every resolution and, if voted in parts, the exact voting record on each part as well. In addition, each volume will contain a topical index, cumulated from volume to volume and an appendix in which "all pertinent and clarifying documents to certain resolutions will be printed in full." Also promised is a "comprehensive and analytical index" at the end of each subseries.

Volume I of the first subseries, *Resolutions Adopted by the General Assembly*, follows the projected format. The body of the work consists of a reprinting of all 189 resolutions passed by the General Assembly in its first two regular and two special sessions, 1946-1948. Since the reprinting is a photographic reproduction of the original documents, their bilingual format, English in the first column and French in the second, is retained. The resolutions are preceded by a table displaying the numerical voting record on each resolution and a roll call vote table which records the votes or abstentions of each member state on the 29 resolutions for which there was a roll call vote. Also preceding the text of the resolutions is a 44 heading Topical Index which provides access to the resolutions by broad subject. Following the resolutions are 14 appendixes containing the text of United Nations documents selected by the editor to clarify or amplify certain resolutions.

At present the Topical Index which precedes the text of the resolutions provides the only subject approach to the body of the work. Until the promised "comprehensive and analytical index" to the subseries appears, one must rely wholly on the Topical Index. This Index with its 44 headings and 5 *see* references provides only a minimal subject approach by general topic (Budget and Finance, Human and Political Rights, Labor and Trade Unions, Refugees, etc.). A Topical Index, useful as it may be, is not an adequate substitute for a comprehensive index. The placement of the resolution number and page number of each of the 189 resolutions under 1 of 44 topics makes for a somewhat difficult search for resolutions on precise subjects. Two of the resolutions do not appear under any topic.

The appendixes contain the full text of 14 of the United Nations documents referred to in certain resolutions. Only those documents have been included which have not already appeared in *Official Records,* although reference to these documents that are not included are listed within the text of the resolutions. This means that the user must consult *Official Records* as well as the 14 appendixes if he wishes to examine all of the background documents referred to in the resolutions. The reproduction of these few documents in the appendixes from among the many noted in the resolutions does not enhance the usefulness of the volume measureably. Most users of this and subsequent volumes will be primarily interested in the text of the resolutions rather than in the supporting documents. Footnotes throughout the book refer to the appendixes when appropriate. Other footnotes referring to previous resolutions also appear when such resolutions are referred to in the text.

It should be noted that the United Nations has recently published an *Index to Resolutions of the General Assembly, 1946-1970.* Part 1, published in 1972, is a numerical list of resolutions. Part 2, published in 1973, is a subject index. Those libraries whose holdings include the *Official Records* of the General Assembly should consider whether they need to purchase a reprinting of the resolutions of this body rather than relying on the new *Index* published by the United Nations. The rather high cost of this series—represented by the volume under review—may in fact be a serious consideration whether or not a library's holdings include the United Nations documents from which the resolutions are reprinted.

The volume is adequately bound and should withstand normal usage well. The margins are wide and will easily permit rebinding without loss of text.

The tables and appendixes are of somewhat larger print than that of the resolutions which are photo-offset reproductions of the original United Nations printed documents. The paper is off-white and non-glare. The volume lies flat when opened.

Final evaluation and recommendation of *United Nations Resolutions* must wait until completion of the set or at least completion of the first subseries with its promised analytical index and its cumulative topic index. Meanwhile, libraries will have to base their decision to purchase on the frequency of calls for United Nations resolutions and the extent to which their holdings of United Nations documents include resolutions of the four major deliberative units. Because of the present difficulty of retrieval of specific resolutions (with the exception of those of the General Assembly, access to which is now made simpler with the publication of the *Index* referred to above) and because of the convenience of having all resolutions compiled numerically in one set, some libraries may wish to purchase this and subsequent volumes despite the per volume cost. *(Nov. 1, 1973, p.250)*

The Ways of Game Fish. Featuring reproductions of paintings by Bob Hines and Fred Sweney and etchings by R. H. Palenske plus numerous photographs of fishing scenes. Text by Russ Williams and Charles H. Cadieux. Edited by Thomas C. Jones. Chicago, J. G. Ferguson Pub. Co. [c1972]; distributed to the book trade by Doubleday & Co. 326p. illus. 34cm. Roxite C-grade cloth $24.95; to schools and libraries 36-41 percent discount.

The Ways of Wildfowl. Featuring the distinguished paintings and etchings of Richard E. Bishop. Text by Russ Williams. Edited by Thomas C. Jones. Chicago, J. G. Ferguson Pub. Co. [c1971]. 260p. illus. maps. 34cm. buckram $24.95; to school and libraries, 36-41 percent discount.

In the past few years, numerous attractive, well-written, heavily-illustrated volumes have been published for the purpose of interesting the general public, and young people in particular, in various aspects of the animal kingdom. The two volumes under review are examples. Although the texts emphasize slightly different viewpoints and are completely independent volumes, they complement each other well. *The Ways of Wildfowl* concentrates on birds; the emphasis in *The Ways of Game Fish* is on fishing.

These two books are original works. Each contains a two-page list of Acknowledgments identifying the agencies and individuals involved in preparing the volume. The authors and contributors are experienced writers and are knowledgeable in their respective fields. Russ Williams, author of *The Ways of Wildfowl* and "Our Fresh-Water Heritage" in *The Ways of Game Fish*, is an advertising man and newspaper reporter with an interest in nature. Charles Cadieux, author of "Salt-Water Fishing" in *The Ways of Game Fish*, was a conservation officer with the North Dakota and U.S. governments for many years and is now Information Chief for the Department of the Interior, Office of Saline Water and is President of the Outdoor Writers Association of America. Richard E. Bishop, principal illustrator of *The Ways of Wildfowl*, is a well-known ornithological artist.

Each volume contains three types of text material: reference sections on the individual species, chapters on related general topics, and narrative stories.

Although the volumes are intended to be "useful and amusing" rather than encyclopedic, they both contain extensive reference sections. About 45 percent of the text of each volume is devoted to such reference material. Each reference chapter covers a particular family and is subdivided into sections, each of which describes the appearance, characteristics, behavior, habitat, and range of an individual species. The data appear to be accurate, although on rare occasions, material is treated as fact which might, in other sources, be qualified by such terms as "probably" or "sometimes." Each reference chapter begins with a list of the common and scientific names of the North American species but only the common terminology is used in the subsection headings and the articles.

Each volume also contains some chapters on important topics that are related to the subject of the book. *The Ways of Game Fish* has very few chapters on related general topics, but it does contain a fairly good article on ocean currents. *The Ways of Wildfowl*, on the other hand, has chapters on migration, each of the major North American flyway systems, the history of wildlife refuges, the creation of suitable habitats, birdbanding techniques, and some of the more important conservation societies. In both volumes, an underlying concern for the preservation of wildlife is readily apparent. In addition, each volume contains chapters explicitly describing the damage being done to the environment although no attempt is made to propose solutions to the problem.

The third type of material in the volumes consists of narratives. In *The Ways of Wildfowl,* these accounts are usually expanded articles which include the author's thoughts and feelings as well as factual material on particular species. A major portion of *The Ways of Game Fish* is comprised of such stories, usually of various fishing expeditions made by the authors. This is particularly true of the chapters on salt-water fishing. Although each article contains one or two interesting facts about the fish, most of the space is devoted to describing how the fish was caught and discussing which tackles and bait are most useful for catching that particular species.

The illustrations are a major feature of the volumes and on the whole they are good. Unfortunately the background colors on some of the paintings in *The Ways of Wildfowl* seem blatant and unrealistic. The birds themselves, however, are all very clearly delineated and colored. These pictures could be used for identification purposes. The black-and-white reproductions are uniformly excellent. All the color reproductions are full page, but there is considerable variation in size of the remaining illustrations, which range from small marginal sketches to full-page etchings and photographs. Within the text of the two volumes, there are only about 15 double pages which totally lack illustrative material. With the exception of a few marginal sketches whose subjects are clearly identifiable by their locations in the text, all the illustrations are captioned and signed. Among the illustrations in *The Ways of Wildfowl* are excellent maps of the North American flyways, showing the major species using them and drawn for the U.S. Fish and Wildlife Service by staff artist Bob Hines.

The volumes are not intended to be scholarly, and this is clearly reflected in the writing. Although the authors tend to be overzealous at times in ascribing personalities to various species, the descriptions are usually powerful and successfully communicate the feelings they are trying to convey. The purpose of the volumes is to express a sense of joy and wonder, as well as concern, for the wildlife around us and this is certainly achieved.

Most of the material in the books is relatively easy to find. The Tables of Contents list the headings of the subsections, although not their pagings, for chapters which are subdivided to cover the individual species. Some of the headings are more catchy than informative and the contents cannot be determined from the titles. There are full listings of all the color reproductions and of those black-and-white illustrations which are more than one-fourth page in size. In *The Ways of Game Fish,* tables of illustrations are placed after the title pages of the sections on fresh-water and salt-water fishing. The maps, charts, and small sketches are not listed in the Table of Contents. Fortunately, this supplementary material can be found through the Index, although sometimes only with difficulty. On the whole, the indexes are quite good. Scientific names are used in the Index but refer only to the pages on which the common and scientific names are listed under the chapter headings. In order to find material on the species, the common name can be used under any of its elements—the black-bellied tree duck is entered under black-bellied, tree, and duck. Places and organizations are entered only under their full proper names but subjects may be found under two or three entries. Both articles and illustrations are indexed, the pagings for illustrations being given in italics. Index entries do not lead to references to the various species within the general articles. There is, for example, no reference from *ducks,* in the Index, to the article on creating a reservoir for ducks. There are no bibliographies, footnotes, or references—even direct quotes are unidentified.

Visually, the volumes are very attractive. They are printed on good quality paper which provides good contrast and no glare. The volumes contain attractive endpapers and have stamped sketches on the front covers. The margins on the printed pages are extremely large; however, rebinding (which should be unnecessary as the volumes are very sturdy) would spoil the full-page illustrations which are bled to the inner edges of the books.

It seems unlikely that these books would be acquired for reference purposes. Even though the contents and arrangement of the texts would facilitate such use, the volumes are clearly not intended for this purpose.

On the whole, *The Ways of Game Fish* and *The Ways of Wildfowl* contain a wide range of material which is accurately and thoroughly covered in a non-technical, popular manner. The writing is clear, interesting, and readable. The illustrations are excellent. The volumes will be of great interest to anyone interested in wildfowl or fishing. Recommended.

    Eleanor MacLean, Librarian
    Blacker-Wood Library of
      Zoology and Ornithology
    McGill University
(Jan. 15, 1974, p.498)

Webster's New Collegiate Dictionary [8th ed.]. Springfield, MA, G. & C. Merriam Co., [c1973]. 32a, 1,536p. 25cm. illus. tables. gray cloth $7.95; red cloth, thumb indexed $8.50; brown Buksyn, thumb indexed $9.95; to schools and libraries, 10-25 percent discount depending on quantity.

The claim that the eighth edition of *Webster's New Collegiate Dictionary* is "the most comprehensive desk dictionary ever published by Merriam" is substantiated by an increase of over 25 percent (i.e., 349 pages) in the length of the volume when compared with the previous edition. As the amount of space devoted to "front" and "back" matter is the same in both editions, the expanded coverage in the new edition is found in the A-Z vocabulary section, the "heart" of the dictionary. The total number of entries in the work has been increased to 152,337, of which 130,578 are vocabulary entries. Thus the number of vocabulary entries in the new edition exceeds the total entries in the seventh edition of the dictionary.

The expansion of the vocabulary section consists primarily of some 22,000 new words and meanings which have come into use since the previous edition of the dictionary was published in 1963. Included are extensive contributions to the language from space science and computer technology, ecology, the drug scene, the black and youth subcultures, and the worlds of politics, fashion, and entertainment.

One must, however, discount the claim that the words *assembler, chord organ,* and *rockabilly* are found "only in *New Collegiate.*" They were included in *Random House Dictionary* as far back as 1966, as was the use of *draft* in relation to sports. Also included for the first time (happily without the fanfare which sometimes accompanies their debut in popular dictionaries) are the common four-letter words omitted from previous editions of the *Collegiate*. For review of the seventh edition, see *The Booklist and Subscription Books Bulletin* July 15, 1963.

Other significant changes applying to the vocabulary entries are the increased use of quotations in context to illustrate usage and a new treatment of synonyms and antonyms. Approximately 3,000 illustrative quotations are included, considerably more than were used in the seventh edition, but relatively few in comparison with the almost 24,000 illustrations of word use supplied by the editors. The quotations are drawn from 1,489 authors ranging from "Shakespeare and Spenser to Barth and Bellow" and are usually identified by author only, although occasionally dates are cited. No explanation is offered for the inconsistency in this respect.

The new treatment of synonyms incorporates an explicit statement of the "shared meaning element" of words included in synonym groups. The 760 synonym groups have also been divided into two types: "words believed to be of interest to the dictionary user" but presenting no problems in use, for which only the shared meaning element is given; and "words believed to present special problems to the dictionary user." Synonym groups of the latter type include discriminated definitions and illustrations of word use.

The inclusion of 1,115 antonyms represents a return to the practice of earlier editions of the dictionary. Antonyms were omitted from the seventh edition of *Collegiate* in accordance with the policy of its parent work, *Webster's Third New International Dictionary* (*The Booklist and Subscription Books Bulletin,* July 1, 1963).

In other respects the vocabulary entries retain the features common to the current Merriam-Webster family of dictionaries. Definitions for words used in more than one sense are arranged in historical order, and etymologies precede the definitions. Stylistic labels are used less frequently than in the past and are less pejorative in character. *Substandard* and *slang* are the two labels most widely used. *Non-standard* is used "for a few words or senses that are disapproved by many but that have some currency in reputable contexts . . . ."

The modified diacritical pronunciation key first introduced in *Webster's Third New International Dictionary* has been retained. The key is printed in full inside the front and back covers and on the page preceding the beginning of the vocabulary entries. An abbreviated version of the key appears at the bottom of each right-hand page in the vocabulary section and also in the supplementary sections listing foreign words and phrases, biographical names, and geographical names. As in the preceding edition, pronunciations for obsolete words are given only if they appear in Shakespeare.

The "Vocabulary of Abbreviations" formerly included as a supplementary section has been incorporated into the main alphabet in the new edition. Nine hundred line drawings, selected for their ability to clarify the verbal definitions, have been placed within the text in the main vocabulary section. While not a notable feature of the volume, the drawings do provide visual illustration of many objects with which users of the dictionary may not be familiar.

Although, as previously noted, the total number of pages which precede and follow the vocabulary entries is the same as in the previous edition, some new material has been added, and some material previously included has been dropped. New to the front matter is a two-page Explanatory Chart which illustrates, by means of a demonstration page, the various points discussed in the Explanatory Notes section which follows. Unfortunately, the large number of items included often results in a wide physical separation between the caption boxes and the examples to which they relate, and the guide lines connecting the two are not always easy to follow. The crowded appearance of the page and the strange effect produced by the use of light gray ink for the text (in order to make the boldface type used for the examples stand out more clearly) weaken the effectiveness of the chart.

The "Guide to Pronunciation," which followed the Explanatory Notes in the seventh edition, has been replaced by a very readable ten-page essay "The English Language and Its History" by W. Nelson Francis, Professor of Linguistics and English at Brown University. (The "serious student" is referred to the "Guide to Pronunciation" in *Webster's Third New International Dictionary* for detailed treatment of the subject. The essay which appeared in the seventh edition of *Collegiate* was an abridgement of that guide.) Professor Francis' essay is followed by a one-page Tabular History of the English Language.

Omitted from the pages following the vocabulary entries are the former supplementary sections covering the rules of spelling and those for the formation of compounds, the list of "Common English Given Names," and the "Vocabulary of Rhymes." As already noted, the alphabetical abbreviations have been transferred to the main alphabet as has the table of proofreaders' marks formerly included in the Signs and Symbols supplement. Other changes in the signs and symbols, which are no longer designated as "arbitrary," include the replacement of the signs and symbols relating to books and music with those used in flowcharts, stamp collecting, and weather mapping.

The inclusion of a supplementary list of Foreign Words and Phrases may create the impression that the editors have returned to the older practice of listing all foreign words and phrases in a separate alphabet. Only in the Preface is the user informed that the 566 words and phrases in this supplementary list "occur frequently in English texts but have not become part of the English vocabulary . . . ." As in the seventh edition, foreign words and phrases which have become "naturalized" (e.g., *caveat emptor, noblesse oblige*) are found in the main English-language vocabulary. This practice is not pointed out in the Preface or in any of the explanatory matter in the dictionary.

Biographical and geographical names continue to be listed in separate supplements rather than in the main alphabet, although other types of proper names (e.g., mythological, literary, and historical) are included there. The number of biographical entries has been increased from 5,196 to 6,051 and the geographical names from 12,345 to 12,485. The introductory paragraphs to both of these sections have been dropped, an omission more objectionable in the case of the geographical names than that of the biographical entries. At least for the United States and Canada, the introductory paragraphs provided an indication of the criterion used for the inclusion of towns and cities (15,000 or more inhabitants) and the census dates for the population figures cited.

The introductory paragraphs to the list of United States and Canadian colleges and universities have also been dropped. While the publishers state that space considerations required the elimination of the introductory material in these supplements, the amount of blank space on the final page of each of these sections suggests that there was ample room for the introductory paragraphs had the editors chosen to include them. The final page of the Biographical Names section, for example, includes only three entries.

The separate supplementary sections covering punctuation, italicization, capitalization, plurals, and forms of address in *Seventh Collegiate* have been combined into a 16-page "Handbook of Style" in the new edition. Also included in the handbook are a brief section on footnotes and one on style in business correspondence. A single-page Index listing the principal matters treated in the dictionary, as well as the 25 tables included in the vocabulary section, is provided on the final page of the volume.

The new dictionary continues the improvement in format which characterized *Seventh Collegiate*. The use of larger type, a new typographical design, and attractive page layouts give the volume a clean, modern appearance and facilitate use. A new system of listing guide words in the vocabulary section makes the location of entries somewhat easier. The dictionary is printed on special smooth-finish dictionary offset paper, and the sturdy, reinforced binding should be able to withstand extensive use.

A brief comparison with the two other major desk dictionaries published within the past five years reveals that both *American Heritage Dictionary* (reviewed in *The Booklist*, February 1, 1972) and *Webster's New World Dictionary of the American Language*, 2d college ed. (New York: World Publishing Co., 1970), include a slightly larger number of entries (155,000 and 157,000 respectively) than does *New Collegiate*. The variety of information included in these other dictionaries appears to be at least comparable to that found in *New Collegiate*, challenging the publisher's statement that the latter contains "the most comprehensive assemblage of dictionary information ever put together in a desktop format."

Both *American Heritage* and *Webster's New World* include the vocabulary and nonlexical entries in a single alphabet, an arrangement preferred by some dictionary users. *New World* arranges multiple definitions in historical order while *American Heritage* presents first the "central meaning about which the other senses may be most logically organized," which may or may not be the earliest sense of the word.

Both *American Heritage* and *New World* place more emphasis on standards of usage than does *New Collegiate*, employing stylistic labels more frequently and calling attention to usages which are in dispute. *New Collegiate*, for example, defines *bimonthly* as either "occurring every two months" or "occurring twice a month." The second meaning is no longer preceded by the mildly qualifying "sometimes" which accompanied this questionable usage when it first appeared in *Webster's Third New International Dictionary.*

American Heritage labels the second meaning *nonstandard* and notes that 84 percent of the dictionary's usage panel voted to reject the usage. *New World* also records the usage but notes that "in this sense, *semimonthly* is the preferred term." Only if the user of *New Collegiate* takes the trouble to look up the prefix *"bi-"* will he be informed that its use in the sense of "coming or occurring two times" is "often disapproved . . . because of the likelihood of confusion" with the customary sense of "coming or occurring every two."

Similarly, *New Collegiate* makes the doubtful assertion that *ain't* is "used orally in most parts of the U.S. by many educated speakers esp. in the phrase *ain't I."* *American Heritage,* which devotes 18 lines to a discussion of the usage of *ain't,* reports that *ain't I* is "unacceptable in writing other than that which is deliberately colloquial, according to 99 per cent of the Panel, and unacceptable in speech to 84 per cent." *Webster's New World* notes that *ain't* "was formerly standard for *am not* and is still defended by some authorities as a proper colloquial contraction for *am not* in interrogated constructions," a statement which would appear to be more defensible than the claim that *ain't* is "used orally . . . by many educated speakers . . . ."

While *New Collegiate* treats *irregardless* merely as a *nonstandard* synonym for *regardless* (implying thereby that the usage has "some currency in reputable contexts"), *American Heritage* holds that it is "Never acceptable except when the intent is clearly humorous," while *New World* defines it as a "substandard or humorous redundancy for *regardless."*

American Heritage places special emphasis on visual material and far outdistances the other two dictionaries in the number and variety of the illustrations provided. The placement of the illustrations in the margins and the use of larger type result in a slightly oversize but not really cumbersome volume. The improved format of the *New Collegiate* significantly narrows the gap between it and *American Heritage* as far as the physical qualities of the volumes are concerned and probably places it ahead of *Webster's New World.*

Webster's New Collegiate Dictionary provides concise, clear definitions, extensive coverage of new vocabulary and a variety of useful information presented in an attractive and serviceable volume. Users who are not prepared to accept the somewhat permissive approach of *New Collegiate* may prefer to rely on one of the more traditionally-oriented dictionaries for guidance in matters of usage. With this caveat, *Webster's New Collegiate Dictionary* is recommended for use in homes, offices, and libraries of all types.

(Nov. 1, 1973, p.251)

Webster's New World Dictionary. David B. Guralnik, editor in chief. [2d college ed.] New York and Cleveland, World Publishing Co., [c1970, 1972]. xxxvi, 1692p. illus. tables. 26cm. cloth deluxe $9.95, thumb indexed $10.95; complete reference $6.95, thumb indexed $7.50, Smyth-sewn $7.25, Smyth-sewn, thumb indexed $7.95; standard $7.95, thumb indexed $8.95.

The first college edition of *Webster's New World Dictionary of the American Language* was reviewed in *Subscription Books Bulletin* October 1953, and recommended as an inexpensive, useful, one-volume desk dictionary. The second edition of this dictionary was published in 1970 and updated in 1972. According to the Foreword, this new edition is a total revision necessitated by "the flood of new terms," "subtle changes in pronunciation," and "changes in group attitudes towards numerous locutions" which have characterized recent decades.

David B. Guralnik, editor in chief, was one of the two general editors of the first edition. Mitford M. Mathews, dean of American lexicographers, served as special consulting editor and editor of Americanisms. The etymological editor, William E. Umbach, is professor of German at the University of Redlands and has been an etymological editor for the World Publishing Company for more than 20 years. He was also etymological editor of the first edition. A staff of 38 editors and special contributors is listed. They are identified as members of university faculties, researchers with industry, or holders of other positions indicating special competence.

New World is a publication of the World Publishing Company, whose dictionaries have no connection with those of similar titles published by the G. & C. Merriam Company.

The editor states that "the vocabulary entered was chosen to meet the needs of students and others in this particular period of history" and contains "a heavier proportion of terms from the sciences than was true for the previous edition." A total of 157,074 entries (about 5,000 more than in the first edition), including thousands of new words and new meanings, is claimed.

In this edition, as before, all entries, including the names of people, places, foreign words and phrases, slang, abbreviations, legendary, Biblical, and classical names, etc., appear in one single alphabetical list, with entry word or words in large boldface type. The vocabulary is arranged letter-by-letter in alphabetical sequence, in two columns per page. The following information is given for each vocabulary entry: pronunciation, part of speech labels, inflected forms if irregular, etymology, and definitions. Variant spellings are given, cross-referred to the spelling most frequently used. Spellings which are British, dialectal, slang, or obsolete are so indicated. Plurals are shown when formed irregularly. Syllabification is indicated and conforms in most instances with rules in use by the United States Government Printing Office. Again etymology is a strong feature, and etymologies are carried back where possible to their Indo-European base. Cognate relationships between words in English and between English words and those in other Indo-European languages are shown. Definitions of words are arranged in semantic order from the original to the most recent meaning. Definitions are clear, precise, and again characterized by simplicity. In many instances illustrations of the use of the words are provided to clarify definitions. Apparently, these were prepared by the editors, as their sources are not given.

The editors claim no authority to permit or disallow any usage, but "believe that one who consults a college dictionary is entitled to the informed collective determination by the staff as to whether a particular term is appropriate to a standard or formal context or is suitable only in an informal context" or as slang, and "whether it is, in spite of widespread usage held in low repute by those who take a stricter view." Usage labels—*colloquial, slang, obsolete, archaic, poetic, dialect, British,* and *Canadian* are included where appropriate. Where a term or sense is generally regarded as vulgar, substandard, or derogatory, and where there is objection to common usage, this opinion is indicated. For example, in the entry block for *who* appears the following note: "The use of *who* rather than *whom* as the object of a verb or preposition (*who* did you see then? *Who* was it written by?), although widespread at all levels of speech is still objected to by some."

The scientific names of plants and animals are indicated with their definitions. Field labels, in italics, indicating specialized fields of knowledge, e.g., medicine, chess, law, appear immediately before the sense involved. *Webster's New World Dictionary* includes many idiomatic phrases; the publisher claims 5,540, and such phrases usually are entered under the keyword.

Pronunciation is shown by diacritical marks and respelling immediately after the word. A key to pronunciation, changed slightly from that used in the first edition, appears at the bottom of every alternate page. There is a detailed explanation of the key in the "Guide to the Use of the Dictionary" appearing in the introductory materials. The key to pronunciation is easy to use. The pronunciations given are "those used by cultivated speakers in normal, relaxed conversation," and it is stated that pronunciations are symbolized so that speakers of every variety of American English can read their own pronunciation into the symbols. Changes in the prevalence of certain pronunciations since the first edition are recorded, (e.g., *harass* is now more often pronounced with the accent on the second syllable, and *acclimate* has its main accent on the first syllable.) Pronunciation is given for the names of persons and places.

According to the publisher, the dictionary contains more than 800 paragraphs in which synonyms are listed. These are entered after the word in the group which is considered the most basic or comprehensive. Distinctions are explained, and frequent examples of use are given. In some instances antonyms are included at the end of the synonymy.

Many small, very clear, line drawings are used to clarify definitions. Some small spot maps are also included. These are placed directly with the entry. Many of the illustrations of tools and instruments show them in use. The size of the animal life illustrated is indicated.

Prefatory material includes a useful six-page guide to the use of the dictionary, a list of the abbreviations and symbols used, and three interesting essays replacing the essay on the English language appearing in the first edition. The new essays are "Language and the Dictionary," a 16-page essay by Charlton Laird, author of *Language in America* (New York: World Publishing Co., 1970); a two-page essay "Etymology" by William Umbach; and "Americanisms" by Mitford M. Mathews, also two pages.

The Appendix includes 23 pages of lists of colleges, universities, and junior colleges in the United States and colleges, universities, and other institutions of higher education in Canada, an expansion over the list in the first edition which did not include Canadian institutions. The following information, supplied by the institution, is provided for each: date of founding, location, general size of enrollment, the principal source of financial control, nature of enrollment, and type of degrees offered. A new, very useful supplementary feature, a "Guide to Punctuation, Mechanics, and Manuscript Form" includes seven pages of regulations for term papers and research papers, generally in accord with those in the *MLA* [*Modern Language Association*] *Style Sheet*. As before, the one-page "Proofreaders Marks," two-page "Tables of Weights and Measures," and three-page "Special Signs and Symbols" the latter section somewhat enlarged, are included in the Appendix. The forms of address section which appeared in the first edition is omitted.

There is broad coverage of geographical, classical, and biographical names although no indication of the basis of selection is given. Population figures are given in round numbers and those for many metropolitan areas are included.

A strong feature of the first edition of *New World* was the inclusion of many American colloquial and slang terms. These are again included in large numbers, and some 14,000 Americanisms are identified. An especially interesting feature is the derivation of many American place-names. For example, *Chicago* is said to be derived from an Algonquian word meaning place of the wild onion. Many new abbreviations have been added, e.g., ROK, SAM, DMZ, although abbreviations for some government agencies, OEO, EEOC, EPA, etc., have not been included.

Omitted are "a handful of old, well-known vulgate terms for sexual and excretory organs and functions" because, the editor says, there is still some objection to their appearance in print and he wishes to avoid the risk of keeping this dictionary out of the hands of some students. Terms of social or ethnic opprobrium are also omitted.

New World is published in three editions—standard, complete reference, and deluxe color. The contents of each are the same except as noted below. The deluxe contains 36 pages of colored illustrations. They are the usual type of page illustrations often found in dictionaries and depict such subjects as state flags, cats, jewels, gems, and crustaceans. These pages are scattered throughout the volume and are listed on the contents page. The illustrations are attractive, but while located near, are not usually adjacent to the page containing the subject illustrated. There are no references to these illustrations in the word entry blocks. In the deluxe edition, the illustrations accompanying the word entries are drawn with blue ink and the running word above each column is printed in blue, causing them to stand out in contrast to the black print. The standard and the deluxe editions have the added feature of illustrated endpapers: a map of the United States showing regional dialects at the front and a chart showing the Indo-European family of languages at the back. The standard, copyrighted in 1970, lacks a few of the new terms included in the two editions copyrighted in 1972. The population statistics given for United States cities in the standard edition are based on pre-1970 census information. These statistics in the complete reference and deluxe editions are based on the 1970 census. In all editions the population statistics for British and Canadian cities are based on the pre-1971 censuses of these countries. The deluxe (eight-and-one-fourth inches by eleven-and-one-half inches) is the largest volume but somewhat oversize for a desk dictionary. The standard (about seven-and-one-fourth inches by ten inches) and the complete reference (seven inches by nine-and-one-half inches) are a suitable size and weight for desk use.

All editions are sturdily bound. The volumes lie flat when opened. The inner margins of the two smaller editions are, however, somewhat narrow. The type in all three is quite clear, and variations in type size facilitate use. The paper is relatively glare free.

A comparison of *New World,* the eighth edition of *Webster's New Collegiate Dictionary,* and *The American Heritage Dictionary* (reviewed in *The Booklist,* February 1, 1972) appears in the review of *Webster's New Collegiate* in *The Booklist,* November 1, 1973. Here it is noted that *New World* contains a larger number of entries, 157,374, as compared with 155,000 in *American Heritage* and 150,000 in *Webster's New Collegiate.* While the variety of information contained in the three dictionaries is said to appear comparable, it should be noted that *New World* contains some new terms and idiomatic phrases not appearing in the other two dictionaries, neither of which identifies Americanisms or gives the derivation of place-names. *New World* also contains many more usage labels, idiomatic phrases, and etymologies. Both *New World* and *American Heritage,* in contrast to *New Collegiate,* emphasize standards of usage, which many users expect a dictionary to provide.

Webster's New World Dictionary of the American Language, college edition, is an up-to-date, inexpensive dictionary. It provides lucid definitions, detailed etymologies, guides to usage, and a variety of interesting and useful information including a large number of idiomatic phrases, slang, and colloquial terms. It is recommended for home, office, and library use.

(Mar. 15, 1974, p.750)

Who Was Who in the USSR: A Biographic Directory Containing 5,015 Biographies of Prominent Soviet Historical Personalities. Comp. by The Institute for the Study of the USSR, Munich, Germany. Ed. by Heinrich E. Schulz, Paul K. Urban, and Andrew I. Lebed. Metuchen, NJ, The Scarecrow Press, Inc., 1972. 677p. 28cm. B grade Arrestox cloth $40.

The directory contains brief biographical information for persons who were active in the Russian and Soviet governments, political parties, and professions, and whose deaths occurred between 1917 and 1967. An Index by Career and Profession supplements the main alphabetical arrangement.

Under the official name Institut zur Erforschung der UdSSR the American-supported organization in Munich employed many emigres and published information about the Soviet Union in Arabic, English, French, German, Spanish, and Turkish from the time of the Institute's founding in 1950 to its closing, as announced by Radio Liberty, in 1971. The Institute's biographical section accumulated an information file on 136,000 persons, according to the Preface.

The volume's principal editor, Dr. Heinrich Eduard Schulz, was the Institute's Director from 1959. Trained in medicine in the Ukraine and in Germany, he is the author of books in the history of medicine. He served as the Institute's head librarian from 1952 through 1958 and was editor of several of its biographical directories.

Of those directories, four general "who's who" volumes were compiled by the Institute: *Biographic Directory of the USSR* (New York: Scarecrow Press, 1958), *Who's Who in the USSR 1961-62* (Toronto: Intercontinental Book and Pub. Co., Ltd., 1962), *Who's Who in the USSR 1965-1966* (Toronto: Intercontinental Book and Pub. Co., Ltd., 1966). The fourth volume was renamed *Prominent Personalities in the USSR* (Metuchen, NJ: Scarecrow Press, 1968). A new feature of the fourth updating, according to its Preface, was that "many" of the persons included "cooperated in correcting and supplementing the information offered about themselves." This edition was supplemented by *Portraits of Prominent USSR Personalities,* a quarterly issued from January 1968 through October 1971, which included younger persons with careers at an earlier stage and cited published sources.

In addition, the Institute issued directories for special groups: *Party and Government Officials of the Soviet Union 1917-1967* (1969), *The Soviet Diplomatic Corps 1917-1967* (1970) and *Soviet Science 1917-1970, Part I: Academy of Sciences of the USSR* (1971), all published by Scarecrow Press.

No statement of sources is provided for the material in the volume under review beyond the one-page Preface general reference to the Institute's library (80,000 volumes) and periodical collection (750 Soviet newspapers and periodicals).

A gauge of the volume's scope is afforded by its Index by Career and Profession. Approximately 34 percent of the biographees are identified primarily with the Communist Party, the government, or the military. About 23 percent had careers in the national economy, science, and education, and somewhat more than 25 percent were prominent in literature, art, music, and theater. Shorter lists make up the remaining 18 percent for persons in the fields of public health, youth and mass organizations, and religion. The latter is subdivided into Clergy (47 names) and Anti-Religious Functionaries (5 names).

The final list of the Index has the caption Resistance. Some major prerevolutionary and emigre figures appear only in this category. The two subheadings are: Politicians of Opposition and other Parties, Factions and Alliances (199 names) and Leading Figures in the Armed Resistance to the Soviet Regime (50 names).

In cases where the biographee died in prison or was executed any subsequent rehabilitation is indicated. A sample suggests that of the persons selected for this directory 11 percent died in prison and 4 percent were executed.

The directory includes a number of academic and political figures who emigrated to Europe or the United States: B. A. Bakhmetyev, David Dalin, P. N. Milyukov, P. B. Struve, I. G. Tsereteli, for example. It omits some internationally known artists and ballet and stage personalities who lived abroad and whose names appear in *Chambers's* and *Webster's* biographical dictionaries, for example: Leon Bakst, Sergei Diaghilev, Vasily Kandinsky, Vaslav Nijinsky, and Anna Pavlova. Also omitted are the authors Leonid Andreyev and Mikhail Artsybashev.

On the average, seven or eight entries appear on a page of two columns. Entries vary in length from three lines to approximately a column each for Bukharin, Pasternak, and Stalin. The form of name by which a biographee is best known is used for the entry and other names are given in parentheses, but there are no cross-references from real name or any variants.

For writers and scientists the amount of space in each entry allotted to major publications is frequently greater than that given to other biographical information such as family background, education, and career. The bibliographic description is abbreviated, however, giving Russian title in Romanized form, followed by English translation of title, and year. The transliteration system resembles that used by journalists, and some difficulties may be expected when names and publications as given in the directory are used in conjunction with most bibliographic and scholarly tools in the United States utilizing the Library of Congress system.

The binding may not be sufficiently strong for a volume of this size if heavily used, but inner margins would permit rebinding.

Who Was Who in the USSR brings together information from scattered sources, including obituaries in periodicals, and makes it accessible in English. For the serious student or researcher with access to published sources primarily in Russian, most of the entries will be found to be too brief and to provide little new information. For reference use in college or larger public libraries where condensed information in English is needed for twentieth-century Russians, this directory is of acceptable quality. Recommended.

(Sept. 1, 1973, p.4)

Who's Who in Government 1972-1973.
Chicago, Marquis Who's Who, Inc., [1972.] 785p. 30cm. Tyvek boards with buckram spine $49.50 cash; $51 charge.

This new biographical directory is intended to serve the needs of businessmen dealing with Federal departments, students researching term paper topics, and other persons interested in government officials. It contains more than 16,000 concise biographies of "key men and women in all branches of the U.S. Federal government" as well as a "selected list of officials in local, state, and international government." Only one requirement for inclusion is stated, "reference value," and this factor "was determined on the basis of career position—reflecting either an individual's level within a hierarchical structure or responsibility of a key nature." A board of 29 advisers made up of such prominent public figures as Carl Albert, Patsy Mink, Mark Hatfield, and John Hannah aided the editors by reviewing and commenting on the contents.

A sampling of entries selected at random from throughout the alphabet reveals that almost one half of these people were also listed in *Who's Who in American Politics*, Taylor's *Encyclopedia of Government*, *Who's Who in America*, *Who's Who of American Women*, or in one of the regional *Who's Whos* published by the Marquis Company. The other individuals could not be located in these standard sources of biographical information. A sampling of 100 biographies also reveals that 93 were for federal officials but only 7 for state or local officials.

All the data were supplied by the officials themselves; all information furnished by the biographee was carefully revised, and prepublication proof was submitted to each biographee for final verification. A careful check of ten entries in other biographical works revealed only one serious error of omission (an M.D. degree not recorded).

The basic format and organization of *Who's Who in Government* conforms to that of most other biographical works published by the Marquis Company as does the type of information supplied: personal facts, education, career data, military service, and professional memberships. A list of abbreviations used in the articles precedes the alphabetical arrangement of the biographical entries. To facilitate the use of this directory the editors have created two detailed indexes, one listing biographees within an alphabetical arrangement of departments, bureaus, and agencies, and the other listing them under such topics as Flood Control, Census Statistics, Radio, and Poverty.

Arranged alphabetically by surname, the entries in the main section of the book are printed in three columns per page on good quality white paper. The type is small but clear; the margins are narrow but adequate, and the binding is buckram over paper boards.

Since *Who's Who in Government* includes many officials not easily located in other standard reference works, it is a desirable purchase for libraries building strong biographical collections. Recommended. *(Feb. 1, 1973, p.499)*

The World Book Encyclopedia. 22v. Chicago, Field Enterprises Educational Corp., [c1965], [c1917-1973]. illus. ports. maps. diagrs. 26cm. standard binding $219.50; school/library $239.50; aristocrat $239.50; renaissance $259.50.

The World Book Encyclopedia, first published as an eight-volume work in 1917, has been reviewed several times in *Subscription Books Bulletin,* beginning in January 1930. The present review will be based, to some extent, on a comparison of the 1973 edition with the edition of 1968, the last to be reviewed in *The Booklist and Subscription Books Bulletin* December 1, 1968.

Designed primarily to meet the reference and study needs of students from elementary school through high school and also as an everyday reference tool for the family and for professional men and women, *World Book* aims to "present information from man's vast reservoir of knowledge in the most accessible and usable form." In order to achieve this goal, the publishers have established an elaborate network of editors, consultants, and contributors. Basic to this network are the Advisory Board, the International Advisors, the Cartographic Advisory Board, and Special Consultants, comprising 27 distinguished men (interestingly, not one woman is included in any of the four groups) representing various fields. The Cartographic Advisory Board is new to the 1973 edition. The International Advisors remain the same as for the 1968 edition, however, five new members were appointed to the Advisory Board to replace five 1968 board members, the best known addition probably being John H. Glenn, Jr., Adviser to NASA. One additional member was appointed to the group of Special Consultants. In addition, there are seven consultant committees consisting of from five to eight members which cover such general areas as biological sciences, humanities, and health and medicine. The actual writing and reviewing of articles however is done by some three thousand scholars and specialists. Supporting the work of all these groups is the permanent editorial staff itself under the direction of Dr. William H. Nault. All persons included in these groups and their qualifications are listed in volume 1. Some of the contributors new since the 1968 edition are: Bernard Rimland, Director of the Institute for Child Behavior Research (Autism); Alan McGowan, Scientific Administration at the Center for Biology of Natural Systems, Washington University (Environmental Pollution); and Tetsur Najita, Associate Professor of History, University of Chicago (Japanese History).

In *The World Book* all articles except the very briefest are signed by contributors. Occasionally an article is signed by two or more contributors or by a contributor and a reviewer, or even by an organization. A few major articles are signed by a group of contributors representing different disciplines. For example, *Latin America* is written by a geographer, a historian, and an art historian, all of whom are experts on Latin America. It should be noted, however, that a number of the listed contributors have been deceased for more than two years, with the term "former" usually preceding their titles. While it is understandable that certain articles written by distinguished persons might very well be retained and need little if any revision, (as for example, *Euripedes* by Moses Hadas, an outstanding classics scholar, who died in 1966,) it would seem that the term "late" might be substituted for "former" in the listing of deceased contributors or perhaps a death date given.

The organization and arrangement of *World Book* generally facilitates the information gathering process. Articles are arranged alphabetically word by word with many cross-references within articles and quite often with further references and a list of related articles found at the ends of articles. Information on specific subjects is found in many separate articles as well as in longer survey articles. Thus a reader can get a concise article on methadone under that heading without having to search a long article on drugs, or if he wants to study methadone in relation to other drugs, there are longer articles on drugs, drug addiction, and drug abuse. Access is also made easier by the use of boldface headings at the top of each page and smaller boldface subheadings throughout the articles.

The most important change from earlier editions of *World Book,* and one that further facilitates easy access, is the addition of an Index. Volume 22, first published in 1972, includes the

Index as well as a section on How To Do Research, and Reading and Study Guides for more than two hundred subjects. While most articles are found under obvious general terms, the user can now locate the main entry and related articles very quickly without looking for *see* and *see also* references within the main article. Under *Time*, for example, one finds the main entry in the T volume, but there are 16 other entries found in such articles as *Chronometer, Relativity,* and *Sun,* that have information on the subject. The Index is extremely simple to use, employing boldface headings for each main entry, a subject identification if necessary, as in *tie* (music) and *tie* (railroad), a reference to pictures, diagrams, or maps is included, and the volumes and page numbers referred to, as for example, S-249 or NO-72.

Interspersed throughout the Index are the Reading and Study Guides which list topics for discussion or further study and sources of more information on the subject. Books are generally selected for their interest and appeal to young people and are listed in two levels, one for easier reading and the second for more advanced study. In the guide for Mental Illness, for example, Green's *I Never Promised You a Rose Garden* and Rubin's *Lisa and David* are listed. In addition, films, filmstrips, and other media, along with names of organizations, are given. A listing of addresses for all publishers, distributors, and organizations is provided at the end of the volume.

World Book follows the unit letter arrangement, except that the C's and S's are each divided into two volumes, and five of the volumes include from two to four letters each. The first and last volumes are large but not unwieldy.

Illustrations for the most part continue to be excellent, especially in the country, state, and natural science articles. They are generally well chosen, clear, and up to date. Many, in fact, were created exclusively for *World Book* by commissioned illustrators and photographers, as for example, photographs of some of the artifacts shown in the *American Indian* article. Also, transparent color overlays are occasionally used for clarifying difficult concepts, as in the article on the human body. While many fine illustrations have been added to the 1973 edition, some have had to be reduced or deleted to make space for new articles or expansion of older articles. Fortunately this has in no way diminished the value of the illustrations.

Children's literature is frequently consulted in a young people's encyclopedia by students, teachers, and librarians alike. Zena Sutherland, an editor at the Center for Children's Books at the University of Chicago is the new contributor of the article *Literature for Children.* The coverage in this article provides a good general reference to the subject for adults, treating the subject historically and by categories of poetry, folk literature, fiction, biography, and information books. The organization of material is improved in the 1973 edition by the attractive format dividing information on Kinds, History, Careers, Selecting Children's Books, and Books to Read by large sectional captions. The length of the text is extended by two pages. Treatment of literature for children by kind, particularly the emphasis on books of information as reflected in the bibliographies, is new to this edition. *History of Children's Literature* is more succinctly treated in the 1973 edition than it was in 1968. Reduced to three pages from the six pages in the 1968 edition, the article shows no appreciable loss except in the cursory treatment of the didactic school.

Current Trends in Children's Literature is omitted from the 1973 edition as a separate heading. However, trends are covered in the body of the text, selection of illustrations, and the bibliographies. The Books to Read section gives a good explanation of grade-level rating as a tool, not a prohibitor, and suggestions for use of the bibliographies it introduces. Bibliographies are arranged by kinds of literature: Beginning Books, Poetry, Folk Literature, Fiction, Biographies and Autobiographies, Information Books, and Books about Children's Literature, with further subdivisions under Folk Literature, Fiction, and Information Books. The organization of book lists is new since the 1968 edition. Previously, books were listed by age group, but in the present edition reading level is given in the annotation for each title. The bibliographies generally reflect a responsiveness to problem areas as is shown in the nonfiction listings which include books treating such problems as ecology, drug abuse, race relations, sex education, and women's rights. Also, titles by a broad range of realistic writers whose work deals with ethical questions are listed in the bibliographies for fiction: Armstrong, Burch, Buars, Carlson, Clymer, Donovan, Fitzhugh, Hentoff, Neville, Townsend, and Wojciechowska. Recent notables omitted, however, are Vera and Bill Cleaver, Fox, and Königsburg.

The nonfiction listings have a separate section on minority groups; almost 25 percent of the titles in Biographies and Autobiographies represent Blacks. Minority groups are strongly represented in the fiction listings. Even in Beginning Books there are three books listed with Black heroes.

Females do not fare as well representatively. In Beginning Books only two titles have females as the main character. In the list of biographies, fewer than 25 percent of the titles are on women. In all the fiction lists, stories featuring girls are outnumbered two to one. This is an improvement, though, over the 1968 edition in which books with females featured in the combined listings of Books for the Intermediate Age and Books for Older Boys and Girls was only one out of five.

The abundant illustrations in full color in the 1973 edition are a fine sampling of the best of past and present in illustrations for children. Prominence is given to illustrations from international children's books with nine full-color illustrations spanning the leading double-page spread for *Literature for Children*. The 56 illustrations, increased from 39 in the 1968 *World Book*, include a fair proportion of illustrations from nonfiction books, many of which show children from minority groups. The illustrations are well placed in relation to both text and book lists. The number, selection, and reproduction of color for illustrations originally appearing in color are all a bonus.

Approximately the same number of American Authors and Illustrators and European Authors and Illustrators appear in the listing of related articles in the two editions with about 25 percent change. Notable deletions are Swift, Stockton, and N. C. Wyeth (two of Wyeth's illustrations appear in the 1973 edition, however). Among overdue additions are Tolkien and E. B. White. The additions are predominantly Newbery and Caldecott Award Winners. With some notable exceptions, few of the illustrators in the related articles are identified as to medium, technique, or style. Also, no reference is made in *World Book* from the illustrators' biographies to coverage of techniques: drawing, engraving, etching, lithography, painting, woodcut, or to the more general article *Illustration*.

Mythology has more than doubled in length in the 1973 edition—from 9 in the 1968 edition to 19 pages—and it is totally new in content and format. Each mythology is described under a separate heading: Egyptian, Greek, Roman, Celtic, Teutonic, Hindu, Mythology of the Pacific Islands, Africa, and American Indian. The new article, attractive in format, broad in scope, and admirable in content, is scholarly. The 1968 article, simply organized by type of myth and concluded with the retelling of three lively myths, probably held greater appeal for intermediate age children. Two new charts, one showing carvings of important divinities in Egyptian mythology, and the other, a comparison of Greek and Roman deities, are helpful. The 21 full-color illustrations from private collections and museums world wide are resplendent. The bibliography for *Mythology,* with notable additions, remains scholarly, as does the *Folklore* bibliography. Neither includes reading level or indication of usefulness to children in the annotations. The Reading and Study Guide on Mythology, found in volume 22, however, does give indication of reading levels.

Storytelling, new in format and content, contains helpful information for the beginning teller of tales: the techniques of the picture book representation, the literary and traditional tale as distinguished in style and teller's delivery, and the environment to make possible a good storytelling experience. The bibliography, condensed to one-and-one-half pages from five pages in the 1968 edition, is divided into Picture Book Editions of Folk and Fairy Tales, Folk and Fairy-Tale Collections, Fiction, Modern Stories for Younger Children, Poetry for Children of All Ages —a helpful encouragement to wider use of materials in storytelling. In addition, a listing of films and recordings about storytelling adds to the improved usefulness for adults new to the art of storytelling.

In spite of the excellent article *Literature for Children* and its major related articles, the relationship between reading interest and the characteristics of the child-in-development is not considered to any extent either in these or other articles in such areas as the child, psychology, educational psychology, or learning.

In its coverage of social sciences and history, *World Book* continues its traditional strength. Among the distinguished contributors in these fields are Kenneth Boulding, Hadley Cantril, Henry Steele Commager, Oscar Handlin, Seymour Martin Lipset, John Diebold, B. F. Skinner, Richard Hofstadter, and Samuel Eliot Morrison.

New articles since the 1968 edition reflect the drastic changes in the social scene that have occurred during the past five years. The Black Panther Party is now represented, and there are new articles on Stokely Carmichael and Malcolm X as well as Shirley Chisholm, Julian Bond, Kenneth B. Clark, and Bayard Rustin.

Developments in domestic politics are reflected in new articles on John B. Connally, Thomas Eagleton, George McGovern, Henry Kissinger, John Mitchell, Ralph Nader, and Cesar Chavez, and revised articles on Richard M. Nixon, John Lindsay, and George Meany.

The changing economic situation has caused new or revised articles to appear for *Balance of Payments, Conglomerate, Food Stamp Program, Foreign Aid, Housing, International Trade, Value Added Tax,* and *National Budget.*

The article *Divorce*, written by John W. Wade of Vanderbilt University Law School, which appeared in the 1968 edition of *World Book,* has been revised and expanded, and the name of a second author, William M. Kephart, Professor of Sociology at the University of Pennsylvania, now appears with Professor Wade's. The article has taken on a strong sociological slant in addition to the almost strictly legalistic treatment it received previously. More recent U.S. statistics on divorce are provided, and the new article generally has a more liberal tone.

A new article on homosexuality by sociologist Carlfred B. Broderick is a clear, sensible, and straightforward exposition of the subject, done in good taste and without the once usual euphemisms. Much the same can be said of the new article on birth control by Leslie Corsa, Jr., Director of the Center for Population Planning at the University of Michigan.

A carefully balanced treatment of *Abortion* is new to *World Book.* It is written by Daniel Callahan, well known as an explicator of the subject. It presents in simplified form the arguments both for and against abortion. *Obscenity and Pornography* is new, but already somewhat outdated in view of the recent Supreme Court decision concerning community standards. The new articles *Social Change* by Harriet Zuckerman of Columbia University and *Social Class* by Seymour Martin Lipset are lucid, readable syntheses of these complex concepts.

In the arts, *Painting* deserves mention. The article has been expanded to include brief descriptions of Expressionism, Fauvism, Dadaism, Op and Pop, and Minimal Arts in addition to formerly omitted information concerning synthetic resins, polymers, acrylics, and newer trends and techniques. Also, overreduced reproductions (e.g., Titian's "Entombment of Christ" and Fra Angelico's "Coronation of the Virgin") found in earlier editions have been removed or replaced by more sensibly sized counterparts. The very impressive color reproductions accompanying the article, 118 in all, include not only the inevitable Botticelli "Venus," but also some not-often-seen illustrations of works by Giotto, Francis Bacon, and Renoir, as for example, the latter's "Children's Afternoon at Wargemont." For this one article, there are six Picassos and two Renoirs. Captions for each illustration provide location data, dates painted, and original dimensions.

The coverage of contemporary crafts, considering the revival of interest in these within the past few years, is somewhat disappointing. For example, Jack Lenar Larsen, the textile designer, Claire Zeisler, Magalena Abakanowicz, Sheila Hicks, and other well-known weavers are not included. The textile article is a precise and effective summary of the industry and its historical development, but it does not cover individual craftsmen. *Weaving* and *Embroidery* are also tightly written historical accounts which slight the current reemergence of interest in individual accomplishments. Consistent with this emphasis, *Handicrafts* is also exclusively concerned with the historical, technical, and vocational aspects of the subject.

In music, new articles appearing since the 1968 edition are *Electronic Music, Rock Music,* and *Country and Western Music.* Surprisingly, there are no entries for stochastic music or Suzuki. Articles for *Conductor* and *Orchestra* are excellent, although in the *Conductor* article it was surprising to note that Sir Georg Solti, who has been music director of the Chicago Symphony since 1969, was not included. The *Harpsichord* article, while adequate, could benefit by incorporating references to pieces in the instrument's repertoire: works by Byrd, Bull, Gibbons, and Domenico Scarlatti through Falla and Carter. The *see also* reference at the end should specify Domenico Scarlatti, the most gifted and prolific writer for the instrument. Also, the accompanying illustration would be more useful if it showed the action mechanism—dampers, jacks, and plectra—rather than an indefinite view of the instrument which fails to convey how it differs from the piano.

Opera is dated and infused with the musical perspective of an earlier generation. For example, the post-1900 operas cited include *Der Rosenkavalier, Girl of the Golden West, Madama Butterfly,* and Britten's *Turn of the Screw.* Some masterpieces of the twentieth century not included are Berg's *Wozzeck* and *Lulu,* Hindemith's *Mathis der Maler,* Britten's best opera, *Peter Grimes,* and Stravinsky's *Rake's Progress.* Mozart's *The Magic Flute,* an especially effective opera for children, is also omitted. Space for synopses of less significant operas might better be given to a straight historical treatment with more emphasis upon opera within our own century and color illustrations of stage settings.

In the biographies of musicians one might hope for more expressive flexibility and more insight into the lives of the musicians to accompany the unstimulating enumeration of works and other dry data. Though Milos Velimirovic's *Mendelssohn, Bizet, Britten, Dvorak,* and *Tchaikovsky,* have a lively style, many of the other contributors' articles are quite bland. *Händel* is overloaded with a discussion about *Messiah* and *Saul.* Händel's *Water Music, Fireworks Music, Concerti Grossi,* and sonatas are omitted. The author seems too exclusively preoccupied with Händel's ability as a composer of choral music. The *Beethoven* article provides a Reading and Study Guide in the Index volume, but it fails to include monographs which appeared in connection with the Beethoven bicentennial in 1970 as, for example, H. C. Robbins Landon's *Beethoven: A Documentary Study* (New York: Macmillan, 1970) and Paul Henry Lang's *The Creative World of Beethoven* (New York: Norton, 1970). While some biographies have been added since the 1968 edition—notably those of Boulez, Messiaen, and Stockhausen—others are conspicuous by their absence: those of Elliott Carter, Hans Werner Henze, Krysztof Penderecki, Edgard Varèse, and Anton Webern.

Motion Picture by Arthur Knight, is replete with excellent color photographs and includes films into the 1970s as, for example, *Shaft* and *M*A*S*H*. The 30-page article more than adequately covers all aspects of motion pictures, including history and production techniques.

Architecture by Edward Durell Stone, also is effectively presented, including terms, design considerations, history, and career possibilities. Too many illustrations do not do justice to the subjects portrayed. For example, St. Peter's in Rome, a TWA promotion picture, is shorn of its square, an essential aesthetic component if one is to appreciate the impact of the structure as it was intended by its creators. Likewise, the flying buttresses of Notre Dame (Paris) are not adequately shown; the Santa Sophia is fuzzy. A series of black-and-white illustrations (pages 584-87) is somewhat cluttered and uneven in quality. Fewer but more effectively arranged illustrations would enhance the usefulness of this article.

In science and technology between 1968 and 1973 the process of rewriting and expanding longer survey articles continues along with the addition of new subjects and the necessary updating of others. Some of the new or revised articles are *Acupuncture, Liquid Crystal, Semiconductor, Spark Chamber,* and *Water Pollution*. The rewritten articles tend to be on a more sophisticated level than those they replace.

Star is almost doubled in length. The illustrations are all new, and several tables and diagrams as well as a bibliography have been added. Although pulsars, quasars, x-ray stars, and a section on the birth and death of a star have been included, there is no mention of the black hole; nor is there a separate article on this subject which is of great interest in astronomy today. *Moon* likewise has been expanded—from 8 pages to 14 pages—with numerous photographs and information from manned exploration of the moon. *Space Travel,* as might be expected, has been brought up to date, including in the second printing of the 1973 edition, an account of the Apollo 17 flight and a note that manned exploration of the moon by the U.S. terminated in 1972.

Technology, expanded from two-and-one-fourth to six pages, now includes not only the benefits of technology but also a discussion of the problems it creates and some of the methods of coping with the problems. *Hydraulics,* somewhat reduced in length, has been rewritten in clearer and more technical language. *Metric System* and *Laser* have been brought up to date with slight additions.

In the biological sciences *Fish* and *Insect* are particularly noteworthy. *Fish* has been expanded from 12 to 31 pages. It has been completely reorganized with much new material, 32 color illustrations (the 1968 edition had only 7 black-and-white photographs) and a classification table added. *Insect* has tripled in length from 8 to 24 pages and now contains 42 color illustrations (the 1968 edition had only 10 black-and-white illustrations). Particularly helpful in this article is the material on anatomy, senses, and behavior. While insects and fish have been given extensive coverage, other classes of animals such as mammals and reptiles are given short, pedestrian treatment.

Insecticide has been rewritten to include a now somewhat out-of-date section on the dangers of insecticides. Examples of other rewritten articles are *Ecology,* which was given more space and includes a diagram of an ecosystem, and *Reproduction,* which has been expanded with several color illustrations and diagrams. *Environmental Pollution* is a major new article, including information on air, soil and water pollution, and the technical, economic, and social causes of and efforts to control pollution. *Automism,* while not a new subject, has been treated in a new article, as have *Techtonics* and *Wankel Engine*. Interestingly, the *Automobile* article has not been changed from the 1968 edition and makes no mention of the Wankel engine.

Geography is another area in which the 1973 *World Book* continues its tradition of excellence. Over 40 articles are either new or completely revised since the 1968 edition. Among these are

Bangladesh, Cuba, Hanoi, and Shanghai. Vietnam was updated in the second 1973 printing to include changes necessitated by the Vietnam cease-fire. All of the major countries, states and cities of the world are covered in comprehensive, up-to-date articles with excellent illustrations and maps. Many of the 2,200 maps were created by a full-time World Book cartographic staff that conducts research on type size, placement, color, symbolization, captioning, scale, and other elements involved in map-making. Others were created especially for World Book by Rand McNally. The maps generally are well placed, adequate in number and type, and show sufficient detail without being cluttered. The inclusion of new urban maps, developed for major U.S. and Canadian cities, adds considerably to the usefulness of the city articles. Statistical data both on maps and in the text have been updated to reflect changing population, resources, and other factors.

The style of World Book continues to be clear, direct, and suited to its audience. The problem of appropriate vocabulary for various grade levels rests largely with the editorial board, which makes decisions based upon reading research and curriculum study. This appropriateness is evident in certain articles that are more frequently sought by younger readers than in those sought by more advanced readers. Tree, for example, is easier to read than Transistor. Longer, comprehensive articles frequently present simpler concepts in the beginning and more sophisticated concepts toward the end of the article. Fish is an example of this. Difficult words are usually given in italics and defined in parentheses in the text immediately following.

The 1973 World Book, available in a variety of bindings, is attractive and durable. The highly legible volume letters and numbers on the spine make it easy to select the proper volume. The addition of the year of the edition on the spine is also a welcome feature. The volumes lie flat when open, but there is only minimum inside margin space. The machine-coated paper provides good legibility, and the print and page layout are attractive and readable.

In summary, the 1973 World Book provides an excellent, up-to-date reference tool for young people. The inclusion of authoritative unbiased material on contemporary social problems and current technology, the clear, well-chosen illustrations, the various guides to further study and reading, and particularly the addition of the Index, make it a valuable set for elementary and high school students and for families in need of a general reference set. It is recommended for all school and public libraries and should be purchased to replace 1968 or earlier editions.

(Dec. 15, 1973, p.399)

World Chronology of Music History. v.I: 4,000B.C.-1594A.D. Compiled and edited by Paul E. Eisler. Dobbs Ferry, NY, Oceana Publications, 1972. 537p. 26cm. cloth $40.

This review of the first volume of an eight to ten-volume project which in itself is an ambitious undertaking, is written because the work is being actively promoted, and it will be published over a long period of time. Volumes II and III will be published in the fall and winter of 1973. The Chronology, which seems to aim at scholars, musicologists, and laymen with specialized interest in music promises to be a very useful tool in music history if the plans of the editor are carried out successfully. It will not be possible for the Committee to reach a conclusive recommendation on the entire set based on examination of this one volume, and the Committee will not review successive volumes until the set, complete with indexes, is finished.

Paul E. Eisler, editor and compiler of the set, teaches music theory and analysis at the Manhattan School of Music. Dr. Fritz Kramer, signer of the Foreword, is also at the Manhattan School of Music, where his field is music history and musicology. According to Dr. Kramer the Chronology is "a concise survey of the art of music, especially its forms, its styles, the development of different theories, the ups and downs of music throughout the centuries and, of course, individual composers. . . . When it is complete, roughly 32,000 years of human evolution and culture will have been covered, starting with the Paleolithic Age and ending with electronic music." In fact, the first seven entries, which are on page 1 of the text, date from c.30,000 B.C. to c.12,000 B.C. and refer to cave paintings, the inference being that if there was painting of a comparatively high order, there was probably music. The first musical entry is for a Neolithic bone flute dating around 7,000 B.C.

The book covers briefly all facets of music: birth and death dates of composers and performers and major events in their lives, appearance of musical works, developments in performance, instruments and their makers, and music publishing. Arrangement is chronological, and "exact dates with month and day were grouped at the start of each year. Following this group, dates for which only the month was available were entered in order of months. Entries with only the year as identification followed, and at the end of this category events, including a range in years, were placed in their proper order. Information preceded by a 'circa' was arranged in the same manner, with those including a range of dates placed at the end of the entries." Arrangement of information for the earlier centuries is fairly simple, since the material is sparse, but beginning with the Renaissance, entries multiply. The 467 entries on the period before Christ occupies 20 pages, while the period A.D. 1500-1594 covers 326 pages with thousands of entries. The nineteenth and twentieth centuries will require even more space.

Within the chronological framework, subject matter is divided roughly as follows. Births and deaths of musical people come first; biographical data, second; and then performances, works, other historical information, births and deaths not connected with music and art, and finally births and deaths of artists other than musicians, and dates of important art works. In some of the entries referring to later dates in the individual's life there are some cross-references, thereby maintaining continuity.

Browsing students will find that the inclusion of historical events outside of music provides a frame of reference and historical connections. In the year 1524, for instance, there is a list of musical compositions having texts by Martin Luther and also of those having music by him published during that year. By browsing one finds that in 1577 Rubens was born, Sir Francis Drake arrived at California on his way around the world, and Monteverdi was writing madrigals influenced by the *Pastor Fido* of Guarini.

If a reader wishes to see pictures of art works mentioned there will be little difficulty in finding them in outside art sources from the fifteenth century on, although no illustrations are included in the volume. However, in the earlier periods when works of art were anonymous, there may be some problems, since some of the entries are very brief. For instance in c.310 B.C. the entry, "Grecian Sculpture: Three Tanagra Figurines," offers no clue as to which of the many Tanagra statues is referred to. On page 5, c.1,400 B.C. the entry reads "Fresco of a Banquet Scene." One is left to suppose that the reference is to the preceding entry of c.1,450 B.C. to the tomb of Nakht in Thebes, which is one of several with banqueting scenes. Incidentally, this scene contains musicians, and so several other references (the one for c.500 B.C. Libation Ritual at the Tomb of the Baron at Tarquinia, for instance), but the entry makes no mention of this fact. When the work of art has a well-known name or location, it can be found in other art sources. The Greek vase with the slaughter of the Niobids, or the Lindisfarne Gospels, or the Amitabha Paradise from Tun-huang are not hard to find, but "Sculptured Figure of an Etruscan Orator" is more difficult to identify. Use of the book would be facilitated if the location or the museum collection to which items belong were included. Later when the artist's name becomes known, there is less difficulty.

The Foreword states that Eastern and Western listings of significant events are included, and there is some Oriental information. Up to 1590, not much is known about Oriental music; so there are not many entries.

The first volume of *World Chronology of Music History* is useful only as a chronology, and information for which the user knows no date can be retrieved only by browsing. This lack of ready access to material in the series will continue until after publication of volume III, when the first interim index is to be published. Dr. Kramer, in his Foreword promises "a separate index volume containing an alphabetical listing of the persons, works and events discussed in the *Chronology*." There is no mention of a bibliography or a listing of the main works consulted. The reader is constantly perplexed by such undocumented statements as the one for 1340, "Manchaut's life is not well documented, but it is known that he sold a horse at this time." A collection of footnotes would be extremely useful and would help establish authority for the work.

There are a few typographical errors and some errors in spelling and punctuation, but these are minor considering the extent of this undertaking. However, it is very difficult to judge the accuracy of much of the material. Events with definite dates (birth and death) can be checked; generally these were accurate. Where the dates are preceded by "circa" and accompanied by a closing date in parentheses, the problem is compounded because statements may be diffuse and difficult to pinpoint in a corroborating source. For instance, on page 214, c.1500, one reads: "In the Sistine Chapel Choir all except three of Dufay's hymns were still performed although they had been composed seventy years earlier." Obviously this is a quotation from one of the numerous sources used by the editor and his contributors. However, since the Committee has no list of sources consulted, we cannot verify the entry.

The format is clear and legible, with two columns to a page. The main date is centered over the column when it appears for the first time, and then is repeated over the first column of each page until a new date occurs. Inclusive dates are given at the beginning of each item, when the date extends over a period of time. There is no variation in size or kind of type. The typewriter printout is light but clear and well-spaced. The red and gray cloth binding is reasonably sturdy. The book is large, but it opens well.

In keeping with Committee policy, final recommendation is deferred until *World Chronology of Music History* is completed. *(Dec. 1, 1973, p.350)*

Worldmark Encyclopedia of the Nations. 4th ed. New York, Worldmark Press, Harper & Row, [c1971]. 5v. illus. maps. 28cm. sturdite $69.95 for set; to schools and libraries, 38 percent discount if ordered directly from Harper & Row.

The fourth edition of the *Worldmark Encyclopedia of the Nations* updates the information, but retains the format of what is now an established reference tool. The first edition was reviewed in the June 15, 1961 issue of *The Booklist and Subscription Books Bulletin*. The second edition was reviewed in the May 1, 1964 issue. The third edition, published in 1967, was not reviewed.

Beginning with the second edition the encyclopedia has appeared in five volumes. There has been little change in design, scope, or content since the first edition, except that the material has been updated. Much of the Committee's praise and criticism accorded to the earlier editions applies as well to this edition.

Moshe Y. Sachs continues as editor and publisher. No author is listed for the first volume, but Louis Barron continues to edit the other four volumes. Each of these four volumes lists contributors along with their subject specialities. Some of the contributors are college professors and authors working in their respective fields. The editorial advisory board of the first edition is listed, but no changes are noted for this edition.

The Preface states the purpose "of this encyclopedia is to offer the reader a portrait of the world—the individual nations and their main meeting ground, the United Nations system." Volume 1 focuses on the United Nations, its origins, structure, and functions. Following introductory material, (a Preface, the table of contents, conversion tables and abbreviations) there is a chart of the United Nations, illustrating the relationship of the various organizations and units with one another. The chart has been redrawn since the third edition and is more pleasing to the eye, but still confusing. The lines between the various units on the chart show a connection, but one must rely on the text to clarify exactly what that relationship is.

The first half of this volume discusses the history and organization of the United Nations. Each chapter reflects revision since the third edition. In almost every instance statistical data have been updated. For instance, the membership list and budget of the United Nations are current for 1971. Revisions and additions have been made. For example, the chapter The Secretariat and the Role of the Secretary-General has been divided into two separate chapters and a section on U Thant's second term, 1966-1971, has been appended. There is new material on narcotics and drug control and an entirely new chapter on human environment. The Bibliography of United Nations publications has been updated. Some older titles have been deleted and new works added.

The second half of the volume devotes a chapter to each of the specialized organizations, such as UNESCO. Background, creation, purposes, membership, structure, budget, activities, and a bibliography of publications are supplied for each. Again there has been extensive revision. Following this section is a list of international organizations outside of the United Nations system which cooperate on a governmental level. Complete with *see* references and a brief activities description, these organizations are arranged alphabetically. A table showing to which organizations each country belongs has been expanded to include both new member countries and new organizations. The concluding Index provides access to all of the articles by the name of the commission or agency and by the subject, including *see* references. Unfortunately, this is the only volume in the set which is indexed.

The other four volumes concentrate on individual countries, volume 2 on Africa, volume 3 on the Americas, volume 4 on Asia and Australasia, and volume 5 on Europe. The authors maintain their stated purpose of trying to view each nation "as it might be reflected in a world mirror and not as seen from the perspective of any one nation." The style of presentation has not changed since the third edition, with each nation given an introductory paragraph and 50 numbered features following. These features range from location and size to a bibliography of works about the country. The number assigned each feature remains constant for each country. The features include climate, flora and fauna, population, history, language, government, mining, economy, education, health, famous persons, libraries, and, in fact, every facet of a nation's personality. Each feature includes at least one, and often several, paragraphs of prose frequently incorporating statistics. There is a key to the arrangement of the features in the front of each volume, but the key itself has no cross-references. The arrangement follows a logical pattern. The parallel arrangement facilitates comparison of one feature from country to country. Although the articles range in length from 4 pages, for such countries as Fiji and Malta, to 36 pages for the United States, all 50 features are uniformly applied to each nation. However, dependencies, such as the Portuguese African Dependencies are treated separately and in abbreviated form.

Black-and-white sketch maps are again provided with each nation's article, but are so small as to indicate only the major cities, rivers, and lakes. They include a locator key to the country's position on the colored maps appearing on the endpapers. In spite of their small size, the sketch maps are legible.

The factual content has been extensively revised. Although some sections are unchanged, these are on static features such as climate. Changing topics, such as balance of payments, health, and education have been rewritten to reflect developments since the third edition, and almost all of the statistical data have been updated since the last edition. The bibliographies have had new works added and older ones deleted.

Those countries which achieved their independence since the third edition of *Worldmark* have now been given their own articles. The total number of country articles in this edition is 146, compared with 141 in the third edition, and 135 in the second.

Worldmark is not revised annually, but this edition brings the data up to date. For instance, Bangladesh is not treated as an independent state, since independence was gained after *Worldmark*'s publication. The article on Pakistan, however, notes the growing dissension in that country. *Worldmark* may be relied on for fairness of coverage and equal treatment for all nations, with reasonably current data.

The print is clear, the paper opaque, and the volumes lie flat when open. Once the user of *Worldmark Encyclopedia of the Nations* is familiar with the arrangement of the subject features, it is convenient to use. It provides clear and readable factual information. *Worldmark*'s coverage of the world is thorough and fair. It will prove a useful reference tool in school, academic, public, and home libraries and is recommended to libraries already holding the older edition also. *(July 1, 1973, p.993)*

The Xerox Intermediate Dictionary.
William Morris, editor in chief. New York, Grosset & Dunlap, Inc., [1973]. Published by arrangement with Xerox Family Education Services. 800p. illus. maps. 29cm. cloth $7.95 plain, $8.95 thumb indexed. *The Xerox Intermediate Dictionary* is also published for school and library use as *The Ginn Intermediate Dictionary* by Ginn and Company, a Xerox Company. ISBN 0-448-02849-2 (trade ed.) 0-448-02905-7 (deluxe ed.)

Xerox Intermediate Dictionary is a somewhat new kind of dictionary which "captures the rhythm of today's language—new meanings, fresh terms and current idioms—and . . . incorporates words nominated by children themselves." Editor-in-chief, William Morris, is editor of *The American Heritage Dictionary of the English Language* (Boston: Houghton Mifflin, 1969) and *Young People's Thesaurus Dictionary,* (New York: Grosset & Dunlap,   ) author of *Your Heritage of Words* (New York: Dell, 1970) and co-author of the *Dictionary of Word and Phrase Origins* (New York: Harper & Row, 1962, 1969). The Advisory Board consists of recognized teachers and professors in such fields as linguistics, mathematics, and elementary curriculum. Morris' editorial staff includes Mary Morris, lexicographer and author, and Norman Hoss, lexicographer and managing editor of *The American Heritage Dictionary* along with the editorial staff for Xerox Family Education Services.

The Xerox Intermediate Dictionary has about 34,000 entries including derived and compound forms. The Introduction states that "many hundreds of young people helped to choose the words . . . indicating what words they use every day—but can't find in their dictionaries." Teachers from all over the United States suggested words for inclusion. Most were affiliated with schools in the East; few teachers from the South reported. In addition to the words suggested by students and teachers, the dictionary contains many words that are commonly used or encountered by upper elementary (grades four to six) school children today. There are geographical entries for the states of the United States, but neither biographical entries nor foreign words or phrases appear.

A publisher's note says that the dictionary "captures the rhythms of today's language—new meanings, fresh terms, and current idioms." There is definitely an emphasis on a contemporary vocabulary as evidenced by the number of current and slang entries. Among the current words are *Black Power, busted play, Chicano, civil rights, hardhat, hoagie, jeans, macrame, minibike, Ms., recycle, space probe.* Among the many slang terms are *bummer, cool it, creep, drag, fork over, grinder, groovy, hassle, jerk, horse (heroin), hot (stolen), meathead, neck, rap, stiff (intoxicated person), turn on, up tight, with it, yak.*

Each entry includes a pronunciation guide (phonetic spelling), variant forms, several meanings of the word arranged by frequency of use, usually a sample sentence using the word and parts of speech. Verb tenses are indicated. The definitions are accurate and easy to comprehend. No synonyms or antonyms are provided.

The key to pronunciation is found near the beginning on page 19 and repeated on the last page, page 800. An essay entitled "Guide to Pronunciation" by Norman Hoss gives reliable information on consonant and vowel sounds and shows that even with pronunciation guides there will be variations in pronouncing some words. Rather than employing the usual accent marks, this dictionary has the accented syllable typeset in small capitals.

Directions for using the dictionary are clear and include numerous examples. These directions cover the locating of words in the dictionary, finding the meanings of words, and spelling and using words correctly. Cross-references are used where there is a preferred spelling. For example: grey (GRAY) noun. See gray. Cross-references are also used for irregular verb forms: e.g., was (WUHZ) verb. See be. Occasionally there is a cross-reference from one entry to an illustration in another part of the dictionary; e.g., pictures of both an alligator and a crocodile are shown at the word *alligator*. The entry for *crocodile* reads: See illustration at alligator.

To indicate which words to use for either general or specific purposes, usage labels are employed except for words in wide general use. Those words used in special ways have appropriate labels in parentheses:

1. (Music), (Sports), (Grammar). To pinpoint "studies or fields in which one meaning of a word has a special or unique application;"

2. (Informal). Identifies words used in everyday or colloquial speech;

3. (Slang). These words may add color to speech but caution is indicated "before you use slang in writing or in talking with people you don't know well";

4. (British);

5. (Rare). Old-fashioned or archaic words.

No etymology is given with individual entries. However, there is an informative article entitled "Latin and Greek Roots" by Margaret D. Parks.

A metric system table is included. Newest state abbreviations are indicated: e.g., California (CA), Massachusetts (MA). Some trade names such as Coke and Kleenex are included.

At the back of the volume are two pages of photograph credits, two pages of Letter Symbols for Sounds, and the Key to Pronunciation.

Most of the illustrations have been "specially drawn or photographed for this book." They are in black and white or in sienna brown and white; they are small in size but for the most part clear. The illustrations are set in the outer margin of each page. Simple outline maps are provided for each state with a dot showing the capital. Scale is not always indicated in the drawings; e.g. a sewing needle is shown as half the size of a knitting needle.

Xerox Dictionary has a washable white cloth cover with black lettering and a colorful illustration of two children reading. The entries appear in two columns to a page; the print is well-spaced and clear on good quality paper. The volume lies flat when opened.

In comparing the *Xerox* volume with the *Thorndike Barnhart Intermediate Dictionary* (New York: Doubleday, c1971, $6.95) for grades 5-8, it was noted that *Thorndike* has more than 56,700 entries, has etymologies, has illustrations integrated into the body of the text, has three-column arrangement with small but clear print, and has the pronunciation guide repeated on every other page. *Thorndike* uses the conventional accent mark, includes biographical entries, contains little if any slang, and indicates some informal usages. The *Thorndike* dictionary offers more in-depth material and would provide easier transition to the use of a collegiate or an adult dictionary.

The *Xerox Intermediate Dictionary* fills its purpose of being up to date with words children use every day, and it proves "that words can be fun." It is, therefore, recommended where contemporaneity and emphasis on current idioms for upper elementary grades are desired. *(June 15, 1974, p.1114)*

Young People's Illustrated Encyclopedia.
20v. Chicago, Children's Pr., [c1972 McGraw-Hill Far Eastern Publishers, Ltd.] illus. 26cm. cloth $93.25; to schools and libraries, $69.95.

Young People's Illustrated Encyclopedia is new on the American market. The 20-volume set is copyrighted by Mc-Graw-Hill Far Eastern Publishers, printed in Singapore, and distributed in the United States by Children's Press. Committee inquiries to Far Eastern and Children's Press have not been answered, and it has therefore been impossible to assemble information on the history of the books. In promotional flyers Children's Press states that "*Young People's Illustrated Encyclopedia* is designed to tie in with the school curriculum while supporting textbooks and other materials used in the classroom." The Press claims to have "worked with prominent educators to develop an encyclopedia set that relates to the schoolwork and interest level of the elementary school student."

The general editorial staff consists of C. J. Tunney, D. S. Sehbai, Rowland Entwistle, and J. I. E. Cooke. Thirty-six contributors are listed with no indication of the particular contribution made. The only identifying information given for the staff and the contributors is the initials for degrees listed after the surnames. Full names are given for the contributors. No authorities are referred to as sources of information. The articles are not signed.

Young People's Illustrated Encyclopedia concentrates on the topics that are of interest to its intended audience, particularly students in grades three to six. The encyclopedia aims to meet curriculum needs, and the social studies are emphasized. According to Children's Press, the set contains 1,570 entries including such contemporary topics as Afro-Americans, drug abuse, poverty, and pollution.

Topics are arranged alphabetically, and information is given under short specific headings. There is scarcely enough information to meet either the curriculum needs or the personal interest needs of the elementary school child. For example *Banks and Banking* in volume 2 consists of one paragraph which explains that banking is a way of protecting and saving money. Other juvenile encyclopedias recommended by the Reference and Subscription Books Review Committee devote five to ten pages of text and illustrations to this important subject. Volume 10 has only 93 pages with 82 entries. Thomas Jefferson is covered in about 300 words as compared with 2,700 word coverage in a recommended juvenile encyclopedia. Comparable inequities occur in the treatment of *Jet Propulsion* and Abraham Lincoln. Where *Young People's Illustrated* covers *Hospital* to *Jazz* in volume 9 (93 pages), the same span of topics in a recommended elementary school encyclopedia requires all of volume 11 and the first three quarters of volume 12 (716 pages).

Not only are the scope and treatment of *Young People's Illustrated* narrow, thereby limiting the amount of information on a subject, but in addition, many subjects important to elementary school children have been omitted entirely. When compared with a similar set, between the entries *Jefferson, Thomas* and *Locomotive,* 76 entries have been omitted from volume 10 of *Young People's.* Among the more important ones omitted are Job; Joffre, Joseph Jacques Césaire; Josephine (French Empress); Joyce, James; June (sixth month); june bug; juvenile court; juvenile organizations; katydid; Kepler, Johannes; Kidd, Captain William; Kiev; kindergartens; kingfisher; Kingsley, Charles; kites; knives; knots; Knoxville; Koch, Robert; Kosygin, Aleksai Nikolaevich; lace; lacquer; Lagerlof, Selma Ottiliana Lovisa; Lamb, Charles; Land, Edwin Herbert (inventor of many optical devices including the Polaroid land camera); and lightning.

It is difficult to determine what criteria were used either in selecting subjects or allotting space. While many important subjects are not included, the word "limerick" is given 300 words and a large illustration of a grandfather clock, because the writer claims that *Hickory, Dickory, Dock* is "probably the oldest surviving limerick." *King and Queen* is an article of 2,000 words. Such lengthy treatment is questionable for so generalized a subject particularly when it occurs at the expense of omitting capitals of states and nations. Land, geography, people, natural resources, manufacturing, and brief history is included for many countries. The map of the United States includes the major cities, rivers, and mountain ranges, but oddly enough, no state boundaries. One chart gives statistics, population, area, bird, flower, tree, and date of admission to the union.

Errors apparent in *Young People's Illustrated Encyclopedia* lead the Committee to doubt the reliability of this encyclopedia. Volume 10, page 861: "In the higher courts, the judge is called justice." This is misleading. In the United States, generally, only a judge of a Supreme Court, either federal or state, is called a justice.

A spot check to determine accuracy for the area in square miles for Colorado, Kansas, South Carolina, and South Dakota revealed that there is a discrepancy between the figures in *Young People's Illustrated* and the 1973 *Statistical Abstract of the United States*.

Other errors were found in a random sampling. In *Liberia* volume 10, pages 915-917, there is a small photograph of children playing in a city street. The caption reads "A residential section on the outskirts of Liberia." Cities rather than countries have outskirts. Volume 14, page 1306 describes porcupine as an animal which when under attack, uses its quills to defend itself and notes that the porcupine has been known to shoot these quills into its enemy from a short distance. *Larousse Encyclopedia of Animal Life* copyright by Paul Hamlyn, Ltd. 1967, page 524 states that the dominant feature of the crested porcupine is the crest of white-tipped quills loosely implanted. They easily become detached. This gave rise to an earlier belief that the porcupine could cast its quills at its enemy like darts. *World Book* states that porcupines defend themselves by striking attackers with their quilled tails. The quills come out easily and stick into the attacker's flesh. Porcupines cannot shoot quills at their enemies as some people believe.

Volume 12, page 1039 states that Monaco covers only six square miles. The 1974 *World Almanac* gives area of Monaco as 433 acres. At 640 acres per square mile the area is more like .6 of a square mile instead of six square miles.

Papyrus page 1228, does not mention any of its uses other than as a writing material. The article completely ignores papyrus' use in boats, baskets, sails, matting, ropes, caulking, fuel and food.

No census dates are given. Information on the individual states of the United States is too brief. *Utah* gives very few basic facts and no population statistics in the text. There is no picture of the state flag. A geographical map shows major cities and their altitudes. There are five small colored pictures and no charts or special guides. By comparison an elementary school encyclopedia recommended by the Committee has a small amount of text but excellent maps and charts. A "Utah profile" shows state flag, tree, bird, seal, motto, and song. The "picture profile" has 13 very good color pictures, and the fact summary covers government, education, agriculture, forest reserves, fishing, farm products, manufacturing, minerals, transportation, and other pertinent information.

There are no special maps showing natural resources and population. There is no key to pronunciation and no indication of pronunciation within the text. In spot checking the Index for accuracy, all entries are listed in proper alphabetical place. However, some Index entries are useless, because the subject cited in the Index is mentioned only briefly in the text.

See and *see also* references and a general Index facilitate locating information in *Young People's Illustrated*. There are no bibliographies and no fact index.

As indicated in the title, *Young People's Illustrated Encyclopedia* is profusely illustrated. However, the illustrations are small and often unclear. There are about 90 photographs for every 50 pages. Most illustrations are in color; they include maps, photographs, and diagrams. In many cases they are inappropriate to the text.

In a chart showing six kinds of skins used to make leather, antelope skin and goat skin appear to be identical. In the *Leaf* article, while it is commendable to provide a diagram of the transverse section of a leaf in 17 parts, the diagram is virtually useless because the function of each part is not discussed in the text.

The format of *Young People's Illustrated Encyclopedia* reveals that the set is intended for the young reader. The books are small, about ten-and-one-half inches by seven-and-one-half inches. The type is large and well leaded. None of the encyclopedias recommended by the Committee for elementary school students has such large type and such spacious pages. The bright red binding is not very sturdy; photographs of unidentified people and places are on both front and back covers. There are no preface or directions on using the encyclopedia.

The producers of *Young People's Illustrated Encyclopedia* fail to meet the curriculum needs of children in grades three to six. It is of extremely limited usefulness. Articles are insufficient in number. They are also inadequate and too brief in coverage. Though profuse, the illustrations are mediocre and often useless for explicating the text or for identification purposes. The finding devices are largely inadequate. Not recommended.

(June 15, 1974, p.1115)

Young Students Encyclopedia. Specially prepared with the staff of *My Weekly Reader*. Editorial Director, George H. Wolfson; managing editor, Mary Lou Kennedy. 15v. plus Parents' Manual. Middletown, CT, American Education Publications, a Xerox Co., [1972]. 2600p. illus. maps. charts. 29cm. mail order sale only. v.1 free, v.2-15, $3.95 each; entire set, $55.30 plus tax, postage and handling.

Young Students Encyclopedia. Editorial director, Harold J. Blum; editor in chief, Jean F. Blashfield. 20v. New York, Funk & Wagnalls, Inc., 1972. 3124p. illus. maps. charts. 26cm. supermarket sale only. v.1 25c, v.2-20, $1.89 each.

Editors of *My Weekly Reader* have joined with book publishers Funk and Wagnalls to create this all new children's encyclopedia in two separate formats, almost identical in content, to be marketed in separate ways—one as a Funk and Wagnalls publication and the other as a Xerox Company, American Education publication. American Education has published periodicals for classroom use for nearly 70 years. Among these magazines are *Current Events, My Weekly Reader* and other curriculum-related publications such as *Read, Current Science,* and *Issues Today.*

The larger 15-volume Xerox edition is bound in washable dark green accented with gold die stamping and will be sold by mail order only. The larger page size with two columns of text provides approximately the same amount of space as is contained in the Funk & Wagnalls 20-volume supermarket edition. Funk & Wagnalls page size is smaller, 7 3/8 inches by 9 3/4 inches compared with 8 1/4 inches by 11 inches, with only one column of text per page. It is bound in bright orange paper over boards with a collage of pictures from the different volumes in the form of a square on the front covers. In both editions, illustrations are arranged in the ample margins; approximately 20 percent more illustrations are included in the Xerox edition.

Separate editorial staffs directed the respective editions. John Schmid is publisher, George Wolfson, editorial director, Mary Lou Kennedy, managing editor, and Richard Harkins, editor of the Xerox edition. None of the staff is listed in any of the standard biographical references. Walter S. Houston, an eminent astronomer, is one of the four curriculum consultants.

For the Funk & Wagnalls edition Leonard Dal Negro is project director, Harold J. Blum, editorial director, and Jean Blashfield, editor in chief. Patricia Markum, juvenile author, is included in a standard biographical reference. No credentials are included with the listing.

The 39 contributors are the same for both encyclopedias. More than 50 percent are authors of juvenile books or articles for children's magazines. Included are such persons as Jocelyn Arundel, Mary Jo Borreson, Frances Cavanah, Martin Keen, Harry Neal, Will Barker and others readily identifiable. Articles are not signed, but names of the authors, their area of contribution, and their qualifications are listed at the beginning of volume 1 in both editions.

"*Young Students Encyclopedia* was published to provide a basic introduction to man's ideas, language, and world for children seven to thirteen years of age. Three fundamental concerns determined its content: coverage of those ideas most often included in the school curriculum, variation in reading ability, and encouragement of active reader participation."—*Foreword*. The material varies only by placement on the page, arrangement of pictures, and an occasional change of adjectives or omission of a sentence or paragraph. The Committee has examined both editions.

The Foreword states that "Approximately 100 categories were chosen for particular emphasis. They represent the prime concepts underlying current elementary school programs of study as well as children's outside interests. These categories serve as a basic introduction and 'umbrella' for the more than 2,400 articles that highlight and explore further various aspects of the major categories." This explanation prepares the user for the broad and balanced coverage. The general fields of science, technology, mathematics, plants, and animals account for approximately 20 percent of the articles, geography 15 percent, and history and government 10 percent. The remaining 55 percent of the space contains an even distribution of articles relating to health and anatomy, economics, arts and crafts, music, education and careers, religion, literature, customs and holidays, transportation and communication, and sports and games.

Choice of the articles for inclusion in the encyclopedia is based on the underlying philosophy that children now can understand certain elements in many subjects at younger ages than formerly; therefore the science entries particularly are far-ranging, limited not in scope and variety but only in the way material is presented. Together with such basic items as electricity, thermometers, magnets, and astronomy are also articles to introduce such concepts as cybernetics, regeneration, genetics, and radioactivity.

Presentation of facts has been geared to the seven- to thirteen-year-old. Experience gained from years of writing for *My Weekly Reader* and other juvenile periodicals written at various interest and reading levels is evident in the editorial policy which realizes that interests and reading levels are not uniform within this age span. Thus the authors have taken into consideration the variations in children's abilities to comprehend. The writing is conversational in style but factual without being condescending or over simplified. This does not result in a strictly definition-type explanation but relates first to something in a child's experience as in the article *Hormone*. "In a circus you may see a man eight feet tall. He became a giant because his body produced too much of the growth *hormone*. Hormones are chemical substances made in the body by endocrine or *ductless* glands." Ten more lines describe the work of hormones and how hormones get into the blood. Subsequent paragraphs describe in more detail the thyroid and pituitary glands and experiments with the effects of hormones on plants and animals. Boxed on the same page is a listing of 12 human hormones, the gland producing each, and the function each hormone performs.

Included are separate entries on each state, each province of Canada, and every country including the new nations of Africa. A uniform format gives brief information about land and climate, historical data, and present-day economic conditions including industry, natural resources, and cultural and tourist opportunities. In a box accompanying each of the state entries is a small map locating the area being described, and listing appropriate facts concerning the state flower, seal, bird, tree, capital with population, area in square miles, total state population, date of statehood, principal river, highest point, and largest city. The box for each nation includes the language, export products, unit of money, and the flag in addition to the map, capital city, area, and population.

Although the source of population statistics is not given, the figures correspond with only slight differences to those in reliable sources. Geographical terms such as isthmus, longitude, and desert are explained.

One of the weaknesses of *Young Students Encyclopedia* is the lack of adequate maps. The article on maps tells how maps are made and gives instructions on how to read road maps and other much more detailed types of maps than those provided in the encyclopedia. Included are: for each continent, a full page relief map which shows the capitals and major cities as well as the large rivers (no tributaries); for each country, an extremely small pinpoint map to be used as a guide for finding the country on the big continent map; for each state and Canadian province a small map, usually less than half a page, shaded to show highlands and plains, and indicating the capital, four or five major cities, principal river and mountain. There is also a climate map for each continent. There is no information about size of cities other than the capital; no gazetteer; no county, state, or even national boundaries shown; and no product or other variety map provided. Source of the maps is the Pictograph Corporation. Scale is given but no date. Since children are familiar with maps and are taught to use them at an early age, the absence of an atlas section or more detailed maps is a handicap in the use of the encyclopedia.

Major subjects are covered in several pages with clearly marked subheads, and at the close of almost all longer articles is a form of cross-reference which advises *For Further Information on:* and then outlines the main areas of interest in the category which the reader may pursue. At the close of briefer articles a heading *Also Read:* guides the user to related topics in the encyclopedia. This chain of cross-references provides effective encouragement to read further on a subject. Examination revealed no false references.

There is no indication how the editors chose articles to be included in the encyclopedia or at what reading level each should be written. Nor is there any information that the vocabulary used was checked against any of the widely accepted reading lists. However, familiarity with the school curriculum and the child's interest and natural curiosity are evidenced in the choice of material. Headings usually are in terms used by children; *Air Pollution,* (not Pollution, Air) *Little League, Roller Coaster, Dog Story, Horse Story, Hoofed Animals, Animal Voices.* There are some debatable listings as *Isabella and Ferdinand* instead of Ferdinand and Isabella.

A unique feature of the encyclopedias is the "learning by doing" activities scattered throughout the pages. Examples of such activities are how to make a compass out of a magnetized needle, cork, and a bowl of water; suggestions for decorating a lemonade stand as a method of advertising; or first steps in starting a stamp collection. Blue type is used to identify these experiments and activities which invite the reader to involve himself in learning by doing.

In addition, challenging questions are asked such as: "What is the make-up of all the substances in the world? How can the make-up of a substance be changed?" These serve as an introduction to chemistry. Sometimes the questions are within the article to encourage the reader to reach his own conclusion. Instructions in the text call attention to illustrations and ask the reader to do his own reasoning. These textbook devices are an effective way to capture the interest of young readers and to involve youngsters, and sometimes their parents, as participants in what they read. However, it is a departure from the usual journalistic style of more comprehensive encyclopedias.

The full instructions for the 59 children's games scattered throughout the entire set are another feature not usually found in such detail in juvenile encyclopedias. Attention is called to games for children in the article *Children's Games*. They are *see* referenced by type, whether outdoor or indoor, pencil and paper, for a group, etc. Some of these games such as Ante-Ante Over, Pussy Wants a Corner, Kick the Can, Tiddly-Winks, Lemonade, Tic-Tac-Toe, Stone, Scissors and Paper are well known, but written instructions are difficult to locate. It is somewhat of a surprise, however, to read under the heading *Rhythm* only the instructions for a game and no reference at all to music or any other usage of the word.

Recreation is well covered with full articles on major sports including ice and field hockey, croquet, archery, Little League baseball, wrestling, judo and karate, fencing, water skiing and skin diving. Some biographies of athletes such as Babe Ruth and Jim Thorpe are included as full articles. A few twentieth-century sports figures such as Jesse Owens are also featured in main articles, but information about many more contemporary athletes is included in the articles *Sports, Professional* and *Olympic Games*.

Model making, puppets, finger painting, tie-dyeing, knitting (but not crocheting), weaving, and stamp collecting are samples of the various craft and needlework articles included "to open the youngster's mind to a wide range of leisure-time enrichment possibilities."

Information about organized groups that are of interest to boys and girls is also included: Boys' Club, Scouts, 4-H Club, Camp Fire Girls, YMCA, YWCA, Red Cross, Salvation Army, Civil Air Patrol, and NAACP. Suggestions about organizing neighborhood clubs are given in the article *Clubs and Societies* and *Parliamentary Procedure*.

Full-color pictures, maps, charts, or tables on colored backgrounds brighten each page. Although there are some drawings, photographs illustrate most of the material because as the editors explain "today's young readers, with their prior experience of visual media, demand photographic accuracy and realism." Most of the photographs are sharp and clear, but there are occasional dark ones, faded ones and out-of-focus illustrations where details are not clear. Space is not wasted in broad expanses of sky or ground. Illustrations vary in size and shape and are positioned on the page near the text referred to. Many of the photographs have children involved in some activity or are of scenes that are of special interest to the age level for which this encyclopedia was intended. A caption accompanies each illustration and even if there is only one picture on the page an arrow directs the reader to the visual for which the caption is intended. The captions are not always statements. Under an inkblot in the article on psychology is the question "What do you see in this inkblot? Think about it, and then ask a friend what he sees." Unfortunately the text provides no information about the significance of this type of test. Some captions encourage comparison without comment as the simple statement under a drawing of an alligator and a crocodile: "The snout of a crocodile is different from that of an alligator." In this case the text on the same page gives details and differences to reinforce what the readers figure out for themselves. The illustrations are well chosen and serve a purpose. It is obvious they were not selected just to fill available space. At the beginning of each volume on a blue page are the acknowledgments for all illustrative materials used in that volume. Most of the photographs have been supplied by Armando Curcio Editore, SpA. Exceptions are listed in alphabetical order by source name with page number given. Pictures have been secured from many sources.

The creative use of color is a pleasing part of the physical makeup of the encyclopedias. In addition to the color photographs and the use of color in the drawings, vivid orange, green, pink, and purple are used as backgrounds for charts and tables; blue forms the background and print for suggested activities and small gold squares form the background for nuggets of information such as "Woodsey the Owl became the nation's new environmental symbol for pollution in September, 1971. His slogan is 'Give a hoot, don't pollute.' Like Smokey the Bear he can be seen on television and on posters." These items, positioned in the outer margins throughout the volumes provide human interest items, comparative statistics, and bits of eye-catching information, but unfortunately there is no reference to them in the Index.

The Index occupies the last 78 pages of volume 20 in the supermarket edition. Two pages of instruction precede the Index pages. There is an explanation of the letter by letter alphabetizing system used throughout the encyclopedia. Examples are given from the Index to illustrate this arrangement. Other paragraphs inform that each Index entry that is the title of an article is listed in boldface with volume and page number following. Under the entry several subentries may be listed. The birth and death of persons listed in the Index are given in parentheses following their names. Scientific groups to which plants and animals belong are listed. Pronunciation of hard-to-pronounce words is also given. Key to pronunciation is found on the page preceding the Index. Illustrations are identified by the word *pic*. Tables and maps are identified by using the full word. *See* references are used mainly with abbreviations to the spelled out word. There are few times when a *see* reference is used from a name not used to a name used such as *Northern Rhodesia* see *Zambia*, *Eire* see *Ireland*. Another use of the *see* reference is to the inverted heading such as *Guinea, Equitorial* see *Equitorial Guinea; Snowman, Abominable* see *Abominable Snowman; South Korea* see *Korea, South*. Occasionally a *see* reference refers to a broader heading such as *Outer Mongolia* see *Mongolia. See also* references are plentiful.

Though the print in the supermarket edition Index is quite small and items are arranged in three closely spaced columns per page, the ample indentation, variation of type, and clearly defined margins between the columns make the Index easy to use. The first word on each double-page spread is used as a guide word. This is positioned a bit off center at the head of the verso. The last word on the recto is also used as a guide word.

An item by item comparison of articles in volumes 7 and 8 in *Young Students Encyclopedia* supermarket edition with corresponding volumes in three other major encyclopedias revealed what was already evident, that there are not as many subjects listed and the treatment of those subjects included is not as comprehensive in *Young Sudents Encyclopedia*. It is the stated intention of the editors that *Young Students Encyclopedia* provide "basic introduction to man's ideas, language, and world" and that "the interlacing chain of cross references after each article guide the young student to related information."

Brevity has been achieved in a number of ways. For example in *The New Book of Knowledge* the article on *Federal Bureau of Investigation* written by J. Edgar Hoover has many statistics—the number of employees, of cases investigated, of offices in the U.S., of fingerprints on file, and the number of fingerprints received each day. The *Young Students Encyclopedia* enumerates these duties and accomplishments but omits all statistics. Another way of abbreviating is by eliminating diagrams and drawings. Under *Fingerprint* an explanation is made of different kinds of prints—loop, arch, whorl, composite—but no drawings to demonstrate these concepts as in other comparable encyclopedias. No drawings showing the cycle of tadpole to frog are included in the article *Frogs and toads*, although this transformation is explained in the text and color photographs of tadpoles and frogs are included. On the other hand, there is an excellent drawing of a fly with all its parts labeled and included also is the drawing of the anatomy of a fish showing the relative size of its brain. Omission of pictures of flags of other countries under *Flags* is a loss, although this information can be found under each individual country. Evolution of the U.S. flag is pictured, but no state flags appear in this article or under each state.

Another way to shorten articles is to omit information. It is understandable that this type of encyclopedia would not provide as much technical, scientific, or historic detail as would standard encyclopedias on such subjects as *Fascism, Fermentation, Fuel* or *Friction*.

Treating only part of a subject is another method of abbreviating articles. This was evident in the article *Forestry*, which was treated from the viewpoint of a career opportunity with little mention of the importance of forests, life in forests, management of forests, or other related information. The same limitation is observed in the article *Foreign*

Service. Other evidence of this type of abbreviation is in the omission of rules in the sports entries. Only general information is given for *Field Hockey*. Basic rules from a spectator's point of view have been provided for *Football*. Rules are provided for many other games including basketball, croquet, and hopscotch. Biographies, too, contain only enough information to identify the persons and to relate their contribution to their fields. Omitted are the controversial or turbulent aspects of a person's life.

These comments should not be considered as adverse criticism of the encyclopedias as a whole since the editors have deliberately intended to include only as much information as the seven to thirteen year olds could absorb and to present it in such a way that the reader would not be inundated in a maze of detail, but rather that this encyclopedia "should provide information beyond the scope of school text books. It should encourage a child to explore —to proceed from one topic to another to make learning a continuing process."

To provide this incentive the editors have included easily located information on such current topics as Bangladesh, electronic music, endangered species (listed under rare animals), the metric system, air pollution, water pollution, housing, insecticides, aerosol, drugs and addiction, ecology, quasar, Wankel engines, unidentified flying objects, Negro history, moon rocks, rock music, Vietnam, gerbils—plus the kinds of articles on history, geography, science, literature, and the fine arts that seven- to thirteen-year-old readers might absorb. Lack of interest or perhaps inability of the reader to comprehend may be the reason for omitting acupuncture, abortion, foreign aid, specific drugs and amphetamines, pornography, and censorship.

Errors and omissions are relatively minor and facts presented, while admittedly brief, are accurate. Emily Dickinson is misspelled in the Index. Two maps seem to have the plains and highlands reversed. The 1972 dates of the death of J. Edgar Hoover and Jackie Robinson are included, but the date of the death of Lyndon Johnson is not. Sometimes the index omits information mentioned in the text.

A Parent's Manual which accompanies the Xerox edition contains eight pages of bibliography listed in various sections of the Manual under headings "Further Reading for Family Well-Being," "Further Reading for Leisure-Time Enrichment," and "Further Reading Beyond the Classroom." The titles for suggested reading are all non-fiction and are subdivided under 14 subjects such as Travel, Nature Study, Literature, Health and Safety. The reading level is indicated and bibliographic information is uniform and complete. There are no annotations, but the selection is appropriate for the intended age group. Titles are available in most libraries or for purchase even though the copyright dates show only two 1970 titles, the others being mainly 1950 or 1960 publications. Apparently this Parent's Manual is not available with the Funk & Wagnalls edition. Therefore, the nearest to a bibliography in this edition is to be found in such articles as *Dog Story* and *Horse Story*. These are composite reviews and include such recent titles as *Sounder* (Armstrong), *Misty of Chincoteague* (Henry), and *Kingdom in a Horse* (Wojciechowska) but do not list publisher or date.

Other suggested reading is included in articles *Children's Literature, Science Fiction, Mythology, Biography, Newbery Award, Caldecott Award, Novel, Nursery Rhyme, Poetry, Short Story, Fable, Fairy Tale, Legend,* and *Animals of Myth and Legend*. Titles of books are also included in biographies of the 94 authors who range from Aesop to Laura Ingalls Wilder and include mainly such literary greats as Shakespeare, the Brownings, Sir Arthur Conan Doyle, Louisa Alcott, Louis Carroll, and Beatrix Potter. Pearl Buck is the most contemporary author listed. Titles enumerated in these articles are sometimes mentioned in the Index. There is no consistency with which titles are indexed.

These listings of titles, wherever they occur, do not substitute adequately for a bibliography in the encyclopedia. The addition of a bibliography would be most useful and in keeping with the editors' intent of "encouraging the child to explore."

Attached to volume 1 of the supermarket edition is a plastic recording entitled *Crazy Fun Trip*, "the excursion that takes you from Africa to the South Pole." Appropriate music and sound effects simulate a jet flight which is intended to be a guided tour through volume 1 of *Young Students Encyclopedia* with page numbers cited to special interest articles and a hint of things to come if future volumes are purchased. This recording is an Auravision product of CBS records with 1972 copyright. Subject to the format limitations of flimsy, plasticized paper, the information is well presented and provides an interesting promotional device.

A wrapper around volume 20 is a certificate which can be mailed to Funk & Wagnalls for a free set of book plates and can also be used as an order for the next annual yearbook when published. The annuals will cost $3.98, may be examined free for 10 days, and will be published for the next three years at least with no advance in price. Funk & Wagnalls intends to update the encyclopedia in this way and by means of continuous revision.

The Funk & Wagnall's pyroxylin-coated paper binding in brilliant orange with varicolored labels, plainly shows off the heavy black print of the title, the volume number, and the combination of three letters indicating inclusive arrangement of subject matter in each book. The binding though attractive is not very sturdy and will soon show signs of wear especially on edges touching the shelves. Inside, the paper is heavy and the print easy to read. One column of text provides ample space on the outer edges for an attractive arrangement of illustrations, "nuggets," or other visual aids. A few illustrations bleed into the inner margins, but there is sufficient room to allow for rebinding. The binding is tight, and therefore the pages do not lie entirely flat when opened. The books have a uniform 160 pages each and are an easy size to hold. Heavier type all in capitals identifies the beginning of each new subject; subheadings in different size type, the italicized new words in the text, guide words at the top of each page, and the abundance of cross-references contribute to making these volumes easy to use.

As clearly stated in the Foreword this encyclopedia is for home purchase and is intended to be used with parental guidance. *Young Students Encyclopedia* has an advantage over other encyclopedias sold in the supermarket at this price in that the information though brief is reliable, reasonably up to date, skillfully written, and attractively presented on quality paper with colorful drawings and photographs. While *Young Students Encyclopedia* will not replace more comprehensive standard encyclopedias for children, it can supplement them when inexpensive additional sets are needed. With this understanding, *Young Students Encyclopedia* is recommended for purchase for home, elementary school, and public library children's departments.

(Feb. 1, 1974, p.551)

NOTES AND COMMENTS

Acronyms and Initialisms Dictionary: A Guide to Alphabetic Designations, Contractions, Acronyms, Initialisms, and Similar Condensed Appellations.
Covering: Aerospace, Associations, Biochemistry, Business and Trade, Domestic and International Affairs, Education, Electronics, Genetics, Government, Labor, Medicine, Military, Pharmacy, Physiology, Politics, Religion, Science, Societies, Sports, Technical Drawings and Specifications, Transportation and Other Fields. Edited by Ellen T. Crowley and Robert C. Thomas. 4th ed. Detroit, Gale Research Co., [c1973]. xv, 635p. 29cm. cloth $27.50. ISBN 0-8103-0500-3.

Gale produced the first *Acronyms Dictionary* of 12,000 entries in 1960. With the second edition of 1965 came a change in title to *Acronyms and Initialisms Dictionary* and expansion to 40,000 entries. The third edition of 1970 contained 80,000 terms, and the current fourth edition has over 102,000 entries. Supplementing the new edition are *New Acronyms and Initialisms: 1974 and 1975 Supplements to Acronyms and Initialisms Dictionary*, 4th ed. covering 12,000 terms and *Reverse Acronyms and Initialisms Dictionary* containing 80,000 entries. These supplements sell for $30 and $27.50 respectively. *Reverse Acronyms* and the *1974 New Acronyms* are available now; the *1975 New Acronyms* is expected off press in February 1975. Editorial policies, organizations and arrangement are clearly explained in the book. The work is easy to use. For acronyms with more than one meaning various meanings are cited. The book is well designed and produced to withstand heavy wear.

(June 1, 1974, p.1069)

African Authors: A Companion to Black African Writing. v.I: 1300-1973. By Donald E. Herdeck; contributors Abiola Irele, Lilyan Kesteloot, Gideon Mangoaela. Washington, DC, Black Orpheus Pr., 1973. 605p. illus. 23cm. grade C natural finish fabric $27.50 postpaid with cash order. ISBN 0-87953-008-1.

Dr. Donald E. Herdeck, School of Foreign Service, Georgetown University, using authoritative primary sources whenever possible and exhibiting impeccable research methods, has undertaken the monumental task of furnishing "the general public with a basic reference guide to a major literature which is little known and even less appreciated in the West." Herdeck also aims "to provide the student and scholar in African studies a kind of base line of information of what is now known of the African literary tradition and its most contemporary productions."—*Introduction*. Not only is *African Authors* a worthy contribution to the literature of Black African writing, but it is also unique in providing biographical information on 594 authors who have written in 37 African vernacular languages and bibliographic information on more than 2,000 works covering a number of literary genres.

The volume under review is the first in a biennial series. According to the publisher, Black Orpheus Press, subsequent volumes will update and correct the previous editions, will add authors and will include new critical original essays by recognized authorities. Cumulative, revised editions are planned for each six-year period.

For each biographee is given a capsule biography including the author's name with variants and pseudonyms in parentheses, birth and death data, genre of writing, and author's profession that may be relevant to his writing (scholar, journalist, teacher). The main biography first paragraph describes the author's schooling, degrees, professional training, travel, positions held, honors won, and general statements on author's relative importance and literary reputation. One or more works usually may be cited and discussed briefly. Length of biographical note agrees with the importance of the writer, with minor authors being covered briefly usually in a single paragraph. Major authors may be covered in several pages with somewhat detailed discussion given to general works. Herdeck attempts to convey the flavor of the author's work by quoting brief passages which give examples of style or method of handling a theme or rhythm.

Herdeck generally limits biographies to creative writers; most of the articles are about writers of the early twentieth century. However, he gives some attention to authors "whose journalistic and historical studies in folklore and oral literature provided later writers with needed inspiration or materials."

The publisher's explanation of the age of some photographs and the difficulty of obtaining others probably accounts for the lack of sharpness of quite a few photographs. Where photographs were completely unacceptable Black Orpheus provided line drawings. The use of book jackets from African authors' publications is particularly effective.

The Appendixes comprise a large part of the book and are a separate reference collection that could stand alone. Part I is comprised of four critical essays by authorities: "The Development of Contemporary African Literature," by Abiola Irele, "Black Writers and the African Revolution," by Lilyan Kesteloot, "Vernacular Writing in Southern Africa," by Gideon Mangoaela, and "Three Key Afro-Caribbean Writers: Aimé Césaire, Leon Damas, René Maran," by Donald Herdeck. Part II contains Authors by Category, Authors by Chronological Period, Authors by Genre, Authors by Country of Origin, Authors by African Languages, Authors by European Languages, and Female Authors. Part III lists Publishers, Journals, Bookshops; Major Publishers of African Literature; Journals Specializing in African Literature; and Bookshops and Book Distributors. The final Appendixes, Part IV list Bibliographies and Critical Studies in African Writing, Anthologies of African Writing in English, French, and Portuguese, and an Analytical Table of Anthologies of African Writing.

African Authors is a basic, authoritative, well-organized reference on the authors and literature of Black Africa. *(Jan. 15, 1974, p.499)*

Afro-American Artists: A Bio-bibliographical Directory. Compiled and edited by Theresa Dickison Cederholm. [Boston], Boston Public Library, 1973. 348p. 24cm. paper $10.

The Committee congratulates Boston Public Library for preparing this much-needed biographical-bibliographical directory of black American artists. This comprehensive directory attempts to fill the void in sources of biographical and bibliographical information on black American artists involved in all phases of the fine arts and crafts—painting, sculpture, photography, printmaking, designing, watercolor, graphics, murals, ceramics, and the like. The book is both retrospective and contemporary, and it covers the period from eighteenth-century slavery to the present. For each artist the following information is given as applicable: name, art medium, year and place of birth, studies, titles of works, exhibitions, sources, collections, awards, membership in organizations, and name of representative. Data were gathered from exhibition catalogs, reviews, periodicals, books, and questionnaires. Collections in 27 institutions like New York Public Library and The Schomberg Collection on Negro Literature and History, Oakland Museum, Detroit Institute of Arts, and Fisk University aided Boston Public Library in the research project, which was funded by the Massachusetts Council on the Arts and Humanities and the National Endowment for the Arts. A useful 23-page Bibliography of sources completes the work. For ease of use the sources are divided into four categories of printed matter: books, exhibition catalogs, magazines, and newspapers. Sources pertinent only to one artist are listed with that artist's sources in his biography and are not repeated in the Bibliography. *(Nov. 15, 1973, p.302)*

American Art Directory 1974. Edited by the Jaques Cattell Press for the American Federation of Arts. New York & London, Jaques Cattell Pr./R. R. Bowker Co.,

c1974. 458p. 28cm. cloth $32 plus shipping and handling.
ISBN 0-8352-0647-5.

The 1974 *American Art Directory* is the 45th edition of a triennial publication which began in 1898. It has appeared under various titles; from 1898 to 1945/48 it was known as *American Art Annual*. From 1936-1947 Part 2 of *American Art Annual* was called *Who's Who in American Art*. The current work lists some 1,500 art organizations and museums in the United States, about 150 in Canada, and 250 museums abroad. Information is organized under seven main headings: Art Organizations, Major Schools, Directors and Supervisors of Art Education in School Systems, Art Magazines, Newspapers with Art Notes and Their Critics, Scholarships and Fellowships, and Travelling Exhibition Booking Agencies. Each section is arranged geographically. Full information including address, telephone number, officers or curators, type of collection or activities, and fees are given for museums and organizations. Entries for art schools and institutions of higher learning with art courses give name, address, telephone number, name of head official, number of instructors, date established, enrollment, entrance requirements, degrees awarded, curricula, cost of tuition, and availability of summer school. The directory is sponsored by the American Federation of Arts, a national not-for-profit organization founded in 1909. An extensive, analytical name/subject Index facilitates finding information. Libraries and practitioners will wish to update and replace their old editions of *American Art Directory*.   *(May 15, 1974, p.1014)*

American Black Women in the Arts and Social Sciences: A Bibliographic Survey.
By Ora Williams. Metuchen, NJ, The Scarecrow Pr., Inc., 1973. xix, 141p. ports. 23cm. cloth $5.
ISBN 0-8108-0615-0.

American Black Women does not pretend to be a comprehensive annotated bibliographic guide to the literature by and about Black women authors, artists, and social scientists in the United States. This small book is a revised and expanded version of an article which appeared originally in the March 1972 *CLA*, a journal of the College Language Association based in Baltimore at Morgan State College. The author hopes *American Black Women* will "serve as a consciousness-raising device acquainting many Americans with the names and talents of some American Black women authors, composers, painters, and sculptors."—*Introduction*. The bibliography claims to contain 1,000 entries covering 2,000 volumes. It is selective in coverage, but there is no statement of the bases of selection or the audience to whom the work is addressed. While it is apparent, therefore, that the Committee cannot judge how well the book adheres to its plan, it is necessary to query a bibliography so narrow in coverage that it lists only nine titles under "encyclopedias, reference books and handbooks" and omits such bibliographic sources as Ploski and Kaiser's *The Negro Almanac* (New York: Bellwether, 1971), *Great Negroes Past and Present* (Chicago: Afro-Am, 1969), *Profiles of Negro Womanhood* v.1 and 2 (Yonkers: Educational Heritage, 1964, 1966), *The Negro in American Literature, An Introduction to Black Literature in America*, and *The Negro in Music and Art* —from *International Library of Negro Life and History* (New York: Publishers Co., 1967-1970), and the three-volume, *Notable American Women 1607-1950* (Cambridge: Harvard Univ. Pr., 1971).

Prepared by a doctoral candidate at University of California, Irvine who teaches at California State University, Long Beach, *American Black Women* barely scratches the surface of a field that needs to be explored in an authoritative manner. The work is useful primarily for its analysis of the ramifications of the involvement of Black American women in literature, the arts, and social sciences. The book scratches the surface by organizing sources under bibliographies (21 titles); encyclopedias (9 titles); autobiographies and biographies (65 titles); arts, including cooking, dancing, music, painting, sculpture, theater (30 titles); anthologies (75 titles); collections (55 titles); plays (38 titles); literature for young readers (45 titles); and novels, short stories, poems, folk literature, historical, and cultural studies with varying numbers of works. There is a section of selected bibliographies for 15 women including Alice Childress, Philippa Duke Schuyler, Dorothy Porter, Shirley Graham DuBois, and Jessie Fauset. Other arts covered are painting, sculpture, illustrations, and music.

Four pages of audiovisual materials list films based on Black women's works, cassette tapes, records, and videotapes. Name and address are given for 26 Black periodicals and 22 Black publishing houses. Black Orpheus of Washington, DC, founded in 1971 is missing from the publisher's list. The 6 and ½-page Index is of limited usefulness, because it omits subjects and lists names only. *(Feb. 15, 1974, p.610)*

American Book Publishing Record: Annual Cumulative 1972. New York and London, R. R. Bowker Co., 1973. 1062p. 29cm. Case-Columbia Bradford D $36.50 plus shipping and handling.

This is the cumulation of the 12 monthly issues of *American Book Publishing Record* issued in 1972. The 34,000 books listed "represent books submitted for listing by American Publishers and by authorized American distributors of current works published in foreign countries and offered for sale here." U.S. government publications from the Government Printing Office are omitted because their volume is too great. *American Book Publishers Record* adheres to the UNESCO definition of a book as a non-periodical publication of 49 pages or more, but pamphlets of sufficient value and interest to merit public attention are also listed.

The work is divided into three separate sections each arranged alphabetically. The first section of 758 pages covers nonfiction arranged under Dewey Decimal Classification, and then alphabetically by author under each classification. Adult fiction is listed on the next 46 pages, and the final section of 31 pages lists juvenile fiction. Included for each entry are author, title, publisher, edition, size in centimeters, indication of illustrations, and binding other than cloth. Price, International Standard Book Number, Library of Congress card number, subject headings, and class numbers are also given, when available. A three-page Subject Index precedes the listings, and author and title indexes follow the listings. Monthly subscriptions to *American Book Publishing Record* are available for $19 annual fee in the United States. The *Record* is particularly useful in updating collections and in preparing up-to-date subject bibliographies.
(Oct. 15, 1973, p.185)

The American Heritage Book of Great Historic Places. By the editors of American Heritage; narrative by Richard M. Ketchum; introduction by Bruce Catton. New York, American Heritage Pub. Co., Inc.; book trade distribution by McGraw-Hill Book Co., [c1957, 1973]. illus. 288p. 28cm. cloth $16.50; deluxe ed. $19. ISBN 07-034413-2 (regular) ISBN 07-34414-0 (deluxe).

The American Heritage Book of Great Historic Places was well received by literary critics when it was first published in 1957. Richard M. Ketchum, editor of *American Heritage* magazine, is responsible for the commentary in the 1973 revised and updated version as well as for the original edition. The text is organized along geographic lines as it was in 1957: New England, Atlantic, Appalacia, the South, the Mississippi River, the Great Lakes and Prairie, the Great Plains, Spanish Southwest, and the Far West. The 407 black-and-white and colored illustrations include reproductions of paintings, lithographs, prints, and drawings. They have been chosen judiciously to illustrate historic places in the United States. The narrative is accurate, authoritative, and unbiased, and the most important historic sites are described. Browsers will enjoy *The American Heritage Book of Great Historic Places*. Libraries that do not have 1957 copies in good condition will wish to acquire this new edition.
(Feb. 15, 1974, p.611)

American Indian Women. By Marion E. Gridley. New York, Hawthorn Books, Inc., [c1974]. vi, 178p. illus. 22cm. cloth $5.95. ISBN 0-80150234.

Marion E. Gridley is a prolific author of books on American Indians. A number of her books, published by various publishing houses, are in print. Her latest work is a short collection of narrative biographies of outstanding American Indian women of both the past and present. Included among the women are Pocahontas, Sacajawea, Susan La Flesche Picotte, Elaine Abraham Ramos, and Maria Montoya Martinez. The facts are accurately recorded, but the stories are not useful for reference purposes, because dates are given rather haphazardly, if at all. For example, the biography of Maria and Marjorie Tallchief cites no birth dates and very few years of other important happenings in their lives. A two-page Bibliography is appended, and an analytical Index facilitates locating facts.
(June 1, 1974, p.1069)

American Malacologists: A National Register of Professional and Amateur Malacologists and Private Shell Collectors: And Biographies of Early American Mollusk Workers Born Between 1618 and 1900. [R. Tucker Abbott, editor in chief.] 1st ed. 1973-1974. Falls Church, VA, American Malacologists, 6314 Waterway Dr., c1973. iv, 494p. 21cm. cloth-grade A $12.50; to libraries, 20 percent discount if payment accompanies order. ISBN 0-0913792-02-0.

American Malacologists (collectors of mollusks or shells) is a first attempt to fill the "need for a register or biographical reference book in the field of malacology, one similar to *American Men and Women of Science* or *Who's Who in America*, but one that would include the lives of amateur conchologists as well as professional college-trained research workers." A second edition is planned for 1976, and *European Malacologists* and *International Malacologists* are projected for the future.

Included in the present work are Geographical Index by State, Census of Professional Researchers 1972-73 (current activities and past interests), Statistical Summary, Occupation Classification, Biographies (Deceased), and Biographies (Living). There is also a list of persons about whom information is wanted. Of the living malacologists listed, about 40 percent are professional, and 60 percent are amateur. For most biographies the following information is given: name, birth date and place, citizenship, occupation, positions held, malacologist memberships, other professional and civic memberships, writing and editorships, research areas, private collections, travel for mollusks, honors, and listings in other reference books. This biographical directory will be of interest to malacologists and to libraries that collect all types of biographical references. The editor is a professional malacologist who holds a Ph.D. from George Washington University. *(May 15, 1974, p.1014)*

American Men and Women of Science. Discipline Index; The Physical and Biological Sciences. 12th ed. Edited by the Jaques Cattell Pr./R. R. Bowker Co., 1973. xi, 536p. 29cm.
pyroxylin-impregnated D grade $25 plus shipping and handling.
ISBN 0-8352-0637-8.

The publisher has at last provided the much-needed dicipline index to the six-volume directory, *American Men and Women of Science*. This makes it possible to locate the top scientists in such fields as astrophysics, food chemistry, physiology, poultry pathology, solid state electronics, toxicology, and animal virology. Altogether more than 1,000 subject fields are included; these conform to the subjects given in the full-length biographies for the 137,500 scientists in the parent work. Biographees with several specialties are listed under each specialization making for ease of identification. Discipline cross-references facilitate locating scientists in related fields. The book is well designed and is printed in very legible type. Inner margins are sufficiently wide to permit rebinding. Libraries with the twelfth edition of *American Men and Women of Science* will find this index indispensable. *(Feb. 15, 1974, p.611)*

American Women: The Standard Biographical Dictionary of Notable Women. v.III 1939-40. Durward Howes, editor; Mary L. Braun [and] Rose Garvey, associate editors. Teaneck, NJ, Zephyrus Pr., Inc., [c1974]. 1083p. 24cm. cloth $37.50. ISBN 0-914264-01-X.

American Women is an exact reprint and reissue of volume III of *American Women* published originally in 1939 by American Publications, Inc. of Los Angeles. That volume was reviewed and recommended by the Committee in the April 1940 *Subscription Books Bulletin*. Volumes I and II had been reviewed in the October 1935 and October 1937 issues respectively. Libraries requiring critical information on the reissued book are referred to the April 1940 review. The only addition to the reprint edition is a one-page Publisher's Foreword to the Reprint Edition.

(July 1, 1974, p.1164)

An Annual of New Art and Artists '73-'74.
Editor in chief, Willem Sandberg. New York, Harry N. Abrams, [1973]. 203p. illus. 30cm. paperbound $12.50. ISBN 8109-9004-0.

Harry N. Abrams of New York has collaborated with seven international publishers (Blume of Barcelona, Contact from Amsterdam, M. Dumont Schauberg of Cologne, Garzanti of Milan, Pierre Horay of Paris, Lindhardt og Ringhot of Copenhagen, and Thames and Hudson of London) to produce an anthology of the works of 53 contemporary artists from 18 countries. Chief editor Willem Sandberg is well qualified by experience and background to supervise the project having directed the City Museum, Amsterdam and the Israel Museum, Jerusalem. Libraries with large art collections will wish to consider this first issue of a major international annual of contemporary art.

(June 1, 1974, p.1069)

Annual Register of Grant Support 1973/74: A Comprehensive Guide to Fellowships, Grant Support Programs of Government Agencies, Foundations, and Business and Professional Organizations.
Deanna Sclar, editor and the Staff of Academic Media. Orange, NJ, Academic Media, [c1973]. xiii, 828p. 29cm. cloth $39.50. ISBN 0-87876-037-7.

This seventh *Annual Register of Grant Support* makes information more accessible than its predecessors, and it includes 1,581 listings. The first *Annual Register, 1969* superseded. *Grant Data Quarterly, 1967-68*. Included among new sources not previously cited are labor unions, major industrial firms, and educational associations. Also new is a fourth index to personnel. The current *Annual Register of Grant Support* aims "to provide the academic and professional community-at-large with the most up-to-date source of information on all existing forms of non-repayable financial aid." The seven major areas for support covered are 1) general 2) humanities 3) social science 4) sciences 5) health and medical sciences 6) area studies and 7) environmental studies.

For each organization both the address of the grant-making organization and the address for submission are listed along with descriptive information on the kind of award, eligibility, duration of the award, the amount of money given, and the names of the trustees, directors, and other officers of the organization. Four indexes facilitate locating information, a Subject Index, Organization Index, Geographic Index, and Personnel Index. The book is extremely well designed for ease of use.

(May 15, 1974, p.1015)

Annual Review of United Nations Affairs, 1971-1972. Compiled by Florence Remz. Dobbs Ferry, Oceana Publications, Inc., 1973. xxvii, 247p. 24cm. cloth $10 ISBN 379-12321-5.

The 1971-1972 *Annual Review of United Nations Affairs* is the twenty-first annual edition. It includes materials "selected because of their significance and to indicate in a necessarily limited way, the wide range of United Nations activities, many of which are carried on without much notice in the information media." In contrast to early volumes, which included the record of the proceedings of the Institute for Annual Review of United Nations Affairs held each summer by the Graduate Program of Studies in United Nations and World Affairs at New York University, this edition contains only actual U.N. documents. The 31 papers and documents have been judiciously selected to include the year's highlights. These include the restoration of rights to the Peoples Republic of China, the United Nations inspired cease-fire in the India/Pakistan conflict, emergence of the new state of Bangladesh, meetings of the Security Council held in Addis Ababa away from United Nations headquarters, the United Nations Conference on Human Environment with the establishment of the global United Nations Environment Programme, and the third session of the United Nations Conference on Trade and Development. The most authoritative sources have been used, and these are cited down to page number. Most documents are from *UN Monthly Chronicle,* but there are a few from *General Assembly Official Records,* and one is an *Outer Space Committee Document.* Libraries will want to acquire this inexpensive record of important United Nations events of 1971-1972. *(Mar. 1, 1974, p.701)*

The Archaeologists' Year Book 1973: An International Directory of Archaeology and Anthropology. [Park Ridge, NJ, Noyes Pr., Noyes Bldg., 1973]. 229p. 23cm. cloth $12.50.

This first *Archaeologists' Year Book* is a directory of names and addresses rather than a book of the year which recounts noteworthy events in archaeology and anthropology. The British emphasis is revealed by the fact that eight of the 14 sections are concerned with Great Britain: British Museums; British Universities; British National Societies; Scottish Societies; British Councils, Committees, Trusts; British Regional Societies, Republic of Ireland Societies; and Laws Relating to Archaeology in Britain. In contrast, four sections are devoted to International Universities, International Museums, International Societies, and International Research Groups. Even the bibliography of recent books on archaeology is of British publications. The books aim "to provide on an International basis, the basic facts on museums, universities, associations, and other institutions whose activities cover the fields of Archaeology, including industrial, Anthropology and Folk-Life studies" is executed with a decided British bias. The bibliography by Stanley E. Thomas is unique, because it is comprised of book reviews listed under the broad headings of archaeological methods and allied studies, general archaeology, science and archaeology, prehistoric and Roman Britain, world and European prehistory, paleolithic archaeology, and regional surveys. In spite of its lack of balanced, comprehensive coverage, the book is worthwhile as a more-or-less up-to-date, accurate directory. *(Dec. 15, 1973, p.402)*

ARTbibliographies Modern. v.4, no.1, 1973. Editor, Peter Fitzgerald; assistant editor, Tony Sloggett; editorial assistant, Katrina Robinson. Santa Barbara, CA, American Bibliographical Center-Clio Pr., [c1973]. vii, 229p. 30cm. paperbound service rate.

ARTbibliographies Modern is an abstracting and annotating art bibliography service covering modern art and design literature since 1800. The present volume contains 2,233 book and periodical entries; it continues and expands *LOMA: Literature on Modern Art* 1969, 1970, and 1971. The bibliography purports to be comprehensive covering worldwide literature in all languages. The material is organized under subjects: Art Theory, Street Art, Mobiles, Naive Art, Suprematisn, Psychotic Art. Peter Fitzgerald, editor of *ARTbibliographies,* is senior lecturer, University of Reading Fine Arts Department. *ARTbibliographies Modern* has a companion series called *ARTbibliographies: Current Titles.* The two services together intend to provide complete art reference service.
(June 1, 1974, p.1069)

Articles on Twentieth Century Literature: An Annotated Bibliography 1954-1970. By David E. Pownall. 3v. of 7v. New York, Kraus-Thompson Organization Ltd., 1973. 26cm. buckram $195 (complete set). ISBN 0-527-72150-6.

Librarian, David E. Pownall, author of this annotated bibliography of twentieth century literature, has a firm grounding in the humanities. The bibliography includes all of "Current Bibliography" in *Twentieth Century Literature,* a quarterly published by IHC Press of Los Angeles, plus 10,000 articles from other sources. The work generally excludes book reviews, review articles, popular journalism, and elementary level articles on teaching literature. Pownall intends to study all authors who actually lived into and published works in the twentieth century. Some few who lived briefly into this century but whose careers were essentially completed before 1900 were excluded. Pownall was aided by editors James R. Baker, Louis Leiter, Warren G. French, 11 assistant editors, and 108 annotators. While most of the articles cited are in English, more than a fourth are in French, Spanish, and German. The annotations are precise descriptive evaluations of the literature cited, and they bear the initials of their authors. Material was selected from some 370 journals. The first three volumes of *Articles on Twentieth Century Literature* cover *Abbe* to *Iwaskiewicz.* The final volume in the series is scheduled for 1974 publication. When the set is completed the Committee will publish a full-length critique.

(Mar. 1, 1974, p.702)

Atlas of Discovery. Text by Gail Roberts; maps by Geographical Projects. New York, Crown Publishers, Inc., [1973]. illus. maps. 192p. 30cm. cloth $9.95. ISBN 0-517-50563-0.

Atlas of Discovery was printed and bound in Spain. Geographical Projects Limited of London produced the historical, relief, and political maps; Aldus Books of London holds the copyright to the work. The maps, which intend to tell the story of exploration from earliest days to the present, are amplified by 13 chapters of text written by Gail Roberts. Due to the arrangement and presentation of material, the atlas will be more useful for browsing than for locating specific facts. Treatment is well suited to the layman without expertise in history and geography. The pleasingly-colored political maps are satisfactory, but the dark colors in some of the relief maps do not allow sufficiently for showing gradation of shading. There are a few good reproductions of historical maps and charts by Mercator, Diego Gutiérrez, and Giacomo Gastaldi. The tight binding will not allow for rebinding without loss of map material which bleeds into the inner margins. *Atlas of Discovery* is a worthwhile library acquisition at the price. *(Feb. 15, 1974, p.611)*

Atlas of Hawaii. [By] Department of Geography. University of Hawaii. [R. Warwick Armstrong, editor and project director]; James A. Bier, cartographer; Sen-dou Chang, gazetteer compiler. Honolulu, The University Press of Hawaii, [1973]. 222p. maps. charts. diagrs. tables. 9″ x 12″ Kivar 3-17 paper $15; to schools and libraries, 10 percent discount. ISBN 0-8248-0259-4.

"The *Atlas of Hawaii* is a general thematic atlas which treats the state of Hawaii as a whole rather than emphasizing a particular island or area."—*Introduction.* The atlas is intended primarily as a reference work, but it will also serve as an inventory of resources and an educational and promotional tool for the state of Hawaii. The atlas was prepared and compiled by 34 authors and contributors, all of whom seem well qualified by position and training to contribute to an accurate, authoritative atlas of Hawaii. The information is primarily in the form of maps, graphs, charts, diagrams, and other illustrations. Short discussions in the text supplement the illustrations; the text is divided into five parts: 1) 15 reference maps with some 3,300 place-names for towns, mountains, bays, and geographic features; 2) natural environment including soils, water, geology, climate, air, plants, birds, insects, and mammals; 3) the cultural environment covering the people, languages, religions, and the arts; 4) the economy describing agriculture, forestry, energy, manufacturing, transportation, and communication; and 5) the appendixes comprised of statistical tables, selected bibliography, references cited, and the gazetteer.

Place-names were checked with the Advisory Committee on Geographical Names, State Department of Planning and Economic Development, and they

were authenticated by comparing with existing maps and gazetteers. Diacritical marks help clarify pronunciation of Hawaiian names. The maps and illustrations are clear. Colors are pleasing. All the maps indicate scale, and the islands are all on the same scale, thus permitting geographical comparison. The data given in illustrations and text is recent, the major source being the 1970 U.S. Census of Population. Most state and county data are for 1971. Most of the maps and diagrams give sources and dates of information. The inner margins of the atlas are sufficiently wide to permit rebinding. The University of Hawaii is commended for producing an authoritative easy-to-use atlas covering all phases of life in Hawaii.
(Feb. 15, 1974, p.611)

Australian Books in Print 1973 (Including Bookbuyers' Reference Book). Editor, Joyce Nicholson. 11th ed. Melbourne, D. W. Thorpe Pty. Ltd.; distributed in the U.S. and Canada by R. R. Bowker Co., 1973. 319p. cloth $15 plus shipping and handling. ISBN 0-909532-01-X.

The 1973 *Australian Books in Print* is the eleventh edition and the first to be hardbound. The work is divided into three sections. Section 1 contains lists of book trade associations, library associations, children's book councils, literary societies and clubs, literary prizes and awards, series of books, and 1,600 Australian magazines. Section 2 lists in an alphabetical author, title, and subject arrangement all Australian books in print. Textbooks, government publications, subscription, and trade books are included. Author, title, publisher, price, number of pages, binding if other than cloth, and size are given for each title. Part 3, printed on blue paper, is a listing of overseas publishers with Australian representatives and agents. While the print is clear and easy to read, the binding leaves much to be desired, and the narrow inner margins would prevent rebinding. Reference and acquisitions departments of libraries requiring current bibliographic data on Australian publishing will wish to acquire the work. *(Feb. 15, 1974, p.612)*

Better Homes and Gardens Encyclopedia of Cooking. 18v. [Editorial director, Don Dooley; managing editor, Malcolm E. Robinson; food editor, Nancy Morton.] New York, Des Moines, Meredith Corp., 1970. illus. 26cm. pre-printed 4-color corvon 120 $31.86 FOB Des Moines.

In these 4,000 recipes the editors of *Better Homes and Gardens Encyclopedia of Cooking* claim to "have put together the culmination of nearly 50 years' of cooking experience" which "guides you confidently through every detail of food shopping, food storing, meal planning, cooking, and serving." —*Cooking by Encyclopedia*. The Reference and Subscription Books Committee has tested a number of the recipes and directions and finds them economical, accurate, and easy to follow. Featured are recipes for Afro-American, Italian, and Creole cookery, appetizers, beverages, bread, canning, freezing, low-calorie cookery, quantity and quick cookery, poultry and fish cooking, and wines and spirits. Mundane, but necessary topics like leftovers, utensils, table settings, and tenderization are also covered. Many of the recipes are accompanied by brightly colored illustrations that entice the user to try the directions.

An easy-to-use 92-page Index in volume 18 facilitates locating all the information in the books. The unusual concept of a multivolume cookbook is well achieved by *Better Homes and Gardens Encyclopedia of Cooking*. These inexpensive books will be most useful to the homemaker. Regardless of experience in the kitchen the reader will find authoritative helpful hints in a well-coordinated compilation.
(Jan. 15, 1974, p.499)

A Bibliography of Finance and Investment. Compiled by Richard A. Brealey and Connie Pyle. Cambridge, MIT Pr., [c1973]. 361p. 25cm. cloth $18.50. ISBN 0-262-02105-6.

Compiler Brealey is author of other MIT publications on securities and risks, and compiler Pyle is reference librarian at Mills College, Oakland, California. Their bibliography lists 3,600 empirical and theoretical studies in

corporate finance and speculative markets that were published in statistical or general economic journals since 1969 primarily in the United States. Works are arranged by author and also under 150 subject headings. The book is well designed for ease of use, and a variety of types and sizes of type has been utilized. Business libraries, public and academic libraries with extensive holdings in economics, and practitioners will find this bibliography a helpful guide to the literature of finance and investment.
(July 15, 1974, p.1213)

A Bibliography of Noise 1965-1970. By Mary K. Floyd. Troy, NY, Whitston Pub. Co., 1973. xxix, 373p. 24cm. cloth $17. ISBN 0-87875-029-0.

"Designed to serve the needs of different kinds of researchers from medical scientists to those with only passing interest in this increasingly severe social problem," this world bibliography of noise is the first in a series. Annual supplements are planned for publication during the fall of each succeeding year. The work intends to cite books and articles dealing with physiological, psychological, sociological, and cultural effects of noise. The author hopes the work will be useful to undergraduate, graduate, and professional students of medicine, psychology, sociology, and the physical and applied sciences, and also to architects, educators, and musicians.

Seventeen serial indexes and abstracts including *Cumulative Book Index, Index Medicus,* and *Index to Legal Periodicals* were used in compiling the bibliography. The Preface explains explicitly the definition of noise as applied to this book: "concerns noise and its effect on people, the culture, and cultural artifacts." One hundred two books, mostly in English, are listed. Author, title, place of publication, publisher, and date are given for each. As would be expected, the major part of the bibliography is devoted to journal articles. For these listings some 300 subject headings are used. Articles appear in two lists. The first is arranged alphabetically by title. Author, periodical, and date are given for each. The second list is arranged alphabetically by the many subjects. Subjects chosen evolve from the nature of the material and are not limited to any standard list like that of the Library of Congress. The publisher informs that the supplement for 1971 is available. Hopefully, succeeding issues can keep better pace with the many new publications on noise.
(May 15, 1974, p.1015)

Biographical Directory of the Comintern. By Branko Lazitch in collaboration with Milorad M. Drachkovitch. Stanford, CA, The Hoover Institution Pr., Stanford Univ., 1973. xxxxii, 458p. 24cm. cloth $15. ISBN 0-8179-1211-8.

Biographical Directory of the Comintern (Communist International 1919-1945) contains more than 700 individual biographies of Comintern personnel and includes 1) some 300 persons in the Comintern's directorate, 2) speakers at the 1919 to 1935 Comintern congresses, 3) members of the Comintern apparatus such as secret emissaries sent abroad and section and division heads, and 4) leaders of the international auxiliary organizations especially the Red Trade Union International and the Communist Youth International. Author Lazitch edits the review *Est et Ouest* in Paris and wrote *Lénine et la IIIe Internationale* and *Tito et la révolucion yougoslave*. Collaborator Drachkovitz is a Senior Fellow, Hoover Institution, who edited *Fifty Years of Communism in Russia* and *Marxism in the Modern World*. This directory supplements *Who Was Who in the USSR* (*Booklist* Sept. 1, 1973) which was recommended for reference use in college or larger public libraries where condensed information is needed on twentieth-century Russians.
(July 15, 1974, p.1214)

The Birds of America. From Original Drawings by John James Audubon, 1827-38; a selection of facsimile plates. v.I. London, The Ariel Pr., c1972. illus. double elephant folio (40" x 27") half linen cloth and boards $400. (Distributed by Voyageur Pr., 3021 Nicollett Ave., Minneapolis, 55408).

The Reference and Subscription Books Review Committee is advised by an expert that the 20 facsimile plates in volume I of this edition of Audubon reproductions bear a fine resemblance to the originals which are in the Meiningen (Germany) State Museum. This reprinting is limited to 250 copies; the second volume is available now from Voyageur Press. Voyageur is both distributor and co-publisher of the second volume which also sells for $400. Dr. Gottfried Mausberger, Berlin wrote the Introduction and the text on the plates for the German edition. Alissa Jaffa translated the Mausberger Introduction into English, and Dr. Elvis J. Stahr, President, National Audubon Society, who is described in the current edition of *Who's Who in America* as an educator, lawyer, and conservationist, and who holds innumerable earned advanced degrees, wrote the Foreword and inspected the proofs.

For this volume from "the most monumental illustrated ornithological work ever to have been undertaken," the selectors have chosen to depict: white-throated sparrow, Baltimore oriole, blue-winged yellow warbler, Carolina parrot, yellow bird or American goldfinch, bunting, red-shouldered hawk, passenger pigeon, le petit caporal, Florida jay, pileated woodpecker, snowy owl, rose-breasted grosbeak, American sparrow hawk, white-crowned pigeon, summer or wood duck, Louisiana tanager, white-winged crossbill, band-tailed pigeon, hairy woodpecker, red-bellied woodpecker, red-shafted woodpecker, Lewis woodpecker and red-breasted woodpecker. The plates are magnificent. On the page opposite each plate is a description which is a direct facsimile of the original. Descriptions cover briefly the habitat, breeding habits, the young, coloring of the bird depicted, and a statement on time and place Audubon executed the original.

(Dec. 1, 1973, p.351)

Black Africa. Hollis Lynch, advisory ed. New York, The New York Times/Arno Pr., 1973. illus. 514p. 29cm. $35. ISBN 0-405-04165-9.

"South African Club to Train White Women in Shooting," "Do White Men Have a Future in Africa?" "U.N. Council Votes Mandatory Curbs on Rhodesia, 11-0," "Kenya Will End Emergency Rule," and "Ethiopians Get New Constitution and Right to Vote for First Time" are headlines typical of those in the compilation of selected *New York Times* articles and feature stories on Africa from 1870 to the present. *Black Africa* is the latest addition to *The New York Times* series entitled *The Great Contemporary Issues*. The Committee commends this book as it did *Women* reviewed November 1, 1973 in *The Booklist*. Both scholars and laymen will find this selected narration of African history invaluable. Two clear, distinct black-and-white maps by Andrew Sabbatini locate countries in Colonial Africa 1885-1898 and in Africa today. Selections from the newspaper are organized under five chapters with chronological arrangement: Imperialism, Independence, Southern Africa, Political and Economic Development, and Africa and the Modern World. The newspaper articles, which are reprinted in their entirety, are followed by a brief summary chronology of Africa's development from September 1876 when "King Leopold of Belgium Forms the International Association for the Exploration and Civilization of Central Africa Leading to Belgium Control of Most of the Congo" to August 1972 when "General Amin of Uganda Orders Expulsion of More Than 50,000 Asians."

The utilitarian suggested reading list covering 29 general books published between 1958 and 1973 is conveniently subdivided geographically: West Africa, Central Africa, East Africa, and South Africa. A few biographies are also listed. Regrettably the Byline Index cited in the Contents is omitted. Libraries expanding their African collections will wish to add this fine source of material. *(Feb. 15, 1974, p.612)*

The Book of Europe: Your Guide to the Best Things To See and Do. Chicago, New York, San Francisco, Rand McNally & Co., [c1973 Mitchell Beazley Ltd.]. 256p. illus. maps. 29cm. fabroleen with meter board $19.95. SBN 528-81965-8.

A vast amount of accurate, concise, well-organized information is packed into this combination atlas and guidebook to Europe. Every aspect of the continent is covered country by country —architecture, parks, natural reserves, fauna, gastronomic and drink specialties, and travel. There are good double-page spreads in color and black and white of major cities and regions of Europe. Twenty-two keyed symbols on the maps depict the diverse cultural and recreational highlights of the continent. A four-page Gazetteer facilitates locating places on the maps. Endpaper maps —Northern Europe on the front and Southern Europe at the back—indicate scale and show highway and major road routes across Europe. *The Book of Europe* is published in collaboration with Mitchell Beazley of London and is produced simultaneously in Europe and in England. The handy size of the book makes it possible for the traveller to carry the work with him for ready consultation. *(Feb. 15, 1974, p.612)*

Books In Print 1973. 2v. New York & London, R. R. Bowker Co., [1973]. 28cm. pyroxylin impregnated-D grade $48.50 plus shipping and handling. ISBN 0-8352-0655-6.

Books In Print, a most useful bibliographic tool for both acquisition and reference work in libraries, has been expanded by 50,000 titles in the just off-the-press 1973 edition. Bowker states that the work contains about 398,000 titles available currently in the United States. *Books In Print* in the now familiar two-volume format, lists in-print titles alphabetically by author in volume 1 and alphabetically by title in volume 2. In this the 26th annual compilation, the following information is given as available: author, coauthor, editor, translator, title, number of volumes, series, language if not in English, whether or not illustrated, school grade range, year of publication, and price. Publisher, ISBN, publisher's order number, imprint, and type of binding if not cloth are also cited.

This year for the first time *Books In Print* cites the Library of Congress order number for most books. This added service allows libraries to order cards at the same time they order books.

Volume 2, Titles, contains the most comprehensive listing of active American publishers available anywhere. According to Bowker, 3,500 publishers are included. The directory gives full name of publisher, complete address, telephone number and ISBN assignment. A good Key to Publishers' Abbreviations of names appearing in the author/title listings, facilitates identifying publishers.

Books In Print is supplemented by several Bowker bibliographies—the new annual *Books In Print Supplement (The Booklist,* Oct. 15, 1973), published about three months before the parent work, *Subject Guide to Books In Print (The Booklist and Subscription Books Bulletin,* July 1, 1958), and the various specialized subject guides in medicine, business, and children's books. *Books in Print 1973* is an indispensable tool for all kinds and sizes of libraries. *(Jan. 15, 1974, p.499)*

Books in Print Supplement, 1972-1973: Authors, Titles, Subjects. New York and London, R. R. Bowker Co., 1973. 2245p. 29cm. Case-D $19.50 plus shipping and handling.

Books in Print Supplement is one of the several current national bibliographies published in 1973 to supplement *Books in Print*. Other useful volumes in the series are *Bowker's Medical Books in Print* ($24.50) and *Scientific and Technical Books in Print* ($28.50). The intent of *Books in Print Supplement* is to bridge "the gap between the annual publication of *Books in Print* and *Subject Guide to Books in Print*." This first midyear supplement claims to list some 37,000 new books published between July 1972 and September 1973, 7,500 titles that have gone out of print since January 1973, and more than 65,000 works which have registered price and other changes since *Books in Print 1972* was published.

Author and title indexes are provided for all the books. New and forthcoming books are also indexed by subject. This comprehensive bibliography gives all pertinent information necessary for ordering: author, title, editor, edition, Library of Congress number, series, grade level, publisher, year of publication, price, binding (if not cloth), and ISBN. Out-of-print works are identified by "o.p."

A directory of publishers represented concludes the volume. Notations indicate changes in names or addresses that have occurred since *Books in Print 1972* was published. This is a welcome addition to current bibliography.
(Oct. 15, 1973, p.185)

British Books In Print, 1973: the Reference Catalogue of Current Literature. 2v. London, J. Whitaker & Sons Ltd.; distributed in U.S. by R. R. Bowker, [1973]. 4451p. 30cm. cloth $45 plus shipping and handling.
ISBN 0-85021-070-4.

Since 1874 when Joseph Whitaker published his first *Reference Catalogue of Current Literature* indexing 35,000 in-print titles for sale in the United Kingdom, *British Books In Print* has grown from an irregularly published serial to an annual which lists 250,000 titles from 7,000 publishers. The 1973 edition is the third computer-generated edition and the third to cite authors, titles, and subjects in one alphabetic arrangement. Data given for each title includes authors, title, subject, publisher, size, price, number of pages, illustrations, edition, series, binding if not cloth, date of publication, and SBN. Use of the book is explained clearly in introductory directions. Many useful lists and tables not usually found in trade bibliographies are included: Table of Book Sizes, List of Abbreviations, List of Publishers, Publisher Identifiers in Numerical Order (each publisher is assigned a number to be used in the Standard Book Number), Guides to British Books and Their Publishers, British Publishers, Overseas Agents and Representatives, and Book Trade Bibliography (books dealing with publishing and book selling). *British Books In Print* is an indispensable tool for library reference, order, and catalog departments. *(Mar. 1, 1974, p.702)*

Business Books in Print 1973. Subject Index, Author Index, Title Index. New York & London, R. R. Bowker Co., [c1973]. 934p. 29cm. cloth $25.50 plus shipping and handling.

Earlier this year R. R. Bowker added to its list of useful in-print bibliographies *Scientific and Technical Books in Print* (*The Booklist* Nov. 1, 1973) and *Medical Books in Print* which the Reference and Subscription Books Review Committee will review Jan. 1, 1974. *Business Books in Print 1973* follows the pattern of the others in being based on *Books in Print* and *Subject Guide to Books in Print*. *Business Books* lists some 31,000 titles of insurance, banking, industrial management, and motivational research books. Scientific, technical, and medical aspects of business were excluded from consideration. For each title the following information is given as available: author, coauthor, editor, coeditor, translator, cotranslator, title, number of volumes, edition, Library of Congress number, series, whether illustrated or not, year of publication, price and type of binding if not cloth over boards, publisher's order number, International Standard Book Number, and publisher's name. The usual Key to Publishers' abbreviations is appended.

Authority for subject headings was Library of Congress catalogs and cards. Ample headings and cross-references are utilized. This book will be most useful to large public and special libraries with clientele seeking ready access to business information.
(Dec. 15, 1973, p.403)

Canadian Reference Sources: A Selective Guide. [By] Dorothy E. Ryder. Ottawa, Canadian Library Association, 1973. 185p. cloth $10. ISBN 0-88802-093-7.

Canadian Reference Sources is the most comprehensive guide to Canadian reference works so far published. This selective bibliography includes over 1,200 items covering Canada, its provinces and territories, and three cities: Mon-

treal, Toronto, and Ottawa. Based to a large extent on the National Library of Canada's holdings, the work attempts to cover reference materials to the end of 1971. Arrangement is under general reference works, history and allied subjects, humanities, science, and social science. Each of these subjects has numerous subdivisions. Full bibliographic data and annotations in English are provided for each entry. There is an author, title and limited subject Index. The first supplement is planned for publication in 1974. Meanwhile "Canadian Reference Works" 1972—a selection by Dorothy E. Ryder appeared in *Canadian Library Journal* v.30, no.4, p.346-351. For all libraries where there is a need for a guide to Canadian reference works supplementary to the information located in *Winchell* and *Walford*, this guide will be indispensable.
(May 15, 1974, p.1015)

The Charles Dickens Encyclopedia.
Compiled by Michael and Mollie Hardwick. New York, Charles Scribner's Sons, [1973]. xi, 531p. 26cm. cloth $15. ISBN 684-13562-0.

The Charles Dickens Encyclopedia was first published in 1973 in Great Britain by Osprey Publishing Ltd. The authors intend "to provide the most comprehensive companion to the works that has yet been attempted, but to include in it only the sort of information that we can imagine being of use or entertainment to someone." The material is accurate, well researched, and well organized. There are eight sections of information: the works—listing all of Dickens' works chronologically with brief critiques and plot summaries; the people—identifying all characters in Dickens' works with descriptive commentary on each character; the places—a selected gazetteer of Dickens' works and life; a Charles Dickens time chart of major events in the life of Dickens and a listing of contemporaneous happenings in the world; Dickens and his circle—listing family, friends, and associates who had the most influence on his life and work, quotations from Dickens, an Index to Quotations, and a Selective Index to the Time Chart which was prepared by Ann Hoffman. The print is quite small, and the inner margins are narrow. However, *The Dickens Encyclopedia* accomplishes its aim and is a welcome addition to references on Dickens.
(April 15, 1974, p.888)

Chicago Negro Almanac and Reference Book: A Reference Book With Wide-Ranging Uses for Scholars, Businessmen, Politicians, Government Officials, Labor Leaders, Human Relations Counselors, Teachers, Librarians and Newspaper Editors. Compiled and edited by Ernest R. Rather. [Chicago, Chicago Negro Almanac Publishing Co., Inc., The LaSalle Hotel, 10 N. LaSalle St., c1972]. xiii, 256, [2]p. illus. charts. tables. 29cm. roxite cloth retail $25.73 including shipping; to schools and libraries, $20 plus shipping.

Ernest R. Rather, publisher, compiler, and editor of *Chicago Negro Almanac* states that this is the first of a series of similar reference works planned for the 10 cities in the United States having the largest Negro population. Rather sets forth his purpose clearly and succinctly in his Publisher's Statement: "the compilation of a volume which chronicles the amazing role played by post-Du Sable Negroes in bringing Chicago to its present pre-eminence." Information in the almanac was gathered from questionnaires, interviews, and printed sources. This compendium has lists (presumably selective) of almost every conceivable activity of Negroes in Chicago, and for good measure a sizeable amount of national material is included. There are 91 photographs of living "distinguished Chicago Negro leaders," and 34 pages of biographies of varying lengths. Among the Johnsons the reader finds E. Marie (psychologist), Eddie C. (associate judge, Cook County circuit court), George E. (Pres., Johnson Products Co.), John H. (Pres., Johnson Publishing Co.), Marie Louise (assoc. dean of women, Circle Campus, University of Illinois), and Robert Edward (editor of *JET* magazine). For politics there are lists of Chicago Negroes serving in the U.S. Ninety-third Congress and Seventy-eighth Illinois General As-

sembly, Negro members of Illinois General Assembly 1876-1974, Chicago Negro ward committeemen, and Chicago's Negro Aldermen 1971-75. Concerning the judicial there are citations for Negro judicial officers in metropolitan Chicago, former Chicago Negro judges, Negro Assistant Corporation Counsels, Chicago Negro Assistant State's Attorneys, and Chicago Negroes in the U.S. Department of Justice. For education the reader can find information on percentage of Negro teachers in Chicago public schools, public school racial survey charts, 1939-1976 Negro members of the Chicago Board of Education, and lists of Negroes holding policy-making and administrative Chicago Board of Education positions. For those needing a Negro Chicago doctor, dentist, pharmacist, or minister, names, addresses, and telephone numbers are given. A January 1974 supplement is planned for the almanac, and the work will be completely rewritten biennially. Such a wide variety of information and facts requires a comprehensive analytical index to provide maximum access to the material. It is regrettable that the only index to this volume is a category index which uses such vague captions as "City of Chicago," "Public Officials," and "Historical Material." The book's narrow inner margins will prevent libraries from rebinding. *Chicago Negro Almanac and Reference Book* is unique in that it brings together under one cover so many current and historical facts about Negroes in Chicago.
(Nov. 15, 1973, p.302)

Chicano Bibliography 1973. Salt Lake City, University of Utah Marriott Library, 1973. 295, [2]p. 29cm. vinyl $8.

Chicano Bibliography is first in a series of ethnic bibliographies to be prepared and published by the University of Utah Marriott Library. According to the University, a bibliography of the Library's materials on blacks is almost completed, and an Indian bibliography is well underway. The purpose of *Chicano Bibliography* "is to enable students, faculty, researchers, and others to have ready access to Mexican American materials in the University of Utah Libraries."

The material is divided into six sections by format, but since the book lacks a table of contents the user gains access to the types of information only by leafing through the book. The greater portion of the bibliography is devoted to books, including a number of titles on microfilm. Books are listed alphabetically by author. Call number, title, publisher, and place and date of publication are cited. A separate section is provided for recently acquired books that have not been processed. Government documents are arranged alphabetically by issuing agency or author. Both juvenile and textbook material in the Educational Resources Information Center are listed separately, and so are periodical articles. A one-page list of periodicals and a page of films conclude the book. This bibliography will be most useful to users of the University of Utah Libraries. It will also have value for those preparing comprehensive bibliographies on Mexican Americans. Well designed, the copy is photographed from typewritten pages.
(Dec. 15, 1973, p.403)

Children's Books In Print 1973: Author Index, Title Index, Illustrator Index. New York & London, R. R. Bowker Co., [c1973]. [5th ed.] 790p. 20cm. Roxite-D grade $17.95 plus shipping and handling (20 percent off on 5 or more). ISBN 0-8352-0651-3.

Subject Guide to Children's Books In Print 1973: A Subject Index to Children's Books in 7,000 Categories. New York & London, R. R. Bowker Co., [c1973]. [4th ed.] 473p. 29cm. Roxite-D grade $17.95 plus shipping and handling (20 percent off on 5 or more). ISBN 0-8352-0687-4.

Lillian N. Gehrhardt, editor in chief of *School Library Journal* has written the Foreword to the fifth edition of *Children's Books In Print* and the fourth edition of *Subject Guide to Children's Books In Print*. Both bibliographies list 40,000 hard and paperbound books for children; 2,000 of these titles are new to these editions. The *Subject Guide* is classified under 7,000 subjects. In conformance with Bowker's other in-print volumes full bibliographic data is given and publishers indexes are provided. Both bibliographies are well designed for ease of use and to withstand heavy usage. *(May 15, 1974, p.1015)*

Coins: An Investor's & Collector s Guide.
[By] Mort Reed. Chicago, Henry Regnery Co., [c1973]. ix, 403p. illus. 24cm. cloth $10.

The Complete Book of Coin Collecting.
4th rev. ed. [By] Joseph Coffin. New York, Coward, McCann & Geoghegan, Inc., [c1973]. plates. 20cm. fictionette cloth $6.95. SBN 698-10539-7.

Coffin's book on coin collecting was well received when it was first published in 1938. Subsequent revisions followed in 1967 and 1970. The edition under review is the fourth. As with its predecessors, this revised edition is intended for those "who know little or nothing" about coin collecting. The work is divided into six chapters: "The Beginning of a Coin Collection," "Collecting United States Money," "Foreign Coins," "Ancient Coins," "Making a Profit from Coin Collecting," and "The Care and Cleaning of Coins." The six-part Appendix will be most useful for reference purposes, because it contains specific, easy-to-retrieve information on coin exhibitions, American and foreign coin dealers, terms used by numismatic dealers and collectors, numismatic periodicals, and clubs and organizations. There is a Table of Contents but no index. Some of the reproductions of coins in the 16 plates pages of plates, which are in the middle of the book, are too dark to be used for identification purposes.

Numismatic expert Mort Reed's guide to coins is well organized and arranged for reference use. Illustrations appear with the text. They are clear, sharp, and sufficiently large to be used for establishing the identity of coins. Part I "The Mechanics of Coin Collecting" contains sections of glossary, an extensive catalog of U.S. coins, commemorative issues, and easy-to-follow suggestions for storing and handling. Part II was written by four practitioners: James F. Ruddy wrote on coin grading, Q. David Bowers on successful investment in rare coins, Max Humbert on investing in modern world proof sets and commemorative issues, and David W. Akers prepared the article on investing in gold coins. Reed's book also has a Table of Contents but no index. In spite of the lack of index, specific facts can be located much easier in the *Investor's and Collector's Guide* than in *The Complete Book of Coin Collecting*. The lists of counterfeit, fake, and altered coins are valuable sources of information. Of the two coin books Reed's is preferred. *(Jan. 1, 1974, p.456)*

Collector's Guide to Antique Porcelain.
[By] Gordon A. Rust. New York, Viking Pr., [c1973]. illus. col. plates. 144p. 23cm. cloth $9.95; to schools and libraries 25 percent discount. SBN 670-22917-2.

Fine black-and-white and colored illustrations, a design checklist of Chinese export porcelain most popular in the Western world and the Appendix lists help Rust's *Collector's Guide to Antique Porcelain* achieve its aim as a concise introductory reference book on antique porcelain from its origins in 1122 B.C. to 1827. The brief text on decorating and identifying porcelain and that on Chinese and Japanese porcelain give useful guidance to the beginning collector. Sixty-one major porcelain factories of the world are cited with history and notation of factory marks. There is a chronology of dates important in the production of porcelain. The six-page Glossary identifies in layman's language such terms as *armorial, biscuit, kaolin, pate dure,* and *willow pattern*. The five-page Bibliography of current basic books cites books for further reading under such classifications as porcelain marks, general works, English, and Oriental porcelain. The listing of antique porcelain public collections in the United States, Great Britain, Europe, and elsewhere provides valuable reference information. Hobbyists and libraries will wish to acquire this handy, reasonably-priced little book.
(Feb. 15, 1974, p.612)

The Common Man Through the Centuries: A Book of Costume Drawings. [By] Max Barsis. New York, Frederick Ungar Pub. Co., [c1973]. illus. 354p. 29cm. A-grade pyroxylin cloth $16; to schools and libraries, $13.60. ISBN 0-8044-10755.

The late Max Barsis, designer for 20th Century-Fox from 1950 to 1957 and illustrator for children's and adult books produced *The Common Man Through the Centuries* for a general audience to meet the needs of researchers for stage and screen, dramatic groups, schools, colleges, and librarians. Barsis defines common people as all those of small or no means—beggars, soldiers, prostitutes, craftsmen, and peasants. The book begins with later Roman days, preceded by a few Greek examples necessary for an understanding of the Roman period, and ends with the French Revolution. The work is limited geographically to Europe from England to the eastern border of the old German Empire. Costumes including headdress, if any, and footgear, are clearly drawn in black and white. Not more than two appear on a page with an identifying label and a brief annotated caption. *The Common Man Through the Centuries* is organized in six sections: Ancient Greece and Rome, Ninth to Fourteenth Centuries, Fifteenth Century, Sixteenth Century, Seventeenth Century, and Eighteenth Century. A five-and-one-half page finding guide facilitates locating specific types of costumes under such captions as *cape, bodice, baker, executioner,* and *servant*. This well-designed, well-illustrated, and well-researched portfolio will add much to the literature of costume. Libraries, particularly those with comprehensive costume collections, will wish to acquire it.

(Mar. 15, 1974, p.752)

The Complete Book of Boating: An Owners Guide to Design, Construction, Piloting, Operation and Maintenance. [By] Ernest A. Zadig. Englewood Cliffs, NJ, Prentice-Hall, Inc., [1972]. 640p. illus. diagrs. charts. plans. 29cm. cloth $12.95. ISBN 0-13-160143-1.

Ernest A. Zadig is contributing editor for *Motorboating and Sailing* and *Boating* magazines, contributor to *Rudder* and *Popular Science,* and author of *Handbook of Modern Marine Materials* and *Inventor's Handbook*. His latest book is concerned with every phase of boating. It is written in a style and language that makes the book easy to read for browsing and convenient to consult for reference purposes. *The Complete Book of Boating* is divided into seven major parts and complemented by an Index and a glossary. Closely related information is kept together thus facilitating comprehension. The parts are divided into chapters. Part I covers the basic boat (hull, motive power, propellers, steering equipment, top and interior, and galley and plumbing) in well-illustrated text. Part II covers compasses, electrical, electronic, heating, refrigeration and air conditioning equipment; part III sailboats; part IV outboard motorboats; part V powerboats; part VI maintenance and repairing of pleasure boats; and part VII has useful instructions on owner's responsibility. The illustrations are informative and are well suited to amplifying the text. Colored maps of Treasure Island and Nantucket occupy the endpapers. Boat hobbyists and libraries will wish to add this well-organized book to their collections.

(Feb. 15, 1974, p.612)

The Complete Encyclopedia of Motorcars 1885 to the Present. Edited by G. N. Georgano. New York, E. P. Dutton & Co. Inc., [c1973]. 751p. illus. 29cm. cloth $30; to schools and libraries, less quantity discounts. ISBN 0-525-08351-0.

G. N. Georgano has established a reputation for writing authoritatively on motorcars. The present revision and updating of *The Complete Encyclopedia of Motorcars* copyright 1968 is no exception. Georgano's intent is "to give balanced biographies of over 4,000 makes of cars that have been offered for sale over the past eighty odd years." The editor clearly explains his limitations: 1) the car must clearly be intended for sale to the public 2) only cars built for private use as passenger vehicles are eligible 3) motorcycles are excluded. The reader must remember that the book makes no attempt to list every model made by a firm. Therefore, Ford's Mach I Mustang and Chevrolet's Vega cannot be located except for brief information under *Ford* and *Chevrolet*. Statistics are given in metric numbers.

Sporting activities of the vehicle are described if they are relevant. Normally the date given is for the year in which the car was made; this follows the practice of the Dating Committee of the Veteran Car Club of Great Britain. Some exceptions are made for American cars announced the season before they hit the market.

The Complete Encyclopedia of Motorcars is liberally illustrated with photographs sufficiently large to show details of each car. Illustrations are placed near the text they explicate, and they occupy one column down the outer margin of each page. Motorcar devotees and libraries with extensive collections on the subject will wish to acquire this volume. *(May 15, 1974, p.1015)*

Comprehensive Dissertation Index, 1861-1972. 37v. Ann Arbor, Xerox University Microfilms, 1973. 29cm. cloth $2,495 for entire set; separate volumes available at various prices.

For years a major frustration of graduate students and librarians in research libraries has been the search for and identification of all doctoral dissertations on a given subject. With the publication of *Comprehensive Dissertation Index*, 1861-1972, this frustration will be largely removed. The bibliographic, editorial, and systems and programming staffs of Xerox University Microfilms have attempted in this 37-volume work to pull together from many sources a complete listing of all dissertations presented in requirement of doctoral degrees from American and some foreign universities from the first three accepted by Yale University in 1861 through the approximately 35,000 accepted by universities in 1972.

Although the total of 417,000 entries does not include every dissertation written during the span of time covered by the set, a fact freely admitted by the editors, it is far and away the most comprehensive listing ever produced. Promised future annual supplements are intended not only to update the set but also to include omitted entries as they become known.

The list of entries was compiled from published and unpublished sources. The published sources include Xerox University Microfilm's own family of publications: *American Doctoral Dissertations* and its predecessor, *Index to American Doctoral Dissertations*, as well as *Dissertation Abstracts International* and its predecessors *Dissertation Abstracts* and *Microfilm Abstracts*. In addition, the citations in the Library of Congress' *List of American Doctoral Dissertations Printed in 1912-1932* and H. W. Wilson's *Doctoral Dissertations Accepted by American Universities 1933/34—1954/55* are included. Importantly, the publishers received the cooperation of over 70 degree granting institutions whose complete list of dissertations had never before been included in any comprehensive published listing.

The first 32 volumes present a subject listing of 22 major disciplines which in turn are usually further divided by academic subject. Volumes 33-37 form an author index. The subject under which a dissertation is listed is that chosen by the author, thus cross disciplinary subjects are listed under only one subject. However, each major subject heading is followed by a list of *see also* references to other major subject areas where closely related or cross disciplinary subjects may be found. In addition, the editors invite users to avail themselves of custom search service from Xerox University Microfilms when necessary, although the cost of such custom search service is not given.

The subject index is a computer-generated keyword index. Keywords appear in boldface in alphabetical order within each subject. Individual dissertation entries having the keyword in their titles are listed under that keyword first by date (beginning with the most recent), then alphabetically by school, and finally alphabetically by author. The editors claim an average of about six principal words in each dissertation title which means an average of six separate subject entries for each title. Every entry, both in the subject and in the author sections, is a full entry providing title, author, degree, date, institution, number of pages, reference to the document from which the citation was obtained, and order number for those dissertations obtainable from Xerox University Microfilms. A keyword index generated by a computer occasionally produces some strange and unnecessarily repetitive entries. In the history volume, for example, the title *'Pig Iron' Kelley, Preacher of Protection* appears under the keywords "pig" and "iron" as well as under "preacher" and "protection," and all entries containing the words "United States" appear under both "united" and "states." Nevertheless, the use of a keyword index for a compilation of dissertation titles is quite appropriate because of the usually precise and descriptive nature of such titles. And of course the project would have been virtually impossible without the utilization of a computer.

Every volume in the set carries the same 21 pages of prefatory material, including a complete table of contents for the entire set, suggestions and instructions for using the index, a list of schools included, a bibliography of sources from which the list was compiled, and instructions for obtaining dissertation copies from Xerox University Microfilms. The explanation of entries and instructions for use of the Index are clear, complete, and helpful. Their inclusion along with the table of contents for all volumes in each volume greatly facilitates ease of use of the set. Running heads appear on every page. When two or more academic divisions are included in one volume, the appropriate subject label appears at the top of every even numbered page. The three-column arrangement of entries is printed in an easily read font of all capital letters with keywords printed in bolder type. The paper and binding are both of high quality which should withstand heavy usage. Inner margins are sufficiently wide to permit rebinding. Spine labelling is clear and easy to read.

Comprehensive Dissertation Index, 1861-1972, which in one index provides a nearly complete listing of all dissertations submitted to American and some foreign graduate schools through 1972, makes available a long-awaited reference tool which will be welcomed by researchers, graduate students, and research librarians alike. While individual volumes by subject area may be purchased separately, most research libraries will want to acquire the entire set as well as the annual supplements which will be published each year.
(July 1, 1974, p.1164)

Compton's Encyclopedia Master Index. 2v. Chicago, F. E. Compton Co., [c1973]. illus. 26cm. cloth $13.95.

The 22 individual fact-indexes found at the back of each volume of *Compton's Encyclopedia* (reviewed in *The Booklist* Jan. 15, 1972) have been combined into a two-volume set, thus providing dual access to the main text of the encyclopedia. This master-index is illustrated and claims to provide more than 25,000 short articles in addition to giving analytical access to the main encyclopedia. *(June 15, 1973, p.956)*

Compton's Young Children's Precyclopedia. 16v. and Teaching Guide and Index. Chicago, F. E. Compton Co., Division of Encyclopaedia Britannica, Inc., 1971. illus. 25cm. Holliston Hexotone $110 to homes, or $80 when purchased in combination with Compton's Encyclopedia; to schools and libraries, $69.95.

The Young Children's Encyclopedia. 16v. Chicago, William Benton, Encyclopaedia Britannica, Inc., 1970. illus. hardbound $59.70, available to homes only through mail order. Orders will not be accepted from schools and libraries.

The Reference and Subscription Books Review Committee has prepared the note which follows in response to many requests for information on the *Young Children's Encyclopedia* and *Compton's Precyclopedia.* The descriptive commentary given here results from a thoroughgoing examination of both of these works and from information provided by Britannica Company and F. E. Compton Company.

The Committee plans a full-length review of *Compton's Precyclopedia* early in 1974, when, according to the Compton Company, extensive revisions, already begun in 1972, will be completed.

Compton's Young Children's Precyclopedia is designed to be a "trainer or browsing encyclopedia" for children approximately four to ten years of age. As noted on the title page of volume 1, *Precyclopedia* is based on a 16-volume Encyclopaedia Britannica publication, the *Young Children's Encyclopedia* whose promotion is directed to the home market. *Young Children's* is sold only through mail order and is not available to schools and libraries. Information from both F. E. Compton Company and Encyclopaedia Britannica, Inc. states that the main text and the illustrations which accompany it are exactly the same in both works.

To the illustrated main text *Precyclopedia* has added "Things to Do," 16 illustrated pages at the beginning of each volume. A 94-page *Teaching Guide and Index* and *Compton's Early Childhood Activities* accompany *Precyclopedia*, while *Young Children's Encyclopedia* has a 128-page *Parent's Manual*.

Harold L. Goodkind is editor in chief of both sets, and the same nine advisers and consultants, among them Clifton Fadiman and Gwendolyn Brooks, serve for both. Three of the nine are directly involved professionally with some type of child-oriented work: Josette Frank as a consultant on children's books for Child Study Association of America, Evelyn Beyler as director of a nursery school for Sarah Lawrence College, and Elizabeth Vernon as program associate for the Institute for Training and Researching Child Mental Health. Aside from Fadiman's 16 poems scattered through *Precyclopedia* under appropriate subject headings, it is impossible to determine the actual contribution of the advisers and consultants to the resulting set.

F. E. Compton Company is known for *Compton's Encyclopedia and Fact Index*, and was a division of Encyclopaedia Britannica, Inc. from 1961 until 1970, after this work was published.

Don Lawson, editor in chief of *Compton's Encyclopedia*, is listed as a general consultant and adviser for *Precyclopedia*. Editors, consultants, advisers, writers, contributors, artists, and production staff responsible for *Precyclopedia* are identified. Chief text editor is Ryerson Johnson, author of textbook material; he is also listed as one of the four staff writers of the main text.

The 16-page introductory sections were created for *Precyclopedia* by Catherine H. W. McKenzie and Joan Zucker. These additional pages constitute the only difference between *Young Children's Encyclopedia* and *Compton's Precyclopedia*.

Precyclopedia lacks preface, foreword, introduction, or other statement to indicate the scope, purpose, intended audience, rationale, range of subject matter, or criteria for inclusion and emphasis for the main text. The publisher defines *Precyclopedia* as "before the encyclopedia," meaning a "starter" or "trainer" encyclopedia for the preschooler and early school-age market, that is, a stepping-stone to the standard children's encyclopedia.

Each *Precyclopedia* volume follows a similar pattern of arrangement. After the 16 activity pages there are 160 pages of main articles. A three-page illustrated table of contents lists the main articles as they appear alphabetically and then the captions for the one or more other entries in the same general area of knowledge. Sometimes there is a little about the articles to entice the browser. There are about 27 main articles per volume; they vary in length from a minimum of a double-page spread to ten or more pages, and from one to five articles for each main entry. At the ends of many of the articles are references to related articles. Articles are unsigned; instead each volume concludes with a page of text and artist credits for that volume. Each article begins on the verso of a page and ends on the recto of one, so that text and illustrations for only one entry are visible regardless of where a volume is opened, a helpful feature for little children.

The name of the main article is not printed as a running head on each page, but only at the top of the first page of each article, necessitating some leafing back and forth. This is a frustration that limits the set's "trainer" value for children learning to use an encyclopedia. Also, for 28 of the main entries about places a question mark is printed inside a box instead of the place-name at the top of the first page of the entry so that the name of the entry has to be ascertained by using the table of contents. Supposedly the child is to read and have fun guessing where the place being described is.

While part of the text is straightforward presentation, some of the articles are written as stories to impart information; others are rhymes that tie in with the subject. About half a dozen use comicstrip format for part of the article; some ask a series of questions leading to a conclusion. Presentation of information is often casual and informal, sometimes chatty, with frequent use of contractions and an imitation of conversational narrative speech. Fragments are often used instead of sentences. Sometimes sentences begin with the word "and" or "but." Condescension has not always been avoided.

Compton Company states, "Topics for the *Precyclopedia* were chosen not so much for their intellectual content but more for their definite appeal to young children." This makes the reference value of *Precyclopedia* of secondary importance. Examination of the text, especially the longer entries, leads one to conclude that well-rounded treatment of subjects and all inclusiveness were not the primary motives of the editors.

There will be differences of opinion in judging the adequacy of inclusion, coverage, and treatment of subjects when appeal to children is the basis for selection. Many of the subjects included would probably interest many children immediately, for instance, how a flashlight works, the Morse code, dolphins, cowboys, volcanoes, masks, puppets, care of pets, the sun, echoes, fireflies, dolls, astronauts, and how a ship model is put in a bottle.

In keeping with the known interests of children in science, there are many more articles on science subjects than from other fields of knowledge. In volume 10, *M*, 13 of the 25 articles are on science subjects while in volume 14, *S*, 19 of the 29 articles are from various sciences. In spite of this, no material was found about magnets. Although there are articles about the sun, the moon, and comets, *Precyclopedia* does not help the stargazer to identify constellations. There are many articles about specific animals, such as beavers, snakes, monkeys, bees, and owls. However, the information is inadequate, and there is no consistent coverage of types of animals within the interest range of young children.

There are articles for several countries or cities for most of the continents; nearly 50 geographic articles were located. More emphasis is on places outside the United States than within; the Amazon river but not the Mississippi, for instance. Of the ten United States entries nearly all are places a family would visit on vacation, such as Mount Rushmore and the Grand Canyon. Articles labeled with a question mark in a box refer the reader to a simple two-page map of the world which outlines the continents and locates the places by numbers. Over half of the geographic entries are sketchy and consist of a page of text and one of illustration.

Traditional literature is included mostly as summaries of plots and can be located in the Index under *fairy tales, mythology, fables,* and *folklore*. There are retellings of "Odysseus and the Cyclops," "The Trojan Horse," "Androcles and the Lion," "The twelve Dancing Princesses," "The Donkey's Shadow," "The Man Who Told Animal Stories," and others selected for the young child.

The set is profusely illustrated with page decorations which do little to amplify the text. Aside from reproductions of famous paintings, the illustrative material is all original artwork in color, and virtually all of it is not captioned or labeled. *(March 15, 1973, p.654)*

Concise Encyclopedia of the Middle East. Mehdi Heravi, editor. Washington, DC, Public Affairs Pr., [c1973]. 336p. 24

cm. cloth $12; discounts depend on quantity purchased. ISBN 81823-130.

Dr. Medhi Heravi, editor of *Concise Encyclopedia of the Middle East*, was educated in Iran, England, and the United States. He taught political science at Tennessee Technical University (Cookeville) and is now on the faculty at Iran-Novin Institute of Political Science and the National University of Iran. Heravi was aided by 100 authorities whose initials accompany the articles for which they are responsible. The encyclopedia gives balanced unbiased treatment for the key people, places, battles, problems, and treaties of the Far East. Emphasis is on current personalities and affairs. Sufficient information is given to place the topic in its proper relation to the Far East. *Concise Encyclopedia of the Middle East* is a handy source of ready reference material. *(June 1, 1974, p.1069)*

Consultants and Consulting Organizations Directory: A Reference Guide to Concerns and Individuals Engaged in Consultation for Business and Industry. Paul Wasserman, managing ed.; Janice McLean, assoc. ed. 2d ed. Detroit, Gale Research Co., 1973. ix, 835p. 29cm. binding? $45. ISBN 0-8103-0350-7.

Dr. Paul Wasserman, Professor, University of Maryland School of Library and Information Services, has updated his *Consultants and Consulting Organizations Directory* first published in 1966 by Cornell University. The second edition of the *Consultants Directory* is planned to be used as a companion with *Who's Who In Consulting,* second edition, which is in preparation. The present work covers almost twice the number of firms and persons covered in the first edition—5,041 compared to 2,612 in 1966. Data were compiled from questionnaires sent to the firms. Biographical details are given about many principals of organizations as well as part-time consultants. The book is arranged in three main sections. The first part is an alphabetically arranged main listing for each organization; code number is given for each. Name, address, city, state, and zip code, date of founding, telephone number, name of principal officer, and a summary of activities is given for each firm. The second part is arranged geographically by state under subject fields, and the last section is an alphabetical index to individuals cited in the first part. The layout of the book is good with information given in two and three columns to a page. Libraries with the now out-of-date first editions of *Consultants and Consulting Directory* will want to replace them. *(May 15, 1974, p.1016)*

Contemporary Games: A Directory and Bibliography Covering Games and Play Situations Used for Instruction and Training by Schools, Colleges and Universities, Government, Business and Management. v.1 Directory. Detroit, Gale Research Co., [c1973]. ix, 560p. 29cm. Columbia Riverside linen grade C $35; 5 percent discount for cash with order.

Volume 1 of *Contemporary Games* is the directory to educational and management games. Volume 2, the accompanying bibliography, will be published in January 1974, and will sell for $25. The directory, "compiled to meet the need for a scholarly bibliographic guide and descriptive index to games regardless of their simplicity or complexity," contains both current and retrospective games and simulations. To qualify for inclusion the games must be of sufficient intellectual content to be used by schools, institutions of higher learning, government, and business for educational purposes. Chess, checkers, games played with 52 cards, games of chance, and games requiring physical skill primarily are excluded. A 33-page list of subject areas into which games are classified precedes the actual explanation of individual games. The subjects are broad rather than specific and include such classes as Anthropology, Political Science, Natural Resources, Thought and Thinking, and War. Nine age and grade breakdowns give broad guidelines as to use of specific games: Early Childhood, Upper Elementary, Elementary Junior High School, Junior High School, Junior High School and Up, High School, High School and Up, College and Adult, and All Ages. The entry

for each game gives as much of the following information as was available: subject, age or grade, playing time, number of players, mode (manual, computer-assisted or computer based), date of origination, name of designer, name of producer, distributing organization, price, and bibliographic citations. Directions for playing are clear and succinct. This directory should be useful to educators at all levels.
(Dec. 1, 1973, p.351)

Dictionary of American Biography Supplement Three 1941-1945. Edward T. James, editor; Philip M. Hosay, Marie Caskey, Philip De Vencentes, assistant editors. New York, Charles Scribner's Sons, [c1973]. viii, 879p. 27cm. cloth $35; to schools and libraries, $28. SBN 684-13199-4. Available only from the publisher by direct subscription; not available to the book trade.

This latest supplement to the original *Dictionary of American Biography* published in 1936 contains biographies of 573 significant figures selected from 2,170 names of outstanding Americans who died during the five-year period between 1941 and 1945. Five hundred expert consultants assisted the editors in making the selection of those "who had made a significant, not merely worthy, contribution to some aspect of American life." Included in this supplement are biographies for Jerome Kern, John H. Kellogg, Albert N. Marquis (founder and publisher of *Who's Who in America),* Manuel Quezon, and Grant Wood. The sketches were written by 475 contributors, and a consolidated list of names in all three supplements is appended. *(June 15, 1974, p.1116)*

Dictionary of Black Culture. By Wade Baskin and Richard N. Rames. New York, Philosophical Library, [c1973]. 493p. 22cm. novelex $15; to schools and libraries, 20 percent discount.

Prepared by Dr. Wade Baskin, Chairman, Classical Languages Department, Southeastern State College, Durant, Oklahoma and Richard N. Runes, a public defender with the Legal Aid Society, New York, this potpourri of brief explanations and identifications of Black leaders, issues, events, and contributions covers a wide range of subjects from Hank Aaron to Youth March. Areas outside the United States are given uneven coverage. Biographies, sometimes without birth and death dates, predominate, but there are materials on federal legislation, judicial decisions, associations and agencies: Compromise of 1850, 14th Amendment, *United States v Cruikshank,* Civil Rights Act of 1960, 1964, 1968, Slaughter House Cases, *Brown v Board of Education;* Black colleges and universities: Fisk, Howard, Meharry, Wilberforce, and Atlanta University publications, but not Morehouse, Spelman, Clark, or Atlanta University; Freedman's and Provident hospitals; beguine (dance), jazz, and blues. Although they are not dictionaries, *The Negro Handbook (The Booklist and Subscription Books Bulletin* Sept. 1, 1962) and *The Negro Almanac (Booklist* March 15, 1972) are both recommended by the Reference and Subscription Books Review Committee and are more comprehensive sources of information on Blacks and their culture.
(Oct. 1, 1973, p.131)

The Dictionary of Foreign Terms in the English Language. [By] David Carroll. New York, Hawthorn Books, Inc., c1973. ix, 212p. 24cm. Devon $9.95.

This dictionary claims to define some 4,000 foreign terms commonly used in English from 30 different languages. Included are foreign words and phrases from law, medicine, psychology, philosophy, science, political science, the arts, religion, and history. Each phrase or term is identified as to language or origin and is either translated, explained, or defined briefly, whichever treatment best fits, e.g., *"eau sucree* [F.] sugar water," *"jefe* [Sp.] the leader; the head; the commander," *"jubilate Deo* [L.] Rejoice in God," but *"ravioli* [It.] Small pasta shells stuffed with spiced meat or cheese and usually covered with a meat sauce," *"spiegeleisen* [G.] A form of pig iron, brittle and hard, containing about 20 percent manganese and used in the production of steel," and *"cloisonné* [F.] A technique of applying enamel in which bands of metal are shaped into patterns and soldered onto the surface of an object, such as a vase; enamel is then placed in these areas, fused, smoothed, and polished." The definitions are accurate, but scholars and writers may prefer Dr. Kevin Guinagh's *Dictionary of Foreign Phrases and Abbreviations* (New York: H. W. Wilson, 1972), because *Guinagh* cites sources and is also more authoritative. *(Dec. 1, 1973, p.351)*

Dictionary of Gypsy Life and Lore. [By] H. E. Wedeck, with the assistance of Wade Baskin. New York, Philosophical Library, [c1973]. vi, 518p. illus. 22cm. cloth $20. SBN 8022-2094-0.

Harry F. Wedeck, of the department of anthropology, New School for Social Research, translator, and prolific writer has had previous books published by Oxford University Press, Sheridan, Littlefield, Blackwell, Putnam, and Citadel. Philosophical Libraries published his *Dictionary of Classical Philosophy* 1956, *Dictionary of Classical Illusions* 1957, *Treasury of Witchcraft* 1961, and *Dictionary of Astrology* 1973. Dr. Wade Baskin, who assisted Wedeck in writing *Dictionary of Gypsy Life and Lore* is Chairman, Classical Languages Department, Southeastern State College, Durant, Oklahoma. Baskin is coauthor of Philosophical Library's *Dictionary of Black Culture* which the Reference and Subscription Books Review Committee reviewed in *The Booklist* October 1, 1973.

The dictionary under review is more a brief, specific-entry encyclopedia than a lexicon on gypsies and their history. There are a number of long articles: *The Gypsies of Modon and the 'Wyne of Romney'* 11 pages, an autobiographical fragment from *Life, Letters, and Literary Remains of Lord Lytton* (1883), by his son, the late Earl 10 pages, *Worship of Mountains Among Gypsies* 9 pages, *Gypsy Tribes in Bulgaria* 2½ pages, and *Restrictive Laws, Dream Book, The Medicine-Seller,* and *Loadstone* 1 page each. In contrast there are shorter identification type articles, e.g., *Eliot, George; Gypsy Courts; Mulé* (souls of the dead); Russia. Several entries are oddly alphabetized under the definite article: *The Traveling Gypsy, The Ubiquitous Gypsy, The Vanishing Gypsy. Aversion to Dissection* is found under "aversion" rather than "dissection," and *Banishment to Africa* is placed in the *B's.* The few full-page plates used to illustrate the text are not sufficiently sharp to enhance the book. Browsers will find *Dictionary of Gypsy Life and Lore* interesting. Students and researchers will require more comprehensive, better balanced coverage. *(Jan. 1, 1974, p.457)*

A Dictionary of Modern Revolution. [By] Edward Hyams. New York, Taplinger Pub. Co., Inc., [1973]. 322p. 22cm. cloth $9.95 paper $4.95; to libraries, 10 percent discount. ISBN 0-8008-2198-X (cloth); 0-8008-2199-8 (paper).

Edward Hyams, prolific author on a number of subjects, intends his *Dictionary of Modern Revolution* to serve as a "thorough guide to modern radical movements, factions and events involved in revolutionary political upheavals of the last 200 years." The coverage is concise but sufficient for identification coverage of personalities like Kurt Eisner, George Jackson, Mohandas Gandhi, Eugene Debs, Fidel Castro, and Chau-En-lai. Such movements as Mau Mau, MIR: Movimento de Izquierda Revolucinaria (Movement of Revolution to the Left), Passive Resistance, Black Panther Party, Black Power, and Trotskyism are described without bias. A person/subject Index facilitates locating information. *Dictionary of Modern Revolution* accomplishes its purpose as an easy to use reference guide. *(June 1, 1974, p.1069)*

A Dictionary of Non-Christian Religions. By Geoffrey Parrinder. Philadelphia, The Westminster Pr., [c1971). 320p. illus. 25cm. cloth $10.95. ISBN 0-664-209815.

Geoffrey Parrinder, Professor of the Comparative Study of Religions, University of London, is a world renowned authority on religion. He has written 20 books on various aspects of the subject. Among those in print in the United States are *African Mythology* (New

York: Tudor), *The Faiths of Mankind* (New York: Apollo, 1972), and *Witchcraft: European and African* (New York: Barnes & Noble, 1970). *Dictionary of Non-Christian Religions* emphasizes the three major non-Christian: Hinduism, Buddhism, and Islam. Also included is information on Judaism, the religion of ancient Persia, Mesopotamia, Egypt, Greece, Rome, the Celts, the Teutons, Scandinavia, ancient America, Australia, and Africa. The dictionary is written and organized so that it can be comprehended by the layman. The book covers deities, gods and goddesses, philosophies and philosophers, names and places, practices, rituals, beliefs, and cults. *A Dictionary of Non-Christian Religions* answers many questions on religion accurately, authoritatively, and comprehensively.

(June 1, 1974, p.1070)

Dictionary of Prehistoric Indian Artifacts of the American Southwest. By Franklin Barnett. [Flagstaff, AZ 86001], Northland Pr., [Box N., 1973]. illus. 24cm. paper $7.95. ISBN 0-87358-120-2.

For the purposes of this dictionary, Southwest is defined as Southeastern Utah, Southwestern Colorado, Arizona, and New Mexico. Artifacts relating to Southwestern open prehistoric sites and caves, but not including ceramic wares, weaving, or woven basketry are defined and illustrated in this little booklet which is a "compendium of terms used by archaeologists and collectors." *Awl, button, ceremonial ax, dart, needle, pestle,* and *whistle* are typical words covered in this general cross-section of material from the various Indian cultures in the Southwest United States. The definitions are clear and sufficiently comprehensive to be helpful to the student. Each definition is illustrated. It is regrettable that the pictures are so small and sometimes not sufficiently sharp. Three colorplates: Use of Gem and Semi-Precious Stone; Pulverized Paint Pigment in Concave Potsherds and Used Pigment Chunks; and Print Pigment, Stone and Mineral add to the usefulness of the work.

The author Franklin Barnett is a surveyer and architectural designer who became interested in archaeology in 1954. He is aided and guided by an authoritative editorial staff. Northland Press is a small trade house that has published works on the Hopi and Navajo. *Dictionary of Prehistoric Indian Artifacts of the American Southwest* is a worthwhile addition to the literature on Southwest Indian culture.

(Jan. 15, 1974, p.500)

The Dictionary of Stamps in Color. [By] James A. Mackay. New York, Macmillan Pub. Co., Inc., [1973]. 296p. illus. 30cm. cloth $19.95.

James A. Mackay, author of *The Dictionary of Stamps,* was Keeper of Stamps at the British Museum before his retirement. He is known throughout the world as an authority on postage stamps. The dictionary was designed, produced, and printed in England. The seven-page Introduction summarizes the history of philately revealing a number of intriguing facts on stamp collecting. One hundred-twenty pages of stamp reproductions in full color add to the attractiveness and utility of the work; stamps reproduced are increased in size 15 percent. The bulk of the work, the dictionary, is arranged by continent, and describes the plates in the sequence in which they appear. For Europe the stamps of 35 nations are covered, for Asia 29, Africa 22, America 23, and for Australia and Polynesia the stamps of 8 countries are reviewed. For each stamp colors, dates, size, and price are given. The four-page currency table with dates will be helpful for reference purposes both to the hobbyist and to the experienced collector. Useful too are the list of Cyrillic inscriptions and the table of stamp printers giving name, city, and country. The four-page Index to text and plates will facilitate locating information and stamps. *The Dictionary of Stamps'* comprehensive, authoritative coverage recommend it to reference collections in homes and libraries.

(Jan. 15, 1974, p.500)

Directory of Consumer Protection and Environmental Agencies. Thaddeus C. Trzyna, editor and the Staff for the Center for California Public Affairs. 1st ed.

Orange, NJ, Academic Media, [1973]. xiii, 627p. 29cm. class A library binding $39.50. ISBN 0-87876-032-6.

The purpose of the *Directory of Consumer Protection & Environmental Agencies* is "to provide a comprehensive, up-to-date source of information on governmental and private organizations concerned with consumer and environmental protection in the United States." Research for the work was done by the Center for California Public Affairs, an affiliate of the Claremont Colleges and the staff of Academic Media. There are two parts; part 1 is devoted to consumer protection and organizations concerned with the rights of the consumer in the marketplace, to safety, freedom of the choice, adequate information, sources of redress, quality, and integrity. Coverage is limited to groups interested in problems related to goods and services usually purchased by consumers. Consumer fraud, unfair and deceptive practices, product testing and safety, labelling, consumer finance, food, drugs, cosmetics, transportation, safety, hazardous household substances, insurance, real estate, public utilities, weights and measures, and broadcasting are treated. U.S. government and national private organizations are listed beginning with Committees of Congress. Each consumer protection agency is listed by name, address, and telephone number. Key personnel are cited; functions of the organization are described, and publications are listed.

Part 2 on environmental protection covers organizations directly concerned with the quality of the natural and physical environment. Included in the scope of this section are problems such as land use management, city and regional planning, preservation of wilderness and material areas, forestry, soil conservation, water resources, management and planning, air and water pollution control, marine resources, the management and protection of flora and fauna, pesticides, radiation, outdoor recreation resources, population planning and control, waste management, transportation planning, noise control, non-renewable resources, and weather modification.

Excluded from both sections were groups whose programs were limited to formal education and research and organizations interested solely for economic return. Emphasis was placed on organizations involved in influencing, formulating, or administering policy in the 50 largest cities in the United States. To aid the user in locating information, there are four indexes: an organization index, a personnel index, a publication index, and a subject index. The book's format is excellent. *Directory of Consumer Protection and Environmental Agencies* is a much needed reference work that libraries requiring such information will wish to acquire.
(May 15, 1974, p.1016)

Directory of Counseling Services, 1973.
Washington, DC, International Association of Counseling Services, Inc., [c1973]. xxii, 273p. 23cm. paper $3.

This is the seventh edition of the directory which was first published in 1948-49 by the Ethical Practices Committee of the National Vocational Guidance Association. This unique work intends to "provide the public with reliable information about reputable counseling services meeting the criteria of the American Personnel and Guidance Association." It will be useful to counselors making referrals and to persons needing competent counseling. Public and school libraries, social welfare agencies, and all types of counseling services will wish to replace their outdated editions with this one. "Criteria for Approval of Certain Counseling Services" precede the list of accredited services which is arranged alphabetically by state. *(Sept. 15, 1973, p.59)*

Directory of Publishing Opportunities: A Guide to Academic, Business, Research, Scientific and Technical Publishing Opportunities. 2d ed. Mary Bucher Ross, editor and the staff of Academic Media. Orange, NJ, Academic Media, [c1973]. x, 722p. 29cm. class A library binding $39.50. ISBN 0-87876-040-7.

Directory of Publishing Opportunities was first published in 1971 as *Directory of Scholarly and Research Publishing Opportunities*. The current edition is the second, and it lists 2,490 periodicals representing real publishing opportunities. In general only periodicals that publish at least a portion of the articles in English are listed. Omitted are abstracting services publications, periodicals that are direct translations of periodicals in foreign languages, and journals prepared by in-house staff. Entries are arranged alphabetically by title in seven major subject areas: general; humanities; social sciences; interdisciplinary and area studies; science and technology; trade, manufactures, and industry; and sports, games, and hobbies. Information was obtained by questionnaire. The amount of information, whether a journal is listed at all, and the accuracy of listing depend in large part on the information provided by the publication. Some 28 specific items of information can be listed for each journal. Depending on the individual character of the various periodicals each entry may include title of journal, subtitle or foreign language, address (either address of publication or editorial address), telephone number, frequency of issue, total paid circulation, cost of annual subscription, name of sponsor, managing editor's name, brief description of purpose and contents, list of subject fields in which manuscripts are accepted, specific style requirements for preparation of manuscripts, preferred length of manuscript, number of copies of manuscript required, copyright information, average time required for editorial decision, and whether or not the manuscript is criticized. Included among the journals are such diverse ones as *Claudel Studies* (University of Dallas), *Interchange* (Ontario Institute for Studies in Education), *Foreign Affairs*, *Indian Political Science Review* (University of Delhi), and *The Mathematical Gazette* (York House, London). The book is well designed with adequate margins. Journalism and general academic libraries will wish to use this reference tool with inquirers seeking publishing opportunities information. *(April 1, 1974, p.836)*

Discover Historic America. [By] Robert B. Konikow. Chicago, New York, San Francisco, Rand McNally & Co., [1973]. illus. maps. 281p. 28cm. hardcover $8.95, $4.95 Frankote C15 paperback; to schools, sliding discount; to libraries, discount on quantity purchase.

Arranged alphabetically under seven geographical regions in the United States, *Discover Historic America* is a handy listing with brief description of some 2,800 places of historic interest in the 50 states and the District of Columbia. The accompanying Rand McNally road maps help the user locate the battlefields, landmarks, historic sites, homes, museums, shrines, monuments, prisons, hospitals, and cemeteries that represent historic America. Pages 269 and 270 contain two reference charts. The first lists the states, their date of entry, capital, and early known explorers. The second cites the nation's presidents chronologically, their dates of birth and death, term of office, birthplace, and residence (state) when elected. An 11-page subject index using such headings as *Civil War; education; government buildings; forts and stockades; religion;* and *stores, taverns, and other commercial buildings* completes the volume. *(Oct. 1, 1973, p.132)*

Ebony Pictorial History of Black America. 4v. Chicago, Johnson Pub. Co., Inc., 1973, 1971. illus. ports. 29cm. imitation leather $27.95 for v.I-III; $10.95 for v.IV.

Drawing on the mass of information and illustrations in the *Ebony* databank, the editors of Ebony and Johnson Publishing Company have produced a three-volume pictorial history of the black experience in the United States. Volume I, *African Past to Civil War*, is composed of nine chapters written in easy-to-comprehend, straightforward narrative style. Covered are such topics as Revolutionary War, slavery, and resistance. Volume II, *Reconstruction to Supreme Court Decision 1954*, is in seven chapters and is equally well written. Volume III, *Civil Rights Movement to Black Revolution* discusses economics, education, politics, and the new world of Afro-America. Picture credits are listed in each volume, but the individual volume indexes are only in the third volume. The material is neither arranged, organized, nor intended for locating specific facts. The books will be most useful for browsing and inspirational reading. Lerone Bennett, Jr., author of *Before the Mayflower, What Manner of Man: A Biography of Martin Luther King, Jr., Black Power USA,* and other books, states it well in the Introduction to the first volume: "What emerges from these volumes is the image of a people with deep and inextricable roots in the soil of America. And that image tells us that the destiny of this land is tied up with the destiny of this people."

Volume IV, *The 1973 Year Book: A Review of the Major Events of 1971-72,* is just off press. It follows the organization plan of the other three volumes in the *Ebony Pictorial History,* being arranged in ten chapters covering politics, economics, education, arts, sports, obituaries, a calendar of 1971-72 events, and two special reports, one on Africa, and one on blacks in films. The yearbook is available separately, and it is indexed. It will be more useful for reference than the other three volumes. It is the only yearbook on blacks in the United States that projects plans for continuing. This one will be published biennially. *(Dec. 1, 1973, p.351)*

Education, U.S.A. James Cass, advisory editor. New York, The New York Times/Arno Pr., 1973. 541p. illus. 29cm. cloth $35 (single copy price) $30 (to series subscribers). ISBN 0-405-04165-9.

"Child Labor Law Has Aided Schools: Prof. John Dewey of Columbia Says Much Should be Done for Young Workers," (Dec. 21, 1913); "Pupils' Time Spent at TV Rivals Hours in Classes," (Mar. 6, 1951); "Why Some 3-Year-Olds Get A's—and Some Get C's," (July 6, 1969); "Civil Rights Suit Over Imbalance in School Fails," (May 5, 1964); "A.B. 'Academic Bureaucracy' A University Professor Complains That a Lush Undergrowth of Nonteaching Administrators is Choking the Groves of Academe," (Oct. 12, 1968); and "Women on the Campus Find a 'Weapon,'" (Jan. 10, 1972) are just a few of the headlines for *New York Times* articles related to education that are reprinted in *Education U.S.A.,* the latest volume in *The Great Contemporary Issues* series. Reprints from the newspaper's archives from 1906 to 1972 are featured to give both a historical overview of education and also an insight into current happenings in education. Reprinted material is organized in six sections: (1) The Background (2) Postwar (World War II) Issues (3) Changes (4) The Minorities (5) The Teachers and (6) Higher Education. A six-page Index facilitates locating information. School, academic, and education department libraries in public libraries and institutional libraries will wish to acquire this thought-provoking compilation of highlights from 67 years of *The New York Times.* *(April 15, 1974, p.888)*

Education Yearbook 1973-74. Bernard Johnston, managing editor; Bob Famighetti, senior editor; Prudence B. Randall, education editor; Jean Paradise, group editorial director. [New York], Macmillan Educational Corp., [c1973]. illus. ix, 630p. 29cm. buckram $49.50. ISBN 02-895430-0.

Education Yearbook 1973-74 is the second up-to-date, comprehensive, well-organized survey of trends and events in education. The work is produced by the publishers of the ten-volume *Encyclopedia of Education* which was reviewed and recommended by the Reference and Subscription Books Review Committee as a well-organized and useful reference set for educators, students, and nonprofessional users. (*See The Booklist* April 15, 1973.) The yearbook proposes to "provide a summary of the major issues that are being discussed and the major events that are taking place in all areas of education.... The topics discussed and debated... reflect the concerns of a variety of scholars and practitioners in both the public and private domains."—*Preface.* Local, state, national, and international sources of information are used. Education throughout the world is covered in five sections: Issues in Education, The Year in Education, Statistical Review, Bibliography of Educational Materials, and Reference Guide.

Issues in Education is comprised of 50 articles arranged under 26 broad topics like busing, exceptional children, international education, performance-based education, staffing, and technology. The articles are mostly reprints from educational journals and conference survey reports. They present in-depth surveys of ideas, theories, issues, and controversies of concern currently to educators and the public. Included are "White Students and Token Desegregation" by Elizabeth Useem, Assistant Professor of Sociology, Boston State College; "Equalizing Education: In Whose Benefit," by Daniel P. Moynihan, currently U.S. Ambassador to India, Assistant Secretary of Labor, 1963-1965, and Assistant to the President for Urban Affairs, 1969-1970; "Learning Disabilities and Juvenile Delinquency: Initial Results of a Neuropsychological Approach," by Allan Berman, Assistant Professor of Psychology, University of Rhode Island and Director, Neuropsychology Laboratory, Rhode Island Training Schools; and "Innovatory Aspects of Cuban Education," by Raul Ferrer Perez, National Adviser for Adult Education, Ministry of Education, Cuba. The articles are well selected from the voluminous writings on education produced in 1972-1973, and they are authored by experts with broad experience and training in the subjects of their articles.

The second portion, Year in Education, presents the most important happenings of the year highlighted under 30 topics such as legislation, media and technology, status of women, and non-public schools. An 80-page state roundup profiles for each state department of education information on finance, curriculum, governance, and personnel. This material was obtained from the chief state school officials or their offices of public information.

Statistical Review, the third section is a compilation of the most current tables available from three authoritative sources: U.S. Office of Education, the National Education Association, and the National Catholic Educational Association. Basic data are supplied for such subjects as early childhood education, elementary and secondary education, higher education, teacher supply and demand, and Catholic schools. There are 57 pages of well-designed, easy-to-interpret tables. Source is cited for each table. Examples of very useful tables are "Number and Percent of Public Secondary Schools Offering Specified Courses and Pupils Enrolled in such Courses, 1970-71," "Student-Teacher Ratios in Catholic Schools, 1970-71," "Cumulative Public School Enrollment by Level, 1962-63 to 1972-73," and "Estimated Public School Revenue and Nonrevenue Receipts, 1972-73."

Section four, Bibliography of Educational Materials is an extensive selected annotated bibliography of recent books, films, and educational texts produced in 1972-73. For convenience in using the material, this section is arranged according to subject categories and alphabetically by author under each category. The bibliography was prepared with the assistance of librarians who are education specialists.

Reference Guide, the final section, is a ten-page directory of educational administrators and policy makers: members of congressional committees on education, officials of the U.S. Office of Education and the National Institute of Education, chief state school officials, and ministers of education in selected foreign countries. A glossary of 19 descriptors compiled by ERIC Clearinghouses throughout the country defines such new terms as *alternative schools, external degree programs, merit pay, neurolinguistics,* and *visual literacy.* A comprehensive index provides ready accessibility to the whole book. School libraries and reference and education departments in public libraries will want to acquire this accurate, authoritative timely source of information on education. *(Mar. 15, 1974, p.752)*

Eerdmans' Handbook to the Bible. Edited by David Alexander [and] Pat Alexander; consulting editors: David Field, Donald Guthrie, Gerald Hughes, Alan Millard, and I. Howard Marshall. Grand Rapids, William B. Eerdmans Pub. Co., 1973. 680p. illus. charts. maps. plates. 23cm. non-woven latex-impregnated pyroxylin

$12.95; to schools and libraries, 20 percent discount. ISBN 0-8028-3436-1.

Eerdmans' Handbook to the Bible is written by 32 authorities representing British, Canadian, or Commonwealth institutions. The contributors are identified as to position, and the materials for which they are responsible are signed. Each has written on subjects for which he is qualified by background and experience. For example, Reverend J. Philip Budd, Lecturer, Trinity Theological College, Bristol wrote *Feasts and Festivals,* George S. Censdale, formerly Superintendent, Zoological Society of London was responsible for *Birds and Beasts, Clean and Unclean Animals,* and *Fishing in Galilee,* and Dr. Richard T. France, Librarian, Tyndale House Library for Biblical Research, Cambridge wrote *Jesus and the Bible, The Religious Background of the New Testament,* and *New Testament Quotations from the Old Testament.*

The Foreword states: "The editors of this book have selected and presented a variety of factual information in a simple, helpful, and visually interesting way. . . . The emphasis is always on the kind of information that is directly relevant for the Bible reader who is trying to increase his understanding of what the text before him has to say." In general, the editors achieve their purpose. The book is designed by arrangement and organization to be consulted for specific information. Part 1 is introductory and sets the stage for Bible study. Part 2 treats the Old Testament, and part 3 covers the New Testament. Part 4 provides several kinds of ready access to information: Key Themes of the Bible, Nations and Peoples of Bible Lands, Who's Who in the Bible, Gazetteer of Places, Prayers of the Bible, and Subjects and Events. The entire text is liberally illustrated with maps, charts, tables, reproductions, and photographs. Users are to be reminded that the version of the Bible used as basis for the text is not specified. *Eerdmans' Handbook to the Bible* will be useful to those who need an easy-to-get-at introduction to Bible literature.

(Feb. 15, 1974, p.613)

Encyclopaedia of Australia. Compiled by Andrew and Nancy Learmonth. 2d ed. London, New York, Frederick Warne & Co. Ltd., [c1973]. 603p. illus. maps. 23cm. cloth list price $15.
ISBN 0-7232-1709-2.

Encyclopedia of Australia is a one-volume updating and revision of the handy concise encyclopedia first published in 1968. The work covers places with 1971 population census figures, persons, history, climate, and wildlife in a well designed volume. Seven colorplates depict such flora and fauna as trees, snakes, birds, butterflies, and moths. Sixteen maps in a separate section at the end show the various regions and climate. The encyclopedia contains some 3,000 articles; among them are 50 special articles on such subjects as *Aborigines* (four pages), *Economy* (one page), *Education* (two-and-one-half pages), *Immigration* (one-and-one-half pages), and *Science* (one-and-one-third pages). The authors have taught in Australia and have written other books on the continent. Homes and libraries will find that *Encyclopedia of Australia* meets the need for ready reference information on Australia.

(July 1, 1974, p.1165)

An Encyclopedia of Chinese Food and Cooking. [By] Wonona W. and Irving B. Chang and Helen W. and Austin K. Kutscher. Edited by Lillian G. Kutscher. New York, Crown Publishers, Inc., [c1970]. x, 534p. 26cm. cloth pre-Xmas $14.95; thereafter $17.50.

An Encyclopedia of Chinese Food and Cooking is all that it sets out to be and in addition is an excellent reference work, well designed and carefully organized for ease of use. Intended "not only for the connoisseur of Chinese cooking who would like to know more about the food he prepares at home . . . but also for the novice who would like to know why certain foods are employed, their characteristics and their contributions to the recipes," the *Encyclopedia of Chinese Food and Cooking* is authoritatively written and gives comprehensive and easy-to-use descriptive information on the four distinctive schools of Chinese cooking representing the geographic areas of Peking, Canton, Shanghai, and Szechuan. The larger portion of the book is comprised of recipes; each recipe is divided into two parts—preparation and cooking—and recipes are separated into categories, e.g., appetizers, pork, vegetables, sauces, salads, desserts. In contrast to some Chinese cookbooks, names of Chinese foods are uniformly romanized. Detailed photographs are given for many ingredients. Constructive information on where and how to purchase and how to store and prepare is given. Useful separate sections of instant dishes, family meals, banquets, and nutrition guide for Chinese ingredients are provided. Unique are the individual dietetic ingredients guides and recipes for low sodium, no sodium, diabetic, and ulcer diets. Tea and wine facts, a list of mail order sources for Chinese foodstuffs in 11 cities, and a checklist of utensils for cooking, serving, and eating are appended as is a good 52-item bibliography. A 26-page analytical index facilitates finding all the material in the encyclopedia. For homes and libraries which collect cooking directions, recipes, and cookbooks, *An Encyclopedia of Chinese Food and Cooking* will become a standard, much-used source. *(Dec. 15, 1973, p.403)*

The Encyclopedia of Dogs: The Canine Breeds. By Firenzo Fiorone. New York, Thomas Y. Crowell Co., [c1970 by Rizzoli Editore;] c1973 translation copyright by Rizzoli Editore. 447p. illus. 31cm. cloth $25. ISBN 0-690-00056-1.

The Encyclopedia of Dogs was first copyrighted and published in Italy in 1970 under the title *Enciclopedia del Cane*. Editorial staff, collaborators, and consultants are mainly Italian. Credit is given to Fédération Cynologique Internationale with its 35 member organizations, the American Kennel Club, and the Société de Vénerie Saint-Hubert, Paris.

The claim that "The work is lavishly illustrated with hundreds of full-color and black-and white photographs showing all American breeds, as well as dogs from Europe, Asia and Africa" is borne out. Dogs are listed by official F.C.I. categories—I. Shepherd dogs, guard dogs, defense and work dogs; II. Hunting dogs; III. Pet dogs; IV. Greyhounds. A short history and lengthy description are given for each of the 308 internationally recognized breeds. Numerous color illustrations add to the book's value.

The Encyclopedia of Dogs is well made, with adequate margins, heavy coated paper, and cloth binding. It includes many breeds not shown in the United States, and will be useful to libraries and homes as a good reference source to be used with the *New Dog Encyclopedia* for comprehensive coverage. *(June 15, 1974, p.1116)*

The Encyclopedia of Floristry. [By] Violet W. Stevenson. New York, Drake Publishers Inc., [1973]. 160, 96p. illus. 23cm. cloth $9.95. ISBN 087749-450-9.

Violet W. Stevenson has written a number of books on flower arranging, gardening, and floristry for publication in Great Britain. *The Encyclopedia of Floristry* was first published in Britain under the title *Treasury of Floristry*. The British edition was similar to the one under review in that it was organized in two parts: Part 1 *The Encyclopedia of Floristry* (160 pages) has 16 black-and-white photographs and 26 line drawings. Part 2 *The Encyclopedia of Christmas and Festival Decorations* (96 pages) contains 21 black-and-white photographs and 13 line drawings. Intended for professional florists or amateurs with considerable floral experience, this work gives step-by-step directions for arranging flowers from acacia to zinnia. Directions are clear and easy to follow. Arrangements like horseshoe bouquets, funeral crosses, crowns for carnival queens, and buttonhole corsages are described fully. Illustrations, like that for tying bow ribbon and wrapping for delivery amplify the text. The section on Christmas and festival decorations has illustrated directions for making floral eggs, valentines, kissing rings, and door and wall garlands. The alphabetical arrangement facilitates locating information, but a general index

would have made facts even easier to find. *The Encyclopedia of Floristry* contains directions for a number of creative floral arrangements. It will be useful to florists and to libraries with comprehensive collections on flowers.
(April 15, 1974, p.888)

Encyclopedia of the Negro in Africa and America. 18v. St. Clair Shores, MI 48080, Negro History Pr., 22929 Industrial Drive East, 1973-? $472.50 prepublication price before Dec. 31, 1973; $425.25 prepaid prepublication price; $540 after Dec. 31, 1973.

Encyclopedia of the Negro in Africa and America, a new encyclopedia, for which no terminal date for publication has been set, is being heavily promoted to public and school libraries, and the Reference and Subscription Books Review Committee has received numerous requests for information on the publication and its publisher. We regret being unable to examine even preview pages of the first volume in time to provide sufficient advance evaluation to guide libraries in deciding to take advantage of the prepublication offer which expires at the end of 1973. Negro History Press was founded in 1969 and is listed in *Literary Market Place* as a reprint publisher of scholarly books. Since the Committee does not review reprints, it is not possible to make a judgment on the quality of the output of the Negro History Press.

The prospectus describes *Encyclopedia of the Negro in Africa and America* as containing "thousands of items of information covering virtually every subject relevant to the study of the Negro." The 18 volumes depicted in the brochure are labelled from v.1-*A* to v.16 *WXYZ;* volume 17 will be the Bibliography, and volume 18, the Index. A sample page of topics includes such subjects as African Civilization, Race Identity, Sickle Cell Syndrome, Ivory Caravans, and Harlem Globetrotters. The prospectus states that the set will be liberally illustrated with charts, figures, and photographs.

Promotional material from the Press gives a partial list of participating editors, but does not indicate what role the editors played in creating the encyclopedia. Such persons as Lorenzo J. Greene of Lincoln University and William Loren Katz of Columbia Teachers College are qualified by experience and background to edit and contribute to an encyclopedia on the Negro. Keith Irvine, listed as general editor, studied at Achimota College, Accra, Gold Coast at intervals prior to 1935. He also studied at the University of Manchester, University of Edinburgh, and Le Sorbonne. He has written material for *Encyclopaedia Britannica, Collier's Encyclopedia,* and *Funk and Wagnalls's Encyclopedia Yearbook.* He has edited *African Weekly* and has been employed in an editorial capacity for British newspapers.

The Committee intends to publish descriptive and evaluative comments on *Encyclopedia of the Negro in Africa and America* as soon as any part of it is made available. We suggest, therefore, that prospective purchasers delay decision until a critical review can be published. *(Dec. 15, 1973, p.403)*

The Encyclopedia of Philosophy. 4v. New York, Macmillan, 1973. diagrs. 29cm. buckram $99.50 plus shipping and handling.

When *The Encyclopedia of Philosophy* was first published in eight volumes, the Reference and Subscription Books Review Committee characterized it as "a much needed authoritative synthesis of mid-twentieth-century philosophy and recommended the work for all academic libraries, medium to large public libraries, and those school libraries where the instructional program requires an encyclopedia with this depth of coverage." (See *The Booklist and Subscription Books Bulletin* Mar. 1, 1969.) The set sold then for $219.50. Now Macmillan has produced the same content in four volumes, each of the four containing two of the original set, and selling at half the price of the original. Libraries with limited funds may now be able to afford this the only major reference work on philosophy in the English language. Its international scope and authoritative treatment commend it. *(Nov. 1, 1973, p.253)*

Encyclopedia of Southern Africa.
Compiled and edited by Eric Rosenthal. 6th ed. London and New York, Frederick Warne & Co. Ltd., [1973]. ix, 662p. drawings. maps. 21cm. linson $15; to schools and libraries, 20 percent discount. ISBN 0-7232-1487-5.

Prolific author, Eric Rosenthal, has completed the sixth revision of his *Encyclopedia of Southern Africa,* which was new in 1961. In its review of the first edition, the Reference and Subscription Books Review Committee recommended the work for public, high school, college, and university libraries because of its wide coverage of subjects dealing with South Africa. The encyclopedia covers the Republic of South Africa, Rhodesia, Zambia, Malawi, South West Africa, Lesotho, Botswana, Swanziland, and Mozambique in 22 long signed articles and some 5,000 briefer ones. Facts on technology, finance, industry, legislation, and education have been updated, and statistics have been revised to take the 1970 population census into account. In most of the articles, even those on plants and animals, South Africa is given more comprehensive treatment than the other countries. The longer articles include *Bantu Peoples of Southern Africa* by Professor D. T. Cole, University of Witwatersrand, Johannesburg (one and a half pages), *Insects of Southern Africa* by Dr. S. H. Skaife, Cape Town, *Mammals of Southern Africa* by C. J. Skead, Kaffrarian Museum, King William's Town, and *Archaeology of Southern Africa* by the late Professor A. J. H. Goodwin, University of Cape Town (all two pages). Libraries with older, out-of-date editions of *Encyclopedia of Southern Africa* will want to replace them with the new 1973 edition.
(Mar. 1, 1974, p.702)

Environmental Atlas of the Greater Anchorage Area Borough, Alaska.
Edited and coordinated by Lidia L. Selkregg with Eugene H. Buck and others. Anchorage, University of Alaska, 1972. vii, 105p. illus. plates. maps. 38 x 45cm. Padjco with multi-ring binding $17.50 postpaid.

The University of Alaska Resource and Science Service, Arctic and Environmental Information and Data Center claims that this first in a series of environmental atlases of Alaska's coastal communities is "the most comprehensive overall study of a metropolitan area ever compiled in the United States." The 69 black-and-white photographs, 67 colored maps, and 16 black-and-white maps depict all facets of the environment of Anchorage, from the slope of the land to the climate, soils, water, fish and wildlife, and vegetation; from natural resources to air and noise pollution; and finally from Anchorage's susceptibility to floods, earthquakes, and volcanoes to the increasing pressure of a fast-growing population. The maps and charts are clear and legible. The book is well designed, and the colors are pleasing. A three-page, up-to-date, authoritative bibliography at the end will aid the searcher for further information. Two other atlases in the series are in preparation—one on the Arctic coastal area and the other on Kodiak Island and its communities.
(Oct. 1, 1973, p.132)

Esquire's Handbook for Hosts. By Roy Andries de Groot. New York, Grosset & Dunlap, [c1973]. xii, 476p. illus. 24cm. cloth $12.95. ISBN 0-448-02167-6.

In *Esquire's Handbook for Hosts,* gourmet-author Roy A. de Groot combines menus and recipes, a survey of wines and spirits of the world, an encyclopedia of mixed drinks, and a reference guide to dining into a complete handbook for the host or hostess entertaining at home or in a restaurant. De Groot is an Oxford University graduate. He was a news commentator for the British Broadcasting Corporation and a war correspondent for the British Ministry of Information and the U.S. State Department. He has also been on the editorial staffs of *Time* and *The New York Times.* De Groot writes the food column for *Esquire* and in 1966 wrote *Feasts for All Seasons* (Knopf). His newest book is divided into five parts: The Art of the Memorable Host, The Host At Home, The Host At A Restaurant, The Host in His Wine Library,

and The Host At His Home Base. Recipes are helpfully arranged giving step-by-step directions with an indication of time required, and a notation of which preparation can be done in advance. De Groot gives difficult-to-find recipes for such foods as sourdough bread, shellfish dinners, Mexican guacamole dip, and brandied and fruited French toast. The sections on wines and mixed drinks are books in themselves. The tips on getting a good meal at a great restaurant and outwitting the wine steward will be useful to the insecure host. A 13-page analytical index facilitates locating information. Interesting to read for its anecdotes and instructive for the host, *Esquire's Handbook for Hosts* is a welcome addition to books on cooking and entertaining. Those who entertain at home will want to purchase it too.
(April 1, 1974, p.837)

Film Literature Index: A Quarterly Author-Subject Periodical Index to the International Literature of Film. Prototype issue/April 1973; Based on Twenty-eight Representative Periodicals for the Year 1971. [Detroit, Information Coordinators, Inc.], 1973. 103p. 24cm. paperbound $125 (four quarterly issues).

Vincent J. Aceto and Fred Silva of the faculty of the State University of New York, Albany have developed the first quarterly index to film literature in 28 periodicals. Their research was made possible by a grant from the New York State Council on Arts to the Upper Hudson Federation, Albany 1971. They have indexed such journals as *Film Comment, Playboy, Sightlines,* and *Take One* under 1,000 subject headings. The print is easy to read, and the book is well designed except for the very narrow inner margin that will not permit rebinding. Film collections will welcome this index to the literature of film periodicals. *(July 1, 1974, p.1165)*

Film Research: A Critical Bibliography with Annotations and Essay. Compiled by Peter J. Bukalski. Boston, G. K. Hall, 1972. 215p. 26cm. cloth $12.50 (U.S.); $13.75 (elsewhere). ISBN 0-8161-0971-0.
Film Research intends to provide a ready reference to motion picture study. A 27-page introductory essay "Film Research" explores the subject and methods of research and lists the major bibliographic sources of information. The main bibliography is arranged in 14 basic categories, e.g., film history, film production, sociology and economics of film, national cinemas, and careers in films. Author, title, place of publication, publisher, and date are cited for each entry. The text is printed in two columns to a page on permanent acid-free paper. Scholars, students, and students of motion pictures will find *Film Research* useful. *(July 15, 1974, p.1214)*

Fine Arts Market Place 73-74. Edited by Paul Cummings. New York & London, R. R. Bowker Co., 1973. vii, 258p. 28cm. paper $16.50 plus shipping and handling.

Paul Cummings, editor of this unique new reference work, states that *"Fine Arts Market Place* is the only national publication to list the thousands of firms, organizations, and individuals involved in the trade with name, location, telephone number, key personnel, and specialties, products, and activities." Cummings, who is Oral Historian, Archives of American Art, Smithsonian Institution, uses his expertise and experience as both art and cultural historian and editor to produce this well-organized, competently-designed, and easy-to-use book. Material included was researched through personal interviews, and was checked by questionnaire or office records. While no claim is made for all-inclusiveness, it is commendable that so great a quantity of information on the fine arts community has been assembled under one cover. Twenty-seven categories of fine arts business are covered under such headings as Services (packers and movers, fine arts printers, restorers and conservators, and insurers), Suppliers (gallery equipment, wholesale art material, and retail art material), Art Press, Art Dealers, Organizations and Associations, and Exhibitions. Entries in the various categories include firm's name, address, telephone, cable or Telex code, major staff members, and a description of the product, service, or activity. The 84-page Index, containing more than 7,200 names, is a reference work in itself, since it gives address, including city, and telephone number for each name. The code number in parentheses following each Index entry locates the section in the directory where each firm is listed. *Fine Arts Market Place* will serve the informational needs not only of those in the fine arts but also the needs of librarians, publishers, curators, and collectors. *(Nov. 15, 1973, p.303)*

Firearms Encyclopedia. By George C. Nonte, Jr. New York, Harper & Row, [c1973 by George C. Nonte, Jr.]. illus. 24cm. cloth $11.95; to schools and libraries, 30 percent discount if ordered direct from Harper & Row. ISBN 0-06-013213-2.

Written by an authority and beautifully illustrated, *Firearms Encyclopedia* gives comprehensive but concise coverage to gun and shooting terms. Major Nonte, the author, is technical editor of *Shooting Times* magazine. He was an ordnance officer in the U.S. Army. Nonte intends to fill the need for "a single-source reference explaining and illustrating the terms generally used by the true enthusiast." The encyclopedia has easy-to-comprehend articles on gunmakers (Peter Paul Mauser, George Luger, Daniel Baird Wesson, Samuel Colt), parts of guns (peep sight, ejector, firing pin, compensator), and technical terms (bullet energy, creasing, smokestack). The 1968 Gun Control Act is explained with its prohibitions. Added to this are a comprehensive annotated bibliography of recent titles arranged by subjects: ballistics and handloading, collectors, general, gunsmithing, handguns, hunting, rifles, shotguns, and periodicals. The useful Appendix contains a list of American and foreign arms associations, directory of goods and services, cartridge interchangeability, table of bullet energies, ballistic charts, useful firearms data, abbreviations, and foreign gun terms. A good Index aids in providing ready access to this wealth of information on guns. The encyclopedia is well designed. *(May 15, 1974, p.1016)*

Foreign Affairs 50-Year Index. Volumes 1-50, 1922-1972. Compiled by Robert J. Palmer. New York & London, Published for the Council on Foreign Relations by R. R. Bowker Co., 1973. xiii, 1279p. 26cm. cloth $34.50 plus shipping and handling. ISBN 0-8352-0490-1.

Finally *Foreign Affairs,* the oldest and probably most prestigious of all journals on international affairs and relations, has been indexed. Robert J. Palmer, indexer, thoroughly explains his methods and the use of this comprehensive analytical Index which not only provides ready access to information about events of 50 years and more than 2,700 articles, essays, editorials and book reviews on foreign affairs, but also traces the relationships between countries, provides an extensive list of minor people, places, committees, and laws, and supplies a useful list of political abbreviations. The format of *Foreign Affairs Index* is well planned. The book is designed for ease of use, and the margins are adequate to permit rebinding. Library subscribers to *Foreign Affairs* will wish to obtain this expertly prepared Index. *(June 1, 1974, p.1070)*

The Foundation Grants Index 1972: A Cumulative Listing of Foundation Grants. Compiled by The Foundation Center, Lee Noe, grants editor. New York, distributed by Columbia University Pr., 1973. xi, 251p. 29cm. cloth $10.

The Foundation Center, with offices in New York and Washington, DC, was founded in 1956 "as an educational organization to acquire, organize, and disseminate information regarding foundations and the grants they award; to collect and make available published information about the foundation field and its relationship to government and society."—*Association Directory*. In addition to *The Foundation Directory* which is in its fourth edition published in 1971 and contains data on 5,454 foundations, the Center publishes *The Foundation Center Information Quarterly* and the listing of foundation grants now under review. The *Grants Index* is the cumulated listing of grants that appear in the separate issues of *Foundation News* of 1972.

The *Grants Index* was prepared by computer from the databank at the

Foundation Center, and it claims to give information on 8,978 grants by 781 foundations with a total monetary volume of $737,868,363. A grant must be in the amount of $10,000 or more in order to be listed. The primary source of information was the donor, but occasionally information from recipients and news sources was used. The list is in four sections with Section I containing the text of grant descriptors arranged alphabetically by state. Information is compressed into a single statement naming the recipient, the amount of the grant, and the purpose. Section II lists the donors by name and location. Section III cites recipients by name and state or country, and Section IV as a helpful subject category classification subdivided by state or country. This compilation will be very useful to those requiring facts on foundation grants. Hopefully it will be updated at least annually. *(Dec. 15, 1973, p.404)*

Frank Schoonmaker's Encyclopedia of Wine. [By Frank Schoonmaker]. [5th rev. ed.] New York, Hastings House Publishers, [c1973]. 454p. maps. cloth $9.95. ISBN 0-8038-1910-2.

Schoonmaker's Encyclopedia of Wine has become a classic among wine books. Since the first edition was published in 1964 the author has constantly updated and revised this encyclopedic dictionary. Schoonmaker gives broad treatment to the wines of Europe and the United States, to wine labels, to vintage years, and to non-technical descriptions of the geographic areas where vineyards are located. The text is readable and authoritative. Schoonmaker himself is well-known as an author of travel books; he wrote his first wine book in 1934, and since then has contributed to *House Beautiful, Holiday, Saturday Review* and *Gourmet Magazine*. The maps are not as useful and legible as those in Simon's *International Wine and Food Society's Encyclopedia of Wines* reviewed by the Reference and Subscription Books Review Committee in *The Booklist* Nov. 15, 1973, but the comprehensive, accurate text makes up for this lack.

(June 1, 1974, p.1070)

Funk & Wagnall's Standard Dictionary of Folklore, Mythology, and Legend. Maria Leach, ed.; Jerome Fried, assoc. ed. New York, Funk & Wagnalls, [c1972, 1950, 1949]. xv, 1236p. Nonelex $17.95; to schools and libraries, 20 percent discount.

This 1972 one-volume edition of *Standard Dictionary of Folklore, Mythology, and Legend* shows only minor revision from the two-volume edition reviewed in *Subscription Books Bulletin,* April 1951. The text itself runs to an identical 1196 pages, and the list of contributors with information supplied for each is the same, with the exception of death dates added after ten of the thirty-four names.

As the Preface indicates, "the significant feature of this one-volume edition is a key to the 2,405 countries, regions, culture areas, peoples, tribes, and ethnic groups presented or discussed." The 37-page key provides access, to some extent, to analytical material within the text entries, but not without some confusion and hardship. In page references, the key entries make no distinction between significant material and mere mention, that is, key words such as "Cameroons" and "Assam" are occasionally used in only a general way in topical articles. Sometimes "Brittany" becomes "coast of western France" or "Hebrews" becomes "Semitic" or "Bible" when located in the text. The key includes references to 12 major religions, but only three of these appear in separate articles: *Buddha, Lamaism,* and *Zoroaster.* For "Hinduism," the reader would have to search through some 300 page references listed in the key to find material. "Christian Church" has been subdivided in the key, but "Hebrews," "Jews," and "Mohammedism" have not. When the key was checked against the text for accuracy, over 10 percent of the references could not be found under any identifiable phrasing. To summarize, the key with its geographical, cultural, and religious orientation only partially succeeds in directing the reader from general to specific information; it does nothing to relate general articles to specific related topical articles.

Standard Dictionary of Folklore remains a standard reference tool for all kinds of libraries. However, since the text of the 1972 edition is basically unchanged and the newly added key is not really an adequate index, this edition is desirable only if the original edition needs replacement or one simply prefers a single-volume edition.
(Nov. 1, 1973, p.253)

The Gallup Poll: Public Opinion 1935-1971. 3v. [Edited by] George H. Gallup. New York, Random House, [c1972]. 2388p. 24cm. buckram $95.

Dr. George H. Gallup, director and founder of the American Institute of Public Opinion and pioneer introducer of new methods of scientific polling in the United States, has compiled for the first time, under one cover, every poll issued by the Institute. The largest number of polls deal with American elections—presidential candidates of all parties, state, congressional and national elections, and all facets of voter preference. Also among the topics researched are Supreme Court, 1935; Negro vote, 1936; income tax and drafting of women, 1941; television and House Un-American Activities Committee, 1949; gun control, 1959; space race, 1965; sexual equality, 1970; and prejudice in politics and college dormitories, 1971. Volume one is prefaced by three essays: "Election Survey Procedures of the Gallup Poll," "Gallup Poll Election Survey Experience, 1959-1960," and "Election Survey Methods," all written by Paul Perry, President, Gallup Organization. Designed and arranged to permit easy access to the material the compilation of opinions on over 20,000 questions will be a useful research tool for social scientists, particularly those interested in the development of sampling procedure as a reliable technique.
(Oct. 15, 1973, p.185)

The Gardener's Basic Book of Trees and Shrubs. [By] Stanley Schuler. New York, Simon and Schuster, [1973]. illus. 319p. 24cm. starch filled spine with tweed print sides $9.95. ISBN 0-671-21481-0.

Stanley Schuler, author of *The Gardener's Basic Book of Trees and Shrubs*, has written prolifically on home remodeling and maintenance and gardening. His books on growing plants and trees include *Gardening in the East* (1969), *Gardening With Ease* (1970), and *Gardens Are for Eating* (1971), all published by Macmillan. His latest work is a popular guide to selecting, acquiring, propagating, planting, watering, fertilizing, pruning, and training trees and shrubs. The book is intended for the layman. In clear, well-illustrated text the author gives easy-to-understand directions for care of trees and shrubs in a home garden. Schuler includes a chapter on controlling pests, climate zone maps, tables on deciduous trees and shrubs, evergreens, trees that grow unusually fast, shrubs for shady places, and lists of hedges. Eight pages of full-colorplates may be used for identification purposes. Four noteworthy tables are included: the 100 best trees, the next best trees, the 100 best shrubs, and the next best shrubs. For each tree and shrub in the tables are given the common name, the botanical name, climate zones, height, sun or shade, and growth speed. A useful Appendix of state agricultural extension services and a fairly comprehensive Index complete the book. Home gardeners and libraries with good gardening collections will wish to acquire this handy inexpensive guide to trees and shrubs.
(Jan. 15, 1974, p.500)

A Gardener's Dictionary of Plant Names: A Handbook on the Origin and Meaning of Some Plant Names. [By] W. A. Smith. rev. and enl. by William T. Stearn [and] Isadore Leighton Luce Smith. New York, St. Martin's Pr., [1972]. xii, 391p. illus. 22cm. cloth $11.95.

Dr. William T. Stearn, botanist at the British Museum (Natural History) and Isadore L. Smith, wife of the late author William Archibald Smith, have revised and enlarged Smith's dictionary which was published in 1963 under the title *A Gardener's Book of Plant Names*. The book accomplishes its aim of providing "in a one-volume work of reference a selection of those plants most likely to be encountered by, or of the greatest interest to, gardeners, horticulturists, and their fellows, professional and amateur." Divided into two parts, the dictionary contains in part 1 some 6,000 botanical names with their origins and meanings, and in part 2, an index of some 3,000 vernacular names. Pages 352-353 have an authoritative bibliography of 37 sources for further information. A number of those works are out of print. *(Sept. 15, 1973, p.60)*

The Golden Book Encyclopedia. Bertha Morris Parker, ed. rev. ed. 16v. New York, Golden Pr., 1973. illus. ports. maps. 27cm. $65 list price; to schools and libraries, $48.50 postpaid.

In keeping with the Reference and Subscription Books Review Committee policy of commenting on in-print general encyclopedias at least once every five years, we are reporting that Western Publishing Company, owner of the work, states that "This current edition has not been revised since the latest review you gave to *The Golden Book Encyclopedia." (The Booklist* Dec. 15, 1970). Until the books have been revised, the Committee endorses its latest evaluation: "While the 1969 *Golden Book Encyclopedia* is improved over the first edition, it still does not reflect enough careful planning, editing, and organization to meet current school reference needs for which it is apparently intended." *(Nov. 1, 1973, p.253)*

The Good Housekeeping Illustrated Encyclopedia of Gardening. Ralph Bailey, editor in chief; Elvin McDonald, executive editor. Compiled under the Auspices of the Editors of Good Housekeeping. 16v. New York, Book Division, Hearst Magazines. c1972. illus. diagrs. 28cm. kivar #6 $59.70. ISBN 0-87851-200-4.

The Good Housekeeping Illustrated Encyclopedia of Gardening has an impressive list of contributors who have prepared these volumes as "an inclusive, readable and graphic guide to all aspects of gardening for pleasure." Among them are not only garden specialists and specialists in bonsai, crafts, organic methods, preservationists, entomologists, landscape architects, and plant pathologists, but also 16 regional editors from the southern shores to Canada. Contents of the 16 volumes include specific entries alphabetically arranged, from *Aaron's Beard* to *Zygote,* with longer articles on the 16 individual regions. Articles vary in length from a few lines to many pages, and there are frequent *see* references, augmented by a good index in the final volume.

Entries for plants follow a definite pattern: pronunciation, simply indicated (vul-gay-tus); common name; habitat; description; and varieties. Some give more specific information on size variations than others. Most of the articles on plants give cultivation and propagation instructions.

Entries for specific types of gardens are practical, e.g. *Water Gardens,* which gives information on water supply and specifications, pool preparation and cleaning, and kinds of plants and their winter protection, with greatest emphasis in both text and illustrations naturally on water lilies. The Japanese influence is apparent in many of the garden articles.

The illustrations whch accompany almost every article consist of 700 drawings for identification and planning techniques and 2,500 photographs, 800 in color. Flowers, both wild and cultivated; gardens; fruits; vegetables; and trees are beautifully photographed and tastefully selected.

The binding is sturdy; the paper is durable and the print clear, with appropriate use of type size and italics. *(April 15, 1974, p.888)*

Great Collectors' Cars. By Gianni Roglatti. New York, Madison Square Pr., Grosset & Dunlap, [1973]. 318p. illus. 29cm. cloth $14.95. ISBN 1914-0.

Great Collectors' Cars was first published in 1970 by Editrice dell'Automobile under the Italian title *Le Piu'- Belle Vettura D'Epoca.* The 1973 edition under review is being published in Canada and the United States. It is also being produced simultaneously in London by the Hamlyn Publishing Group under the title *Period Cars.* The author, Gianni Roglatti, is an engineer who contributes to motor car journals; he also wrote *The Ferrari* (New York: Crowell, 1973). More than 130 collector's vehicles are described and illustrated in the current volume. Included are discussions of the Maserati type 26B, Alfa Romeo type B, Renault Grand Prix, Benz Mylord Coupe, and the Panhard et Levassor M2E. A brief Index provides ready access to the material. Automotive buffs and libraries with extensive collections on the subject will wish to purchase this inexpensive, well-illustrated book.

(April 1, 1974, p.837)

The Great Ideas Today 1973. Editors in chief, Robert M. Hutchins and Mortimer J. Adler; executive editor, John Van Doren. Chicago, London. Encyclopaedia Britannica, Inc., [c1973]. 474p. 24cm. cloth $9.55; to schools and libraries, $8.95. ISBN 0-85229-286-4.

The Great Ideas Today is published annually as a service to subscribers of the 54-volume *Great Books of the Western World*. The symposium featured in the 1973 issue is entitled "The Hero and the Heroic Idea"; participants are S. L. A. Marshall, military critic, editorial writer, and author; Ron Dorfman, editor, Chicago *Journalism Review;* Josef Pieper, philosopher and author; Joy Gould Boyum, teacher, author, and film critic for *Wall Street Journal;* Sidney Hook, philosopher and author; and Chaim Potok, novelist.

Part two, Reviews of the Arts and Sciences contains articles on twentieth-century philosophy by W. T. Jones, justice in taxation by Walter J. Blum and Harry Kalven, Jr., and one on Copernicus by Owen Gingerich. Part three features a review of the *Canterbury Tales* by Mark Van Doren, and part four features an essay on freedom by Charles Van Doren.

Part five covers four additions to the *Great Books Library*: *In Defense of Socrates, The Song of Roland, Religio Medici,* and *She Stoops to Conquer.* The *1973 Great Ideas Today* achieves its intended purpose of relating contemporary thought to the *Great Books*.

(July 15, 1974, p.1214)

The Grosset World Atlas. New York, Grosset & Dunlap, [c1973 by Hammond Inc.]. 52p. illus. 29cm. 4/c printed "B" grade pyroxylin impregnated $2.99 library edition.

Grosset World Atlas appears to be identical to *Hammond Headline World Atlas* published in a tag cover and sold for $1. *Headline* was reviewed by the Reference and Subscription Books Committee in the May 1, 1972 *Booklist* in an omnibus review with six other new Hammond atlases. The Committee characterized *Headline* as an inexpensive atlas with almost no frills or extras and recommended it as a good bargain at the price of $1. Now the Committee endorses its opinion of *Headline* if it is still in print at the price. For the price of the *Grosset World Atlas,* the Committee would recommend instead *Hammond's Globemaster Atlas* which sold for $2.95 when it was reviewed in 1972 and which consisted of two atlases under one cover—*Headline* and a Road Atlas and Travel Guide to the United States. *(Dec. 15, 1973, p.404)*

Guide to Current British Journals. Edited by David P. Woodworth. 2d ed. 2v. London, The Library Association, 1973; distributed in U.S. by R. R. Bowker Co. 30cm. cloth $37.50 plus shipping and handling. ISBN 0-85365-204-4.

The new second edition of *Guide to Current British Journals* is a successful updating and expansion of the first edition published in 1970/71. Volume I contains some 4,700 entries for trade, student, popular, professional, ecclesiastical, research, and institutional journals arranged according to the 10 major Universal Dewey Classification subject areas. David P. Woodworth, editor, who lectures at the School of Librarianship, Loughborough, cites five types of exclusions: (1) parish magazines (2) some "pin-up" journals (3) daily press (4) some children's periodicals, especially comics, and (5) student publications, unless containing serious material. For each title the following information is given as applicable: current title, former title (if any), year first published under current title, circulation, subscription fee, frequency, name and address of publisher, aspects of the subject stressed, inclusion of book reviews, articles, letters, obituary notices, notices of new books or products, where journal is abstracted or indexed, level of readership appeal, and average number of advertising and text pages. An alphabetically arranged title index containing both current and superseded titles, a list of journals produced by about 1,000 societies, and a list of discontinued titles conclude the volume.

For the purposes of this work "British" is defined as including England, Wales, Scotland, Northern Ireland and the Isle of Man, and the Channel Islands. A few journals from the Irish Republic are also included. The second volume is an easy-to-use index to almost 3,000 British periodical publishers. Current addresses are cited, and the titles issued by each publisher are listed. Acquisitions and reference departments of academic and large public libraries will wish to acquire this well designed set.

(April 15, 1974, p.889)

Hammond Nature Atlas. By Roland C. Clement. Maplewood, NJ, Hammond Inc., [1973]. 255p. illus. 30cm. pyroxylin coated stock $17.95. ISBN 0-8437-3511-2.

In 1952 Hammond Inc. first published a *Hammond Nature Atlas*. The 1952 atlas was reprinted without revision for years. It also appeared under the title *Nature Atlas of America*. The 1973 atlas is basically a new work with new design, format, author, and contents. Roland C. Clement, author of the 1973 *Hammond Nature Atlas,* is an officer of the National Audubon Society; chairman of the U.S. Army Corps of Engineers' Advisory Committee on the Environment; chairman of the U.S. section, International Council for Bird Preservation; and author of *American Birds* (New York: Bantam, 1973). The *Nature Atlas* "is a primer on American nature for the automobile age in which we live . . . . It is designed to satisfy initial curiosity and to arouse international delving more deeply."—*Our American Land*. In text and five color maps produced by Hammond cartographers the atlas covers eight phases of U.S. natural environment: rocks and minerals, trees, wildflowers, mammals, birds, reptiles and amphibians, fishes, and insects. The illustrations are colorful, accurate, and graphic. Particularly noteworthy are the special maps: A Naturalist's America, which shows national and state parks, forests, grasslands, seashores, swamps, mountains, and wildlife sanctuaries; Gealogy and Tectonics, which locates sedimentary, igneous, and metamorphic rocks, volcanic cones, and salt domes in the 50 states; Natural Vegetation, which depicts the families of trees in the 50 states; Rainfall and Sunshine, which shows the factors that make wildflowers possible; and the Range Maps of Mammals, Birds, Reptiles, and Amphibians, which locate the habitats of the various species in the 50 states. Written in clear, succinct language readily understood by the student or layman *Hammond Nature Atlas* is an excellent introduction to the ecology of the United States.

(Feb. 1, 1974, p.555)

Handbook of Austrian Literature.
Introduced and edited by Frederick Ungar. New York, Frederick Ungar Publishing Co., [1973]. xvi, 296p. 24cm. A-grade pyroxylin linen $12.50; to schools and libraries, $10.62. ISBN 0-8044-2929-4.

Author, editor, publisher Frederick Ungar has produced the first English-language bio-critical reference book devoted to Austrian literature. His *Handbook of Austrian Literature* is mostly translated from Hermann Junisch's *Handbuch der deutschen Gegenwartsliteratur* (München: Nymphenburger Verlagshandlung, 1965). The article for Peter Altenberg by Franz H. Mautner is reprinted from the *Columbia Dictionary of Modern Literature* (New York: Columbia Univ. Pr., 1947), and the remaining articles were prepared especially for this book. Each of the 79 articles is written and signed by an author with expertise in Austrian literature. Ungar himself wrote three—those on Ernst Waldinger, Otto Stoessl, and Karl Kraus. Literature is interpreted broadly to include persons like Freud, not commonly known for his literary accomplishments. Included, of course, are Rilke, Luckas, Werfel, von Hofmannsthal, and Zweig. Each article is comprised of a relatively long critique and biography, a list of the author's works, and a good bibliography for further reading. A detailed name Index makes all references to a given person readily accessible. Libraries owe a debt of gratitude to Ungar for making portions of Junisch's handbook available in English. This compact guide to Austrian literature is not expensive either.

(April 15, 1974, p.889)

Handbook of English Costume in the Twentieth Century, 1900-1950. By Alan Mansfield and Phillis Cunnington. Boston, Plays, Inc., [c1973]. [Printed in Great Britain by Robert MacLehose and Co., Ltd., The University Pr., Glasgow.] illus. 371p. 23cm. cloth $12.95.
ISBN 0-8238-0143-8.

The final volume in a series on English costume by C. Willett Cunnington and Phillis Cunnington, *Handbook of English Costume in the Twentieth Century* presents an overview of men's fashions and women's fashions, including accessories, for each decade, 1900 to 1950. Numerous illustrations from contemporary sources show representative clothing, but no photographs are included. Appended supplementary material such as clothes rationing information, a short Glossary, Sources of Information, a Bibliography, and an Index complete the work. Useful to the theatrical designer and student of social history, but not comprehensive enough to be a really satisfactory reference tool for American libraries.

(Mar. 15, 1974, p.753)

Handbook of the World's Religions. Edited by A. M. Zehavi. New York, Franklin Watts, Inc. 1973; [c1963-1973 by Grolier Inc.]. vii, 203p. illus. 26cm. cloth $8.95. discounts are available depending on quantity. SBN 531-02644-2.

The purpose of *Handbook of the World's Religions* is "to facilitate access to basic information on the organized religions of the world . . . presents the casual reader with a concise introduction to the subject and to the student it offers details . . ."—*Introduction.* According to the publisher, the handbook consists of sections on religion from Grolier's *Encyclopedia International.* Comparison with pertinent sections of the encyclopedia reveals that the handbook reprints paragraphs and sections verbatim. Information in the handbook is organized into seven chapters: 1. Christianity 2. Judaism 3. Buddhism 4. Islam 5. Hinduism 6. Other Religions 7. Religion: A Summary. The first five chapters consist of general discussion of the specific religions: denominations, personalities, terms, holidays, and literature. Under other religions Babi (Bahai), Ethical Culture, Jainism, Shinto, Sikhs, Taoism, and Zoroastrianism are described.

The summary has a brief discussion of primitive religions and concise articles on 15 terms pertaining to religion. Deism, monism, gnosticism, mysticism, and theosophy are among the terms meriting attention. This material, too, is taken from *Encyclopedia International.* The handbook, therefore, carries with it the authority and accuracy of the signed articles which appear in the encyclopedia. Ample access to the information is provided by a good analytical Index. Editor Zehavi has done well in selecting material for the handbook; the book serves its intended purpose.

(May 15, 1974, p.1016)

Harper's Bible Dictionary. By Madeleine S. Miller and J. Lane Miller, revised by eminent authorities. 8th ed. New York, Evanston, Harper & Row Publishers, [c1952-1973]. ix, 853p. illus. maps. 24cm. cloth $12.50; $14.50 (thumb indexed); to schools, 30 percent discount on direct orders. ISBN 0-06-065673-5, thumb indexed 0-06-065674-3.

In 1953 the Reference and Subscription Books Review Committee reviewed and recommended the first edition of *Harper's Bible Dictionary* to supplement but not supersede Hastings *Dictionary of the Bible.* The review pointed out the usefulness of *Harper's* to a wide audience of laymen, students, and teachers. This latest revision of Harper's is the most complete one produced to date.

Articles have been revised, reedited, rewritten, corrected, and expanded. Tables have been revamped and changed to bring them up to date, to correct information altered in the light of more recent study, and to provide as much information as possible. Ten percent of the 500 illustrations are new, and maps have been changed to substitute new place-names and to reflect recent archaeological findings and the research of biblical scholars.

The articles in the eighth edition of *Harper's* are written by authorities, and are signed with the initials of both the original writers and revisers. The 12 contributors are listed near the front of the book. The many small but clear illustrations amplify the text. Besides maps in the text there is an indexed 17-page section of colored maps at the end. Owners of older editions of *Harper's* will wish to replace them with this improved, up-to-date new *Harper's Bible Dictionary*. *(May 15, 1974, p.1017)*

Illustrated Dictionary of Practical Pottery. [By] Robert Fournier; photographs by John Anderson; diagrams by Sheila Fournier. New York, Van Nostrand Reinhold Co., [1973]. illus. diagrs. plates. 256p. 26cm. linson (paper) $12.50; to schools and libraries, $10.
ISBN 0-442-29950-8.

Illustrated Dictionary of Practical Pottery contains 1,200 entries with 450 illustrations arranged alphabetically for student, amateur, or professional craft potters. Effective use of the book requires some orientation and practice in ceramics. There are analyses, charts, descriptions, definitions, formulas, materials and equipment, recipes, step-by-step instructions on processes, and definitions of terms used in ceramics. Historical references are minimal; aesthetics is covered only when it is inseparable from the rest of the discussion, and industrial and archaic terms are omitted. The charts, diagrams, and illustrated directions amplify and elucidate the text. Definitions are sufficiently long to give clear explanations. Cross references to other entries that might help clarify a discussion are printed in italics. Atomic or molecular weights are given for elements, oxides, or minerals. The author, Robert Fournier, has maintained his own pottery in Great Britain since 1947. He has made four films on pottery and has issued several hundred slides on modern and ancient pots. Libraries building collections on crafts will wish to consider this easy-to-use, inexpensive dictionary.
(Mar. 1, 1974, p.702)

The Illustrated Library of Science, Nature & Man's Environment. 18v. [Chicago, J. G. Ferguson, 1972]. illus. 29cm. cloth $69.50. v.1 Beginning Science, Science Experiments, Light and Color; v.2 The Moon, Planets and Interplanetary Travel, Stars; v.3 Chemistry, the Human Body, Oceanography; v.4 Our Earth, Rocks and Minerals, Weather; v.5 Flight, Rockets and Missiles, Atomic Energy; v.6 Magnets and Magnetism, Microscope, Machines; v.7 Sound, Mathematics, Electricity; v.8 Birds, Ants and Bees, Wild Flowers; v.9 Butterflies and Moths, Insects, Fish; v.10 Trees, Ecology, Air and Water; v.11 Deserts, Polar Regions, North America; v.12 Dinosaurs, Prehistoric Mammals, Primitive Man; v.13 Basic Inventions, Electronics, Famous Scientists; v.14 Sea Shells, Mushrooms, Ferns and Mosses, Reptiles; v.15 Time, Lost Cities, Caves and Skyscrapers; v.16 Ships and Boats, Railroads, Building; v.17 Dogs, Horses, Wild Animals; v.18 The Environment and You and Index.

J. G. Ferguson Company has reprinted 52 of the "How and Why Wonder Books" originally published by Grosset and Dunlap between 1960 and 1971 in an 18-volume indexed set. Each book is an independent unit, separately paged and written by its own author. Volumes 1 to 17 of *The Illustrated Library* contain three "How and Why Wonder Books" each. Volume 18 is the *Environment and You* and Index. The set is "designed to stimulate curiosity through short articles, hundreds of pictures, ideas for things to make and do." The selections are written in nontechnical language easily understood by elementary and junior high school students. In organization, arrangement, and treatment *The Illustrated Library of Science,*

Nature & Man's Environment differs from other young people's science sets on the market today.
(June 15, 1973, p.956)

Index to the Contemporary Scene: An Analytical Guide to the Contents of 322 Recent Monographs, Collections, Symposia, Anthologies, Handbooks, Guides, Surveys, and Other Works of Nonfiction Dealing with Topics of Current Interest. Prepared by David W. Brunton. v.1. Detroit, Gale Research Co., [c1973]. 122p. 29cm. buckram $14; 5 percent discount for cash with order.

Given its unusual criteria for selection, this first annual *Index to the Contemporary Scene* accomplishes its purpose reasonably well. The work intends to analyze the contents of works on "currently important topics in the social sciences and popular culture" that have not been adequately classified or given sufficient subject headings on Library of Congress cards. The author, David W. Brunton, holds a degree in history and one in library science. He has served as a cataloger and head librarian and is presently employed at the Longmount, Colorado Public Library.

Three hundred titles, which were reviewed in the "standard media during 1971" and which the author thought "would have been purchased by medium-sized libraries," have been analyzed as to contents. Collections of writing by several authors have been given particular attention. The List of Books Indexed appears at the front of the book; each title is cited by author, title, publisher, publication date, price, and Library of Congress card number, and each work is assigned a code number from A 01 to Z 01. Entries are listed alphabetically by author, title, or subject, but there are no directions explaining the arrangement or the reference to code numbers for individual works. Examination proves that the author's claim to sparing use of cross-references is justified, but the claim for generous utilization of synonyms is not borne out. For example, the excerpt from E. Franklin Frazier's *The Black Bourgeoise,* which appears in Ducas and Van Doren's compilation *Great Documents in Black American History,* is entered both under author Frazier and title, but James Baldwin's *The Fire Next Time* which is in the same anthology is listed only under title. The only entry for Baldwin cited for *Ducas and Van Doren* is his letter to his nephew. The intent of *Index to the Contemporary Scene* is a worthy one, but lack of guidance in effective use of the book and dearth of in-depth analysis which the reader is led to expect, prevent the book from achieving its aim.
(Dec. 1, 1973, p.352)

Index to Literature on the American Indian, 1971. San Francisco, The Indian Historian Pr., [1972]. 230p. 23cm. paper $7.

For years access to the mass of literature on the Indians of North, South, and Central America has been impeded by the lack of a ready index. The 1971 *Index to Literature on the American Indian* is the second annual index to current books, periodical articles, government documents, and theses on the American Indian prepared by the all-Indian American Indian Historical Society. The Society, founded in 1964, evaluates and corrects textbooks, oversees awarding of scholarships to American Indians, and maintains a publishing program. Literature "reflected in the so-called 'western magazines' has been deliberately eliminated from indexing consideration." The material cited in the *Index* is mostly from 294 journals ranging from *Ramparts* to *Christian Century* and from *Senior Scholastic* to *Harvard Law Review.* The publications are classified under 134 subjects and under these subjects are listed by author. Illustrations and bibliographic references are cited where included in the articles or books indexed. The work has several serious shortcomings. Prices are not given; nor does the *Index* evaluate the materials. Descriptive annotations are not supplied either. Works covering more than one subject appear under related subjects giving full bibliographic data. The Committee hopes that the future issues of the *Index*

"will expand both subjects chosen for indexing and content."
(Oct. 15, 1973, p.186)

Index to Plays in Periodicals Supplement. By Dean H. Keller. Metuchen, NJ, The Scarecrow Pr., Inc., 1973. x, 263p. 22cm. cloth $7.50.
ISBN 0-8108-0335-6.

When Dean Keller produced the original *Index to Plays in Periodicals* in 1971, he indexed only 103 journals. The present supplement continues the indexing from 1969 through 1971 and in addition indexes several important periodicals for the first time. This brings the total journals indexed to 2,334. The features of the original are retained in the supplement, and the arrangement is in two parts: Author Index and Subject Index. In evaluating the Supplement to *Index to Plays in Periodicals* the Reference and Subscription Books Review Committee endorses and expands its recommendation of the parent volume to school libraries with an extensive periodical file and college and university libraries as well as public libraries. *(June 15, 1974, p.1117)*

International Bibliography of Directories. International Bibliographie der Fachadressbücher. 5th rev. ed. Pullach/München, Verlag Dokumentation, 1973; New York & London, R. R. Bowker Co. xv, 536p. 22cm. cloth $31 plus shipping and handling.
ISBN 3-7940-1156-2.

International Bibliography of Directories, compiled "to simplify the user's search for information," contains over 6,000 titles divided into 15 main subjects and more than 80 subgroups. Each entry includes the full title, publisher, place of publication, price, and mailing address. A lengthy key word index and an alphabetical geographic index increase the usefulness of this work for reference librarians. The subjects covered range from hospitals and factories to museums and dentists. The individual directories include such diverse groups as shopping centers in New York, bars in Ghana, and antique dealers in the Pennsylvania Dutch Country.

Verlag Dokumentation was established at Munich several years ago as a publisher of works in library and information science. Its publications are handled in the United States by the R. R. Bowker Company. This fifth edition of *International Bibliography of Directories* has been completely revised with the cooperation of librarians and publishers. Correction questionnaires were sent out to remove errors; older titles no longer in print have been dropped, and new publications added.

The format of this book is adequate. The binding is cloth on light binder boards. The paper is opaque white with two columns on each page. The type is clear and readable, but the margins are too narrow to permit rebinding. This bibliography should be useful to reference librarians in special libraries as well as in those larger research libraries that need a comprehensive coverage of directories. *(July 1, 1974, p.1165)*

International Bibliography of the Book Trade and Librarianship: Fachliteratur zum Buch-und Bibliothekswesen. 10th ed. 2v. New York & London, R. R. Bowker Co., Pullach/Munich, Verlag Dokumentation, 1973. 818p. 22cm. cloth $45 plus shipping and handling.
ISBN 3-7940-1127-9.

The tenth edition of *International Bibliography of the Book Trade and Librarianship* cites 10,000 monographs issued mostly between 1969 and 1972 and which concern present and past developments in publishing, library science, and book selling. Part 1, the first volume, concerns Europe; Part 2 describes activities in Africa, the Americas, Asia, and Oceania. Each volume is arranged geographically by country. One hundred nine countries are covered. Each entry cites the author, title, publisher, year of publication, and price of the work. Author and subject indexes and a geographically-arranged directory of publishers facilitate locating information. The format of the volume is good, but the narrowness of the inner margins would preclude rebinding.
(July 15, 1974, p.1214)

International Bibliography, Information, Documentation. v.1-   . New York, R. R. Bowker Co. and Unipub., Inc., 1973- quarterly. 28cm. paper $15 per year in U.S. and Canada, $17.50 elsewhere. ISSN 0000-0329.

International Bibliography, Information, Documentation is a quarterly which began publication in March 1973. The work is the only existing single source of information covering the publications of the United Nations and its 18 autonomous intergovernmental agencies. This bibliographic guide covers books, monographs, periodicals, audiovisual materials, and microforms which will be of use to subject specialists, librarians, educators, researchers, government officials, and businessmen needing information. Each issue of *International Bibliography, Information, Documentation* is organized into three principal sections. Section 1, Information and News, has background information on the organizations of the United Nations system. The main section, Bibliographic Record, is arranged under some 40 subject groupings, and the final section, the Periodicals Record, is arranged by titles of the periodicals. The publication is beautifully designed for ease of use. *(July 15, 1974, p.1214)*

International Bibliography to the Sociology and Psychology of Reading. Compiled by Eymar Fertig; edited by Heing Steinberg. Berlin, Verlag Dokumentation; New York, R. R. Bowker Co., 1971 München-Pullich. 230p. 21cm. cloth $12.95. ISBN 3-7940-3192-X.

The current *International Bibliography to the Sociology and Psychology of Reading* is the third edition of the work produced in Germany. The Introduction and section captions are given both in German and in English. This bibliography, which excludes all entries of pedagogical, economic, technical, aesthetic, historical, and theological examinations unless these are determined by sociological and psychological methods, is divided into three main sections: Communications, Bookselling, and Libraries, and each major section is subdivided under theory and empirical observations. More than one thousand pieces of literature are cited, including books, journal articles, and pamphlets. A comprehensive variety of sources is cited: theses and dissertations (Emory University, Columbia University, University of North Carolina, College of Cape Coast Ghana, Innsbruck, Atlanta University, Indiana University), proceedings of conferences (National Academy of Sciences, Reading Habits in Pakistan), polls (Elmer Roper Associates on Public's Attitude Toward Television and Other Media), research reports (MIT), papers (Occasional Papers University of Illinois Library School), journals *(Public Opinion Quarterly, College and Research Libraries)*, and encyclopedia articles *(Encyclopaedia Britannica)*.

The period covered begins at the end of World War II and ends May 15, 1971. A few obvious pioneers published before 1945 are cited. These include William S. Gray's and Ruth Monroe's *The Reading Interests and Habits of Adults* (Chicago: Macmillan, 1929) and Douglas Waples' and Ralph Tyler's *What People Want to Read About* (Chicago: American Library Association and University of Chicago, 1931).

Entries are arranged alphabetically by author, and they appear in the language of the country of origin. Some of the languages noted are the predominating German and English, then Swedish, Hungarian, Danish, French, and Polish. For each entry the following data is given when applicable: author, coauthor, editor, coeditor, title, number of pages, date of publication, series, and name of publisher or sponsor. Titles that do not reveal the content of a work are briefly annotated in German. Helpful subject and personal indexes facilitate locating the material. This bibliography of the all-important sociology and psychology of reading will be valuable to students, booksellers, and librarians. *(Jan. 15, 1974, p.500)*

International Index to Film Periodicals 1972. Edited by Karen Jones. New York & London, R. R. Bowker Co., 1973. xv, 344p. 29cm. cloth $17.95 plus shipping and handling. ISBN 0-8352-0582-7.

The contents of more than 60 film periodicals have been analyzed in this first *International Index to Film Periodicals*, which is edited by Karen Jones of the Danish Film Museum. The project was produced under the direction of the International Federation of Film Archives whose Documentation Commission numbers nine persons of international repute. Twenty-four archives located in various parts of the world participated in the compilation: American Film Institute, Los Angeles; Cinémathèque de Toulouse; Gosfilmofond of Moscow; and National Film Archive, London. The project was two years in the making, and the results appeared in two stages; first, publication and distribution of 7,000 entries on cards and second, publication of the present annual volume. Michael Moulds will edit the next annual from London.

The purpose of the *International Index to Film Periodicals* is to pool the labor and resources of individual archives that had been indexing periodicals independently. This cooperative venture is largely successful. The *Index* is divided into eight major areas of information: General Reference Material; Film Industry; Distribution, Exhibition; Society and Cinema; Film Education; Aesthetics, Theory, Criticism; History of the Cinema; and Institutions, Festivals, Conferences. Each article has at least one entry, and articles dealing with several topics are entered under each pertinent subject. The following information is given for each, as applicable: name of author, title of article, journal title, volume, issue, page numbers, and an indication of type of item whether article, film review, or interview.

Individual films, uncompleted films and projects, and unrealized scripts are listed in a separate section. Collected and individual biography citations are given for actors, cameramen, critics, directors, and stuntmen.

Periodicals indexed include *Cinema Nuovo* (Florence), *Films in Review* (New York), *Fant* (Oslo), *Focus on Film* (London), and *Telecine* (Paris). The book is well reproduced from typewritten copy. It will be an essential reference for researchers as well as libraries with comprehensive film collections. *(Jan. 1, 1974, p.457)*

The International Jewish Encyclopedia.
By Ben Isaacson and Deborah Wigoder. Jerusalem, Massada Pr.; Englewood Cliffs, NJ, Prentice-Hall, 1973. 336p. illus. colorplates. 27cm. cloth $10.95. ISBN 0-13-473066-6.

This large-type, long-article (averaging a page to each entry) encyclopedia has about 200, often irrelevant illustrations, 12 colorplates, 2 maps, and 2 charts to accompany its 332 articles. One of the maps is a loose "Mini-Touring Map" available from any travel agent. The illustrations are not indexed and the text is inadequately indexed. The focus is on Israel, and the word "international" in the title is misleading. Though interestingly written and attractive, it is simply not in the same class as *The Junior Jewish Encyclopedia* (edited by Naomi ben Asher and Hayim Leaf; 7th rev. ed.; N.Y.: Shengold, 1970; 350p.; $8.95) or *The New Standard Jewish Encyclopedia* (edited by Cecil Roth and Geoffrey Wigoder; 4th new, rev. ed.; Garden City, NY: Doubleday, 1970; 2028 cols.; $19.95), the best one-volume Jewish encyclopedias for children and adults respectively. *(June 15, 1974, p.1117)*

International Organization: An Interdisciplinary Bibliography. (Hoover Institution Bibliographical Series XL1). Compiled by Michael Haas. Stanford, CA, Hoover Institution Pr., Stanford University c1971, published 1973. xxiv, 944p. 27cm. cloth $35. ISBN 0-8179-2411-6.

Michael Haas, compiler of *International Organization*, is professor of political science at the University of Hawaii. The book's Foreword proclaims it as the "most comprehensive and well-organized listing of scholarly works to yet become available in the international organization field." The bibliography "aims to break free from a parochial and topical orientation in order to provide historical depth along with contributions from all the social sciences. The major use of the bibliography, accordingly, will be to facilitate cross-historical comparative analysis and an accumulation of evidence in the tradition of historical sociology."

The bibliography of more than 8,000 references classified into some 300 divisions is organized into seven major parts: A. International Organizations B. Early International Organizations (dating back to classical civilization C. League of Nations System D. United Nations System E. Regional International Organizations F. Non-Governmental Organizations G. Proposals for World Government. Most sources used are secondary; only some of the most important documentary series and other primary sources from international institutions are listed. Books are given broader coverage than periodical articles. The articles that are cited are primarily from 50 scholarly journals. Unpublished dissertations, polemical tracts, popular pamphlets, working papers, and newspaper and magazine articles were outside the scope of the work. For each entry are given the author, title, place, publisher, date, and number of pages. The book is extremely well designed for ease of use. An Author Index and a Subject Index facilitate locating specific references. *(May 15, 1974, p.1017)*

The International Wine and Food Society's Encyclopedia of Wines. By André L. Simon. [New York,] Quadrangle Books, [1973, c1972]. maps. 25cm. 312p. cloth $15.

André L. Simon, French-born authority and writer on food and wine, was reputed to have written more than 70 books when he died in 1970. *Encyclopedia of Wines,* his last book, was revised and updated by Simon's friends between 1970 and 1972. The encyclopedia was first published under the title *The International Wine and Food Society's Gazetteer of Wines.* The version under review is the first American edition, and it was produced and printed in England. A brief Introduction sets the stage for discussion of the Major Vineyards of the World and Other Vineyards of the World. The major text is a 191-page gazetteer of wines. Arranged alphabetically, the geographical entries are keyed to the maps which follow in a separate section, and they either give an exact location or a nearby location. The maps locate only the better-known vineyards and towns. For countries like Japan, which produce small quantities of wine, there are no individual maps, and the world map or a map of a much larger area must be consulted. Identifications in the gazetteer are brief, e.g., *Burgen* "Moselle valley; village between Valwig and Kobern. Fair white table wine. West Germany" or *Premoureux, Les* "Jura., Salino vineyard. Ordinary to fair red table wine. France." This brevity contributes to ease of use of the book. There are some 7,000 such concise entries, unique in that they comprise the first such list ever brought together under one cover. A 15-item bibliography of titles published between 1963 and 1971 directs the reader to other reference books for further information particularly for information on national and regional viticulture. The broad coverage of this useful reference work recommends it.
(Nov. 15, 1973, p.303)

Investment Methods: A Bibliographic Guide. [By] James B. Woy. New York & London, R. R. Bowker Co., 1973. viii, 220p. 24cm. cloth $11.95 plus shipping and handling. ISBN 08352-0631-9.

Investment Methods is a dictionary-bibliography of some 150 investment terms, concepts, and strategies "intended primarily for use by the individual nonprofessional investor." Defined in clear easy-to-understand language are such terms as *dormant bottoms, treasury bills, stop-loss orders, hedge funds,* and *high-low index.* Each definition in the first section is followed by an annotated descriptive/critical bibliography of sources of relevant information. Author, title, chapter title, page, and publication date are given for each book. The six-page bibliography which lists all 100 titles cited also lists the name of publisher and price. A second major section lists the same 150 investment terms, concepts, and strategies relating them to pertinent periodical references which are very briefly annotated. Complete bibliographic data is given for each journal article. A list of 42 journals cited gives complete information on each magazine including frequency and price. Separate author, title, and subject indexes complete the volume and provide three-way access to the material. Author James Woy is an author and librarian with wide experience in business books. *Investment Methods* accomplishes its aim. Business libraries and lay investors will wish to purchase this up-to-date bibliographic dictionary. *(Mar. 1, 1974, p.703)*

Latin America in the Nineteenth Century: A Selected Bibliography of Books of Travel and Description Published in English. By A. Curtis Wilgus. Metuchen, NJ, Scarecrow, 1973. 174p. 23cm. cloth-B grade $5. ISBN 0-8108-0634-7.

Dr. A. Curtis Wilgus, author of this selected bibliography on Latin American travel and description is a prolific author and editor of books on Latin America and the Caribbean. He is Emeritus Director, School of Inter-American Studies, University of Florida. Wilgus defines travel and description broadly to include guidebooks, geographies, some histories, diaries, letters, memoirs and reminiscences, autobiographies, personal collections of private and public papers, and some relevant fiction. Items are numbered consecutively by author's surname. There are 1,182 entries in all which give the usual bibliographic data when it was available. When acceptable, short titles are used for a few very long titles. If a book has been reprinted and is in print in such form, this is indicated. A Geographical Index by Gilberto V. Fort of Miami Dade Junior College helps the reader locate titles by country. A 17-page Selected List of References concludes this authoritative bibliography. *(May 15, 1974, p.1017)*

The Library Journal Book Review 1972. New York & London, R. R. Bowker Co., 1973. 820p. 29cm. Case-Columbia/Grade C $19.95 plus shipping and handling.

This sixth annual cumulation of reviews of adult books that appeared in *Library Journal* in 1972 contains 5,700 succinct descriptions and evaluations. As with its predecessors, the book is arranged to provide easy access to the reviews: reference books precede 20 non-fiction subject categories, and fiction, recently revised editions, and library science follow. A helpful Author-Title Index concludes the work. The reviews are arranged alphabetically by author under the main subject headings, and they are reprinted exactly as they were published originally.

Janet Fletcher, Book Review Editor, *Library Journal,* sets forth criteria for reviewers in the Preface: "LJ's reviewers represent a broad range of personal, professional, and geographic backgrounds, and are chosen for their ability to convey in limited space a sense of each book's essential quality, its ideas, and to render a reliable assessment of its merits and demerits, its place in the literature of its field. Many are librarians with experience in book selection at the public or academic level; the others are specialists from a host of disciplines." *(Nov. 1, 1973, p.253)*

The Life Cycle Library for Young People. 6v. Chicago, Parent and Child Institute, [c1969-1971]; distributed by J. G. Ferguson Pub. Co. col. illus. 25cm. Corvon 120 $19.95.

The first three volumes of this series are intended for young people. They discuss birth, growth, sexual development and behavior, the reproductive process, love, and marriage. Divided into easy-to-read chapters they cover such topics as "Necking, Petting, Sexual Feelings," "How Do You Know When It's Love," "How a Baby is Born," and "What is Normal." The publishers state that doctors, psychiatrists, educators, and clergymen checked the information. Volume 4, which is continuously paged with volumes 1-3, is a glossary of such terms as *abortion, husband, sodomy, hormone, masochism,* and *prophylactic.* The definitions are far more comprehensive than those in abridged and unabridged dictionaries, and they are accurate. The fifth volume is a parents' answer book on a variety of subjects, and volume 6 is entitled *Parents' Answer Book on Drugs.* The seven chapters on drugs give an overview of the drug scene, discuss the legal aspects of illegal drug use, present a drug glossary, and two pages on the literature of drugs. *The Life Cycle Library* will be useful in schools and homes. *(Oct. 1, 1973, p.132)*

Literary and Library Prizes. 8th ed. Rev. and ed. by Jeanne J. Henderson and Brenda G. Piggins. New York & London, R. R. Bowker Co., 1973. 480p. 24cm. cloth $16.50 plus shipping and handling. ISBN 0-8352-0645-9.

Literary and Library Prizes has been published under various titles since its first edition of 1935. In 1935 and 1939 it was called *Famous Literary Prizes and Their Winners.* The third edition of 1946 was entitled *Literary Prizes and Their Winners.* Since the fourth edition of 1959 it has appeared under its present title. The book is organized under four categories: International Prizes, American Prizes, British Prizes, and Canadian Prizes. For each prize the following information is given: a succinct history, a description, and if the prize is cash the amount is cited, eligibility requirements, and procedure for determining the winner. The book includes a list of winning books and authors from the inception of the prize through 1973. Prizes discontinued since the seventh edition of *Literary and Library Prizes* in 1970 also listed with cessation date of the prize. The Library Prizes section is 40 pages long, contains all the expected awards and many that will be known to few readers. The Index to awards, recipients, and donors helps provide maximum access to the wealth of material in the book. The work is up to date and is commendable for its accuracy.
(Jan. 1, 1974, p.457)

Literature By and About the American Indian: An Annotated Bibliography for Junior and Senior High School Students. By Anna Lee Stensland. [Urbana], National Council of Teachers of English, [c1973]. x, 208p. 23cm. paperbound $3.95; to NCTE individual and institutional members, $3.65. ISBN 0-8141-4203-7.

Dr. Anna L. Stensland is a professor of English in the Department of Education at the University of Minnesota. Her bibliography of books by and about American Indians is intended to be used primarily by junior and senior high school English teachers. The work will also be useful in libraries. The 350-book bibliography is introduced by an 18-page prefatory essay "Books By and About the American Indian." Covered in this exposition are sections on Indian stereotypes in literature and criteria for selection. The bibliography proper consists of descriptive narratives about the books. For convenience the works are classified by subject: myth, legend, oratory, and poetry; fiction, drama, biography and autobiography; history; anthropology and archaeology; modern life and problems; and music, arts and crafts. Works are arranged within the subject classification alphabetically by author. Title, publisher, date of publication, price, and indication of paper binding is given for each.

Sixty-one pages of helpful information for the teacher and librarian complete the work. Included are: study guides to nine selected books, biographies of American Indian authors, a list of basic books for a collection, a listing of additional sources of material, a directory of publishers, an author Index, and a title Index. This is a well-researched bibliography and a much-needed reference tool.
(May 15, 1974, p.1017)

Living Black American Authors: A Biographical Directory. [By] Ann Allen Shockley and Sue P. Chandler. New York & London, R. R. Bowker Co., 1973. xv, 220p. 24cm. roxite-B grade $12.95 plus shipping and handling.
ISBN 0-8352-0662-9.

Editors Ann Allen Shockley and Sue P. Chandler are respectively Associate Librarian and Head of Special Collections and Assistant Librarian of Special Collections at Fisk University Library. Aware of the paucity of information about living black American authors, their intent with *Living Black American Authors* is to identify and provide information on both famous black authors and the many less familiar authors who are omitted from standard biographical references about contemporary authors. The editors include in their definition of "author" those who have written books, who have works in progress, who have published in newspapers, journals, or periodicals, editors, and authors of plays, television scripts, and filmstrips. Some 450 authors are included. For each author is provided as much of the following information as was accessible: name (including real name) and occupation, place and date of birth, education, family, professional experience, membership, awards, publications, and mailing address. It was necessary to take information for some authors from printed sources.

A list of 20 black publishers with addresses is appended as a convenience. Book titles cited in the biographies are listed in a Title Index at the end of the book. Each title is identified as to author, place of publication, publisher, and date. In print status is not indicated. *Living Black American Authors* is a welcome addition to biographical collections in libraries.

(March 15, 1974, p.753)

Man and the Environment: A Bibliography of the Selected Publications of the United Nations System 1946-1971. Compiled and edited by Harry N. M. Winton. New York & London, Unipub, Inc./R. R. Bowker Co., 1972. 305p. 24cm. case A $12.95 plus shipping and handling.

The aim of this annotated bibliography of 1,219 publications of the United Nations and such related agencies as World Health Organization, International Labour Organization, International Atomic Energy Agency, and International Telecommunications Union "is to call attention to the generally valuable kinds of information and publications emanating from the United Nations system." Monographs, dictionaries and glossaries, bibliographies, directories, yearbooks, periodicals, and filmstrips and other visual aids are listed alphabetically under 59 headings such as seismology, nutrition, vital and health statistics, animal resources, and water resources. Items are numbered consecutively and arranged chronologically, and for each are given: title, subtitle, author, editor, edition, number of pages, series, publisher/distributor, price, format, indication of illustrations, binding, and publication date. Four indexes facilitate use and study of this international approach to environmental problems: a personal and corporate name Author Index, a Series and Serials Index, a Title Index of monograph titles, and a Subject Index. This book is a useful source of comparative information for the countries of the United Nations, and it brings together the results of 25 years of extensive research on all aspects of global environment.

(Nov. 1, 1973, p.254)

The Middle East and North Africa, 1973-74. 20th ed. London, Europa Publications Ltd.; distributed in America by Gale Research Co., [1973]. xxiv, 872p. 26cm. maps. cloth $32.
ISBN 0-900-36Z60-X.

The first edition of *Middle East and North Africa* entitled *Middle East* was published by Europa in 1948. The Reference and Subscription Books Review Committee recommended it for libraries needing detailed current statistics and factual information on the countries in that part of the world. With the improvements made over the years the Committee reiterates its endorsement of this comprehensive, up-to-date, authoritative reference work. A wealth of information is organized in four parts. Part One is comprised of general survey articles on the religions (Islam, Christianity, Judaism) of the Middle East and North Africa, the Arab-Israeli confrontation 1967-1973, the Jerusalem issue, documents on Palestine, Palestine organizations, background of the current energy/oil crisis, and the Suez Canal. Part Two lists regional organizations, their officers, statistics, finances, and activities. Included are Organization of Arab Petroleum Exporting Countries, International Bank for Reconstruction and Development, and Federation of Arab Republics. Part Three contains extensive surveys of Afghanistan, Algeria, Bahrain, Cyprus, Egypt, Iran, Iraq, Israel, Jordan, Kuwait, Lebanon, Libya, Morocco, Oman, Qatar, Saudi Arabia, Spanish North Africa, Sudan, Syria, Tunisia, Turkey, United Arab Emirates, Yemen Arab Republic, and Yemen People's Democratic Republic. Part Four contains a Who's Who of the Middle East and North Africa, calendars, excellent bibliographies, and a list of international institutes and associations studying the Middle East and North Africa. There is no index.

A great wealth of information is in the country surveys. Acknowledgment is made to 37 foreign ministries, embassies, national statistical offices, and other bodies who provided information. A bibliography and facts on geography, history, the economy, and statistics are given for each nation.

A comparison between *The Middle East and North Africa* and *The Statesman's Year Book 1973/1974* revealed that many more kinds of data are given in the Europa publication. For example, for Saudi Arabia *Statesman's* cites government and constitution, area and population, education, welfare, finance, defense, agriculture, commerce, shipping, diplomats, roads, railways, aviation, telecommunication, and banking. For the same country, *Middle East* has information on physical features, climate, economic life, race, language, seven surveys of history including events since 1967, area and population, agriculture, oil, other industries, transport, foreign trade, finance, budget, statistical surveys of such matters as area and pilgrimages to Mecca, constitution and government, diplomatic representatives, defense, judicial system, religion, the press, publishers, radio and television, finance, trade and industry, transport, atomic energy, and education. Libraries and individuals requiring current, comprehensive facts on the Middle East and North Africa will find *The Middle East and North Africa* more useful than *The Statesman's Yearbook*.
(Feb. 15, 1974, p.613)

Military Aircraft of the World. [By] John W. R. Taylor and Gordon Swanborough. [rev. ed.] New York, Charles Scribner's Sons, [c1973]. 240p. illus. 23cm. cloth $5.95. SBN 684-13367-9.

The first *Military Aircraft of the World* was published in 1971 "to fill the need for a 'quick reference' guide to the equipment of the world's air forces." The current edition depicts and describes 30 newly adapted types of military aircraft and shows changes in the craft illustrated in the first edition. Each airplane is clearly identified by title. Facts are given on the type of engine, length, span, empty weight, gross weight, speed, and type of armament. Each craft is also identified by country of origin. A good index facilitates locating aircraft by name. Model makers and libraries which serve the aviation industry will be interested in this well illustrated reference tool.
(June 15, 1974, p.1117)

Military Dress of North America 1665-1970. [By] Martin Windrow & Gerry Embleton. New York, Charles Scribner's Sons, [c1973]. 159p. illus. maps. plates. ports. 24cm. binding? $10.
ISBN 0-684-13551-5.

Military Dress of North America 1665-1970 was first published in London by Ian Allen, Ltd. The work is organized chronologically in eight chapters. Each chapter has summarizing text which precedes plates of beautifully illustrated uniforms. Each uniform is identified as to name and date and is described in sufficient detail for the student or researcher. The bibliography of 28 sources will provide additional material for the interested reader. Libraries with extensive costume and military collections will wish to acquire this illustrated history of North American military dress. *(May 15, 1974, p.1018)*

Motion Picture Directors: A Bibliography of Magazine and Periodical Articles, 1900-1972. Compiled by Mel Schuster. Metuchen, NJ, The Scarecrow Pr., Inc., 1973. xxii, 418p. 22cm. B-grade cloth $12.50. ISBN 0-8108-0590-1.

This bibliography of English-language magazine and periodical articles on 2,300 motion picture directors, filmmakers, and animators brings together biographical references in one compact form. *Current Film Periodicals in English*, privately published by Adam Reilly in 1970, and its revised edition of 1972 were used as sources for journal titles. In the book's Introduction Mel Schuster explains the virtual impossibility of determining criteria for selection. More than 850 directors on whom no information was available are listed. The major portion of the book is devoted to the list of 388 directors for whom information is available in magazines and periodicals. There are as few as one citation for Henri Diament Berger and Gordon Douglas to 106 for Ingemar Bergman to 317 for Charlie Chaplin. The bibliography is arranged alphabetically by director and chronologically under director with the oldest reference appearing first. Each citation gives as much bibliographic data as was available to Schuster. There are two appendixes, one listing the 340 periodicals researched and the other providing a key to abbreviations. Libraries with extensive holdings on filmmaking will find this compilation useful and timesaving. *(Jan. 1, 1974, p.458)*

Museum Media: A Biennial Directory and Index of Publications and Audiovisuals Available from United States and Canadian Institutions. 1st ed. Paul Wasserman, managing editor; Esther Heiman, associate editor. Detroit, Gale Research Co., 1973. vii, 453p. hardbound $48. ISBN 0-8103-0385-X.

Prolific author/editor Professor Paul Wasserman of the University of Maryland School of Library and Information Services edited this first edition of *Museum Media* with Esther Herman. The book intends to provide comprehensive access to the significant materials covered in the books, booklets, exhibit catalogs, films, and other media that are sold or distributed by museums, galleries, art institutes, and similar institutions in the United States and Canada. From the 2,000 institutions sent questionnaires, 732 were selected for inclusion. The main part of the book lists institutions and their media alphabetically. As much of the following information as is applicable is given: books, booklets, monographs (title, author, publication date, number of pages, illustrations, and price); catalogs of exhibits, collections, and showings (title, author, publication date, number of pages, illustrations, and price); films (title, size of film, running time, color or black and white, sound or silent, and availability); filmstrips (title, size, running time, color or black and white, sound or silent, terms of availability, sale price, and rental fee); pamphlets and leaflets (title, author, date, number of pages, illustrations, and price); and other media available (form and descriptive details). A 245-page Title and Keyword Index, a 9-page Subject Index, and an 8-page Geographic Index facilitate locating information in the body of the book. *Museum Media* is both a reference and an acquisitions source for libraries, students, and those interested in materials currently available from museums. Format and layout of the book are good. *(April 15, 1974, p.889)*

The National Directory for the Performing Arts and Civic Centers 1974. [By] Beatrice Handel; editors Janet Spencer [and] Nolanda Turner. Dallas, Handel & Co., Inc., 2800 Routh, Suite 231, [1973]. 604p. 25cm. cloth $24. ISBN 0-913766-00-3.

Beatrice Handel, a Dallas business woman, conceived and wrote the first annual directory to the dance, theater, and vocal and instrumental music arts in all 50 states. Initial lists were compiled from such sources as states arts councils and commissions, chambers of commerce, governor's and mayor's offices, and state tourist bureaus. Based on the preliminary investigation 5,000 questionnaires were sent out. The directory is arranged alphabetically state by state and by city under the states. All types of performing arts activities are identified. Facilities for performing are cited by name, address including zip code, and telephone number. Other pertinent information given includes date of founding, name of manager and directors, type of organization (civic, profit, non-profit), season, sources of income, and seating capacity. Facts checked by the Committee are accurate. The book is extremely well designed for readability and easy access to the information. The inner margins are sufficiently wide to permit rebinding. *The National Directory for the Performing Arts and Civic Centers* is a much-needed reference tool which achieves its purpose of identifying everything that is happening in theater, music, and dance

in the United States. The fact that it will be updated, revised, and improved annually is in its favor. Libraries will wish to provide students and others interested in the performing arts with this accurate reference book.
(Feb. 15, 1974, p.613)

National Security Affairs: A Guide to Information Sources. [By] Arthur D. Larson. Detroit, Gale Research Co., [c1973]. Management Information Guide 27. 411p. 23cm. grade C linen $14.50.

National Security Affairs is compiled by Arthur D. Larson, formerly of Cornell and University of Maryland and now on the faculty, University of Wisconsin, Parkside. "While this bibliography will be of use to specialists and non-specialists alike, it is intended primarily to serve the needs of the latter—the officials, the practitioners, teachers, students, and educated laymen who through work, education or general interest are involved in national security affairs."—*Introduction*. The work is divided into seven sections: I. The World Setting of National Security, II. U.S. National Security Affairs, III. National Security and Domestic Affairs of Other Nations, IV. Theory, Research, Concepts and Study, V. Reference Material, VI. Periodicals, VII. Research and Educational Organizations. Three thousand eight hundred twenty two books are listed. Pertinent bibliographic data are given, and the citations are not annotated. A 58-page Key Word Index facilitates locating material. *National Security Affairs* is a very well-designed reference tool. *(July 15, 1974, p.1214)*

The Naturalists' Directory. 41st ed. 1972 and Supplement Sept. 1, 1973. South Orange, NJ 07079, PCL Publications, Inc. [1972, 1973]. 178p. and 58p. 20cm. paperbound $5 (41st ed.) $2.50 (supp).

The Naturalists' Directory is international in scope and was founded in 1878. The present edition has names, addresses, discipline, and other information on more than 3,500 naturalists in 60 countries. It also contains lists of natural history museums, societies, and associations and a listing of natural science journals. The supplement contains new information, changes of address, and notices of death. Universities, students, government agencies, and hobbyists requiring information of the natural sciences will need the updated *Naturalists' Directory* and *Supplement*.
(July 1, 1974, p.1166)

The New Dog Encyclopedia: Completely Revised and Expanded Updating of the Henry P. Davis Classic *Modern Dog Encyclopedia.* Harrisburg, Stackpole Books, c1970; second printing March 1973. 736p. illus. 30cm. linen $24.95; to schools and libraries, 20 percent discount; cash 10 percent discount. ISBN 0-8117-1064-5.

The New Dog Encyclopedia is the revised, enlarged, and retitled *Modern Dog Encyclopedia* first published in 1949. Other editions were published in 1956 and 1958. The present edition claims to be a completely updated and revised one. Individual articles are not signed, but a list of well-qualified contributors and consultants is given in the front of the book. An extensive table of contents and a lengthy Index, with *see also* references, add to the book's usefulness.

Coverage is very broad. Feeding, training, care, and breeding are well covered. Origin, history and use of the dog, as well as early classification systems precede many international classification schemes. History, description, and standards for the more than 100 breeds recognized by the American Kennel Club are included in the latter half of the book, as are the AKC rules and regulations and a directory of member clubs.

The print is very clear and easy to read. Illustrations are in black and white, numerous, and well-placed in relation to subject. The margins are wide; the book lies flat when open; and the stitching is sturdy, but the linen binding on one review copy already shows some wear on the bottom edge of backstrip. The heavy book is apt to require a sturdier binding, since a 1970 reference copy used by the Committee is badly worn. Both the pet owner and breeder will find useful up-to-date information in this large volume.
(June 15, 1974, p.1117)

The New York Times Book Review (1896-1972). New York, The New York Times/Arno Pr., 1972. v. illus. 32cm. buckram 1896-1971 $4670 (entire set); $6830 (purchased individually); 1972 $85.

This complete reprint of 76 years of weekly literary supplements to *The New York Times* serves both as an archive of modern literature and a history of contemporary reporting and literary criticism. The collection also provides a cumulative record of social, economic, political, scientific, and artistic trends in the United States as they were characterized in literature and criticism. Reviews of the years 1896-1919 are reprinted in one volume per year; those of 1920-1972 are covered in two volumes per year. Volumes are bound sturdily to withstand heavy use, and the quality of the reprint on permanent paper is far superior to that in other *New York Times* reprints. *The New York Times Book Reviews* will be useful to libraries wishing to maintain a permanent collection or to replace worn issues of the newspaper.
(Nov. 1, 1973, p.253)

The New York Times Book Review Index 1896-1970: v.I Author Index, v.II Title Index, v.III Byline Index, v.IV Subject Index, v.V Category Index. New York, The New York Times/Arno Pr., 1973. 30cm. D grade buckram pyroxylin coated $600.

The New York Times Book Review Index 1896-1970 a well-designed and well-edited reference work not only provides complete access to 75 years of *The New York Times Book Review,* but it also gives students, scholars, and researchers a history of literary trends, events, and developments in the United States during the period covered by the reviews. The index, comprising 800,000 entries on 50,000 pages, is monumental and covers everything in *The New York Times Book Review* except advertisements and queries to the editor. This means that comprehensive access is provided not only to the full-length book reviews but also to the brief reviews and biographical sketches, letters to the editor, brief comments, and notes and anecdotal items. As cited in the heading to this note, the work is arranged in five separate indexes not only the to-be-expected author, title, and subject indexes but also two bonus indexes, one for bylines and one for categories. The Author Index lists author, title, reviewer, and date and page reference to the review. The Title Index lists works alphabetically by distinctive title, collective title, series title, and subtitle. Titles with several significant words appear under each such word. Letters, commentary on a book, and every significant mention of a title in *The New York Times Book Review* are cited.

The Byline Index lists reviewers, authors of essays, articles, columns, letters, or any other item. The terms used in the Subject Index generally conform to those in the *Times Thesaurus of Descriptors* and ranges from Aachen, Germany to Krystyna Zywulska. This index is mostly limited to general articles, letters, columns, and reviews of nonfiction books. Under each subject, entries are given in chronological order. For example, *Amphibians* cites the 1915 *Reptiles and Batrachians,* the 1950 *Frogs and Toads,* the 1956 *Book of Reptiles and Amphibians,* and the 1957 *Boys Books of Frogs, Toads and Salamanders.*

The Category Index is unique because it places books under 16 literary genres and socio-historical categories like anthologies; mystery, detective, and spy fiction; reference works; self-help books; and westerns. Categories are listed alphabetically, and under the category entries are chronological. Only full-length reviews are indexed.

Printed on acid-free paper, production of *The New York Times Book Review Index* was facilitated by use of advanced computer technology. This work will become one of the most useful book reviewing reference works produced to date. *(Dec. 15, 1973, p.404)*

New York Times Everyday Reader's Dictionary of Misunderstood, Misused, Mispronounced Words. Laurence Urdang, ed. New York, Quadrangle Books, [c1972]. 377p. cloth $7.95.

This compilation of uncommon words by a professional lexicographer is

unique, but any reputable general dictionary serves just as well this book's stated purposes: 1) looking up pronunciations and meanings and 2) browsing to enlarge one's vocabulary. Generally, scientific and technical terms have been omitted, with the exception of anatomical terms and diseases. Words such as *gallstone, gamesmanship, gastrolith, migraine, milky way, totem pole,* and *xerography* have been included, but better, more precise and more complete definitions for these words are found in general dictionaries. Many words which librarians are frequently asked about have been omitted, e.g., abdomen, exorbitant, frag, prerogative, reich, and tragedy. The word selection here is based on personal choice; the result is not a unique reference tool.
(Oct. 15, 1973, p.186)

Paperbound Books in Print with 114,500 Titles, November 1973. New York & London, R. R. Bowker Co., [c1973]. 2625p. 28cm. Tyver $19.50 plus shipping and handling. ISBN 0-8352-0686-6.

The current *Paperbound Books in Print* lists some 114,500 inexpensive paperbacks. Works are listed by author, title, and subject. This conveniently arranged bibliography is published three times each year—in April, July, and November. Each entry provides author, title, publisher, price, and ISBN. Notes indicate illustrations and when the paperbound is an original publication. A useful directory of publishers is appended. The 26 major subject headings devised by the American Booksellers Association and the National Association of College Bookstores are listed. These major classifications are adhered to in the classified section of *Paperbound Books in Print.* A more detailed breakdown of subjects is also listed in the book. Pages are cited. The inner margins on many of the pages will not allow for rebinding, but for the library that purchases the three volumes a year, rebinding of out-of-date books would not be necessary. *(May 15, 1974, p.1018)*

Performing Arts Books in Print: An Annotated Bibliography. By Ralph Newman Schoolcraft. New York, Drama Book Specialists Publishers, [c1973]. 761p. 29cm. cloth $32.50.

This well-researched, well-designed annotated bibliography of 12,000 in-print books on the theater, drama, motion pictures, televison, radio, the mass media, dance, and music is welcome as a revision and updating of *Theatre Books in Print,* first published in 1963 and revised in 1966. Criteria for selection are clearly defined: books currently available in the United States, almost without exception in English, and among plays, only Shakespeare's plays or "those scholarly editions which provide, in addition to text, as extensive study of the background, the style, the playwright's intent." There are two major sections in the book; the first includes work published before December 31, 1970, and the second lists books published during or after 1971 and also those published before 1971 that were not previously known to the author. Each section of the book is organized into four parts: Books on Theatre and Drama; Books on the Technical Arts of the Theatre; Books on Motion Pictures, Televison, and Radio; and Books on the Mass Media and the Popular Arts. For each entry is given author, title, publisher, year of publication, pagination, and price. A brief annotation describing the contents follows. The easy-to-follow classification scheme facilitates access to the various types of books. Books are classified into general reference works, philosophy of theatre, world theatre, Greek and Roman theatre, Shakespeare, national theatres, biographies, musical theatre, and dance. This bibliography will be valuable in high school, academic, and public libraries.
(Dec. 15, 1973, p.404)

Periodicals for School Libraries: A Guide to Magazines, Newspapers, and Periodical Indexes. Compiled and edited by Marian H. Scott, rev. ed. Chicago, American Library Association, 1973. xvi, 269p. 21cm. paper $4.95. ISBN 0-8389-0139-5.

The revised edition of *Periodicals for School Libraries* updates the first edition of 1969. It covers 500 journals and newspapers for school libraries at all levels from kindergarten through high school, and it intends to serve the "needs of school librarians and teachers." Only works recommended for school selection are listed in this annotated buying guide. Full bibliographic information is given, and the annotated descriptions are sufficiently long and evaluative to place each work in proper perspective. *Periodicals for School Libraries* is revised, corrected, and updated with periodic listings in *The Booklist*. Libraries will use this selection tool with William Katz's *Magazines for Libraries,* second edition, which will be reviewed by the Reference and Subscription Books Review Committee in the current volume of *The Booklist*. *(May 15, 1974, p.1018)*

Pest Control in Buildings: A Guide to the Meaning of Terms. [By] P. B. Cornwell. London, [Hutchinson & Co. Ltd., 1973]; St. Martins Pr., U.S. distributor. 192p. illus. 24cm. cloth $10.

Wood Preservation: A Guide to the Meaning of Terms. [By] Norman E. Hickin. London, [Hutchinson & Co. Ltd., 1971]; St. Martins Pr., U.S. distributor. 109p. illus. 24cm. cloth $10.

These companion volumes aim to provide current, detailed, and comprehensive references to terms in wood preservation and pest control. Both books are of British origin. They are organized similarly, and the well-designed format is equally good in both. While some of the terms defined may be found in general dictionaries and even in science dictionaries, such terms are more clearly and comprehensively covered in these two dictionaries. For example, in the *Pest Control* dictionary the definition of *bait* is 21 lines long, and it is fortified by coverage of six related terms *bait block, bait box, bait shyness, bait station, bait tray,* and *bait tunnel. Ambrosia beetles* are given encyclopedic treatment in 23 lines in the *Wood Preservation* dictionary. The chief genera are named, and habits, effects, and fungi of the species are detailed. The practitioner in pest control or wood preservation will find relevant definitions not available elsewhere for terms such as *card process* (preservation process), *contact dust* (a rodenticidal powder), and *full-cell process* (wood preservation).

Authors Hickin and Cornwell are respectively Scientific Director and Director of Research at Rentokil Laboratories in Great Britain. Rentokil has prepared a library of eight other books including *Household Insect Pests* and *Termites. (Dec. 15, 1973, p.405)*

Pictorial Travel Atlas of Scenic America. bicentennial ed. By E. L. Jordan. New York, Chicago, Boston, Hammond Inc. [c1973]. 256, 32p. illus. maps. 29cm. crown linen $14.95 to schools and libraries, 25 percent discount.

The author of this revised travel atlas, Dr. Emil Leopold Jordan, had been a faculty member at Rutgers University for 24 years when he wrote the original edition of this work in 1955. For this edition Dr. Jordan has rewritten the entire text; Hammond has provided new maps, and the editors have secured new illustrations. Dr. Jordan is author of several college texts and books on ecology. Five preliminary pages of hints on travel, descriptions of regional foods of the United States, Puerto Rico, and Hawaii, and a key to America's regions precede the main text which is as in 1955, organized into six regional sections: Northeast, Southeast, North Central, South Central, Northwest, and Southwest. A double-page colored map of the area introduces each section. These maps are keyed to the more detailed maps which follow, and they show larger lakes and rivers, large cities, major highways, local, state and national recreation areas, and points of interest. The 91 articles which cover the featured areas are practical and helpful for the traveller regardless of his means of transportation. The Committee is pleased to note that in contrast to the 1955 edition which lacked an index, access to the information is facilitated by a five-page gazetteer Index. In honor of the bicentennial of the United States, the final 32 pages are devoted to "1776 Revisited—See and Relive the American Revolution," interesting brief historical narrative enlivened by colored maps. *(Nov. 15, 1973, p.303)*

Plot Summary Index. Compiled by Carol L. Koehmstedt. Metuchen, NJ, The Scarecrow Pr., Inc., 1973. 312p. 22cm. cloth $8.50. ISBN 0-8108-0584-7.

Plot Summary Index, by North Dakota State University Reference Librarian Carol L. Koehmstedt, began as an index to the *Masterplots* series available in North Dakota State University Library. The present work indexes all 15 existing *Masterplots* compilations plus 10 others, including Springhorn's *20th Century Plays in Synopsis* (New York: Crowell, 1966) and Grazier's *Plot Outlines of 101 Best Novels* (New York: Barnes & Noble, 1962). *Plot Summary Index* is arranged in two sections, a Title Index and an Author Index. High school, college and university, and public libraries serving students who require summaries of literary works will wish to purchase this handy reference. *(July 1, 1974, p.1166)*

Publications of the United Nations System: A Reference Guide. Compiled and edited by Harry N. M. Winton. New York & London, R. R. Bowker Co., 1972, xi, 202p. 24cm. Case-A $10.95 plus shipping and handling.

Publications of the United Nations System intends to "present a brief overview of the organizations of the United Nations and their publications, to call attention to a number of valuable reference works published by these organizations, and to provide a comprehensive list of their periodicals and selected other recurrent publications." This book fulfills a long-standing need for a comprehensive bibliography for locating the many reference works published by the United Nations and its member agencies.

Publications of the United Nations System is divided into three major parts. Part I, "The Organizations of the United Nations System and Their Publications," surveys the United Nations and each of the related international organizations briefly giving headquarters address, aims and membership, structure, and a listing of publications and documents, together with information on availability and name and address of Canadian and United States distributor.

Part II, "Reference Guide to Publications of the United Nations System," is a selected bibliography of statistical publications, directories of institutions, collections of laws and treaties, dictionaries and glossaries, classification schemes, and bibliographies, abstracts, and catalogs. These references are grouped under 29 broad subjects, e.g., demography, peace and armament, treaties and international agreements, and postal and telecommunication services.

Part III, "Periodicals of the United Nations System," is a comprehensive listing of periodicals and series. Included are both subscription and priced material. Titles are arranged in alphabetical order. Each entry gives information on periodicity, availability, year of initial issue, and language(s) of publication. The brief subject analysis provided for each periodical is very useful. A 14-page Subject Index concludes this well-researched work. *(Oct. 1, 1973, p.132)*

The Puerto Ricans: An Annotated Bibliography. Edited by Paquita Vivó. New York & London, R. R. Bowker Co., 1973 [c by Puerto Rican Research and Resources Center, Inc.]. xv, 299p. 26cm. cloth A $14.95 plus shipping and handling.

This much-needed bibliography of materials was prepared by the Puerto Rican Research and Resources Center, 1766 Church Street, Washington, D.C. The work was edited by Paquita Vivó and researched by Lourdes Miranda King, both of the Research and Resources Center. The 2,600-entry bibliography proposes to "offer light to Puerto Ricans in search of their own roots and their cultural heritage. The bibliography will also serve as a resource to non-Puerto Ricans in the society who should and do want to know about their fellow citizens." The Center, established in February 1971, fathered the concept for Universidad Boricua, learning centers to be established for Puerto Ricans in all parts of the United States. The first arm of the university will open in New York City in October or November 1973. The Washington Center has done studies on Puerto Rican dropouts, migration, and civil rights. According to Miss King in an interview conducted by the Committee, its goal is to identify through research pressing problems that confront Puerto Ricans.

Primary sources at the world's largest and best collections of Puerto Ricana were used in the compilation of the bibliography: Library of Congress, University of Puerto Rico Library, Ateneo Puertorriqueno, Centro de Investigaciones Historicas of the University of Puerto Rico, New York Public Library, and Instituto de Cultura Puertorriqueno in Puerto Rico. All items listed are either in print or are relatively easy to obtain in libraries in the United States and Puerto Rico. When both English and Spanish versions of a work exist, the title is entered in English with reference to the Spanish edition. Most of the titles are in English.

The Puerto Ricans is easy to use and is divided into four sections: Books, Pamphlets, and Dissertations subdivided into 21 subject classifications; Government Documents with Puerto Rican documents separated from those of the United States; Periodical Literature with a list of selected periodicals appearing before the bibliography of journal articles; and Audiovisual Materials classified into motion pictures and filmstrips. Book and periodical entries are arranged alphabetically by title. Government documents are listed by title under the name of the issuing agency, and audiovisual materials are cited by title. Full bibliographic information is given, and in most instances clear, concise annotations describe and evaluate the title. Grade level recommendations are also made. A helpful list of publishers and distributors, and author, title, and subject indexes conclude the work. Teachers, librarians, social workers, and others who serve the Puerto Rican community will wish to acquire this authoritative, utilitarian reference work. *(Nov. 15, 1973, p.303)*

Ralph Nader Congress Project: Citizens Look at Congress. 9v. Wash., DC, Grossman Publishers Congress Project, Box 19281, Wash., DC 20036, 1972- tables. charts. 29cm. Spring post looseleaf vinyl $450 full set; $1 per profile postage paid.

The *Ralph Nader Congress Project* portion one, profiles of 484 United States senators and representatives, was prepared by more than one thousand of Nader's researchers "to provide detailed, specific information about members of Congress." The profiles, which vary in length from 20 to 40 pages, were reviewed by Nader's editors and verifiers, and according to the publisher, in most cases were reviewed by the Congress member or his or her staff prior to publication. Each profile is signed by the author responsible for the writing. There are profiles available for all members of the 93rd Congress except those elected for the first time in November 1972 or those who retired or lost primary elections in 1972.

For each member of Congress, information in succinct, easy-to-retrieve form is provided on positions and votes on key issues, votes in committees, financial interests and campaign contributions (if available), legislative interests, supporters in Washington and elsewhere, ratings by major groups, communication with constituents, and very brief personal and political biography. Facts are presented in unbiased language that is notable for its economy of words. The sets, arranged alphabetically by state, should be useful in all libraries requiring information on the political record of congressmen. Profiles of individuals are also available.

The second phase of the Nader Congress Project will be devoted to volumes on the major congressional committees and such topics as campaign financing, lobbying, Congressional rules and procedures, relationship with the Executive branch, and a citizens handbook. *(Oct. 15, 1973, p.186)*

Rand McNally Popular World Atlas. Desk ed. Chicago, New York, San Francisco, Rand McNally & Co., [c1972]. 46A, 201p. col. illus. col. maps. 32cm. paper $4.95.

Rand McNally advises the Committee that *Popular World Atlas* is a paper-

back version of *Worldmaster Atlas* which was reviewed and recommended in an omnibus review of Rand McNally atlases December 1, 1972. For libraries and homes that cannot afford the $6.95 *Worldmaster,* the paperbound version is a good buy at $4.95.
(Feb. 15, 1974, p.614)

Record and Tape Reviews Index 1972. Compiled by Antoinette O. Maleady. Metuchen, NJ, The Scarecrow Pr., Inc., c1973. ix, 509p. 23cm. B-grade cloth $12.50. ISBN 0-8108-0672-X.

Antoinette O. Maleady is Acquisition Librarian, Somona State College, Rohnert Park, California. Her 1972 *Index* cites reviews of classical music on discs, tapes, cassettes, and spoken recorded works in 18 periodicals among them *High Fidelity, Music Quarterly,* and *Records and Recordings.* The work is organized into four sections; section I is an alphabetical listing by composer; section II, Music in Collections, cites records and tapes with several composers on one disc or tape; section III lists reviews of spoken recordings; and section IV is a performer index. The 1972 *Index* is the second such work by Mrs. Maleady; the first one covers 1971. In each section sufficient information is provided for identification of sources, recordings, and performers. The indication of the reviewer's evaluation of each recording is an aid to those needing to evaluate classical records and tapes. The book is well designed for ease of use.
(July 15, 1974, p.1215)

Records in Review, 1973 Edition: The Eighteenth High Fidelity Annual. Great Barrington, MA, The Wyeth Pr.; New York, Charles Scribner's Sons, [1973]. 459p. 22cm. cloth $9.95.

The 1973 *Records in Review* is the eighteenth annual reprinting of record reviews from *High Fidelity* magazine. *High Fidelity* is well-known among musicians and record collectors for the superior quality of its reviews prepared and signed by authorities. For ease of reference use reviews in the present compilation are organized alphabetically by composer. For frequently recorded composers further subdivision is made under categories such as Chamber Music, Vocal Music, and Orchestral Music. Composers' dates are recorded; participants on the record are cited by name, and the recording company and number of discs are noted. Each review is initialed by its writer; full names of reviewers are given at the front of the volume.

Since the 1973 edition contains reviews of 1972 productions, libraries and music lovers must wait almost a year for the reprinting of 1973 reviews. *Records in Review* is well designed and is a priority purchase for those who consider it "the bible for record collectors."
(April 15, 1974, p.889)

The Scolma Directory of Libraries and Special Collections on Africa. Compiled by Robert Collison and revised by John Roe. [Hamden, CT], Archon Books 1973. 118p. 22cm. cloth $7.50. ISBN 0-208-01332-6.

Scolma Directory is the third edition of the (British) Standing Conference on Library Materials on Africa's *Directory of Libraries and Special Collections on Africa,* and it is based on librarian-indexer-bibliographer Robert Collison's original edition and is revised by John Roe. The edition under review was first published in Great Britain by SCOLMA. "The Standing Conference on Library Materials on Africa was set up in April 1962 to facilitate the acquisition and preservation of library materials needed for African studies, and to assist in the recording and use of these materials." The Conference has published *African Research and Documentation* (a newsletter) 1962- , *Theses on Africa Accepted by Universities in the United Kingdom* (1964), *U.K. Publications and Theses on Africa* (an annual) 1963- , *Conference on Acquisition of Material from Africa, Univ. of Birmingham* 1970, and *Debates of African Legislatures* (1972). The 93-page directory is arranged alphabetically by town. Under each library or collection is given the name, address, telephone number, name of librarian, hours, and a brief description of the collection. The description also tells how a user gains access to the collection and names publications of the institution. A good 18-page Index helps provide maximum access to the information. Libraries with substantial Africa collections will wish to acquire this new British directory of libraries and special collections on Africa.

(Jan. 1, 1974, p.458)

Selected Guide to Make-It, Fix-It, Do-It-Yourself Books. Susan Nueckel, editor. New York, Fleet Press Corp., [1973]. 213p. 24cm. cloth $14.50; to schools and libraries, $11.60. ISBN 0-8303-0125-9.

Selected Guide to Make-It, Fix-It, Do-It-Yourself Books is a convenient guide to do-it-yourself books on 82 subjects such as psychology, sex education, childbirth, occult, needlecraft, health, and home repairs and maintenance. Broad subjects are further classified, e.g., cooking has 36 classifications; home repairs and maintenance is subdivided under air conditioning and refrigeration, appliances, electrical, general repairs, plumbing, and roofing. Information given for each title includes author, publisher, price, type of binding (hard cover or paperback), and number of pages. A simple one-line descriptive annotation is given for each book. Each title is also classified as to juvenile or adult audience. This will be helpful to the user who is unfamiliar with the individual titles. No dates of publication are cited, but the Committee assumes that the editor intends the book as a list of in-print titles, since a list of 179 publishers with addresses is appended to the guide. To provide maximum access to the material there is a nine-page analytical index and a table of contents arranged alphabetically by subject. For public libraries requiring an index to do-it-yourself books this guide will be useful. *(Mar. 1, 1974, p.703)*

The Statesman's Year-Book: Statistical and Historical Annual of the States of the World for the Year 1973-1974. Edited by John Paxton. New York, St. Martin's Pr., [c1973]. xxviii, 1566p. maps (part fold.; part col.) 21cm. cloth $13.95; to schools and libraries, 20 percent discount.

This 110th edition of "the most useful of all the general yearbooks—indispensable in any type of library" presents reliable current descriptive facts and statistical data on governments of the world. In this edition changes have been made to update information: Sri Lanka replaces the name Ceylon; Bangladesh is correctly placed in the Commonwealth section while Pakistan has been transferred to the general section on nations outside the Commonwealth. Maps reflect changes in the county boundaries of England and Wales, and there is a new map of world shipping routes and container ports. Featured in the 1973/1974 *Statesman's Yearbook* are a new section of information on the Council of Mutual Economic Assistance and statistical tables of international reserves of member countries of the International Monetary Fund. The valuable feature of selected reference books on each country is retained.

(July 1, 1974, p.1166)

String Music In Print. [By] Margaret K. Farish. 2d ed. New York & London, R. R. Bowker Co., 1973. xv, 464p. 26cm. buckram-C grade $34.50 plus shipping and handling. ISBN 0-8352-0596-7.

In 1965 Margaret Farish, Evanston, Illinois musician and music teacher, edited the first bibliography of *String Music In Print*. A supplement followed in 1968. Now she has updated the original and supplement retaining the old works still in print and adding 6,000 new works. This second edition guide to music for violin, viola, violoncello, double bass and viols intends to provide a practical reference for teachers and performers. In order to avoid an excessively long volume, contents of large collections are omitted. The book is well organized for ease of use. Sixteen sections arrange the citations primarily by number of instruments required (solos, quartets, quintets), and subdivisions are based on specific instruments necessary. Except for folksongs listings are arranged alphabetically by composer. For each work the composer, title, publisher, and publisher's order number are given.

An index to composers and a directory of publishers are appended. Performers, teachers, and music libraries who want to avoid culling publishers' catalogs will appreciate the new *String Music In Print*. *(May 15, 1974, p.1018)*

Subject Guide to Books in Print 1973. 2v. New York & London, R. R. Bowker Co., [1973]. 4150p. 29cm. pyroxylin-impregnated B grade $44.50 plus shipping and handling. ISBN 0-8352-0681-5.

When the Reference and Subscription Books Review Committee reviewed the first edition of *Subject Guide to Books in Print* in *The Booklist and Subscription Books Bulletin* July 1, 1958, the Committee noted that the work had the reference value of a printed subject catalog in a good-sized library. The *Subject Guide* is now in its seventeenth annual edition. The number of titles covered has expanded from 91,000 in 1957 to 337,000 in 1973. With this latest, improved edition the Committee endorses its commendation of the first edition. The guide will be useful to libraries in selecting replacements in subject fields, and it will aid readers who need to identify a book whose subject is known, but whose author and title are vague.

Books are classified under 62,000 of the latest Library of Congress subject headings; titles are listed where the user is most likely to look for them, with as many additional references as are necessary. Only fiction, except when the work's historical, biographical or other background is extensive, poetry and drama, and bibles as such are excluded. Full bibliographic detail including ISBN are given. Explicit directions for use are noted. The list of publishers is comprehensive. This worthwhile complement to *Books In Print* 1973 recommended by the Committee in January 15. 1974 *Booklist* is a primary purchase for libraries, particularly for those that do not need or cannot afford Bowker's special subject guides in business and medicine. *(Feb. 15, 1974, p.614)*

Subject Guide to Microforms in Print, 1973. [Washington, DC, Microcard Editions, c1973]. xii, 202p. 28cm. paperbound. $6.

In 1961 Microcard Editions published the first annual *Guide to Microforms in Print*. A year later a companion *Subject Guide* followed. The *Subject Guide* is biennial and classifies materials available on microfilm and other microforms by 135 Library of Congress classifications. Each classification is assigned a number thus making it easier to locate related works. The output of more than 100 publishers is cited; theses and dissertations are excluded. Use of the *Subject Guide* is clearly explained in the book's forematter. Purchasing information and price are given for each item cited. The format of the guide is good; margins are sufficiently wide to permit rebinding. Libraries needing an up-to-date listing of microform publications offered for sale on a regular basis will wish to acquire this latest *Subject Guide*. *(June 15, 1974, p.1117)*

Webster's Biographical Dictionary. Springfield, Mass., G. & C. Merriam Co. Publishers, [c1972]. 1697p. 26cm. sturdite sold with two other Webster dictionaries to schools and libraries, $29.95 plus shipping and handling for the three.

Webster's New Geographical Dictionary. Springfield, Mass., G. & C. Merriam Co., Publishers, [c1972]. 1370p. maps. 26cm. sturdite sold with two other Webster dictionaries to schools and libraries, $29.95 plus shipping and handling for the three.

Webster's Seventh New Collegiate Dictionary. Springfield, Mass., G. & C. Merriam Co., Publishers, [c1972]. 1224p. illus. 26cm. sturdite sold with two other Webster dictionaries to schools and libraries $29.95 plus shipping and handling for the three.

Encyclopaedia Britannica Educational Corporation has prepared a special classroom edition of the three major desk dictionaries produced by Merriam-Webster, a fully-owned subsidiary of Encyclopaedia Britannica Inc. In previous editions all three dictionaries have been recommended by the Reference and Subscription Books Review Committee—*Webster's Biographical*

Dictionary (*The Booklist* July 15, 1970), *Webster's Seventh New Collegiate Dictionary* (*The Booklist and Subscription Books Bulletin* July 15, 1963), and *Webster's Geographical Dictionary* (*Subscription Books Bulletin* July 1950). Prospective purchasers will wish to note that the *Collegiate Dictionary* has been superseded this spring by a new edition. In the present package *Collegiate* has 130,000 entries; the new edition claims to have 150,000. The *Biographical Dictionary* has 40,000 entries, and the *Geographical* has almost 48,000 entries. *(June 1, 1973, p.917)*

Who Was Who in Florida. Written and compiled by Henry S. Marks. Huntsville, AL, Strode Publishers, [c1973]. 276p. 27cm. cloth $14.95; to schools and libraries, 10 percent discount. ISBN 87397-039-X.

Who Was Who in Florida is a retrospective biographical directory of "outstanding residents or developers of Florida who have passed away. Our main conception has been to provide pertinent information about the major events or importance of as many people as possible to present in a single volume." The period covered is from the earliest date of recorded history to November 30, 1972. Prominent Florida residents from all walks of life are included; an attempt has been made to provide information on persons librarians and historians are likely to be asked about. Pertinent facts of biographees' lives are given with a minimum of eulogizing. For those requiring additional information a Bibliography of sources used is provided. Henry S. Marks is author of Strode's *Who Was Who in Alabama* (1972). *(July 1, 1974, p.1166)*

Who's Who In Dickens. [By] John Greaves. New York, Taplinger, [1973]. 232p. 21cm. cloth $6.95; to libraries, 10 percent discount. ISBN 0-8008-8266-0.

John Greaves, lecturer on Dickens and Secretary of the Dickens Fellowship for 25 years, is author of this addition to Taplinger's *Who's Who in Literature Series*. *Who's Who in Dickens* is an alphabetically arranged handbook to all of Dickens characters. Sufficient identification and description are given to place each character, and reference is made to the work in which each appears. This handy compendium will be useful to students and others interested in Dickens. *(July 15, 1974, p.1215)*

Who's Who in Shakespeare. [By] Peter Quennell and Hamish Johnson. New York, William Morrow & Co., Inc. [c1973]. 288p. illus. 26cm. cloth $14.95.
ISBN 0-688-001920.

Peter Quennell, British author, biographer, and critic has used as sourcebook for his guide to Shakespeare characters C. J. Sisson's edition of *William Shakespeare: The Complete Works*. The book is intended "for the reader of the huge Shakespearian cannon who wishes to recollect where such-and-such a character occurs, and the function he or she performs." In addition to the plays one would expect to cover are characters from *Pericles* and *Henry VIII*, because both plays are usually attributed to Shakespeare. *Sir Thomas More* and *The Two Noble Kinsmen* are omitted. Entries are arranged alphabetically and are liberally illustrated with playbills and photographs. Each entry describes the character and establishes the character's importance in the plays. For most important Shakespeare characters, quotations are included from famous early critics such as Jonson, Coleridge, and Hazlitt. Quennell's *Who's Who in Shakespeare* is superior in coverage and treatment to the work bearing the same title by Robin May, described below.
(May 15, 1974, p.1018)

Who's Who in Shakespeare. [By Robin May]. With a foreword by Judi Dench. New York, Taplinger Pub. Co., [1973]. xi, 190p. 20cm. cloth $6.50; to libraries 20 percent discount. ISBN 0-8008-8269-5.

Robin May is an author and former actor. He claims that this biographical dictionary "contains all Shakespeare's characters except for some of the smallest fry." The text is arranged alphabetically and identifies each character briefly and concisely. As an aid to the user 40 Shakespearian plays are listed

at the end of the book with major characters identified by act and scene. This little handbook can serve as a companion to Alan Dent's *World of Shakespeare: Animals and Monsters* and *World of Shakespeare: Plants* also published by Taplinger.
(May 15, 1974, p.1018)

Women: Their Changing Roles. Elizabeth Janeway, advisory ed. New York, The New York Times/Arno Pr., [c1928-1972]. illus. 556p. 29cm. $35; to series subscribers, $30.

Women: Their Changing Roles is the latest in "The Great Contemporary Issues" series spin-offs from *The New York Times*. Already published in the series are *Labor and Management, Drugs, Mass Media and Politics,* and *China*. Also planned for this reference series are *Black Africa; Education in America; Values Americans Live By; Religion; The Sexual Revolution; Environment, Medical Care and Health; Japan; Middle East;* and *Crime and Justice*. Elizabeth Janeway, advisory editor of *Women* is an author of novels, short stories, and critical articles.

Comprised of reprints from *The New York Times,* the book is divided into nine sections depicting the best output of the newspaper's articles on "Social Feminism," "The Twenties," "The Thirties," "Women and World War II," "The Postwar Period," "Women in the Arts," "Sexual Emancipation," "Radical Feminism," and "Challenge and Change." A good 27-item suggested reading list is appended. Included are such works as Simone de Beauvoir's *Second Sex*, Margaret Sanger's *Women and the New Race*, and Eli Ginzberg's *Life Styles of Educated Women*. A 14-page Subject Index and a 2-page By-Line Index facilitate location of material. While the quality of reproduction both of illustrations and text leaves much to be desired, the quality of the selections themselves as eyewitness reports and commentaries warrants commendation. *(Nov. 1, 1973, p.254)*

World Communism: A Handbook, 1918-1965. Edited by Witold S. Sworakowski. Stanford, Hoover Institution Pr., Stanford University, 1973. xv, 576p. 26cm. cloth $25. ISBN 0-8179-1081-3.

World Communism Handbook is a companion to the latest *International Yearbook on Communist Affairs* (*The Booklist* Nov. 15, 1973). The handbook gives detailed encyclopedic treatment to past events in the history of the Communist Party, and it provides the basic information for the current yearbook. Both works are published by The Hoover Institution on War, Revolution and Peace, Stanford University. Although the Institution disclaims responsibility for views expressed in the two books, the handbook attempts to meet the need for "a succinct historical background for every communist party that existed anywhere in the world up to the end of 1965, and it covers the developments leading to the founding of each party and the most important activities of each."—*Preface*.

The handbook consists of authoritative signed articles by 53 scholars from all over the world. In many instances the writing is based on firsthand knowledge. Following most of the articles is a paragraph on important party records, documents, party press organs, a list of party congresses, and a short bibliography. Since no books are available on the newly-founded parties in Africa and other locales, the bibliographies for such parties consist almost exclusively of journal articles.

Witold S. Sworakowski, editor of *World Communism Handbook*, is Professor Emeritus and Consultant to the Director, Hoover Institution. The handbook can be best used in conjunction with the yearbook. For libraries which cannot afford both books, it is advisable to purchase the yearbook, because it is more easily consulted for specific items of information. *(Jan. 15, 1974, p.501)*

World Directory of Environmental Education Programs: Post-Secondary Study and Training in 70 Countries. Prepared by International Institute for Environmental Affairs in Cooperation with the Institute of International Education; edited by Philip W. Quigg. New York &

London, R. R. Bowker Co., 1973. xlii, 289p. 23cm. roxite-B grade $14.95 plus shipping and handling. ISBN 0-8352-0689-0.

Publication of this first directory of more than 1,100 environmental education programs in some 750 institutions in 70 countries was made possible by grants from the Henry Luce Foundation, the U.S. Environmental Protection Agency, the General Services Foundation, Exxon Corporation, the Ford Motor Company, and the Mobil Oil Company. The Foreword states that this directory attempts to provide "the kind of information which educators, institutions of learning, research institutes, and all groups and people interested in environmental management can use as they begin to examine the studies and curricula needed in this new field." Information was obtained through questionnaires in English, French, or Spanish sent to every identifiable institution of higher learning throughout the world, as well as to training institutes and many government ministries. Only one group is listed for Union of Soviet Socialist Republic—Nauchni Sovet Ozhzani Pzipodi Akademi Nauk Azmensi (Scientific Council of Conservation of Nature of the Armenian Academy of Sciences), while 53 are listed for the United Kingdom, and 444 for the United States. Nonresponding institutions known to have environmental programs were sent follow-up requests for information. Criteria for determining which programs warranted inclusion were kept flexible intentionally. A typical entry cites the name and address of the institution, date of establishment of the program, number of enrollees, number of faculty, name of director, and type of degrees offered. Listings are arranged geographically by country, and alphabetically by political division within the country. Seven Appendixes provide ready access to definite items of information: Subject Index (Institutions by Fields of Emphasis or Specialization), Integrated Degree Programs, Specialized Degree Programs, Cognate and Cooperative Programs, Training Programs, Short-Term Programs, and Other Miscellaneous Programs. The directory is well designed for ease of use. It will add to the meager supply of information on environmental education programs now available.

(Mar. 15, 1974, p.753)

World Historical Fiction Guide: An Annotated Chronological, Geographical and Topical List of Selected Historical Novels. 2d ed. By Daniel D. McGarry and Sarah Harriman White. Metuchen, NJ, The Scarecrow Pr., Inc., 1973. xxi, 629p. 23cm. B-grade cloth $15. ISBN 0-8108-0616-9.

The first edition of *World Historical Guide* published in 1963 was accepted in the library world as a standard. It covered the period from ancient times to 1900, was selective, annotated, and cited 5,000 fiction titles. The new edition covers more than 6,400 titles, covers the same period in history and provides brief sentence fragment annotations for each entry. For the purpose of this bibliography the authors define historical fiction to include references to customs, conditions, identifiable persons, or events in the past. The work is selective and intends to include only better works of fiction meeting such criteria as literary excellence, readability, and historical value. Although designed especially for use by adults and students in senior high schools, colleges, and universities, the bibliography can also be used by students at the junior high school level. Books suitable for such grades are identified as "Y.A." The book is arranged chronologically under historical periods: Antiquity (to about 400 A.D.), Middle Ages and Early Renaissance (c.400-1500), and Modern World (c.1500-1900). Each chronological period is geographically subdivided. Daniel D. McGarry is Professor of History, St. Louis University and has written several historical works. Sarah H. White is a graduate of St. Louis University. Libraries will wish to acquire the new edition of *World Historical Fiction Guide*. *(July 15, 1974, p.1215)*

World of Shakespeare: Animals & Monsters. By Alan Dent. With a foreword by Sir Ralph Richardson. New York, Taplinger Pub. Co., [1973, c1972]. 160p. 20cm. fabrikoid $5.50; to schools, 40 percent discount on text orders from schools' bookstores; to libraries, 10 percent discount. ISBN 0-8008-0274-8.

World of Shakespeare: Plants. [By] Alan Dent. With a foreword by Sir Michael Redgrave. New York, Taplinger Pub. Co., [1973, c1972]. 126p. 20cm. fabrikoid $5.50; to schools, 40 percent on text orders from schools' bookstore; to libraries, 10 percent discount. ISBN 0-8008-6313-5.

British author, editor, journalist, lecturer, and theater critic Alan Dent has produced two handy companion handbooks on Shakespeare's animals and plants. They complement and supplement Taplinger's *Who's Who in Shakespeare* described above. In these two authoritatively written reference works the reader will find concise yet comprehensive critiques on *Anchovies and Herrings, Fleas, Flies, and Gnats, Mermaids and Neptune, Bats and Leeches, Onions and Garlic, Mushrooms and Toadstools, Flowers in General,* and *Aconite.* The animal and monster handbook contains 109 entries, and the plant handbook consists of 110 articles. Both are alphabetically arranged. Both identify Shakespeare reference by play, act, and scene and include exact quotations from Shakespeare. Refreshing to read, and easy to use, these two little books will be valuable for reference purposes. *(May 15, 1974, p.1019)*

The World This Year 1973: Supplement to the Political Handbook and Atlas of the World: Government and Intergovernmental Organizations as of January 1, 1973. Edited by Richard P. Stebbins and Alba Amora with the collaboration of Sheila Low-Beer. [New York], Council on Foreign Relations, [1973]; distributed by Simon and Schuster. viii, 184p. 29cm., 3-piece case Arrestox C on spine; elephant hide on sides $11.95.

Compiled by Richard P. Stebbins and Alba Amoia, both of whom are well qualified by training and experience to prepare such a work, *The World This Year 1973* can stand on its own as a guide to present-day political affairs and will also provide a good updating and supplementary source for the forty-third edition of *Political Handbook and Atlas of the World,* published in 1970. The 133-page governments section provides pertinent information on 149 countries and major political units listing area, population (with sources), official language, political leader, legislative body, political parties, and a summary of current (up to 1973) politics. A section on Intergovernmental Organizations gives facts on origins, purposes, membership, principal organs, and current activities of 54 leading international agencies like United Arab Emirates, Council of Europe, and East African Community.

Appendix I lists members of the United Nations and related agencies; Appendix II lists rates of exchange of selected currencies as of April 1973. A two-part Index helps provide ready access to all the information. This volume will prove to be a utilitarian source of easy-to-get-at information on political units of the world.
(Dec. 15, 1973, p.405)

World's Great Men of Color. [By] J. A. Rogers. 2v. New York, The Macmillan Co., [c1946, 1972]. illus. 21cm. cloth $8.95 each; paper $3.95 each.

World's Great Men of Color was first published in a small private edition in 1947. Written by the late Joel A. Rogers, journalist, anthropologist, historian, and pioneer in black studies, the biographies cover the period from B.C. 3,000 to 1946 A.D. Volume I treats Asia, Africa, and historical figures before Christ; volume II covers famous Negroes of Europe and the New World. This new edition has been updated with an introduction, commentaries and bibliographical notes by John Henrik Clarke, author and editor of books on the Negro. The author's intention "not to write highly critical and psychoanalytical, or even literary essays, but rather principally success stories, chiefly for Negro youth" has been carried out. *World's Great Men of Color* is valuable for its international scope and treatment of the lives of persons neglected in the pages of history. *(June 15, 1973, p.957)*

Worldwide Directory of Computer Companies 1973-1974. Marie B. Waters, editor and the Staff of Academic Media. Orange, NJ, Academic Media, [c1973]. viii, 631p. 29cm. cloth $39.50. ISBN 0-87876-033-4.

Libraries with need for up-to-date information on computer companies currently active will wish to update their reference sources with the new *Worldwide Directory of Computer Companies*. The current directory updates, expands, and revises *World Directory of Computer Companies* published in 1970, and according to Academic Media it lists 2,000 new companies. An innovation for this edition is the provision of the full financial profile of all public companies and of the private and nonprofit companies for which such information was available. The text is arranged alphabetically by company, and the amount of information given for each company varies. Name, address, telephone number, subsidiaries, ownership, number of employees, officers, and sales may be cited.

For the purposes of *Worldwide Directory of Computer Companies* 14 major business sectors were isolated and defined: communications, components, conglomerates, education, leasing, mainframes, peripherals, optics, production automation, service, software, supplies, technology, and timesharing. Four indexes (name, activity, business sector, and geographic) provide good access to the material. *(June 1, 1974, p.1070)*

The Writers' and Artists' Year Book 1973: A Directory for Writers, Artists, Playwrights, Writers for Film, Radio and Television, Photographers and Composers. Boston, The Writer, Inc., [cA & C Black, London, 1973]. 426p. 21cm. fabrikoid $6.95; to schools and libraries, 20 percent discount.

This is the sixty-sixth issue of *The Writers' and Artists' Year Book,* a useful compendium of all kinds of information for creators of literature, art, music, drama, and film. It is divided into five sections, each of which treats a different phase of creativity. "Writing for Newspapers, Magazines," pages 1-133, includes lists of British, Irish, American, Australian, Canadian, East and Central African, Indian, New Zealand, Bangladesh, Pakistani, and South African journals and magazines; a classified index of journals; and a list of news and press agency syndicates.

"Writing Books," pages 134-230 lists book publishers of Britain and Ireland, the United States, Australia, Canada, India, New Zealand, the British Commonwealth, and South Africa. Also given are a brief explanation of publishers' agreements, a list of British book clubs, a summary of the Florence Agreement, suggestions on preparing and submitting typescript, proofreaders' signs, and a brief description of vanity publishing.

"Writing for Theatre, Films, Radio and Television," pages 231-271, gives useful information on London and provincial markets for plays; a list of play publishers; signed articles on markets for screenplays; screenplays for films and writing for television; lists of British radio and television networks; information on Australian, Canadian, Indian, New Zealand and South African broadcasting; lists of British play, film, television, and radio agents; British and American music publishers; and material on Mechanical-Copyright Protection Society, Ltd. and the Performing Right Society, Ltd.

"Artists, Designers, and Photographers," pages 272-295, has suggestions for free-lance artists and photographers; lists of British art agents, commercial art studios, photographic agencies, and picture libraries; Artists and Designers Code of Professional Conduct issued by the Society of Industrial Artists and Designers, Ltd.; and an article on picture research by Judith Bryne, complete with list of sources.

"General," the final section, pages 296-423, has signed articles on copyright, U.S. copyright, subsidiary rights, libel, the writer and income tax liability, and the writer and artist and national insurance. There are brief lists of British, American, and foreign literary agents; literary prizes; a bibliography for writers; and information on translation, indexing, and press cutting agencies. The three-page Index at the end of the book provides limited access to the wealth of material. The book will be useful as an up-to-date source of names and addresses. *(Nov. 1, 1973, p.254)*

The Year Book of Social Policy in Britain 1972. Edited by Kathleen Jones. London and Boston, Routledge & Kegan Paul, [1973]. x, 240p. 24cm. plastic coated $13.95.

Year Book of Social Policy, the second such yearbook, is comprised of 16 signed papers contributed by persons qualified by background and experience to write on the subjects for which they are responsible. The book is divided into two sections, the first of which is devoted to education. Such subjects as developments in nursery schools, polytechnical training, and teacher education and training are covered. The seven papers in section II relate to new developments and are entitled "Uganda Asians in Britain," "Social Policy in Northern Ireland," "The Proposals for a Tax Credit System," "Seeking Out the Disabled," "A New System of Housing Subsidies," "Community Work in 1972," and "The Centre for Studies in Social Policy."

The editor, Kathleen Jones, is Professor of Social Administration at University of York. She holds a doctorate from the University of London and has a number of publications on health, mental health, and social policy to her credit. The essays are written in language comprehendible by the average reader and have references appended. The volume will benefit those seeking a brief analysis of social groups in Great Britain during 1972.
(Dec. 15, 1973, p.405)

The Year Book of World Affairs 1973. [Editors: George W. Keeton and Georg Schwarzenberger]. New York, Washington, Praeger Publishers; published under the auspices of the London Institute of World Affairs, 1973. vii, 462p. 26cm. cloth $19.50. ISBN 0-275-33140-X.

The 1973 Year Book of World Affairs is co-published in England with Sweet & Maxwell. The yearbooks began in 1947 with the intent of producing an annual survey on international affairs comprised of authoritative research articles on important current topics. The 1973 editorial concerns Columbia University professor Wolfgang Friedmann, who was murdered in the vicinity of the University September 1972. The editorial is followed by a classified bibliography of trends and events organized under trends in comtemporary world society, strategic arms limitation, international law and order, international economy and international economic law, Middle East, South East Asia and the far East, and World Portraits (Adenauer, U Thant, and De Gaulle).

The bulk of the work is comprised of 22 signed articles written by authors with firm grounding and expertise in their subjects. For example, G. W. Choudhury, Visiting Fellow, Southern Asian Institute, Columbia University wrote "The Emergence of Bangla Desh and the South Asian Triangle," George Ginsburgs, Professor, Department of Political Science, Graduate Faculty, New School for Social Research is responsible for "The Constitutional Foundations of the 'Socialist Commonwealth:' Some Theoretical and Organizational Principles," and Ivor H. Mills, Professor of Medicine, Department of Investigative Medicine, Cambridge is author of "The Biological Factor in International Relations." A comprehensive analytical Index provides ready access to the material.
(May 15, 1974, p.1019)

Yearbook of Higher Education 1973/74: A Comprehensive Up-to-Date Guide to the World of Higher Education. Jon S. Greene, editor; Paul Richard Gibson, associate editor and the staff of Academic Media. Orange, NJ, Academic Media, [1973]. ix, 570p. 29cm. buckram $39.50. ISBN 0-87876-038-5.

The *1973-74 Yearbook of Higher Education* is the fifth annual yearbook; the first was published in 1969. The scope of the current yearbook has been broadened to cover Canada. The aim of the work is to "provide the professional higher education community—faculty, administrators and higher education personnel—with a comprehensive up-to-date guide to the world of higher education." The book is divided into two parts: Part One—Directory of Higher Education and Part Two—Statistics of Higher Education. Information for the directory was obtained through questionnaires sent to 3,000 colleges and universities in the United States and Canada and from secondary sources. The first section cites 30,000 department chairmen, 30,000 academic deans, and other administrators by name. Each institution of higher learning is identified by address, type of control, makeup of student body, type of calendar year, enrollment, and for the first time, by telephone number including area code. An alphabetical School Name Index facilitates locating information on specific institutions. Part Two contains 70 tables and 16 figures. Covered are such subjects as "Number of First-Professional Degrees Conferred in Dentistry, Medicine, and Law, by Sex"; "Number of Institutions of Higher Education by Type, Control, and State: Fall 1971"; "Physical Plant Value Per Student in Institutions of Higher Education, By Control and By Level: United States 1967-68 and 1969-70"; and "Earned Master's Degrees By Field of Study." Source of data is identified for each table. In general U.S. Department of Health, Education, and Welfare statistics are used. High school, academic, and public libraries will need to update their files on higher education with the new *1973-74 Yearbook of Higher Education. (April 1, 1974, p.837)*

Yearbook on International Communist Affairs, 1973. Editor: Richard F. Staar. Stanford, Hoover Institution Pr., 1973. xvii, 651p. B-grade cloth $25; paper $9.50.

The Hoover Institution on War, Revolution and Peace, founded at Stanford University in 1919 by the late President Herbert Hoover, is "a center for advanced study and research on public and international affairs in the twentieth century." The views expressed in the yearbook under review and in the Institute's other publications are not necessarily those of the Institute. This seventh consecutive *Yearbook on International Communist Affairs* is similar in organization, content, and purpose to its predecessors. The 1973 yearbook aims "to provide . . . a comprehensive survey covering the calendar year 1972 about the organizational structure, internal developments, domestic and foreign policies, and activity of communist parties throughout the world." Sections on communist parties in Eastern Europe and the Soviet Union (9 parties), Western Europe (22), Middle East and Africa (15), Western Hemisphere (26), and Asia and the Pacific (20) give primary source based data on the founding date, domestic conditions under which the party operates, membership figures, electoral support and participation, organization and leadership, domestic and political programs, decisions on key problems of communist ideology, views on major international issues, and orientation in the international communist party movement.

There are 32 pages of information on 10 communist front organizations: Afro-Asian Writers' Permanent Bureau, International Association of Democratic Lawyers, International Federation of Resistance Fighters, International Organization of Journalists, International Union of Students, Women's International Democratic Federation, World Federation of Democratic Youth, World Federation of Scientific Workers, World Federation of Trade Unions, and World Peace Council. A good 23-page classified selected unannotated bibliography follows the discussion, and a 13-page Index of Persons completes the volume. *(Nov. 15, 1973, p.304)*

BIOGRAPHICAL DICTIONARIES

Biographical dictionaries are among the most frequently used of all reference books for several reasons. People want to know about their forebears in order better to understand the past. In this complex modern society, they need to know who is doing what in fields other than their own. Furthermore, when asked to supply biographical sketches for inclusion in directories, they need to verify the reliability and objectivity of such books. Constance M. Winchell in *Guide to Reference Books* (Chicago: American Library Association, 1967, 1968) states that "Unscrupulous publishers will sometimes include padded or unduly eulogistic articles on comparatively unknown persons, with the expectation, or on condition, that these persons will pay for inclusion or will subscribe for the book. The inclusion of such articles puts the book in the commercial or 'vanity' class and casts doubt on the authority of all articles. Such books are not necessarily to be rejected if they happen to be the only ones in their field, but they must always be used with caution." This article seeks to provide information on judging the merits of biographical dictionaries. Summaries of the characteristics of a number of such works currently on the market are appended to this article. Citation to the most recent Reference and Subscription Books Committee review of each biographical dictionary is also given.

TYPES

Biographical works are of several different types: They may be retrospective or current or a combination of the two. *Dictionary of American Biography* is retrospective; *Who's Who in America*, current; and *Webster's Biographical Dictionary*, a combination of the two. There are also four main categories of biographical references (1) general or universal; (2) professional or occupational; (3) national or regional; (4) special groups. Hyamson's *A Dictionary of Universal Biography* is general or universal; *American Men and Women of Science*, professional or occupational; *Who's Who in the East*, national or regional; and *Who's Who of American Women*, special groups.

FREQUENCY OF PUBLICATION

Of course no biographical dictionary is ever completely current. It is reasonable to expect, however, that both retrospective and contemporary works be revised on a regular basis. It is only in the field of membership directories in which more than name, title, and address are rarely given that yearly compilations such as *ALA Membership Directory* (Chicago: American Library Association, 1949-   ) are possible. Only biographical dictionaries attempt to keep up to date by continuous revision as in *Webster's Biographical Dictionary* or by issuing supplements, such as those for *Current Biography*.

Publishers of biographical reference works use three methods to update their works and add newly eligible subjects: by issuing new editions biennially (Marquis *Who's Whos*); by revising volumes continuously (Bowker's *American Men and Women of Science*); or by adding new volumes (*Dictionary of American Biography* and *Contemporary Authors*). A new copyright date does not necessarily indicate substantial revision. If such dates are used as a judge of currency, careful comparison of the previous and the latest editions must be made.

COVERAGE

There are several questions to ask about the coverage of any biographical dictionary: (1) are persons of interest included? (2) are notables within the particular fields or groups for which the work claims coverage represented fully? (3) does the work duplicate information already available in another source? An example of a work which is both comprehensive and representative as well as unique in coverage is *Biographical Directory of the American Congress, 1774-1971*. It includes all U.S. Congressmen for the dates indicated; the biographies are complete and have reference value, and the collected information cannot be found in such complete form in any other biographical dictionary. On the other hand, U.S. Library of Congress *A Catalogue of Books Represented by Library of Congress Printed Cards, Issued to July 31, 1942* (Ann Arbor: Edwards, 1942-1946. v.162, p.597) describes *Who's Who in Maryland: A Biographical Dictionary of Leading Living Men & Women of the States of Maryland, Pennsylvania, New Jersey, Delaware and West Virginia*. This work appeared some time ago and contained a who's who volume for several of the states; yet all volumes were identical except for the title pages. Published by A. N. Marquis Company of Chicago, it was reprinted under the titles *Who's Who in Delaware*, *Who's Who in New Jersey*, *Who's Who in Pennsylvania*, and *Who's Who in West Virginia*. The publisher admitted that the text, imprint, and price of all five were the same, but claimed that "The different titles were used for legal purposes." Of course, this is not to be confused with the very creditable present practice of Marquis Who's Who, the successor company, of printing some 19,000 biographies in the 1972-1973 edition of *Who's Who in the East*, and, in addition, providing a regional supplement listing the names of Easterners who appear in *Who's Who in America*. The reader then has a complete record of coverage of the East in these two works.

PUBLISHER

It is difficult to judge the reputation of a publisher. Date of founding sometimes helps, because old, well-established publishers generally have reputations for integrity and good editing. Better Business Bureaus may be a source of information particularly if complaints about misleading advertising or questionable sales have been received.

TEXT

Probably the most important test of all is careful examination of the text. The reader needs to know whether the information was contributed by the biographee or written by a research staff, if the information is as complete as possible, whether the material is padded, and if it is well edited. A large number of contemporary biographical works are compiled from questionnaires or other materials supplied by the biographee. This is often a means of enlivening the sketch with personal reminiscences such as those in *Current Biography* and *Contemporary Authors*. This practice may, however, lead to omission of pertinent information, padding, or misinformation. For instance, *Official Congressional Directory* is often of little reference value because the biographee released insufficient data, supplied the wrong birth year, or neglected to check the information for accuracy. Padding is of two kinds: (1) enumeration of trivia or, (2) insertion of fabricated events to impress the reader. On the other hand, the use of unfamiliar abbreviations, acronyms, and symbols to conserve space can frustrate the reader by forcing him to leaf back and forth from keys to text.

ILLUSTRATIONS

Although illustrations are useful, they are not the rule in biographical dictionaries. For many years *Appleton's Cyclopedia of American Biography*, 7v. (New York: Appleton, 1887-1900) and *National Cyclopedia of American Biography* (New York: White, 1892-   ) have been used to locate both portraits and signatures of distinguished Americans. *Current Biography* is an example of good use of photographs. Some vanity publications such as *Encyclopedia of American Biography* make charges, some of them exorbitant, for inclusion of portraits.

BIBLIOGRAPHIES

Bibliographies found in biographical dictionaries are of two kinds—those by and those about the biographee. Bibliographies of works by the subject of the entry are included if his writings have formed an important part of his life. Bibliographies of the sources of the information found in the sketch are also sometimes provided.

INDEX

Use of the index is essential in locating information in any work that is not alphabetically arranged, such as *National Cyclopedia of American Biography*. It is also convenient to have a cumulative index to dictionaries that have supplements, e.g., *Who Was Who* and *Contemporary Authors*. It is also very helpful to have special indexes like *Index to Principal Businesses and Key Executives* appearing in *Who's Who in Finance and Industry*.

PRICE AND SALES PRACTICES

Most biographical works are not overpriced in comparison to other reference works being published at the same time. Yet, more frequently than would be suspected, works appear on the market that can be classified only as vanity publications, because they expect biographees to pay for an article and subscribe to the work. Often a reliable review will warn against these objectionable prices and sales practices. Reviews are discussed in the next section of this article.

REVIEWS

Only reviews of the Reference and Subscription Books Review Committee are cited in the summaries accompanying this article. The American Library Association has assigned this agency the responsibility of accumulating "information about books sold on the subscription basis *(not in bookstores but in the home, by mail, etc.)* and about comparable publications"; preparing "reviews and editorial comments about such books in the Reference and Subscription Books Reviews section of *The Booklist*"; receiving "reports of questionable sales practices affecting such books" and transmitting "substantiated facts to such agencies as Better Business Bureaus and the Federal Trade Commission." The Committee calls particular attention to the December 15, 1966 review of the now defunct *Encyclopedia of American Biography*, which does not appear in the summaries. This review gives insight into the methods of promoting commercial vanity publications. Readers will also find useful such guides to reference books as *Winchell* previously mentioned, *The Reader's Adviser* (New York: Bowker, 1969, v.2), *The Readers Guide* (New York: Bowker, 1969), Walford's *Guide to Reference Materials*, 3v. (London: The Library Association, 1973-   and Chicago: American Library Association, 1974), and book reviews indexed in *Book Review Digest* (New York: Wilson, 1905-   ) and *Book Review Index* (Detroit; Gale, 1965-   ).

> Reference and Subscription Books Review Subcommittee to Study Omnibus Reviews, Articles, and Editorials: Thomas S. Shaw, Chairman, Retired, Professor of Library Science, Louisiana State University, Baton Rouge, LA; Lynne M. Birlem, Wm. A. Bradford Library, Quincy High & Voc. Tech. Schools, Quincy, MA; Dr. Richard S. Halsey, Associate Professor, State Univ. of New York, School of Library & Information Science, Albany, NY; Mrs. Pauline Robinson, Coordinator of Children's Services, Denver Public Library, Denver, CO; and Dr. Wiley J. Williams, Associate Professor, Peabody Library School, Nashville, TN.

SUMMARY REVIEW OF BIOGRAPHICAL REFERENCES

In order not unduly to extend the annotated list of titles which follows, only the major established retrospective and current biographical dictionaries in English are cited, and coverage of those devoted to special groups is highly selective. Information on special groups and foreign-language biographical compilations may be found in *Winchell* and *Walford*, the *Bulletin of the Public Affairs Information Service* (PAIS) under directories, and in Robert B. Slocum's *Biographical Dictionaries and Related Works* (Detroit: Gale, 1967). In quoting prices the Committee used publisher-supplied quotations; for a few works it was necessary to obtain price information from printed bibliographies. The following biographical works are described and categorized in individual notes: *The Academic Who's Who; American Architects Directory; American Authors, 1600-1900; American Men of Science; American Men and Women of Science; Asimov's Biographical Encyclopedia of Science and Technology; Baker's Biographical Dictionary of Musicians; Biographical Directory of the American Congress; Biographical Directory of Fellows and Members of the American Psychiatric Association as of October 1, 1967; A Biographical Directory of Librarians in the United States and Canada; Biographical Directory of the United States Executive Branch, 1774-1971; The Biographical Encyclopaedia and Who's Who of the American Theatre; The Blue Book; British Authors Before 1800; British Authors of the Nineteenth Century; The Canadian Who's Who With Which is Incorporated Canadian Men & Women of the Time; Celebrity Register; Chambers's Biographical Dictionary; Chambers's Dictionary of Scientists; Composers Since 1900; Concise Dictionary of American Biography; Contemporary Authors; Contemporary Dramatists; Contemporary Novelists of the English Language; Contemporary Poets of the English Language; County Authors Today; Current Biography Yearbook; Dictionary of American Biography; Dictionary of Canadian Biography; A Dictionary of Contemporary American Artists; Dictionary of International Biography; Dictionary of National Biography; Dictionary of Scandinavian Biography; Dictionary of Scientific Biography; Dictionary of South African Biography; A Dictionary of Universal Biography of All Ages and of All People; Directory of American Scholars; Directory of Medical Specialists Holding Certification by American Specialty Boards; European Authors, 1000-1900; Everyman's Dictionary of European Writers; Everyman's Dictionary of Literary Biography; Foremost Women in Communications; Great Composers, 1300-1900; The International Who's Who; International Who's Who in Poetry, 1972-1973; The International Year Book and Statesman's Who's Who, 1973; The Junior Book of Authors; More Junior Authors, 1963; Third Book of Junior Authors, 1972; Leaders in Education; McGraw-Hill Modern Men of Science; National Cyclopedia of American Biography; New Century Cyclopedia of Names; Notable American Women 1607-1950; Popular American Composers; Something About the Author; Twentieth Century Authors; Webster's Biographical Dictionary; Who Was Who; Who Was Who in America; Who Was Who in the USSR; Who's Who, 1973-1974; Who's Who in Advertising; Who's Who in America; Who's Who in American Art; Who's Who in American Politics; Who's Who in the East; Who's Who in Finance and Industry; Who's Who in Government; Who's Who in the Midwest; Who's Who in the South and Southwest; Who's Who in the Theatre; Who's Who in the West; Who's Who in the World; Who's Who of American Women; Women Artists in America; World Who's Who in Science;* and *The World Who's Who of Women, 1973.* For convenience a list of publishers is appended.

The Academic Who's Who: University Teachers in the British Isles in Arts, Education and Social Sciences. 1st ed. 1973-1974. London, Adam & Charles Black, 1973- . Distributed in the U.S. by R. R. Bowker Co. 521p. cloth $21.95. ISBN 0-7136-1340-8.

Frequency: The *Academic Who's Who* is published once every other year.
Scope: Only contemporary biographees are cited.
Coverage: There are fifty-two hun-

dred entries for teachers above the rank of senior lecturer and who have held a university appointment for five years or more. Actively supported by Anglo-American Associates, the work contains information collected from biographical forms sent to subjects. Entries are concise and abbreviated. A second volume concerned with scientists and engineers is under consideration.

Bibliography: Writings of biographees are listed in sketches.

Arrangement and Index: Arrangement is alphabetical. Abbreviations used in book are listed.

American Architects Directory. Edited by John F. Gane, and editor emeritus George S. Koyl. 3d ed. Published under the sponsorship of the American Institute of Architects. New York & London, R. R. Bowker Co., 1955-   . 1126p. hardcover $38.95. ISBN 0-8352-0281-X.

Frequency: 1956, 1962, 1970.

Scope: Only contemporary biographees from the United States are listed.

Coverage: Two forms were used to collect the information for the 23,000 brief abbreviated sketches: Biographical Questionnaire and Firm Listing. Prepublication proofs are sent to biographees. A group of listed Associate Editors representing each state assisted the editor in the selection. Members of the American Institute of Architects are included. The architectural firms listings include address of main and branch office, and professional status of firm principals. Individual sketches include lists of biographees' main works and achievements.

Bibliography: Publications of biographees are listed in their sketches.

Arrangement and Index: Arrangement is alphabetical. Appended are American Institute of Architects, Officers, Honorary Members and Fellows, College of Fellows, Medals and Awards, Officers and Conventions 1857-   ; Abbreviations; Addenda; Geographical Section; Necrology; Appendix; National Council of Architectural Boards; and Association of Collegiate Schools of Architecture.

RSBR Review: The Booklist and Subscription Books Bulletin, Nov. 1, 1956, p.105.

American Authors, 1600-1900: A Biographical Dictionary of American Literature, Complete in One Volume with 1300 Biographies and 400 Portraits.
Edited by Stanley J. Kunitz and Howard Haycraft. New York, The H. W. Wilson Co., 1938-   . cloth $12. ISBN 0-8242-0001-2.

Frequency: Foundation volume was published 1938 with printings in 1940, 1949, 1955, 1960, 1964, and 1968.

Scope: American Authors is retrospective—1607 to the close of the nineteenth century.

Coverage: Entries for both major and minor figures are from 150 to 2,500 words in length. Some persons such as educators, statesmen, orators, jurists, and clergymen not known primarily for literary expertise are also included. List of persons who assisted the editors in the selection of the names and in the research is included.

Bibliography: Principal works of and biographical and critical works about the authors are included.

Arrangement and Index: Arrangement is alphabetical with cross-references from variations of the name.

American Men of Science: A Biographical Directory, the Social & Behavioral Sciences. 2v. Edited by The Jaques Cattell Pr. 11th ed. New York & London, R. R. Bowker Co., 1956-   . cloth $25 per v. ISBN 0-8352-0293-3. (Since the ninth edition of *American Men of Science* [1956], the social and behavioral sciences and the physical and biological sciences have been issued in separate volumes.)

Frequency: Editions were published in 1956, 1962, 1968, and November 1973.

Scope: Includes biographies for contemporary United States and Canadian scientists.

Coverage: The twelfth edition (Nov. 1973) is expected to have some 31,000 brief biographic entries of outstanding figures in the fields of psychology, political sciences, sociology, economics, anthropology, geography, and statistics. Selection was based on: (1) achievement by reason of experience or training to the equivalent of that associated with the doctoral degree, coupled with continuing activity; (2) or research activity of high quality as evidenced by publication; (3) or attainment of a position of substantial responsibility requiring scientific training and ability equivalent to that required in (1) and (2). The books are sponsored by the Social Science Research Council; a distinguished advisory committee is listed by name, as are the editors appointed by the publisher.

Bibliography: Publications of the biographees are listed in sketches.

Arrangement and Index: Arrangement is alphabetical; abbreviations are listed.

RSBR Review: The Booklist and Subscription Books Bulletin, Oct. 1, 1962, p.89.

American Men and Women of Science: Formerly American Men of Science, a Biographical Directory Founded in 1906. Edited by the Jaques Cattell Pr. 12th ed., 1971-1973. 6v. Physical and Biological Sciences. New York & London, R. R. Bowker Co., 1906-   . cloth $37.50 per v. v.1 (A-C) 1971, ISBN 0-8352-0500-2; v.2 (D-G) 1972, ISBN . . . 0501-0; v.3 (H-K) 1972, ISBN . . . 0502-9; v.4 (L-O) 1972, ISBN . . . 0503-7; v.5 (P-Sr) 1972, ISBN . . . 0504-5; v.6 (St-Z) ISBN . . . 0505-3.

Frequency: American Men and Women of Science is published irregularly.

Scope: Contemporary United States and Canadian scientists are listed; there is a necrology list.

Coverage: Edited by the Jaques Cattell Press, the current edition gives brief sketches of some 138,500 persons working in agriculture, astronomy, biochemistry, botany, chemistry, engineering, genetics, geology, medicine, nucleonics, physics, and zoology. Names were selected with the assistance of an advisory board of distinguished scientists, and questionnaires were used to provide the information, which was edited by the Press. Selection for entry was on the basis of experience and training, research activity, or attainment of a position of substantial responsibility.

Arrangement and Index: Arrangement is alphabetical; appended are list of abbreviations, addendum of late additions, and necrology.

RSBR Review: The Booklist and Subscription Books Bulletin, Oct. 1, 1962, p.89.

Asimov's Biographical Encyclopedia of Science and Technology: The Lives and Achievements of 1195 Great Scientists from Ancient Times to the Present Chronologically Arranged. By Isaac Asimov. New rev. ed. Garden City, NY, Doubleday, 1972. 805p. cloth $12.95. ISBN 0-385-04693-6.

Frequency: The first edition was published in 1964.

Scope: Asimov covers technologists and scientists through the ages.

Coverage: Narrative sketches give the living stories of the biographees. Information on all selected for inclusion is written by Asimov who is an authority on the subject. Each sketch is headed by essential facts such as field, birth, and death in abbreviated form. Pronunciation of names is a valuable asset to this work.

Illustrations: There are 79 portraits several to a plate.

Bibliography: Author's works are listed in his biography.

Arrangement and Index: Since the arrangement is chronological, item numbers are given to the entries from 1-1195. These numbers instead of pages are referred to in the name and subject indexes. There are numerous cross-references in text.

Baker's Biographical Dictionary of Musicians. Edited by Nicolas Slonimsky. 5th ed. 1971. 1855, 262p. New York & London, G. Schirmer, 1900-   . cloth $35 with 1971 supp.; $7.50 for separate supp. ISBN 0-911320-62-8; supp. ISBN . . . 06-7.

Frequency: Baker's was published in 1900, 1905, 1919, 1940, 1958, and 1971.

Scope: Universal in scope, *Baker's* is both retrospective and contemporary.

Coverage: Baker's contains compact biographies strong in factual data and corrected from the earlier editions by modern research. As in the case of other biographical dictionaries with a long life span and distinguished editors, (Nicolas Slonimsky is present editor), a reliable bank of information is presented to the reader. Many corrections have been made for this edition, and composers of the avant-garde are given special attention, as are stars of popular modern music: Beatles, crooners, guitar strummers, and country music balladeers.

Bibliography: Works by and about biographees, including important magazine articles, are listed in their entries.

Arrangement and Index: Arrangement is alphabetical.

Biographical Directory of the American Congress, 1774-1971. The Continental Congress, September 5, 1774 to October 21, 1788 and The Congress of the United States from the First Through the Ninety-First Congress, March 4, 1789, to January 3, 1971, Inclusive. 11th ed., 1971-1972. Washington, Govt. Print. Off., 1859- . (91st Cong., 1st Sess: Senate Document no.92-8). cloth $15.75.

Frequency: Eleven editions were published between 1859 and 1971.

Scope: Biographical Directory of the American Congress is both contemporary and retrospective.

Coverage: The directory contains (1) the composition by name of both the Continental Congress and the U.S. Congress by Congress and Session; (2) Complete biographies of all the names mentioned above in brief form. Also data are compiled under the direction of the Joint Committee on Printing by a Compilation Staff which is identified by name. Names of the Officials of the Executive Branch of the Government are cited through the years.

Arrangement and Index: Part I: Chart form for each session; Part II: Alphabetical by surname. See also Companion volume: *Biographical Directory of the United States Executive Branch, 1774-1971* below.

Biographical Directory of Fellows & Members of the American Psychiatric Association as of October 1, 1967. 5th ed. 832p. New York & London, published for the APA by R. R. Bowker Co., 1968. cloth $38.50. ISBN 0-8352-0028-0.

Frequency: Biographical Directory of Fellows and Members of the American Psychiatric Association is published once every five years; the next edition was due in 1973.

Scope: The directory is contemporary covering United States with some Canadian and other foreign biographees.

Coverage: There are 13,000 very brief sketches supplied mainly by the American Board of Psychiatry and Neurology, Inc. and the Royal College of Physicians and Surgeons of Canada. Names of editorial staff of Bowker and others who assisted in compilation are listed. The work does not indicate fields of specialization or endeavor of biographees. Prepublication proofs are sent to biographees for accuracy check.

Bibliography: Publications of subjects are listed in entries.

Arrangement and Index: Arrangement is alphabetical. Appended are Development of the American Psychiatric Association, Presidents of the Association, Vice Presidents of the Association, Secretaries of the Association, Treasurers of the Association, Medical Directors, Deputy Medical Directors, Editors of the American Journal of Psychiatry, Assembly of District Branches, List of and Key to Abbreviations, Addenda, and Geographical Index.

Method of Purchase: Prepublication offer is made to biographees for sale by direct mail.

A Biographical Directory of Librarians in the United States and Canada. Edited by Lee Ash. 5th ed. Chicago, American Library Association, 1970. 1250p. cloth $45. ISBN 0-8389-0084-4.

Frequency: The directory under the title *Who's Who in Library Service* was published in 1933, 1943, 1955, 1966 with various editors and publishers. The present title was adopted in 1970.

Scope: Contemporary librarians in the United States and Canada are listed.

Coverage: Sponsored by the Council of National Library Associations and edited by Lee Ash, this concise work lists some 20,000 librarians, archivists, information scientists, and persons in related fields. By advisory board decision all with a bachelor's or higher level degree in library science or five years of progressive and recognized work experience are included. Information was collected by questionnaires, and the book was produced by the Shoe String Press. In future editions the American Library Association Publishing Board will assume responsibility for the work. Errors and omissions have been reported.

Bibliography: Works of biographees appear in entries.

Arrangement and Index: Arrangement is alphabetical. There is an appendix listing names of persons appearing in the fourth edition that did not return or update questionnaires.

Biographical Directory of the United States Executive Branch, 1774-1971.
Robert Sobel, editor in chief. Westport, CT, Greenwood Pub. Co., 1971. 493p. Columbia Riverside vellum, pyroxylin impregnated. $27.50. ISBN 0-8371-5173-2.

Frequency: Biographical Directory of the United States Executive Branch was first published in 1971.

Scope: See above.

Coverage: There are 500 career biographies of Presidents, Vice Presidents, Presidents of the Continental Congress, and of the men and women who served in the U.S. Cabinet. This is a companion volume to the invaluable *Biographical Directory of the American Congress, 1774-1961.*

Bibliography: Works by and about the biographees are included in the sketches.

Arrangement and Index: Arrangement is alphabetical. These indexes are appended: Presidential Administration, Heads of State and Cabinet Officials, Other Federal Government Service; State, County, and Municipal Government Service; Military Service by Branch, Education, Place of Birth, and Marital Information.

The Biographical Encyclopaedia and

Who's Who of the American Theatre.
Edited by Walter Rigdon. New York Heineman, 1966. 1101p. cloth $82.50.

Frequency: There is no indication of frequency.

Scope: Contemporary for biographies.

Coverage: There are detailed sketches of some 3,350 living actors, playwrights, directors, and designers of the American theater. Editors who compiled their information mainly from the New York Public Library Theatre Collection are listed.

Bibliography: Works by biographees are listed in their sketches. There are also lists of biographies of theater personalities and theater recordings.

Arrangement and Index: An international necrology of some 9,000 figures from stage history is provided as well as New York City drama productions 1900-1964. There are a chronological listing of playbills of New York City play productions as well as other related openings, 1959-64, abbreviated histories of United States theater groups and New York theater buildings, awards and recipients.

The Blue Book: Leaders of the English-Speaking World. 1973-1974. London, St. James Pr.; New York, St. Martin's Pr., 1973- . 1586p. cloth $30. ISBN 0-900997-14-1.

Frequency: The Blue Book is an annual. One thousand names are expected to be added each year, and no one is dropped unless he dies.

Scope: Contemporary persons of the United Kingdom, Ireland, Australia, New Zealand, Canada, and the United States are included.

Coverage: There are brief biographies of 16,000 persons who have achieved distinction in the arts, sciences, business, and the professions. Selection is made by a group of British and American ex-teachers whose names are not listed. Most of the information was obtained through questionnaires sent to the biographees. Biographies for those who did not respond were researched by the staff, and the completed sketch sent to the subject for correction and approval. Information of a doubtful nature supplied by biographee was checked in primary sources. The work leans heavily on government personnel with business and the arts represented particularly by those with international reputations.

Bibliography: Books written or edited by the subjects are cited in their sketches.

Arrangement and Index: Arrangement is alphabetical. Appended are a list of abbreviations used, list of orders of chivalry, and an obituary section.

British Authors Before 1800: A Biographical Dictionary: Complete in One Volume with 650 Biographies and 250 Portraits. Edited by Stanley J. Kunitz & Howard Haycraft. New York, The H. W. Wilson Co., 1952. 584p. illus. buckram $10. ISBN 0-8242-0006-3.

British Authors of the Nineteenth Century: Complete in One Volume with 1,000 Biographies and 350 Portraits. Edited by Stanley J. Kunitz and Howard Haycraft. New York, H. W. Wilson Co., 1936-1964. 677p. illus. waverly $12. ISBN 0-8242-0007-1.

Frequency: Authors Before 1800 was printed in 1952, 1956, 1961, and 1966; *Nineteenth Century Authors* was printed in 1936, 1940, 1948, 1955, 1960, and 1964.

Scope: Before 1800 begins with the dawn of literature in England and ends with Robert Burns. *Nineteenth Century Authors* covers William Blake to Aubrey Beardsley.

Coverage: Selected by the editors, a small, named research staff assisted in the preparation of the sketches of the biographees chosen. Acknowledgements of assistance are mentioned in the *Before 1800* volume. Biographies consist as a rule of long essay-type critical sketches written in a popular style, but there are some short summaries of famous writers in other than literary fields that have proven valuable.

Bibliography: List of principal works of authors and biographical and critical sources about them are cited in each entry.

Illustrations: Portraits are included when available.

Arrangement and Index: Arrangement is alphabetical with cross-references from variant name forms.

The Canadian Who's Who With Which is Incorporated Canadian Men & Women of the Time: A Biographical Dictionary of Notable Living Men and Women. v.XII, 1970-1972. Toronto, Who's Who Canadian Publications, 1910- cloth $47.50.

Frequency: The *Canadian Who's Who* is published once every three years; supplements follow at six month intervals.

Scope: Only living Canadians are included.

Coverage: There are over 8,000 sketches (some in the French language) in abbreviated form similar to that used in *Who's Who in America*. The *Canadian Who's Who* covers all fields of endeavor, but the method of selection is not stated other than the statement that no persons paid their way into the work. The work is compiled from questionnaires to the biographees which are checked by the editorial staff for accuracy.

Bibliography: Works of authors are listed in their sketches.

Arrangement and Index: Arrangement is alphabetical. Appended are deaths reported during the course of printing, publisher's note, Who's What Canadians, and abbreviations.

Celebrity Register. Edited by Earl Blackwell. 3d ed., 1973. 562p. New York, Simon & Schuster, 1959- . cloth $29.95.

Frequency: Frequency is irregular.

Scope: Only contemporary celebrities are covered.

Coverage: Cleveland Amory, the general editor, thinks that there is a difference between a celebrity and a VIP, the dissimilarity being that a celebrity must be known outside his field while the VIP is always known in connection with his job. Editors and chief writers are listed. The abbreviated sketches often contain biographees' personal remarks of interest. There is no indication of how information is obtained.

Bibliography: Works of biographees are included.

Illustrations: A portrait from photograph of each biographee is shown.

Arrangement and Index: Arrangement is alphabetical; a Directory of Addresses is appended.

Chambers's Biographical Dictionary. Edited by J. O. Thorne. rev. ed. New York, St. Martin's Pr., 1969. v, 1432p. buckram $17.50; to schools and libraries, 20 percent discount.

Frequency: Chambers's was published in 1897 and 1929 with revised editions in 1946, 1961, and 1968.

Scope: Chambers's is both retrospective and contemporary.

Coverage: Spanning all nations, ages, and fields to the present time, its 15,000 biographies are not bound by categories or prestige but by whether the person is likely to be looked up. While *Chambers's* entries are short, the bare facts are presented with interesting critical observations making them more readable and sometimes more useful than the regular abbreviated form used in most concise biographical directories. Since the W. & R. Chambers Co. has put some 70 years into selecting and weeding names for its various editions, a base of names of persons of importance has resulted. *Chambers's* stresses names from the English-speaking world with emphasis on nineteenth- and twentieth-century figures. Pronunciation is given for difficult names.

Bibliography: Works by and about biographees are cited.

Arrangement and Index: Arrangement is alphabetical. An unpaged supplement of new biographies precedes main work.

RSBR Review: The Booklist, Feb. 1, 1974, p.550. (See also page 20 herein.)

Chambers's Dictionary of Scientists. Edited by A. V. Howard. London & Edinburgh, W. & R. Chambers, Ltd., 1951; distributed in U.S. by E. P. Dutton & Co., Inc. 499p. illus. cloth $6.95. ISBN 0-525-07925-4.

Frequency: 1951, reprinted 1956, 1964.

Scope: Retrospective and contemporary. Universal.

Coverage: A. V. Howard, B. Sc. selected the names and wrote the concise, interpretative biographies of the 1,400 leading figures, including some living persons, in the history of science. The aim is to compile sketches of essential facts for those who do not have the time or opportunity to read further, and to focus attention on the path and rate of progress of scientific knowledge. Difficulty of assessing the value of contemporary work prevented the number of living scientists from being much greater. English-speaking subjects predominate. Pronunciation is given for difficult names.

Bibliography: Important publications of biographees included in sketches.

Arrangement and Index: Arrangement is alphabetical except in case of successive generations of the same family, then chronological. Index to Illustrations; Nobel Laureates in physics, chemistry, medicine, 1901-1964; subject alphabet. Nineteen-page supplement of new names (1956 reprint had similar four-page supplement).

Illustrations: Seventy halftone portraits (none in supplement).

RSBR Review: Subscription Books Bulletin, Oct. 1952. p.45.

Composers Since 1900: A Biographical and Critical Guide. Compiled and edited by David Ewen. New York, H. W. Wilson Co., 1969. Replaces *Composers of Today* (1934-1954); *American Composers Today* (1949) and *European Composers Today* (1954) by the same author. 639p. group C-1 pyroxylin $17. ISBN 0-8242-0400-X.

Scope: Composers Since 1900 is both retrospective and contemporary.

Coverage: Seventy persons from North and South America, 147 from Europe, and 3 from Australia were selected by the compiler and editor who is an authority in the field. Almost half of these persons were interviewed by him. Selection was based on the importance of the composers' work, the frequency with which the compositions have been heard, and the interest that the musicians have aroused for their music and their lives. Entries are interpretive and critical in narrative form usually with a description of the appearance of the composer and some direct quotations from conversations.

Bibliography: Major compositions without dates and list of works about the composer are listed.

Illustrations: A portrait of each musician is included in text.

RSBR Review: The Booklist, July 1, 1970, p.1290.

Concise Dictionary of American Biography. Edited by Joseph G. Hopkins. New York, Charles Scribner's Sons, 1964. 1273p. cloth $25. ISBN 0-684-10266-8.

Frequency: There is no indication in Preface of plans for supplements or revisions.

Scope: Concise Dictionary of American Biography contains short biographies of all those in *Dictionary of American Biography* and its first two supplements. It provides essential facts of articles in parent volume for ready reference by anyone who wishes to inform himself quickly about minor and major American figures. The concise edition has three types of entries: (1) Minimal: bare facts; (2) Medium: bare facts plus some critical comment on accomplishments; (3) Extended entries: content, style, and spirit of the original biographies.

Arrangement and Index: Arrangement is alphabetical. Appended are lists of the American Council of Learned Societies' Committee on *Dictionary of American Biography,* Advisory Editorial Board, and Important Note to Users.

RSBR Review: The Booklist and Subscription Books Bulletin, Sept. 1, 1964, p.2.

Contemporary Authors: A Bio-Bibliographical Guide to Current Authors and Their Works. Clare D. Kinsman and Mary Ann Tennenhouse, editors. Detroit, Gale, 1962-   . v.1-32 (1962-1972). Semiannual v. 1972 to date.

Available in four-volume units, cloth $25 per unit; annual subscription $25.

Frequency: New editions are published twice annually; annual volumes cumulate into units of four volumes in one.

Scope: Contemporary Authors gives full bio-bibliographical information on 28,000 of today's active writers (excluding scientific, medical, and technical authors) of the world most of whom are hard to locate in other printed materials. Seventy-five percent are not in major biographical reference works. Data were compiled from questionnaires and personal correspondence with the biographees or from secondary sources, these last being indicated by an asterisk. In addition to regular abbreviated biographical information, work in progress and sidelights of interesting personal information are generally supplied.

Bibliography: Writings are given a separate paragraph in each entry, and sometimes biographical/critical sources appear.

Arrangement and Index: Arrangement is alphabetical. Appended are List of Contributing Authors, Writers, Indexers, and Editorial Assistants. There are annual indexes and cumulative indexes from v.1 to date in latest bound volume of the four volumes in one unit.

RSBR Review: The Booklist and Subscription Books Bulletin, Feb. 1, 1965, p.491.

Contemporary Dramatists. James Vinson, editor. London, St. James Pr.; New York, St. Martin's Pr., 1973. 926p. cloth $30. ISBN 0-900997-17-6.

Frequency: Contemporary Dramatists is published at three-year intervals.

Coverage: Coverage is contemporary.

Scope: There are nearly 300 abbreviated entries for playwrights in the English language selected by recommendation or advisors who are listed. Besides the biographical information, there is commentary by the dramatist on his plays, and a signed critical essay on his work.

Bibliography: Included are a full list of works by the playwright and playwright-related references to criticisms of his work. The first production of each work is noted.

Arrangement and Index: Arrangement is alphabetical. Included are lists of Screen Writers, Radio Writers, Television Writers, Musical Librettists, The Theatre of Mixed Means, Theatre Collections, Notes on Advisors and Contributors.

Contemporary Novelists of the English Language. James Vinson, ed. New York, St. Martin's Pr., 1972. 1444p. cloth $30. SBN 900997-12-5.

Frequency: Contemporary Novelists is published at three-year intervals.

Scope: Contemporary figures of international importance are listed, with emphasis on the British Commonwealth and the United States.

Coverage: More than 600 biographees receive unique treatment different from that in most biographical dictionaries. Each entry consists of a biography, a comment by the author on his fiction, and a signed critical essay on his work. Selection of writers was made by an advisory board whose names are listed.

Bibliography: All novels, but, with few exceptions, only those uncollected short stories specifically referred to, and those critical studies recommended by the entrant have been included. British and United States editions of all books have been listed; other editions are listed only if they are the first editions.

Arrangement and Index: Arrangement is alphabetical with no cross-references from real names to pen names. Advisors and contributors are listed, and notes are given on advisors and contributors.

Contemporary Poets of the English Language. Rosalie Murphy, editor; James Vinson, deputy editor. London, St. James Pr.; New York, St. Martin's Pr., 1971. 1243p. cloth $25. ISBN 0-900997-6-0.

Frequency: Three-year intervals.

Scope: More than 1,100 poets who write in English are represented. Universal in coverage, selection was made on the advice of critics and editors who are listed for each country. Abbreviated sketches may also include comment by the author about his work. Also, there may be a critical signed article that explains about the poet and his work. English-speaking poets of the world predominate.

Bibliography: There is a list of the biographee's works in chronological order. Sometimes author-selected critical statements are also listed.

Arrangement and Index: Arrangement is alphabetical under each geographical area. Contributors of critical articles, and advisors and consultants are listed.

RSBR Review: The Booklist, Mar. 1, 1972, p.537.

Contemporary Writers of the English Language Series, *see:* Contemporary Dramatists, Contemporary Novelists, Contemporary Poets.

County Authors Today. (A Planned Series of 20v., Intended Basically as Checklists With Easy Reference to Place of Birth and Present Address, to Cover All the Counties in the United Kingdom of Great Britain and Northern Ireland.) London, Eddison Pr., Ltd., 1971- Distributed in U.S. by Rowman & Littlefield. Balacron cloth $6.25 a v.

Frequency: Four volumes have been published to date: Lancashire (1971); Yorkshire, Wales, and Scottish (1972). The projected series containing biographies of 15,000 living authors was to be completed in 1973.

Scope: County Authors is contemporary.

Coverage: Selection is made by county, city, borough, and district librarians. The very brief entries contain only name, birth, education, profession, honors, and address.

Bibliography: Reference books consulted are cited.

Arrangement and Index: Arrangement is alphabetical.

Current Biography Yearbook. Charles Moritz; associate editors Evelyn Lohr, Henry Sloan, Kieran Dugan, Donna Lambson. New York, H. W. Wilson Co., 1941-   . 483p. buckram $10. ISBN 0-8342-0463-8.

Frequency: Current Biography Yearbook is published annually.

Scope: Only contemporary biographees are chosen from all over the world.

Coverage: The yearbook contains 300 to 350 biographies of leaders in all fields of human accomplishment. Questionnaires filled out by the biographees are the main source of information, and the editors choose those to be selected for inclusion with the help of the readers of *Current Biography.* Many have become prominent only recently and are therefore barely identified in other biographical works. Pronunciation of names is given, and earlier biographies in previous volumes are updated as the subject's career progresses. Deceased biographees are noted. The yearbook is composed of the yearly cumulation of biographies appearing in *Current Biography.*

Bibliography: Principal works of the subject and publications about his life are appended as are biographical references, and periodicals and newspapers consulted.

Arrangement and Index: Arrangement is alphabetical with cross-references from variations in surname. Appended are Key to Abbreviations and Pronunciation, Photo Credits, Necrology, Classification by Profession, Cumulative Index-1971 (Cumulative Index 1940-1951 in 1950 Yearbook, 1951-1961 in 1960 Yearbook, and 1961-1970 in 1970 Yearbook.)

Illustrations: There is a portrait for each biographee.

RSBR Review: Subscription Books Bulletin, April 1941, p.19.

Dictionary of American Biography. 20v. and Index. Published under the Auspices of the American Council of Learned Societies. Supplement 3, 1941-1945. New York, Charles Scribner's Sons, 1928-1937. (Reprints: 1943, 21v.; 1946, 11v. on thin paper) See also: *Concise Dictionary of American Biography.* cloth $325.

Frequency: Foundation volumes were published 1928-1937; reprints were made in 1943 and 1946. Supplements were put out in 1935 (first supplement), 1936-1940 (second supplement), and 1941-1945 (third supplement).

Scope: Dictionary of American Biography is retrospective covering those who lived in the present boundaries of the United States.

Coverage: The dictionary is comprised of signed long essay-type articles on persons who have made a distinctive positive or negative contribution on some aspect of American life. Experts in each field chose those to be included. Each sketch attempts to evaluate the biographee's place in progress in his endeavors. Most of the articles are compiled and written with distinction. There are very few errors. Together with supplements 14,890 persons were covered.

Bibliography: Principal works of biographees and excellent list of publications about them are appended to each sketch.

Arrangement and Index: Arrangement is alphabetical. There are six separate indexes: (1) Names of subjects of biographies with authors; (2) Contributors, with names of subjects of their articles; (3) Birthplaces arranged alphabetically by states and foreign countries; (4) Occupations; (5) Schools and Colleges attended; (6) Topics.

RSBR Review: Subscription Books Bulletin, Oct. 1938, p.43.

Dictionary of Canadian Biography: Dictionnaire Biographique du Canada.
Toronto, University of Toronto Pr.; Quebec, Les Presses de l'Universite Laval, 1966- . (20v. projected) buckram $20 per v.

Frequency: v.1, 1966; v.2, 1969; v.3, 1972.

Scope: The purpose is to supply full, accurate, and concise biographies of all deceased inhabitants of the Dominion of Canada. Scholars from all fields helped select the names for inclusion. British and American as well as Canadian leading scholars contributed the articles. The articles generally range from 200 to 10,000 words, and many obscure, but historically important persons are covered here that have not hitherto been in print.

Bibliography: Scholarly references including manuscript material are cited. Works of biographee are included in his entry. General bibliography: archival and manuscript sources describe holdings of collections; comprehensive list of primary sources; reference works and studies cited.

Arrangement and Indexes: Although similar in content to the *Dictionary of National Biography* and the *Dictionary of American Biography,* the arrangement is by period of history (v.1: 1000-1700; v.2: 1701-1940; v.3: 1871-1880). The death date not the birth date of the biographee must fall within these periods. Cumulative name index is in each new volume, but there are no subject indexes.

RSBR Review: The Booklist, July 15, 1966, p.1056.

A Dictionary of Contemporary American Artists. By Paul Cummings. 2d ed. 1971. New York, St. Martin's Pr., 1966- cloth $25.

Frequency: A Dictionary of Contemporary American Artists was published in 1966 and 1971.

Scope: Only contemporary artists in the United States are included.

Coverage: Containing concise information on 787 painters, sculptors, and printmakers, every entry is updated from the first 1966 edition with 98 completely new entries. The names were selected by the author, and information was collected from questionnaires, personal interviews, and intensive research. Artists are chosen by these criteria: representation in museum, public, and private collections; representation in major American or international exhibitions; influence as teachers; recognition that they have received from fellow-artists, dealers, critics, and others with professional interest in the fine arts.

Bibliography: Pages 342-368 contain a reading list of specialized and general books on the fine arts with references at the end of entries to this bibliography.

Arrangement and Index: Arrangement is alphabetical; appended are How to Use This Book, Key to Museums and Institutions and Their Schools, and Galleries.

Illustrations: There are 100 newly selected black-and-white illustrations in the text with index and picture credits.

RSBR Review: The Booklist and Subscription Books Bulletin, April 15, 1967, p.867.

Dictionary of International Biography: A Biographical Record of Contemporary Achievement Together with a Key to Biographical Notes. 8th ed. 1972. 3v. London and Dartmouth, Melrose Pr., 1963-   . Distributed in U.S. by Rowman & Littlefield. $57.50 pre-pub. to biographees, royal morocco ed. of 50 copies handbound linson $75. SBN 900332-09-3.

Frequency: Dictionary of International Biography is an annual publication.

Scope: Living persons from 100 countries are treated.

Coverage: There are 15,000 concise entries of biographees selected on merit from all fields by the editor, by researchers in all parts of the world, and by reference to other works. Information is obtained by questionnaires, and internal checks are made to assure that the information so furnished is correct. Indication is given for the other biographical works in which the subject appears. In each edition a Head of State in the World is honored with a dedication, a portrait, and a memoir of his life (H. M. Bhumibol Adulyadej, King of Thailand in 1972 edition).

Bibliography: Works by subjects are listed in their sketches.

Illustrations: There is a portrait frontispiece of head of state honored in volume.

Arrangement and Index: Arrangement is alphabetical. Coding used, numbering of reference books mentioned, and a table of abbreviations are appended.

Dictionary of National Biography: From Earliest Time to 1900 (and continuation). New York, Oxford, 1885-   . 22v. including 1st Supp. Reprint 1938, $310; 2d Supp., 1901-1911, 3v. in 1, $25.50; 3d Supp., 1912-1921, $17; 4th Supp., 1922-1930, $17; 5th Supp., 1931-1940,

$20.50; 6th Supp., 1941-1950, $25.50; 7th Supp., 1951-1960, $32.25.

Frequency: Dictionary of National Biography is published every ten years.

Scope: The work is retrospective.

Coverage: The father, and perhaps the most famous of all the national biographical works, *Dictionary of National Biography* presents long signed sketches of prominent personages of all eras in Great Britain and her colonies including America. Biographies are written by scholars familiar with each field. A *Concise Dictionary* containing all the names in the original work through 1950 with abbreviated sketches is available for $18.75 from Oxford. Also, G. K. Hall Company of Boston has published the $25 list of corrections and additions to this work prepared by the Institute of Historical Research of the University of London which is essential to the best usage of the work since no general revision is contemplated.

Bibliography: Excellent bibliographies are appended to each article for many primary sources. Works of authors are listed in their sketches.

Arrangement and Index: The first 21 volumes are in one alphabet; the main works and supplements each have their own indexes with a cumulative index for the years 1901-1960 in the latest supplement (1951-1960). Lists of contributors and editors are identified by initials in the main set and supplements.

Dictionary of Scandinavian Biography.
General editor, Ernest Kay. v.1. London, Melrose Pr., Ltd., 1972. Distributed in U.S. by Rowman & Littlefield. 467p. linson $27.50. SBN 900332-20-4.

Frequency: Dictionary of Scandinavian Biography appears annually.

Scope: Only living persons are cited.

Coverage: The dictionary contains some 3,600 concise abbreviated factual biographical sketches of outstanding persons in all fields from Denmark, Finland, Iceland, Norway, and Sweden, selected under the supervision of F. W. K. Wendt, Secretary-General of the Danish Delegation to the Nordic Council, an interparliamentary union designed to promote cooperation among these countries; their embassies in London; and many private and public bodies in the places covered. The only suggestion given regarding how the subjects were chosen is: "this edition contains a biographical sketch on every participant in the Nordic Council sessions in 1971, and many other persons prominent in the work of Scandinavian cooperation." Despite this claim, however, selection is not predominately political.

Bibliography: Books by biographees are listed in sketches.

Arrangement and Index: Arrangement is alphabetical. A note on filing of Nordic names should be consulted on p.xxiv-xxxv.

Dictionary of Scientific Biography.
Charles Coulston Gillispie, editor in chief. v.7. New York, Charles Scribner's Sons, 1970-   . 622p. bancroft and buckram $35 per v.
ISBN v.1 0-684-10112-2; v.2 . . . 10113-0; v.3 . . . 10114-9; v.4 . . . 10115-7; v.5 . . . 10116-5; v.6 . . . 10117-3; v.7 . . . 10118-1.

Frequency: The projected 13 volumes are expected to be completed in 1975.

Scope: Only deceased scientists are listed.

Coverage: Edited by Charles Coulston Gillispie, Professor of the History of Science, Princeton, the dictionary has many distinguished contributors who sign their articles and are listed in each volume. Sponsored by the American Council of Learned Societies and financially supported by the U.S. National Science Foundation, the work is universal in coverage. A Board of outstanding persons in all fields of science aimed to select "figures whose contributions to science were sufficiently distinctive to make an identifiable difference to the profession or community of knowledge." Technology, medicine, the behavioral and social sciences, and philosophy are excluded unless they are intrinsically related to the sciences of nature or to mathematics. The long articles adhere closely to the details of the person's contribution to the subject with a brief outline of other activities. Twentieth-century figures are proportionately few. Personages from India, China, Japan, Babylon, and Egypt are to be treated in essay form in the final volume.

Bibliography: Works about the biographee are listed.

Arrangement and Index: Arrangement is alphabetical, and a subject index is promised for final volume.

RSBR Review: The Booklist, Nov. 1, 1970, p.185.

Dictionary of South African Biography.
W. H. de Kock, editor in chief until 1970; D. Kruger since 1971. Pretoria, Published for the National Council for Social Research, Dept. of Higher Education, by Nasionale Boekhandel BPK., 1968- . cloth (Price varies with each volume as it appears.)

Frequency: Two volumes have been published to date. When coverage to 1950 is completed, a new volume will appear every ten years.

Scope: Dictionary of South African Biography from before the fifteenth century to 1950 is retrospective.

Coverage: Dictionary of South African Biography is projected to include 2,500 to 3,000 biographees selected from all available sources by the intellectual community of South Africa. The long sketches are chiefly written by specialists in the subject's fields and signed by initials. (Key to initials appears in each volume.) Volumes are published as soon as about 600 sketches are completed. Articles are included for those in every field who have contributed to the development of the country although they may never have resided there. *Dictionary of South African Biography* is similar to *Dictionary of American Biography* in content of sketches and is strong on genealogical material.

Bibliography: Long bibliographies are generally appended to each article, and works of authors are listed in their sketches. There is one page of general bibliography.

Arrangement and Index: Each volume is arranged alphabetically with a cumulative index in each succeeding volume. Contains also Board of Control, Contributors, Glossary, Corrigenda et Addenda in volume 2, and Abbreviations.

A Dictionary of Universal Biography of All Ages and of All People. [By Albert M. Hyamson]. 2d ed., entirely rewritten, 1951. London, Routledge and Kegan Paul, Ltd.; New York, E. P. Dutton & Co., Inc., 1916- . 680p. cloth $19.50.
ISBN 0-525-09302-8.

Frequency: Hyamson's dictionary was published in 1916 and 1951.

Scope: No living persons are cited.

Coverage: Generally *Hyamson's* is comprised of a one-line identification of the biographee, but in the case of some, major authors in particular, principal works are listed. Entries are selected by the editor. *Hyamson's* is not a biographical dictionary; it is primarily an index to persons appearing in the major biographical dictionaries of the principal countries of the world.

Bibliography: Hyamson's lists major works supplying the names and cites works of authors listed.

Arrangement and Index: Arrangement is alphabetical. Appended are List of Abbreviations, Key to References, and Addenda.

RSBR Review: Subscription Books Bulletin, July 1952, p.39.

Directory of American Scholars: A Biographical Dictionary. Edited by the Jaques Cattell Pr. 4v. New York & London, R. R. Bowker Co., 1942- cloth $27.50 per v. ISBN v.1 History 0-8352-0239-9; v.2 English, Speech and Drama . . . 0240-2; v.3 Foreign Languages, Linguists and Philology . . . 0241-0; v.4 Philosophy, Religion and Law . . . 0242-9.

Frequency: Five editions were published between 1942 and 1969; a sixth edition has been announced for 1974.

Scope: Directory of American Scholars covers only living persons.

Coverage: There are 33,500 factual concise biographies in the fields of v.1: History (606p.); v.2; Speech and Drama (606p.); v.3: Foreign Languages, Linguistics and Philology (453p.); and v.4: Philosophy, Religion and Law (559p.). Scholars in fields such as fine arts, which have their own substantial directories, are not included. The directory is edited by the Jaques Cattell Press with the cooperation of the American Council of Learned Societies, and the biographees are selected because of sustained achievement to that associated with a doctor's degree, through publication of scholarly works, or through attainment of a position high in the field of administration equivalent to the doctoral degree. Information was obtained by questionnaires sent to those selected for entry. An attempt was made to list all scholars with more than local reputations.

Bibliography: Works of biographees are entered.

Arrangement and Index: Arrangement is alphabetical. There is a cumulative index for all four volumes in volume 4. There are biographies at the end of each volume for persons who responded too late for inclusion in the main text.

RSBR Review: The Booklist, Feb. 15, 1970, p.677.

Directory of Medical Specialists Holding Certification by American Specialty Boards. 15th ed., 1972. 2v. Chicago, Marquis Who's Who, Inc., 1939- arrestox buckram $49.50. ISBN 0-8379-0515-X.

Frequency: Directory of Medical Specialists is published once every two years.

Scope: Only contemporary medical specialists mainly from the United States, but some from Canada, and foreign countries are included.

Coverage: There are entries for 120,000 specialists whose certification was reported before October 1971. Authorized by the American Board of Medical Specialists who verify the certifications, the biographical data is furnished by the practitioners themselves, and only active physicians are listed. The sketches are very brief.

Arrangement: Arrangement is according to specialty boards, listed in alphabetical sequence. Within each of these sections, arrangement is by state, city, and then by surname of doctor.

Appended are Abbreviations, Key to Information in This Directory, Members of American Board of Medical Specialists, Latest Listings, Supplemental Listings, and Alphabetical List of Diplomats (foreign specialists).

European Authors, 1000-1900: A Biographical Dictionary of European Literature. Edited by Stanley J. Kunitz and Vineta Colby. 1968. New York, H. W. Wilson Co., 1967- . 1,016p. illus. buckram $24. ISBN 0-8242-0013-6.

Frequency: The foundation work was published in 1967; a second printing was made in 1968.

Scope: Popular in appeal, *European Authors* covers almost 1,000 years of literary tradition of continental Europe and omits ancient writers. The editors, Stanley J. Kunitz and Vineta Colby, have selected nearly 1,000 authors each of whom occupies a place in the history of literature. The essay-type sketches vary from 350 to 2,500 words in length and include no authors that died since 1925. Thirty-one different literatures are represented. List of contributors is given; initials of writers are used after the biographical sketches they compiled.

Bibliography: Principal works of and about the authors are cited at the end of each sketch.

Illustrations: There are more than 300 portraits.

Arrangement and Index: Arrangement is alphabetical; where name forms are debatable, the editors have tended to follow the popular usage with cross-references from one to the other. A key to pronunciation is provided.

Everyman's Dictionary of European Writers. By W. N. Hargreaves-Mawdsley. London, J. M. Dent & Sons, Inc.; New York, E. P. Dutton & Co., Inc., 1968. 561p. cloth $8.50. SBN 460-03019-1.

Frequency: No mention is made of new editions.

Scope: Everyman's is both retrospective and contemporary. Over 20 major countries are represented.

Coverage: There are concise entries for over 2,000 subjects with length determined by importance. Biographees are chosen for: (1) historical value showing the life of his day; (2) influence on a large public; or (3) creation of a literary movement or inspiration of an author greater than himself, although he himself produced no work of great importance. Foreign titles translated into English are noted, and all titles requiring such treatment have been translated into the English alphabet.

Bibliography: Principal works of authors are cited in their entries.

Arrangement and Index: Arrangement is alphabetical with cross-references from variations.

Everyman's Dictionary of Literary Biography: English & American.
Compiled after John W. Cousin by D. C. Browning. 3d ed., 1969 (with supplement). London, J. M. Dent & Sons, Ltd.; New York, E. P. Dutton & Co., Inc., 1958- 812p. cloth $6. SBN 460-03008-6.

Frequency: First published in 1958, *Everyman's Dictionary of Literary Biography* was revised in 1960, 1962, 1965, and 1969 (with supp.). The dictionary supercedes *Biographical Dictionary of English Literature* by John W. Cousin.

Scope: Everyman's is both retrospective and contemporary.

Coverage: There are about 2,300 concise literary biographies of which 1,300 are entirely new, and 650 treat subjects not dealt with at all in older volumes. Popular and sophisticated authors are admitted on same terms. The text is readable.

Bibliography: Main works of subjects are listed in their entries.

Arrangement and Index: Arrangement is alphabetical with cross-references from pen names.

Foremost Women in Communications: A Biographical Reference Work on Accomplished Women in Broadcasting, Publishing, Advertising, Public Relations, and Allied Professions.
Barbara J. Love, editor. New York, Foremost American Pub. Corp. in association with R. R. Bowker Co., 1970-   . 788p. cloth $28.50. ISBN 0-8352-0414-6.

Frequency: There is no stated term of issue.

Scope: Living women from the United States are listed.

Coverage: There are nearly 8,000 brief abbreviated entries for women named, for their professional accomplishments, works of merit, and contributions to communications and to the public. Selection is made by an editorial advisory board, editorial staff, and others.

Illustrations: There are portraits of editorial advisory board members.

Bibliography: Works by biographees are cited in the sketches.

Arrangement and Index: Arrangement is alphabetical. Appended are lists of Editorial Advisory Board, Editorial Staff, Abbreviations, Foremost Women in Communications, and Geographical and Subject Cross-Index.

Great Composers, 1300-1900: A Biographical and Critical Guide, 1968.
Compiled and edited by David Ewen. New York, H. W. Wilson Co., 1966-
(Replacement of *Composers of Yesterday,* Wilson, 1937). 429p. pyroxylin $12. ISBN 0-8242-0018-7.

Frequency: The foundation work, *Composers of Yesterday* was published in 1937; the present work, *Great Composers,* was first printed in 1966 with second printing in 1968.

Scope: Deceased composers from all over the world are cited.

Coverage: Great Composers consists of historical, analytical, critical, and personal sketches of 200 great and some minor composers written by the editor and compiler, who is an eminent music critic and historian in his own right. The articles are written in essay form.

Bibliography: Principal works by and biographical and critical works about the subjects are listed.

Illustrations: There are 152 clear portraits.

Arrangement and Index: Arrangement is alphabetical with cross-references from variations. Appended are a Chronological Listing of Composers and Composers Grouped by Nationality.

The International Who's Who. 37th ed., 1973-74. 1879p. London, Europa, 1935- . Distributed in U.S. by International Publications Service, Collings, Inc., New York. cloth $39.50. ISBN 0-900-36259-6.

Frequency: The International Who's Who is published annually.

Scope: Biographies are contemporary.

Coverage: There are abbreviated sketches of some 16,000 persons of international importance in all fields; nearly 900 are new to this edition. No indication of selectors or methods of selection are indicated, but the information is collected from questionnaires, and proofs of the finished sketches are read by the biographees. After many years of issue, the editors appear to have acquired the ability to select for inclusion the majority of most important international personalities.

Bibliography: Works of biographees are listed in their articles.

Arrangement and Index: Arrangement is alphabetical. Abbreviations, Reigning Royal Families, and Obituary are appended.

Purchase Information: The International Who's Who may be purchased from the International Publications Service, 114 E. 32d St., New York, NY 10016.

International Who's Who in Poetry, 1972-1973. Edited by Ernest Kay. London and Dartmouth, International Who's Who in Poetry, 1958- ; distributed in U.S. by Rowman & Littlefield. 716p. linson royal ed. $100; deluxe ed. $50; standard ed. $27.50. SBN 900332-19-0.

Frequency: Three editions were published between 1958 and 1972.

Scope: International Who's Who in Poetry lists living poets of international importance.

Coverage: The copyright for this work is held by the Melrose Press, publishers of *Dictionary of International Biography*. The *Poetry Who's Who* consists of some 3,000 concise abbreviated biographies selected by the editor and an advisory committee. The United States appears to be well represented. The work is compiled from carefully checked questionnaires containing information supplied by the biographees.

Bibliography: Works by the subjects are listed in their sketches. Poetry references are named.

Arrangement and Index: Arrangement is alphabetical with cross-references from pen names. Appended are Addendum, Poetry Awards, Poetry Societies and Magazines (International), Poetry Publishers in Britain and U.S., and Poetry on Record and Tape.

Illustrations: There are 31 full pages of portraits of mainly minor selected poets appended.

The International Year Book and Statesman's Who's Who. 1973. 909p. London, Burke's Peerage, 1953- . cloth $35. SBN 85011-016-5.

Frequency: The International Year Book and Statesman's Who's Who is published annually.

Scope: Coverage is contemporary.

Coverage: The directory covers more than 10,000 biographies, in abbreviated form not only of people in government, but also of those in business, education, and other fields. No method of editing or selection is stated, but the information given is compiled from questionnaires, and suggestions for additional names for inclusion are requested of those already included.

Arrangement and Index: The biographical section is arranged alphabetically. The work is organized in parts: Pt. I: Abbreviations, International Organizations; Pt. II: Colored Maps of States of World; Pt. III: Biographical Section, General Index.

Purchasing Information: The International Year Book and Statesman's Who's Who may be purchased from the British Book Centre, Maxwell House; Fairview Park, Elmsford, NY 10523.

The Junior Book of Authors. Edited by Stanley J. Kunitz and Howard Haycraft. 2d rev. ed., 1951. 5th printing 1965. New York, H. W. Wilson Co., 1932. 309p. illus. buckram $8. ISBN 0-8242-0028-4.

More Junior Authors, 1963. Edited by Muriel Fuller. 3d printing 1969. New York, H. W. Wilson Co., 1963-   . 235p. illus. buckram $8. ISBN 0-8242-0036-5.

Third Book of Junior Authors, 1972. Edited by Doris De Monreville and Donna Hill. New York, H. W. Wilson Co., 1972. 320p. illus. buckram $10.50. ISBN 0-8242-0408-5.

Frequency: Editions were published in 1951, 1963, and 1972. (First and second editions of *The Junior Book of Authors* contain some of same names.)

Scope: The three books of juvenile authors cover both contemporary and retrospective writers of works for young people. The works are intended to be contemporary, but some of the biographees have died over the long span of years of coverage.

Coverage: In the same general format the three volumes contain sketches of approximately 900 persons. For the first two titles selection was made by vote of librarians and specialists in children's literature whose names are listed, and for the third title the editors and named advisory committee made the choices. *Third Book of Junior Authors* also gives names of children's book editors who assisted with information. Most of the sketches are comparatively long, autobiographical, informal, essay-form notes written by the biographees. Pronunciation is given for difficult names. All three books are suitable for use in school libraries as well as other types of libraries.

Bibliography: In *The Junior Book of Authors* and *More Junior Authors* works of authors are mentioned in the text; *Third Book of Junior Authors* lists selected works, and works about the authors are appended to each sketch.

Arrangement and Index: Arrangement is alphabetical by surname best known to reader with cross-references to actual name. *The Junior Book of Authors* has list of Death Dates; *More Junior Authors* has Cumulative Index of Authors and Illustrators, and *Third Book of Junior Authors* has list of Death Dates.

Illustrations: Each article in all three volumes has a passport-size portrait.

Leaders in Education: A Biographical Directory, 1971. Edited by the Jaques Cattell Pr. 4th ed. New York & London, Jaques Cattell Pr./R. R. Bowker Co., 1932-   . 1097p. cloth $40.50. ISBN 0-83520-434-0.

Frequency: Leaders in Education was published in 1932, 1941, 1948, and 1971.

Scope: There are 15,000 concise biographies of leading educators in the United States and Canada who were selected because of achievement by experience and training, by reason of achievement as evidenced by research activities and publications in the field, or by attainment of a position of substantial responsibility. Selection was made through efforts of educational associations and staff, some of whom are listed by name. Subjects verified their entries in proof form unless, in cases where the form was not returned, material submitted within the scope of the established criteria had been included.

Bibliography: Writings of subjects are cited in biographies.

Arrangement and Index: Arrangement is alphabetical. Appended are Abbreviations, Addenda, and Geographic Index.

RSBR Review: Subscription Books Bulletin, July 1941, p.44.

McGraw-Hill Modern Men of Science: Leading Contemporary Scientists. v.2. New York, McGraw-Hill, 1966-   . 679p. buckram $22.50 per v.; $14.50 to subscribers to *McGraw-Hill Encyclopedia of Science and Technology.*

Frequency: Volume 1 was published in 1966 (620p.), volume 2 in 1968 (679p.).

Coverage: The first two volumes contain 846 entries which are international in scope with stress on scientists of the United States and Great Britain. Selection of the names was made by a distinguished group whose names are published in each volume. The majority of the articles are autobiographical and are indicated by an asterisk. The articles include an account of how each subject solved the problems of his research and an assessment of the results. The relatively few articles not marked by an asterisk are written by the staff of the encyclopedia cited below when autobiographical material was not available for a subject. The aim is "to provide, for a substantial number of contemporary scientists, both essential biographical data and extended descriptions of their most significant achievements . . . ," to "tell what each man did but also describe the background of his work, the problems he faced and how he solved them . . . ." *Modern Men of Science* is designed to supplement the *McGraw-Hill Encyclopedia of Science and Technology* which contains no purely biographical articles. The editors of the encyclopedia edited the biographical work and updated some articles from volume 1 in volume 2. *Modern Men of Science* provides little information on other than scientific details of the biographee's life.

Bibliography: Biographee's publications are listed in articles.

Arrangement and Index: Each volume is arranged alphabetically, and an analytical and classified index is appended.

Illustrations: There are a drawing and a portrait of each biographee.

RSBR Review: The Booklist, Nov. 1, 1970, p.185.

Marquis Biographical Library see also *The Directory of Medical Specialists, Who Was Who in America with World Notables, Who's Who in America, Who's Who in the East, Who's Who in Government, Who's Who in the Midwest, Who's Who in the South and Southwest, Who's Who in the West, Who's Who in the World, Who's Who of American Women, World Who's Who in Finance and Industry,* and *World Who's Who in Science.*

More Junior Authors see *The Junior Book of Authors.*

National Cyclopedia of American Biography. Clifton, NJ, James T. White Co.; Ann Arbor, MI, University Microfilms, 1892-1973 (in progress) cloth v.1-54 to date; first 50v. $980 from University Microfilms; v.51-54 price varies from White. Current series, v.A-K, price varies from White, 1930-1967 (in progress).

Frequency: The *National Cyclopedia of American Biography* is published irregularly.

Scope: Permanent volumes 1-54 and continuation are retrospective; current series volume A and continuations are contemporary.

Coverage: The permanent volumes containing only deceased person's biographies, and the current volumes containing biographies only of those living now comprise 65 volumes containing over 55,000 entries. While this work falls somewhat within the vanity class and is less selective and limited than *Dictionary of American Biography,* it is nevertheless the most comprehensive retrospective American work available. Compiled from questionnaires and family interviews the unabbreviated sketches not only assist in the discovery of information regarding the biographee's career, but his ancestry as well making it useful to the genealogist as well.

Bibliography: Works by biographees are listed in their sketches.

Illustrations: The *National Cyclopedia of American Biography* is a good source for full-page portraits and photographs in the text. The biographee or his family pays extra for inclusion of portraits. Many autographs also are reproduced making the *Cyclopedia* a valuable source for authenticating signatures.

Arrangement: The *National Cyclopedia* is not arranged alphabetically in either series. Name indexes are in each volume. There is an index volume for the first 50 volumes and cumulative indexes for more recent material.

New Century Cyclopedia of Names.
Edited by Clarence L. Barnhart; assistant editor, William D. Halsey. 3v. New York, Appleton-Century-Crofts, 1954. cloth $47.45; $15.80 per v. ISBN 0-390-66835-4.

Frequency: The *New Century Cyclopedia of Names* appeared previously as v.11, *Century Dictionary* (1914).

Scope: The work is both retrospective and contemporary.

Coverage: Completely revised and updated, the *New Century Cyclopedia of Names* contains over 100,000 proper names, many of them biographical. Very brief, abbreviated entries with pronunciation. Names from all centuries and all walks of life were selected by the editors, special writers, and editorial staff of the publisher. Names are selected if information about the person is likely to be needed. Supplements contain many tables; those of biographical interest are List of Rulers, Chiefs of State and Other Notables by Country, Genealogical Charts, Members of the United Nations, and Table of Popes.

Bibliography: Only best-known works of biographee are listed.

Arrangement and Index: Arrangement is alphabetical. Included are Key to Pronunciation and List of Prenames Used in This Work with Pronunciations.

Notable American Women 1607-1950: A Biographical Dictionary. Edward T. James, editor; Janet Wilson James, associate editor; Paul S. Boyer, assistant editor. 3v. Cambridge, MA, The Belknap Pr. of Harvard Univ. Pr., 1971. Columbia Riverside linen C grade $75.
ISBN 0-674-62731-8.

Frequency: No supplements are mentioned.

Scope: Only notable women of the United States are cited.

Coverage: The book is made up of long essay-type sketches interpretive as well as factual in nature similar to those in *Dictionary of American Biography.* One thousand three hundred fifty nine subjects are selected from a large number of names gathered from all important sources by the editors with the advice of a distinguished committee of listed consultants. The articles were written by experts in the fields covered and are signed.

Bibliography: Works by and about subjects are listed in entries.

Arrangement and Index: Arrangement is alphabetical with cross-references to variations in name. There is a Classified List of Selected Biographies.

RSBR Review: The Booklist, July 15, 1972, p.948.

Popular American Composers; From Revolutionary Times to the Present: A Biographical and Critical Guide and first supp., 1972. Compiled and edited by David Ewen. New York, H. W. Wilson Co., 1962-1972. 217, 121p. illus. cloth $8 (parent v.); $6 (supp.).
ISBN 0-8242-0040-3; supp. . . . 0436-0.

Frequency: Popular American Composers was published in 1962 and 1972.

Scope: Contemporary composers are listed.

Coverage: The work is comprised of 161 informal editor written essay sketches of persons selected by the editor, who is well known for his accuracy and critical ability. In most cases the information is firsthand from the composers themselves or was obtained by mail, and many of the rough drafts of the entries were corrected by the musicians themselves.

Bibliography: Works by and about the biographees are listed.

Illustrations: There are portraits of each subject many of them furnished by the biographees themselves.

Arrangement and Index: Arrangement is alphabetical. Appended are Chronological List of Popular Composers and Index to Songs and Other Compositions.

Something About the Author: Facts and Pictures about Contemporary Authors and Illustrators of Books for Young People. Anne Commire, editor. 2v. Detroit, Gale Research Co., 1971- illus. grade C cloth $15 per v.

Frequency: Volumes 1 and 2 were published in 1971; volume 3 is in preparation.

Scope: Living authors chiefly from the United States are listed.

Coverage: The interpretative sketches describe not only the life but also work in progress and cite intimate sidelights of the author's life and works. Selection is made by the editor based on librarian and teacher recommendations. *Something About the Author* is written for young readers. There are no abbreviations in sketches. Some of the entries have appeared in the publisher's *Contemporary Authors* series.

Illustrations: There are portraits of authors and illustrations from their works. Photograph credits and artists' acknowledgments are listed.

Bibliography: Works of authors are listed in sketches; lists of works are appended to entries.

Arrangement and Index: Arrangement is alphabetical. A Cumulative Index to all entries is in the latest volume.

RSBR Review: The Booklist, Feb. 1, 1972, p.483.

Twentieth Century Authors: A Biographical Dictionary of Modern Literature. Edited by Stanley J. Kunitz and Howard Haycraft. 1st supp. 1955. New York, H. W. Wilson Co., 1942- (4th printing, 1967). 1,123p. 1,577p. buckram $22 (basic v.); 1st supp. $18. ISBN 0-8242-0049-7; supp. . . . 0050-0.

Frequency: The parent volume was published in 1942; reprints were made in 1944, 1950, 1956, 1961, 1966. A first supplement was distributed in 1955, 1959, 1963, and 1967.

Scope: Twentieth Century Authors treats living authors from all over the world.

Coverage: The main volume and the supplement contain some 2,550 biographical and autobiographical sketches of the lives of modern writers in whom readers are interested. Selection of biographees is by the editors. Sketches range in length from 300 to 800 words. Often written by the subject himself, the articles are in essay style. Death dates have been noted in the latest reprint of the main work and in the fourth printing of the supplement for those who appeared in the first printing of that volume.

Bibliography: Principal works and works about are listed in each entry.

Illustrations: There are 2,370 portraits in main work and supplement.

Arrangement and Index: Arrangement is alphabetical with cross-references from variations of the name.

Principal works by and works about the subjects are appended to each sketch.

RSBR Review: Subscription Books Bulletin, Jan. 1943, p.13.

Webster's Biographical Dictionary. Springfield, MA, G. & C. Merriam, 1972. 1697p. B grade pyroxylin impregnated $12.95; to schools and libraries, 10 percent discount. ISBN 0-87779-143-0.

Frequency: The first edition was printed in 1943; slight revisions were made 1948, 1951, 1953, 1956, 1957, 1958, 1960, 1961, 1962, 1963, 1965, 1966, 1969, 1970, and 1971.

Scope: Webster's Biographical Dictionary is both contemporary and retrospective.

Coverage: Forty thousand people of historical importance from all countries selected by the permanent editorial board listed on p.vi-vii and consultant editors cited on p.vii-viii are given brief concise factual treatment. The work treats fully persons prominent in all fields except sports, motion pictures, contemporary theater, and radio entries for which were cut to the minimum. Syllabication and pronunciation is given for surnames. American and British subjects receive the fullest treatment. Names are chosen from a large file, the accumulation of many years of reading newspapers and a list of reference books noted on p.vi. *Webster's* has lost much of its value as a contemporary source, because of the slight revisions since the first 1943 edition.

Bibliography: There are lists of works of biographees.

RSBR Review: The Booklist, July 15, 1970, p.1353. (See also page 354 herein.)

Who Was Who: A Companion to Who's Who Containing the Biographies of Those Who Died 1897-1970. v.6, 1961-1970. London, Adam & Charles Black; New York, St. Martin's Pr., 1929- . 1243p. cloth v.1, 1897-1915 $17; v.2, 1916-1928 $17; v.3, 1929-1940 $17; v.4, 1941-1950 $16; v.5, 1951-1960 $17; v.6, 1961-1970 $30. SBN v.1 7136-0168-X; v.2 . . . 0169-8; v.3 . . . 0170-1; v.4 . . . 0171-X; v.5 . . . 0172-8; v.6 . . . 1202-9.

Frequency: Who Was Who was published 1897-1915, 1916-1928, 1929-1940, 1941-1950, 1951-1960, and 1961-1970.

Scope: The work is retrospective and is comprised of biographies removed from *Who's Who* on account of death.

Coverage: Who Was Who consists of brief biographies of thousands of notable men and women in every walk of life who died during the period 1897-1970. The details of each entry were obtained from the biographee originally and revised by him or her each year. Checked and supplemented editorially from many sources, the information rates high in accuracy. This standard has made *Who's Who* a national British institution. A few prominent names of persons outside Great Britain are included.

Bibliography: Works of authors are listed.

Arrangement and Index: Arrangement is alphabetical. There are Addenda of biographies of persons belonging in other volumes because of their death dates and those belonging in the latest volume while it was in process.

RSBR Review: Subscription Books Bulletin, Jan. 1943, p.13.

Who Was Who in America. v.4, 1961-1968. Chicago, Marquis Who's Who, Inc., 1943-   . cloth $34.50. (A component title: *Who's Who in American History* is also used by the publisher to cover this set.) ISBN 0-8379-0315-7.

Frequency: Who Was Who in America is generally published every seven years.

Scope: The work is retrospective and chiefly covers the United States.

Coverage: There are concise biographies of persons who have contributed to every phase of American history. All the volumes contain some 90,000 biographical entries. The historical volume covering 1607-1896 contains biographies of persons selected and written by the publisher's staff and has omissions and errors. The entries in the other volumes (1—1897-1942 and 4—1961-1968) are for deceased persons who were listed in *Who's Who in America*

and other Marquis publications. Therefore, the publisher's staff has made the selections with advisory board help at times, and most of the information has been supplied by the biographees.

Bibliography: Publications of biographee are listed in sketch.

Arrangement and Index: Arrangement is alphabetical. An alphabetical index to all volumes keys each name to the volume containing the biography. Abbreviations are listed.

Method of Purchase: Who Was Who in America may be purchased by direct mail and direct sale through representatives.

RSBR Review: Subscription Books Bulletin, Oct. 1943, p.53. Historical volume. *The Booklist and Subscription Books Bulletin,* Oct. 1, 1964, p.106.

Who Was Who in American History see *Who Was Who in America.*

Who Was Who in the USSR: A Biographic Directory Containing 5,015 Biographies of Prominent Soviet Historical Personalities. Edited by Heinrich E. Schulz & Paul K. Urban. 1972. Metuchen, NJ, Scarecrow Pr., 1972-   . 677p. arrestox $40. ISBN 0-8108-0441-7.

Scope: Who Was Who in the USSR is retrospective covering 1917-1967.

Coverage: The work is compiled by the Institute for the Study of USSR of Munich, Germany; the editors selected subjects from detailed biographical information on more than 135,000 Soviet citizens, an 80,000-volume library, and 750 USSR newspapers. The sketches are concise and factual and attempt to represent "prominent individuals who have made major contributions to political, intellectual, scientific, social and economic life of the country."

Bibliography: Works of subjects are listed in their sketches.

Arrangement and Index: Arrangement is alphabetical and there is an Index by Career and Profession.

RSBR Review: The Booklist, Sept. 1, 1973, p.4. (See also page 270 herein.)

Who's Who, 1973-1974: An Annual Biographical Dictionary. New York, St.

Martin's Pr., 1849- . 3600p. cloth $52.50. SBN 7136-1348-3.

Frequency: Who's Who is an annual.

Scope: Scope is world-wide with emphasis on persons in Great Britain and the British Commonwealth.

Coverage: In its 125th year, *Who's Who* is the pioneer of all works using the title who's who. This accurate compilation covers persons of distinction in all fields of endeavor. Sketches are abbreviated and contain information edited by the publisher's staff from questionnaires filled out by the biographees with final proof approved by them. Names of selection and editorial board are not given, but constant use by librarians for a number of years has demonstrated that the choice is excellent. Biographies are dropped if they drop from public interest or do not answer the questionnaire. Deceased entrants appear in *Who Was Who*.

Bibliography: Publications of biographees are listed in their respective sketches.

Arrangement and Index: Arrangement is alphabetical. Abbreviations, Obituary, The Royal Family, and Supplement are included.

Who's Who in Advertising. Editor, Robert S. Morgan. 2d ed. Rye, NY, Redfield Pub. Co., 1963-1972. 764p. pyroxylin impregnated $42.50 cover price; to schools and libraries, $24.50.

Frequency: Who's Who in Advertising is published once every two years.

Scope: Only living subjects from the United States and Canada are cited.

Coverage: Nearly 6,500 key advertising and marketing executives representing more than 3,800 companies have been selected for inclusion because of title, agency billings, and background in business. Entries were selected by the editors, and the information was collected on questionnaires filled in by the subjects. Those who did not respond are not included. Sketches are concise.

Biography: Writings of biographees are included in their sketches.

Arrangement and Index: Arrangement is alphabetical. Appended are How to Use Who's Who in Advertising, Addendum, Acknowledgements, Advertising Hall of Fame, Advertising Council, Abbreviations, Cross-Index to Companies and Personnel, and Cross-Index by Canadian Companies and Personnel.

RSBR Review: The Booklist and Subscription Books Bulletin, Feb. 15, 1964, p.504.

Who's Who in America. 37th ed. 2v. Chicago, Marquis Who's Who, Inc., 1899- . Joanna Western C grade cloth $69.50. ISBN 0-8379-0137-5.

Frequency: Who's Who in America is published every other year.

Scope: The work covers only contemporaries chiefly from the United States, but some foreigners such as heads of states, diplomatic corps to this country, and others of high responsibility are included.

Coverage: Individuals selected for inclusion are chosen by the unlisted Marquis staff and a listed Board of Advisors. Marquis Company claims the biographees have "current reference value because of meritorious achievement." Biographees submit information on a questionnaire which is staff edited for publication and returned to the subject for final approval. An asterisk after an entry denotes that the biographee did not return the questionnaire, but that he was sufficiently important to be included, and a staff member researched and wrote the sketch. There are 64,200 persons in the present edition.

Bibliographies: Books by biographees are listed.

Arrangement and Index: Arrangement is alphabetical. Appended are lists of Board of Directors, Citations for Significant Contribution to Society, Key to Information in this Directory, Tables of Abbreviations, Alphabetical Practices, and Latest Listings.

Method of Purchase: Pre-publication offers are made to biographees. Sale is by direct mail and direct sale from representatives.

RSBR Review: Subscription Books Bulletin, July 1950, p.43.

Who's Who in American Art. Edited by the Jaques Cattell Pr. Foreword by Wilder

Green. 11th ed., 1973. New York & London, Jaques Cattell Pr./R. R. Bowker Co., 1947- . 895p. cloth $34.50. ISBN 0-8352-0611-4.

Frequency: Who's Who in American Art is published once every three years.

Scope: Only living artists from the United States and Canada are chosen for inclusion.

Coverage: There are biographies of some 6,500 professional painters, sculptors, illustrators, craftsmen, graphic artists, executives, collectors, patrons, scholars, critics, and others in art. The book is sponsored by the American Federation of Arts, and the information was collected by questionnaires. The work's intent is to include relevant material with accuracy. Prepublication proofs were sent to the biographees.

Bibliography: A bibliography of works by and about the subjects is featured in many entries.

Arrangement and Index: Arrangement is alphabetical. Appended are geographical and specialty indexes, directory of regional state and national exhibitions, and obituary.

RSBR Review: Subscription Books Bulletin, Jan. 1954, p.13.

Who's Who in American Politics: A Biographical Directory of United States Political Leaders. Compiled by the Jaques Cattell Pr. Edited by Paul A. Theis and Edmund L. Henshaw, Jr. 3d ed. 1971-72. London & New York, R. R. Bowker Co., 1967- . 1171p. cloth $37.50. ISBN 0-8352-0617-3.

Frequency: Who's Who in American Politics is revised every other year. The fourth edition was due November 1973.

Scope: The work covers contemporary politicians living in the United States.

Coverage: The new fourth edition is expected to have over 19,000 notables covering the entire span of American political life from the President and key federal, state, and local officials to non-officeholders who are politically active and influential. Concise entries are compiled from questionnaires which are edited into final copy and approved by the biographee. If biographical forms were not returned, and the prominence of the individual warranted inclusion, material was gathered from other sources, and proof sent to the subject for verification of content. Editorial Advisory Committee and key editors of the Cattell staff are named.

Arrangement and Index: Arrangement is alphabetical. Appended are lists of Editorial Advisory Committee, The President and Members of His Cabinet, State Delegations to the 92d Congress, Governors of the States, Lists of Abbreviations, Addenda, and Geographical Index.

Bibliography: Writings of biographees are listed in their sketches.

Who's Who in the East: Including Connecticut, Delaware, Maine, Maryland, Massachusetts, New Hampshire, New Jersey, New York, Pennsylvania, Rhode Island, Vermont, West Virginia, and in Canada the provinces of New Brunswick, Newfoundland, Nova Scotia, Prince Edward Island, Quebec, and the Eastern half of Ontario. 13th ed., 1972-1973. Chicago, Marquis Who's Who, Inc., 1947- . 855p. tyvek over binders board with buckram spine $34.50. ISBN 0-8379-0613-X.

Scope: Who's Who in the East covers lives of contemporaries in the Eastern United States and Canada.

Coverage: Nineteen thousand abbreviated entries were selected by unnamed Marquis Editors, because: (1) persons are of regional reference importance, and (2) individuals are of national reference and also of regional and local importance. The vast majority furnished the information on biographical data forms. However, information on those prominent citizens who did not respond was researched and authored by the Marquis staff.

Bibliographies: Lists of published works of the biographees are included.

Arrangement and Index: Arrangement is alphabetical. Appended are Key to Information in this Directory, Table of Abbreviations, Alphabetical Practices, and Eastern Biographees in *Who's Who in America.*

Method of Purchase: Prepublication

offer is made to biographees. Sale is by direct mail or direct sale through representatives.

RSBR Review: Subscription Books Bulletin, Oct. 1948, p.66.

Who's Who in Finance and Industry. 17th ed., 1972-1973. Chicago, Marquis Who's Who, Inc., 1936- . 978p. tyvek over binders board with buckram spine $44.50. ISBN 0-8379-0318-1. (Title varies: *Who's Who in Commerce and Industry; World Who's Who in Commerce and Industry*.)

Frequency: Who's Who in Finance and Industry is published once every two years.

Scope: Living persons from all over the world are included.

Coverage: The work consists of concise abbreviated biographies of the executives of over 1,000 of the largest firms and many smaller but important ones reaching a total of 25,000 sketches. Selected by the staff of the publisher with the assistance of expert consultants (none of which are listed), the information was gathered by questionnaires sent to the biographees, and the sketches written by the Marquis staff were reviewed by the subjects before publication. An asterisk indicates that the questionnaire for the biographee was not returned, but that the editors thought that the subject was important enough to have a biography researched and written by staff. Biographees selected fall into two groups: (1) those who have accomplished some conspicuous achievement, and (2) because of positions held.

Bibliographies: Books by subjects are listed in their sketches.

Arrangement and Index: Arrangement is alphabetical. Appended are Key to Information in Sketches, Table of Abbreviations, Alphabetical Practices, Index to Principal Businesses and Their Key Executives, and Who's Who in America Biographies Other than Those Sketched Herein.

Method of Purchase: The work is sold prepublication to biographees and direct by mail and direct sale through representatives.

RSBR Review: Subscription Books Bulletin, July 1947, p.42.

Who's Who in Government. 1st ed., 1972-1973. Chicago, Marquis Who's Who, Inc., 1972- . tyvek over binders board with buckram spine $49.50. ISBN 0-8379-1201-6.

Frequency: Who's Who in Government is published every other year.

Scope: Contemporary statesmen in the United States and a few other countries are listed.

Coverage: Fifteen thousand entries were selected by the staff and a distinguished advisory board of key officials of all branches of the Federal government plus selected state, local, and international government officials. The book is intended to serve not only as a biographical dictionary but also as a directory, through the indexes, where the reader may find the proper government office and individual to answer his inquiries. Information was obtained by questionnaires. Biographies for those who did not reply, but who were considered essential to the completeness of the work were researched and written by the staff. These biographies are marked with an asterisk. All biographies were read and approved by the subjects before publication.

Bibliography: Titles by the biographees are listed in entries.

Arrangement and Index: Arrangement is alphabetical. Appended are Abbreviations, Key to Information, Advisory Board, Alphabetical Practice, and Index of Biographees by Topics, and Index of Biographees by Departments.

Method of Purchase: Prepublication offer is made to biographees; sale is by direct mail and direct sale through representatives.

RSBR Review: The Booklist, Feb. 1, 1973, p.499. (See also page 272 herein.)

Who's Who in the Midwest. 12th ed., 1970-1971. Chicago, Marquis Who's Who, 1948- . 774p. tyvek over binders board with buckram spine $34.50. ISBN 0-8379-0712-8.

Frequency: Who's Who in the Midwest is published every two years.

Scope: Only living persons are included.

Coverage: There are biographies for noteworthy men and women of Illinois, Indiana, Iowa, Kansas, Michigan, Minnesota, Missouri, Nebraska, North Dakota, South Dakota, Wisconsin, Manitoba, and Western Ontario. Seventeen thousand entries were selected by the publisher's unnamed editorial staff, because they are national or regional leaders in their respective fields. The work is compiled in concise factual form from information supplied by subjects, edited by the staff, and final review is by the biographee. Those who are prominent but did not answer the questionnaire are covered by articles written by the staff from their own research. These entries are marked with an asterisk.

Bibliography: Books by biographee are listed in sketch.

Arrangement and Index: Arrangement is alphabetical with Index to Who's Who Biographies, Midwestern Section appended.

Method of Purchase: Biographee can purchase at a prepublication rate; others may buy through direct mail.

RSBR Review: Subscription Books Bulletin, July 1947, p.43. Title was *Who's Who in the Central States.*

Who's Who in the South and Southwest.
13th ed., 1973-1974. Chicago, Marquis Who's Who, Inc., 1949- . 864p. tyvek over binders board with buckram spine $34.50. ISBN 0-8379-0812-4.

Frequency: Who's Who in the South and Southwest is published every other year.

Scope: Living persons in the South and Southwest United States and Mexico are cited.

Coverage: More than 16,000 persons from Alabama, Arkansas, the District of Columbia, Florida, Georgia, Kentucky, Louisiana, Mississippi, North Carolina, Oklahoma, South Carolina, Tennessee, Texas, Virginia, Puerto Rico, and the Virgin Islands as well as Mexico are included. These biographees are (1) persons who are of regional reference importance and (2) those of national importance who have great regional significance as well. The names of the selection board members are not listed, but the completed questionnaires are edited by the Marquis staff and finally approved by the subject, and those of sufficient importance who did not return the biographical forms are researched and sketches are written by the staff. Entries are abbreviated and brief.

Bibliographies: Lists of works of biographees appear in their sketches.

Arrangement and Index: Arrangement is alphabetical. Appended are Key to Information in Directory, Table of Abbreviations, Alphabetical Practices, and Southern and Southwestern Biographees in *Who's Who in America.*

Method of Purchase: Prepublication offer is made to biographee. Sale is by direct mail and direct sale through representatives.

Who's Who in the Theatre: A Biographical Record of the Contemporary Stage. Edited by John Parker. 15th ed., 1972. 1725p. London, Pitman, 1912- cloth $32.50. SBN 273-31528-5.

Frequency: Who's Who in the Theatre is published irregularly.

Scope: Contemporary.

Coverage: Who's Who in the Theatre covers all persons connected with the theater, including actors and directors. In recent years attempt has been made to cover many more biographees living outside Great Britain; 600 new names were added in the last edition and particular efforts were made to cover the American field. Abbreviated sketches are given for biographees selected by listed editors.

Bibliography: Works of biographees and appearances in works of others are listed.

Arrangement and Index: Arrangement is alphabetical. New York, London, and other playbills are listed with indexes as are Theatre Associations and Movements, Names in Previous Editions, Obituary, Long Runs, and Working Dimensions of British Stages.

Who's Who in the West: An Extension of Who's Who in America and a Component Volume of the Marquis Biographical

Library. 12th ed., 1970-1971. Chicago, Marquis Who's Who, 1970- . 705p. tyvek over binders board with buckram spine $44.50. SBN 8379-0912-1.

Frequency: Who's Who in the West is published every other year.

Scope: Persons living in Alaska, Arizona, California, Colorado, Hawaii, Idaho, Montana, Nevada, New Mexico, Oregon, Utah, Washington, and Wyoming in the United States, and Alberta, British Columbia, and Saskatchewan in Canada are included.

Coverage: There are concise biographies of 14,400 persons selected by the publisher's staff because of their regional or national reference interest. The vast majority of the sketches were compiled by the staff from information supplied by the biographees on Marquis biographical questionnaires. Those of special noteworthy achievement who did not reply were researched and compiled by the staff. Biographees reviewed their sketches in proof before publication.

Bibliography: Published works of the subjects are listed in entries.

Arrangement and Index: Arrangement is alphabetical. There is an Index of *Who's Who in America* Biographies in the Western Section.

Method of Purchase: Prepublication offer is made to biographees. Purchase may also be made by direct mail and direct sale through representatives.

Who's Who in the World. v.1, 1971-1972. Chicago, Marquis Who's Who, 1970- 1060p. tyvek over binders board with buckram spine $44.95. ISBN 0-8379-1101-X.

Frequency: Who's Who in the World is published every two years.

Scope: Only living persons are included.

Coverage: There is abbreviated concise factual information for about 25,000 names selected by the Marquis staff (not listed) after "extensive research into every significant field of human endeavor throughout the world." (150 countries). A Board of Advisors (listed p.vi) composed of ambassadors from 50 countries, reviewed the names selected. Most of the information was supplied by the biographees, but for those eminent persons not replying to the questionnaire and deemed essential to the work, entries were researched and written by the staff. These are marked with an asterisk. All who submitted information had the opportunity to review the final draft after editing of their material. There are more names from the United States and Great Britain than any other countries.

Bibliography: Books by biographees are listed in their sketches.

Arrangement and Index: Arrangement is alphabetical, but rules for filing foreign names must be read in order to find certain names. Index to Biographees by Countries and Index of Latest Listings are appended.

RSBR Review: The Booklist, July 15, 1971, p.911.

Who's Who of American Women. 7th ed., 1972-1973. Chicago, Marquis Who's Who, Inc., 1957- . 1017p. tyvek over binders board with buckram for spine $39.50. ISBN 0-8379-0407-2.

Frequency: Who's Who of American Women is published once every other year.

Scope: Only contemporary women chiefly from the United States are cited. A few foreign heads of state and other dignitaries are included.

Coverage: Twenty-four thousand two hundred entries were selected by the publisher's staff with the aid of unnamed international expert consultants. Selection was based on either or both of two factors: (1) positions of responsibility held, (2) level of achievement attained. Most biographees supplied their own information which was edited into brief sketches by the staff and resubmitted to the biographee for final approval. Of those who did not respond, only the most outstanding are included; in such cases staff members edited and wrote the sketches and appended an asterisk to so indicate.

Bibliographies: There are lists of published books written by the biographees.

Arrangement and Index: Arrangement is alphabetical. Appended are Key to Information in this Directory, Table of Abbreviations, and Alphabetical Practices.

Method of Purchase: Prepublication offer is made to biographees. Sale is by direct mail and direct sale through representatives.

RSBR Review: The Booklist and Subscription Books Bulletin, Jan. 1, 1963, p.329.

Women Artists in America: Eighteenth Century to the Present. By J. L. Collins. Chattanooga, Dept. of Art, Univ. of Tennessee, 1973. 430p. buckram $15; to libraries $10.

Frequency: No revision is contemplated.

Scope: Covers only women artists in the United States.

Coverage: The work contains more than 4,000 biographies of painters, sculptresses, and printers. Brief sketches suffer because only year of birth, death, and other events is cited. In fact, some are not identified even by year. Other information is so weak that this work can scarcely be used for more than identification purposes.

Bibliography: No publications of artists are listed.

Arrangement and Index: Arrangement is alphabetical.

Illustrations: There are 29 full-page illustrations: a symbol by the artist's name indicates that her work is illustrated.

World Who's Who in Science: A Biographical Dictionary of Notable Scientists From Antiquity to the Present. 1st ed., 1968. Chicago, Marquis Who's Who, Inc., 1968-   . 1855p. cloth $60. ISBN 0-8379-1001-3.

Frequency: There will be other editions.

Scope: World Who's Who in Science is both retrospective and contemporary. While the work is universal in scope, it is in fact, strongly United States and Western Europe.

Coverage: Brief biographies of 30,000 prominent persons and their achievements. The Marquis staff, Advisory Council, and other consultants assisted in the selection of the names to be included and the editing of the text. The publisher's staff, supplemented by graduate students in the Chicago area, researched and compiled the data in the retrospective sketches, and questionnaires were sent to the living scientists included. From this data most of the contemporary sketches were written by the staff and approved by the biographees. In cases where very eminent scientists did not answer the biographical form, the staff researched and wrote a biography.

Bibliographies: Selected Bibliography lists sources of further information. Articles list works published by subjects.

Arrangement and Index: Arrangement is alphabetical. Appended are Court Decision of "Who's Who," Table of Abbreviations, and Addendum.

Method of Sale: Purchase is by direct mail and direct sale through representatives.

RSBR Review: The Booklist, Dec. 1, 1969, p.417.

The World Who's Who of Women, 1973. Ernest Kay, general editor. Cambridge and London, Melrose Pr., Ltd., 1973- (From 1969 to 1972 *Two Thousand Women of Achievement.*) Distributed in U.S. by Rowman & Littlefield. cloth $49.50.

Frequency: The World Who's Who of Women is published once every eighteen months.

Scope: Only contemporary biographees are listed.

Coverage: The work contains 6,800 abbreviated sketches of outstanding women in all walks of life. Material is compiled by the editorial staff of the International Biographical Center at Cambridge, England from questionnaires filled out by the biographees. Some persons from the selection and editorial boards are mentioned in the Preface. Those few sketches compiled by the staff are preceded by an asterisk. Avid women's liberation supporters who have protested an all-woman volume have been omitted at their request.

Illustrations: There are more than 5,000 portrait photographs.

Bibliography: Works by biographees are listed in their respective sketches.

Arrangement and Index: Arrangement is alphabetical; addendum is appended.

DIRECTORY OF PUBLISHERS CITED

American Library Assn., 50 E. Huron St., Chicago, IL 60611.

Appleton-Century-Crofts, 440 Park Ave. S., New York, NY 10016.

Adam & Charles Black, Ltd., 4, 5, & 6 Soho Sq., London, W1V 6AD, England.

R. R. Bowker Co., 1180 Ave. of the Americas, New York, NY 10036.

British Book Centre, Inc., 996 Lexington Ave., New York, NY 10021.

Burke's Peerage, Ltd., Mercury House, Waterloo Rd., London SE1 8UL, England.

Jaques Cattell Pr., Div. of R. R. Bowker Co., Box 25001, Tempe, AZ 85281.

W. R. Chambers, Ltd., 6 Dean St., London W.1, England.

J. M. Dent & Sons, Ltd., Aldine House, 10-13 Bedford St., London, WC2, England.

Doubleday & Co., Inc., Garden City, NY 11530.

E. P. Dutton & Co., Inc., 201 Park Ave. S., New York, NY 10003.

Eddison Pr., Ltd., Artillery Mansions, Victoria St., London SW1H OJE, England.

Foremost Americans Pub. Corp., Suite 628 Empire State Building, 350 Fifth Ave., New York, NY 10001.

Gale Research Co., Book Tower, Detroit, MI 48226.

Greenwood Pr., Inc., 51 Riverside Ave., Westport, CT 06880.

Harvard Univ. Pr., 79 Garden St., Cambridge, MA 02138.

Heinemann Educational Books, Ltd., 48 Charles St., London W1X 8AH, England.

International Publications Serv., 114 E. 32d St., New York, NY 10016.

International Who's Who in Poetry, Artillery Mansions, Victoria St., London SW1, England.

McGraw-Hill, Inc., 1221 Ave. of the Americas, New York, NY 10020.

Marquis Who's Who, Inc., 200 E. Ohio St., Chicago, IL 60611.

Melrose Pr., Artillery Mansions, Victoria St., London SW1, England.

G. & C. Merriam, 47 Federal St., Springfield, MA 01101.

Nasionale Boekhandel BPK, Pretoria, South Africa.

Oxford Univ. Pr., Inc., 200 Madison Ave., New York, NY 10016.

Sir Isaac Pitman & Sons, Ltd., Pitman House, Parker St., Kingsway, London, WC2B 5PB, England.

Redfield Pub. Co., P.O. Box 556, Rye, NY 10580.

Routledge & Kegan Paul, Ltd., Broadway House, 68-74 Carter Lane, London EC4V, England.

Rowman & Littlefield, Div. of Littlefield, Adams & Co., 81 Adams Drive, Totowa, NJ 07512.

St. James Pr., 178 Gloucester Place, London NW1, England.

St. Martin's Pr., Inc., 175 Fifth Ave., New York, NY 10010.

Scarecrow Pr., Inc., 52 Liberty St., Metuchen, NJ 08840.

G. Schirmer, Inc., 866 Third Ave., New York, NY 10022.

Charles Scribner's Sons, 597 Fifth Ave., New York, NY 10017.

Simon & Schuster, Inc., 630 Fifth Ave., New York, NY 10020.

U.S. Government Printing Office, Washington, DC 20402.

Univ. of Tennessee, Dept. of Art, Chattanooga, TN 37401.

Univ. of Toronto Pr., Toronto, Ontario, Canada.

James T. White & Co., 1700 State Highway 3, Clifton, NJ 07013.

Who's Who Canadian Publications, Toronto, Ontario, Canada.

The H. W. Wilson Co., 950 University Ave., Bronx, NY 10452.

Xerox University Microfilms, 300 N. Zeeb Rd., Ann Arbor, MI 48106.

(May 1, 1974, p.946)

Ref
Z
1035.1
S922
1972/74

AUG 26 1975